International Management Behavior

Dedication

To all the friends who have helped me learn about other cultures, and my own.

Henry W. Lane

To my parents and grandparents, whose combined legacy of deep pride in our Old World roots and openness to New World diversity has provided me with a wonderfully rich cultural life.

Joseph J. DiStefano

To Katie and Julianna, to help them inspire the next generation.

Martha L. Maznevski

International Management Behavior
Text, Readings, and Cases

Fifth Edition

Henry W. Lane

Darla and Frederick Brodsky Trustee Professor in International Business, Northeastern University, and Professor Emeritus, Richard Ivey School of Business, University of Western Ontario

Joseph J. DiStefano

Professor Emeritus, IMD, Lausanne, Switzerland, and Richard Ivey School of Business, University of Western Ontario

Martha L. Maznevski

IMD, Lausanne, Switzerland

Blackwell Publishing

© 2006 by Henry W. Lane, Joseph J. DiStefano, and Martha L. Maznevski

BLACKWELL PUBLISHING
350 Main Street, Malden, MA 02148-5020, USA
9600 Garsington Road, Oxford OX4 2DQ, UK
550 Swanston Street, Carlton, Victoria 3053, Australia

First edition published 1988 by Nelson Canada
Second edition published 1992 by PWS-Kent Publishing Company
Third edition published 1997
Fourth edition published 2000
Fifth edition published 2006 by Blackwell Publishing Ltd

4   2008

Library of Congress Cataloging-in-Publication Data

Lane, Henry W., 1942–
    International management behavior : text, readings, and cases / Henry W. Lane, Joseph J.
DiStefano, Martha L. Maznevski.—5th ed.
        p. cm.
    Includes bibliographical references and index.
    ISBN: 978-1-4051-2671-7 (pbk. : alk. paper)
    1. International business enterprises—Management. 2. Organizational behavior. 3.
Culture. I. DiStefano, Joseph J., 1940– II. Maznevski, Martha L. III. Title.

    HD62.4.L36 2006
    658′.049—dc22

                                                                                    2005006159

A catalogue record for this title is available from the British Library.

Set in 10/12 pt Baskerville
by Graphicraft Limited, Hong Kong
Printed in Singapore
by Fabulous Printers Pte Ltd

The publisher's policy is to use permanent paper from mills that operate a sustainable forestry
policy, and which has been manufactured from pulp processed using acid-free and elementary
chlorine-free practices. Furthermore, the publisher ensures that the text paper and cover board
used have met acceptable environmental accreditation standards.

For further information on
Blackwell Publishing, visit our website:
www.blackwellpublishing.com

Brief Contents

Contents

Contributors

Henry W. Lane   Darla and Frederick Brodsky Trustee Professor in International Business, Northeastern University, and Professor Emeritus, Richard Ivey School of Business, University of Western Ontario

Joseph J. DiStefano   Professor Emeritus, IMD, Lausanne, Switzerland, and Richard Ivey School of Business, University of Western Ontario

Martha L. Maznevski   IMD, Lausanne, Switzerland

Neil Abramson   Simon Fraser University

Nancy J. Adler   McGill University

Nicholas Athanassiou   Northeastern University

Paul W. Beamish   Richard Ivey School of Business, University of Western Ontario

Allan Bird   University of Missouri

J. Stewart Black   University of Michigan

R. William Blake   Queen's University, Kingston, Ontario

Michael Brown

Paula Caligiuri   Rutgers University

Daniel D. Campbell   Argo Management Partners, Toronto

Archie B. Carroll   University of Georgia

Wayne F. Cascio   University of Colorado-Denver

Jamie Collins   Texas A&M University

Cary L. Cooper   Manchester School of Management, Manchester, UK

Joerg Dietz   Richard Ivey School of Business, University of Western Ontario

Jonathan P. Doh   Center for Responsible Leadership and Governance, Villanova University

Lorraine Eden   Texas A&M University

Gail Ellement   Richard Ivey School of Business, University of Western Ontario

Donna Everatt   Richard Ivey School of Business, University of Western Ontario

Jay Galbraith   IMD, Lausanne, Switzerland

J. Michael Geringer   California Polytechnic State University

Tom Gleave   IMD, Lausanne, Switzerland

Brian Golden   University of Toronto

Hal B. Gregerson   Brigham Young University, Utah

Laura Pincus Hartman   DePaul University

Geert Hofstede   University of Tilburg, The Netherlands

Colleen Lief   IMD, Lausanne, Switzerland

Jeanne M. McNett   Assumption College

Joyce Miller   Lausanne, Switzerland

Chantell Nicholls   Toronto

Anne-Valerie Ohlsson   IMD, Lausanne, Switzerland

Fernando Olivera   Richard Ivey School of Business, University of Western Ontario

Elizabeth O'Neil

Joyce S. Osland   San Jose State University

Peter Rodriguez   Darden Graduate School of Business, University of Virginia

Philip M. Rosenzweig   IMD, Lausanne, Switzerland

Juan I. Sanchez   Florida International University

Christine Shea   University of New Hampshire

Donald G. Simpson   Toronto

Bert Spector   Northeastern University

Paul E. Spector   University of South Florida

Francis Spital   Northeastern University

Linda Klebe Treviño   SMEAL College of Business, Pennsylvania State University

Klaus Uhlenbruck   Mays Business School, Texas A&M University

David T. A. Wesley   Northeastern University

Lorna L. Wright   York University

Xin Zhang   Dell (China) Ltd, Xiamen, China

Foreword

Nancy J. Adler

[handwritten: Cultural awareness – supports managers in creating effective world-wide human networks and systems –]

[handwritten: Great Quote ! ✗ →]

> *Japanese and American management is 95 percent the same and differs in all important respects.*
> – *T. Fujisawa, Cofounder, Honda Motor Corporation*

Managing the global enterprise and modern business management have become synonymous. "International" can no longer be relegated to a category of organizations or to a division within a company. Definitions of societal and business success, now highly interwoven, transcend national borders. In fact, the very concept of domestic business has become anachronistic. As the authors aptly describe, "The modern business enterprise has no place to hide. It has no place to go but everywhere."

To succeed, organizations and companies must use global strategies. The last decade of the twentieth century made the importance of such recognition commonplace, at least among leading firms and management scholars. New approaches to managing research *[handwritten: and Logistics]* and development (R&D), information technologies, production, marketing, and finance, incorporating today's complex global dynamics have evolved rapidly. Yet only much more recently has an equivalent evolution in managing global human resource systems begun to emerge. Although other functional areas increasingly use strategies that were largely unheard of – or that would have been inappropriate – only one and two decades ago, many firms still conduct the worldwide management of people as if neither the external economic and technological environment, nor the internal structure and organization of the firm, had changed.

In focusing on global strategies and management approaches from the perspectives of people and culture, this book supports us, as managers and scholars, in creating effective worldwide human networks and resource systems. The new fifth edition of

Nancy J. Adler is an international management professor at McGill University, Montreal, Canada. She conducts research and consults on global management and leadership issues worldwide. She has published numerous articles and books, including *From Boston to Beijing: Managing with a Worldview* (2002), *International Dimensions of Organizational Behavior*, 4th edition (2002), and *Competitive Frontiers: Women Managers in a Global Economy* (Blackwell, 1994). She revised this foreword for this edition.

International Management Behavior allows us to examine the influence of national culture on organizational functioning. Rather than becoming trapped within the more commonly asked, and unfortunately misleading, question of *if* organizational dynamics are universal or culturally specific, the authors ask us to focus on the crucially important question of *when* to be sensitive to national culture and and *how* to benefit from cultural diversity. They allow us to investigate the implications of global approaches for traditional human resource management decisions, as well as for those decisions that will only make sense from the global perspective of firms operating in the twenty-first century.

How important are cultural differences to organizational effectiveness? Some observers of corporate behavior say "not at all," while others claim that cultural differences are and will remain extremely important. The first group, those adhering to a cultural convergence perspective, argue that organizational characteristics across nations are free, or are becoming free, from the particularities of specific cultures. Their position suggests that as an outcome of "common industrial logic" – most notably of technological origin – institutional frameworks, patterns, and structures of organizations, and management practices across countries are converging (Adler and Doktor, 1986, pp. 300–1). In counter-distinction, other managers and scholars argue that organizations are culture-bound, rather than culture-free, and are remaining so. These scholars conclude that there is no one best way to manage; that is, the principle of equifinality applies to organizations functioning in different cultures. Their research findings indicate that there are many equally effective ways for people to manage and for organizations to succeed, with the most effective depending, among other influences, on the array of cultures involved (Adler and Doktor, 1986, p. 301).

Perhaps this dilemma has not been resolved because we have been asking the wrong question. If we ask what the influence of cultural diversity is on transnational organizational and multinational firms, we realize that the importance and the extent of the impact of national cultural differences depend on the historical stage of development of the firm, the industry, and the world economy. Thus, the relevant question to ask is when and how does culture influence organizational functioning rather than if it does or does not. Observing the development of business enterprises over the past half-century, one can deduce distinct variations in the relative importance of cultural diversity and, consequently, equally distinct variations in the most appropriate approaches to managing people worldwide.

Up through the middle of the last century, firms operated primarily from an ethnocentric perspective. Most firms produced unique goods and services that they offered almost exclusively to their own domestic market. The uniqueness of the products and services offered, along with the relative absence of international competition, negated most firms' need to demonstrate sensitivity to cultural differences. When organizations exported goods, they often did so without adapting them to overseas markets. Any cultural differences, if recognized at all, were expected to be absorbed by the overseas buyers, not by the home country's product-design, manufacturing, or marketing teams. In some ways, the implicit message to foreigners was, "We will allow you to buy our products and services" and, of course, the assumption was that foreigners would want to buy. During this initial phase, home-country nationals and home-country philosophies dominated business strategy. Culture and global human resource management were perceived as irrelevant.

Growing international competition ushered in phase two, and with it the beginning of a need to market and to produce overseas. Totally unlike the first phase, sensitivity to cultural differences became critical in implementing effective business strategies. The first phase's emphasis on product design and service creation shifted to a market orientation, with the range of national domestic markets each needing to be addressed separately and differently. Whereas the uniqueness of products fits well with firms' all-too-common ethnocentric "one-best-way" approaches, by phase two firms began to change assumptions and to use an equifinality approach; that is, they began to recognize that there were many good ways to manage, with each dependent on the particular national culture involved. Successful companies no longer expected foreigners to adapt to cultural mismatches between buyers and sellers. Rather, home-country representatives had to modify their approach to fit with that of their clients and colleagues in each country's market. Moreover, while cultural differences became important in designing and marketing culturally appropriate goods and services, they became critical in manufacturing them in locations around the world. Managers had to learn culturally appropriate ways to manage their human resource systems in each of the countries in which they operated.

By the 1980s, many industries had entered a third phase. The environment for these industries had changed again, and with it the demands for cultural sensitivity also changed. Characteristic of phase three industries, many companies produced very similar products (almost commodities), with the only salient and significant competition being based on price. From this perspective of the dominance of price sensitivity, managers assumed that the need for cultural sensitivity was of minimal importance, and organizations' cultural awareness fell. Price competition among almost identical goods and services produced by numerous multinational competitors appear to negate the importance of most cultural differences and any potential advantage to be gained by cultural sensitivity. The primary product design and marketing assumption was no longer "one best way" or even "many best ways," but rather "one least-cost way." Primary markets had gone global, and most companies saw little to no need for significant geographic market segmentation, and almost no need for market segmentation based on cultural variation. Firms believed that they could only gain competitive advantage through increasingly refined process engineering, sourcing critical factors on a least-cost worldwide basis, and deriving maximum benefits from economies of scale. Price competition reduced cultures' perceived influence to negligible.

While many observers believed that the third phase was the ultimate phase, it was not; a fourth phase, with completely different dynamics, emerged. In it, top-quality, least-possible-cost goods and services became the baseline, the minimally acceptable standard. Firms increasingly gain competitive advantage, not from least-cost strategies (no matter how well executed), but rather from constant innovation, mass customization, and organizational strategies that are inherently flexible enough to thrive in rapidly changing, complex, and chaotic environments. In this fourth phase, product ideas are drawn from sources all over the world. Similarly, the factors and locations of production are distributed worldwide. Organizations, however, tailor their final goods and services and their marketing to very discrete market niches. One of the critical components of this global market segmentation, again, becomes culture. Successful phase four firms quickly learn how to understand their potential clients' needs, translate those needs into goods and services, produce the goods and services on a least-cost basis, and deliver them to clients worldwide using culturally appropriate means. By this fourth phase, the single-focus product, sales, or price orientation of the prior phases almost completely disappears. These past orientations are replaced with an integrated, strategic, and culturally responsive design orientation accompanied by a quick, least-cost production function. Needless to say, culture is critically important to this current stage. The ability to manage cross-cultural interaction, multinational teams, and global alliances becomes fundamental to businesses' initial and continued success. Whereas effective global human resource management strategies in the past varied from being irrelevant to helpful, by the fourth phase they become essential, a minimum requirement for organizational survival and success.

International Management Behavior addresses questions involving people, culture, and the corporation. It allows us, as readers, to examine the implications of alternative approaches to managing people from around the world and to leveraging cultural diversity. The authors encourage us to maintain a global perspective. More than merely being interesting and important, the fifth edition of *International Management Behavior* is fundamental to our understanding of management in the twenty-first century.

BIBLIOGRAPHY

Adler, Nancy J., and R. Doktor (in collaboration with S. G. Redding), "From the Atlantic to the Pacific Century: Cross-Cultural Management Reviewed," *Journal of Management*, 12(2) (1986): 295–318.

Adler, Nancy J., and Fariborz Ghadar, "Strategic Human Resource Management: A Global Perspective," in Rudiger Pieper (ed.), *Human Resource Management in International Comparison* (Berlin: de Gruyter, 1990), pp. 235–60.

Vernon, R., "International Investment and International Trade in the Product Cycle," *Quarterly Journal of Economics* (May 1966).

Acknowledgments

The fifth edition of this book has involved a major revision of many of its elements, including the acknowledgments. Both Professors Lane and DiStefano appreciate the support for their work on international business shown by their colleagues and research associates over the years at the Ivey Business School. Professor Maznevski, who graduated from Ivey's PhD program, also acknowledges the broad support and assistance from the Ivey Business School, financial and otherwise, that contributed to her development and to this book. All of us owe a special debt to our professors, colleagues, and friends who shaped our interests and knowledge. We are grateful to: Deans C. B. Johnston, Adrian Ryans, and Larry Tapp; Professors Jim Hatch, Terry Deutscher, and Ken Hardy; the directors of Research and Publications at the Ivey Business School; and especially the donors of the Donald F. Hunter professorship (a Maclean Hunter endowment) and the Royal Bank professorship, which provided extra time for Professors Lane and DiStefano to undertake much of the initial work in developing this text.

After the third edition Professor DiStefano moved to Hong Kong to launch the Ivey EMBA program there and acknowledges with thanks Ivey alumnus, Alexander Chan, for support in the form of the Shirley Chan Memorial Professorship of International Business. In particular this made possible the addition of new Asian cases. In this regard we must also recognize the Richard and Jean Ivey fund of London, Ontario, for funding the development of Asian case studies, some of which appear in this new edition. Professor Lane assumed responsibility for Ivey's Americas Program and is grateful to Ivey for the support that made possible the development of many new Latin American cases, including the ones in this edition. In September 1999 Professor Lane moved to Northeastern University, where he is the Darla and Frederick Brodsky Trustee Professor in International Business. The generous endowment of Darla and Frederick Brodsky has contributed to making this fifth edition possible. In January 2000, Professor DiStefano joined IMD in Lausanne, Switzerland and would like to thank President Peter Lorange and the IMD research directors for their support in writing the fifth edition.

Professor Maznevski thanks the McIntire School of Commerce and her colleagues there, in particular Dean Carl Zeithaml. The commitment of the school to making its programs global provided substantial support for her involvement in developing material for this book. In 2001 Professor Maznevski joined Professor DiStefano at IMD, and with him thanks the administration and colleagues there.

To this list of acknowledgments we need to add a large number of people and institutions from around the world who have broadened and informed our experience: managers in both the public and private sectors; colleagues at other universities and institutes; companies who have provided access to their operations for the purpose of writing cases; and a number of former students and research assistants who worked with us to develop material for this and previous editions. Among the former research assistants, a special note of thanks is due to Professor Bill Blake of Queen's University and to Professor Lorna Wright of York University. We would also like to thank Professor David Ager of Harvard University, Dan Campbell, David Wesley, and Karsten Jonson for their substantial contributions.

The restructuring that has taken place in the publishing industry adds considerably to this list of acknowledgments. A series of acquisitions and reorganizations has led to our experience with five publishers and editors during the writing of the four editions. Our sincere thanks go to Joerg Klauck who was at Methuen, Ric Kitowski who was at Nelson Canada, Rolf Janke who was at PWS-Kent and then Blackwell, and Catriona King at Blackwell. All were strong believers in, and advocates for, this book. We are delighted to be working now with Rosemary Nixon at Blackwell, who also has proven to be a strong supporter of our work, as well as to be continuing our relationship with Blackwell Publishing. We also express our appreciation to colleagues who have provided the publishers, and us, with helpful critiques. To Bob Moran, Ed Miller, Bob Dennehy, Jerry O'Connell, John Stanbury, Christa Walck, Nick Athanassiou, Jeanne McNett, Bruce Stening, and Peter Steane we say thanks for the reviews and suggestions, which shaped this, and earlier, editions. Students and managers who have worked with our materials, and colleagues who have adopted our book and have written to us with thanks and suggestions, all have helped us and others learn. To them we also add our gratitude.

Our assistants, past and present, deserve our appreciation for the multiple tests of patience which they have endured gracefully over the years of our efforts: thanks to Sue O'Driscoll, Linda Minutillo, Beth Sinclair, and Jeannette Weston of the Ivey Business School, Cindy Hoeffer, the rest of the McIntire support group and Laurence Vagnières at IMD. Professor DiStefano adds his thanks to Anne-Marie Tassi for her indefatigable support over the last five years.

Last, but hardly least, we thank our families who have supported our learning and the publishing of what we have learned. This has meant time away from home, time spent alone writing, and time and energy devoted to the many visitors and friends from around the world who have been entertained at home. All have been critical to our development. Our spouses, Anne, Lynne, and Brian, have been more than patient; they have contributed significantly to our understanding and commitment, as have all our children. We thank them all for their love and assistance. Notwithstanding this lengthy list of personal acknowledgments, we close with the usual caveat that we alone remain responsible for the contents of this book.

H. W. Lane
Boston, MA

J. J. DiStefano
Lausanne, Switzerland

M. L. Maznevski
Lausanne, Switzerland

January 2005

The authors and publisher gratefully acknowledge the permission granted to reproduce the copyright material in this book:

Beamish, Paul W., Alan Morrison, Andrew Inkpen, and Phillip Rosenweig, "The design and management of international joint ventures," chapter 7 from *International Management*, 5th edition (Irwin McGraw Hill, 2003). Reproduced with permission of the McGraw-Hill Companies.

Black, J. Stewart, and Hal B. Gregersen, "Serving two masters: Managing the dual allegiance of expatriate employees," *Sloan Management Review*, (Summer 1992): 61–71. Reprinted by permission of the publisher. Copyright © 1992 by Sloan Management Review Association. All rights reserved.

Blake, R. William, "Footwear International." Reproduced with the permission of the author. © R. William Blake, Faculty of Business Administration, Memorial University of Newfoundland, St John's, Newfoundland, Canada.

Caligiuri, Paula, and Wayne F. Cascio, "Can we send her there? Maximizing the success of Western women on global assignments," *Journal of World Business*, 33(4) (Winter 1998): 394–419. Reprinted by permission of Elsevier.

Carroll, Archie B., "In search of the moral manager," *Business Horizons* (March/April 1987): 7–15. Reprinted by permission of Elsevier.

Doh, Jonathan P., Peter Rodriguez, Klaus Uhlenbruck, Jamie Collins, and Lorraine Eden, "Coping with corruption in foreign markets," *Academy of Management Executive*, 17(3) (August 2003): 114–27. Reprinted by permission of *Academy of Management Executive*.

Galbraith, Jay, "Building organizations around the global customer." Reprint Number 9B01TE02, *Ivey Business Journal*, September/October 2001, 66(1). Ivey Management Services prohibits any form of reproduction, storage, or transmittal of this material without its written permission. This material is not covered under authorization from any reproduction rights organization. Copyright © 2001 Ivey Management Services. One time permission to reproduce granted by Ivey Management Services on July 23, 2004.

Hofstede, Geert, "Cultural constraints in management theories," *Academy of Management Executive*, 7(1) (1993): 81–94. Reprinted by permission of *Academy of Management Executive*.

Hofstede, Geert, table (the 40 countries) and figures 5, 6, and 7 from "Motivation, leadership and organization: Do American theories apply abroad?," *Organizational Dynamics* (Summer 1980): 42–63. Reprinted by permission of Geert Hofstede.

Hofstede, Geert, and M. H. Bond, Exhibit 2 from "The Confucius connection: From cultural roots to economic growth," *Organizational Dynamics*, 16(4): 4–21. Reprinted by permission of Geert Hofstede.

International Institute for Management Development (IMD) for "Johannes van den Bosch Sends an Email," "Vodafone: Building a Global Organization," "Schneider Electric Global Account Management," "Facing a Crisis: Lars Kruse Thomsen Starts His New Job (A)," and "Dealing with Crisis: Lars Kruse Thomsen Moves to Solve Problems (B)." All rights reserved. Not to be used or reproduced without written permission directly from IMD, Lausanne, Switzerland.

Ivey Management Services for "David Shorter," "Bob Chen," "Japanese American Seating Inc. (A)," "Footwear International," "Hazelton International," "An International Project Manager's Day (A)," "Monsanto Europe (A)," "Five Star Beer – Pay for Performance," "Moscow Aerostar," "Ellen Moore (A): Living and Working in Korea," "The Leo Burnett Company Ltd.: Virtual Team Management," "Global Multi-Products Chile," "Marconi Telecommunications Mexico," "Blue Ridge Spain," "NES China: Business Ethics (A)," "Yahoo v. Survivors of the Holocaust," "Valley Farms International (A)," "Enron – What Went Wrong?" and "Building Products International – A Crisis Management Strategy (A)." One time permission to reproduce granted by Ivey Management Services on May 28, 2004.

Lane, Henry W., and Donald G. Simpson, "Bribery in international business: Whose problem is it?," *Journal of Business Ethics*, 3(1) (1984): 35–42. With kind permission of Kluwer Academic Publishers.

Osland, Joyce S., and Allan Bird, "Beyond sophisticated stereotyping: Cultural sensemaking in context," *Academy of Management Executive*, 14(1) (February 2000): 65–79. Reprinted by permission of *Academy of Management Executive*.

Sanchez, Juan I., Paul E. Spector, and Cary L. Cooper, "Adapting to a boundaryless world: A developmental expatriate model," *Academy of Management Executive*, 14(2) (May 2000): 96–106. Reprinted by permission of *Academy of Management Executive*.

Treviño, Linda Klebe, Laura Pincus Hartman, and Michael Brown, "Moral person and moral manager: How executives develop a reputation for ethical leadership," from *California Management Review*, 42(4). Copyright © 2000, by The Regents of the University of California. Reprinted from the *California Management Review* by permission of The Regents.

Every effort has been made to trace copyright holders and to obtain their permission for the use of copyright material. The publisher apologizes for any errors or omissions in the above list and would be grateful if notified of any corrections that should be incorporated in future reprints or editions of this book.

Global Mindset and Culture

people

The real voyage of discovery consists not in seeking new landscapes, but in having new eyes.
– Marcel Proust

This book is not just a book about global business. It is about *people who conduct business globally*. It illustrates and explores typical situations that managers encounter: the problems and opportunities, the joys and frustrations, the successes and failures, and the decisions they must make. The case studies in this book describe situations that anybody could confront while pursuing an international business career. You don't have to wait until you are the chief executive officer or president of a company to experience these situations.

We focus on the implementation of management decisions and the resulting operating issues and problems – and not just on theory. Our aim is to help you develop an understanding of the practice – the doing – of global business and management. There's a difference between studying a subject from a theoretical perspective and studying it in an applied way. In the first instance, you are able to talk about the subject. In the second instance, you are able to do it. Someone may be extremely knowledgeable about art, music, or drama – a real student of these activities. However, this doesn't mean that he or she is a good artist, musician, or actress. In the same way, knowing and talking about global management are not the same as managing globally. Being a good manager requires knowledge of theory and concepts, but it also requires skills and practice. This book provides both knowledge and opportunities for practice to develop important global management skills.

International business is not impersonal, so international business should not be studied solely in an impersonal way. It is useful to understand trade theories; to know how to hedge the future value of currencies in which a corporation is dealing; to be able to weigh the pros and cons of exporting versus licensing; and to understand the advantages of a joint venture versus a wholly owned subsidiary. Although such knowledge is important, it is not enough. Eventually, the conceptualizing, the strategizing, and debating of alternatives must give way to action. A manager must leave his headquarters to implement a project, sell a product, or negotiate an alliance – in other words, to interact with colleagues, customers, and suppliers from other places, to try to get other people to do things, and to experience what it really means to do business globally. In this book we focus on the interactions, on getting things done with and through other people in a global context.

In this part of the text, we introduce the global mindset and show how important it is to effective management. We then describe the cultural perspective and its place in international management behavior. Next, we outline and discuss four types of expertise required by global managers, and show how this book aims to help you develop that expertise. We then describe in more detail some important aspects of the book, including the purpose of the three parts of text, readings, and cases, and we provide some notes on cases in general. We close with some personal observations on the joys and value of developing global management expertise.

A GLOBAL MINDSET[1]

As the global economy continues to develop, managers must learn how to function as effectively in other countries as they do in their own and to build bridges across the world by leveraging both similarities and differences. In the broadest terms, this means reorganizing the way one thinks as a manager and as a student of management. As one executive put it, "to think globally really requires an alteration of our mindset."[2] Thinking globally means extending concepts and models from one-to-one relationships (we to them) to holding multiple realities and relationships in mind simultaneously, and then acting skillfully on this more complex reality.

Managers need to develop a *global mindset*. A global mindset enables a person to adapt to the changing needs of global business. It is not simply a set of facts, which is useful in the present but perhaps not in the long-term future. It is a set of attitudes and skills for developing and acting on knowledge in a dynamic world. The heart of the global mindset is the ability to see and understand the world differently than one has been conditioned to see and understand it, and yet still to make sense of the world to act appropriately. With a global mindset, a manager can function successfully in new and unknown situations and integrate this new understanding with other existing skills and knowledge bases. Our definition of a global mindset is

> The ability to develop and interpret criteria for personal and business performance that are independent from the assumptions of a single country, culture, or context; and to implement those criteria appropriately in different countries, cultures, and contexts.

For example, we know a company that was implementing self-managed teams throughout the organization for its new modular-based production facilities. In this more dynamic and interdependent environment, the company believed it was important to have decision-making authority with the people who had the most immediate information to make the decisions, and who had to implement the decisions. The company developed a model of how self-managed teams should work, piloted it in their home country, then rolled out the new structure around the world. However, they met resistance in many sites. In many parts of the world, the idea of teams managing themselves, without a specific boss to lead them, is completely unheard of. Some plant managers pushed through the self-managed teams program to greater and greater dissatisfaction; others gave up and just kept the more rigid and hierarchical teams.

Some managers, however, did something rather different. They looked at the two most important criteria for identifying who should make a decision in this new manufacturing context: the people who have the information, and the people who have to implement it. They also realized that manufacturing would not achieve its potential unless there was more interdependence among the various parts of the process. Then they questioned whether the only way to accomplish this was the self-managed team model that headquarters dictated. They met with their managers and teams, and developed a way to achieve the required working relationships and decision processes that fit with the local teams' preferences and context. In some cases this had more hierarchy, in others it had fewer specific roles and more fluidity, and in others it had more individual responsibility. In all cases, it achieved the performance goals.

These last managers were working with a global mindset. They were able to separate performance criteria, such as "people with the information make the decisions," from contextual preferences, such as "self-managed teams." Then they found a way to achieve the performance criteria in different contexts.

Four components of a global mindset

A global mindset is a framework about global business that enables a person to pay attention, interpret, and behave effectively. It has four main components, as shown in Figure 1. To be effective globally, a manager must develop knowledge in each of the quadrants, and act on that knowledge.

The crux of developing a global mindset is achieving *self-awareness* and *other-awareness* and, more specifically, the relationship between context – institutions, cultures, professions, and so on – and characteristics of the self and others. Second, it is important for managers to see themselves and others both as individuals and as members of collaborative units, and to develop insights about individual and social behavior and perspectives.

FIGURE 1   Components of a Global Mindset

	Individual	Organizational
Self	**Quadrant 1 Myself** Understand myself and how who I am is associated with the context I am in	**Quadrant 3 Own Organizations** Understand my own organizations and how their characteristics and effectiveness are associated with the context we are in
Other	**Quadrant 2 Others** Understand how characteristics of people from other countries, cultures, and contexts are associated with the context they are in	**Quadrant 4 Other Organizations** Understand how characteristics and effectiveness of organizations from other countries, cultures, and contexts are associated with the context they are in

A global mindset continually adapts universals of business to contextual contingencies. Since doing business globally is filled with uncertainty, amplified by numerous differences from country to country, abilities to tolerate ambiguity and to learn from new situations are critical to the global mindset.

The text, readings, and cases in this book have been written and selected to help you develop knowledge in each of the quadrants, and to practice applying it to specific business situations. As you go through the material, focus both on building awareness of yourself in your own context, as well as learning about others in their contexts. Question your assumptions and those of others, and test the application of your knowledge in different contexts. These actions will help you build a global mindset.

THE CULTURAL PERSPECTIVE

One of our basic premises is that there is a link between successful global business and cultural awareness and sensitivity. Why do we make this the central core of the book? There are many people who argue that this perspective is misleading. They assert that cultures around the world are converging, that business is business everywhere, and that people are basically the same all over. Of course, there is some truth to each of these statements. People around the world wear jeans and European designer fashions, eat at McDonald's, talk on Nokia phones, and listen to Sony Walkmen. Currencies are traded globally every moment, and there are global infrastructures for conducting business. Everyone has the same basic physiological and psychological needs.

However, as we argued above, developing a global mindset requires an understanding of the relationship between people and their contexts. And one of the most important elements of the context – especially for understanding people and their behavior – is culture. The meaning of behaviors and how business is conducted differ dramatically from one culture to another. These differences may not be important on the surface or in a quick interaction, but they deeply affect commitments, relationships, cooperative decision-making, and other critical elements of social interaction. Take the McDonald's example. Not only does McDonald's change its menu in different parts of the world – serving beer in Germany, a McLobster sandwich on Canada's east coast, and tropical shakes in Hong Kong – but the meaning of eating at McDonald's changes from one culture to another. As a Malaysian student said to her American peers:

> In Kuala Lumpur, we don't eat at McDonald's for convenience like people in the United States do. And we rarely take the food out to eat. We eat at McDonald's when we feel like having a hamburger, the same way you might eat at a Chinese restaurant when you feel like you want Chinese food. To say that we're becoming Westernized because McDonald's does well there is like saying the United States is becoming Easternized because there are a lot of Chinese restaurants.

We will define culture more specifically in the next part of the book, but for now let us say that culture is an implicit agreement among a group of people concerning what people's actions mean. Most cultures agree on some basic principles, but there is much variation in the details. The agreement on basic principles makes it appear as if cultures are converging. It allows mergers and acquisitions to be negotiated, money and goods to be traded, and employees to stay briefly in overseas countries without too much trouble. It allows us to work together, at least on the surface. However, the differences become apparent when people have to interact more intensively with each other on a day-to-day basis. This is when the synergy anticipated from the mergers and acquisitions is more elusive than anticipated,[3] when the goods traded for the money don't arrive on time or are not in the condition expected, or when the stay in the overseas country is prolonged.

Not surprisingly, research shows clearly that culture influences the practice of management. Many management concepts, techniques, and systems developed and taught in business schools are based on cultural beliefs, values, and assumptions about how managers should behave, and they work well in the countries in which they were developed. However, these concepts, techniques, and systems may not work as intended in other cultures. If they are transferred to another country and used improperly, they can compound managers' problems. For example, management by objectives (MBO), a standard North American management tool, is based on an assumption that subordinates will share their objectives with their superior. This is an unrealistic assumption in many cultures that have strong status differentials and that maintain hierarchies. A recent study showed that in Spain, subordinates strongly prefer that their bosses supervise their work directly, and feel very uncomfortable making their own decisions or telling the boss what the decision should be.[4] Another comparative study of preferences for different performance appraisal practices showed that Taiwanese respondents preferred to focus more on group performance than individual performance and also preferred less direct and open relations between supervisors and subordinates than did North American respondents.[5] MBO probably would have to be implemented very differently in these countries than in the United States, where it was "invented."

Cultural differences, if not understood, can also pose significant barriers to the implementation and success of a business venture. For example, there tends to be less emphasis on personal relationships between suppliers and customers in the United States, Canada, and parts of northern Europe, where business is usually the primary focus and a personal relationship might develop from the business relationship. In most of the rest of the world, however, people want to establish the personal relationship first, and from that relationship business may develop. Even in the initial negotiations, customers in many countries are at least as interested in personal relationships with the company's after-sales-service providers as they are in the product itself. These customers want a product and a supplier they trust, and believe it will come only from people they trust. An executive once told us that this advice only means "paying attention to the customer's needs and wants is just good business." Most certainly! Understanding your customers and their culture is simply good business practice. However, in our own culture, either intuitively or through experience, we tend to know what a customer in our culture needs or wants. The point is, in international business more time must be spent to find out what the customer in his or her own environment wants or needs.

Good business practice, coupled with good intercultural skills, is an unbeatable combination. This is the global mindset. It would be nice if good business practice automatically included good intercultural skills. Unfortunately, this is not always the case, and therefore both need to be stressed. In this book, we combine knowledge and concepts from the areas of cultural studies and international business so you can improve your global management skills.

THE EXPERTISE OF A GLOBAL MANAGER

In this book, we use the terms "international" and "global" interchangeably. It is important, however, to understand the difference that has evolved in their meanings. An international perspective tends to describe interactions between two countries – the home country and one other – or rather straightforward interaction among more countries but in which each country is treated completely separately. Until recently, this has been an adequate model for much of the world's international business activity. However, globalization has come to mean transforming our international perspective to a global perspective, one that does not see national borders as being contiguous with business borders. For example, an international company will have mostly autonomous units in each country or region, but a global company may split the activities of a single product's value chain across several countries and treat the globe as one unit for that product. Daimler Chrysler sources parts for its Mercedes cars from the United States, western Europe, eastern Europe, and Asia. These are partially assembled into components in different countries, and final assembly takes place in German plants (among others).

In spite of our tendency to use both terms, our philosophy is emphatically global because the most effective managers, whatever their company's approach, manage as if the company were global. They make strategic decisions, taking into account what is best for the business and for the customer, wherever that customer is, and they implement ideas in the ways that are best for the people carrying out the decisions. They select the best people to do the jobs, whoever they are and wherever they're from, and they manage those people in a manner consistent with their values and culture. Not every executive needs to have a global mindset, but the senior executives of a global company like Nestlé have to be internationally minded and skilled, while also comfortable with their nations of origin.

But increasingly the globalization of business requires more of a global mindset from more managers, even those without formal global responsibility. The shift means that even if a manager has a regional responsibility for marketing for Central and South America, she or he will not only have to understand Latin cultures and speak Spanish and Portuguese, but also may have to deal with research and development (R&D) labs in Japan, Europe, and North America to provide customer information and to get updates on emerging new products. The same manager may have to discuss product problems with manufacturers in Southeast Asia late at night, South American time, and then send a fax about the potential solution to an alternative supplier in eastern Europe.[6]

In addition to a global mindset with a cultural perspective, the global manager must act differently, must organize the complexity of the management task in a new way.[7] Since it is impossible to know and control all aspects of the job, the manager's role must become much more one of facilitating processes, ideas, and behaviors of others. To do this, a global manager needs four types of expertise: *strategic, adaptive, interpersonal,* and *cross-cultural.*[8] Each type of expertise incorporates a high level of both knowledge and skills. The four types are closely related to each other, but it is useful to focus on each separately for a clearer understanding of their roles in effective global management.

Global
Perspective
sees
borders
differently

why you
need this →

Global strategic expertise

A global manager must be both highly knowledgeable about global business, and able to integrate new knowledge into a "big-picture" view of the company, its industry, and its environment. The new global economy is shaped and driven by flows of money, goods, services, and people around the world. Often it is characterized by volatile foreign exchange, changing government policies, resistance to standardized products, and new economies of scale.

Managers who understand these flows and what causes them to change will be better equipped to respond to the changes, predict them, and even influence them. A working knowledge of international relationships and foreign affairs, including global financial markets and exchange-rate movements, is critical. Managers who have strong knowledge of and experience with a broad range of strategic responses will be able to implement strategy more effectively. Major players in the new global environment will have a fast-response capability and be entrepreneurial and flexible. They will also embrace global responsibilities to take advantage of manufacturing rationalization, mass customization of products, and low-cost, global sourcing. Managers with this global perspective will need to strike a balance between national responsiveness and exploitation of global economies of scale. This is the vaunted ability to "think globally, but act locally."

Global success, therefore, is contingent on striking a balance between capitalizing on resources and needs within national boundaries and the ability to capture a vision of a world without boundaries. One aspect of managing this balance often includes moving decision-making authority as close to the customer as possible to ensure that local requirements are satisfied. Thus the global manager's job, as mentioned earlier, becomes one of facilitating the work of local managers within the context of the overall strategy. But even local managers will perform better if they understand the global strategy, enacting it within the context of their local environment.

Although the purpose of this book is not to focus on building global strategic expertise (other books do that well), the other three types of expertise – which *are* the focus of the book – are best developed within the context and understanding of global strategy. The decision-making situations provided in the cases in this book, as well as examples throughout the text, are intended to help you develop this global strategic context.

Adaptive expertise

Global managers need to be able to create adaptation, change, and flexibility in themselves and in their organization.

Adaptive and flexible as individuals   They will be sailing in a sea of change that they must somehow navigate, and the ability to adapt oneself is a fundamental prerequisite. Managers who are globally competent are deeply curious about the world and other people, and they are effective learners. They have broad interests, are open to a variety of experiences, and are willing to experiment and to take risks. Their enthusiasm is

Renessance Man

contagious, and they share their knowledge and learning with others effectively through-out the organization.

A few years ago, a visiting scholar from the People's Republic of China typified these characteristics for us. She soon knew more people than several other scholars who had been at our school for many months. Although her specialty was finance, she audited classes from all disciplines. She interviewed the old-timers, secretaries, researchers, students, and seasoned teachers. Nor were her interactions confined to work. She learned our humor, visited churches, traveled across the country by air, bus, train, and boat, went to country fairs, and even insisted on trying golf! By the end of her year, she understood the institution better than most faculty members who had been there for several years; she understood the country almost as well as any native. Then, she transferred her knowledge to her colleagues in China and overseas through an extraordinary report[9] and a series of lectures and seminars. Then she leveraged her knowledge and skill into a thriving consulting business. Subsequently she earned her PhD doing research on distance learning, and then joined the World Bank, where her expertise and broadened global mindset are highly valued.

One of the most unexpected personal experiences of global managers is the difficulty of adapting to different cultural environments. Although the figures have decreased somewhat over the last ten years, still fully 25 percent of expatriates return to their home country earlier than anticipated, and the single most frequent reason for early return is failure to adapt to the other culture, on the part of either the expatriate manager or the manager's family.[10]

Often, when thinking about international business, places like London, Paris, Frankfurt, Geneva, Sydney, Singapore, Hong Kong, Tokyo, New York, and Vancouver come to mind. But business does not always take place in these cities, and living and working in another country is not always glamorous. Nor is business only conducted in industrialized countries. Corporations pursue business opportunities in remote places and under difficult conditions. Some countries in which large corporations operate and earn substantial revenue have difficult economic, political, and living conditions. Global managers often have to travel to these places, in spite of the increasing use of communications technology, and they and their families often live in these locations. Personal learning, adaptation, and flexibility are critical to developing and sustaining an effective career in global management.

Manage organizations to be adaptive and flexible   An individual manager alone cannot be expected to develop and use all the diverse skills required for successful global management. The organization itself, then, must assist global managers as much as possible, and global managers must design and operate the very organizations that will help them to be more effective. These new organizations are characterized by flexibility and multidimensionality. Networks, alliances, outsourcing, virtual departments are all currently implemented in global organizations with varying degrees of frequency and effectiveness. Managers are creating borderless organizations where the ability to learn, to be responsive, and to be efficient is well established within the firm's administrative heritage. We will describe these new organizations in more detail in Part 2. For now, the point is that these new structures are operated best by a cadre of managers with strong personal adaptive expertise.

Not only must global managers build the organizations to be flexible and adaptable, but they must also manage them in a dynamic way, constantly changing to respond to and influence the movements in the industry. The shortening of product life cycles, driven by technological change in the products and how they are manufactured and delivered, contributes to the acceleration of change. Managing change in an unstable environment is a constant challenge. Forever fine-tuning the balance between global and local pressures under changing competitive conditions, global managers must frequently reorganize resources, human networks, technology, and marketing and distribution systems.

As difficult as these constant changes are to manage, the overall transition to global operations represents a formidable challenge in itself. Existing international operations, often marked by standardization of products and uniformity of procedures, may be a barrier to effective globalization. There are many mechanisms for making the transition. For example, flexible factories, which can produce "mass-customized" products, are a potential response to the "think globally–act locally" axiom. However, they may be difficult to invest in and effectively operate if the company has a long history of mass-producing standard products. Another method of making the transition to global operations is through the formation of a strategic alliance or network to reduce the high cost of R&D or to enter a new market, for example. Most firms find that forming these alliances is much easier than running them, however. These and all other organizational responses to globalization require built-in flexibility and effective management of change and transition.

For a successful transition to global operations, it is also important that managers in different countries share a common view of the strategy and are all committed to it. If poorly implemented, the move to globalization can pit headquarters managers against country or field managers. If global strategy is perceived as a move toward the centralization of responsibility, a local manager's role may become less strategic. Autonomous units in a firm often try to protect their own turf, and subsidiary managers who joined a company because of its commitment to preserving local autonomy and adapting products to local environments may become disenchanted or even leave the organization. So effective global managers need the skills to manage the transition from independence or dependence to interdependence, from control to coordination and cooperation, and from symmetry to differentiation.

Learning, too, can be done at an organizational level. In fact, the best global companies distinguish themselves by systematizing learning systems and opportunities for the company as a whole to develop and leverage knowledge and experience. Operating managers are encouraged to look for opportunities in one country that can be transferred elsewhere. These opportunities or experiments usually are the responsibility of national managers, while their transfer is the responsibility of corporate management. The use of cross-national task forces for problems of corporate concern, such as significant expense-reduction, is another way global companies try to learn and to take advantage of their global experience.

The ability of people and organizations to learn, to adapt, and to manage change will only increase in importance as markets continue to globalize. In this book, the skills addressed will help you develop adaptive expertise both for yourself and for the organization. The cases present situations that require adaptability and flexibility, and provide opportunities to explore and practice this important skill-building.

This Class!

Cross-cultural expertise

3.

Global managers must recognize that culture influences themselves, as well as others, and they must be able not only to overcome the barriers raised by those differences but to leverage them for higher performance. That means having strong knowledge about their own and other cultures, and also using this knowledge constructively when interacting with others, designing organizational systems, and making and implementing strategic decisions.

Cross-cultural incidents: costs and opportunities

Some famous examples of a lack of cross-cultural understanding and adaptation in marketing and product development demonstrate the obvious need for a basic level of cross-cultural expertise. For example, Procter & Gamble's (P&G's) liquid detergent failed in Europe when it was introduced in the early 1980s because European washing machines were not equipped for liquid detergent. Modifications to the detergent were made, and sales subsequently improved. Moreover, additional features that were introduced specifically for the European market, such as low-sudsing action, were incorporated into the global product and launched successfully elsewhere. In another product area, P&G introduced Pampers in Japan and was delighted with the initial success. But the P&G marketing managers did not know that Japanese do their laundry daily and were using Pampers only at night. Mooney, a Japanese company, introduced a disposable diaper with reusable parts, which appealed greatly to the savings-conscious Japanese. P&G's market share for disposable diapers dropped from 90 percent to 10 percent almost overnight. P&G regained share by retaliating with a smaller, thinner diaper. Then, as it did with the liquid detergent, using a global-learning approach, P&G brought that diaper to other markets.

These are very smart & skilled companies

Even Wal-Mart is not immune from these problems. It had difficulty in Argentina when it tried to transfer its winning business formula away from home. The *New York Times* noted:

> So with typical Yankee can-do confidence – some would call arrogance – Wal-Mart entered the Argentine market with a team of American managers and the same basic store model that worked from Des Moines to Dallas.[11]

The miscalculations included the merchandise mix (e.g., 110-volt appliances for a country that uses 220 volts), to the customer traffic and the physical widths of store aisles.

In the food industry, as mentioned earlier, McDonald's has adapted and has different menus in different countries. Recently the company has improved its flagging sales with a health-oriented product line, reflecting adaptation to cultural change.

we are literally more isolated

The recognition of cultural differences in global management does not necessarily come easily to North American managers, who often have less exposure to multicultural realities in their workplace than, for instance, their European or Asian counterparts. Having sensitivity to cultural differences, however, doesn't automatically mean that executives can avoid problems. The head of human resources (HR) at a Netherlands-based global bank recently led an effort to improve their performance-management system worldwide.[12] He wanted to standardize as much as possible to reflect corporate values and priorities consistently around the world; but being aware of the need to reflect local differences, he circulated a request for ideas to his HR colleagues and line managers in the country organizations. The suggestions from the Dutch managers put strong emphasis on measuring activities that supported high performance, such as the number of innovative proposals put forward by the corporate bankers, the number of presentations made to new clients, and so forth. The US managers said that the level of goals *set and achieved* should be the focus of performance measurement. When he suggested to each group that the ideas of the other had merit and that combining their approaches would be useful, both groups strongly objected! In Part 1, we will show that each set of ideas was rooted in their cultural preferences: for the Dutch, analytic thinking and understanding the complex causes of performance; for the Americans, doing, taking action, and mastering events. So having a map of cultural differences can help anticipate misunderstandings and deal better with those that occur. A core part of Part 1 of this book describes a Mapping, Bridging, and Integrating model designed to do exactly that.

In reporting on Siemens, the *Wall Street Journal* said that its "fast growing operation was putting pressure on rigid German structure." It was just one of a "parade of big German companies that have struggled to adapt a centralized, deliberate German corporate structure to a more flexible and faster-moving business environment in the US."[13]

Language training, cross-cultural and expatriate experiences early in careers, membership on international task forces, and global content in all management training programs are among the ways to counter the ethnocentricity of domestic managers, regardless of their country of origin.

One country can be multicultural Learning to manage global cultural diversity effectively can start with the recognition of cultural diversity at home. As a result of global movement of people through both voluntary (e.g., immigration) and involuntary (e.g., refugees) modes, most countries now have a vastly more diverse domestic labor market than they did only a decade ago. Toronto in Canada, for example, is one of the most ethnically diverse cities in the world – home to almost all the world's culture groups, where over 100 languages are spoken. The 2001 census showed that almost 40 percent of the city's population are from visible minorities.

Many large offices in Toronto employ people from dozens of countries. A typical team we worked with at a Toronto bank had 16 members who had been born in 14 countries across Asia, Africa, Latin America, and Europe. Only two members had been born in Canada. Other large cities around the world may not yet reflect this extreme multiculturalism, but they are still experiencing a shift in demographics to incorporate more cultural diversity. In France, Germany, and Italy the influx of significant numbers of Muslim immigrants has meant a challenge to the dominant values among the host societies. The degree to which adaptations are made by both the "newcomers" and the "locals" varies both within and across these societies, causing new changes to both communities. So the opportunities to gain insight and experience in managing cultural diversity are local as well as global; the need for skillful managing of this diversity is evident in the daily news.

As we discussed earlier, the cultural perspective is key to understanding global management, and cross-cultural expertise must be incorporated into the other three types of global management expertise. The text, readings, and cases in this book provide knowledge and opportunities for practice of this critical skill.

Interpersonal expertise

Because global management has become, more than ever, an exercise in cooperative decision-making and action as well as the facilitation of others' ideas and actions, interpersonal expertise continues to increase in importance. The two main types of interpersonal expertise we will discuss here are communication and teamwork, but they incorporate other interpersonal skills such as negotiation, conflict resolution, and leadership.

Communicate for two-way understanding   Communicating effectively means getting your message across the way you want to, and understanding others the way they want you to. Even in domestic organizations, communication is a critical skill, and most interpersonal problems can be attributed at least in part to miscommunication. In a global organization, effective communication is both more important and more difficult. It is more important, because the cost of miscommunication is extremely high. In a now infamous example, Chevrolet tried to introduce a new automobile, the Nova model, in Latin America without realizing that "no va" in Spanish means "it doesn't go." A little research and communication effectiveness would have prevented this miscue.

Even successful companies have to be continually alert to avoid problems related to communication effectiveness, as the following example makes clear. In 1997, Nike, Inc. apologized to the Islamic community and recalled more than 38,000 pairs of athletic shoes with a logo that Muslims claimed resembled the Arabic word for *Allah*, or God.[14] Nike was not the first shoe company to have this problem, and it could have been prevented through more effective research into what it takes to communicate effectively in a global marketplace.

In addition to the skills necessary for effective interpersonal communication and advertising, managers need to take advantage of the increasingly global communications technology and systems. New modes of communicating through technology reduce the need for travel, but create their own challenges. Communications through technological media are much less rich than a face-to-face interaction, and miscommunication is much easier.

People from different cultures prefer different media, and prefer using them in different ways. A multi-site global R&D team we worked with finally met face-to-face for the first time after working for more than a year and a half together. One of the first items on their agenda was agreeing on a protocol for the use of email. The different usages associated with the different cultures had resulted in a large number of miscommunications over the previous year, many associated with negative outcomes. But they felt they had to build personal relationships before talking about how to communicate electronically.

Besides the direct positive effects of good communication skills among colleagues and with customers, this latter example highlights another advantage of effective communication. Sensitive communication builds trust and strong relationships over time and these relationships help reinforce commitment in the company's direction and decisions. Moreover, strong relations reduce many of the negative effects of cultural mistakes. A mistake made with a friend is more easily forgiven and overcome than one with a stranger. In the R&D team referred to above, the time spent talking together in person made electronic communication easier, but also generally facilitated virtual decision-making as team members began to trust each others' motives.

Teamwork is everywhere   In addition to good communication skills, global managers also require effective team skills. Even before the advent of global companies, effective teamwork was becoming essential for managerial success. As the specialization of people and differentiation in organizations increased (often driven by technological improvements, fragmentation of markets, explosions in product variations, and so on), there was a concomitant increased need for integration: for putting the specialized units back together in the service of the organization's objectives. Teams, committees, and task forces were among the devices used to accomplish the desired integration.

With the increased complexity of global operations, the ability to function in work teams – especially in culturally diverse groups – is even more important. A Conference Board report on the experiences of 30 major multinational corporations (MNCs) in building teams to further their global interests showed the following: teams used solely for communication or providing advice and counsel still exist, but more and more firms are also using teams in different and more participative and powerful ways. Global teamwork can do more than provide improved market and technological intelligence. It can yield more flexible business planning, stronger commitment to achieving worldwide goals, and closer collaboration in carrying out strategic change.[15] Teams that span internal organizational boundaries or the company's external boundary (joint-venture partners, suppliers, customers) are often required.

Interestingly, the need for transnational teamwork shows up in different ways in different functions. Consider, for example, the different assumptions about the nature and purpose of accounting and auditing in various parts of the world. In one country, financial statements are meant to reflect fundamental economic reality and the audit function is to ensure that this is so. In another country, the audit is to check the accuracy of the financial statements vis-à-vis the economic records. In yet another country, it is to make sure legal requirements have been met.[16] Imagine, then, the need for cross-cultural understanding and sensitivity in auditing an international subsidiary, or the teamwork needed to develop international audit standards,[17] or the resentment generated by unilateral imposition of requirements such as Sarbanes-Oxley.[18]

Other functions pick up the teamwork theme differently. In production, teams need to develop system-sensitive outlooks and processes and personal relationships across subsidiaries. HR managers must develop capabilities for leading multinational teams in flexible and responsible ways. Global marketing managers need the ability to take advantage of a local execution strategy, where "not invented here" becomes "now improved here." Using this strategy, a core international team gathers ideas and passes them to local levels where the final marketing decisions are made and implemented.

In R&D, culturally diverse teams have been a reality for a long time. For example, in one American subsidiary of the French-based manufacturer of electrical distribution systems, Schneider Electric, a research team is composed of two Americans, two Mexicans, a Pole, a Russian, a Frenchman, a Chinese, an Iranian, and an Indian; another consists of two Americans, a Belgian, a Thai, a Filipino, a Chinese, and a Mexican. The first team is headed by the Belgian and the second by the Polish scientist. The manager to whom they report is an American who is working closely with the team leaders to understand the cultural complexity in their daily lives.

Virtual Teams →

The advent of better and cheaper global communications technology means global teams can operate even when the members are not physically in one place. In early 1995, Ford reorganized its product development into five "vehicle platform centers" charged with designing automobiles for both North America and Europe. Using computer technology and satellite communications, a designer in Cologne can alter a fender shape formulated by a colleague in Dearborn and get an immediate response to his revision via an audio and video hookup.[19] Since the advent of these organizational changes, rapid advances in technological support for synchronous communication among members of global teams has facilitated their operations. But issues of cross-cultural and interpersonal skills remain.

The ability to communicate effectively and work with other people in teams is so critical to the successful implementation of a global strategy that participation in global teams should occur early in the careers of managers to transform these people into potential global leaders.[20] In fact, we believe interpersonal skills represent such a cornerstone for the rest of the global manager's skills that we begin Part 1 by focusing on these skills, and build on this foundation throughout the rest of the book.

SUMMARY

This review might lead you to conclude that an effective global manager is superhuman. But the prospect of acquiring strategic, adaptive, cross-cultural, and interpersonal skills can be seen as an exciting challenge rather than an impossible task. Developing these skills is a lifelong journey, and it is unlikely that a single executive will master all of them. Effective teams and organizational design will support both skill development and also global management itself.

Notes

1 This section is based on Martha Maznevski and Henry Lane, "Shaping the Global Mindset: Designing Educational Experiences for Effective Global Thinking and Action," in N. Boyacigiller, R. Goodman, and M. Phillips (eds.), *Crossing Cultures: Insights from Master Teachers* (London: Routledge, 2003): 343–71.

2 Bernard Daniel, Secretary-General, Nestlé, Vevey, Switzerland, personal communication.

3 See Mark Mendenhall and Guenter Stahl (eds.), *Culture and Human Resources in Mergers and Acquisitions* (Stanford: Stanford University Press, 2005).

4 Lena Zander, "The License to Lead," PhD dissertation, International Institute of Business, Stockholm School of Economics, 1997: 175.

5 G. M. McEvoy and W. F. Cascio, "The United States and Taiwan: Two Different Cultures Look at Performance Appraisal," *Research in Personnel and Human Resources Management*, Supplement 2 (1990): 201–19.

6   As two of the authors were revising this section, they were sitting in a Global Innovation Centre for a major food multinational. In the next office was a videoconference coordinated among managers on five continents planning details of a new product launch. The new product had a global brand image, but local adaptation depending on the tastes of different markets. These managers considered what they were doing to be "normal business practice."

7   H. W. Lane, M. L. Maznevski, M. Mendenhall, and J. McNett (eds.), *Blackwell Handbook of Global Management: A Guide to Managing Complexity* (Oxford: Blackwell, 2004).

8   The following section was based heavily on research conducted by Brenda McMillan, Joseph J. DiStefano, and James C. Rush, published in "Requisite Skills for Global Managers," Working Paper, National Centre for Management Research and Development, Ivey Business School, University of Western Ontario, London, Canada.

9   Jiping Zhang, "The Building and Operation of a North American Business School" (in Chinese; Beijing: Tsinghua University Press, 1990; early English version published in 1987 by the Ivey Business School, University of Western Ontario, London, Canada).

10 "Don't Be an Ugly-American Manager", *Fortune*, October 16, 1995: 225.

11 Clifford Krauss, "Selling to Argentina" (as translated from the French), *New York Times*, December 5, 1999, Section 3: 7.

12 This example was provided to two of the authors by the bank HR executive during a research Discovery Event at IMD, May 4, 2004.

13 Matthew Karnitschnig, "For Siemens, Move Into U.S. Causes Waves Back Home," The Wall Street Journal Online, September 8, 2003.

14 http://isgkc.org/nike_pix.htm

15 Ruth G. Shaeffer, "Building Global Teamwork for Growth and Survival," *Conference Board Research Bulletin*: 228.

16 Leslie G. Campbell, *International Auditing* (New York: St Martin's Press, 1985): 141.

17 William S. Albrecht, Hugh L. Marsh, Jr., and Frederick H. Bentzel, Jr., "Auditing an International Subsidiary," *Internal Auditor* 45(5) (1988): 22–6; Joseph Soeters and Hein Schreuder, "The Interaction Between National and Organizational Cultures in Accounting Firms," *Accounting, Organizations and Society* 13(1) (1988): 75–85; and Nicholas M. Zacchea, "The Multinational Auditor: Overcoming Cultural Differences to Apply Audit Standards," *Internal Auditor* 45(5) (1988): 16–21.

18 The Sarbanes-Oxley Act of 2002 was passed to restore confidence in publicly traded companies in the United States after the Enron and other accounting scandals. The legislation affects corporate governance, financial disclosure, the practice of public accounting, executive compensation, and the use of independent directors and requires CEOs to personally approve a company's financial statements. It was intended to improve the transparency of US public companies but it applies to foreign firms as well if they are listed on a US stock exchange or have 300 or more shareholders in the United States. Although the Securities and Exchange Commission has modified some of the rules for foreign companies, the law still is a source of contention.

19 *Globe and Mail*, January 10, 1995: B9.

20 Martha L. Maznevski and Joseph J. DiStefano, "Global Leaders Are Team Players: Developing Global Leaders Through Membership on Global Teams," *Human Resource Management Journal*, 39(2 & 3) (Summer/Fall 2000): 195–20.

About this Book

This book is designed to help develop the knowledge, perspective, and skills that global managers need to function effectively in different cultural environments and to work effectively with people from other cultures. Our intention is to develop, to the extent possible using this medium, an appreciation of what it is like to work with people from other cultures and to work in other countries. In short, we intend to help you develop a global mindset: adaptive, cross-cultural, and interpersonal expertise within the context of global strategy.

In this description of the book, we begin with a discussion of our orientation to the teaching of international management behavior and how it is reflected in the text. We then outline the book and provide some specific notes on cases and using them as a learning tool.

ORIENTATIONS TO TEACHING INTERNATIONAL MANAGEMENT BEHAVIOR

These orientations describe perspectives that have been developed, refined, and tested in our teaching a course of this type for over 30 years to undergraduates, graduate students, and practicing managers around the world. We have found that a combination of conceptual knowledge and contextually based skill-building opportunities provides an effective learning package. As well as drawing on the research of others we have conducted our own research on the issues and skills relevant to international management, and also on how best to train global managers. The result is a set of statements that reflect our approach to teaching international management behavior.

Management orientation

This book presents a problem-solving approach to international business. The implications of cultural differences and similarities for management can be examined, not isolated from business realities, but embedded in actual management situations where an appreciation of cultural influences on behavior can make a difference in outcome and performance. It is only in this context that future global managers can learn to generalize and apply the skills more broadly.

Behavioral orientation

The human element in managing effectively across cultures is just as important as, and sometimes more important than, the technical or business elements. However, interpersonal skills are likely to be less developed in managers than are technical or business skills. People chosen to work in the international side of business generally have already developed a basic set of business or technical skills as a prerequisite for the assignment. These people need to complement the basic skills with people skills; if they don't, they may never get the opportunity to use the business or technical skills. The material here acknowledges that business and technical skills are necessary for effectiveness, but their development is not emphasized. This book focuses on the interpersonal behavioral skills.

Process orientation

Related to the behavioral orientation is a process orientation – behaving, interacting, learning, and moving forward to meet objectives. We think this perspective is an important contributor to success in a global market. It is the "currency" of implementation, or actually putting policy decisions into practice.

Richard Pascale contrasted the Japanese "proceeding" with the American "deciding" mentality:

> The process of "proceeding" in turn generates further information; you move toward your goal through a sequence of tentative steps rather than bold-stroke actions. The distinction is between having enough data to decide and having enough data to proceed."[1]

Conducting business in other countries and cultures is an activity filled with ambiguity and uncertainty. In this type of situation, "proceeding" may be the appropriate mode of operation. Too often the focus is on quick decisions and end results rather than on the activities necessary to achieve the end results. This achievement focus very often obscures the fact that one needs to proceed, to get better information, and to make progress – rather than come to a quick resolution of the issue – to achieve desired results. Information must be collected to put pieces of the puzzle together. An orientation that moves one closer to his or her objectives is needed, accomplished through "process," or a series of interactions with other people.

The term "process" conjures up words that are active and interactive: words like exporting, managing, trading, negotiating, licensing, and joint-venturing or partnering; selecting, training, entering, leaving, and relating. The interactions and relationships with other people in other organizations in other countries are necessary in order to be a successful exporter, manager, trader, or negotiator. The cases in this book focus on process. Often, you will not be able to "find a solution" or "come to a decision," but will have to suggest and outline a process. This reflects the reality of international management.

Intercultural orientation

The material in this text focuses primarily on the interaction between people of different cultures in work settings. This intercultural orientation is distinct from a comparative approach, in which management practices of individual countries or cultures are examined and compared. The intercultural perspective has been chosen because it is in the interaction of cultures that managers experience difficulties. Although the study of practices within a single culture may be helpful, it is the interaction of people with different beliefs and management practices that has an impact on managers.

Culture-general orientation

This book is intended for general managers (meaning management generalists rather than the specific position) and international staff who must function effectively in a realm of cultural diversity. It is also useful for people who aspire to such positions in global management and staff of multinational or transnational corporations. A culture-general perspective provides a framework within which country-specific learning can take place more rapidly, as necessary. It helps you know what questions to ask and how to interpret the answers received when conducting business globally or helping others to do the same. It makes the learner become more effective at learning and adapting to other cultures. As such, the book does not focus on culture-specific learning: you will not become an expert in any one culture or be able to operate in a given culture flawlessly. This is not to say that culture-specific learning will not take place. The cases and readings will convey information and knowledge specific to given cultures. However, in-depth culture-specific training is more appropriate when someone is assigned to a specific country, and may also be appropriate for staff specialists concentrating on a particular country or a limited regional area. But any kind of culture-specific training is strongly enhanced by this culture-general orientation.

OUTLINE OF THE BOOK

The book has three main parts after this Introduction: Intercultural Effectiveness in Global Management; Implementing Strategy, Structure, and Systems; and Competing with Integrity in Global Business. The first two parts build the basics of global management

CSR

expertise, while the third part raises some critical issues about making competitive choices that affect the social and environmental context.

Each part comprises a text, a set of readings, and a set of cases. The text is a summary of the main knowledge required by global managers. It is drawn from our own research and experience and that of many others. The readings were selected carefully to complement our perspectives and add more depth that is informative and insightful. Together, the text and readings provide the conceptual background needed to address the situations in the cases and in your real-life experiences.

The cases put you in the position of a manager interacting with people from other cultures. Of course, studying a few cases in a book is not a substitute for experience. However, cases provide initial practice, and a mechanism for comparing previous experiences to others'. In taking a manager's role, you psychologically put yourself into another person's place and situation, sort out the issues involved in that situation, and plan action. In this way, you can simulate experience. A combination of the knowledge and the experience gained from immersion in the case situations improves the judgment and skills of managers. The cases in this book are specifically intended to increase sensitivity to important cultural differences and assumptions underlying management behavior, and to issues managers are likely to encounter.

We have been involved in writing many of the cases for this book. We have lived in, or traveled to many of the locations in the cases while working as teachers, consultants, managers, or specifically for case writing. We have worked with the managers described in the cases and have tried to bring the flavor, feeling, and tempo of these people and the countries in which they live into the classroom and to you, the reader.

The situations described in this book may seem like unusual dilemmas to a reader with no international business experience. But before one jumps too quickly to say, "I'll never go to those countries," or "I will never find myself in these situations," some individual experiences should be recounted. One person was completing a management training program and, as part of that program, a speaker came from the firm's operation in Germany to address the class. As the speaker discussed all of the problems and hassles associated with the operation, the listener was thinking, "I'm glad I'll never be sent there." He was quite surprised when, soon afterwards, he was sent to Germany as a manager. He wished he had listened more carefully to the speaker. Another manager, who appears in a case later in this book, dismissed as irrelevant a cross-cultural case taught at an executive development session. But on his first day back at the office he faced a very similar situation. He, too, wished he had paid more attention to the class discussion. In an effort to increase others' international management skills, he and the subordinate involved participated in developing a powerful case series about the situation. These cases, "David Shorter" and "Bob Chen," are included in this book.

Disguised cases

Ideally, we would prefer to use the real names of companies, countries, and places portrayed in the cases. However, there are many reasons why this cannot always be done. Often, the issues involved are sensitive or are perceived to be sensitive by the people in the company who have cooperated in writing the case. Also, some of the comments made about other people or other countries are not always flattering. Many of the companies depicted have ongoing business relationships with these same people and countries, and do not wish to cause offense. In allowing others to write and use these cases, some companies have insisted on disguising the names of people, places, and countries. Because the companies and people involved in these cases have cooperated with the case authors in order that students may benefit from their experience, their requests are honored.

Sometimes, the management of a company is sensitive only to seeing the real names of people and the company in print. In such cases, a thin disguise can be used in which all the remaining information is real. Companies may also be sensitive to financial data in a case and want these as well. In these situations, the data have been slightly altered, but the important relationships are maintained. Occasionally, sensitivity to all the issues contained in a case is very high, and therefore in these instances mythical countries have been created so that no one is offended. There is nothing mythical about the situation described in such a case, only the name of the country. The number of such mythical countries has been kept to a minimum.

Though it might be preferable for the cases not to be disguised, the disguise is not a critical issue with a culture-general orientation. The emphasis should be on identifying the important issues and analyzing the problems. Many of the situations described are classic and may be found in South America, Africa, or Europe. For example, one disguised case that we wrote was used in a company training program, and five experienced and knowledgeable people who read the case identified it as a project they had intimate knowledge of. Yet all five projects that these people were working on were different projects in different countries, and none was the one in the disguised case!

We have indicated on cases whether they have been disguised. The important point is that, despite the disguise, the essential elements of the problems are intact, and the cases faithfully describe the reality experienced by managers in the actual situations.

Terminology: gender

The gender of the people in the cases is the same as the actual people in the real situations. We recognize that in some societies men are given preferential treatment in organizational life and that in other societies there are attempts to provide equal opportunity to men and women managers. The cases represent the current reality in international business, not what is necessarily desirable. The text portions of the book have been written in gender-neutral or inclusive language.

A FINAL NOTE

This book is based on the philosophy that learning is a lifelong, continuous process. Rather than provide an illusion of mastery, we hope it stimulates and facilitates even more learning about other cultures and how to work effectively with others. For some of you, the material in this book may represent a first encounter with different cultures. Others may have been exposed to different cultures through previous courses or personal experience. For those with prior exposure to other people and places, the journey continues with a new level of insight. For those without prior experiences, welcome to an interesting journey!

Note

1   Richard Tanner Pascale, "Zen and the Art of Management," *Harvard Business Review*, 56(2) (1978).

PART 1

Intercultural Effectiveness in Global Management

[handwritten: Global Management is complex – 3 levels – Home country / Host country and international]

> *Reforms, when the ground has not been prepared for them, especially if they are institutions copied from abroad, do nothing but mischief.*
>
> **Dostoyevsky, The Brothers Karamazov,** *in which the Devil speaks to Ivan in his nightmare about changes in Hell*

A fundamental part of the global manager's reality is its intercultural nature. Interactions within our own culture are difficult enough to manage effectively. Interactions with people from different cultures present an even greater potential for distortion or misunderstanding. The greatest challenge in global management is avoiding the "mischief," and being able to handle it well when it is unavoidable. On paper, a new product line, a new distribution strategy, or a new alliance may move the company way ahead of its competition. But unless the ground has been prepared properly, managers may experience nothing but mischief and unrealized goals.

[handwritten: Avoid problems if you can – handle them gracefully if you can't]

In this part of the book we address the most immediate task that international managers face when executing strategy: effective interpersonal interaction. We focus on ideas and skills to prevent misunderstandings and problems so that you can implement ideas and reforms effectively. We do not suggest reducing or eliminating differences; there is creative potential inherent in those differences. What might be seen as "mischief" or "not doing it our way" by the home-country organization may in fact show a creative response to a situation. Multinational organizations have access to a wealth of knowledge and unique perspectives that can contribute to excellence and innovation. Rather than diminish or negate these differences, the best companies develop synergies to take advantage of them. They recognize that some "mischief" may be constructive and a source of competitive advantage.

We begin by defining culture, then describing the influence of cultural assumptions on our thinking and action. We next outline the dynamics of typical cross-cultural situations, or the interaction of different sets of assumptions. How do people usually respond when faced with the inconsistencies of different cultural perspectives? What tends to happen in groups with members from different cultural backgrounds? Although the most frequent responses in individuals and groups are negative or at best neutral, some people and teams grow and improve with these interactions. We turn next, therefore, to the knowledge and skills needed to learn from and be highly effective in cross-cultural interaction. We explore the nature of culture through a Cultural Orientations Framework, and identify its implications for management. We finally describe our Mapping/Bridging/Integration (MBI) model and the skills that managers need to achieve those elusive synergies. The readings then provide more in-depth discussions on these issues, and the cases present opportunities to see the concepts in action and practice the skills.

CULTURE – ITS NATURE, FUNCTION, AND INFLUENCE

Think about the following examples of cultures: Nigerian, Japanese, Québécois, soccer (football) fans, golfers, snowboarders, wine connoisseurs, Generation X, engineers, artists, Nestlé Corporation, and Matsushita Electric. What other examples have you come across? What do they have in common? What makes each a culture?

Culture is the set of assumptions and values that are shared by a group of people and that guide that group of people's interaction with each other. To paraphrase Florence Kluckhohn and Fred Strodtbeck, culture consists of a shared, commonly held body of general beliefs and values that define the "shoulds" and the "oughts" of life. These beliefs and values are taught to people so early and so unobtrusively that they are usually unaware of their influence. In a similar way, Geert Hofstede defines culture as "the collective programming of the mind which distinguishes one group or category of people from another."[1]

Culture is most readily seen in norms and practices, such as language, clothing, and behavior; however, its meaning and important influence are much deeper than these surface manifestations. Speaking French and eating *poutine* do not make one automatically Québécois; watching the World Cup and wearing a football jersey do not make one automatically part of the soccer (football) culture. A new employee at either Nestlé or Matsushita becomes part of the culture slowly.

we learn most of our culture in Quinters

And in Jr. High School

The assumptions and values that define culture – the ones that are held by members of the culture – are those that identify what is successful and what isn't, what is to be prioritized, and how people should behave in the world and toward each other. These assumptions and values are learned by passing them on from one generation to the next in both formal ways, such as school or orientation programs, and informal ways, such as storytelling and social reinforcement.

Culture serves two important functions for groups. First, it makes action more simple and efficient. When people know what to prioritize and how to interact with each other, business and social interactions take place quickly and easily. There is no need to question each action. Members of the Japanese culture can produce and interpret each level of bowing without conscious thought; engineers can easily proceed together using standardized work methods and mathematics. *1.*

Second, culture provides an important source of social identity for its members. Humans have a basic need to belong to social groups. Belonging to a culture – as demonstrated by acting in accordance with the norms and values – brings safety and security from the group, and separates the group from outsiders who are different and perhaps even threatening. *2.*

Culture and individuals interact in many ways. Culture is a characteristic of groups, and is defined in terms of what group members share. However, individuals within the culture are all different, and subscribe to the culture's assumptions and values to a greater or lesser degree. We are all members of many cultures – cultures related to our national, regional, professional, organizational, age, gender, hobby, and other identities.[2] The culture we identify with most closely in a given situation influences that set of assumptions and values we prioritize in that situation. When a Nigerian oil engineer is working at the company's Norwegian headquarters office as an internal consultant, she may identify most closely with her professional and corporate cultures and act with the priorities and assumptions of a corporate engineer. When she is working in her home country on the oil rig supervising local employees, she may identify more with her national culture and interpret events and act according to Nigerian cultural assumptions.

In this book we focus on national or ethnic cultures – those cultures we become part of as children and whose assumptions and values are reinforced strongly throughout our formative years. It is these cultures that have the greatest impact in international management both as barriers to effective interaction and as opportunities for innovation and synergy. All of the analysis we present, however, is equally applicable to other types of culture. *←**

The world as we see it

To understand culture's influence, we need to understand first the basic role of *assumptions* and *perceptions* in influencing our own thoughts and actions. This allows us to see our own culture's influence on us, and why cross-cultural encounters are both so difficult to understand and so interesting.[3]

An assumption is an unquestioned, taken-for-granted belief about the world and how it works. Assumptions help create our worldview, or the cognitive environment in which we operate. They come in many different varieties. Some are so deeply ingrained and

def-

Assume

unquestioned that it is difficult ever to surface them, and even when surfaced they are not testable. For example, assumptions about the basic nature of humans are normally surfaced and questioned only by philosophers and religious leaders, and even they cannot test them in an unambiguous way. Culture incorporates many of these deep assumptions, and we will elaborate on more of them presently.

Other assumptions are learned at various stages of our lives, and, once learned, are taken for granted without further questioning. A child comes into the world with no knowledge of it, yet in the first few years learns to take so much for granted: day and night follow each other; manipulating switches makes things work or turns them off; things that move are either alive or powered by something; living things need nourishment; and, today, whenever you need to know something you can find it out on the Internet. As we develop through life, we learn more and more, and each lesson becomes a basic building block for adding new skills and competencies.

A financial analyst valuing companies takes for granted certain assumptions about efficient markets and develops analyses that affect the companies' ability to obtain resources. An advertising account manager takes for granted certain assumptions about human motivations, and produces advertising campaigns that play to those motivations and invoke them.

Assumptions influence the process of perception, or what we notice and how we interpret events and behaviors. Assumptions influence our perceptions themselves, our interpretations of events and behaviors, or the meaning that the events and behaviors have for us. The expression "we see what we want to see and hear what we want to hear" is a reflection of how our assumptions affect our perceptions. Karl Weick, a social psychologist, suggests that "I'll see it when I believe it" is more accurate than proclaiming "I'll believe it when I see it."[4]

The financial analyst focuses on financial ratios, earnings growth, or dividends, but may not notice programs with long lead-times that may enhance the company's reputation for social responsibility. If she did notice this information, she would likely interpret it as something admirable but nothing that should influence stock price or ability to borrow money today. The advertising account manager will likely notice only product features that fit into his framework of assumptions about motivation for the target audience, and miss other implications of those features. The first marketing campaigns for cellphones focused exclusively on the business audience. The next generation of campaigns realized that the same features were equally important for families involved in multiple activities, and attractive to teenagers wanting to stay in touch with their friends. If marketers' assumptions had not focused exclusively on business, they may have tapped this broader consumer market much earlier.

Assumptions are necessary. If we did not make innumerable assumptions about the world, we would be constantly paralyzed by the need to inquire about the meaning of events and the motives of others. The more others share our assumptions, the more easily we can interact and communicate effectively with each other. It is not surprising that our assumptions are generally effective when we operate within our own culture.

A simple way to remember this process of social perception is captured in the acronym DIE, which stands for *Describe, Interpret,* and *Evaluate*. We observe something and take note of its characteristics, or describe it. In describing something we stay with the objective facts. What we are inclined to notice is influenced in part by our assumptions of what is important. We then interpret those facts, or give them meaning, again based on our assumptions. Finally, we evaluate the facts and take action based upon our evaluation.

When selecting a potential supplier for specialty chemicals, a purchasing agent may notice that different companies offer different prices for the same grade of chemical. The purchasing agent will compile a table comparing the different suppliers, *describing* their price ranges. The purchasing agent may not notice that the suppliers offer different types of technical assistance or compound customization, because his assumptions about priorities do not include this. Although price is sometimes an indicator of quality, the purchasing agent may interpret the chemical grade as the quality information. As long as prices are identified for the same chemical grade, the purchasing agent *interprets* that he is comparing them on an equal basis. Finally, the purchasing agent *evaluates* the lowest price compound as good for the company. He takes action and buys this compound.

Just like the purchasing agent, we all act based on the world we perceive, the world we see through the *Describe, Interpret, Evaluate* sequence. Since the sequence builds so heavily on our assumptions of the world and how it works, those assumptions end up influencing our own actions and what we think of others' actions.

Culture influences our worldview

Figure 1 shows the influence pattern of culture on assumptions, perceptions, and management behavior, and demonstrates why culture and assumptions play such a large role in cross-cultural encounters. The cultural assumptions and the factors that contribute to their development represent the hidden bedrock upon which the guiding imperatives of activities rest. As one moves through levels from the abstract and general elements

FIGURE 1 Culture and Individual Behavior

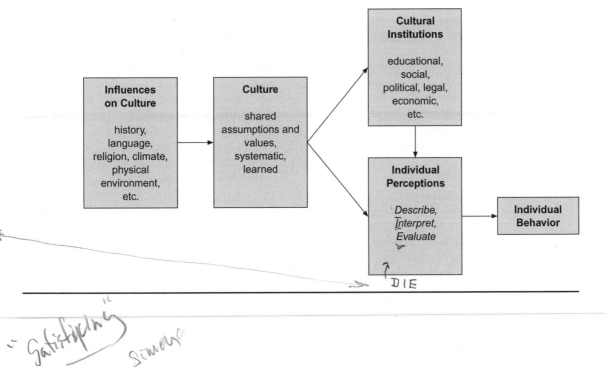

of culture to their concrete and specific manifestations (e.g., in institutions), the influence of the cultural assumptions pervades one's ways of thinking and behaving.

A good way to identify someone's cultural assumptions is to ask a series of "why" questions. For example, consider the following conversation:

> *Colleague*:   We should adjust our incentive scheme for salespeople so they have more commission.
> *You*:   Why?
> *Colleague*:   That way they'll be more motivated to sell the products.
> *You*:   Why will it work?
> *Colleague*:   Because they'll see that if they sell more products, they'll get more money.
> *You*:   Why will they change their behavior?
> *Colleague* (getting frustrated with you):   Because everyone wants more money!
> *You*:   Why?
> *Colleague* (not believing he is part of this conversation):   Just because!

When you get to this response, "Just because," you have reached the level of assumptions. These assumptions are often provided by the person's culture. You can also identify assumptions by giving people examples of situations that involve the assumption and asking them how they would respond. For example, people may not be conscious enough about their basic belief about human nature to articulate it. However, ask someone, "What do you expect someone to do if she found a large amount of money in an unidentified package on the street?" and "What type of system should be put in place to prevent dishonest employees from stealing money?" Your respondent would probably be able to reply easily, and this will give you clues about his assumptions regarding human nature. In general, people are more consciously aware of how they ought to behave in situations that are specific and concrete; but people are not usually aware of where those "oughts" originate. Often, they come from culture.

When cultures meet – question the other or question ourselves?

If culture is a set of shared deep-level assumptions and values, and these assumptions and values influence thoughts and behavior, what happens when people from two or more different cultures meet or work together? Their assumption and value systems (cultures) may direct them to perceive the same situation differently, interpret what they notice differently, evaluate the situation differently, and take different actions.

This sets up a potential conflict situation. From our own point of view, the other person is thinking and behaving in a way that is inconsistent with our assumptions about the world (assumptions which we are not conscious of holding). When assumptions are consistent with perceptions, we experience a neutral feeling, or perhaps comfort or harmony. We are able to function, to get our work done, to produce. But what happens when we encounter something that contradicts our assumptions? What if the purchasing agent assumes that all compounds within the same chemical grade are equal, then the chemical engineer tells him they are not? These encounters set up a condition described by psychologists as "cognitive dissonance." It is an uncomfortable feeling of imbalance.

Because we seek pleasure and avoid pain, we are motivated to reduce the imbalance to achieve consistency again.

There are two ways to regain consistency: change our perceptions of the evidence to match the assumptions (question the other), or change our assumptions to match the evidence (question ourselves). We are much more inclined to invoke the first method than the second; it requires a great deal less energy, is reinforced by others who hold the same assumptions, and is less confusing. We usually do this by distorting what we've perceived to make it consistent with our assumptions. The purchasing agent tells the engineer that she is just seeing the engineering point of view and doesn't understand the strategic picture.

Although the usual mode of reducing the gap between assumptions and perceptions is to distort perceptions, there is another option: altering one's own assumptions. The purchasing agent may question the engineer about time and other costs related to technical assistance for new product development associated with different suppliers, and shift his assumptions about purchasing priorities to include such investment. Unfortunately, this is usually an unexamined alternative. Furthermore, the closer the relationship between the assumptions in question and one's identity or concept of self, the less likely one is to consider changing assumptions.

This tendency to make perceptions congruent with assumptions is often a source of misunderstanding between people in the same cultural milieu. It is an even bigger problem in an intercultural context where there is a lack of shared assumptions. Recall that definitions of how one ought to behave and, therefore, the explanations of why a person is behaving in a particular way often differ from one culture to another. People get into difficulty by making inaccurate assumptions about a person or situation in a different culture. Consider this short exchange:

> **Susan** *(British)*:   Pablo, the company has decided to transfer you to the regional headquarters in São Paulo.
>
> **Pablo** *(Chilean)*:   That will be very difficult. May I decline?

There is an awkward pause. What are both thinking? If each is thinking from their own assumption set, Susan is probably wondering whether Pablo is really interested in developing his career: "A transfer to regional headquarters is an important promotion. Maybe he's not as ambitious as I thought. It's too bad to waste such talent." Pablo may wonder why Susan or the company would transfer him: "My family and my life is here. Why would I want to go to Brazil? I don't speak Portuguese; I could not have a life there. How can the company do this to me?"

With this interpretation, both are making assumption about the other's motivations and values, based on their own assumption set. Moreover, because we make interpretations from our own assumption set, we are prone to ethnocentric error. Ethnocentrism is the evaluation of differences between groups, seeing "us" as better and "them" as worse. We have a strong tendency to use our own group's assumptions as the benchmark when viewing other groups, placing our group at the top of a hierarchy, and ranking all others as lower.[5] Susan's thoughts may continue with, "No wonder the Chilean economy is still struggling." Pablo might think, "This is just another example of Anglo values colonizing the rest of the world – and we'll end up as robots without heart and loyalty to our families."

FIGURE 2   When People from Two Cultures Meet

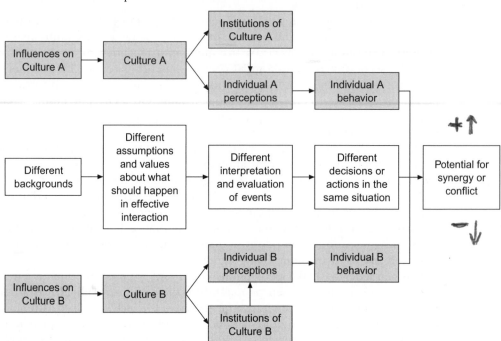

The dynamics of what happens when cultures meet are shown in Figure 2. The same perceptual process occurs as described earlier and shown in Figure 1, but in this case two different people are acting based on two different sets of cultural assumptions. The resulting different decisions or behaviors set up the conditions for conflict – or synergy, as discussed below.

If assumptions can be identified and understood, the capacity to verify their accuracy increases. Differences in assumptions might be anticipated, and errors in perception might be avoided. This process is similar to Samuel Coleridge's requirement for readers of poetry: "the willing suspension of disbelief." In the case of poetry, the poet's power of insight often enables him to juxtapose two images or ideas that most people do not normally associate with each other. The reader of poetry should not let her assumptions overwhelm the poet's creativity in linking the elements (to disbelieve the unusual association). The challenge is to be open intellectually to the poet's assumptions about what is normal. The reward is a new vision. However, the more unusual the poet's perception of what belongs together, the more the readers' assumptions are challenged and the less likely that the poet will be appreciated or understood. The more abstract the poet, the less likely the reader is to even try to understand his or her perception. Even more regrettable is the likelihood that the reader will justify her assumptions by dismissing the poet as "impenetrable," "impossible," "weird," or some other favorite pejorative.

In intercultural situations, a similar process is often employed. People from the other culture say things and behave in ways that are not at all familiar to us, and we stereotype the other culture as "primitive," "lazy," or some other negative stereotype. As with the poetry example, ethnocentric behavior is a major stumbling block in intercultural interaction.

People tend to become aware of how their assumptions shape perceptions, values, and behavior only as they confront a different set of assumptions guiding the views and practices of other people. If people are exposed to new experiences under the right circumstances (including the person's own motivation), part of their response will include an examination of their own guiding values. The next stage of Susan and Pablo's hypothetical conversation could easily have been one of open dialogue about reasons for moving or not, and how those were related to different values. Both could be enriched by the conversation.

What about when it comes to groups? How does this assumptions–perceptions process tend to play out in multicultural group settings? Not surprisingly, usually quite badly. A study reported by Nancy Adler showed that, compared with culturally homogeneous groups, multicultural groups either performed worse or better, and that more performed worse than better.[6] Every manager with whom we have worked has confirmed this result. Looking at a wide variety of diversity characteristics including gender, age, organizational tenure, and profession, research has found that the more diverse a group is, the less satisfied members are with their membership, the lower the cohesion, and the higher the absenteeism and/or turnover.[7] The experiences that lead to negative evaluations and actions tend to multiply with the number of people and intensity of the task, resulting in a disaster in terms of group relations. In our experience, the most common reaction of teams to diversity is to suppress it; to impose a set of norms that represent the dominant culture or the lowest common denominator in terms of skills and abilities. This creates enough shared assumptions to operate, but is not a stable or productive solution.

For a while, the standard recommendation to managers was to avoid putting together diverse groups whenever possible. However, given the trends in demographics and global business in general outlined in the Introduction, this approach is unrealistic. Global organizations inevitably have multicultural teams even within single "domestic" units, and they need multicultural teams across units.

On the positive side, some studies have shown that multicultural groups provide some advantages. Compared with culturally homogeneous groups, multicultural ones have been shown to be more creative, and to develop more and better alternatives for resolving a problem and more and better criteria for evaluating the alternatives.[8] However, even in these studies multicultural teams, on average, didn't perform as well as the more homogeneous ones. Of course, there are some high-performing diverse teams. They are the ones that capture the different perspectives offered by their broad membership and weave them into a synergy of innovative, effective responses to management challenges. In fact, high-performing diverse teams do outperform high-performing homogeneous teams. Their path to success is described in the next section.

MAP, BRIDGE, INTEGRATE: MANAGING CULTURAL DIVERSITY FOR PERSONAL AND TEAM EFFECTIVENESS

The discussion that follows is based on our research on individual and team interactions in organizations. It is centered around three basic skills: Mapping to understand cultural

FIGURE 3 The MBI Model

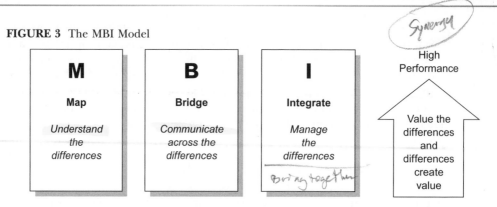

Synergy

High
Performance

M

Map

*Understand
the
differences*

B

Bridge

*Communicate
across the
differences*

I

Integrate

*Manage
the
differences*

Bring together

Value the
differences
and
differences
create
value

differences among members; Bridging to communicate effectively among members; and Integrating to bring perspectives together and build on them. When these three skills are executed well, interactions between individuals or among team members result in high performance.[9] The basic model is shown in Figure 3. We have used this approach in a wide variety of countries, situations, organizational levels, and functions, and those using it have found it helped them achieve high effectiveness with cultural diversity.

Integrating leads directly to success, but Bridging accounts for more than two-thirds of a team's success in Integrating. In other words, if Bridging is done well, Integrating follows naturally. Moreover, Bridging cannot be done without good Mapping, no matter how skilled or well intentioned the team members are. We begin with an extensive discussion of Mapping, then discuss the skills needed for good Bridging and Integrating.

Mapping

We are all familiar with maps and their use. A good geographic map accurately provides all the information the user needs to conduct the task at hand, whether it is navigating a vacation or drilling for oil. But it contains no extraneous detail. For example, a road map does not show underlying geological formations, and a geological map does not show the location of rest stops. The skill of using a map is knowing how to find oneself on the map, and then using it in relation to the terrain to help decide where to go next.

A cultural map, rather than showing streets and highways, provides information about a group's characteristics and behavior. It is based on objective data, and is updated with new information and changes in the culture. A good cultural map for international managers provides accurate information about the cultural differences that are important to international business. It simplifies those differences enough to avoid an overabundance of detail but still permit comparisons between cultures. The skill of cultural mapping involves being able to describe oneself and others in terms of the map, predicting and explaining characteristics and behaviors in terms of the map, and being able to move from the map to the real territory.

Another kind of a model !

Just as a good geographer uses different types or scales of maps for different purposes, a good international manager has access to several cultural maps. Each map shows different dimensions of culture, and allows different types of cultural comparisons. Edward T.

Hall has written several books and articles describing elements of culture that are relevant to business. In his classic article, "The Silent Language in Overseas Business," he describes cultural differences relating to the dimensions below and their impact on interpersonal behavior:[10]

- Time
- Space
- Things
- Friendships
- Agreements

Geert Hofstede has developed the most extensively researched framework or cultural map.[11] He identified four basic value patterns of cultures around the world:

- Individualism
- Power distance
- Uncertainty avoidance
- Masculinity

He also linked these dimensions to management theories and practice. Later, with colleague Michael Bond, he identified a fifth value of *Confucian Dynamism,* or Long-Term Orientation. Hofstede's framework is presented in more detail in Reading 1, "Cultural Constraints in Management Theories" and Reading 2, "Maps of Cultural Dimensions by Country."

Following Hofstede, but incorporating more dimensions developed in sociology and anthropology, Fons Trompenaars developed a map of seven dimensions.[12] These are:

- Universalism versus Particularism
- Collectivism versus Individualism
- Affective versus Neutral Relationships
- Specificity versus Diffuseness
- Achievement versus Ascription
- Orientation Toward Time
- Internal versus External Control

Trompenaars's framework has become quite popular among managers. Space limitations prevent us from including it in detail in this book. However, if you are interested we encourage you to pursue it in more depth through the books he has authored or co-authored.

A fourth framework, developed by anthropologists Florence Kluckhohn and Fred Strodtbeck, identifies six value orientations (or dimensions) and their respective variations in different cultures.[13] Since this is the framework we use to illustrate the mapping component of the MBI model, we will discuss it in much more detail below.

Unfortunately, cultural maps are not as ubiquitous as road maps. An international manager may also have a role as a cartographer and through his or her experience help create a map of the important features of a culture. People who live for a long time in a new culture eventually develop their own maps, often unconsciously. Using a formal framework (a mapping tool) to help organize what you learn accelerates the learning enormously.

The Cultural Orientation Framework   The basic premise underlying Kluckhohn and Strodtbeck's Cultural Orientation Framework (COF) is that there are common themes in the issues or problems that different societies have faced throughout time, and that these universal issues provide a way of viewing culture more objectively.[14] Kluckhohn and Strodtbeck produced their framework by analyzing hundreds of ethnographic descriptions of worldwide cultures conducted by researchers from many different backgrounds. They identified six problems or issues that all societies throughout recorded history face, but different societies developed different ways of coping with these issues. The six issues are referred to as cultural orientations, and the different responses to each issue are called variations. The six issues are:

1   Relation to the environment
2   Relationships among people
3   Mode of human activity
4   Belief about basic human nature
5   Orientation to time
6   Use of space

For each of the six issues, we will explain the nature of the underlying assumptions and describe the variations that occur. We will also give examples of how the orientation might influence general managerial activities. We will often use country as a shorthand indicator for culture, but remember that there are many other levels of culture as well, and not every person in a culture will behave in accordance with the culture's dominant pattern.

1 Relation to the environment

The issue of people's relationship to the environment reflects how people in a society orient themselves to the world around them and to the supernatural. What do people direct their attention to, and what do they see as their role in the environment? Three main variations seem to exist in the human experience.

VARIATIONS IN RELATION TO ENVIRONMENT

The first variation is *harmony* with the environment: the imperative to behave in concert with the physical environment and other systems in the world around us, to see the environment and ourselves within it as a systemic whole and to keep the system in balance. To a Native American in the Southwest, this may mean designing a road to skirt a clump of trees on a lovely hill. Harmony with the environment is not equivalent to the current meaning of strong environmentalism. Native Americans, for example, are traditionally hunters as well as gatherers. But their traditions also incorporate strong norms of studying the ecosystem to ensure that no more game is hunted than the system can tolerate without becoming unbalanced, and utilizing every single part of the animal to provide for their own needs, with no waste whatsoever. Their social traditions encourage and, in fact, regulate harmony within the tribe.

In contrast, an Anglo-Saxon civil engineer designing a road might alter the terrain by leveling the trees and the hill. In doing so, the engineer would exhibit the second variation and dominant North American value: *mastery* over the environment. A good example of the mastery orientation was the goal of landing a person on the moon when the technology did not exist for accomplishing the task. The audacity of announcing that this mission was to be achieved by the end of the 1960s reflected not only a politically astute move to recapture America's confidence after the Russians launched the Sputnik satellite, but also a profound belief that if enough time, money, and brains are applied to a goal, nearly anything is achievable. This is the meaning of the mastery notion.

The third variation is *subjugation* to the environment: people see themselves as dominated by physical forces and/or subject to the will of a Supreme Being. Life in this context is viewed as predetermined or preordained, or an exercise in chance. It is felt that one should not try to alter the inevitable by acts of will, for such actions will be futile at best and blasphemous at worst. To a devout Muslim, the expression *Insh'allah*, which has the same meaning as "God willing," reflects a dominant worldview that plans can be made, but will only take place according to the will of God.

People who do not come from societies with an appreciation for subjugation often view it as a variant of fatalism: why bother working hard, for example, if everything is preordained anyway? However, this quotation from a Muslim friend of one of the authors helps explain subjugation as a non-fatalist orientation:

> Through meditation and prayer, I am to understand what it is that Allah has planned for me – what role I am to play in His plan. Then it is my own responsibility to fulfill that role as well as I can. If I understand my role well and work hard to be effective in it, then if something happens to prevent me from doing it well, I know that act was meant to happen and is part of Allah's larger plan. If I do not understand my role – which may be because I have not communicated well with Allah – and something happens to prevent me from doing it well, that act might be predetermined to help me understand my role better. If I do understand my role but I am lazy and don't work well towards it, and something happens to prevent me from fulfilling my role, that act may be my own responsibility. So it's a lot more complicated than "God determines everything," meaning every detail.

Much of the basis of culture is manifested in religious writings and literary works. International managers would be well advised to read the literature of the countries in which they operate for clues to understanding the cultural roots of the managerial practices that they may experience in the workplace. For example, the influence of this cultural dimension on perceptions of events is often shown in the language used to describe them. When Sir Edmund Hillary reached the summit of Everest, headlines throughout the English-speaking world screamed "MAN CONQUERS EVEREST." Chinese colleagues have said that the same event reported in Mandarin would have been translated as "man befriends the mountain." Religious writings also reflect culture's influence. The mastery notion seems to pervade Genesis 26, which states: "Let them have dominion over all the Earth." In contrast, the Tao Te Ching states: "Those who would take over the Earth and shape it to their will, never, I notice, succeed."

Management impact

The impact of this orientation is not just on the physical environment, but on all aspects of the environment including the competitive, the economic, the social, and so on. Because of its pervasive scope, the environment orientation influences managerial activity in many ways.

One is in *goal-setting*, or identifying the objectives of a set of actions. A cross-border manufacturing team we worked with had Asian members who were stronger on harmony than mastery, and North American members who were stronger on mastery than harmony. The team was asked to work together to improve the production quality of a plant. The harmony-oriented Asian members defined the task as analyzing the whole production system and improving linkages among the parts; the mastery-oriented North American members defined the task as identifying the one or two most important quality problems and fixing them.

This pattern is consistent with how the different cultures view goals. Harmony cultures tend to identify system-wide goals, and to link sets of goals to each other. Goals are seen as a way of articulating the ideal system. Mastery cultures tend to identify specific achievements as goals, and see goals as intentions of control over a situation. If the team had subjugation-oriented members, they may have taken either set of goals, but the meaning of "goal" would have been different. In a subjugation culture, if the goals are not achieved after a good attempt then they might be recognized as the wrong goals, or it might be decided that production improvement is not the right thing to do at this point.

Which approach should the team take? From the company's point of view, a combination of all three is best. This is the opportunity for cultural synergy! Unfortunately in this case, the team became very divided on this issue and neither the harmony nor the mastery goals were achieved.

A second managerial activity affected by orientation to the environment is *budgeting*. One study reported the differences between French and US subsidiaries of a large multi-national corporation (MNC) with a supposedly uniform budget system.[15] This budgeting system had volumes of procedures, rules, forms, schedules, and deadlines to be followed worldwide. The French subsidiaries, that showed a very weak preference for the mastery orientation over the harmony orientation, considered the budget system an elegant exercise. They treated only the actual accounting results as real. The US subsidiaries, which showed a strong preference for the mastery orientation over the harmony orientation, treated the budget as real, relevant, and useful. They were confident of their ability to control (or at least influence) events by using this managerial tool.

Forcing this budget system on a subsidiary operating in a subjugation-oriented cultural context might be a futile exercise. The outcomes of the system, intended to assist managers to shape events, would be seen as predetermined by local employees in such a setting. Local managers would likely complete the forms involved either reluctantly or randomly. Some managers we know have reported such experiences with Indonesian managers.

A third way the environment orientation influences management activity is in the *attribution of problems and successes*. A European consumer goods company was trying to understand why product sales had not met targets. The British mastery-oriented manager was sure it was because the company's salespeople had not executed the strategy the right way; in other words, the company had not controlled actions and the environment appropriately. The Norwegian harmony-oriented manager was sure it was because conditions were not what they had predicted when the goals had been set; the current relationships between customers, salespeople, competition, and the economic environment were not consistent with the goals. The Russian manager, who was both harmony- and subjugation-oriented, could not understand the importance of the discussion. Sales were what they were, and she wanted to move on and discuss how to get more from the current system. When results are successful, people in mastery-oriented cultures tend to attribute the success to their own actions and how they controlled or influenced other parties' behavior; people in harmony-oriented cultures tend to attribute the success to their ability to align the system; people in subjugation-oriented cultures tend to acknowledge the success and try to understand the conditions it has created.

A dramatic example of these variations in orientation to environment occurred when a civil engineer in a large North American construction company was given responsibility to select a site and design and construct a fish-processing plant in a West African country. The engineer classified potential sites according to the availability of reliable power, closeness to transportation, nearness to the river for access by fishing boats from the Atlantic Ocean, location near the main markets, and availability of housing and people for employment. After evaluating these criteria and ranking the few sites in the final list, the engineer chose the optimum location. Just prior to requesting bids from local contractors for some of the site preparation, the engineer discovered, in talking to local authorities, that the site was located on ground considered sacred by the local people. These people believed this site was the place where their gods resided. None of the local people on whom the engineer was depending to staff the plant would ever consider working there! The engineer quickly revised the priorities and relocated the plant. In this case, it was lucky that the ignorance of a significant cultural barrier was discovered prior to construction. Too often these errors are realized only after a project has been completed. This true story points out the hidden workings of culture and also demonstrates that having a prior framework can assist in avoiding the problems of culturally bounded criteria for decision making.

MASTERY AND HARMONY ARE DOMINANT VARIATIONS

In our own research measuring these orientations we have yet to encounter any cultural group – ethnic, national, professional – that has had subjugation as its dominant orientation to the environment. Some groups definitely have a stronger belief in subjugation than others did: groups from Arab and Muslim cultures and many Eastern European groups tend to have higher subjugation scores, and groups from North America and Australia and some industries such as biotechnology and manufacturing tend to have very low subjugation scores. We have not yet seen a group with subjugation higher than either mastery or harmony, although a number of individuals we have worked with have had subjugation as a dominant value.

The important cultural differences on this variation seem to be whether mastery or harmony is dominant, and the degree to which subjugation is assumed, in a relative way, rather than whether it is preferred to the other variations in an absolute way.

FIGURE 4 Variations in Relation to the Environment and Examples of Management Impact

Management Impact	Harmony	Mastery	Subjugation
Goal-setting	Systems-oriented, define the whole	Specific, aimed at control and influence	Not meaningful for directing behavior
Budget systems	Budgets are ways of describing the actions of the system	Budgets guide behavior and lead to results	Budgets are guidelines but not meaningful for directing behavior
Attributing causes of problems	Problems arise from imbalances in the system	Problems arise when we don't control things well enough	Problems arise when we identify the wrong things to do, or when it is fate or God's will

in no group is this dominant

SUMMARY

The relation to the environment orientation is summarized in Figure 4. Under each of the variations are examples of how the cultural values manifest themselves in managerial spheres of activity.

2 Relationships among people

The orientation of relationships among people is concerned with issues of power and responsibility. What responsibility do people have for the welfare of others? Who has power over us, and over whom do we have power?

VARIATIONS IN RELATIONSHIPS AMONG PEOPLE

One variation is that we should take care of ourselves: *individualism*. Individualism is a belief that if individuals look after themselves, and if no one has absolute power over anyone else, then we will all be better off. Individuals should make their own decisions, and live with the consequences of them.

This attitude is dominant in North America, Australia and New Zealand, and parts of Europe. The nuclear family tends to be the outer limit of formal responsibility, and even that changes after children reach the age of majority. Independence is valued, and "Stand on your own two feet!" is the injunction. Except in unusual circumstances, such as a poor economy, parents whose children are still living with them past the age of 25 or so have failed in their obligations to instill the "rugged individualism that made this country great!"

Another variation of relationships among people is *collectivism*, which is dominant in many Mediterranean, South American, and Asian cultures. In this type of society, one's allegiance and loyalty are to the extended family or group of which one is a part. In such a culture, cousins are treated with as much concern and love as siblings are in an individualistic culture. In fact in many languages the same word is used for the English pairs grandfather/uncle, grandmother/aunt, sister/cousin, and brother/cousin; and no distinction is made between the two relationships. The group tends to be clearly defined, and the group's members have an ultimate obligation to help and care for each other.

An important corollary in collective cultures is that if a person is *not* part of one's own group, one has no obligation to help or care for the other person. These are out-group members, as opposed to the in-group members of one's own family or circle of friends. It is assumed his or her own group will look after the other person. On the other hand, if someone treats a stranger with the concern normally reserved for a member of one's group, then the person so treated for all intents and purposes becomes a member of the group, with all the rights and responsibilities associated with such membership.

This complexity of collectivism can give rise to many misunderstandings. They are exemplified by the apocryphal story of an American who assisted a pedestrian knocked down by a passing car in a busy street in an Asian city. Appalled at the lack of attention shown to the injured stranger, the American yelled at a nearby police officer, provided first aid, and insisted on hailing and paying for a taxi to take the person to a hospital. Afterward, the American muttered about the inhumanity of the local population and concluded that the incident confirmed his personal theory, "How cheap human life is in the over-populated Asian cities." Meanwhile, the police officer's family listened, appalled, as the officer told of the American who was so dumb as to treat a stranger like a family member. Then he was so indifferent as to send the person off in a taxi, rather than accompany him to the hospital personally and to attend to him properly afterwards.

A further variation on the relationship dimension is *hierarchy*. In this variation, relationships of power and responsibility are arranged such that those higher in the hierarchy have power over those lower in the hierarchy. In return, they are expected to look after and provide for those lower down in the hierarchy. The hierarchy tends to be stable over time, such that most people remain in the same general level of the hierarchy throughout their lives. Many hierarchical societies also develop a strong collective orientation within hierarchical levels. This is characteristic of aristocratic society and caste systems. One looks after one's own kind, but knows where one's kind stands on the status ladder. The status systems within cultures with a strong hierarchical value tend to be multi-layered and clearly defined; cultures with a low hierarchical value tend to have fewer layers whose boundaries are more penetrable by the members.

MANAGEMENT IMPACT

Managing a business requires managing relationships among people; therefore, the relationship variable has a pervasive influence on managerial practice and policy. Organizational structures, communication and influence patterns, reward systems, teamwork, and other managerial processes are all influenced by the relationship orientation.

In individualistic cultures, *organizational structures* are seen as a set of roles that individuals fit into. Individuals can move in and out of roles and should perform whichever behaviors are necessary for that role. Although organizational structures show power relationships, people in individualistic cultures see the lines in the organizational chart as guidelines for decision-making authority and communication, not as strict power relationships. The arrangement of relationships is treated informally, and behavior within the structures is flexible. It is very common for someone to talk to his boss's boss about a particular decision, or to give direct feedback to the CEO. Two-boss relationships are possible, as in a matrix organization. In Perret's study of the budgeting procedure, managers in the individualistic American subsidiary reported budget-related information to anyone who had an interest in the data, regardless of his or her position in the structure.

In a group-dominated culture, more attention is given to horizontal differentiation. Differences between groups are the preoccupation, and the structures of work organizations reflect this concern. Formal communication patterns are focused within divisions. In collective cultures there is a strong focus on relationship-building. Relationships are seen as ends in themselves, not as means to ends. Once relationships are built, they are often used for business purposes. So although formal communication in collective cultures follows division or department lines, informal communication follows the lines of relationships built among managers. An individualistic Dutch manager implementing a change in Latin America had great difficulty understanding how information about the change was traveling so quickly through the organization when all the information was discussed in separate departmental meetings. Then he remembered that many of the middle managers socialized together frequently in the evenings, and realized that the information was being shared in this setting.

Hierarchical cultures emphasize vertical differentiation. Of all variations, the most rigidly obeyed structures are found in hierarchical cultures. In Marie Perret's study of budgeting procedures, the hierarchical French managers could not conceive of working in a matrix structure and faithfully reported any budget anomalies exclusively to their immediate superior, even if there were serious implications for lateral departments.[16] André Laurent experienced the same phenomenon in teaching and research he conducted at INSEAD in France. The thought of reporting to two bosses was alien to French managers and the consideration of such an organizing principle was an impossible exercise.[17] This is also true in Japan and Brazil.

Similarly, the relationship variations have an impact on *reward systems*. In individualistic cultures, rewards that are based mostly on individual contributions are deemed to be most fair. Why should I be paid for something that someone else does? In collective cultures, group-based reward systems are seen as more fair, because everyone is assumed to contribute what they can to the group. Without all of us the group could not perform, so we should all be compensated for the group's performance. In hierarchical cultures, status-based pay is seen as most fair. In one hierarchical company we worked with there are almost one hundred different salary grades for managers, each associated with a position level in the company. If the company has extensive and elaborate criteria for assignment to a particular position, then pay is automatically associated with the hierarchical level.

Teamwork is also affected by a culture's orientation to relationships among people. It is a common misconception that collective cultures engage in more teamwork than individualistic cultures do. In fact, all cultures work in teams; they just do it differently.[18] In individualistic cultures, team members have specific roles and responsibilities, and the team can identify each person's contribution. The leadership role may change depending on which part of the task needs to be emphasized. When something goes wrong, everyone knows whose responsibility it is to fix it. Members' loyalty is as much to the task as to the other people. Membership may change frequently, depending on the needs of the task or of the individuals on the team with respect to other tasks. In collective cultures, roles are much more fluid and commitment is to the team itself. Each person may have a specific contribution to make, but each person is also responsible for helping the group as a whole to function well. When something goes wrong, everyone is responsible for fixing it. Membership is less likely to change. In hierarchical cultures, team members have specific levels and roles in the hierarchy, and the team is directed clearly by the leader. People contribute to meetings and discussions in accordance with their place in the hierarchy.

The reputation of the Japanese for skilled group management deserves mention. Careful examination of Japanese culture shows a more complex pattern than the popular literature leads one to believe.[19] In Japan, collectivism is combined with a strong sense of hierarchy. This coexists with an educational and social system that depends on merit (doing orientation to activity, see below) rather than class-consciousness. This combination of cultural characteristics gives rise to a very specific type of group decision-making: decisions made by group consensus and executed uniformly. These groups are supervised by a superior, who is invariably an older, experienced manager with greater practice and skill in managing groups. Japanese managers are encouraged to move laterally and diagonally through the organization during their careers. This is partly due to their skills in managing groups of functional experts and partly because companies can depend on investment in such experience paying off in the future (because of the tradition – now eroding – of lifetime employment). *long-term time orientation*

INDIVIDUALISM AND COLLECTIVISM ARE DOMINANT VARIATIONS

In the survey data we have gathered, almost all the cultures and subcultures have preferred either individualism or collectivism, with the other of this pair second. Hierarchy has almost always been preferred least. Anglo cultures tend to prefer individualism the most, followed very closely by collectivism. Latin American, Southern European, and Asian cultures tend to prefer collectivism most, followed by individualism. Hierarchy was the highest of the three variations in only two settings: a group of Japanese senior managers and a group of Brazilian senior managers. Our data collection has focused on industrialized settings, so it is possible that this reflects a cultural convergence or commonality for industrialized cultures. Research has consistently shown that the more hierarchical an organization is, the more difficulty it has adapting to change. In today's dynamic environment, perhaps it is impossible to have an organization with a dominant preference for hierarchy over the long term.

Even though hierarchy was always the least preferred arrangement of responsibility, there were strong differences between countries and between subcultures within the same country. Hierarchy tends to be much higher than average in Latin American, southern European, Indian, and Japanese cultures, and much lower in Anglo and northern European cultures. We have found some company cultures to be much more hierarchical than others, regardless of geographical location. One US company we worked with was extremely low on hierarchy. The headquarters managers of this company had a very difficult time with its subsidiary in India, which had a relatively high preference for hierarchy (although still lower than individualism or collectivism). The American managers were frustrated that their Indian subordinates would not embrace empowerment and make

FIGURE 5   Variations in Relationships Among People and Examples of Management Impact

Management Impact	Individualism	Collectivism	Hierarchy
Organizational structures	Informal, flexible behavior with respect to structures	Attention to horizontal differentiation, informal relationships across groups	Strong attention to vertical dimension
Communications and relationships	Many relationships in different places; open communication	In-group relationships most important; communication respects group members' feelings	Authority-based hierarchy, communicate freely down; junior people speak only when asked by senior
Reward systems	Individually based	Group-based	Status-based
Teamwork	Individual roles and responsibilities, revolving leadership based on task, loyalty to task	Group-oriented roles and responsibilities; loyalty to the group	Regulated, formal, clear leadership and norms based on status of members

decisions. The Indian subordinates were frustrated that their American bosses were so inefficient and were taking so much time to discuss simple decisions with everyone, when just telling everyone what to do and then letting them go about their business would be much faster. On the other hand, we found a sample of US loan officers to be higher on the hierarchy orientation than the general US business population, with potential implications for how they processed loan applications.

SUMMARY

The relationships among people orientation is summarized in Figure 5.

3 Mode of Human Activity   *being — doing — thinking*

The activity orientation does not refer to a state of activity or passivity, but rather the desirable focus of activity. There are three variations of activity found in cultures.

VARIATIONS IN HUMAN ACTIVITY MODES

Note that's referring to greek gods is a western cultural assumption

The *being* variation is characterized by spontaneity. One is expected to act out feelings as they are experienced. This is the Dionysian mode (named after Dionysus, the Greek god of wine and celebrations). In being-oriented cultures, the present is experienced to its fullest. Being-oriented cultures, such as many Latin American ones, have a polychronic sense of time: many things are done at once, and time is seen as elastic, bending and stretching to fit the needs of the situation. Punctuality is not an important value; attending to the moment without rushing off to the next activity is very important (for more on this, see "Orientation to Time," below).

The *doing* variation is the Promethean mode. Prometheus stole fire from Olympus and gave it to humans to use. As punishment, he was chained to a rock and tormented by vultures. Throughout eternity, he strained to break free of his chains, but whenever he was successful, new chains constantly reappeared. The relentless striving to achieve and compulsive attempts to accomplish are the core of the "doing" orientation. The doing variation is often associated with the Protestant work ethic, which dictates that hard work is pure, and is seen in many western European and Anglo cultures. Marxism, too, argues that work is part of humans' identity, and goes so far as to say that the problem with capitalism is a separation of the identity of work from the person through management ownership.

In addition to the being and doing approaches we find the *thinking* variation. This is the Apollonian mode, in which the senses are moderated by thought, and mind and body are balanced. Thinking-oriented cultures place a high value on being rational and carefully thinking everything through before taking action. At the extreme, they may value the beauty of an elegant argument at least as much as the results it creates. Most academic and research institutions have thinking-oriented cultures.

MANAGEMENT IMPACT

The activity dimension affects how a culture's members approach work and leisure, the importance of work, and the extent to which work-related concerns pervade other parts of their lives. In a strongly doing-oriented culture, people view work and work-related activities as a central focus to their existence. Decisions tend to be made with pragmatic criteria, reward systems are results-based, and there is a compulsive concern for achieving tangible performance measures. These are the cultures that invented "to do" lists and extensive personal calendars that allow people to track their activities and accomplishments. In work and team settings, meetings are used to make decisions and close with everyone committing to action points.

In a being-oriented culture, people say they "work to live, not live to work." Work is a means to an end – an enjoyable life – and not an end in itself. For this reason, emotional criteria are included in decision-making. A manager may choose between two relatively equal decisions based on which one he likes, rather than conducting further analysis to see which brings a slightly higher marginal return. The definition of performance is much broader than specific accomplishments. The company may not reach the highest possible economic performance, but people ask whether it helps all its employees make a good living for their families, and whether it creates services that others in the community want. The degree of concern for output and performance is variable, a function of individual spontaneity.

In cultures with a dominant thinking orientation, decisions are more likely to be based on rational criteria, rewards are distributed logically, and output is measured against balanced objectives such as long- and short-term profitability, quality as well as quantity of production, and so on. While companies from all cultures create Balanced Scorecards to assess performance, companies with thinking-oriented cultures excel at them. They spend more time designing the process to identify what goes on the scorecard, tracking indicators with detailed measures, assessing the extent to which indicators relate to other dimensions of performance, and designing reward systems that fit the performance shown by the indicators.

We observed an interesting meeting among three managers: a doing-oriented Canadian, a thinking-oriented Indian, and a being-oriented Spaniard. The three were discussing potential partners for a strategic supplier relationship. The Spaniard arrived 20 minutes after the scheduled start of the meeting. The other two rolled their eyes, knowing that the Spaniard was likely to be late. If they had asked him what he was doing, he would have replied that he met someone on the way to the meeting who had good information about one of the potential suppliers and he stopped to find out more; however, they did not ask, they just assumed that their meeting was unimportant to him. During the meeting the Canadian wanted to make a decision on a shortlist of potential suppliers, while the Indian argued for setting up a procedure to assess the validity of the current information about each potential supplier and gather more information to compare. As the meeting was moving toward its scheduled closing time, the two started to bring their ideas together (with the help of the Spaniard) to both create a shortlist and assess further information for better decision-making. Just at that point, however, the Canadian realized the time and said, "Oh, we have to stop now. Well, we've made good progress. Let's schedule our next meeting and get the action points done before we have to go." The Indian was also getting out her calendar when the Spaniard spoke up in disbelief. "What? Stop now? We're just getting to the good ideas. Why should we stop now? Let's keep going!" The next appointment on the calendar was not as important to him as continuing a discussion that was going somewhere – whether it was toward achievements or rationality!

DOING AND THINKING ARE DOMINANT VARIATIONS

In our own research, we have only encountered cultures that were highest on being in two situations: a few R&D groups within a large multinational corporation, and undergraduate university students. In all of the other groups we have surveyed, either thinking or doing was highest, and the other of this pair was most often second highest. It would be very difficult for a large company dominated by a being-orientation to engage in business over the long term. The R&D groups with the high being-orientation were some of the hardest working in the company – they happened to love their work passionately. Their strength was producing high-quality innovations, but not coordinating with the rest of the company. Undergraduate university students' main purpose is to pursue ideas with each other and with professors in a learning community, which is consistent with a being-oriented culture. We have found different country, organization, and subculture groups to prefer different levels of being-oriented activity, with some quite high; however, at least one of doing or thinking was almost always higher.

In general, we find that Anglo and northern European countries are more doing-oriented while other countries are more thinking-oriented. On this orientation we tend to find more systematic industry organizational culture differences than the previous two orientations. Engineering-oriented companies such as manufacturing firms tend to have thinking-oriented cultures, and consumer products firms tend to have doing-oriented cultures. Even within large companies we see differences across functional departments, with engineering and accounting departments being thinking-oriented and sales departments being doing- (and often being-) oriented.

FIGURE 6   Variations in Activity Orientation and Examples of Management Impact

Management Impact	Doing	Thinking	Being
Role of work; concern for output	Work is central in life, compulsive, must get to action	Balanced objectives, rational approach to work and life	Work to live; the moment is important; output may or may not be important
Decision criteria	Pragmatic, anything that gets to action	Highly logic-based, create a good argument	Emotional, spontaneous, context-based
Information and measurement systems	Simple, operational, the fewest indices that are most useful	Complete, in-depth, complex, broad, balanced	Vague, feeling-based, intuitive

SUMMARY

The variations in mode of human activity are shown in Figure 6.

4 Belief about Basic Human Nature   (Groups – not individual)

The belief about basic human nature does not reflect how one thinks about individuals, but rather one's belief about the inherent character of the human species. What is the fundamental nature of infants before they are affected by their environment? What would humans be like if they all had the "right" environment? Can you trust strangers?

VARIATIONS IN THE NATURE OF HUMAN BEINGS

This orientation asks two basic questions. First, are humans primarily *evil, good, neutral* (neither good nor evil), or *mixed* (a combination of good and evil)? Note that this is not a question about *behavior*, but about the basic nature. For example, in Christian faiths the story of Adam and Eve in the Garden of Eden is pertinent. Adam's eating of forbidden fruit symbolizes the "fall of man," as Adam gave in to the devil. This incident shows (to Christians) that the basic nature of humans is evil. However, the Christian faith teaches that it is important for people to *behave* in ways that are good. The main task of a Christian is to overcome this basic nature, to resist temptation, and to behave according to the model of Christ, who was good. Some of today's more secular Christian perspectives tend to hold a more neutral or mixed orientation – "There is good in everyone." Our own understanding of Muslim and Shinto faiths and personal communications from Arab and Japanese proponents suggest that orientations emerging from these traditions are closer to the "good" end of the spectrum. The Baha'i view "begins with the notion that human beings are essentially good, and that evil is a corruption of our true human nature."[20] This same orientation is reported by a Taiwanese manager to be the main theme of a very popular Chinese children's story.

The second question is whether the fundamental nature of people is *changeable or unchangeable.* For example, in Christianity men and women are perfectible if they follow and worship God.[21] We see this debate frequently around political campaigns, foreign affairs discussions, and criminal litigation: can someone who has shown his or her nature to be bad change and become good? Note that we cannot "prove" either answer except through faith or argument; these are assumptions we make that affect our thoughts and behaviors.

MANAGEMENT IMPACT

The most obvious impact on business of the human nature orientation is *control systems.* In cultures that believe humans are essentially evil, people are not to be trusted unless they are well known. A dominant evil orientation is associated with tight control system based on an underlying suspicion of people. An article in the *Wall Street Journal* stated that American workers were "among the world's most watched."[22] The primary reason employers gave for electronic monitoring were checking on productivity and investigating theft and industrial espionage. Among the most monitored industries were retail sales, banking and finance, and telecommunications. Managers who operate with the assumption that goodness is the basic human trait favor control systems based primarily on the need for management information, rather than for surveillance, checking, and control. Flexible work arrangements – in which people can come and go from the office as they wish provided they achieve work goals – are more predominant in organizational cultures characterized by a dominant good orientation. Cultural orientations dominated by a neutral or mixed value produce moderately tight controls, with modifications based on managers' experience with the people involved.

An executive who was negotiating a large contract in Saudi Arabia was shopping in an open-air market. Stepping up to a currency exchange booth, the executive was very surprised to see about a quarter of a million dollars clipped to a board in the stall. The currency dealer wandered away from the board to get some coffee after completing a transaction. The executive was stunned that such a large amount of money should be left unattended, but then he remembered the Islamic code's punishment for stealing – cutting off the right hand at the wrist. The severity of the punishment explained the apparently cavalier behavior of the money dealer. The executive also assumed, erroneously, that Saudis viewed basic human nature the same way as North Americans. This assumption led the executive to believe the punishment and the punishers were inhumane. However, consider an alternative explanation. If the Saudis hold human nature to be basically good, then it may follow that anyone who behaves evilly is less than human. If one is not behaving according to the expectations of what is human, then one may deserve to be identified as such by having a hand cut off.

Note that this value orientation may explain the executive's feelings toward crime and the punishment system. To most North Americans and Europeans, people's basic nature is, at best, mixed. Therefore, one should not be surprised if money were to be stolen from a neglected stall in an open-air market. A North American or European would feel that a violator should be punished, but not severely. (They tend to slap the wrist, not cut it off!) In fact, in these places, the currency dealer would probably be examined for mental stability for leaving money unattended. Simply put, control and punishment systems are created based on expectations about behavior, and the expectations are based on cultural values.[23]   `Laws - rules - audits - security`

An ironic end to this story occurred when, after the executive had signed the contract, the employees who were to go to Saudi Arabia to implement the deal were sent to a cross-cultural training session in Canada for a week. The first program was held at a hotel. Soon after the executive made the speech about the unattended money, the hotel, as part of a chain-wide campaign to reduce customer theft, put a sign on the bathroom counters in each room. The sign read: "Love is leaving the towels here when you leave!" All employees about to embark on their first trip into a markedly different culture had their own culture's view of human nature reinforced just before they left home.

The value orientation regarding basic human nature affects other areas of management, such as *management style*. A culture with a dominant evil orientation supports autocratic managers with very close supervision (Theory X). Neutral or mixed dominant orientations encourage moderate supervision and consultative managers. At the good end of the spectrum, managers are encouraged to engage in a laissez-faire style or to practice participative management (Theory Y). An organization's *climate* may also be consistent with the culture's orientation on the human-nature dimension. At one extreme is an adversarial climate and a stress on contractual relations. At the other extreme, collaborative and informal relations may exist. Organizational climates are consistent generally with control systems and management styles. This consistency is at least partially explained by their common roots in a particular cultural orientation.

SUMMARY

Figure 7 summarizes this human-nature orientation and its variations and potential influence on managerial practices.

5 Orientation to Time

There are two ways to think about time. The first involves a general orientation toward time; the second is about how people think about or use specific units of time.[24]

VARIATIONS IN GENERAL ORIENTATION TO TIME

A culture's general orientation to time reflects the time-related criteria used to make decisions, interpret events, or prioritize actions. For example, in a *past*-oriented culture,

FIGURE 7   Variations in Human Nature Orientation and Examples of Management Impact

Management Impact	Evil	Neutral or mixed	Good
Control system	Tight; suspicion-based	Moderate; experience-based	Loose; information-based
Management style	Close supervision; authoritarian	Moderate supervision; consultative	Empowering, delegating; participative
Organizational climate	Adversarial; contractual		Collaborative; informal

people respond to a new challenge by looking to tradition and wondering, "How have others dealt with this kind of problem before?" If people primarily consider the immediate effects of an action, then the dominant orientation is more likely to be *present*-oriented. If the chief concern is "What are the long-term consequences of this choice?" then the dominant orientation can be described as *future*-oriented.

One author of this text remembers vividly his Sicilian grandfather's answers to questions. The grandfather would invariably frame his answers in the form of vignettes and start with: "Well, I remember that my father would always tell me . . ." In contrast, the author's father, who had been born in the United States, almost always answered: "What is it that you want to accomplish?" Then he would give his advice, usually in the form of alternatives rather than answers. This example also illustrates that generations within a culture often subscribe to different subcultures!

MANAGEMENT IMPACT

The *planning horizon* is this cultural variable's most obvious point of impact for managers. Past-oriented cultures are more likely to re-create past behavior when planning, while present-oriented managers will have shorter-term concerns, and future-oriented managers are more likely to consider long-term effects. The influence of precedence, current realities, or effects desired in the future may also influence decision-making. *Reward systems*, too, may fall under the hidden effects of time orientation. Rewards in past-oriented cultures are more likely to be based on historically determined systems. An emphasis on currently contracted arrangements, which can be revised to reflect new realities, is more likely to be found in cultures where the present-time orientation is dominant. Bonus systems and other incentive schemes tend to reflect a short-term future orientation, and systems that reward training and skills tend to reflect a longer-term future orientation. However, since rewards are also mediated by other variables, there are exceptions, and there is not a simple one-to-one relationship between a value orientation and a management system.

Perception of one's own time orientation may be a source of distortion. Most North American managers would like to think of themselves as being a future-oriented culture, for whom planning is an important part of the managerial function. However, North American culture is much more present-oriented than many think. There is a decline in the corporate planning departments, and financial analysts focus on quarterly results in their assessments of company value. Although it may make more sense for line managers to do strategic planning, Henry Mintzberg demonstrated long ago how short the cycle time of activities is even for senior executives and how little planning is done as a percentage of time available.[25] With the increasing speed of global dynamics, this is even more true today.

In addition, the meaning and implications of North America's propensity to send planeloads of politicians, government bureaucrats, and business executives on trade missions to overseas countries should be pondered. One such mission targeted several Brazilian cities with a blitz of government officials and business executives. On their return two weeks later, one of the managers remarked that the travel had been a waste of time since no orders had been secured during the whole trip. Even if orders were received, it reflects a predominant time orientation of now and fast.

At the other extreme is the example of Konosuke Matsushita, founder of the large Japanese manufacturer, who on the fourteenth anniversary of the company announced a 250-year corporate plan divided into ten 25-year sections.[26] That is future-oriented planning! Although such a plan is no longer realistic, the company's emphasis is still on building a future society far into the future.

Perhaps a more practical example is that of a Japanese manager who was sent to Rio de Janeiro by a company who gave the manager a simple mission: "Get to know the people and learn Portuguese during your first year there. Then worry about starting the business." Of course, the measurement system of the Japanese company did not require their expatriates to recoup the overseas investment in the first year. Part of the reason is the traditional structure of the Japanese economy and the close links between companies, government, banks, and investors. But the confluence of factors facilitating the longer-term planning of Japanese companies, as compared to their North American counterparts, is not entirely an accident. Even with the extended period of economic stagnation in Japan, Japanese companies have been trying to find ways to maintain their long-range approach. Neither is it an accident that North American managers are constrained in their planning horizons by concern for quarterly earnings per share and even by daily shifts in stock prices. A good example of the influence of North Americans' present-time orientation on management behavior was the decision of Levi Strauss to privatize the company. Their motivation was significantly related to shareholders' pressure to maximize profitability in the short term. The executives believed that this pressure constrained future-oriented strategic decision-making that would be more beneficial to the company in the longer run.

Some effects of these preoccupations are useful; some are detrimental. The important points are to understand that some of the forces that shape such behavior are cultural, that these forces operate in several spheres that tend to reinforce each other, and that these forces are not easily altered.

MONOCHRONIC AND POLYCHRONIC TIME ORIENTATIONS

There is another aspect of time orientation that strongly influences behavior and also appears to be related to the activity orientation. This dimension asks the questions: "What are the most important units of time?" and "How does time flow?" In some cultures, time is broken up into small, specific, equal units, and it flows in a linear fashion. These cultures are called *monochronic* cultures. In these cultures, such as most Anglo cultures, time is a valuable commodity. People save, spend, and waste time. People live by their schedules, and punctuality is valued. North Americans, with their present/future orientation, divide the hour into quarters, but some subcultures treat five-minute intervals as the appropriate guide to behavior. Punctuality is defined by the most natural division of time. Pay attention to when people start to explain why they are late, or offer an apology for their tardiness, and you will have a clue to what is the natural division of time for that society.

In *polychronic* cultures, time is seen as elastic. Units may be small or large, depending on what is being done or experienced at the time. Several timelines flow in parallel, and people believe it is natural to be doing many things at the same time. Arab and Latin cultures are typical polychronic cultures. In these cultures, time schedules are less critical. It might be 45 minutes to an hour before an apology or explanation for being late is expected, and among friends no explanation is ever needed.

In polychronic cultures, individuals who are driven to meet schedules and deadlines are seen as lacking patience, tact, or perseverance. Polychronic cultures are often also collective, and they use the less hurried pace as a way to build relationships. Someone from a monochronic, individualistic culture may want to "get down to business" quickly, which prevents taking the time to develop relationships. Many Americans and western Europeans have stories of how they have destroyed opportunities to conduct business or negotiate contracts by underestimating the combination of collectivism and polychronic time orientation!

We are not suggesting that it is wrong to establish schedules or deadlines when they are reasonable. However, "reasonable" is a cultural variable. Since much of the world has elastic and relaxed attitudes toward time, others have to learn what is reasonable in those countries and adapt to their definitions, especially when these countries act as hosts. Otherwise, at best one will rush from one country, city, or meeting to another without ever taking sufficient time to build relationships before attempting to close deals. At worst, one offends others with insensitivity and risks erecting permanent barriers to doing business.

SUMMARY

Figure 8 summarizes the time orientation and points of potential managerial impact.

6 Use of Space

The variable in space orientation has to do with how one is oriented toward surrounding space.[27] How does one view its use, especially the sense of "ownership" of space relative to others? This dimension is also related to ownership of whatever is in the space, including information and resources.

FIGURE 8 Variations in Time Orientation and Examples of Management Impact

Management Impact	Past	Present	Future
Planning	Extension of past behavior	Short-term results prioritized	Long-term results prioritized
Decision criteria	Past precedents	Current impact	Desired effects
Reward systems	Historically determined	Currently contracted	Contingent on long-term performance
	Monochronic		*Polychronic*
Punctuality	Very important		Much less important
Interactions	Singular, linear		Parallel, many at once

Variations in use of space

The *private* perspective holds that space is for the exclusive use of an occupant, and that information and resources are privately owned. Space is for an occupant's benefit, and it defines a large area surrounding the occupant as part of that person's territory. Protective action is taken if this larger area is "invaded" by others. In contrast, the *public* orientation sees space as available for anyone's use. The sense of territory is small, and defensive action to guard against invasion is taken only in the immediate area around the occupant. The *mixed* orientation is a blend of the private and public perspectives – an intermediate position.

Management impact

The spatial dimension can have an impact on communication, influence, and interaction patterns and on physical realities such as office and building layout. On one hand, managers operating in a culture dominated by a private orientation are more likely to find themselves *communicating* on a one-to-one basis in a closed, serial pattern. Physically, these managers are most comfortable having a fair amount of distance between them when talking directly to each other. On the other hand, managers interacting in a culture dominated by a public orientation are more likely to engage in a wide variety of interactions using an open style. Their conversations may involve several people simultaneously, and physically close relations will not be uncommon. Gestures will be broad and will use space expansively. Cultures with a mixed orientation influence managers to be more selective in their communications, with moderately separated space between people and somewhat more organized, semiprivate arrangements.

The *office layout,* or the space within which interactions occur at work, shows parallel effects of the dominant orientation to space. Barriers characterize private orientations. Office doors are closed; private offices are favored; large desks and formal spaces are usual. In public-oriented cultures, offices are more likely to be arranged in an open manner. Where private offices do exist, doors are more likely to be left open and fewer barriers, such as office furniture, will appear in them. The mixed orientation features a blend of these characteristics – for example, an office containing specialized spaces. Part of the layout may be formal, with an official desk providing a barrier between the occupant and visitors. An adjoining space in the same office may be furnished with more comfortable, informal furniture.

The perils of ignoring the cultural factors of space can be extremely costly. One Canadian government ministry, caught in the grips of architectural fads, decided it would modernize its office space and save money at the same time. The ministry planned to consolidate several departments in a new building and use an open-plan office layout. Not wishing to traumatize the managers, they decided that movable partitions would provide the appropriate degree of privacy in the new situation. The move involved a total of 1,300 people. Arrangements were made to purchase sufficient dividers for all, even though the merger was to be accomplished in several steps. The first move involved 300 people, but partitions allotted for 800 people were requisitioned from storage. Puzzled, the planners went to inspect and found that most people had insisted on their own dividers.

Poorly executed!

Duplicate partitions had been placed back-to-back to satisfy the managers' need for privacy and ownership!

In another situation, the new CEO of a large insurance company was frustrated by the inability of divisions in the company to better integrate their efforts. The CEO was surprised when a consultant who had been in the company for a total of only 14 hours began to introduce several of the 120 headquarters executives to each other. Closer scrutiny of the office layouts revealed a highly private orientation that explained both situations. Long corridors in the company formed a maze that separated people from each other. The suites of offices off the corridors all closed the doors accessing the reception areas. Inside, each of the offices that formed the group of suites also closed all their doors. The company had operated in a French-speaking milieu for over a century. However, the company was staunchly British in its culture, and the private orientation to space overwhelmed the CEO's wish for stronger integration among the departments. Even the language used in the company acknowledged the dominance of privacy; the executives openly referred to the high degree of isolation between business units as "functional solitudes." The senior management of the company, including those who used this highly descriptive language in reference to their own situation, seemed genuinely puzzled about their failure to achieve the desired degree of integration. They were, in short, oblivious to the ways their own company culture, firmly embedded in their own broader cultural values, affected the management processes. In a highly regulated environment in which the company originated, its processes were adequate. As deregulation changed the industry, though, greater integration, flexibility, and speed were required and the old cultural values impeded adaptation to the new realities.

Know yourself !

In addition to this spatial sense, the space-orientation value also applies to physical goods, property, or information. People with a dominantly private orientation are likely to have a strong sense of ownership of things as well as space. This manifests itself in the degree to which physical items are shared or viewed as community property.

SUMMARY

copiers / printers / vehicles etc.

Figure 9 summarizes the spatial orientation.

FIGURE 9   Variations in Spatial Orientation and Examples of Management Impact

Management Impact	Private	Mixed	Public
Communication and influence patterns	One-to-one, private	Selective, semi-private	Wide, open
Office layout	Emphasis on barriers; closed doors, large desks, etc.	Specialized spaces; e.g., informal furniture next to formal desk	Open concept
Interaction patterns	Physically distant, one-to-one, serial	Moderately spaced, moderated numbers, organized	Physically close, frequent touching, multiple relations

Key -

FIGURE 10   Completed and Summarized Cultural Orientations Framework

Issue	Variations		
Relation to the environment (to the complete environment and to life and work in general)	**Subjugation** • Predetermined • Inevitable • Accepting • External control • Dependent • Fate	**Harmony** • Interdependent • Coexist • Live together with	**Mastery** • Control events/situation • Make happen • Independent • Internal control
Relationships among people (power and responsibility)	**Hierarchical** • Vertical differentiation • Authority • Status (age, family, seniority, etc.)	**Group** • Horizontal differentiation • In-group out-group distinction	**Individual** • Informal • Variable • Status (personal achievement) • Egalitarianism
Mode of human activity (mode of action)	**Being** • Spontaneous • Act on feelings	**Thinking** • Think and feel • Work and self • Seeking, becoming • Control self	**Doing** • Achieving/striving • Compulsive • Performance • Work is central focus
Basic human nature changeable? unchangeable?	**Bad** • Suspicion • Close supervision • Theory X	**Mixed/neutral** • Product of social environment • Consultation	**Good** • Information • Participation • Collaborative • Theory Y
Time – general orientation	**Past** • Respect tradition and proven ways • Precedence • Maintain continuity	**Present** • Current realities • Near-term • Respond to change	**Future** • Longer-term • Anticipate change
Time – activities	**Polychronic** • Relaxed • Elastic • Less critical	**Monochronic** • Tight schedules • Punctual • Hectic	
Use of space Personal ownership	**Private** • Closed • Secretive • Distant	**Mixed**	**Public** • Open • Physically close

Completed framework

The discussion of each of the orientations in the Cultural Orientation Framework has demonstrated the variety of ways in which the effects of values seep into one's assumptions and perceptions and influence managerial life. Figure 10 shows the full matrix with examples of each of the variations within the cells.

It is important to remember that the dominant values on one dimension are independent of dominant values on another. When inspecting the overall matrix in Figure 10, it is tempting to impose a correlation of dominant values that seem to cluster together naturally. This tendency to associate values across the dimensions as fitting with each other is a result of our own cultural conditioning. Thus, North Americans may feel that mastery, present/future, mixed/neutral, doing, individualistic, and mixed space values belong together, while Chinese readers may feel that harmony, future, good, thinking, group, and public space belong together. However, the associations are based only on what we are used to seeing, not inevitably brought about by natural law. Subcultures with all different combinations exist in society, and in our research and teaching we have seen individuals with a wide variety of combinations of value variations.

is there a natural law?

The skill of mapping   Being able to map involves more than the knowledge of the framework. It requires *using* the framework to explain and predict others' attitudes and behavior. Mapping creates awareness and appreciation of differences and their implications in a structured and consistent way. It begins a conversation about similarities and differences using a common language and framework, and allows the conversation to move quickly and constructively to individual and situational differences. Just like any other skill, managers can practice mapping and improve their ability to map. With practice, they begin to see patterns in the values and actions of other people, and to understand those patterns from the other people's own perspectives. It is this level of mapping skill that provides a foundation for effective *bridging*.

Beyond mapping: navigating across cultures intelligently   Mapping is a good first step to cross-cultural understanding, but it is important to recognize its limits. In its most basic form, mapping is sophisticated stereotyping. Sophisticated stereotyping is describing cultures using objective, non-evaluative data to predict thinking and behavior patterns of the culture's members.[28] As we illustrated above, sophisticated stereotyping is extremely helpful when we enter new situations or try to understand unexpected events. People who go into new countries and cultures without sophisticated stereotypes, saying, "I have no expectations, I have an open mind," are really assuming "I think they will be like me." This is due to the basic human processes related to the assumptions and perceptions described earlier in Part 1. As research has shown, when people go into a new situation with a map of expectations concerning how the others are likely to be different from oneself – sophisticated stereotypes – they are more prepared for differences in thinking and behavior and they manage those differences much better.[29]

Using maps to identify the main features of a new landscape to get yourself oriented is an essential skill. But as you become more active and experienced, you need to go further and learn to navigate the territory well. Reality is always more complex than the map.

The limits of maps

There are three important reasons why maps are limited. The first is that *individuals do not always conform to their cultures*. Variety and unpredictability are both the beauty and the complexity of human nature. We are all different, and we do not always behave as

FIGURE 11   Mastery Orientation: People's Republic of China and the United States

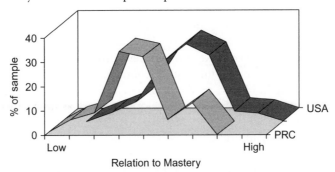

predicted! Within cultures, some people hold more strongly to the cultural norms than others. Furthermore, personality and environmental factors influence individual behavior. Even people who are strong proponents of their culture's values do not always behave in a way that is consistent with those values.[30] This limitation is called the *ecological fallacy*: by knowing the culture (ecological level) you cannot always predict individuals; by knowing an individual, you cannot automatically predict the culture. Figure 11 illustrates this principle with data from our research. In this figure you can see that there are individuals who are *atypical* of their cultural group, and others who cluster around the norm. You can see that there are differences between the two cultural groups, but there are overlaps, too. Some individuals in each cultural group are more like those in the *other cultural group*! And in the sample of managers from the People's Republic of China there are two distinct subgroups. Think about yourself; are you more or less typical of the cultural group you identify yourself with? If you are like most, you *think* you are atypical. But that may be true only of one or two important values. Think again!

2. Second, cultures are much more *complex* than can be described by six orientations with their aggregate variations. The configuration of preferences themselves leads to complex differences. Mastery combined with doing, for example, looks different from mastery combined with thinking. Mastery–doing is associated with obsessive task activity for accomplishment; mastery–thinking is associated with more depth in analysis before controlling. More importantly, the dimensions cannot ever capture the richness of cultures. We have provided examples of poetry and stories to illustrate some of the principles, but the art, music, traditions, practices, and beliefs of cultures go far beyond these dimensions. As we discussed earlier, multiple cultures exist simultaneously in the same social "space." The existence of subcultures and complementary cultures also adds to the complexity of culture.

3. Third, cultures are *dynamic*, always changing. In fact, Kluckhohn and Strodtbeck argued that cultures must change or they will stagnate and die (and that change is made possible by the variation of individuals within cultures and the existence of subcultures).[31] Usually change is quite slow, but sometimes external and internal events combine to create fast change. For example, it is impossible to describe *a* culture of Russia right now.

Navigating with cultural intelligence

Cultural intelligence is going beyond mapping to navigate within the territory in a successful way.[32] It involves recognizing and accepting cultural differences, but then putting them in the context of individuals involved, companies, and other aspects of the situation. It means being mindful of people and situations as dynamic and complex, and behaving in a fluid and responsive way. Osland and Bird's article on cultural sense-making and cultural paradoxes develops these ideas much further and is included here as Reading 3.

We prefer the Cultural Orientations Framework to other maps of culture partly because it provides good maps, but also because it provides a springboard to move from mapping to navigating. It is more comprehensive and complex than other culture-general maps. Unlike other frameworks, the Cultural Orientations Framework assumes that all three variations of an orientation exist in all cultures, and that there are no bipolar dimensions. For example, all cultures have all of individualism, collectivism, and hierarchy, and individualism is not the opposite of collectivism. The comprehensive nature covers a broad range of issues and can serve as a brainstorming tool for developing navigational questions. However, it is still a map that provides sophisticated stereotypes.

Remember: the map is not the territory. Managers must learn to be navigators as well as cartographers. Developing good Bridging and Integrating skills are an important way to do this.

Bridging differences through communication

Understanding the lens through which others see the world is an enormous aid to intercultural effectiveness. But this understanding provides little benefit as long as it remains latent. It must be put into use to help the flow of ideas among people in a conversation, a team, or an organization. The goal of these interpersonal flows is effective communication, or the transfer of meaning from one person to another as it was intended by the first person. Most managers recognize that effective communication within one's own culture is difficult enough. Interactions with people from different cultures are even more difficult. The challenge is to interpret correctly what a person from a different culture means by his or her words and actions. Even if interaction is aided by slowing speech, speaking more distinctly, listening more carefully, or asking more questions, there still remains the problem of interpreting the message. Resolving miscommunication depends, in large part, on a manager's willingness to explain the problem rather than to blame the other person. And the quality of the explanation depends, in large part, on the manager's ability to map the other person's culture with respect to his or her own.

Although language is an important part of communication, communication is not simply a matter of understanding and speaking a language. Communication is broader than language alone. Someone who is able to speak three different languages still may not be able to understand the issues from the viewpoint of those from another culture. Or, put more eloquently by an eastern European manager in an executive program, "I can speak to you in your language, but I can't always tell you what I am thinking in my own language."

FIGURE 12 The MBI Model – Bridging Emphasized

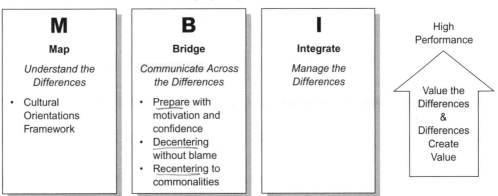

There are three skills important to effective communication in a cross-cultural setting: preparing, decentering, and recentering.[33] While it is true that these three skills help improve all communication, in interactions within a single culture the parties can generally assume the same set of background assumptions, so the steps can be conducted implicitly. The more culturally diverse the setting, however, the more difficult it is to accomplish these steps, and the more explicit they should be. But they also result in bigger payoffs. This component of the MBI model is summarized in Figure 12.

Prepare Preparing is about setting the ground for communication. The most important place to set the ground is in one's own mind. Two attitudes are especially predictive of effective communication: motivation and confidence. Motivation is having the will to communicate across a cultural boundary both to be understood and to understand others. We are usually very good at the former, but not as good at the latter. The confidence part of preparing is to believe that it is possible to overcome any barriers and communicate effectively. Ironically, people with little cross-cultural experience and those who have never tried to understand others from their own perspective tend to have high confidence, and confidence is decreased with the first increments of experience and insight. However, with practice and success – as aided, for example, by the tools described here – confidence increases rapidly, and this later confidence has a much more realistic foundation.

These attitudes may sound simple to control, but their manifestation is complicated by some psychological tendencies we all have. They are inherent to our nature and normally serve us well, but tend to slip us up in cross-cultural interaction. More specifically, we tend to assume:[34]

1 The other person sees the situation the same way we do.
2 The other person is making the same assumptions we are.
3 The other person is (or should be) experiencing the same feelings as we are.
4 The communication situation has no relationship to past events.
5 The other person's understanding is (or should be) based on our own logic, not their feelings.

6   If a problem occurs, it is the other person is the one who has the "problem" or does
    not understand the logic of the situation.
7   Other cultures are changing and becoming, or want to become, more like our cul-
    ture and, therefore, the other person is becoming more like us.

While reading a book it may seem easy to keep these in mind, but in the rush and pressure of making decisions we often forget to withhold judgment. However, there are some
simple things we can do to facilitate the process, aside from just trying to remember to
be motivated and confident. For example, expatriates who spend most of their time in
the company of other expatriates often have little motivation to bridge the cultural communication gaps. They manifest their motivation by the company they keep. When they
do run into difficulties at work, they have little practice at resolving them in more relaxed
settings. A more positive sign of motivation to communicate cross-culturally is learning
the language of those with whom one is working. Nothing is more likely to signal your
motivation for cross-cultural communication than such an effort. Of course, having
confidence that you can learn the language and that, in doing so, you will be more effective, is in itself a boost to the motivation to learn. These two elements create a positive,
reinforcing circle, since having the motivation to learn will probably also boost confidence
in the possibility of improving cross-cultural communication.

    Even without language training, there are ways of developing motivation and confidence
in cross-cultural skills. Reading and studying about the host country's culture, meeting locals and asking them to help immerse oneself in the country, and learning to
apply other parts of this model are examples of how to increase confidence in one's
cross-cultural communication ability and how to demonstrate the motivation to do so.
Mastering a cultural framework or "map," such as the one described in the variations
in value orientation section, is another way. This gives you the motivation and confidence to ask questions that will be especially helpful in preparing yourself for future
understanding. Our research shows that it is possible to learn enough about the MBI
model in a two-day training program to improve performance. Therefore, there is
ample reason for managers to feel both motivated and confident that preparation for
bridging cultures can make a difference.

Decenter   Decentering is actively pushing yourself away from your own "center" and
moving into the mind of the other person to send messages in a way the other will understand, and to listen in a way that allows you to understand them from their own point
of view. Thus, one has a bicultural tongue and bicultural ears. The fundamental idea
of decentering is empathy: feeling and understanding as another person does. But in
the context of the communication model, decentering requires *using* one's empathy
in hearing and speaking. We all know people who understand exactly how we feel, but
nevertheless go ahead and say or do something hurtful anyway. This is practicing
empathy without decentering.

    There are two main elements to decentering. The first is perspective-taking, which is
the skill of being able to see things from the other person's point of view to the extent
that you can speak and listen that way. The second is explaining without blame. When
problems in communication do occur, it is critical that no one blames the other in a

personal way, but that all parties seek an explanation in the situation – the differences in initial starting assumptions. This last point cannot be emphasized enough. In our research this emerged as the single best predictor of effective cross-cultural interaction. Teams that withhold blame and search for situation-based explanations of miscommunication almost inevitably have more effective interaction. Does this mean that all you have to do is explain without blame? No. But look at the sequence of events initiated when blame is suspended. This simple act leads a group into a positive cycle of decentering, exploring alternatives to build a shared reality, developing trust and common rules, and building confidence in the group's ability to use different perspectives productively. This conversation not only resolves the present miscommunication, but also prevents some further ones and provides ideas for creative synergy.

Good decentering is largely dependent on good mapping. The map warns you that surprises and problems may have different explanations, and also provides you with some alternatives to explore. The describe–interpret–evaluate framework identified earlier is very helpful here. When differences are encountered, the people involved should try to come to a point where they can agree on a description: what are the tangible, concrete facts we are talking about? Next they should explore their different interpretations – what do those facts mean to each person, and why? This is where the map provides a common language for sharing the analysis of interpretations. Finally, they should try to understand the different evaluations of the facts – why do some people see something as an opportunity and others as a threat? In cross-cultural situations, the greater the tendency to judge events, the greater the probability of making errors. Resisting the interpretive and evaluative modes while maintaining a descriptive posture for as long as possible is the best protection against cultural gaffes. While this may be difficult to do, it is still to be encouraged.

Recenter   The final step to effective communication is recentering, or establishing a common reality and agreeing on common rules. Like the other elements, establishing a common reality is easier said than done. But it is much easier to see the need to do so, if one is aware of the types of differences between your own values and those of others. For example, the implicit definition and purpose of "a meeting" varies from one culture to the next, with some cultures using meetings to discuss perspectives and come to a joint decision, and other cultures using meetings to publicly formalize decisions that were discussed informally among smaller subgroups of a team. A multicultural team that has not addressed even this basic definition is bound to find at least some members very frustrated with the first meeting. Again, good mapping helps to find a common definition and give the team a point of leverage. For example, members of a multi-site global R&D team differed enormously on relationships and environment orientations, but virtually all preferred thinking strongly over any other mode of activity. They were able to use their common ground of the need to plan and be rational to discuss their differences and work together. A team managing a strategic alliance in a manufacturing technology firm consisted of members from all over Europe, North America, and Asia. Like the R&D scientists they had strong differences on many cultural orientations. Coincidentally, though, all were engineers for at least some part of their career, and they shared the same mastery orientation to the environment. Their common reality was based on what had to be done (changed and controlled), and they used this point to launch discussions about how to divide the work and what task processes to use.

Common norms for interacting must also be established. However, what is critical here is not necessarily agreeing on the same norms for everyone, but rather agreeing what the acceptable norms are to be. It is futile to expect someone to behave in a way that is uncomfortable to them, yet still expect them to participate to their full potential. Asking someone with a predominantly thinking orientation to constantly jump in and "do" because that is the dominant mode and "you'll just have to adapt" is tantamount to asking that person not to bother contributing his or her best ideas to the group. The most effective groups find ways of allowing different members to work with the group differently. Finding these norms is a creative process. It takes time, and relies on strong relationships and trust within the group. But, like good preparing and decentering, the effort is well worth it. When the processes are not explored or discussed to find common ground, serious misunderstandings can occur, even when the cultures are not dramatically different, as exemplified by the following exchange between the Finnish operating head and a senior Swedish executive of a software company grown by a series of acquisitions across the Nordic countries. The SVP Finn was explaining the decision process in the company:

> We reach our decisions by informal consultation "feeling out" positions, evolving into a common view of what should be done – what is possible, what alterations to each others' views are necessary, etc. This all occurs during the "feeling-out" process. Then when I think every-thing is clear I put the issue on the agenda of a meeting that ratifies the result of this process.

His Swedish colleague, who had been working as part of the senior executive team for nearly two years, interrupted and exclaimed heatedly:

> This is exactly the problem with you Finns! It [annoys] me very much when I don't have the opportunity to contribute . . . or even worse, I come to the meeting expecting it to be the first of a series of discussions and after I talk, you Finns give a PowerPoint presentation with the decision already included!! Don't insult me by pretending to ask for my involve-ment and opinion when you've already made up your mind!!

When he calmed down he explained more mildly:

> We Swedes expect a series of meetings, each an opportunity for extensive discussion among the participants, with all involved, until a consensus is achieved or an *explicit* decision is taken. Since Finns occupy many of the senior posts at headquarters, we often find ourselves really annoyed by the process. Now I know why!!

More examples   We captured a classic example of cross-cultural communication when we videotaped a group of executives discussing the possibility of their company acquir-ing another firm. The group consisted of senior managers from the United States, the United Kingdom, Belgium, Japan, and Uruguay. After studying various aspects of the potential deal, they came together to make a recommendation. After 20 minutes of dis-cussion, the British manager stood up in the room and went to the flip chart and wrote: "Do Nothing!" He punctuated his writing by saying, "I don't usually entertain this option, which is always raised as a 'straw man' by business school profs, but I really think in this situation it is our best choice. The deal is far from being ready to make for a whole host of reasons." There was a moment of silence, followed by the Japanese manager clearing his throat and quietly murmuring, "Wait." The others thought that he was asking for a chance to discuss the "Do Nothing" option, but only a silence ensued. After a barely discernible pause, the British manager crossed out "Do Nothing" and wrote next to it, "Wait," and then proceeded with his next point.

Yet the Japanese manager's "Wait" was not the same as the British executive's "Do Nothing." There was no common reality established. The British executive literally meant "don't do anything more; proceed to look for other deals until the other party indicates a change in the conditions." In contrast, the Japanese executive's "Wait" was filled with subtle actions including continuing to get to know the other parties, extending attempts to get more information about their business, and so on. If either of the speakers (or any of the other managers on the team) had been aware that, in terms of the activity dimension of the value orientation, the British executive was operating out of a dominant doing orientation, while the Japanese manager was expressing a thinking mode, then a chance for establishing a common reality might have occurred.

The business consequences would likely have been quite different if they (a) had a map of cultural differences; (b) seen that their orientations were different and defined different realities for the acquisition situation; and (c) acted to explore their differences until they could agree on a common definition of situation. Had they done so, a different course of action (or in the British manager's sense, inaction) might have followed. In addition, both would have added to their understanding of the other's culture and its manifestation in business activity. As it was, only a review of the videotape revealed this missed opportunity. Although the Japanese manager did know that he had been misunderstood when the original incident had occurred, he had not called it to the others' attention.

In the same discussion, in the 20 minutes before the British manager wrote his recommendation to do nothing, there were three failed attempts by the manager from Uruguay to introduce the issue of who would constitute the top executive team should the deal be struck. Would the buying company or the acquired organization supply the key executives for the merged entity? He thought that this question was pertinent to the decision of whether or not to buy the organization. But each time he tried to raise the issue, the two American and the British managers, who were citing the lack of compatible strategies and financial problems in the negotiations, brushed his comments aside. Soon their dominance in the discussion extinguished the South American's view of what was important. This, too, exemplifies the lack of a common reality. To the Latin manager, relationships were highly relevant to the deal; to the Anglo-American managers, quantitative and strategic issues were what mattered. Again, having a cultural map might have helped. The difference in relative emphasis on relationships versus mastery and doing led to a missed opportunity to reach common ground. Note also that, in both cases, it was the view of the majority of the managers present that was acted on without the other perspective even being noticed, much less engaged. In these two real examples from a single meeting, it becomes evident that having a framework to understand one's own culture and to map the differences of others can provide a way of testing whether there is a common reality or not and of building one if it is needed.

[handwritten margin note: A good facilitator would have brought each position out!]

Similarly, the map helps in establishing common rules for communicating and interacting. The two examples noted above illustrate this component of the model as well as the common reality dimension. In the first situation, the Japanese manager did not call the British manager's attention to his misinterpretation of "Wait." In Japan, such a comment would have meant a loss of face for the British manager. So the rule of communication is silence. But if the British manager knew he had been misunderstood, it is much more likely that he would have at least clarified what he had meant, and might have added that he had been misinterpreted. His rule for interaction is direct communication. The roots of these different rules are in varying preferences for individualism, doing, and mastery on one side versus group, thinking, and harmony modes on the other.

The example of the Uruguayan's attempt to introduce people into the acquisition equation provides another illustration of the common rules theme. Two aspects of uncommon rules were visible in that series of exchanges. First, each time he wanted to speak, the manager from Uruguay waited until there was a brief pause in the conversation; in contrast, the American and British managers often interrupted each other. Another contrast was in how the issues were raised by the two sides; the Uruguayan posed his idea tentatively, twice putting it in the form of a question ("Don't you think we should explore from which company the top officers will be drawn?"). The Anglo-Americans were much more definite and assertive in their phrasing ("That's irrelevant until we get the financials and strategy agreed to!"). Again, no common rules of interaction were established for the two parties. Until some common modes of interaction are understood and acknowledged by both parties, cross-cultural communication will be problematic.

So, if the American in this team knew that the Uruguayan was likely to value relationships more, he would have been more likely to hear the suggestion to consider the issue of the top executive team the first time it was made. And he would be less likely to feel and show the irritation that was evident when the videotape captured his tone of condescension the third time the Uruguayan tried to pose his idea.

Integrating to manage and build on the differences

Figure 13 introduces the final component of the MBI model, integrating the differences. It is not sufficient to have a way of understanding cultural differences and bridging the gaps by effective communication. One also needs to manage the differences effectively if they are to result in higher performance of the people who are working together. There are three main integration skills: building participation, resolving conflicts, and building on ideas.

To realize the benefits of different perspectives and ideas (the latent possibilities among the multicultural membership of a group), it is necessary to express the ideas. Not all cultures are equally predisposed to offer their ideas openly. People from cultures with a strong hierarchical orientation, for example, are not likely to put forward their ideas in a group containing a direct superior or a higher-status person. In contrast, people from individualistic cultures are more likely to assert their ideas. The first challenge for a multicultural group, then, is to ensure that all the ideas are heard.

It is especially helpful if someone on the team monitors participation to notice whether there are systematic differences in participation rates. Figure 14 shows the pattern of participation in the meeting described above (group 2) and a parallel meeting with

FIGURE 13 The MBI Model – Integration Emphasized

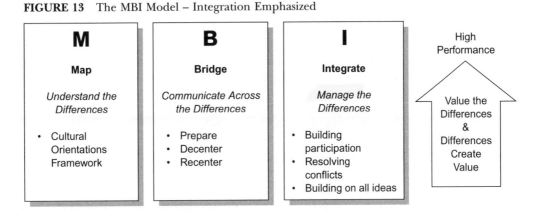

FIGURE 14 Participation by Individuals in Two Group Discussions

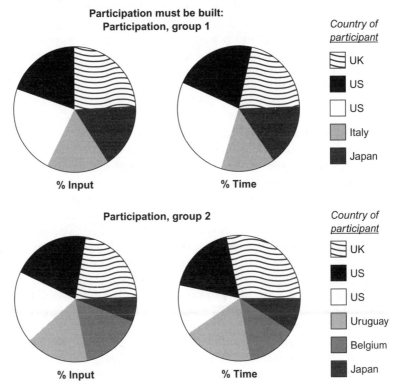

different individuals, first in proportion of contributions by number, then in percentage of time. If there were no differences in the rates, each shaded area would be equal in size. Aggregating the UK and US data shows a clear dominance of executives from these countries in both groups for both percentages of inputs and time. This pattern is especially clear in the second group.

There are ways of engaging all group members and facilitating their participation. In the example given earlier, the Japanese manager hardly spoke in the first half-hour; his "Wait" was his lone contribution during the first 20 minutes. Yet later, when the Texan in the group noticed his silence, he invited participation by saying, "If I recall, Sugano-san, a couple of years ago you had some experience in a merger similar to the one we are discussing. What do you think about this situation?" What followed was a highly relevant and cogent discourse, fluidly expressed, which had a big impact on the shape of the group's recommendation. When his involvement was sought, this otherwise infrequent participant made an important contribution.

To avoid relying solely on the observational power of a group member to notice the absence of participation, the group can set up routines to facilitate everyone's participation. For example, the group can decide that, on all important issues, a process of going around the table will be used to produce as many ideas as possible before discussion starts. Or one person can be charged with ensuring that all members have been included before an important decision is made. Another way of facilitating participation is to vary the modes of input. It might be easier, for example, for an otherwise reticent member to provide written input than to appear to be dominating or advancing his or her own interest by speaking in the group. Or it might be easier to provide ideas outside the context of formal meetings: in a private, face-to-face setting instead of a group meeting where the status issues (including the ambiguity of roles) may inhibit easy communication. Once they accept the possibility of having different norms for group members, most groups find creative ways to get everyone's input.

Resolving disagreements   As more ideas from various viewpoints are expressed, there is an increasing likelihood that there will be disagreements. The way these conflicts are handled, then, becomes the next cross-cultural challenge. Even the way conflict gets expressed, quite apart from how it gets resolved, varies in different cultural traditions. In many cultures it is deemed inappropriate to express conflict openly. So for a manager from a culture where open expression of disagreement is valued, the first problem becomes detecting the existence of the conflict. In high-context cultures, a disagreement may be expressed very subtly or indirectly through a third party. In low-context cultures, conflict is more likely to be stated bluntly, in words of little ambiguity. When these norms (rules of communication from the earlier component of the model) are not understood, frustration or anger are likely to be the result. If I express conflict more directly, I may be frustrated by behavior that I read as sending "mixed signals" or conclude the other person is confused or cannot make up his or her mind. If I expect indirect expression of conflict, I might feel insulted by what I experience as impolite or crass comments from the other person who feels she or he is "just putting the issue on the table."

One way to deal with these issues is to use the map and communication components of the model noted in the previous section. The mapping framework provides a way to anticipate when the conflict gaps may occur; the communication techniques give tools for reaching a common understanding and a common set of rules or norms for resolving the conflicts and avoiding them in the future. Effective communication is more than half of effective conflict resolution. The map of cultural differences may provide clues as to the other person's preferred ways of dealing with conflict. By decentering, you can

FIGURE 15   The Completed MBI Model

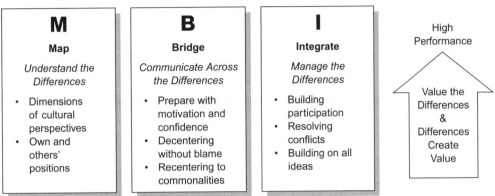

adapt to the other's perspective without falling into the ethnocentric trap of blaming _Trap_
the other person or misinterpreting the meaning of actions by referencing your own
cultural codes.

Building on ideas   Even if the mapping framework is well understood, the communication skills are well developed, and participation and conflict issues are managed effectively, there is still a key component to realizing the potential of a multicultural group,
namely, moving forward and building on the ideas. There are cultural barriers in this
phase of activity, too. As mentioned earlier, some cultural preferences would lead a
person to push one's ideas (individualism), while another orientation (hierarchical) is
more likely to lead to deference to authority. If you are in a group with several cultures,
there might be an agreement (common rules of interaction) to surface ideas without
attributing them to individuals or using an individual's ideas as a starting point for discussion. The main idea is to encourage the exploration of ideas with the conscious attempt
to invent new ideas, to build on the ideas initially surfaced. A real stimulus to innovation is to try to do more than combine ideas and to avoid compromises. Finally, striving to find solutions to issues or problems that are acceptable to all (another rule for
interaction or norm for behavior) is another way to increase the probability of getting
synergy from the diversity in the group. Trying to invent new ideas from those available
and reaching for solutions to which everyone can agree are ideals that are difficult to
accomplish. But even setting them as objectives will help a multicultural team achieve
its potential for high performance.

Figure 15 shows the completed MBI model for interpersonal and team effectiveness.

APPLYING THE MBI IN SIX ARENAS

Six types of situations require that managers understand their own culture and how it
differs from others (see Figure 16). In each of these situations, decisions must be made
and implemented across cultural boundaries. At the individual level (Arenas 1 and 2),

FIGURE 16 Six Arenas for Synergy in International Management

	One-way	*Multi-way*
Individual level	Arena 1 *Expatriate* • Individual manager going to another country to manage a business unit or perform a specialist job	Arena 2 *Multicultural team* • Group from many countries, often cross-functional, managing across units or a multi-country project
Organizational level	Arena 3 *Export system* • Take a human resources, information system, or other practice or strategy from one country into another	Arena 4 *Global system* • Develop human resources systems, organizational structures or strategies, to be implemented in many countries
External to organization	Arena 5 *External relationships* • Customer, supplier, marketing, or other information developed in one market, adapt to another market	Arena 6 *Multilateral systems* • Conglomerates, lobbying or trade agreements, professional organizations

managers must interact effectively with individuals from other cultures. People from different cultures will bring with them diverse expectations about the interaction, and effectiveness depends on understanding and building on these differences. At the organizational level (Arenas 3 and 4), managers must design systems of interaction that guide the coordinated behavior of many people. It is important for managers to know whether these systems will be consistent or contradictory with the cultural system in place. External to the organization (Arenas 5 and 6), managers work with customers, suppliers, and other stakeholders in partnerships, complex negotiations, and indirectly through marketing and advertising efforts. In one-way transactions (Arenas 1, 3, and 5), managers need to take something that has been developed in one culture and put it into another one. Successful execution is based on an understanding of how things will be interpreted in the new context. In multi-way transactions (Arenas 2, 4, and 6), managers must take into account many cultural and contextual systems at the same time. Unless the differences are understood, conflict and division will characterize the situation.

To anticipate and avoid cross-cultural problems at any of the three levels, appropriate preparation is needed. For example, if a manager is going to another country, that manager should be oriented to the culture in which she will operate. She can organize the information, observations, and advice provided in such an orientation by using the cultural variations of the map described as the first component of the MBI model. The manager can then evaluate her own dominant value orientations, analyze those of the destination culture, and then decide where the main differences exist. For each value dimension where there are differences, she can deduce the likely areas of managerial problems by examining the examples from Figures 4–10, combined with careful thought.

A similar approach can be taken if a manager in a multinational corporation (MNC) is attempting to introduce organizational structures or systems from headquarters into an overseas subsidiary (Part 2 of this book provides a more detailed treatment of these issues). The difference here is that the issues involved include organizational design elements rather than people

If a manager is involved with external relationships or has to manage multilateral relationships and systems, the application of the MBI model is that much more complex.

In any of the arenas tabulated in Figure 16, the usefulness of applying the model depends upon:

1 Being explicit about one's own culture.
2 Organizing what is known about another culture.
3 Providing for a systematic comparison of dominant values.
4 Noting value differences and using them to predict the areas in which managerial problems are likely to arise.
5 Actively working through the key elements of bridging and integrating.

Even though areas of potential managerial and personal problems may be predicted, the international executive still has to make a basic choice. For each kind of problem, he or she can make plans to avoid it using a dominant approach (deciding which culturally defined management practice should be followed) or a mixed strategy (blending the practices of different origins). Executives can also develop a synergistic approach to management and organization that "transcends the distinct cultures of [its] members" using the tools of communication and integration described in the overall model.[35]

It is probably unwise to select a single strategy for all kinds of problems. Some situations may require different approaches. For example, the Canadian National Railway found it necessary to insist that Inuit employees, who run their trains on a single-line track, always call in by radio if they stopped to rest.[36] (An Inuit harmony and being value is: "When tired, sleep.") In this situation, safety demanded that a dominant strategy be adopted. But when oil companies in the Arctic found that native people failed to show up for work in order to go hunting when geese were migrating (again, a harmony-influenced behavior) or when they felt like visiting relatives (a being- and group-oriented behavior), the companies hired more workers than needed and paid them only when they worked. Rather than complain about "unreliable" employees, they adopted a synergistic solution.[37]

In addition to choosing among dominant, mixed, and synergistic strategies, there is the additional issue of deciding which party needs to adapt. A number of factors influence the decision of who should adapt and how the adaptation should be made. As a general rule, the onus for adaptation rests with the party who is seen as the foreigner. The sheer force of numbers probably influences this. But this rule of the majority also misses significant opportunities for learning and inventing, as we saw in the example of the culturally mixed team of managers discussing the acquisition.

Location is another strong factor. Everything else being equal (which is rarely the case), the guest is expected to adapt to the host. Technological dependence may alter this equation. A German joint venture in Beijing may choose to emphasize German cultural values and management practice in spite of the location and overwhelming majority of Chinese population, simply as a recognition of the need to acquire information. In fact, the power of resources in general has a strong influence on who is expected to adapt. The buyer almost always expects the seller to adapt, unless the seller has something extremely rare for which there are many willing buyers.

Individual preference may also enter the equation. An expatriate dealing with Chinese in Beijing may attempt to adapt to Chinese traditions, even though there is no necessity to do so. The motives for adaptation in this situation may range from showing courtesy to a desire to learn and to increase one's own repertoire of behavior. Furthermore, no matter where a company is operating, an attempt to adapt to others' customs will be appreciated and will have a positive influence on relations.

In the variety of examples we have discussed, the range of behavior serves as a reminder that several different values can influence people simultaneously. This makes the use of a framework even more valuable in that it provides a checklist against which to analyze a situation for cultural causes. Fixating on single explanations for events can lead to missing the complexity of the causes involved. This can lead to errors in framing the solutions to problems.

Although everyone attempts to avoid problems, international managers often find themselves immersed in problems that they failed to anticipate and now must resolve. In such cases, the manager must avoid the tendency to blame the other party, as we noted earlier in the discussion of blame-free explanations. You should seek many alternative explanations for a problem, and be especially wary of interpreting events from only one perspective when people from more than one culture are involved. If it appears that there is a cross-cultural component to a problem, then the choice of strategy remains as described earlier. The key factor, however, is the careful analysis of the causes of a problem and the isolation of those elements that are cultural in nature. If there are no culturally linked causes, then conventional approaches can be followed to resolve the problems.

PERFORMANCE OF DIVERSE TEAMS USING THE MBI MODEL

Since the publication of the fourth edition of this book, we have assisted a large number of teams, each responsible for a wide variety of tasks, from a wide variety of industries. We selected seventeen of these teams for which we had the most reliable data on their membership characteristics and their mapping, bridging, and integrating applications, and then compiled a matrix of the data together with our best estimates of their performance or success on the tasks for which they were responsible.[38]

These data are presented in the accompanying box. Five of the seventeen teams were classified as having high to very high performance; eight had medium to medium high performance and four were classified as having low to very low performance. Within these categories of performance the patterns of application of the MBI model strongly support the principles we described earlier in this section of the book.

Among the high performing teams, all exhibited high motivation and four of the five also demonstrated high confidence. They engaged in medium to high decentering, with four of the five exhibiting low blame, a key characteristic of high-performing groups (the fifth group had medium low blame behavior). In addition, four of the five showed medium to high recentering behavior. In terms of the integrating elements in the model, all of the high-performing teams had high participation, widely distributed over the members. They also demonstrated medium to high conflict resolution (though one had very little conflict to resolve!). They all were medium to high in behaviors that helped them to build on each other's ideas.

In contrast, the low-performing teams showed the opposite kinds of behaviors. Three of the four were classic in having high blame orientation (one was medium in this characteristic). Their overall decentering was low in three of the four cases, and three of the four also had low motivation and confidence. Their recentering was either low in frequency or in quality; for example, two of the teams displayed a façade of recentering. None of the four systematically built on the ideas expressed by their members. Three had low conflict resolution and the other team had trouble even detecting the conflict that was bubbling beneath the surface. Their participation patterns were either mixed or skewed or one-way in the direction of the dominant person or subgroup.

The mixed performance groups had mixed patterns of MBI behaviors, with no clear pattern of either very high or very low behavior on the variables in the model.

These results match very well the systematic, controlled studies from which the model was derived and tested. They strongly suggest that it would be worth your effort to apply the ideas we have described in this section.

Multi-Cultural Teams: Learning from Experience

Type of Team	Level of Diversity	Mapping Function	Bridging Function	Integrating Function	Face-to-Face v. Virtual	Level of Success
Special Full-Time Task Forces (4 teams)	High Culture & Personality	Culture & Personality (CPQ & FIRO)	High Motivation & Confidence, Medium Decentering, **Low Blame**, Medium–High Recentering	**High Participation**, Medium Conflict Resolution, **High Building on Ideas**	Face-to-face daily	**Very High**
Bank Back Office Processing Team (self managed)	High Culture & Personality	Culture only (CPQ)	High Motivation & Confidence, High Decentering, **Low Blame**, High Recentering	**High Participation**, Low Conflict so Resolution not relevant **High Building on Ideas**	Face-to-face	**Very High**
Research & Development (self-managed)	High Culture & Personality + large team)	Culture only (CPQ)	All elements high, except **Low Blame**	**All elements high**	Virtual	**High**
National Account Teams	High Personality	Personality only	High Motivation & Confidence, Medium Decentering, **Low Blame**, High Recentering	**High Participation**, Medium Conflict Resolution, **Medium Building on Ideas**	Face-to-face for 1 week & 2x/year + virtual as needed	**High**
Executive Team	High Culture & Personality	Culture & Personality (CPQ & MBTI)	High Motivation & Medium Confidence, **Medium–Low Blame**, Medium Decentering & Recentering	**High Participation**, Medium Conflict Resolution, **High Building on Ideas**	Face-to-face daily	**High**

Multi-Cultural Teams: Learning from Experience (*cont'd*)

Type of Team	*Level of Diversity*	*Mapping Function*	*Bridging Function*	*Integrating Function*	*Face-to-Face v. Virtual*	*Level of Success*
Task Force for Merger & Acquisitions	High Culture & Personality	Culture & Leadership (CPQ & LBI)	Medium Motivation & Confidence, High & Low Decentering, **Low Blame**, Medium Recentering	**High Participation**, Medium Conflict Resolution, **Medium Building on Ideas**	Face-to-face daily for 2 weeks	**Medium–High**
Global Account Team (MNC)	High Culture	Culture only (CPQ)	Medium Motivation, Low Confidence, Medium Decentering, **Low Blame**, Medium Recentering	**Medium Participation**, Medium Conflict Resolution, **Medium–High Building on Ideas**	Face-to-face, 1/year, virtual often	**Medium–High**
Executive Team (Regional Company)	Medium (2 local, 2 from region, 1 expat from headquarters country	Intuitive Mapping *post facto*	Medium Motivation & Confidence, Medium Decentering, **Medium Blame**, Medium Recentering (expatriate exception)	**High Participation**, Medium Conflict Resolution, **Low Building on Ideas**	Face-to-face weekly	**Medium (expatriate resigned)**
Exec + Regional Team (MNC)	Low in Top Executive Team, High in Regional Team	Culture only (CPQ)	High Motivation & Confidence, Medium Decentering, **Low Blame**, Medium Recentering	**High Participation**, Medium Conflict Resolution, **Medium High Building on Ideas**	Executive Team Face-to-face often, Regional Team F2F 1/year, Low Virtual	**Medium**
Executive Team (Domestic)	Low Culture, Medium Personality	Culture & Personality (CPQ & MBTI)	Medium Motivation & Confidence, Medium Decentering, **Medium Blame**, Medium Recentering	**High Participation**, Medium Conflict Resolution, Medium Building on Ideas	Face-to-face weekly	**Medium**
Executive Team (Global Reach, but Headquarters Expats Dominate)	Medium (14 local Culture, 2 from largest market)	Culture only (CPQ)	High Motivation & Confidence, Medium Decentering, **Low Blame**, High Recentering	**Mixed Participation, (local culture is High Context Culture)**, Medium Conflict Resolution, **Medium Building on Ideas**	Monthly Face-to-face for 2 days each month	**Medium**

Multi-Cultural Teams: Learning from Experience (*cont'd*)

Type of Team	Level of Diversity	Mapping Function	Bridging Function	Integrating Function	Face-to-Face v. Virtual	Level of Success
Executive Team + Direct Reports (Multi Domestic)	Ethnic Diversity within Domestic Culture	Culture & Personality (CPQ & MBTI)	High Motivation & Medium Confidence, Medium Decentering, **Medium Blame**, Medium Recentering	**High Participation**, Medium Conflict Resolution **Medium High Building on Ideas**	Executive Team Face-to-face daily, Direct Reports Face-to-face once a quarter	**Medium**
Exec Team & Multi-Functional Teams (2)	High (Culture & Personality)	Culture & Personality (CPQ & MBTI)	**All elements**	**All elements**	Face-to-face & Virtual	**Medium (met expectations)**
Executive Board (Multi-Domestic firm)	Very Low (same Culture but high variation in Personality)	Personality only (MBTI)	Low Motivation and Confidence, Low Decentering, **High Blame**, Facade of Recentering	**Mixed Participation**, Low Conflict Resolution, **Low Building on Ideas**	Weekly Face-to-face with frequent one-to-one meetings of different pairs	**Low**
Executive Team (Regional of MNC)	Medium (Top positions all American expatriates; rest of team from region)	Culture only	Low Motivation and Confidence, Medium Decentering, **Medium Blame**, Recentering on top expatriate American	**Skewed Participation**, Low Conflict Resolution, **Low Building on Ideas**	Face-to-face bimonthly	**Low**
Global Account Team (MNC)	High Culture, Moderate Personality	None	Low Motivation, Low Decentering, **High Blame**, Low Recentering	**One way Participation**, Low Conflict Resolution, **Low Building on Ideas**	Virtual, low richness technology used	**Low**
Financial Services Team	High Culture & Personality	**Intuitive Culture & Personality map, but inaccurate (stereotype)**	High Motivation, Low Confidence, Low Decentering, **High Blame** Low Recentering	**One-sided Participation, Low Detection of Conflict, Low Building on Ideas**	Face-to-face, but infrequent	**Very Low (Critical Person Quit)**

A FINAL CAUTION: KNOWLEDGE DOES NOT EQUAL SKILL

This chapter discusses the impact of culture on management and intercultural effectiveness in an analytic and almost impersonal way. It is important to know how culture works – how it affects behavior and what some of its dimensions are. It is equally important to know the components of bridging and integrating skills. Knowledge and understanding should be the bases from which one takes action. There is a danger, however, in assuming that because one has learned something, one can take such action automatically.

Intellectual understanding may not translate directly into a high degree of skill. Skills take practice. Imagine hearing someone explain, using physics and mathematical equations, how to ride a bicycle. Undoubtedly, the explanation would be correct and would display a thorough understanding of the facts and laws that would have to be observed for a person to ride a bicycle successfully. But no one would stand a chance of riding a bicycle for the first time after such a scientific lecture. Parents, teaching their son or daughter to ride a bicycle, talk about balance, turning the handlebars (and therefore the front wheel) gently, pedaling fast enough to keep the bicycle upright, and so on. Keeping these principles in mind and practicing these principles usually leads to success.

Putting knowledge into action is a skill. It is this skill that brings success. Just as the notion of "lecture and ride" is naive, so is "read and go." The child riding the bicycle has reality (hills, bumps, sand on sidewalks, other bicycles) to deal with, and so do managers working in other cultures. Managers who will conduct business in another culture cannot be told about all the hills and bumps they will face. An open mind and a willingness to learn from experiences will help the international manager get over many problems and adapt to new cultures. However, in the process of adapting, one can expect to fall off one's bicycle occasionally. We hope that the ideas presented here will decrease the number of falls and cushion their impact.

Notes

1   Geert Hofstede, *Cultures and Organizations: Software of the mind* (Maidenhead, Berkshire, England: McGraw-Hill Book Company Europe, 1991).
2   For an elegant and powerful work on the risks of defining oneself with only a single identity (or allowing others to define you as having only one identity) see Amin Maalouf, *In the Name of Identity* (New York: Penguin, 2000).
3   M. Erez and P. C. Earley, *Culture, Self-Identity, And Work* (Oxford: Oxford University Press, 1993).
4   Karl Weick, *The Social Psychology of Organizing* (Reading, MA: Addison-Wesley, 1979).
5   John Berry et al., *Cross Cultural Psychology: Research and Applications* (Cambridge: Cambridge University Press, 1992): 8.
6   Nancy Adler, *International Dimensions of Organizational Behavior*, 4th edn. (Cincinnati: South-Western, 2000).
7   Susan E. Jackson, "Team Composition in Organizational Settings: Issues in Managing an Increasingly Diverse Workforce," in S. Worchel, W. Wood, and J. A. Simpson (eds.), *Group Process and Productivity* (Newbury Park, CA: Sage, 1991), pp. 138–73; F. J. Milliken and L. Martins, "Searching for Common Threads: Understanding the Multiple Effects of Diversity in Organizational Groups," *Academy of Management Journal*, 21 (1996): 402–33.

8   S. C. Ling, "The Effects of Group Cultural Composition and Cultural Attitudes on Performance," doctoral dissertation, London, Canada: University of Western Ontario, 1990; P. L. McLeod and S. A. Lobel, "The Effects of Ethnic Diversity on Idea Generation in Small Groups," *Academy of Management Annual Meeting Best Papers Proceeding* (1992): 227–31; W. E. Watson, K. Kumar, and L. K. Michaelson, "Cultural Diversity's Impact on Interaction Process and Performance: Comparing Homogeneous and Diverse Task Groups," *Academy of Management Journal*, 36 (1993): 590–602.

9   Martha Maznevski, "Synergy and Performance in Multicultural Teams," doctoral dissertation, London, Canada: University of Western Ontario, 1994; Martha Maznevski, "Understanding our Differences: Performance in Decision-making Groups with Diverse Members," *Human Relations*, 47 (1994): 531–52. Joseph DiStefano and Martha Maznevski, "Creating Value with Diverse Teams in Global Management," *Organizational Dynamics*, 29 (2000): 45–63.

10 Edward T. Hall, "The Silent Language in Overseas Business," *Harvard Business Review*, 38(3) (1960): 87–96.

11 Geert Hofstede, *Culture's Consequences: International Differences in Work-related Values* (La Jolla, CA: Sage, 1980) and "Motivation, Leadership and Organization: Do American Theories Apply Abroad?," *Organizational Dynamics*, 9(1) (1980): 42–63.

12 Charles Hampden-Turner and Fons Trompenaars, *The Seven Cultures of Capitalism* (New York: Currency Doubleday, 1993). Also Fons Trompenaars and Charles Hampden-Turner, *Riding the Waves of Culture: Understanding Cultural Diversity in Global Business*, 2nd edn. (New York: Irwin Professional, 1998).

13 F. R. Kluckhohn and F. L. Strodtbeck, *Variations in Value Orientations* (New York: Row, Peterson, 1961).

14 This premise itself is a manifestation of the culture from which the two anthropologists were operating. The assumption that such common themes can be found, or even ought to be sought, reflects "doing" orientation and a sense that it is possible, even desirable, to "master" one's environment. The meaning of these labels and the cultural roots of the scheme will become apparent as the reader proceeds through the framework.

15 Marie Solange Perret, "The Impact of Cultural Differences on Budgeting," doctoral dissertation, London, Canada: University of Western Ontario, 1982.

16 Ibid.

17 André Laurent, "The Cultural Diversity of Western Conceptions of Management," *International Studies of Management and Organization*, 13(1–2) 1983: 75–96.

18 C. B. Gibson and M. Zellmer-Bruhn, "Metaphor and Meaning: An Intercultural Analysis of the Concept of Teamwork," *Administrative Science Quarterly*, 46 (2001): 274–303.

19 Although the specific examples are becoming dated, one of the most readable and thorough studies remains Edwin O. Reischauer's *The Japanese* (Cambridge, MA: Harvard University Press, 1977).

20 "Introduction," *To the Peoples of the World – A Statement on Peace* (Thornhill, Ont.: Baha'i Council of Canada, 1990).

21 Note that if one believes that by following the religious tenets only the *behavior* of people changes but not the fundamental *nature* (which remains marked by original sin), then the orientation would be evil/unchangeable.

22 Asra Q. Nomani, "'Labor Letter.' A special news report on people and their jobs in offices, fields and factories," *Wall Street Journal*, August 2, 1994: A1.

23 Another example of this kind of reasoning is available in Huston Smith, *The World's Religions* (New York: HarperCollins, 1991). According to traditional Hindu tenets, punishment varied by the caste of the offender. For the same offense, a Follower (unskilled laborer) would receive *x* punishment, a Producer (craftsman, farmer, artisan) would receive *2x*, an Administrator

(organizer, doer, man of affairs) would receive *4x*, and a Brahmin (intellectual and spiritual leader) would receive *8x* to *16x.*

24   For a more complete treatment of the time variable, see Edward T. Hall, *The Silent Language* (New York: Doubleday, 1959).

25   Henry Mintzberg, *The Nature of Managerial Work* (Englewood Cliffs, NJ: Prentice-Hall, 1980).

26   Robert W. Lightfoot and Christopher A. Bartlett, "Phillips and Matsushita: A Portrait of Two Evolving Companies," in Christopher A. Bartlett and Sumantra Ghoshal (eds.), *Transnational Management: Text, Cases and Readings in Cross-border Management* (Homewood, IL: Richard D. Irwin, 1992): 82.

27   Hall, *The Silent Language*. In Edward T. Hall, *The Hidden Dimension* (Garden City, NY: Doubleday, 1966), the subject of space is even more fully developed.

28   Allan Bird and Joyce Osland, "Beyond Sophisticated Stereotyping: Cultural Sense-making in Context," *Academy of Management Executive*, 14 (2000): 65–79.

29   I. Ratiu, "Thinking Internationally: A Comparison of How International Executives Learn," *International Studies of Management and Organization*, 13(1–2) (1983): 139–50.

30   C. B. Gibson, M. L. Maznevski, and B. L. Kirkman, "When Does Culture Matter?," in K. Leung (ed.), *New Directions in Cross-Cultural Research*, JIBS Macmillan Research Series Vol. I (2004).

31   Kluckhohn and Strodtbeck, *Variations in Value Orientations*.

32   David C. Thomas and Kerr Inkson, *Cultural Intelligence* (San Francisco: Berrett Koehler, 2004).

33   This scheme was adapted from the groundbreaking work of Rolv M. Blakar. See Blakar, "Towards a Theory of Communication in Terms of Preconditions: A Conceptual Framework and Some Empirical Explorations," in H. Giles and R. N. St. Clair (eds.), *Recent Advances in Language, Communication, and Social Psychology* (London: Lawrence Erlbaum, 1985): 10–40.

34   The first five of these are drawn from Richard E. Porter and Larry A. Samovar, "Approaching Intercultural Communication," in Larry A. Samovar and Richard E. Porter (eds.), *Intercultural Communications: A Reader*, 5th edn. (Belmont, CA: Wadsworth, 1988): 15–30. The last two are corollaries of the first five that, according to our observations, are particularly critical to cross-cultural communication.

35   Adler, *International Dimensions of Organizational Behavior*. For a more full description of cultural synergy, see Adler's text, which devotes a full chapter to this topic. For another extensive treatment, see Robert T. Moran and Philip R. Harris, *Managing Cultural Differences*, 4th edn. (Houston: Gulf, 1996).

36   See "The Great Slave Lake Railway," Case 9-71-C011, Case and Publications, Richard Ivey School of Business, University of Western Ontario, London, Canada.

37   Although the example given was set in the Arctic, oil companies in Chad are finding the need to develop similarly creative solutions to employment issues that they face.

38   This is obviously not a closely controlled or measured set of studies. But we did attempt to avoid bias in our estimates of performance. For example, we did the descriptions and assessments by similar types of groups (e.g., project teams, executive teams, etc.) and ordered the groups from high to low performance only *after* all the data had been assembled.

READING 1

Cultural Constraints in Management Theories

Geert Hofstede

Lewis Carroll's *Alice in Wonderland* contains the famous story of Alice's croquet game with the Queen of Hearts.

> Alice thought she had never seen such a curious croquet-ground in all her life; it was all ridges and furrows; the balls were live hedgehogs, the mallets live flamingoes, and the soldiers had to double themselves up and to stand on their hands and feet, to make the arches.

You probably know how the story goes: Alice's flamingo mallet turns its head whenever she wants to strike with it; her hedgehog ball runs away; and the doubled-up soldier arches walk around all the time. The only rule seems to be that the Queen of Hearts always wins.

Alice's croquet-playing problems are good analogies to attempts to build culture-free theories of management. Concepts available for this purpose are themselves alive with culture, having been developed within a particular cultural context. They have a tendency to guide our thinking toward our desired conclusion.

As the same reasoning may also be applied to the arguments in this article, I better tell you my conclusion before I continue – so that the rules of my game are understood. In this article we take a trip around the world to demonstrate that there are no such things as universal management theories.

Diversity in management *practices* as we go around the world has been recognized in US management literature for more than 30 years. The term "comparative management" has been used since the 1960s. However, it has taken much longer for the US academic community to accept that not only practices but also the validity of *theories* may stop at national borders, and I wonder whether even today everybody would agree with this statement.

An article I published in *Organizational Dynamics* in 1980 entitled "Do American Theories Apply Abroad?" created more controversy than I expected. The article argued, with empirical support, that generally accepted US theories like those of Maslow,

Herzberg, McClelland, Vroom, McGregor, Likert, Blake, and Mouton may not or only very partly apply outside the borders of their country of origin – assuming they do apply within those borders. Among the requests for reprints, a larger number were from Canada than from the United States.

MANAGEMENT THEORISTS ARE HUMAN

as contrasted with parts in an army.

Employees and managers are human. Employees as humans were "discovered" in the 1930s, with the human relations school. Managers as humans were introduced in the late 1940s by Herbert Simon's "bounded rationality" and elaborated in Richard Cyert and James March's *Behavioral Theory of the Firm* (1963, and recently republished in a second edition). My argument is that management scientists, theorists, and writers are human too: they grew up in a particular society in a particular period, and their ideas cannot help but reflect the constraints of their environment.

The idea that the validity of a theory is constrained by national borders is more obvious in Europe, with all its borders, than in a huge borderless country like the United States. Already in the sixteenth century, Michel de Montaigne, a Frenchman, wrote a statement which was made famous by Blaise Pascal about a century later: "*Vérité en-deca des Pyrenées, erreur au-delà.*" There are truths on this side of the Pyrenées which are falsehoods on the other.

FROM DON ARMADO'S LOVE TO TAYLOR'S SCIENCE

According to the comprehensive ten-volume *Oxford English Dictionary* (1971), the words "manage," "management," and "manager" appeared in the English language in the sixteenth century. The oldest recorded use of the word "manager" is in Shakespeare's *Love's Labour's Lost*, dating from 1588, in which Don Adriano de Armado, "a fantastical Spaniard," exclaims (Act I, scene ii, 188): "Adieu, valour! rust, rapier! be still, drum! for your manager is in love; yea, he loveth."

The linguistic origin of the word is from Latin *manus*, hand, via the Italian *maneggiare*, which is the training of horses in the *manege*; subsequently its meaning was extended to skillful handling in general, like of arms and musical instruments, as Don Armado illustrates. However, the word also became associated with the French *menage*, household, as an equivalent of "husbandry" in its sense of the art of running a household. The theater of present-day management contains elements of both *manege* and different managers and cultures may use different accents.

The founder of the science of economics, the Scot Adam Smith, in his 1776 book *The Wealth of Nations*, used "manage," "management" (even "bad management"), and "manager" when dealing with the process and the persons involved in operating joint stock companies. British economist John Stuart Mill (1806–73) followed Smith in this use and clearly expressed his distrust of such hired people who were not driven by ownership. Since the 1880s, the word "management" appeared occasionally in writings by American engineers, until it was canonized as a modern science by Frederick W. Taylor in *Shop Management* in 1903 and in *The Principles of Scientific Management* in 1911.

While Smith and Mill used "management" to describe a process and "managers" for the persons involved, "management" in the American sense – which has since been taken back by the British – refers not only to the process but also to the managers as a class of people. This class (1) does not own a business but sells its skills to act on behalf of the owners, and (2) does not produce personally but is indispensable for making others produce, through motivation. Members of this class carry a high status, and many American boys and girls aspire to the role. In the United States, the manager is a cultural hero.

Let us now turn to other parts of the world. We will look at management in its context in other successful modern economies: Germany, Japan, France, Holland, and among the overseas Chinese. Then we will examine management in the much larger part of the world that is still poor, especially Southeast Asia and Africa, and in the new political configurations of Eastern Europe, and Russia in particular. We will then return to the United States via mainland China.

Germany

del.

The manager is not a cultural hero in Germany. If anybody, it is the engineer who fills the hero role. Frederick Taylor's *Scientific Management* was conceived in a society of immigrants – where large numbers of workers with diverse backgrounds and skills had to work together. In Germany, this heterogeneity never existed.

Elements of the medieval guild system have survived in historical continuity in Germany until the present day. In particular, a very effective apprenticeship system exists both on the shop floor and in the office, which alternates practical work and class-room courses. At the end of the apprenticeship the worker receives a certificate, the *Facharbeiterbrief*, which is recognized throughout the country. About two-thirds of the German-worker population holds such a certificate and a corresponding occupational pride. In fact, quite a few German company presidents have worked their way up from the ranks through an apprenticeship. In comparison, two-thirds of the worker population in Britain have no occupational qualification at all.

The highly skilled and responsible German workers do not necessarily need a manager, American-style, to "motivate" them. They expect their boss or *Meister* to assign their tasks and to be the expert in resolving technical problems. Comparisons of similar German, British, and French organizations show the Germans as having the highest rate of personnel in productive roles and the lowest both in leadership and staff roles.

 Flat organization / *line vs staff*

Business schools are virtually unknown in Germany. Native German management theories concentrate on formal systems. The inapplicability of American concepts of management was quite apparent in 1973 when the US consulting firm of Booz, Allen, and Hamilton, commissioned by the German Ministry of Economic Affairs, wrote a study of German management from an American viewpoint. The report is highly critical and writes among other things that "Germans simply do not have a very strong concept of management." Since 1973, from my personal experience, the situation has not changed much. However, during this period the German economy has performed in a superior fashion to the United States in virtually all respects, so a strong concept of management might have been a liability rather than an asset.

American style

Japan

The American type of manager is also missing in Japan. In the United States, the core of the enterprise is the managerial class. The core of the Japanese enterprise is the permanent worker group; workers who for all practical purposes are tenured and who aspire to life-long employment. They are distinct from the non-permanent employees – most women and subcontracted teams led by gang bosses, to be laid off in slack periods. University graduates in Japan first join the permanent worker group and subsequently fill various positions, moving from line to staff as the need occurs while paid according to seniority rather than position. They take part in Japanese-style group consultation sessions for important decisions, which extend the decision-making period but guarantee fast implementation afterwards. Japanese are to a large extent controlled by their peer group rather than by their manager.

Three researchers from the East-West Center of the University of Hawaii, Joseph Tobin, David Wu, and Dana Danielson, did an observational study of typical preschools in three countries: China, Japan, and the United States. Their results have been published both as a book and as a video. In the Japanese preschool, one teacher handled 28 four-year olds. The video shows one particularly obnoxious boy, Hiroki, who fights with other children and throws teaching materials down from the balcony. When a little girl tries to alarm the teacher, the latter answers: "What are you calling me for? Do something about it!" In the US preschool, there is one adult for every nine children. This class has its problem child too, Glen, who refuses to clear away his toys. One of the teachers has a long talk with him and isolates him in a corner, until he changes his mind. It doesn't take much imagination to realize that managing Hiroki 30 years later will be a different process from managing Glen.

American theories of leadership are ill-suited for the Japanese group-controlled situation. During the past two decades, the Japanese have developed their own "PM" theory of leadership, in which P stands for performance and M for maintenance. The latter is less a concern for individual employees than for maintaining social stability. In view of the amazing success of the Japanese economy in the past 30 years, many Americans have sought the secrets of Japanese management hoping to copy them.

France

The manager, US-style, does not exist in France either. In a very enlightening book, unfortunately not yet translated into English, the French researcher Philippe d'Iribarne describes the results of in-depth observation and interview studies of management methods in three subsidiary plants of the same French multinational: in France; the United States; and Holland. He relates what he finds to information about the three societies in general. Where necessary, he goes back in history to trace the roots of the strikingly different behaviors in the completion of the same tasks. He identifies three kinds of basic principles (*logiques*) of management. In the United States, the principle is the *fair contract* between employer and employee, which gives the manager considerable prerogatives, but within its limits. This is really a *labor market* in which the worker sells

US

his or her labor for a price. In France, the principle is the *honor* of each class in a society which has always been and remains extremely stratified, in which superiors behave as superior beings and subordinates accept and expect this, conscious of their own lower level in the national hierarchy but also of the honor of their own class. The French do not think in terms of managers versus non-managers but in terms of *cadres* versus *noncadres*; one becomes cadre by attending the proper schools and one remains it forever; regardless of their actual task, cadres have the privileges of a higher social class, and it is very rare for a non-cadre to cross the ranks.

The conflict between French and American theories of management became apparent at the beginning of the twentieth century, in a criticism by the great French management pioneer Henri Fayol (1841–1925) on his US colleague and contemporary Frederick W. Taylor (1856–1915). The difference in career paths of the two men is striking. Fayol was a French engineer whose career as a *cadre supérieur* culminated in the position of Président-Directeur-Général of a mining company. After his retirement he formulated his experiences in a pathbreaking text on organization: *Administration industrielle et générale,* in which he focused on the sources of authority. Taylor was an American engineer who started his career in industry as a worker and attained his academic qualifications through evening studies. From chief engineer in a steel company, he became one of the first management consultants. Taylor was not really concerned with the issue of authority at all; his focus was on efficiency. He proposed to split the task of the first-line boss into eight specialisms, each exercised by a different person; an idea which eventually led to the idea of a matrix organization.

Taylor's work appeared in a French translation in 1913, and Fayol read it and showed himself generally impressed but shocked by Taylor's "denial of the principle of the Unity of Command" in the case of the eight-boss system.

Seventy years later André Laurent, another of Fayol's compatriots, found that French managers in a survey reacted very strongly against a suggestion that one employee could report to two different bosses, while US managers in the same survey showed fewer misgivings. Matrix organization has never become as popular in France as it has in the United States.

Holland

In my own country, Holland, or as it is officially called, the Netherlands, the study by Philippe d'Iribarne found the management principle to be a need for *consensus* among all parties, neither predetermined by a contractual relationship nor by class distinctions, but based on an open-ended exchange of views and a balancing of interests. In terms of the different origins of the word "manager," the organization in Holland is more *ménage* (household), while in the United States it is more *manège* (horse drill).

At my university, the University of Limburg at Maastricht, every semester we receive a class of American business students who take a program in European studies. We asked both the Americans and a matched group of Dutch students to describe their ideal job after graduation, using a list of 22 job characteristics. The Americans attached significantly more importance than the Dutch to earnings, advancement, benefits, a good working relationship with their boss, and security of employment. The Dutch attached more importance to freedom to adopt their own approach to the job, being consulted by their boss in his or her decisions, training opportunities, contributing to the success of their organization, fully using their skills and abilities, and helping others. This list confirms d'Iribarne's findings of a contractual employment relationship in the United States, based on earnings and career opportunities, against a consensual relationship in Holland. The latter has centuries-old roots; the Netherlands were the first republic in Western Europe (1609–1810), and a model for the American republic. The country has been and still is governed by a careful balancing of interests in a multi-party system.

In terms of management theories, both motivation and leadership in Holland are different from what they are in the United States. Leadership in Holland presupposes modesty, as opposed to assertiveness in the United States. No US leadership theory has room for that. Working in Holland is not a constant feast, however. There is a built-in premium on mediocrity and jealousy, as well as time-consuming ritual consultations to maintain the appearance of consensus and the pretense of modesty. There is unfortunately another side to every coin.

The overseas Chinese

Among the champions of economic development in the past 30 years, we find three countries mainly populated by Chinese living outside the Chinese mainland: Taiwan, Hong Kong, and Singapore. Moreover, overseas Chinese play a very important role in the economies of Indonesia, Malaysia, the Philippines, and Thailand, where they form an ethnic minority. If anything, the little dragons – Taiwan, Hong Kong, and Singapore – have been more economically successful than Japan, moving from rags to riches and now counted among the world's wealthy industrial countries. Yet very little attention has been paid to the way in which their enterprises have been managed. *The Spirit of Chinese Capitalism* by Gordon Redding (1990), the British dean of the Hong Kong Business School, is an excellent book about Chinese business. He bases his insights on personal acquaintance and in-depth discussions with a large number of overseas Chinese businesspeople.

Overseas Chinese-American enterprises lack almost all characteristics of modern management. They tend to be small, cooperating for essential functions with other small organizations through networks based on personal relations. They are family-owned, without the separation between ownership and management typical in the West, or even in Japan and Korea. They normally focus on one product or market, with growth by opportunistic diversification; in this, they are extremely flexible. Decision making is centralized in the hands of one dominant family member, but other family members may be given new ventures to try their skills on. They are low-profile and extremely cost-conscious, applying Confucian virtues of thrift and persistence. Their size is kept small by the assumed lack of loyalty of non-family employees, who, if they are any good, will just wait and save until they can start their own family business.

Overseas Chinese prefer economic activities in which great gains can be made with little manpower, like commodity trading and real estate. They employ few professional managers, except their sons and sometimes daughters who have been sent to prestigious business schools abroad, but who upon return continue to run the family business the Chinese way.

The origin of this system, or – in the Western view – this lack of system, is found in the history of Chinese society, in which there were no formal laws, only formal networks of powerful people guided by general principles of Confucian virtue. The favors of the authorities could change daily, so nobody could be trusted except one's kinfolk – of whom, fortunately, there used to be many, in an extended family structure. The overseas Chinese way of doing business is also very well adapted to their position in the countries in which they form ethnic minorities, often envied and threatened by ethnic violence.

Overseas Chinese businesses following this unprofessional approach command a collective gross national product of some 200 to 300 billion US dollars, exceeding the GNP of Australia. There is no denying that it works.

MANAGEMENT TRANSFER TO POOR COUNTRIES

Four-fifths of the world population live in countries that are not rich but poor. After World War II and decolonization, the stated purpose of the United Nations and the World Bank has been to promote the development of all the world's countries in a war on poverty. After 40 years, it looks very much like we are losing this war. If one thing has become clear, it is that the export of Western – mostly American – management practices and theories to poor countries has contributed little or nothing to their development. There has been no lack of effort and money spent for this purpose: students from poor countries have been trained in this country, and teachers and Peace Corps workers have been sent to the poor countries. If nothing else, the general lack of success in economic development of other countries should be sufficient argument to doubt the validity of Western management theories in non-Western environments.

If we examine different parts of the world, the development picture is not equally bleak, and history is often a better predictor than economic factors for what happens today. There is a broad regional pecking order with East Asia leading. The little dragons have passed into the camp of the wealthy; then follow Southeast Asia (with its overseas Chinese minorities), Latin America (in spite of the debt crisis), South Asia, and Africa always trails behind. Several African countries have only become poorer since decolonization.

Regions of the world with a history of large-scale political integration and civilization generally have done better than regions in which no large-scale political and cultural infrastructure existed, even if the old civilizations had decayed or been suppressed by colonizers. It has become painfully clear that development cannot be pressure-cooked; it presumes a cultural infrastructure that takes time to grow. Local management is part of this infrastructure; it cannot be imported in package form. Assuming that with so-called modern management techniques and theories outsiders can develop a country has proven a deplorable arrogance. At best, one can hope for a dialogue between equals with the locals, in which the Western partner acts as the expert in Western technology and the local partner as the expert in local culture, habits, and feelings.

Russia and China

The crumbling of the former Eastern bloc has left us with a scattering of states and would-be states of which the political and economic future is extremely uncertain. The best predictions are those based on a knowledge of history, because historical trends have taken revenge on the arrogance of the Soviet rulers who believed they could turn them around by brute power. One obvious fact is that the former bloc is extremely heterogeneous, including countries traditionally closely linked with the West by trade and travel, like the Czech Republic, Hungary, Slovenia, and the Baltic states, as well as others with a Byzantine or Turkish past; some having been prosperous, others always extremely poor.

Let me limit myself to the Russian republic, a huge territory with some 140 million inhabitants, mainly Russians. We know quite a bit about the Russians as their country was a world power for several hundred years before communism, and in the nineteenth century it has produced some of the greatest writers in world literature. If I want to understand the Russians – including how they could so long support the Soviet regime – I tend to reread Lev Nikolayevich Tolstoy. In his most famous novel *Anna Karenina* (1876), one of the main characters is a landowner, Levin, whom Tolstoy uses to express his own views and convictions about his people. Russian peasants used to be serfs; serfdom had been abolished in 1861, but the peasants, now tenants, remained as passive as before. Levin wanted to break this passivity by dividing the land among his peasants in exchange for a share of the crops; but the peasants only let the land deteriorate further. Here follows a quote:

> (Levin) read political economy and socialistic works . . . but, as he had expected, found nothing in them related to his undertaking. In the political economy books – in [John Stuart] Mill, for instance, whom he studied first and with great ardour, hoping every minute to find an answer to the questions that were engrossing him – he found only certain laws deduced from the state of agriculture in Europe; but he could not for the life of him see why these laws, which did not apply to Russia, should be considered universal. . . . Political economy told him that the laws by which Europe had developed and was developing her wealth were universal and absolute. Socialist teaching told him that development along those lines leads to ruin. And neither of them offered the smallest enlightenment as to what he, Levin, and all the Russian peasants and landowners were to do with their millions of hands and millions of acres, to make them as productive as possible for the common good.

In the summer of 1991, the Russian lands yielded a record harvest, but a large share of it rotted in the fields because no people were to be found for harvesting. The passivity is still there, and not only among the peasants. And the heirs of John Stuart Mill (whom we met before as one of the early analysts of "management") again present their universal recipes which simply do not apply.

Citing Tolstoy, I implicitly suggest that management theorists cannot neglect the great literature of the countries they want their ideas to apply to. The greatest novel in the Chinese literature is considered Cao Xueqin's *The Story of the Stone*, also known as *The Dream of the Red Chamber*, which appeared around 1760. It describes the rise and fall of two branches of an aristocratic family in Beijing, who live in adjacent plots in the capital. Their plots are joined by a magnificent garden with several pavilions in it, and the young, mostly female members of both families are allowed to live in them. One day the management of the garden is taken over by a young woman, Tan-Chun, who states:

> I think we ought to pick out a few experienced trustworthy old women from among the ones who work in the Garden – women who know something about gardening already – and put the upkeep of the Garden into their hands. We needn't ask them to pay us rent; all we need ask them for is an annual share of the produce. There would be four advantages in this arrangement. In the first place, if we have people whose sole occupation is to look after trees and flowers and so on, the condition of the Garden will improve gradually year after year and there will be no more of those long periods of neglect followed by bursts of feverish activity when things have been allowed to get out of hand. Secondly, there won't be the spoiling and wastage we get at present. Thirdly, the women themselves will gain a little extra to add to their incomes which will compensate them for the hard work they put in throughout the year. And fourthly, there's no reason why we shouldn't use the money we should otherwise have spent on nurserymen, rockery specialists, horticultural cleaners, and so on for other purposes.

As the story goes on, the capitalist privatization – because that is what it is – of the Garden is carried through, and it works. When in the 1980s, Deng Xiaoping allowed privatization in the Chinese villages, it also worked. It worked so well that its effects started to be felt in politics and threatened the existing political order; hence the crackdown at Tienanmen Square of June 1989. But it seems that the forces of privatization are getting the upper hand again in China. If we remember what Chinese entrepreneurs are able to do once they have become overseas Chinese, we should not be too surprised. But what works in China – and worked two centuries ago – does not have to work in Russia, not in Tolstoy's days and not today. I am not offering a solution; I only protest against a naive universalism that knows only one recipe for development, the one supposed to have worked in the United States.

A THEORY OF CULTURE IN MANAGEMENT

Our trip around the world is over and we are back in the United States. What have we learned? There is something in all countries called "management," but its meaning differs to a larger or smaller extent from one country to the other, and it takes considerable historical and cultural insight into local conditions to understand its processes, philosophies, and problems. If already the word may mean so many different things, how can we expect one country's theories of management to apply abroad? One should be extremely careful in making this assumption, and test it before considering it proven. Management is not a phenomenon that can be isolated from other processes taking place in a society. During our trip around the world, we saw that it interacts with what happens in the family, at school, in politics, and government. It is obviously also related to religion and to beliefs about science. Theories of management always had to be interdisciplinary, but if we cross national borders they should become more interdisciplinary than ever.

Cultural differences between nations can be, to some extent, described using first four, and now five, bipolar *dimensions*. The position of a country on these dimensions allows us to make some predictions of the way their society operates, including their management processes and the kind of theories applicable to their management.

As the word culture plays such an important role in my theory, let me give you my definition, which differs from some other very respectable definitions. Culture to me is *the collective programming of the mind which distinguishes one group or category of people from another.* In the part of my work I am referring to now, the category of people is the nation.

Culture is a *construct*, that means it is "not directly accessible to observation but inferable from verbal statements and other behaviors and useful in predicting still other observable and measurable verbal and non-verbal behavior." It should not be reified; it is an auxiliary concept that should be used as long as it proves useful but bypassed where we can predict behaviors without it.

The same applies to the *dimensions* I introduced. They are constructs too that should not be reified. They do not "exist;" they are tools for analysis which may or may not clarify a situation. In my statistical analysis of empirical data the first four dimensions together explain 49 percent of the variance in the data. The other 51 percent remain specific to individual countries.

The first four dimensions were initially detected through a comparison of the values of similar people (employees and managers) in 64 national subsidiaries of the IBM Corporation. People working for the same multinational, but in different countries, represent very well-matched samples from the populations of their countries, similar in all respects except nationality.

The first dimension is labelled *power distance*, and it can be defined as the degree of inequality among people which the population of a country considers as normal: from relatively equal (that is, small power distance) to extremely unequal (large power distance). All societies are unequal, but some are more unequal than others.

The second dimension is labelled *individualism*, and it is the degree to which people in a country prefer to act as individuals rather than as members of groups. The opposite of individualism can be called *collectivism*, so collectivism is low individualism. The way I use the word, it has no political connotations. In collectivist societies, a child learns to respect the group to which it belongs, usually the family, and to differentiate between in-group members and out-group members (that is, all other people). When children grow up they remain members of their group, and they expect the group to protect them when they are in trouble. In return, they have to remain loyal to their group throughout life. In individualist societies, a child learns very early to think of itself as "I" instead of as part of "we." It expects one day to have to stand on its own feet and not to get protection from its group any more; and therefore it also does not feel a need for strong loyalty.

The third dimension is called *masculinity* and its opposite pole *femininity*. It is the degree to which tough values like assertiveness, performance, success, and competition, which in nearly all societies are associated with the role of men, prevail over tender values like the quality of life, maintaining warm personal relationships, service, care for the weak, and solidarity, which in nearly all societies are more associated with women's roles. Women's roles differ from men's roles in all countries; but in tough societies, the differences are larger than in tender ones.

The fourth dimension is labelled *uncertainty avoidance*, and it can be defined as the degree to which people in a country prefer structured over unstructured situations. Structured situations are those in which there are clear rules as to how one should behave. These rules can be written down, but they can also be unwritten and imposed by tradition. In countries which score high on uncertainty avoidance, people tend to show more nervous energy, while in countries which score low, people are more easy-going. A (national) society with strong uncertainty avoidance can be called rigid; one with weak uncertainty avoidance, flexible. In countries where uncertainty avoidance is strong a feeling prevails of "what is different is dangerous." In weak uncertainty avoidance societies, the feeling would rather be "what is different is curious."

The fifth dimension was added on the basis of a study of the values of students in 23 countries carried out by Michael Harris Bond, a Canadian working in Hong Kong. He and I had cooperated in another study of students' values which had yielded the same four dimensions as the IBM data. However, we wondered to what extent our common findings in two studies could be the effect of a Western bias introduced by the common Western background of the researchers: remember Alice's croquet game. Michael Bond resolved this dilemma by deliberately introducing an Eastern bias. He used a questionnaire prepared at his request by his Chinese colleagues, the *Chinese Value Survey* (CVS), which was translated from Chinese into different languages and answered by 50 male and 50 female students in each of 23 countries in all five continents. Analysis of the CVS data produced three dimensions significantly correlated with the three IBM dimensions of power distance, individualism, and masculinity. There was also a fourth dimension, but it did not resemble uncertainty avoidance. It was composed, both on the positive and on the negative side, from items that had not been included in the IBM studies but were present in the Chinese Value Survey because they were rooted in the teachings of Confucius. I labelled this dimension: *Long-term* versus *short-term orientation*. On the long-term side, one finds values oriented towards the future, like thrift (saving) and persistence. On the short-term side, one finds values rather oriented towards the past and present, like respect for tradition and fulfilling social obligations.

Table 1 lists the scores on all five dimensions for the United States and for the other countries we just discussed. The table shows that each country has its own configuration

TABLE 1 Culture dimension scores for ten countries

	PD		ID		MA		UA		LT	
United States	40	L	91	H	62	H	46	L	29	L
Germany	35	L	67	H	66	H	65	M	31	M
Japan	54	M	46	M	95	H	92	H	80	H
France	68	H	71	H	43	M	86	H	30*	L
Netherlands	38	L	80	H	14	L	53	M	44	M
Hong Kong	68	H	25	L	57	H	29	L	96	H
Indonesia	78	H	14	L	46	M	48	L	25	L
West Africa	77	H	20	L	46	M	54	M	16	L
Russia	95*	H	50*	M	40*	L	90*	H	10*	L
China	80*	H	20*	L	50*	M	60*	M	118	H

* estimated

Note: PD = power distance; ID = individualism; MA = masculinity; UA = uncertainty avoidance; LT = long-term orientation; H = top third, M = medium third, L = bottom third (among 53 countries and regions for the first four dimensions; among 23 countries for the fifth).

on the four dimensions. Some of the values in the table have been estimated based on imperfect replications or personal impressions. The different dimension scores do not "explain" all the differences in management I described earlier. To understand management in a country, one should have both knowledge of and empathy with the entire local scene. However, the scores should make us aware that people in other countries may think, feel, and act very differently from us when confronted with basic problems of society.

IDIOSYNCRASIES OF AMERICAN MANAGEMENT THEORIES

In comparison to other countries, the US culture profile presents itself as below average on power distance and uncertainty avoidance, highly individualistic, fairly masculine, and short-term oriented. The Germans show a stronger uncertainty avoidance and less extreme individualism; the Japanese are different on all dimensions, least on power distance; the French show larger power distance and uncertainty avoidance, but are less individualistic and somewhat feminine; the Dutch resemble the Americans on the first three dimensions, but score extremely feminine and relatively long-term oriented; Hong Kong Chinese combine large power distance with weak uncertainty avoidance, collectivism, and are very long-term oriented; and so on.

The American culture profile is reflected in American management theories. I will just mention three elements not necessarily present in other countries: the stress on market processes; the stress on the individual; and the focus on managers rather than on workers.

The stress on market processes

During the 1970s and 80s it has become fashionable in the United States to look at organizations from a "transaction costs" viewpoint. Economist Oliver Williamson has opposed "hierarchies" to "markets." The reasoning is that human social life consists of economic transactions between individuals. We found the same in d'Iribarne's description of the US principle of the contract between employer and employee, the labor market in which the worker sells his or her labor for a price. These individuals will form hierarchical organizations when the cost of the economic transactions (such as getting information, finding out whom to trust, and so on) is lower in a hierarchy than when all transactions would take place in a free market.

From a cultural perspective the important point is that the "*market*" *is the point of departure or base model*, and the organization is explained from market failure. A culture that produces such a theory is likely to prefer organizations that internally resemble markets to organizations that internally resemble more structured models, like those in Germany or France. The ideal principle of control in organizations in the market philosophy is *competition* between individuals. This philosophy fits a society that combines a not-too-large power distance with a not-too-strong uncertainty avoidance and individualism; besides the United States, it will fit all other Anglo countries.

The stress on the individual

I find this constantly in the design of research projects and hypotheses; also in the fact that in the US psychology is clearly a more respectable discipline in management circles than sociology. Culture however is a collective phenomenon. Although we may get our information about culture from individuals, we have to interpret it at the level of collectivities. There are snags here known as the "ecological fallacy" and the "reverse ecological fallacy." None of the US college textbooks on methodology I know deals sufficiently with the problem of multilevel analysis.

A striking example is found in the otherwise excellent book *Organizational Culture and Leadership* by Edgar H. Schein (1985). On the basis of his consulting experience, he compares two large companies, nicknamed "Action" and "Multi." He explains the differences in culture between these companies by the group dynamics in their respective boardrooms. Nowhere in the book are any conclusions drawn from the fact that the first company is an American-based computer firm, and the second a Swiss-based pharmaceutics firm. This information is not even mentioned. A stress on interactions among individuals obviously fits a culture identified as the most individualistic in the world, but it will not be so well understood by the four-fifths of the world population for whom the group prevails over the individual.

One of the conclusions of my own multilevel research has been that culture at the national level and culture at the organizational level – corporate culture – are two very different phenomena and that the use of a common term for both is confusing. If we do use the common term, we should also pay attention to the occupational and the gender level of culture. National cultures differ primarily in the fundamental, invisible values held by a majority of their members, acquired in early childhood, whereas organizational cultures are a much more superficial phenomenon residing mainly in the visible practices of the organization, acquired by socialization of the new members who join as young adults. National cultures change only very slowly if at all; organizational cultures may be consciously changed, although this is not necessarily easy. This difference between the two types of culture is the secret of the existence of multinational corporations that employ, as I showed in the IBM case, employees with extremely different national cultural values. What keeps them together is a corporate culture based on common practices.

The stress on managers rather than workers

The core element of a work organization around the world is the people who do the work. All the rest is superstructure, and I hope to have demonstrated to you that it may take many different shapes. In the US literature on work organization, however, the core element, if not explicitly then implicitly, is considered the manager. This may well be the result of the combination of extreme individualism with fairly strong masculinity, which has turned the manager into a culture hero of almost mythical proportions. For example, he – not really she – is supposed to make decisions all the time. Those of you who are or have been managers must know that this is a fable. Very few management decisions are just "made" as the myth suggests it. Managers are much more involved in maintaining networks; if anything, it is the rank-and-file worker who can really make decisions on his or her own, albeit on a relatively simple level.

An amusing effect of the US focus on managers is that in at least ten American books and articles on management I have been misquoted as having studied IBM *managers* in my research, whereas the book clearly describes that the answers were from IBM *employees*. My observation may be biased, but I get the impression that compared to 20 or 30 years ago less research in this country is done among employees and more on managers. But managers derive their *raison d'être* from the people managed: culturally, they are the followers of the people they lead, and their effectiveness depends on the latter. In other parts of the world, this exclusive focus on the manager is less strong, with Japan as the supreme example.

CONCLUSION

This article started with *Alice in Wonderland*. In fact, the management theorist who ventures outside his or her own country into other parts of the world is like Alice in Wonderland. He or she will meet strange beings, customs, ways of organizing or disorganizing, and theories that are clearly stupid, old-fashioned, or even immoral – yet they may work, or at least they may not fail more frequently than corresponding theories do at home. Then, after the first culture shock, the traveller to Wonderland will feel enlightened, and may be able to take his or her experiences home and use them advantageously. All great ideas in science, politics, and management have travelled from one country to another, and been enriched by foreign influences. The roots of American management theories are mainly in Europe: with Adam Smith, John Stuart Mill, Lev Tolstoy, Max Weber, Henri Fayol, Sigmund Freud, Kurt Lewin, and many others. These theories were replanted here, and they developed and bore fruit. The same may happen again. The last thing we need is a Monroe doctrine for management ideas.

All Great Ideas Travel! From Country to Country!

Table, Figures 5, 6 and 7, and Exhibit 2

Geert Hofstede

The 40 countries (showing abbreviations used in Figures 5, 6 and 7)

ARG	Argentina	HOK	Hong Kong	PHI	Philippines
AUL	Australia	IND	India	POR	Portugal
AUT	Austria	IRA	Iran	SAF	South Africa
BEL	Belgium	IRE	Ireland	SIN	Singapore
BRA	Brazil	ISR	Israel	SPA	Spain
CAN	Canada	ITA	Italy	SWE	Sweden
CHL	Chile	JAP	Japan	SWI	Switzerland
COL	Colombia	MEX	Mexico	TAI	Taiwan
DEN	Denmark	NET	Netherlands	THA	Thailand
FIN	Finland	NOR	Norway	TUR	Turkey
FRA	France	NZL	New Zealand	USA	United States
GBR	Great Britain	PAK	Pakistan	VEN	Venezuela
GER	Germany (West)	PER	Peru	YUG	Yugoslavia
GRE	Greece				

From "Motivation, Leadership and Organization: Do American Theories Apply Abroad?" by Geert Hofstede, *Organizational Dynamics*, Summer 1980, pp. 42–63. Hofstede, Geert, and M. H. Bond, Exhibit 2 from "The Confucius connection: From cultural roots to economic growth," *Organizational Dynamics*, 16(4): 4–21. Reprinted by permission of Geert Hofstede.

FIGURE 5 The Position of the 40 Countries on the Power Distance and Uncertainty Avoidance Scales
Power Distance Index

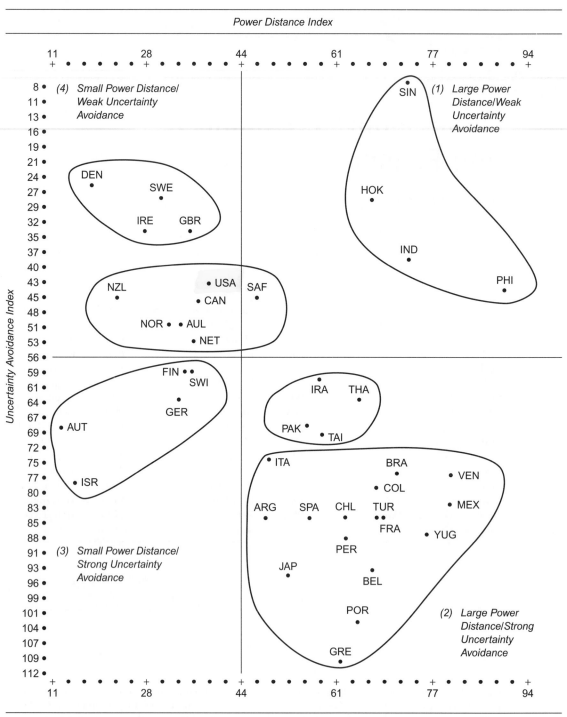

FIGURE 6 The Position of the 40 Countries on the Power Distance and Individualism Scales
Power Distance Index

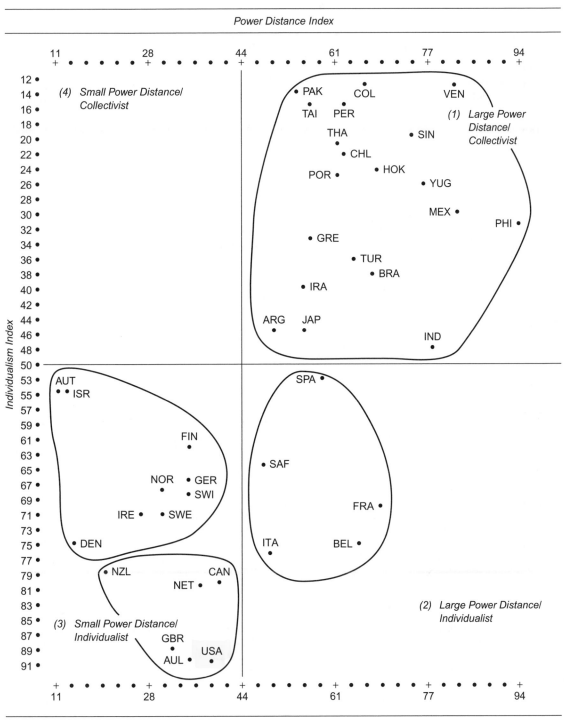

FIGURE 7 The Position of the 40 Countries on the Uncertainty Avoidance and Masculinity Scales

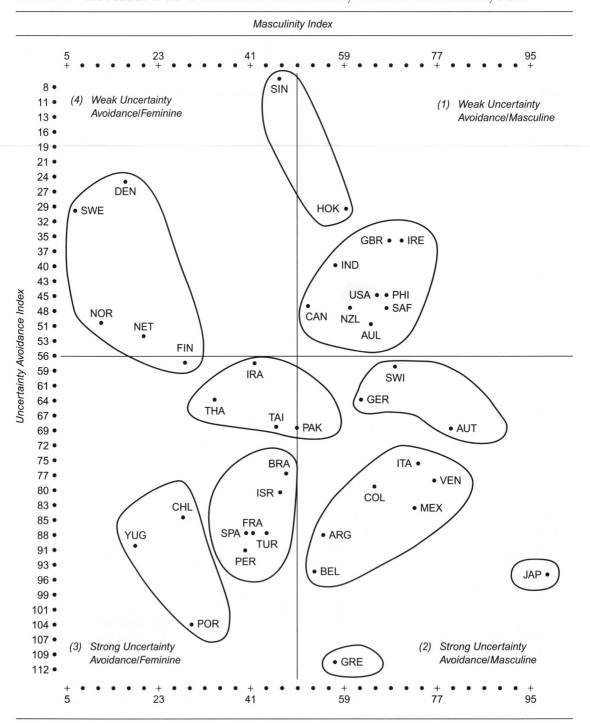

EXHIBIT 2 Scores on Five Dimensions for Fifty Countries and Three Regions in IBM's International Employee Attitude Survey

Country	Power Distance		Individualism		Masculinity		Uncertainty Avoidance		Confucian Dynamism	
	Index	*Rank*	*Index*	*Rank*	*Index*	*Rank*	*Index*	*Rank*	*Index*	*Rank*
Argentina	49	35–36	46	22–23	56	20–21	86	10–15		
Australia	36	41	90	2	61	16	51	37	31	11–12
Austria	11	53	55	18	79	2	70	24–25		
Belgium	65	20	75	8	54	22	94	5–6		
Brazil	69	14	38	26–27	49	27	76	21–22	65	5
Canada	39	39	80	4–5	52	24	48	41–42	23	17
Chile	63	24–25	23	38	28	46	86	10–15		
Colombia	67	17	13	49	64	11–12	80	20		
Costa Rica	35	42–44	15	46	21	48–49	86	10–15		
Denmark	18	51	74	9	16	50	23	51		
Ecuador	78	8–9	8	52	63	13–14	67	28		
Finland	33	46	63	17	26	47	59	31–32		
France	68	15–16	71	10–11	43	35–36	86	10–15		
Germany (FR)	35	42–44	67	15	66	9–10	65	29	31	11–12
Great Britain	35	42–44	89	3	66	9–10	35	47–48	25	15–16
Greece	60	27–28	35	30	57	18–19	112	1		
Guatemala	95	2–3	6	53	37	43	101	3		
Hong Kong	68	15–16	25	37	57	18–19	29	49–50	96	1
Indonesia	78	8–9	14	47–48	46	30–31	48	41–42		
India	77	10–11	48	21	56	20–21	40	45	61	6
Iran	58	19–20	41	24	43	35–36	59	31–32		
Ireland	28	49	70	12	68	7–8	35	47–48		
Israel	13	52	54	19	47	29	81	19		
Italy	50	34	76	7	70	4–5	75	23		
Jamaica	45	37	39	25	68	7–8	13	52		
Japan	54	33	46	22–23	95	1	92	7	80	3
Korea (S)	60	27–28	18	43	39	41	85	16–17	75	4
Malaysia	104	1	26	36	50	25–26	36	46		
Mexico	81	5–6	30	32	69	6	82	18		
Netherlands	38	40	80	4–5	14	51	53	35	44	9
Norway	31	47–48	69	13	8	52	50	38		
New Zealand	22	50	79	6	58	17	49	39–40	30	13
Pakistan	55	32	14	47–48	50	25–26	70	24–25	0	20
Panama	95	2–3	11	51	44	34	86	10–15		
Peru	64	21–23	16	45	42	37–38	87	9		
Philippines	94	4	32	31	64	11–12	44	44	19	18
Portugal	63	24–25	27	33–35	31	45	104	2		
South Africa	49	36–37	65	16	63	13–14	49	39–40		
Salvador	66	18–19	19	42	40	40	94	5–6		
Singapore	74	13	20	39–41	48	28	8	53	48	8
Spain	57	31	51	20	42	37–38	86	10–15		
Sweden	31	47–48	71	10–11	5	52	29	49–50	33	10
Switzerland	34	45	68	14	70	4–5	58	33		
Taiwan	58	29–30	17	44	45	32–33	69	26	87	2
Thailand	64	21–23	20	39–41	34	44	64	30	56	7
Turkey	66	18–19	37	28	45	31–33	85	16–17		

EXHIBIT 2 *(cont'd)*

Country	Power Distance		Individualism		Masculinity		Uncertainty Avoidance		Confucian Dynamism	
	Index	Rank	Index	Rank	Index	Rank	Index	Rank	Index	Rank
Uruguay	61	26	36	29	38	42	100	4		
United States	40	38	91	1	62	15	46	43	29	14
Venezuela	81	5–6	12	50	73	3	76	21–22		
Yugoslavia	76	12	27	33–35	21	48–49	88	8		
Regions:										
East Africa	64	21–23	27	33–35	41	39	52	36	25	15–16
West Africa	77	10–11	20	39–41	46	30–31	54	34	15	19
Arab Ctrs.	80	7	38	26–27	53	23	68	27		

Rank Numbers: 1 = Highest; 53 = Lowest (For Confucian Dynamism: 20 = Lowest)
From "The Confucius Connection: From Cultural Roots to Economic Growth", G. Hofstede and M. H. Bond, *Organizational Dynamics*, Vol. 16, No. 4, pp. 4–21.

Beyond Sophisticated Stereotyping: Cultural Sensemaking in Context

Joyce S. Osland and Allan Bird

If US Americans are so individualistic and believe so deeply in self-reliance, why do they have the highest percentage of charitable giving in the world and readily volunteer their help to community projects and emergencies?

In a 1991 survey, many Costa Rican customers preferred automatic tellers over human tellers because "at least the machines are programmed to say 'good morning' and 'thank you.' "[1] Why is it that so many Latin American cultures are noted for warm interpersonal relationships and a cultural script of *simpatía* (positive social behavior),[2] while simultaneously exhibiting seeming indifference as service workers in both the private and public sectors?

Based on Hofstede's[3] value dimension of Uncertainty Avoidance, the Japanese have a low tolerance for uncertainty while Americans have a high tolerance. Why then do the Japanese intentionally incorporate ambiguous clauses in their business contracts, which are unusually short, while Americans dot every i, cross every t, and painstakingly spell out every possible contingency?

Many people trained to work in these cultures found such situations to be paradoxical when they first encountered them. These examples often contradict and confound our attempts to neatly categorize cultures. They violate our conceptions of what we think particular cultures are like. Constrained, stereotypical thinking is not the only problem, however. The more exposure and understanding one gains about any culture, the more paradoxical it often becomes. For example, US Americans are individualistic in some situations (e.g., "the most comprehensive of rights and the right most valued is the right to be left alone"[4]) and collectivist in others (e.g., school fundraising events).

Academy of Management Executive, 14(1) (February 2000): 65–79. Reprinted by permission of *Academy of Management Executive*.

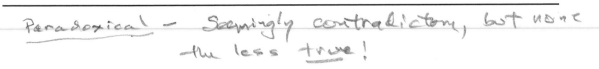

Paradoxical – Seemingly contradictory, but none the less true!

Long-term sojourners and serious cultural scholars find it difficult to make useful generalizations since so many exceptions and qualifications to the stereotypes, on both a cultural and individual level, come to mind. These cultural paradoxes are defined as situations that exhibit an apparently contradictory nature.

Surprisingly, there is little mention of cultural paradoxes in the management literature.[5] Our long-term sojourns as expatriates (a combined total of 22 years), as well as our experience in teaching cross-cultural management, preparing expatriates to go overseas, and doing comparative research, has led us to feel increasingly frustrated with the accepted conceptualizations of culture. Thus, our purpose is to focus attention on cultural paradoxes, explain why they have been overlooked and why they exist, and present a framework for making sense of them. Our intent is to initiate a dialogue that will eventually provide teachers, researchers, and people who work across cultures with a more useful way to understand culture.

A look at the comparative literature reveals that cultures are described in somewhat limited terms.[6] There are 22 dimensions commonly used to compare cultures, typically presented in the form of bipolar continua, with midpoints in the first examples, as shown in Table 1. These dimensions were developed to yield greater cultural understanding

TABLE 1   Common Cultural Dimensions

Subjugation to nature	Harmony	Mastery of nature
Past	Present	Future
Being	Containing and controlling	Doing
Hierarchical relationships	Group	Individualistic
Private space	Mixed	Public
Evil human nature	Neutral or mixed	Good
Human nature as changeable		Human nature as unchangeable
Monochronic time		Polychronic time
High-context language		Low-context language
Low uncertainty avoidance		High uncertainty avoidance
Low power distance		High power distance
Short-term orientation		Long-term orientation
Individualism		Collectivism
Masculinity		Femininity
Universalism		Particularism
Neutral		Emotional
Diffuse		Specific
Achievement		Ascription
Individualism		Organization
Inner-directed		Outer-directed
Individualism (competition)		Group-organization (collusion)
Analyzing (reductivist)		Synthesizing (larger, integrated wholes)

Sources: Kluckhohn & Strodtbeck (1961); Hall & Hall (1990) (see n. 6); Hofstede (1980) (see n. 3); Parsons & Shils (1951); Trompenaars & Hampden Turner (1993) (see n. 6); Fons Trompenaars, *Riding the Waves of Culture: Understanding Diversity in Global Business* (Burr Ridge, IL: Irhin). The dimensions are bipolar continua, with the first six containing midpoints.

and allow for cross-cultural comparisons. An unanticipated consequence of using these dimensions, however, is the danger of stereotyping entire cultures.

SOPHISTICATED STEREOTYPING

In many parts of the world, one hears a generic stereotype for a disliked neighboring ethnic group – "The (fill in the blank) are lazy, dirty thieves, and their women are promiscuous." This is a low-level form of stereotyping, often based on lack of personal contact and an irrational dislike of people who are different from oneself. Professors and trainers work very hard to dispel such stereotypes. Rarely, however, do we stop to consider whether we are supplanting one form of stereotyping for another. For example, when we teach students and managers how to perceive the Israelis using Hofstede's[7] cultural dimensions, they may come to think of Israelis in terms of small power distance, strong uncertainty avoidance, moderate femininity, and moderate individualism. The result is to reduce a complex culture to a shorthand description they may be tempted to apply to all Israelis. We call this sophisticated stereotyping, because it is based on theoretical concepts and lacks the negative attributions often associated with its lower-level counterpart. Nevertheless, it is still limiting in the way it constrains individuals' perceptions of behavior in another culture.

Do we recommend against teaching the cultural dimensions shown in Table 1 so as to avoid sophisticated stereotyping? Not at all. These dimensions are useful tools in explaining cultural behavior. Indeed, cultural stereotypes can be helpful – provided we acknowledge their limitations. They are more beneficial, for example, in making comparisons between cultures than in understanding the wide variations of behavior within a single culture. Adler[8] encourages the use of "helpful stereotypes," which have the following limitations: They are consciously held, descriptive rather than evaluative, accurate in their description of a behavioral norm, the first best guess about a group prior to having direct information about the specific people involved, and modified based on further observations and experience. As teachers, researchers, and managers in cross-cultural contexts, we need to recognize that our original characterizations of other cultures are best guesses that we need to modify as we gain more experience.

For understandable, systemic reasons, business schools tend to teach culture in simple-minded terms, glossing over nuances and ignoring complexities. An examination of the latest crop of organizational behavior and international business textbooks revealed that most authors present only Hofstede's cultural dimensions, occasionally supplemented by Hall's theory of high- and low-context cultures.[9] Although these disciplines are not charged with the responsibility of teaching culture in great depth, these are the principal courses in many curricula where business students are exposed to cross-cultural concepts. Another handicap is that many business professors do not receive a thorough grounding in culture in their own disciplines and doctoral programs. One could further argue that we are joined in this conspiracy to give culture a quick-and-dirty treatment by practitioners and students who are looking for ways to simplify and make sense of the world.

The limitations of sophisticated stereotyping become most evident when we confront cultural paradoxes. This is the moment we realize our understanding is incomplete, misleading, and potentially dangerous. Perhaps because cultural paradoxes reveal the limitations in our thinking, they are often left unmentioned, even though virtually any-one with experience in another culture can usually identify one or two after only a moment's reflection.

WHY DON'T WE KNOW MORE ABOUT CULTURAL PARADOXES?

With one exception,[10] the cross-cultural literature contains no mention or explanation of cultural paradoxes. This absence can be explained by:

Near-sightedness

- homegrown perceptual schemas that result in cultural myopia
- lack of cultural experience that leads to misinterpretation and failure to comprehend the entire picture
- cultural learning that plateaus before complete understanding is achieved
- Western dualism that generates theories with no room for paradox or holistic maps
- features of cross-cultural research that encourage simplicity over complexity
- a between-culture research approach that is less likely to capture cultural paradoxes than a within-culture approach.

Perceptual schemas

When outsiders look at another culture, they inevitably interpret its institutions and customs using their own lenses and schemas; cultural myopia and lack of experience prevent them from seeing all the nuances of another culture.

In particular, a lack of experience with the new culture creates difficulties for new expatriates trying to make sense of what they encounter. The situation is analogous to putting together a jigsaw puzzle. Though one may have the picture on the puzzle box as a guide, making sense of each individual piece and understanding where and how it fits is exceedingly difficult. As more pieces are put into place, however, it is easier to see the bigger picture and understand how individual pieces mesh. Similarly, as one acquires more and varied experiences in the new culture, one can develop an appreciation for how certain attitudes and behaviors fit the puzzle and create an internal logic of the new culture.

Excellent analogy!

The danger with sophisticated stereotyping is that it may lead individuals to think that the number of shapes that pieces may take is limited and that pieces fit together rather easily. As Barnlund notes: "Rarely do the descriptions of a political structure or religious faith explain precisely when and why certain topics are avoided or why specific gestures carry such radically different meanings according to the context in which they appear."[11]

Early conclusions may be wrong

Expatriates and researchers alike tend to focus first on cultural differences and make initial conclusions that are not always modified in light of subsequent evidence.[12] Proactive learning about another culture often stops once a survival threshold is attained, perhaps because of an instinctive inclination to simplify a complex world. This may lead us to seek black-and-white answers rather than tolerate the continued ambiguity that typifies a more complete understanding of another culture.

One of the best descriptions of the peeling away of layers that characterizes deeper cultural understanding is found in a fictionalized account of expatriate life written by an expatriate manager, Robert Collins.[13] He outlines ascending levels on a Westerner's perception scale of Japanese culture that alternate, in daisy-petal-plucking fashion, between seeing the Japanese as significantly different or not really that different at all:

> The initial Level on a Westerner's perception scale clearly indicates a "difference" of great significance. The Japanese speak a language unlike any other human tongue . . . they write the language in symbols that reason alone cannot decipher. The airport customs officers all wear neckties, everyone is in a hurry, and there are long lines everywhere.
>
> Level Two is represented by the sudden awareness that the Japanese are not different at all. Not at all. They ride in elevators, have a dynamic industrial/trade/financial system, own great chunks of the United States, and serve cornflakes in the Hotel Okura.
>
> Level Three is the "hey, wait a minute" stage. The Japanese come to all the meetings, smile politely, nod in agreement with everything said, but do the opposite of what's expected. And they do it all together. They really are different.
>
> But are they? Level Four understanding recognizes the strong group dynamics, common education and training, and the general sense of loyalty to the family – which in their case is Japan itself. That's not so unusual, things are just organized on a larger scale than any social unit in the West. Nothing is fundamentally different.
>
> Level Five can blow one's mind, however. Bank presidents skipping through streets dressed as dragons at festival time; single ladies placing garlands of flowers around huge, and remarkably graphic, stone phallic symbols; Ministry of Finance officials rearranging their bedrooms so as to sleep in a "lucky" direction; it is all somewhat odd. At least, by Western standards. There is something different in the air.
>
> And so on. Some Westerners, the old Japan hands, have gotten as far as Levels 37 or 38.[14]

The point of Collins's description is that it takes time and experience to make sense of another culture. The various levels he describes reflect differing levels of awareness as more and more pieces of the puzzle are put into place. Time and experience are essential because culture is embedded in the context. Without context it makes little sense to talk about culture. Yet just as its lower-order counterpart does, sophisticated stereotyping tends to strip away or ignore context. Thus, cognitive schemas prevent sojourners and researchers from seeing and correctly interpreting paradoxical behavior outside their own cultures.

Theoretical Limitations

Another reason for the inattention to cultural paradoxes stems from the intersection between cognitive schemas and theory. Westerners have a tendency to perceive stimuli in terms of dichotomies and dualisms rather than paradoxes or holistic pictures.[15] The idea of paradox is a fairly recent wrinkle on the intellectual landscape of management theorists[16] and has not yet been incorporated into cultural theories in a managerial context.

Cross-cultural research is generally held to be more difficult than domestic studies. Hofstede's[17] work represented a major step forward and launched a deluge of studies utilizing his dimensions. Hundreds of studies have used one or more of Hofstede's dimensions to explore similarities and differences across cultures regarding numerous aspects of business and management. However, Hofstede himself warned against expecting too much of these dimensions and of using them incorrectly. For example, he defended the individualism-collectivism dimension as a useful construct, but then went on to say: "This does not mean, of course, that a country's Individual Index score tells all there is to be known about the backgrounds and structure of relationship patterns in that country. It is an abstraction that should not be extended beyond its limited area of usefulness."[18]

When we fail to specify under what conditions a culture measures low or high on any of the common cultural dimensions, or to take into consideration the impact of organizational culture, it misleads rather than increases our understanding of comparisons of culture and business practices. Such an approach prevents rather than opens up opportunities for learning and exploration.

A final explanation for the failure to address cultural paradoxes can be traced to the emic/etic distinction commonly used in the cultural literature. An emic perspective looks at a culture from within its boundaries, whereas an etic perspective stands outside and compares two or more cultures. To make between-culture differences more prominent, the etic approach minimizes the inconsistencies within a culture. Most cultural approaches in management adopt a between-culture approach, playing down the within-culture differences that expatriates must understand in order to work successfully in the host country.

Anthropologist Claude Lévi-Strauss warned that explanation does not consist of reducing the complex to the simple, but of substituting a more intelligible complexity for one that is less intelligible.[19] In failing to acknowledge cultural paradoxes or the complexity surrounding cultural dimensions, we may settle for simplistic, rather than intelligently complex, explanations.

SOURCES OF PARADOX IN CULTURAL BEHAVIOR

Behavior that looks paradoxical to an expatriate in the initial stages of cultural awareness may simply reflect the variance in behavioral norms for individuals, organizational cultures, subcultures, as well as generational differences and changing sections of the society. In addition, expatriates may also form microcultures[20] with specific members of the host culture. The cultural synergy of such microcultures may not be reflective of the national culture. These false paradoxes need to be discarded before more substantive paradoxes can be evaluated.

Based on an analysis of all the paradoxes we could find, we have identified six possible explanations for cultural behaviors that appear truly paradoxical. They are:

- the tendency for observers to confuse individual with group values
- unresolved cultural issues
- bipolar patterns
- role differences
- real versus espoused values
- value trumping, a recognition that in specific contexts certain sets of values take precedence over others.

Confusing individual with group values is exemplified by the personality dimension labeled allocentrism versus idiocentrism, which is the psychological, individual-level analog to the individualism-collectivism dimension at the level of culture.[21] Allocentric people, those who pay primary attention to the needs of a group, can be found in individualistic cultures, and idiocentric people, those who pay more attention to their own needs than to the needs of others, in collectivist cultures. What we perceive as cultural paradox may not reflect contradictions in cultural values, but instead may reveal the natural diversity within any culture that reflects individual personality and variation.

Unresolved cultural issues are rooted in the definition of culture as a learned response to problems. Some paradoxes come from problems for which there is no clear, happy solution. Cultures may manifest a split personality with regard to an unresolved problem.[22] As a result, they shuttle back and forth from one extreme to the other on a behavioral continuum. US Americans, for example, have ambivalent views about sex, and, as one journalist recently noted: "Our society is a stew of prurience and prudery."[23] Censorship, fears about sex education, and sexual taboos coexist uncomfortably with increasingly graphic films and TV shows and women's magazines that never go to press without a feature article devoted to sex. This melange is more than a reflection of a diverse society that has both hedonists and fundamentalists with differing views of sex; both groups manifest inconsistent behaviors and attitudes about sex, signaling an enduring cultural inability to resolve this issue.

Bipolar patterns make cultural behavior appear paradoxical because cultural dimensions are often framed, perhaps inaccurately, as dualistic, either-or continua. Cultures frequently exhibit one of these paired dimensions more than the other, but it is probable that both ends of the dimensions are found in cultures – but only in particular contexts. For example, in Latin America, ascribed status, derived from class and family background, is more important than its polar opposite, achieved status, which is based on talent and hard work. When it comes to professional soccer, however, achieved status trumps class and ascription.

Good example

Often some groups and roles appear to deviate from cultural stereotypes. For example, in the United States, autocratic behavior is frequently tolerated in CEOs, even though the United States is characterized as an egalitarian culture. Such behavior may also be an example of a high power distance context in a low power distance culture: We accept that CEOs possess an unequal degree of power and that they will behave in a different manner than most US Americans.

There is also a difference between real versus espoused values. All cultures express preferences for ideal behaviors – for what should be valued and how people should act. Nevertheless, people do not always act consistently with ideal behaviors and values. For example, US Americans may simultaneously pay lip service to the importance of equality (an espoused value), while trying to acquire more power or influence for themselves (a real value).

A final possible explanation of cultural paradoxes derives from a holistic, contextual view of culture in which values co-exist as a constellation, but their salience differs depending on the situation. Using the Gestalt concept of figure-ground, at times a particular value becomes dominant (figure), while in other circumstances, this same value recedes into the background (ground).[24] In India, for example, collectivism is figural when individuals are expected to make sacrifices for their families or for the larger society –

such as Hindu sons who postpone marriage until their sisters marry, or daughters who stay single to care for their parents. In other circumstances, however, collectivism fades into the background and individualism comes to the fore and is figural when Indians focus more upon self-realization – for example, elderly men who detach themselves from their family to seek salvation.[25] Taking the figure-ground analogy a step further, depending on the context, one cultural value might trump another, lessening the influence another value normally exerts.[26] For example, we find it useful to view culture as a series of card games in which cultural values or dimensions are individual cards. Depending on the game, previous play, and the hand one is dealt, players respond by choosing specific cards that seem most appropriate in a given situation. Sometimes a particular card trumps the others; in another round, it does not. In a given context, specific cultural values come into play and have more importance than other values. To a foreigner who does not understand enough about the cultural context to interpret why or when one value takes precedence over another, such behavior looks paradoxical. Members of the culture learn these nuances more or less automatically. For example, children learn in what context a socially acceptable white lie is more important than always telling the truth. A true understanding of the logic of another culture includes comprehending the inter-relationships among values, or how values relate to one another in a given context.

A MODEL OF CULTURAL SENSEMAKING

To make sense of cultural paradoxes and convey a holistic understanding of culture, we propose a model of cultural sensemaking. The model shown in Figure 1 helps explain how culture is embedded in context.[27] Cultural sensemaking is a cycle of sequential events:

- **Indexing Context.** The process begins when an individual identifies a context and then engages in indexing behavior, which involves noticing or attending to stimuli 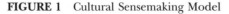 that provide cues about the situation. For example, to index the context of a meeting

FIGURE 1   Cultural Sensemaking Model

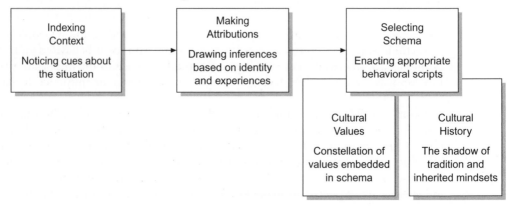

with a subordinate, we consider characteristics such as prior events (recent extensive layoffs), the nature of the boss-subordinate relationship within and without work (golfing partner), the specific topic under discussion (employee morale), and the location of the interaction (boss's office).

- **Making Attributions.** The next step is attribution, a process in which contextual cues are analyzed in order to match the context with appropriate schema. The matching process is moderated or influenced by one's social identity (e.g., ethnic or religious background, gender, social class, organizational affiliation) and one's history (e.g., experiences and chronology). A senior US American manager who fought against the Japanese in World War II will make different attributions about context and employ different schema when he meets with a Japanese manager than will a Japanese-American manager of his generation, or a junior US manager whose personal experience with Japan is limited to automobiles, electronics, and sushi.

- **Selecting Schema.** Schemas are cultural scripts, "a pattern of social interaction that is characteristic of a particular cultural group."[28] They are accepted and appropriate ways of behaving, specifying certain patterns of interaction. From personal or vicarious experience, we learn how to select schema. By watching and working with bosses, for example, we develop scripts for how to act when we take on that role ourselves. We learn appropriate vocabulary and gestures, which then elicit a fairly predictable response from others.

- **The Influence of Cultural Values.** Schemas reflect an underlying hierarchy of cultural values. For example, people working for US managers who have a relaxed and casual style and who openly share information and provide opportunities to make independent decisions will learn specific scripts for managing in this fashion. The configuration of values embedded in this management style consists of informality, honesty, equality, and individualism. At some point, however, these same managers may withhold information about a sensitive personnel situation because privacy, fairness, and legal concerns would trump honesty and equality in this context. This trumping action explains why the constellation of values related to specific schema is hierarchical.

- **The Influence of Cultural History.** When decoding schema, we may also find vestiges of cultural history and tradition. Mindsets inherited from previous generations explain how history is remembered.[29] For example, perceptions about a colonial era may still have an impact on schemas, particularly those involving interactions with foreigners, even though a country gained its independence centuries ago.

SOME ILLUSTRATIONS OF SENSEMAKING

Sensemaking involves placing stimuli into a framework that enables people "to comprehend, understand, explain, attribute, extrapolate, and predict."[30] Let's analyze each of the cultural paradoxes presented in the introduction using the sensemaking model. In the United States, when a charity requests money, when deserving people are in need, or when disaster hits a community (indexing contexts), many US Americans (e.g., religious, allocentric people making attributions) respond by donating their money, goods, or time (selecting schema). The values underlying this schema are humanitarian concern for

FIGURE 2   Making Sense of Paradoxical Behavior: Seemingly Indifferent Customer Service in a Culture Characterized by Positive, Warm Relations

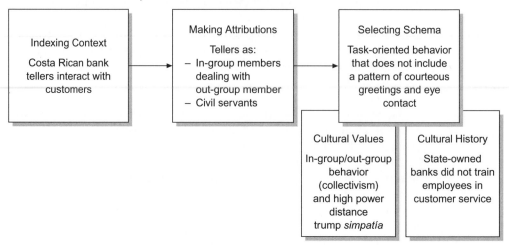

others, altruism,[31] and collectivism (cultural values). Thus, individualism (a sophisticated stereotype) is moderated by a communal tradition that has its roots in religious and cultural origins (cultural history).

Fukuyama[32] writes that US society has never been as individualistic as its citizens thought, because of the culture's relatively high level of trust and resultant social capital. The United States "has always possessed a rich network of voluntary associations and community structures to which individuals have subordinated their narrow interests."[33] Under normal conditions, one should take responsibility for oneself and not rely on others. However, some circumstances and tasks can overwhelm individual initiative and ingenuity. When that happens, people should help those in need, a lesson forged on the American frontier (cultural history). To further underscore the complexity of culture, in the same contexts noted above, the tax code and prestige associated with philanthropy (cultural history) may be the primary motivations for some citizens (e.g., idiocentric, upwardly ambitious people making attributions) to act charitably (selecting schema), but the value underlying the schema would be individualism.

The Costa Rican example is illustrated in Figure 2. When bank tellers interact with clients (indexing context) many of them (e.g., members of various in-groups, civil servants making attributions) do not greet customers and make eye contact, but concentrate solely on their paperwork (selecting schema). The values that underlie this schema are in-group-out-group behavior[34] and power (cultural values). In collectivist cultures such as Costa Rica, members identify strongly with their in-group and treat members with warmth and cooperation. In stark contrast, out-group members are often treated with hostility, distrust, and a lack of cooperation. Customers are considered as strangers and out-group members who do not warrant the special treatment given to in-group members (family and friends). One of the few exceptions to *simpatía* and personal dignity in Costa Rica, and Latin America generally, is rudeness sometimes expressed by people in positions of power.[35] In this context, the cultural value of high power distance (the extent to which a society accepts the fact that power in institutions and organizations is distributed unequally)[36] trumps *simpatía*. Whereas *simpatía* lessens the distance between people, the opposite behavior increases the distance between the powerful and the powerless. Unlike many other contexts in Costa Rica, bank telling does not elicit a cultural script of *simpatía*, and state-owned banks did not have a history of training employees in friendly customer service (cultural history) at this time.

In the third cultural example, when Japanese business people make contracts (indexing context), they (e.g., business people making attributions) opt for ambiguous contracts (selecting schema). The dominant value underlying this schema is collectivism (cultural value). In this context, collectivism is manifested as a belief that those entering into agreement are joined together and share something in common; thus, they should rely on and trust one another. Collectivism trumps high uncertainty avoidance (sophisticated stereotype) in this context, but uncertainty avoidance is not completely absent. Some of the uncertainty surrounding the contract is dealt with upstream in the process by carefully choosing and getting to know business partners, and by using third parties. An additional consideration is that many Japanese like flexible contracts, because they have a greater recognition of the limits of contracts and the difficulties of foreseeing all contingencies (cultural history). Even though US Americans are typically more tolerant of uncertainty (sophisticated stereotype), they value pragmatism and do not like to take unnecessary risks (cultural values). If a deal falls through, they rely on the legal system for a resolution (cultural history).

WORKING FROM A SENSEMAKING APPROACH

Sophisticated stereotypes are useful in the initial stages of making sense of complex behaviors within cultures. However, rather than stereotyping cultures somewhere along a continuum, we can advance understanding by thinking in terms of specific contexts that feature particular cultural values that then govern behavior. Geertz maintains that "culture is best seen not as complexes of concrete behavior patterns – customs, usages, traditions, habit clusters – as has by and large been the case up to now, but as a set of control mechanisms – plans, recipes, rules, instructions (what computer engineers call 'programs') – for the governing of behavior."[37]

Understanding the control mechanisms within a culture requires the acquisition of attributional knowledge, the awareness of contextually appropriate behavior.[38] This is in contrast to factual knowledge and conceptual knowledge. Factual knowledge consists of descriptions of behaviors and attitudes. For example, it is a fact that Japanese use small groups extensively in the workplace. Conceptual knowledge consists of a culture's views and values about central concerns. Sophisticated stereotyping operates in the realm of conceptual knowledge. This category of knowledge is an organizing tool, but it is not sufficient for true cultural understanding. Knowing that the Japanese are a communal society (conceptual knowledge) does not explain the noncommunal activities that exist in Japanese organizations or when the Japanese will or will not be communal. For example, why are quality control circles used in some work settings and not in others? Factual and conceptual knowledge about Japanese culture cannot answer that question; only attributional knowledge can.

Managers can acquire attributional knowledge from personal experience, vicariously from others' experience, and from cultural mentoring. The personal experience method involves carefully observing how people from another culture act and react, and then formulating and reformulating hypotheses and cultural explanations for the observed behavior. When expatriates test their hypotheses and find them valid, they form schemas about specific events in the host culture.

One can learn vicariously by reading about other cultures, but the best form of vicarious learning is via cultural assimilator exercises.[39] These are critical incidents of cross-cultural encounters, accompanied by alternative explanations for the behavior of people from the foreign culture. After choosing what they perceive as the most likely answer, trainees then read expert opinions relating why each answer is adequate or inadequate. These opinions are validated by cross-cultural experts and include information about the relative importance of cultural dimensions or context-specific customs in the culture in question.

A cultural mentor can be viewed as a hybrid of vicarious and personal acquisition of attributional knowledge – a sort of live cultural assimilator. Cultural mentors are usually long-term expatriates or members of the foreign culture. The latter are often helpful souls who have lived abroad themselves and understand the challenge of mastering another culture or people not totally in step with their own culture.[40] "They interpret the local culture for expatriates and guide them through its shoals, as well as providing them with the necessary encouragement when it feels like the expatriates will never 'break the code' of another culture and fit in comfortably."[41] Reading an explanation from a book or working through a series of cultural assimilators is different from receiving an explanation of an experience the expatriate has personally lived through and now wishes to understand. Cultural mentors can correct inaccurate hypotheses about the local culture. Expatriates who had cultural mentors overseas have been found to fare better than those who did not have such mentors: They were more fluent in the foreign language; they perceived themselves as better adapted to their work and general living conditions abroad; they were more aware of the paradoxes of expatriate life, indicating a higher degree of acculturation and understanding of the other culture; and they received higher performance appraisal ratings from both their superiors and themselves.[42]

In spite of the benefits of mentoring, few multinationals formally assign a cultural mentor to their expatriates. Yet another way of developing an expatriate's attributional knowledge is to provide more training in the host country rather than relying solely on predeparture culture "inoculations."

Admittedly, there are trade-offs to developing attributional knowledge. The acquisition of cultural knowledge takes a good deal of time and energy, which is not available to all managers. Nor is it reasonable to expect employees who work with people from various cultures on a daily basis to master each culture. Nevertheless, organizing the knowledge they do acquire as context-specific schemas can speed up cultural learning and prevent confusion and errors in making sense of cultural paradoxes.

If we accept that cultures are paradoxical, then it follows that learning another culture occurs in a dialectical fashion – thesis, antithesis, and synthesis. Thesis entails a hypothesis involving a sophisticated stereotype; antithesis is the identification of an apparently oppositional cultural paradox. Synthesis involves making sense of contradictory behavior – understanding why certain values are more important in certain contexts. Behavior appears less paradoxical once the foreigner learns to index contexts and match them with the appropriate schemas in the same way that members of the host culture do. Collins's description of the Westerner's Perception Scale in comprehending Japanese culture[43] illustrates one form of dialectical culture learning, an upwardly spiraling cycle of cultural comprehension.

USING THE MODEL

Because this cultural sensemaking model provides a more complex way of understanding culture, it has clear implications for those who teach culture, for those who work across cultures, and for organizations that send expatriates overseas.

Teaching about Cultural Understanding

Sophisticated stereotyping should be the beginning of cultural learning, not the end, as is so often the case when teaching or learning about culture. Recognition of a more complex, holistic, sensemaking model of culture allows us to respond more effectively when students or trainees provide examples of paradoxes that seem to contradict cultural dimensions. The model also requires a somewhat different teaching approach. We have developed a sequential method that has been effective in our teaching:

What I should be doing in this class

- **Help students understand the complexity of their own culture.** To acquaint students with the vast challenge of comprehending culture, we begin with a thorough understanding of the internal logic of one's own culture and its socioeconomic, political, and historical roots. We add complexity by pointing out paradoxes as well as identifying regional, ethnic, religious, organizational, and individual variations in behavior. For example, when Thai students describe their culture as friendly, we ask the following series of questions: "Are all Thais friendly? Are Thais always friendly? Under what circumstances would Thais not exhibit friendly behavior? Why?"
- **Give students cultural dimensions and values as well as sophisticated stereotypes as basic tools.** These dimensions, including the values listed in Table 1, can then be used to explain contrasting behavior from two or more different cultures (e.g., what can sample obituaries from the United States and Mexico reveal about cultural values? What is the typical response of businesses in both countries when a member of an employee's family dies?). Students practice recognizing cultural dimensions in cross-cultural dialogues and cases and learn sophisticated stereotypes. This helps them gain conceptual knowledge about different cultures so they can make between-culture distinctions.
- **Develop students' skills in cultural observation and behavioral flexibility.** One of the difficulties expatriates confront in making sense of a new culture is the contradiction between the expected culture, the sophisticated stereotype taught in predeparture training or gleaned from others, and the manifest culture, the one actually enacted in a situation.[44] To help students become skilled at observing and decoding other cultures, teach them to think more like anthropologists and give them practice in

honing observational and interpretive skills. To help students develop the behavioral flexibility needed to adapt to unanticipated situations, role-playing and videos of cross-cultural interactions can be used.

- **Have students do an in-depth study or experience with one culture.** To go beyond sophisticated stereotypes, students learn the internal logic and cultural history of a single culture. They acquire attributional knowledge from cultural mentors and/or cultural immersion, in addition to extensive research.

- **Focus on learning context-appropriate behavior in other cultures and developing cultural hypotheses and explanations for paradoxical behavior.** Once students have mastered the preceding steps, the emphasis changes to learning schemas for different contexts. For example, student teams are instructed to deliberately demonstrate incorrect behavior; they ask others to point out the mistakes and then replay the scene using correct behavior. To model the crucial behavior of asking for help in understanding cultural mysteries,[45] students use cultural mentors to explain situations they choose to learn about (e.g., "How do managers in _____ encourage employees to perform at high levels? Why does that work for them?"). The variation in the mentors' answers ("Some managers are successful doing this while others . . .") and the qualified answers ("This seems to work unless . . . ; it depends on . . .") helps students develop more complex understandings of the other culture. To highlight the message of moving beyond cultural stereotypes, use language that focuses on forming and testing hypotheses about contextual behavior: "What are your hypotheses about why a French employee behaves this way in this situation? How can you find out if these hypotheses are correct?"

Sensemaking for Individuals Working across Cultures

After the training program, and once on assignment in a new culture, this cultural sensemaking approach has other practical implications.

- **Approach learning another culture more like a scientist who holds conscious stereotypes and hypotheses in order to test them.** One of the key differences between managers who were identified by their fellow MBA students as the "most internationally effective" and the "least internationally effective" is that the former changed their stereotypes of other nationalities as they interacted with them while the latter did not.[46]

- **Seek out cultural mentors and people who possess attributional knowledge about cultures.** Perhaps one of the basic lessons of cross-cultural interaction is that tolerance and effectiveness result from greater understanding of another culture. Making sense of a culture's internal logic and decoding cultural paradoxes is easiest with the aid of a willing and knowledgeable informant.

- **Analyze disconfirming evidence and instances that defy cultural stereotypes.** Even people with a great deal of experience in another culture can benefit from analyzing cultural paradoxes. For instance, the question, "In what circumstances do Latin Americans fail to exhibit *simpatía*?" led to a more complex cultural understanding for one of the authors, who had already spent nine curious years in that region. Once expatriates can function reasonably well in another culture, it is easy for them to reach plateaus in their cultural understanding and mistakenly assume that they comprehend the entire puzzle. This presents a danger when expatriates inadvertently pass on inaccurate information about the local culture, or make faulty, and even expensive, business decisions based on partial understandings.

- **Learn cultural schemas that will help you be effective.** Knowing how to act appropriately in specific cross-cultural settings results in self-confidence and effectiveness. One cannot memorize all the rules in another culture, but understanding the values that underlie most schemas can often prevent us from making serious mistakes.

How Multinational Organizations Can Use the Sensemaking Model

The cultural sensemaking model also has practical implications for multinational organizations.

All part of the organizational the culture of an Culture of an effective company

- **Use cognitive complexity as a selection criterion for expatriates and people in international positions.** Avoid black-and-white thinkers in favor of people who exhibit cognitive complexity, which involves the ability to handle ambiguity and multiple viewpoints. This skill is better suited to a thesis-antithesis approach to understanding the paradoxical nature of culture.
- **Provide in-country cultural training for expatriates that goes beyond factual and conceptual knowledge.** Predeparture cultural training is complemented by on-site training, which has the advantage of good timing. In-country culture training takes place when expatriates are highly motivated to find answers to real cultural dilemmas and when they are ready for greater complexity.[47]
- **Gauge the cultural knowledge possessed by expatriates within a country.** The accuracy and depth of one's cultural understanding is not always linked to the time one has spent in another country; it depends on the degree of involvement with the other culture as well as cultural curiosity and desire to learn. Nevertheless, when companies determine the optimum length of overseas assignments, they should consider how much time is generally necessary to function effectively in a particular culture. If a firm's expatriates stay abroad for only two years, it is less likely that a deep understanding of the culture will be shared among them than if they were to stay for longer periods. As long as the longer-term expatriates do not stop at a low-level plateau of cultural learning, mixing short-term (2–3 years) with longer-term expatriates (6–7 years) with permanent expatriates could produce more shared organizational learning about the culture. It is also essential to recognize that expatriates working for the same organization may be at different levels of cultural understanding.
- **Act like learning organizations with regard to cultural knowledge.** Multinationals benefit from formal mechanisms to develop a more complex understanding of the cultures where they do business through such methods as cultural mentors and in-country cultural training. There should also be mechanisms for sharing cultural knowledge. For example, having returned expatriates give formal debriefing sessions in which they report what they learned in their assignment increases the company's collective cultural knowledge and eases the expatriates' transition home by helping them make sense of a highly significant experience.[48]

ACKNOWLEDGMENT

The authors would like to thank the UCLA CIBER Cross Cultural Collegium for its contributions to the article. Dr Osland's research is partially funded by a grant from the Robert B. Pamplin Jr. Corporation.

Notes

1   This was one of the findings of a class research project on the acceptance of ATMs by Dr Osland's graduate students at INCAE's (Central American Institute of Business Administration) Banking Program in 1991.

2   Triandis, J. C., Marin, G., Lisansky, J., & Betancourt, H. 1984. *Simpatía* as a cultural script of hispanics. *Journal of Personality and Social Psychology,* 47(6): 1363–1375.

3   Hofstede, G. 1980. *Culture's consequences: International differences in work related values.* Beverly Hills: Sage.

4   Olmstead v. United States, 277 U.S. 438, 478 (1928) (Brandeis, J., dissenting).

5   The descriptions of cultural metaphors in *Understanding global cultures: Metaphorical journeys through 17 countries* (Thousand Oaks, CA: Sage, 1994) by Martin Gannon and his associates, contain passing references to paradoxes, but do not address the issue directly.

6   Parsons, T. & Shils, E. 1951. *Toward a general theory of action.* Cambridge: Harvard University Press; Kluckhohn, F. & Strodtbeck, F. L. 1961. *Variations in value orientations.* Evanston, IL: Row, Peterson; Hofstede, op. cit.; Triandis, H. C. 1982. Dimensions of cultural variations as parameters of organizational theories. *International Studies of Management and Organization,* 12(4): 139–169; Ronen, S. & Shenkar, O. (1985). Clustering countries on attitudinal dimensions: A review and synthesis. *Academy of Management Review,* 10: 435–454; Hall, E. T. & Hall, M. R. 1990. *Understanding cultural differences.* Yarmouth, ME: Intercultural Press; Fiske, A. P. 1992. The four elementary forms of sociality: Framework for a unified theory of social relations. *Psychological Review,* 99(4), 689–723; Schwartz, S. 1992. Universals in the content and structure of values: Theoretical advances and empirical tests in 20 countries. In M. Zanna (Ed.), *Advances in experimental social psychology,* 25: 1–66. New York, NY: Academic Press; Trompenaars, F. & Hampden Turner, C. 1993. *The seven cultures of capitalism.* New York: Doubleday.

7   Hofstede, op. cit.

8   Adler, N. 1997. *International dimensions of organizational behavior,* 3rd ed. Cincinnati: South-Western, 75–76.

9   Hall & Hall, op. cit.

10 Gannon, op. cit.

11 Barnlund, D. 1975. *Public and private self in Japan and the United States.* Yarmouth, ME: Intercultural Press, 6.

12 Osland, J. S. 1995. *The adventure of working abroad: Hero tales from the global frontier.* San Francisco: Jossey-Bass.

13 Collins, R. J. 1987. *Max Danger: The adventures of an expat in Tokyo.* Rutland, VT: Charles E. Tuttle Co.

14 Ibid., 14–15.

15 Tripathi, R. C. 1988. *Aligning development to values in India.* In D. Sinha & H. S. R. Kao (Eds.), Social values and development: Asian perspectives: 315–333. New Delhi: Sage; Wilbur, J. 1995. *A brief history of everything.* New York: Shambala.

16 Quinn, R. & Cameron, K. S. (Eds.) 1988. *Paradox and transformation.* Cambridge, MA: Ballinger; Smith, K. K. & Berg, D. N. 1987. *Paradoxes of group life.* San Francisco: Jossey-Bass.

17 Hofstede, op. cit.

18 Hofstede, G. 1994. In U. Kim, H. S. Triandis, C. Kâgitçibasi, S. Choi & G. Yoon (Eds.), *Individualism and collectivism*. Thousand Oaks, CA: Sage, xi.

19 Lévi-Strauss, C. 1962. *La pensée sauvage*. Paris: Adler's Foreign Books, Inc.

20 Fontaine, G. 1989. *Managing international assignments: The strategy for success*. Englewood Cliffs, NJ: Prentice Hall.

21 Triandis, H. C., Bontempo, R., Villareal, M. J., Asai, M., & Lucca, N. 1988. Individualism and collectivism: Cross-cultural perspectives on self-ingroup relationships. *Journal of Personality and Social Psychology*, 54(2): 323–338,

22 Bateson, G. 1973. *Steps to an ecology of mind*. London: Paladin Books.

23 Haught, J. 1993. What does sex have to do with it? *Oregonian*, December 29, 1993, D7.

24 Tripathi, Marin, op. cit.

25 Ibid.

26 Bird, A., Osland, J. S., Mendenhall, M., & Schneider, S. 1999. Adapting and adjusting to other cultures: What we know but don't always tell. *Journal of Management Inquiry*, 8(2): 152–165.

27 Context is also embedded in culture, so one could argue that the entire model is situated within the broader culture. For simplicity's sake, however, we chose to focus only on the sensemaking that occurs in deciphering cultural paradoxes.

28 Triandis, Marin, et al., op. cit.

29 Fisher, G. 1997. *Mindsets: The role of culture and perception in international relations*. Yarmouth, ME: Intercultural Press.

30 Starbuck, W. H. & Milliken, F. J. 1988. *Executives' personal filters: What they notice and how they make sense*. In D. Hambrick (Ed.), The executive effect: Concepts and methods for studying top managers. Greenwich, CT: JAI Press, 51.

31 Barnlund, op. cit.

32 Fukuyama, F. 1996. *Trust*. New York: Penguin Books.

33 Ibid., 29.

34 Triandis, et al., op. cit.

35 Osland, J. S., De Franco, S., & Osland, A. 1999. Organizational implications of Latin American culture: Lessons for the expatriate manager. *Journal of Management Inquiry*, 8(2): 219–234.

36 Hofstede, *Culture's consequences*, op. cit.

37 Geertz, C. 1973. *The interpretation of cultures*. New York: HarperCollins Basic Books, 44.

38 Bird, A., Heinbuch, S., Dunbar, R., & McNulty, M. 1993. A conceptual model of the effects of area studies training programs and a preliminary investigation of the model's hypothesized relationships. *International Journal of Intercultural Relations*, 17(4): 415–436.

39 The original cultural assimilators were developed by Harry Triandis at the University of Illinois. A recent collection is found in *Intercultural interactions: A practical guide*, by R. Brislin, K. Cushner, C. Cherrie, & Yong, M., Thousand Oaks, CA: Sage, 1986 and 1996 (second edition).

40 Osland, *Working abroad*, op. cit.

41 Ibid., 68.

42 Ibid., 74.

43 Collins, op. cit.

44 Schermerhorn, Jr., J. & Bond, M. H. 1997. Cross-cultural leadership dynamics in collectivism and high power distance settings. *Leadership & Organization Development Journal*, 18(4): 187–193.

45 On occasion we have heard frustrated cross-cultural trainers grumble that some expatriates view seeking out cultural explanations with the same disdain they reserve for stopping to ask for driving directions.

46 Ratiu, I. 1983. Thinking internationally: A comparison of how international students learn. *International Studies of Management and Organization*, 13: 139–150.

47 Bird, Osland, et al., op. cit.

48 Osland, *Working Abroad*, op. cit.

CASE **1**

David Shorter

Joseph J. DiStefano and Neil Abramson

David Shorter sat back in his chair and thought about what he should say to Bob Chen when they met in a few minutes. Three weeks ago when David had left for holiday, he had regarded Bob as an up-and-coming member of the James-Williams team. David had seen Bob as a solid performer who wanted a career at James-Williams and who could be developed over time into a manager and perhaps eventually into a partner. David had even thought that Bob could help attract to James-Williams some of the new entrepreneurial Hong Kong companies that were coming to Toronto. Now David heard from Bob's managing partner, Jane Klinck, that Bob was threatening to resign.

DAVID'S FIRST DAY BACK

David thought about the steady stream of people who had been in to see him this first morning back in the office. Jane Klinck was worried and upset. She felt that Bob was acting "crazy" and that there might be some sort of personality conflict between Bob and Mike McLeod. She hoped that David would be able to sort out the problem and find a solution that would keep Bob in the company. Mike McLeod had been in to see David, too. Mike was a fairly new partner who attracted a lot of business to James-Williams.

Neil Abramson prepared this case under the supervision of Professor J. J. DiStefano solely to provide material for class discussion. The authors do not intend to illustrate either effective or ineffective handling of a managerial situation. The authors may have disguised certain names and other identifying information to protect confidentiality.

He felt that he had not only been through the proper channels to have Bob assigned to the Softdisk Computer audit, but that he had been extremely patient with Bob. Mike said the other partners were shaking their heads about his behaviour, wondering why he was being so patient when it was standard procedure for partners to make such an assignment. Joe Silverman had been in as well. Joe was the tax partner Bob would report to starting in September, just five weeks from now. Joe hotly protested Bob's behaviour:

> We can't have staff refusing assignments! Bob is way out of line! The customers must come first and this behaviour sheds a poor light on Bob. If he doesn't take the Softdisk job, he should be fired!

THE NEW ENTERPRISE GROUP AT JAMES-WILLIAMS

David Shorter was the Practice Director of the New Enterprise Group at James-Williams. James-Williams was one of the six largest public accounting firms in Canada with 400 partners practising in 30 Canadian cities. James-Williams was the sole Canadian member of James-Williams International which provided audit, tax, consulting and other services to individuals, private businesses and governments in the Americas, Europe, the Middle East, Africa, Asia, and the Pacific.

The New Enterprise Group had been set up seven years ago to provide service to smaller growth companies managed by entrepreneurs. David had been the Practice Director for the past four years. James-Williams believed that companies with gross annual revenues of between $5 million and $100 million were often neglected as potential customers by Canadian public accounting firms because of their small size. Yet these companies had need of a variety of services that could be provided by James-Williams and these companies would pay high fees for their relative size. When these companies had grown beyond gross revenues of $100 million, their business could be transferred from the New Enterprise Group to the main auditing and consulting services of James-Williams and a solid relationship would exist. This was an important consideration in a mature industry where public accounting firms competed on service, reputation and price. Often, it was a long-term relationship that kept a client with a public accounting firm. These relationships enabled partners of the public accounting firms to have such an intimate knowledge of their clients' activities that they could anticipate problems and become indispensable to their clients' planning process.

The New Enterprise Group provided a range of consulting services geared to the needs of growing entrepreneurial companies. In addition to accounting and auditing services, the partners acted as principal business advisors. Client companies were particularly interested in the subjects of corporate finance and tax consulting, as well as the problems of acquisition and divestiture. Consulting was also available on strategic planning, development of business plans, marketing, human resource management, and information systems.

The New Enterprise Group was organized as a collegial system of partners who managed their own clients and activities within the performance objectives established by James-Williams, and under the general supervision of the Practice Director, who was also a partner (see Exhibit 1). Staff members below the partner level were organized on the staff system. A staff usually consisted of one or two senior staff accountants and

EXHIBIT 1 James-Williams: The New Enterprise Group Organizational Chart (Reporting Relationships prior to Bob Chen's Reassignment to Tax)

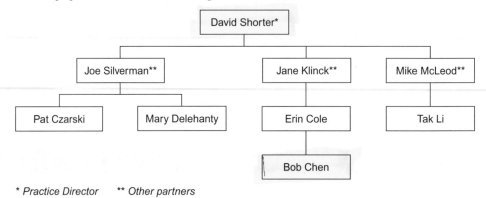

* *Practice Director*   ** *Other partners*

several intermediate or junior staff accountants under a manager. A partner would have one, two or three managers and several staff reporting to him/her.

Most of the staff were either chartered accountants or in the process of becoming chartered accountants. Usually, staff would be hired out of business school as junior staff accountants and would work on staff over a two-year period while they studied for their chartered accountant examinations. At the beginning of their second year, they were promoted to intermediate staff accountants at which level they remained until they passed the chartered accountant exams. At the beginning of their third year they wrote their exams, and, if they passed, they were promoted to senior staff accountants. If they did not pass, which was fairly common, they would have another year to prepare for a final chance at the exams.

The normal promotion process at James-Williams was for staff to remain as senior staff accountants for two years while they developed a consulting specialty of their choice. Then they might be promoted to manager and supervise six to nine staff. Most partners were selected from the ranks of the managers after they had been with the firm for 10 to 11 years.

BOB CHEN'S BACKGROUND WITH NEW ENTERPRISE GROUP

Bob Chen was born in Hong Kong and came to Toronto as a high school student for Grade 13. He graduated with a Bachelor of Commerce from Queen's University in Kingston. At Queen's he achieved an overall grade point average of 75 percent[1] and was the treasurer of the Chinese Students' Society. He was recruited for James-Williams in the spring of his final year at Queen's, and began as a junior staff accountant at the New Enterprise Group in the following September.

Bob was seen as quiet and soft-spoken. One of his managers described him as "shy and accommodating. He does what he is asked to do and a bit more. Casual requests get immediate results." He was also a very private person whose politeness often meant not saying exactly what he wanted out of a situation or from another person. His civility may have masked from his colleagues his strongly felt desire for success and strongly held views about his possible contribution to the firm.

Bob was well liked by the people around him, most of whom viewed him as Westernized. Some partners and staff thought that Bob "was fairly outgoing for an Oriental" and had much better oral communications skills than previous staff from Hong Kong hired by the firm. His colleagues believed that Bob had good potential with James-Williams and hoped he would stay with the firm.

PREVIOUS CONTACTS BETWEEN DAVID AND BOB

Two years after joining the firm, Bob wrote his chartered accountant examinations and in the following December learned the good news that he had passed. He was transferred as an audit senior to Jane Klinck, because the partner Bob had previously reported to was leaving the company. Bob was to report to Erin Cole who was the manager working under Jane.

Early in the new year, David Shorter followed his usual custom of having one-on-one meetings with staff who had passed their examinations and been promoted to senior staff accountant positions. The purpose of the meetings was not only to congratulate them on their success, but also to begin to identify their interests in professional specialization so that David could plan appropriate assignments for them within the New Enterprise Group. New assignments were usually announced after the annual performance appraisal in May, and were effective by September.

When he met with Bob in January, David was pleased with Bob's success because he had thought that Bob was a solid, but average performer and might not pass his examination the first time he wrote it. Now David decided that Bob might have higher potential within the New Enterprise Group and suggested that Bob might like to work to build a practice around attracting entrepreneurial, Hong Kong-based companies to use the New Enterprise Group's services. David explained:

> One of our goals is to build up our business with Hong Kong companies. Up to now, we haven't had much success because most Hong Kong money has been invested in real estate. Now, however, Hong Kong money is being invested in businesses which are in the New Enterprise Group's target market.

To be able to attract a Hong Kong practice, Bob would have to build up his auditing skills for another year, because audit was the initial function which brought companies to the New Enterprise Group and stimulated their interest in other consulting services. David remembered that he had two goals in suggesting further auditing experience for Bob. First, the New Enterprise Group had a shortage of senior auditors for this year. Second, he felt that Bob was a "keeper" who could have a long and mutually valuable future with the firm. Bob's auditing skills needed strengthening since he had done very little auditing in his first two years. David had seen previous staff with similar limitations fail as both managers and partners, because without auditing experience they could not understand the practical nature of most business problems. David noted, "Without more seasoning, he would not be as valuable to us. He would get weeded out as a technician."

But Bob had other ideas; he indicated to David that now that he had his CA designation, he wanted to develop a specialization in tax. He was open to the idea of developing a Hong Kong practice, but in the meantime he wanted an assignment that would teach him tax. David told Bob that he didn't believe Bob was ready for a tax assignment, because tax was a practical discipline that needed the ability to find creative tax solutions to business problems. Without a firm grounding in audit, staff had a tendency to quote tax regulations, rather than use the tax regulations to the advantage of their clients.

> I didn't think he was ready and believed that his chargeable activity time would fall. I was under pressure to keep up the chargeable activity time of all staff.

David thought that by the end of the interview he had convinced Bob of the soundness of his argument and that Bob had agreed to defer his request for a tax position.

In May, Jane conducted Bob's annual performance appraisal during which time Bob repeated his request for an assignment in tax. Her reply was similar to David's earlier commentary. Jane told Bob that she thought he needed another year of auditing work.

> He had one year of decent audit work with me, but his junior year had not been enlightening in the area of audit. I thought he agreed that his junior year had not been productive in the area of audit.

Jane asked David to review the performance appraisal because Bob had only been transferred to her in December. When David met with Bob in June, Bob again asked for an assignment in tax. David said no, reiterating his earlier argument that Bob needed more auditing experience. He added that Jane supported this recommendation. It was both David's and Jane's opinion that Bob was only now doing his first and second comprehensive audits. Bob seemed to accept this judgment, though he did not appear to be satisfied by it.

Over the next month, Bob requested and received two more interviews with David to request a tax assignment. David was pleased to talk with Bob because he felt that Bob's concern showed he was highly interested in his career and also highly committed to James-Williams. At the first meeting, David offered the compromise that if Bob would continue as an auditor for a year, then David would send Bob on a comprehensive three-year tax training program that was a much prized opportunity among tax consultants. "I offered to send him on this expensive course fully funded by the firm if he would agree to wait another year for a tax assignment." Bob seemed initially to agree but then asked for another meeting. At the second meeting, David finally agreed to assign Bob to a tax partner, Joe Silverman, to work in tax starting in September.

> I told him that even though he could make the move into tax in September, he'd have to do some audits during his first year in tax. The firm needed to take advantage of his auditing skills as a senior. It would also keep his activities time up.

Bob agreed to the conditions and David left for holidays shortly after.

EVENTS OCCURRING DURING DAVID SHORTER'S ABSENCE

David Shorter left the New Enterprise Group to attend a Partner Development Program and for holidays at the beginning of July. During this time, Mike McLeod realized his upcoming need for a senior auditor for an important account, the Softdisk Computer Company. Softdisk's year-end required that the audit had to be done in September and October. The audit would fully occupy the time of the senior auditor during those two months. In order to make preparations for the job, the senior auditor had to be assigned to the audit by the end of July at the latest. It was more desirable for the senior auditor to be in place by July 13 in order to attend the client's physical inventory being conducted on that date. This would also provide an opportunity for the client and senior auditor to meet each other and work together prior to the actual audit.

Mike found that Bob Chen was the only senior auditor in the New Enterprise Group who might be available in September and October. Policy in the New Enterprise Group was to use internal staff as senior auditors whenever possible because the cost for hours of internal staff was less than if an auditor had to be "rented" from another division of James-Williams. Also, it would be easier for Mike to manage someone from inside the New Enterprise Group.

Since the actual audit work was to be conducted in the fall, Bob would be "officially" working for Joe Silverman in tax. Mike approached Joe Silverman and his manager, Pat Czarski, to see whether he could use Bob Chen for the audit. Joe and Pat told him that Bob was to be assigned to Joe's other manager, Mary Delehanty, who was away on holiday. But Joe and Pat thought it was a very good idea to assign Bob to the audit. The arrangements for Bob to be transferred to Joe had only been made in June and there was no tax work available for him. Further, with Mary on holiday, it was unlikely that she could find tax work for Bob to do in September and the Softdisk audit would keep Bob's billable hours at an acceptable level until they could use his services effectively.

With this approval, Mike approached Bob on July 10. He asked Bob to take the Softdisk audit and provided Bob with information on the company. In particular, Mike wanted Bob to know that the Softdisk audit would fit in with Bob's career path in tax. The audit would include international multi-jurisdictional tax issues, tax problems concerning research and development being done in Quebec, and a high technology emphasis much valued by staff who worked in the New Enterprise Group. The tax issues were so complex and interesting that the audit had been supervised last year by a tax partner who was now in New York. Mike reassured Bob that this partner would be available for consultation if Bob had problems. Further, once Bob had done the audit, he would have first call on any further, special tax work which might be required by Softdisk. Mike suggested that Bob should contact Dominick Sousa, a manager in the New Enterprise Group who had acted as senior auditor for Softdisk last year, to confirm these details.

Mike also noted that because the prior year's work with Softdisk had been a first audit by James-Williams, extra efforts had been taken. Therefore Bob would benefit from a better planning package being in place and a high client commitment for the second year. In addition, two James-Williams staff members from last year's audit would be carried over to Bob's team, further strengthening the continuity. Finally, Mike assured Bob that Mike and Tak Li would also be available to assist as needed. Altogether, he sought to assure Bob that taking on this audit would be consistent with his professed career objectives.

It was Mike's impression that Bob had agreed to do the Softdisk audit once he had confirmed the information Mike had given him with "due diligence."

> He didn't refuse. Basically, he did not say yes, but he said "Yes, I'll consider it and will talk to the people." I was led to believe that he would seriously consider it and I got the impression he would do it. I thought we had a reasonable exchange and that we were both being open with each other.

Bob agreed to attend the physical inventory conducted on July 13. The key contact at Softdisk was also of Chinese origin, liked Bob and was pleased to have him for the audit.

Then Mike heard from Pat Czarski and from his own manager, Tak Li, that Bob had told them privately that he did not intend to do the audit. Given that Mike had thought the matter settled, he was shocked by this turn of events. He was especially surprised because Bob's attendance at the physical inventory sent a clear signal to Mike of Bob's acceptance of the assignment. Over the next week when Mike saw Bob in the office corridor or in the washroom, he checked if Bob was planning to do the audit and got the impression that Bob was still agreeable to the arrangements made earlier. But then he would hear more second hand reports from Pat and Tak that Bob was not planning to do the audit. So Mike decided to be more direct.

> I guess that I precipitated a crisis from Bob's perspective. I said, "Don't BS me. Tell me up front. What are you going to do instead?" We had frequent contact in the hallways. I would ask him if he had a chance to talk to Dominick Sousa. But Bob wouldn't say anything about it.

At this point, Mike decided that Bob was not being straight with him. He asked Pat and Tak to act as agents to see how Bob was reacting to the Softdisk project. "They would report one day that he was committed. Then the next day he had thought about it and wasn't committed any more."

This situation frustrated Mike immensely. His parents had lived in Hong Kong while Mike was growing up. His sister still lived there.

> I have a better than average knowledge of cultural differences between Canadians and people from Hong Kong. I thought I was being effective.

Mike decided an open discussion was necessary and wondered if Bob had not understood what a developmental opportunity the Softdisk audit was for furthering his professed career interest in tax consulting. Mike needed a fast and firm resolution to the problem because an auditor had to be in place by the end of July. If Bob would not do the job, then Mike would have to borrow a senior auditor from another James-Williams office, and the time pressure to brief such a replacement adequately would be extreme.

Mike decided to call a meeting with Bob, Pat, and Tak for July 20.

> I didn't want a fight but I wasn't going to take any BS. Tak and Pat weren't getting the same story that I was. Bob was telling them "no" and me "maybe." I wanted to get all four of us in a room and finally get some straight answers. I was going to tell Bob, "You want to be a tax consultant. Well, here is the opportunity."

On July 19, Bob met with Jane and asked for her help. Jane had supported Bob at partners' meetings and he felt she was an ally. Bob told Jane that he wanted to refuse the Softdisk job. He said he was concerned that the amount of planning time required for the Softdisk audit would interfere with a complex audit he was currently doing with a film company. He was afraid he might have to take leave from the film company audit. Jane asked if scheduling was his only concern.

> Bob told me there was a bigger problem than scheduling. He didn't want to do the audit. He said he couldn't work for Mike but he wouldn't say why.

Jane told Bob that he was crazy and not to do anything rash.

On July 20, Mike, Pat, Tak and Bob met for three hours. Most of the discussion centred around Mike's re-emphasizing how the Softdisk job fit with Bob's career goals in tax consulting.

> I kept dragging Bob back to the career goals he said he had and showing him that if he was serious about tax then this was an opportunity. I answered all of his objections. Pat, Tak and I left the meeting once again thinking that Bob had agreed to do the job.

Meanwhile, Joe Silverman had heard about the situation and started to have doubts about the desirability of Bob joining his tax group in the fall. Since he had never worked with Bob, he approached Jane and asked for more information. Joe said the grapevine was giving him a poor impression of Bob. In Joe's view, not only was it out of line for staff to refuse assignments from partners, but also the clients' interests were the number one concern of the firm. Yet Bob did not seem to be acknowledging either of these values. If Bob would not do the Softdisk audit, then Joe thought Bob should be forced out.

Jane agreed with Joe. She was shocked by Bob's behaviour and felt, as Bob's key backer in partners' meetings, very unhappy to be caught in the middle. She called Bob into her office and told him that both Mike and Joe were furious. She told Bob that his behaviour had put him in a bad position with Joe, who was to be Bob's new managing partner. Joe was very client-oriented and was unlikely to give Bob the benefit of the doubt, because he had never seen Bob's hard work first-hand.

> I told him that it didn't seem to be the right time for taking a stand. He said he believed it was a serious enough problem to resist. He was willing to leave the firm rather than work with Mike on the audit. I was shocked. I thought he enjoyed working for the firm and that he saw himself as having a good long-term career here. I don't know if he had a personal problem about working with Mike. I've talked to Mike and he doesn't know either.

On Sunday night, July 22, Bob phoned Pat to say that he would not do the Softdisk audit. Pat informed Mike, who washed his hands of the matter and obtained another senior auditor from the Richmond Hill office of James-Williams.

On the morning of July 23, Bob came to see Jane. He said he would have to resign because he could not work for Mike. He also said he realized he had ruined his relationships with the partners and could not expect good performance appraisals even if he did do the audit. Jane told him he was crazy to throw away his career at James-Williams. Jane thought that maybe he was right about getting a poor performance appraisal because

Joe "was fit to be tied," but she suggested that Bob wait and talk to David who was returning from holiday the next day. Perhaps David could transfer Bob since David had a high opinion of Bob's worth to the company.

DAVID'S DECISION

David Shorter returned from vacation on July 23. His first day back he met with Jane Klinck and Mike McLeod who briefed him about the trouble with Bob. He also met with Joe Silverman who came to express his outrage about Bob's behaviour.

On July 24, David sat at his desk thinking. Bob would be here in a few minutes. David had some decisions to make. He knew that Bob was threatening to resign rather than do the Softdisk audit. He knew that both Mike and Joe were furious, but if Bob worked hard in the future, he did not think that Joe would give Bob poor performance appraisals. He knew that Jane had a high opinion of Bob and could not understand what was causing Bob to act this way.

David knew he had to make a decision that balanced the needs of all the people involved. On the one hand, Bob had offended some fairly important partners with whom David had to work and maintain good relationships. David was under no illusion that he could tell these partners what to do or think. They were all partners together, and they decided together. Besides, David agreed with them that it was inappropriate to let an employee with the capacity and the time to do a job refuse it. The Softdisk job also looked like a good opportunity for someone who wanted to specialize in tax. David did not know why Bob had turned it down.

On the other hand, Bob was a valuable employee given his skills and his potential for helping the New Enterprise Group attract business from Hong Kong investors. In addition to his knowledge, as reflected by his passing the uniform C.A. exam on his first attempt, he spoke and wrote Chinese fluently, skills relevant to James-Williams's stated goal of attracting Hong Kong business. That objective was one reason why the James-Williams office had been opened in Hong Kong. Yet the office had not done well and was now closed, so David was uncertain of the importance of Bob to the Canadian strategy.

There was the possibility of a transfer. The "Tower" (James-Williams's main group in Toronto) had been requesting that seniors interested in specializing in tax be transferred to them because they anticipated a future demand for tax specialists. Maybe that was what Bob was hoping for. David suspected that some of Bob's friends had been transferred to the Tower without any audit responsibilities and that Bob had been comparing notes with them.

David was sure of one thing. He did not want to offend the other partners in the New Enterprise Group. Perhaps he could persuade Bob to stay, and do the job, and then start tax work. Bob was an emotional kind of guy. Maybe David could get him to see reason.

Note

1   In Canada the grade point system follows the British model. At Queen's a 75 average is a B+ and is considered evidence of high achievement.

Bob Chen

Joseph J. DiStefano and Neil Abramson

Bob Chen prepared himself for his meeting with David Shorter, Practice Director of the New Enterprise Group at James-Williams. In a few minutes, Bob might feel it necessary to resign from James-Williams. Bob had no other job to go to, and with a recession looming, it might be hard to find other employment. Nevertheless, Bob felt that his career was at stake if he was not firm.

THE NEW ENTERPRISE GROUP AT JAMES-WILLIAMS

The New Enterprise Group was a division of James-Williams located in Toronto. James-Williams was one of the six largest public accounting firms in Canada with 400 partners practising in 30 Canadian cities. James-Williams was the sole Canadian member of James-Williams International which provided audit, tax, consulting and other services to individuals, private businesses and governments in the Americas, Europe, the Middle East, Africa, Asia, and the Pacific.

The New Enterprise Group had been set up seven years ago to provide service to smaller growth companies managed by entrepreneurs. David Shorter had been the Practice Director for the past four years. James-Williams believed that companies with gross annual

IVEY

Neil Abramson prepared this case under the supervision of Professor J. J. DiStefano solely to provide material for class discussion. The authors do not intend to illustrate either effective or ineffective handling of a managerial situation. The authors may have disguised certain names and other identifying information to protect confidentiality.

revenues of between $5 million and $100 million were often neglected as potential customers by Canadian public accounting firms because of their small size. Yet these companies had need of a variety of services that could be provided by James-Williams and these companies would pay high fees for their relative size. When these companies had grown beyond gross revenues of $100 million, their business could be transferred from the New Enterprise Group to the main auditing and consulting services of James-Williams and a solid relationship would exist. This was an important consideration in a mature industry where public accounting firms competed on service, reputation and price. Often, it was a long-term relationship that kept a client with a public accounting firm. These relationships enabled partners of the public accounting firms to have such an intimate knowledge of their clients' activities that they could anticipate problems and become indispensable to their clients' planning process.

The New Enterprise Group provided a range of consulting services geared to the needs of growing entrepreneurial companies. In addition to accounting and auditing services, the partners acted as principal business advisors. Client companies were particularly interested in corporate finance, tax consulting, and the problems of acquisition and divestiture. Consulting was also available on strategic planning, developing business plans, marketing, human resource management, and information systems.

The New Enterprise Group was organized as a collegial system of partners who managed their own clients and activities within the performance objectives established by James-Williams, and under the general supervision of the Practice Director who was also a partner (see Exhibit 1). Staff members below the partner level were organized on the staff system. A staff usually consisted of one or two senior staff accountants and several intermediate or junior staff accountants under a manager. A partner would have one, two or three managers and several staff reporting to him/her.

Most of the staff were either chartered accountants or in the process of becoming chartered accountants. Usually, staff would be hired out of business school as junior staff accountants and would work on staff over a two-year period while they studied for their chartered accountant examinations. At the beginning of their second year, they were promoted to intermediate staff accountants at which level they remained until they passed

EXHIBIT 1   James-Williams: The New Enterprise Group Organizational Chart (Reporting Relationships prior to Bob Chen's Reassignment to Tax)

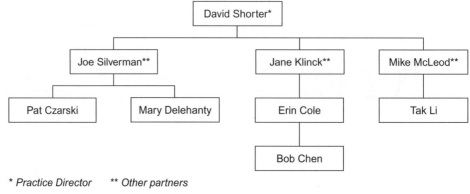

* Practice Director   *** Other partners*

the chartered accountant exams. At the beginning of their third year, they wrote their exams, and, if they passed, they were promoted to senior staff accountants. If they did not pass, which was fairly common, they would have another year to prepare for a final chance at the exams.

The normal promotion process at James-Williams was for staff to remain as senior staff accountants for two years while they developed a consulting specialty of their choice. Then they might be promoted to manager and supervise six to nine staff. Most partners were selected from the ranks of the managers after they had been with the firm for 10 to 11 years.

BOB CHEN'S BACKGROUND AT JAMES-WILLIAMS

Bob Chen was born in Hong Kong and came to Toronto as a high school student for Grade 13. He graduated with a Bachelor of Commerce from Queen's University in Kingston. At Queen's he achieved an overall grade point average of 75 percent[1] and was the treasurer of the Chinese Students' Society. He was recruited for James-Williams in the spring of his final year at Queen's, and began as a junior staff accountant at the New Enterprise Group in the following September.

Early in his final year at Queen's, Bob's father, living in Hong Kong, suggested he find a job in Canada because Hong Kong would revert to the People's Republic of China in 1997. His father believed Bob's future would be better in Canada. Bob applied to a number of major Canadian public accounting firms and was told to reapply if he was able to obtain landed immigrant status. These companies did not seem to realize that it was very hard to obtain landed immigrant status unless one had a job offer.

One firm, James-Williams, offered Bob a job. He accepted. Afterwards Bob felt very loyal to the company because their offer had made it possible for him to remain in Canada.

In September after graduation, Bob started with James-Williams in the New Enterprise Group as a junior staff accountant, doing accounting work and studying for his chartered accountant exams which were scheduled for two years hence. In the following fall he was promoted to intermediate staff accountant as was standard for all second-year staff at James-Williams. During his first two years with the New Enterprise Group, Bob worked under the supervision of several managers including Tak Li and a partner named Lara Witmer. Due to turnover of staff in the New Enterprise Group during those years, Bob was attached for various jobs to a number of managers and partners. About the time that Bob was scheduled to write his CA exams, he learned that Lara Witmer had been asked to leave the firm. Bob would be assigned to work for Jane Klinck under the project supervision of Erin Cole.

In the New Enterprise Group Bob was seen as quiet and soft-spoken. One of his managers described him as "shy and accommodating. He does what he is asked to do and a bit more. Casual requests get immediate results." He was also a very private person whose politeness often meant not saying exactly what he wanted out of a situation or from another person. His civility may have masked from his colleagues his strongly felt desire for success and strongly held views about his possible contribution to the firm.

Bob was well liked by the people around him. Some partners and staff thought that Bob was fairly outgoing and had much better oral communications skills than previous staff from Hong Kong hired by the company. His colleagues believed that Bob had good potential with James-Williams and hoped he would stay with the company.

THE BEGINNINGS OF A PROBLEM

Early in his employment at James-Williams, Bob decided he would like to specialize as a tax consultant. He knew that the normal procedure at James-Williams was for intermediate staff to wait until they had passed their chartered accountant exams before approaching the Practice Director with indications of their specialization interests. However, tax was a very popular choice, and some intermediate staff in the New Enterprise Group went to David Shorter before they had passed their exams so that David would have enough time to find them assignments in their preferred areas.

Nine months after joining the New Enterprise Group, Bob met formally with David Shorter when David reviewed Bob's annual performance appraisal. At that meeting, Bob told David about his interest in becoming a tax specialist. Bob's impression of the meeting was that David had agreed to see what he could do to further Bob's interests. Bob expected that he would receive some tax assignments over the next year while he was studying for his chartered accountant exams, but no such assignments materialized.

In September, Bob wrote his exams and, in December, he received the good news that he had passed on his first attempt. The following January David Shorter called Bob in for an interview during which he congratulated Bob on passing his CA exam and asked what Bob would like to specialize in. Bob again asked for an assignment to tax, but David told him that he wasn't ready for tax because his auditing skills were not strong enough. David asked Bob to work as a senior auditor for a year in order to provide a stronger base for his tax specialization. David also asked Bob to consider the idea of specializing in Hong Kong-based entrepreneurial companies. Bob said he would think about it.

Bob was aware that the New Enterprise Group had a shortage of senior auditors. He felt that he was being asked not to pursue his career interests because of this shortage and not because of any weakness he had as an auditor. When Bob had originally mentioned his interest in tax during his first interview with David, David said he would see what he could do and had not indicated that Bob was weak in auditing. This also suggested to Bob that the main problem was the shortage.

> I wanted to choose tax but I had the feeling that the partners didn't want me to because of the need for continuity in audit. I was maybe the only CA under Jane Klinck. Partners want qualified CAs on their jobs. Maybe Jane didn't want me to go to tax.

Bob was also aware that he had a reputation for doing what he was told. He tried to anticipate the needs of his supervisors and his clients, and he worked extra hard to accommodate their wishes. Partly this was his natural tendency, but he also felt a strong loyalty to the firm for hiring him and thereby providing a way for him to stay in Canada. Now he wondered if David thought he would not make a fuss if he held back in auditing for another year. "I did not usually express myself. I wondered if he thought I was too easygoing and would do whatever he wanted."

When David reviewed his annual performance appraisal in June after Bob had passed his CA exams, Bob again asked David for an assignment to tax. And again David refused, indicating that Bob needed more experience in audit. Bob did not accept this judgment and felt that he had once again been too easygoing and had failed to express himself forcefully enough.

Therefore, in late June, Bob approached David once more and after extensive discussion got David to compromise that if Bob would agree to stay in audit for the year, David would arrange to send Bob on a three-year tax training program. Bob initially agreed, but when he talked to friends in tax, they told him that the course would not teach him tax. Becoming a tax consultant required hands-on experience and the opportunity to deal with the tax problems of real companies in real situations. "I initially agreed, but decided later that it wasn't a good compromise because I wouldn't learn tax technique."

Once again Bob approached David with his concerns and David finally agreed to assign Bob to Joe Silverman, a tax consultant, in September as long as Bob agreed to finish his current audit work and was willing to accept one major audit assignment in January and February. Bob agreed and David made the arrangements for transferring Bob to Joe's tax group starting in September.

THE SOFTDISK AUDIT

On July 10, soon after this series of conversations with David Shorter, Bob was approached by Mike McLeod, another partner in the New Enterprise Group, to be the senior on an audit of the Softdisk Computer Company. The audit would require Bob's full time attention in September and October. Bob was extremely wary. He believed if he accepted the Softdisk audit, he would have very little opportunity to specialize in tax for the entire year. The problem, as Bob saw it, was that it now looked as if he might be required to do audit for six of the next eight months. He was currently doing an audit of a film company for his present managing partner, Jane Klinck. This audit had been scheduled for completion in early July, but the company's books were a mess and Bob thought he might have to continue on that job through August. In August, he would have to begin an interim audit of Softdisk. The Softdisk audit would occupy September and October. Then in January and February, he was required to do another major audit for Jane Klinck as part of his agreement with David. This left November and December for tax work, but December was a slow month due to Christmas. It didn't seem fair to Bob. He had friends who had also passed their CA exams and had been transferred directly into the Tax Department at James-Williams's main group in Toronto without having to agree to any further auditing responsibilities.

Consequently, Bob decided not to do the Softdisk audit. He told Mike McLeod that he would help out because there were no other senior auditors currently available in the New Enterprise Group. He went to the physical inventory at Softdisk in mid-July because no one else seemed to be available. At the time, he told Jane's staff manager, Erin Cole, that he would not do the Softdisk audit even though he went to observe the physical inventory.

Mike had tried to entice Bob into the audit by indicating the possibilities of learning about tax because of the intricate tax situation at the company. Bob talked about these possible advantages with others and decided that Softdisk was not as good an opportunity as Mike was describing. For one thing, Softdisk's tax complexities had been sorted out the year before by a senior tax manager, and Bob would simply be following the procedures developed at that time. Yet the situation wasn't risk free. Bob did not have adequate expertise in tax yet, and he was concerned that if he did encounter a difficult problem and made a serious mistake, he would be blamed and it would damage his career.

Bob tried to break the news gently that he would not be doing the Softdisk audit. He approached Tak Li, who now worked for Mike McLeod as a manager, and told Tak that he did not want to do the job. He also told Pat Czarski, a manager reporting to his new managing partner, Joe Silverman. Somehow the message did not seem to get through to Mike McLeod and over the next week Mike would stop Bob in the halls or in the men's room and ask if Bob had made a decision, or if Bob had any reservations that Mike could help him resolve. Mike seemed to be convinced that Bob would eventually take the job. Bob began to feel trapped. Since David Shorter had gone on vacation, he could not help sort out the situation.

> I knew that Mike was quite influential in the New Enterprises Group because he had many bigger clients. He was persuasive and forceful. I wondered, "Why is this happening to me? Why is he so determined to make me give in and take this job? Why is he going around to other partners and managers trying to get them to persuade me? He wants me to bow on this issue and I don't want to."

The final straw for Bob was a meeting called by Mike, including himself, Pat, Tak, and Bob on July 20. Bob felt that the sole purpose of the meeting was to coerce him into taking on the Softdisk audit. After hours of pressure, Bob said he would do the job, just to end the meeting. However, he felt that he had been unfairly treated in the meeting and that he did not have to honour his agreement. "I felt isolated, like it was three against one."

OTHER FACTORS

After his meeting with Mike, Pat, and Tak, Bob reviewed his situation and prospects. He knew that he had offended Mike McLeod. He had heard from Jane Klinck that he had also offended Joe Silverman, who was scheduled to be his new managing partner in tax. Bob did not feel that he had a career potential with the New Enterprise Group any more.

In addition, the New Enterprise Group did not seem committed to supporting his desire to become a tax consultant. They appeared more concerned with their shortage of senior auditors. Bob felt less inclined to be loyal to a company which was not loyal to him.

Bob felt that he had the security to find another job. He had his chartered accountant designation. He was a Canadian citizen. He had money saved and his family would support him if he got into financial difficulties. He also had contacts from a management recruiting company that had tried to hire him for another company after he passed his chartered accountant exams. He decided to resign and told Jane of his intention. She discouraged him from acting rashly and convinced him to at least talk with David Shorter again when he returned from vacation on July 24.

Jane seemed to be shocked when I said I was thinking of resigning. She said, "But you're usually so easy going!" I thought maybe they were picking on me because I'm easy going and never complain.

A FINAL MEETING WITH DAVID SHORTER

Bob expected no miracles from David before his upcoming meeting of July 24. He expected David to tell him that he was doing good work and to ask him to stay. He also expected David to ask him to do the Softdisk audit and to "tough out" the situation. Although Bob was prepared to listen, he thought he might have to resign unless David was willing to work out an acceptable alternative for him. Bob hoped David could come up with something. In the final analysis, Bob did not really want to leave. He just wanted to do tax.

Note

1   In Canada the grade point system follows the British model. At Queen's a 75 average is a B+ and is considered evidence of high achievement.

Johannes van den Bosch Sends an Email

Joseph J. DiStefano

After having had several email exchanges with his Mexican counterpart over several weeks without getting the expected actions and results, Johannes van den Bosch was getting a tongue-lashing from his British MNC client, who was furious at the lack of progress. Van den Bosch, in the Rotterdam office of BigFiveFirm, and his colleague in the Mexico City office, Pablo Menendez, were both seasoned veterans, and van den Bosch couldn't understand the lack of responsiveness.

A week earlier, the client, Malcolm Smythe-Jones, had visited his office to express his mounting frustration. But this morning he had called with a stream of verbal abuse. His patience was exhausted.

Feeling angry himself, van den Bosch composed a strongly worded message to Menendez, and then decided to cool off. A half hour later, he edited it to "stick to the facts" while still communicating the appropriate level of urgency. As he clicked to send the message, he hoped that it would finally provoke some action to assuage his client with the reports he had been waiting for.

He reread the email, and as he saved it to the mounting record in Smythe-Jones's file, he thought, "I'm going to be happy when this project is over for another year!"

Professor Joe DiStefano prepared this mini-case as a basis for class discussion rather than to illustrate either effective or ineffective handling of a business situation.

The mini-case reports events as they occurred. The email exchanges in both cases are reported verbatim, except for the names, which have been changed. Professor DiStefano acknowledges with thanks the cooperation of "Johannes van den Bosch" in providing this information and his generous permission to use the material for executive development.

IMD Lansanne, Switzerland   *GM963*

Message for Pablo Menendez

Subject:	*IAS 1998 Financial statements*
Author:	*Johannes van den Bosch (Rotterdam)*
Date:	*10/12/99 1:51 p.m.*

Dear Pablo,

This morning I had a conversation with Mr Smythe-Jones (CFO) and Mr Parker (Controller) re the finalization of certain 1998 financial statements. Mr Smythe-Jones was not in a very good mood.

He told me that he was very unpleased by the fact that the 1998 IAS financial statements of the Mexican subsidiary still has not been finalized. At the moment he holds us responsible for this process. Although he recognizes that local management is responsible for such financial statements, he blames us for not being responsive on this matter and inform him about the process adequately. I believe he also recognizes that we have been instructed by Mr Whyte (CEO) not to do any handholding, but that should not keep us from monitoring the process and inform him about the progress.

He asked me to provide him tomorrow with an update on the status of the IAS report and other reports pending.

Therefore I would like to get the following information from you today:

- *What has to be done to finalize the Mexican subsidiary's IAS financials;*
- *Who has to do it (local management, B&FF Mexico, client headquarters, B&FF Rotterdam);*
- *A timetable when things have to be done in order to finalize within a couple of weeks or sooner;*
- *A brief overview why it takes so long to prepare and audit the IAS f/s;*
- *Are there any other reports for 1998 pending (local gaap, tax), if so the above is also applicable for those reports.*

As of today I would like to receive an update of the status every week. If an major problems arise during the finalization process I would like to be informed immediately. The next status update is due January 12, 2000.

Mr Smythe-Jones also indicated that in the future all reports (US GAAP, local GAAP and IAS) should be normally finalized within 60 days after the balance sheet date. He will hold local auditors responsible for monitoring this process.

Best regards and best wishes for 2000.

Johannes

CASE **4**

Japanese-American Seating Inc. (A)

Joyce Miller and J. Michael Geringer

In mid-January 1991, Jim Needham was facing one of the first challenges of his new position as general manager at Japanese-American Seating Inc. (JASI). Located in southwestern Ontario, JASI was a joint venture between a Japanese seat manufacturer and a Michigan-based seat assembler. When Needham arrived at the beginning of the year, the JASI plant had been through 20 months of commercial production under his predecessor, Bill Stanton. After several hours of discussion in a recent meeting about how to strengthen project management, Needham's Japanese managers had finally gotten his agreement to hire a project coordinator who would report to the materials manager and schedule and control engineering projects. But the more he considered the situation, the more uneasy Needham felt about enlarging the role of the materials department. Could he renege on his earlier decision, or should he just let this one go?

THE NORTH AMERICAN AUTOMOTIVE INDUSTRY

The automotive industry accounted for a large part of manufacturing activity in both Canada and the United States, and contributed significantly to the expansion and recession of these economies. In the past decade, the "Big Three" US automakers had

EXHIBIT 1   The Big Three Automakers and the North American Automotive Industry, 1973–1989

	1973	1978	1987	1988	1989
General Motors Corporation					
Quality (defects per 100 cars)	–	–	176	165	158
Productivity (cars per person per year)	11.4	12.1	11.3	12.9	12.6
Inventory turns	5.4	6.7	18.0	18.8	20.0
Profit per unit ($)	490	684	435	692	645
Return on sales (%)	6.7	5.5	3.5	4.4	3.8
Market share (%)	51.5	47.3	34.7	34.9	35.0
Ford Motor Company					
Quality (defects per 100 cars)	–	–	156	169	143
Productivity (cars per person per year)	13.7	13.8	18.7	19.9	20.9
Inventory turns	5.3	6.5	15.6	17.3	18.0
Profit per unit ($)	260	360	1,023	1,014	663
Return on sales (%)	3.9	3.7	6.4	5.7	3.9
Market share (%)	29.8	26.5	23.1	23.7	24.6
Chrysler Corporation					
Quality (defects per 100 cars)	–	–	178	202	169
Productivity (cars per person per year)	13.0	13.1	16.2	18.0	19.5
Inventory turns	5.6	6.3	16.8	21.6	26.3
Profit per unit ($)	127	(129)	853	649	649
Return on sales (%)	2.1	(1.5)	4.5	3.0	1.0
Market share (%)	15.6	11.2	12.3	13.9	13.7

Source: Annual reports and industry sources.

experienced an unprecedented decline in market share and profitability, and they continued to battle against foreign car companies (Exhibit 1). A recent study noted that sales of vehicles made by North American manufacturers had dropped dramatically as the popularity of overseas models increased, particularly those from Japan, Taiwan, and South Korea. In the 1984–1989 period, annual North American vehicle production was relatively flat at about 13 million units, roughly 30 percent of global production. Captive imports represented a growing phenomenon, and accounted for nearly five percent of North American motor vehicle sales in 1990. Pure imports accounted for an additional 24 percent of 1990 sales. Captive imports were vehicles imported by American companies. For instance, Chevrolet marketed the Isuzu I-Mark as the Spectrum, General Motors' LeMans and Optima were manufactured in Korea by Daewoo, and Chrysler imported several products made in Thailand by Mitsubishi.

Overall, foreign nameplates had captured about a third of the North American automobile market, despite trade barriers designed to keep them at bay. Honda now claimed 10 percent of the North American passenger vehicle market, and Toyota had a 7.5 percent share. These companies beat the quotas by agreeing to voluntary restraints, and building plants in North America, sometimes in conjunction with domestic producers. These operations were called "transplants." The total transplant production in Canada for 1991–1992 was forecast at 460,000 units or 16 percent of Canadian capacity, an explosive increase since 1988, when transplants represented only 3 percent and 9.5 percent, respectively, of total Canadian and US production capacity. Under the Auto Pact, vehicles manufactured in Canada and having at least 50 percent Canadian or US content could be exported duty-free to the United States. This also applied to vehicles built by transplant operations.

In response to the challenge posed by foreign manufacturers, the Big Three had invested over US$8 billion in the past five years to upgrade capacity and launch quality programs aimed at matching the Japanese. As well, they were streamlining the manufacturing process by using just-in-time (JIT) principles and contracting out subassemblies. Outsourcing was part of an industry-wide effort to reduce costs. Where car makers used to retool and redesign components almost annually, they were now pushing the burden of design and engineering down to parts suppliers.

These developments had a dramatic effect on organizations supplying seats to the automotive manufacturers. Until the early 1980s, the seat industry was highly fragmented, and could be described as a series of hand-offs, from engineering through to marketing. Each supplier concentrated on one or two areas, such as headrests or suspension systems. The automakers handled most of the "cut-and-sew" activities in-house. By 1991, however, 40 percent of seat production was being outsourced to suppliers who designed and manufactured complete seating systems. A complete system included the frame, foam pads, cover, seat tracks, lumbar support, recliner, headrest, and trim. At this time, to cut overhead and increase quality control, the automakers were reducing the number of suppliers, and the seat industry was becoming more competitive.

JAPANESE-AMERICAN SEATING INC. (JASI)

In 1987, Kasai Kogyo Ltd, a seat manufacturer based in Tokyo, and Banting Seat Corporation, a seat assembler headquartered in a Detroit suburb, formed a 65–35 joint venture to exclusively supply seats on a JIT basis to Orion Manufacturing Corporation. JASI was one of several companies established in southwestern Ontario as dedicated suppliers to Orion. Located 15 kilometres away, Orion was a recently negotiated Japanese-American joint venture which expected to begin producing four cylinder subcompact cars in early 1989. The Orion plant would have the capacity to produce 200,000 vehicles annually, most of which would be shipped to the United States. Actual production volumes would depend on the market's acceptance of these vehicles as well as cyclical movements of the industry.

Banting and Kasai were leaders in automotive seating in their respective countries. Banting employed about 5,000 people in their North American operations and another 2,000 abroad. They were an established supplier to the Big Three with over $1 billion in annual revenues. After several years of reorganization, Banting had shed all of their non-automotive businesses, and were focused exclusively on seating (approximately 70 percent of revenues) and other automotive interior parts. Banting's objective was to attain a position of leadership in the automobile seating industry. During the late 1980s, they had invested heavily in R&D and manufacturing facilities in the United States, as well as acquiring several smaller European producers of automotive seating and interior components.

Kasai employed about 4,200 people and had $1.5 billion in annual sales. Nearly 80 percent of Kasai's revenues were from the automotive industry, with the remainder coming from office and communications equipment, chemical products, building materials, and miscellaneous machinery. Overall, while heavily involved in their traditional business of automobile parts, Kasai's objective was to achieve greater growth and stability through product diversification and overseas market expansion.

While Banting relied on a myriad of raw materials suppliers to assemble their seating systems, Kasai had a more vertically integrated operation. Kasai owned 12 plants and 26 affiliated companies in Japan, most of them involved in auto-related activities. By applying just-in-time principles to seat production, Kasai had gained a strong reputation within the Japanese auto parts industry. In the 1980s, in an effort to follow their customers and to increase penetration of international markets, Kasai had aggressively expanded their sales network throughout the world, with regional sales headquarters in the United States, Canada, Spain, Brazil, Taiwan, and Thailand. Although Kasai had also pursued international manufacturing through eleven joint ventures worldwide, the JASI operation marked the company's entry into North American production. The JASI venture was initiated, in part, to help Kasai maintain its supplier relationship with the Japanese firm which was the majority partner in Orion.

The venture was to be run as a profit centre. Banting held the minority participation, and JASI would supply Orion on an exclusive basis for a five-year period. The contract called for three to five percent annual price cuts. Construction on the 120,000 square foot facility began in mid-1988, and was completed in early 1989. An investment of $20 million was required and breakeven was expected within four years. The plant had the capacity to produce 245,000 seats annually and would eventually employ 220 people on two shifts.

JASI's start-up

Under the terms of the joint venture agreement, Banting would design the plant, contribute a general manager, and negotiate the purchase of major raw materials and components. Kasai would contribute their expertise in production and process technology and provide a President to head the venture. Orion placed great value on having an important representative from Japan on-site.

The start-up team was composed of Sumio Imai, president, Bill Stanton, general manager, Akira Hoshino, finance, Tadashi Abe, Orion design engineer, Katsuhiko Ito, engineering, and Yuji Yamanaka, manufacturing/quality director (Exhibits 2 and 3 have organization charts for mid-1989 and January 1991). This was the first time any of the Japanese managers had worked in North America. The Japanese who went abroad were typically on a five-year rotation. Rotating people to gain a cross-section of experience within a company was a widely accepted practice and was, in fact, the foundation of management training and development in Japan. Lifetime employment was still the common practice in Kasai.

Except for Imai, all the Japanese managers brought their families to Canada. Imai, who chose to return to Tokyo three or four times a year for three-week periods, commented:

EXHIBIT 2   Organization Chart, May 1989

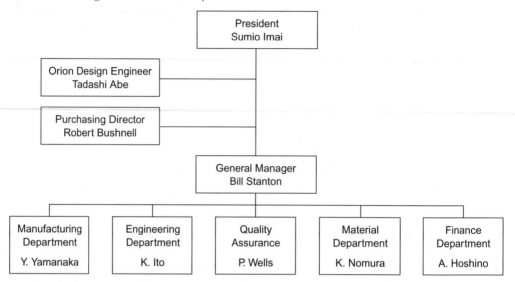

EXHIBIT 3   Organization Chart, January 1991

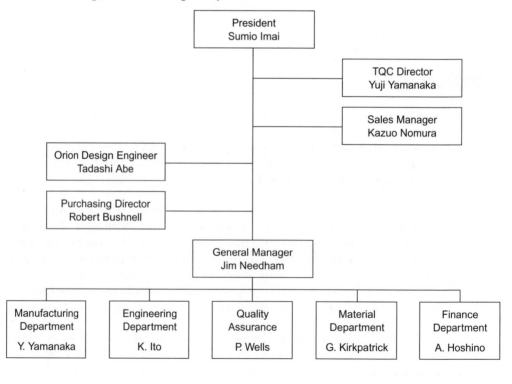

My children are finished university and are working; it made sense to do it this way. I go back regularly to spend time with my family and to maintain business connections. The biggest challenge of going on rotation is actually returning. I mean this in a couple of ways. First, companies are dynamic, always changing, and it is important to know the organization. This takes time. It is not uncommon for people to spend many evenings after work socializing with colleagues, building up networks. Second, those who relocate their families to another country often find returning quite an adjustment. They get used to the lower cost of living and the bigger houses. Some people have difficulty getting their children back on track for the best universities. There is a sense that they have gained "bad habits" abroad.

JASI adopted the principles of the JIT production system known as "kanban," which was considered to be Toyota's invention. As one Japanese manager remarked:

> Toyota has been doing it for 30 years and is seen as the master of the kanban system. In Japan, everybody likes and lives under kanban.

Where the conventional production system was built on an earlier process continuously forwarding products to a later process regardless of its requirements, the kanban system was built on reversing this conception. To supply parts used in assembly under this system, the later process traced back to an earlier process, and withdrew materials only when they were needed. In this way, wasteful inventory could be eliminated. Imai was an early champion in applying the kanban system to the production of seats at Kasai.

In JASI's case, the kanban referred to a triangular vinyl envelope which accompanied parts and products as they moved through the plant. The kanban provided information about picking up or receiving an order so that only what was needed would be produced. The kanban controlled the flow of goods by serving as a withdrawal order, a work order, and an order for conveyance. Associates picked and replaced parts in small batches according to the kanban.

Work cells contained several machines designed for quick, easy changes and short set-up times so that a single operator could do a series of tasks. At any one time, there was no more than four to eight hours of inventory in the plant, from parts through to the seats waiting on the rack for shipping. Seat storage and shipping were geared to the "live broadcast" of cars coming out of Orion's paint section which fixed the order through final trim and assembly. To meet JIT requirements, units were shipped sequentially based on material and other options according to Orion's production schedule. JASI typically had a 3.5- to four-hour window to deliver a particular seat set to Orion. There was a substantial financial penalty for late or incorrect delivery. Incoming seats were transferred directly to the final assembly line in the correct position without having to sort through an entire truckload to locate a specific unit. An industry analyst observed:

> Kanban systems require a lot of training: training workers to monitor inventory levels and training suppliers to operate under JIT principles. Suppliers have to understand the concept of delivering 50 pieces at 10 AM, not before, not after, and not 49. It's about supplying the right quantities of the right product at the right time. It's changing the philosophy away from protecting business behind the delivery door; it's about partnerships.

JASI had approximately 100 suppliers of small stampings, nuts and bolts, cloth, foam, frame, recliners, and other raw materials. At some point, certain activities like manufacturing foam might be brought in-house in a separate facility.

In September 1988, Kazuo Nomura joined the company as materials manager. Following the Japanese model, Nomura had both purchasing and sales responsibilities, and oversaw all aspects of cost, material, and production control. In addition to being a liaison with Orion, handling suppliers, and scheduling incoming materials, he controlled engineering projects. However, expediting materials was taking up an extraordinary amount of his time. Nomura explained:

> North American suppliers don't give us the kind of support we're used to in Japan. I'd end up having regular quarrels with suppliers just trying to explain the kanban process. It was taking longer than I expected to get them to buy in, to deliver small quantity shipments on a JIT basis, and I was getting frustrated. It was hard to handle everything. Our reputation with Orion was key, and I was dedicated to building this relationship. In January 1990, I became sales manager, and JASI hired a Canadian, George Kirkpatrick, to take over materials. By this time, many of my responsibilities had been parcelled out to other departments. Kirkpatrick would schedule parts in and products out, keep suppliers on-stream, ensure manufacturing had the products to keep the plant going, and interact with Orion regarding product sequencing and shipping.

During start-up, the management team generally worked well together despite some differences in management style. Stanton had designed the plant, knowing nothing about Japanese management and production principles that would be used to operate it. Over a six-month period beginning in November 1988, three groups of two or three salaried managers and technicians went to Japan to learn about Kasai's production system, and see the same seats they would be making being built at the Tokyo facility. Throughout this time, JASI was producing pilot seats, programming and debugging the numerically controlled metal benders and robot welders, and training people how to properly fit seat covers.

Overall, there were few technical problems or difficulties with the non-unionized workforce. The area had an abundant labor pool, particularly with the recent influx of East European and Southeast Asian immigrants. Stanton's policy was to recruit young people without industry experience, and have them work in teams and cross-train. With a monthly absenteeism rate of three percent, where the industry average was five percent, JASI was considered a highly successful venture, especially on the interpersonal side.

JASI began commercial production in April 1989, coinciding with Orion's start-up. Over the next 20 months, the company made steady progress in training their workforce and suppliers, containing costs, and meeting the price cuts scheduled into the contract with Orion. From the start, JASI had adopted the Japanese concept of "kaizen." Literally translated, this meant continuous improvement. This philosophy encouraged associates to submit ideas for new methods, rationalized setups, more efficient ways of operating machinery, and so on.

The Japanese managers considered that JASI operated relatively autonomously from both parent companies, particularly Kasai. Their communications with Kasai were principally about issues of product quality; major problems with customers, especially regarding product quality issues; engineering changes, and the development and testing of prototypes; and proposed investments. For example, in response to model changes at Orion, they would send samples of parts prototypes for testing in Kasai's labs, since JASI lacked the required capabilities. Interactions with Banting often involved operational details such as purchasing materials, changing suppliers, and introducing new products. They also communicated with Banting regarding cultural issues which the Japanese managers were unfamiliar with, such as donations to a local charity, or staging a company party for employees and their families.

On a monthly basis, both parent companies received a statement outlining the venture's general financial status. While Kasai had never requested additional detailed financial data, Banting had occasionally asked for figures on overtime, production costs and output, particularly during the venture's start-up. JASI's managers were strictly required to consult with both parents, including detailed documentation, whenever funding was required for new investments. One Japanese manager noted that requests for investment funds had never been rejected, and parent inquiries associated with these requests had diminished substantially as the venture became more established. However, he noted that where Kasai would allow the venture to have a negative cash flow for five years, Banting had a significantly shorter horizon and seemed to require stricter budgetary control.

As a sole supplier of a major component, quality or delivery problems on JASI's part could shut down Orion's plant. Of all of Orion's suppliers, JASI believed it faced the greatest potential for problems; the fabric, foam, and weave of the knit all affected the final product. Most returns were because of variances within tolerances. Nomura was the key liaison between the two companies, and he met daily with Imai to report current issues. He travelled frequently to the Orion site, and was in daily contact with the purchasing, engineering, and quality departments to feed information back into the JASI plant. Nomura explained:

> For minor problems, Orion's quality department talks directly with our quality area. If problems are deeper, I get involved. I'll set up a meeting with people from both sides to analyze the current system and get at the root cause, then I report back to Orion about how we're implementing improvements. Everyone has their own mind on corrective action and there's a lot of informal communication. We're still small enough to respond fast. When significant new investment is required, I'll get the president and general manager involved. Otherwise, it's up to me.

Showing a high degree of responsiveness and taking quick action to correct returns had enabled JASI to build an excellent reputation to the extent that the company had recently been taken off Orion's regular quality audit list, which meant that performance reviews would only be conducted every six months. By this time, a strongly knit culture had developed, in both management and on the plant floor.

When Orion geared up production in September 1990, JASI brought on a second shift which added 100 people to the payroll. Work groups had to be split up to train the new associates. Defects increased and productivity deteriorated significantly during this period. At this time, the Canadian Auto Workers (CAW) made a successful bid to unionize the workforce. In October, the CAW was certified as the official bargaining unit and began negotiations with JASI management.

JIM NEEDHAM'S ARRIVAL

In Fall 1990, Banting finalized a deal to acquire a German seat assembler, giving the firm entry into the country which represented about one-third of the automotive manufacturing market in Europe. European seat makers had traditionally sold foam and metal components, but there was increasing pressure from the car makers to deliver complete seating systems on a JIT basis. Stanton was asked to take over the management of the plant in Germany, and Jim Needham was offered the general manager position at JASI, a promotion from his current position managing a seat assembly plant in Michigan. Needham, age 41, expected to spend at least three years at JASI. He reflected:

> Bill took the job in Germany because he felt he couldn't do much more here; he was ready to take on a new challenge. I accepted the job in mid-November and started commuting back and forth several times a week. A lot of my time was taken up with paperwork and immigration matters. I had to buy a house, move my family here at the beginning of the year, and get my two kids settled into new schools. My wife and 12-year-old son seemed to make the transition okay. But my 16-year-old daughter wasn't exactly thrilled about moving to a small rural town in another country. At first, it seemed like there was just one brick on my back after another.

Needham had worked for Banting for the past six years, coming up through the ranks from manufacturing manager. He continued:

> I'm an old factory nut, and I was really impressed with the JASI plant: how well it was laid out, the robotics and metal bending capabilities, the high tech product testing. JASI was making all their own frames whereas the plants I'd worked in before were building seats with purchased parts. I'd been through some consensus training but I had limited experience working with the Japanese. In Michigan, we were doing JIT, we had cards on the seats and were scheduling the replacement of batches. We thought we were doing a lot, but I've never seen kanban worked as thoroughly through the production process as here. It's hard to learn how to make kanban work, and making it work right is a real trick.
>
> Right now, I'm concerned about the union negotiations. I'd worked with the United Auto Workers in the past but the CAW has the reputation of being a more militant organization. I hope that we won't get into the typical adversarial relationship. JASI's wage structure is good and the benefits package is solid. We have a progressive-thinking union rep who seems open to a different approach. I'm not anticipating a lot of restrictions; the union knows our relationship with Orion, that the company will be growing.
>
> I think Bill took the decision to unionize quite personally. Bill put everything he had into this plant, and he had a strong feeling of personal ownership here. He was into all the details. Once he was convinced of something, he went all out to make it happen. He has quite a forceful personality with a decisive, direct style, even authoritarian at times.

Needham did not have a lot of preparation before taking on his new position. He remarked:

> I only had three or four days with Bill, and I spent that time trying to get down the mechanics of the organization. I knew that I was coming into a tightly knit group. And I was coming into a situation where I couldn't even speak directly with my own boss and some of my key

managers. Nomura and Hoshino had a working knowledge of English, but I'm not sure how much the other Japanese comprehend. They spend a lot of time together interpreting for each other. I suspect that Imai understands more than what he can express in English. Whenever Imai has a meeting with an Anglo, he'll always have someone else there, usually Nomura, to interpret. Still, I have to be careful. What gets said may be just the best way someone knew how to say it and not necessarily their intent.

It's hard to figure out the dynamics of the management group. Imai is gregarious and outgoing while Yamanaka gravitates towards the role of the "keeper"; he keeps situations in control, he's more grounded. Nomura seems to be the linking pin in the whole operation. Bill tried not to tell me too much; he didn't want to predispose me to certain individuals. One thing Bill emphasized was the need to maintain operational control, especially in order to achieve better cost/benefit ratios. He gave the example that the Japanese continually look for improvements and might request that eight people be assigned to the task of rearranging a work cell. They'll justify it as being for the good of the company, but the benefit might not come until four or five years later. Bill noted that this could generate problems at Banting, since Mr. Begar, an Executive Vice President at Banting and their senior representative on JASI's board, as well as other key executives at headquarters would expect me to regularly report key production data as Bill had done, and they would not be pleased if the figures varied substantially from budget.

I'm mostly learning as I go along. I realize that I can't do things the same way I did before. I didn't think people could tolerate an American coming in swinging. The last thing I want anyone to think is that I'm a dictator; I've worked for those types before, and it never works. I want to take the long view; changes will come over time. At the beginning, the important thing is to not make too many quick judgments or life-threatening decisions, to just get involved where you really need to.

I'm starting to have some interaction with Hoshino on the budget, and it's possible that he could be a window into the Japanese group, someone who I can put the sticky questions to and find out about personalities and political ramifications in Japan. At the moment, I'm very much the new guy. I have a sense that people might be looking for changes in the way things get done. I bring a new set of ears, and ideas that didn't get through before will be resubmitted. People are redefining relationships, and this isn't necessarily a bad thing. There are good reasons for making changes at this level: there's the saying that you can't change the players but you can sometimes change the coach. Maybe I'll have a chance to make the improvements my predecessor couldn't crack.

Shortly after Needham's arrival, the media reported that early January 1991 sales of North American vehicles had plunged as worries about the faltering economy and the Persian Gulf crisis continued to erode consumer confidence.

MANAGING IN A CROSS-CULTURAL ENVIRONMENT

Needham knew that his job at JASI would be more difficult, at least initially, than those he had gone into previously. He recounted:

I'm used to reading a situation quicker. I come from a system where a good boss listens to his managers, then makes a decision; his people understand it and follow it. The Japanese look for consensus, and this is hard to get to. Management meetings are long. Recently, we spent an hour only to find that we had two versions of the same vacation policy, one for the Japanese and one for the North Americans. We spent another two hours trying to hammer out a single policy. There's always a risk that everyone will nod their heads, and then the Japanese will go off and run the business their way and the North Americans will go off and do things differently. People forget that they're supposed to be learning from each other; there's always some tension, and sometimes it's hard to get over the humps. The North Americans aren't familiar with the kanban system and sometimes they don't go far enough; they had something that worked before. Put that against the Japanese guys who know and believe in their system.

    I see my role as bringing up issues for discussion. If I walked in with the solution to a problem, there would be immediate resistance. We need the extra step here, and I'm patient enough to go through it.

Through a series of conversations, Needham discovered that the Japanese were used to relying heavily on their technicians. In Japan, once these people were told the rules, there was apparently little need to follow up. However, he noticed that JASI's floor technicians were not consistently enforcing such simple things as wearing safety glasses. Shop rules and discipline seemed to be foreign ideas to his Japanese managers. Needham elaborated:

> The Japanese don't seem to recognize that the workforce might slip; they aren't trained to look for such problems. Even if they become aware of something, they appear to overlook it. I don't know if it's just a cultural difference, a case of not feeling comfortable dealing with the situation. For instance, it recently happened that someone was stealing and my Japanese guys didn't seem to realize that a person who behaved this way would have to be fired.

Another difference between the Japanese and North American systems was the role of the materials department. In Japan, this department was a large, central hub which ran new engineering and information programs, and scheduled and controlled all aspects of projects. In North America, these activities were typically handled by engineering or manufacturing. As a whole, JASI's Japanese management group felt strongly that the company needed to get better at project management to achieve continuing quality improvements and cost reductions.

THE JANUARY MEETING

On January 11, 1991, Jim Needham convened a two-hour meeting with virtually the entire management team, including Imai, to discuss the project management situation. Project management was intimately linked with costs. The decisions made in this meeting would affect everyone. The Japanese managers felt strongly that the materials department should enlarge its role and regain its original status. As the venture had moved toward commercial production, many of the responsibilities Nomura originally had as materials manager had been dispersed across departments as he dedicated more of his time to building JASI's relationship with Orion. The Japanese felt that the key to better project management was to centralize this function back in materials. They argued adamantly that a project coordinator needed to be hired in.

    Reporting to the materials manager, the project coordinator would launch projects and follow them through to completion. For example, if an engineering study proposed joining three pieces to bolt onto a seat, the project coordinator would find parts suppliers and obtain quotes to facilitate a make or buy decision. This person would also interact with engineering, quality, and manufacturing to ensure each department carried out its responsibilities on the project. The Japanese contended that creating such a position would mean that everyone was informed of the status of ongoing projects. Starting up new projects would be smoother, less costly, and better quality. Needham responded:

> I kept telling people I wasn't convinced that we needed to add an extra person. This hadn't been slotted in and I didn't want to bastardize the budget within the first month. I thought that the job could be handled by someone else already in the organization. I had recently talked to the quality manager, Paul Wells, and he was willing to schedule and follow up projects. This wouldn't make for as big a role for the materials department as the Japanese wanted: the real responsibility would still be with the pieces, but I didn't feel comfortable giving up some of my own authority when I still didn't completely understand the operation. My Japanese managers persisted. One even remarked that when I went to Japan in April, I'd learn why project management should be done in materials. After several hours of discussion, I finally relented.
>
> I suspected that Imai and the others were pleased with the outcome. They were comfortable that I went after consensus, and I had a feeling they would like JASI to operate even more like a Japanese organization.

A few days after agreeing to hire a project coordinator, Needham was having serious second thoughts. Besides concerns that the company was still too small to warrant this additional person and the accompanying costs, he did not feel that the materials department was ready to take on this level of responsibility, and ultimately, he was not comfortable defining the department as largely as it was in Japanese operations. Delegating this additional authority to lower-level managers before he was comfortable in his new position might also limit his own decision-making authority in the future. But what could he do now?

Needham was to meet with Imai at 8:00 AM tomorrow for their weekly meeting, and the agenda which Imai had sent to him was quite full. In addition to addressing several important strategic and operational issues, such as improving integration of local suppliers within JASI's kanban system, production planning and quality control issues, and finalizing a strategy for upcoming negotiations with union representatives, Needham and Imai had been asked by the materials manager to formally approve the proposal to hire a project coordinator, including funding to retain a personnel recruiting firm and placement of position advertisements. In fact, this latter issue was the first item on their agenda, along with review of the quality control report for the prior two weeks, which showed a continuing decline in production defects. Could he change his mind? And how would he even go about doing it?

Footwear International

R. William Blake

John Carlson frowned as he studied the translation of the front-page story from the afternoon's edition of the *Meillat*, a fundamentalist newspaper with close ties to an opposition political party. The story, titled "Footwear's Unpardonable Audacity," suggested that the company was knowingly insulting Islam by including the name of Allah in a design used on the insoles of sandals it was manufacturing. To compound the problem, the paper had run a photograph of one of the offending sandals on the front page. As a result, student groups were calling for public demonstrations against Footwear the next day. As Managing Director of Footwear Bangladesh, Carlson knew he would have to act quickly to defuse a potentially explosive situation.

FOOTWEAR INTERNATIONAL

Footwear International is a multinational manufacturer and marketer of footwear. Operations span the globe and include more than 83 companies in 70 countries. These include shoe factories, tanneries, engineering plants producing shoe machinery and moulds, product development studios, hosiery factories, quality control laboratories, and approximately 6,300 retail stores and 50,000 independent retailers.

Footwear employs more than 67,000 people and produces and sells in excess of 270,000,000 pairs of shoes every year. Head office acts as a service center and is staffed with specialists drawn from all over the world. These specialists, in areas such as marketing, retailing, product development, communications, store design, electronic data processing, and business administration, travel for much of the year to share their expertise with the various companies. Training and technical education, offered through company-run colleges and the training facility at headquarters, provide the latest skills to employees from around the world.

Although Footwear requires standardization in technology and the design of facilities, it also encourages a high degree of decentralization and autonomy in its operations. The companies are virtually self-governing, which means their allegiance belongs to the countries in which they operate. Each is answerable to a board of directors which includes representatives from the local business community. The concept of "partnership" at the local level has made the company welcome internationally and has allowed it to operate successfully in countries where other multinationals have been unable to survive.

BANGLADESH

With a population approaching 110,000,000 in an area of 143,998 square kilometers (see Figure 1), Bangladesh is the most densely populated country in the world. It is also among the most impoverished, with a 1987 per capita gross national product of US$160 and a high reliance on foreign aid. More than 40% of the gross domestic product is generated by agriculture and more than 60% of its economically active population works in

FIGURE 1   Bangladesh

the agriculture sector. Although the land in Bangladesh is fertile, the country has a trop-ical monsoon climate and suffers from the ravages of periodic cyclones. In 1988, the country experienced the worst floods in recorded history.

The population of Bangladesh is 85% Moslem, and Islam was made the official state religion in 1988. Approximately 95% of the population speaks Bengali with most of the remainder speaking tribal dialects.

Bangladesh has had a turbulent history in the twentieth century. Most of the country was part of the British-ruled East Bengal until 1947. In that year it joined with Assam to become East Pakistan, a province of the newly created country of Pakistan. East Pakistan was separated from the four provinces of West Pakistan by 1,600 kilometers of Indian territory and, although the East was more populous, the national capital was established in West Pakistan. Over the following years widespread discontent built in the East, whose people felt that they received a disproportionately small amount of development fund-ing and were underrepresented in government.

Following a period of unrest starting in 1969, the Awami League, the leading polit-ical party in East Pakistan, won an overwhelming victory in local elections held in 1970. The victory promised to give the league, which was pro-independence, control in the National Assembly. To prevent that happening the national government suspended the convening of the Assembly indefinitely. On March 26, 1971, the Awami League proclaimed the independence of the People's Republic of Bangladesh and civil war quickly followed. In the ensuing conflict hundreds of thousands of refugees fled to safety across the border in India. In December India, which supported the independence of Bangladesh, declared war and twelve days later Pakistan surrendered. Bangladesh had won its inde-pendence, and the capital of the new country was established at Dhaka. In the years immediately following independence industrial output declined in major industries as the result of the departure of many of the largely non-Bengali financier and mana-gerial class.

Throughout the subsequent years, political stability proved elusive for Bangladesh. Although elections were held, stability was threatened by the terrorist tactics resorted to by opposition groups from both political extremes. Coups and counter coups, assassina-tions, and suspension of civil liberties became regular occurrences.

Since 1983, Bangladesh had been ruled by the self-proclaimed President General H. M. Ershad. Despite demonstrations in 1987, which led to a state of emergency being declared, Ershad managed to retain power in elections held the following year. The country remains politically volatile, however. Dozens of political parties continually maneuver for position and alliances and coalitions are the order of the day. The principal opposition party is the Awami League, an alliance of eight political parties. Many of the parties are closely linked with so-called opposition newspapers, which promote their political positions. Strikes and demonstrations are frequent and often result from cooperation among opposition political parties, student groups, and unions.

FOOTWEAR BANGLADESH

Footwear became active in what was then East Bengal in the 1930s. In 1962 the first major investment took place with the construction of a footwear manufacturing facility at Tongi, an industrial town located thirty kilometers north of Dhaka. During the following years the company expanded its presence in both conventional and unconventional ways. In 1971, the then Managing Director became a freedom fighter, while continuing to oversee operations. He subsequently became the only foreigner to be decorated by the government with the "Bir Protik" in recognition of both his and the company's contribution to the independence of Bangladesh.

In 1985, Footwear Bangladesh went public and two years later spearheaded the largest private-sector foreign investment in the country, a tannery and footwear factory at Dhamrai. The new tannery produced leather for local Footwear needs and the export market, and the factory produced a variety of footwear for the local market.

By 1988, Footwear Bangladesh employed 1,800 employees and sold through eighty-one stores and fifty-four agencies. The company introduced approximately 300 new products a year to the market using their in-house design and development capability. Footwear managers were particularly proud of the capability of the personnel in these departments, all of whom were Bangladeshi.

Annual sales in excess of 10,000,000 pairs of footwear gave the company 15% of the national market in 1988. Revenues exceeded US$30 million and after tax profit was approximately US$1 million. Financially, the company was considered a medium contributor within the Footwear organization. With a population approaching 110,000,000, and per capita consumption of one pair of shoes every two years, Bangladesh was perceived as offering Footwear enormous potential for growth both through consumer education and competitive pressure.

The managing director of Footwear Bangladesh was John Carlson, one of only four foreigners working for the company. The others were the managers of production, marketing, and sales. All had extensive and varied experience within the Footwear organization.

THE INCIDENT

On Thursday, June 22, 1989, John Carlson was shown a copy of that day's *Meillat*, a well-known opposition newspaper with pro-Libyan leanings. Under the headline "Footwear's Unpardonable Audacity," the writer suggested that the design on the insole of one model of sandal produced by the company included the Arabic spelling of the word "Allah" (see Figure 2). The story went on to suggest that Footwear was under Jewish ownership and to link the alleged offense with the gunning down of many people in Palestine by Jews. The story highlighted the fact that the design was on the insole of the sandal and therefore, next to the bottom of the foot, a sign of great disrespect to Moslems.

Carlson immediately contacted the supervisor of the design department and asked for any information he could provide on the design on the sandals. He already knew that they were from a medium-priced line of women's footwear that had the design on the insole changed often as a marketing feature. Following his investigation the supervisor reported that the design had been based on a set of Chinese temple bells that the designer had purchased in the local market. Pleased by the appearance of the bells, she had used them as the basis for a stylized design, which she submitted to her supervisor for consideration and approval (see Figure 3).

FIGURE 2   Translation of the *Meillat* Story*

Unpardonable Audacity of Footwear

In Bangladesh a Sandal with Allah as Footwear trade mark in Arabic designed in calligraphy has been marketed although last year Islam was made the State Religion in Bangladesh. The Sandal in black and white contains Allah in black. Prima facie it appears it has been designed and the Alif "the first letter in Arabic" has been jointly written. Excluding Alif it reads LILLAH. In Bangladesh after the Satan Rushdies Satanic Verses† which has brought unprecedented demonstration and innumerable strikes (Hartels). This International shoe manufacturing organization under Jewish ownership with the design of Allah has made religious offence. Where for sanctity of Islam one million people of Afghanistan have sacrificed their lives and wherein occupied Palestine many people have been gunned down by Jews for sanctity of Islam in this country the word Allah under this guise has been put under feet.

 Last night a group of students from Dhaka university came to Meillat office with a couple of pairs of Sandal. The management staff of Footwear was not available over telephone. This sandal has got two straps made of foam.

---

* The translation is identical to that with which Carlson was given to work.
† Salman Rushdie was the author of the controversial book *The Satanic Verses*. The author had been sentenced to death, in absentia, by Ayatollah Khomenei, the leader of Iran, for crimes against Islam.

All the employees in the development and marketing department were Moslems. The supervisor reported that the woman who had produced the offending design was a devout Bengali Moslem who spoke and read no Arabic. The same was true of almost all the employees in the department. The supervisor confirmed to Carlson that numerous people in the department had seen the new design prior to its approval and no one had seen any problem or raised any objection to it. Following the conversation Carlson compared the design to the word Allah, which he had arranged to have written in Arabic (see Figure 4).

Carlson was perplexed by the article and its timing. The sandals in question were not new to the market and had not been subject to prior complaints. As he reread the translation of the *Meillat* article, he wondered why the Jewish reference had been made when the family that owned Footwear International was Christian. He also wondered if the fact that students from the university had taken the sandals to the paper was significant.

As the day progressed the situation got worse. Carlson was shown a translation of a proclamation that had been circulated by two youth groups calling for demonstrations against Footwear to be held the next day (see Figure 5). The proclamation linked Footwear, Salman Rushdie, and the Jewish community and ominously stated that "even at the cost of our lives we have to protest against this conspiracy."

More bad news followed. Calls had been made for charges to be laid against Carlson and four others under a section of the criminal code that forbade "deliberate and malicious acts intended to outrage feelings of any class by insulting its religion or religious believers" (see Figure 6). A short time later Carlson received a copy of a statement that had been filed by a local lawyer, although no warrants were immediately forthcoming (see Figure 7).

FIGURE 3   The Temple Bells and the Design Used on the Sandal

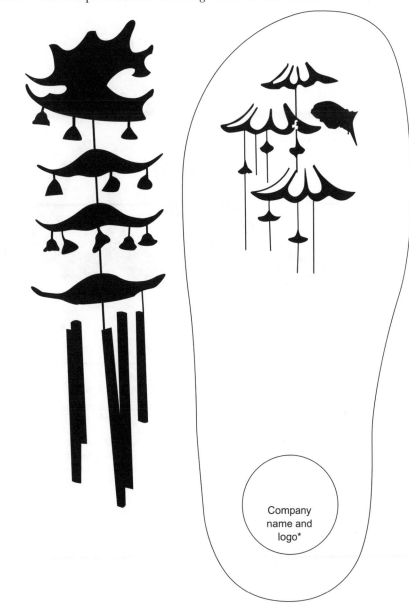

* The company's name and logo appeared prominently on the insole of the sandal. Both of the images in the exhibit were redrawn from copies of facsimiles sent to headquarters by John Carlson.

FIGURE 4   The Arabic Spelling of *Allah* (was redrawn from a facsimile sent to headquarters by John Carlson)

FIGURE 5   Translation of the Student Group's Proclamation*

The audacity through the use of the name "Allah" in a sandal.
Let Rushdies Jewish Footwear Company be prohibited in Bangladesh.

Dear people who believe in one God It is announced in the holy Quran Allahs name is above everything but shoe manufacturing Jewish Footwear Shoe Company has used the name Allah and shown disrespect of unprecedented nature and also unpardonable audacity. After the failure of Rushdies efforts to destroy the beliefs of Moslems in the Quran, Islam and the prophet (SM) who is the writer of Satanic verses the Jewish People have started offending the Moslems. This time it is a fight against Allah. In fact Daud Haider, Salman Rushdie Viking Penguin and Footwear Shoe Company all are supported and financed by Jewish community. Therefore no compromise with them. Even at the cost of our lives we have to protest against this conspiracy.

For this procession and demonstration will be held on 23rd. June Friday after Jumma prayer from Baitul Mukarram Mosque south gate. Please join this procession and announce we will not pardon Footwear Shoe Companys audacity Footwear Shoe Company has to be prohibited, don't buy Jewish products and Footwear shoes. Be aware Rushdies partner.

Issued by Bangladesh Islamic Jubashibir (Youth Student Forum) and Bangladesh Islamic Satrashbir (Student Forum).

* The translation is identical to that with which Carlson was given to work.

While he was reviewing the situation Carlson was interrupted by his secretary. In an excited voice she informed him that the Prime Minister was being quoted as calling the sandal incident an "unforgivable crime." The seriousness of the incident seemed to be escalating rapidly and Carlson wondered what he should do to try to minimize the damage.

FIGURE 6   Section 295 of the Criminal Code

[295-A. *Deliberate ar   ⋯⋯⋯⋯ *religious feelings* of any class by insulting its
religion or religious   on of outraging the religious
feelings of any clas   )ken or written, or by visible
representations insu   that class, shall be punished
with imprisonment.

. . . In order to br   er of discourse or the written
expression but also   ds the expressions should be
such as are bound   iive and provocative and mali-
ciously and delibera   ns. . . . If the injurious act was
done voluntarily witk

FIGURE 7   The

The plaintiff most r

(1)   The plaintiff is   Islam. He is basically a devout
      Moslem. Accc   work.
(2)   The first accu: e Company, the second accused
      is the Product   e Marketing Manager, the fourth
      accused is th   d is the Sales Manager of the
      said company   aving shoe business in different
      countries.
(3)   The accused   Muslims by engraving the calli-
      graphy of "Al   of majority this Muslim Country.
      By marketing   ffended the religious feelings of
      millions of M   of every devout Muslim to protect
      the sanctity   alligraphy on 22nd June 1989 at
      Elephant roa

The accused pe   iy under the feet thereby to offend
the religion of mir   under provisions of section 295A
of the Penal Cod

Therefore unde   e accused persons be issued with
warrant of arrest

The names of
(1)
(2)
(3)

CASE 6

Hazelton International

Henry W. Lane and Lorna L. Wright

Dan Simpson, the incoming project manager of the Maralinga-Ladawan Highway Project, was both anxious and excited as he drove with John Anderson in their jeep up the rutted road to the river where they would wait for the ferry. John was the current manager and was taking Dan, his replacement, on a three-day site check of the project. During this trip John was also going to brief Dan on the history of the project and the problems he would encounter. Dan was anxious about the project because he had heard there were a number of messy problems, but was excited about the challenge of managing it.

Hazelton, a consulting engineering firm, was an adviser on the project and so far had little success in getting the client to heed its advice. After two years of operation, only 17 kilometres of the 245-kilometre highway were under construction.

BACKGROUND

Since 1965, Hazelton had successfully completed assignments in 46 countries across Africa, Asia, Europe, South and Central America, and the Caribbean region. A large proportion of the projects had been in Africa but the company was now turning attention to

Henry W. Lane and Lorna L. Wright prepared this case solely to provide material for class discussion. The authors do not intend to illustrate either effective or ineffective handling of a managerial situation. The authors may have disguised certain names and other identifying information to protect confidentiality.

developing its Asian operations. Since the beginning, Hazelton had done only 10 projects in Asia – less than 10 percent of all its projects.

Hazelton provided consulting services in transportation, housing and urban development, structural engineering, and municipal and environmental engineering, to both government and corporate clients around the world. Specific services included technical and economic feasibility studies, financing, planning, architecture, preliminary and final engineering design, maintenance programming, construction supervision, project management, and equipment procurement.

Projects ranged from extremely large (building an international airport) to very small, requiring the skill of only a single expert (advising on a housing project in Malaysia). The majority of these projects were funded by international lending agencies (ILAs) such as the World Bank, the African Development Bank, and aid agencies like the US Agency for International Development (USAID) and the Canadian International Development Agency (CIDA). The previous year Hazelton's worldwide annual fee volume exceeded US$40 million.

Hazelton staffed its overseas projects with senior members of its permanent staff. In addition, experts with international experience and capabilities in the applicable language were used whenever possible. Both these principles had been adhered to in the Maralinga-Ladawan Project.

MARALINGA-LADAWAN HIGHWAY PROJECT

Soronga was a nation of islands in the Pacific Ocean. This project required design and construction supervision services for a 245-kilometre highway along the western coast of the island of Tola from Maralinga in the north to Ladawan in the south (see Exhibit 1). Sections of the highway past Ladawan were being reconstructed by other firms funded by aid agencies from Japan and Australia.

In addition to supervising the project, Hazelton was responsible for a major training program for Sorongan engineers, mechanics, operators, and administrative staff.

This was the fifth largest project ($1.6 million in fees) Hazelton had ever undertaken (see Exhibit 2). It was a joint venture with two other firms, Beauval Ltd and McPherson Brothers International (MBI), whom Hazelton involved to strengthen its proposal. Hazelton acted as the lead firm on behalf of the consortium and assumed overall responsibility for the work. Over the life of the project, the three firms would send 22 expatriates, including highway designers, engineers, mechanics, and operators.

MBI was involved because it was a contractor and Hazelton felt it might need those types of skills when dealing with a "force account" project. Usually, Hazelton supervised the project and left the actual construction to experienced contractors. This project was different. Force account meant that the construction workers would be government employees who would not be experienced in construction work.

Beauval had been working in Asia for 17 years and had established a base of operations in Kildona. It had done several projects on the island of Hako, but this would be the first on the island of Tola. This local experience helped the proposal gain acceptance both in the eyes of the financing agency, and the client, the Sorongan Highway Department (SHD).

EXHIBIT 1 Map of Soronga (not to scale)

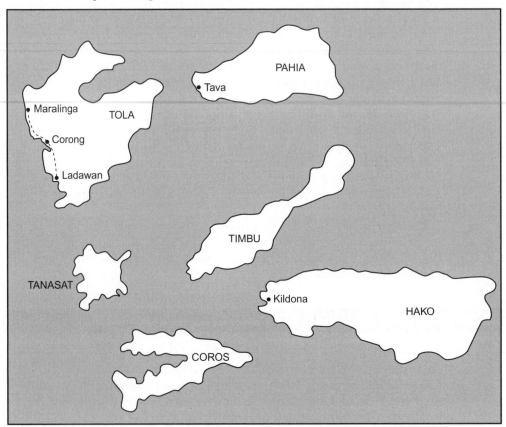

EXHIBIT 2 Hazelton's Six Largest Projects

Project	Location	Fee
1 International airport	Africa	$4 million
2 Highway supervision	South America	$3.4 million
3 Highway feasibility	South America	$2.25 million
4 Highway design	South America	$2.25 million
5 Highway betterment	Soronga	$1.63 million
6 Secondary roads: graveling	Africa	$1.32 million

The financing agency provided a combination loan and grant for the project and played a significant role in the selection of the winning proposal. The grant portion paid for the salaries of the expatriates working on the project while the loan funds were for necessary equipment.

Under the contract's terms of reference, Hazelton personnel were sent as advisers on the techniques of road construction and equipment maintenance. The training component was to be the major part of the project with the actual construction being the training vehicle. The project was to last five years with Hazelton phasing out its experts in about four years. The Sorongans would be trained by that point to take over the project themselves. The training program would use formal classroom instruction and a system of counterparts. Each expatriate engineer or manager would have a counterpart Sorongan engineer or manager who worked closely with him in order for the expertise to be passed on. At the mechanic and operator levels, training programs would be set up involving both in-class instruction and on-the-job training.

SHD's responsibilities included providing counterpart staff, ensuring that there was housing built for the expatriates, and providing fuel and spare parts for the equipment that would be coming from Canada.

It was thought that a force account project – with government staff doing the work – would be the best way to marry the financial agency's objective of training with the Sorongan government's aim of building a road. It was one of the first times that SHD had found itself in the role of contractor.

Hazelton was in the position of supervising one arm of the organization on behalf of another arm. It was working for the client as a supervising engineer, but the client also ran the construction. Hazelton was in the middle.

In Soronga's development plans, this project was part of the emphasis on developing the transportation and communications sector. It was classed as a *betterment* project, meaning that Soronga did not want undue resources going toward a "perfect" road in engineering terms; merely one that was better than the present one and that would last. An important objective also was to provide employment in Tola and permit easier access to the rest of Soronga, because the province was a politically sensitive area and isolated from the rest of the country.

TOLA

Tola was the most westerly island of the Sorongan archipelago. It was isolated from the rest of the country because of rough terrain and poor roads. It was a socially conservative province and fundamentalist in religion. The majority of Tolanese were very strict Moslems. The ulamas (Moslem religious leaders) played an important role in Tolanese society, perhaps more so than in any other part of Soronga.

Economically, the province lagged behind Hako, the main island. The economy was still dominated by labor-intensive agriculture. Large-scale industry was a very recent development with timbering providing the biggest share of exports. A liquefied natural gas plant and a cement factory were two new industries begun within the past two years.

From its earliest history, Tola had enjoyed a high degree of autonomy. In 1821, it signed a treaty with a European country guaranteeing its autonomy in commerce. This was revoked in 1871 when that European country signed a treaty with another European colonial power, recognizing the latter's sovereignty over the whole of Soronga. The Tolanese understood the implications of this treaty and tried to negotiate with their new master to retain Tola's autonomous standing. Neither side was willing to compromise, however, and in 1873 the European country declared war on Tola. This war continued for 50 years, and the fierce resistance of the Tolanese against colonization became a model for Soronga's own fight for independence later. Even after the Tolanese officially surrendered, this did not mean peace. Guerrilla warfare continued, led by the ulamas. With the advent of the Second World War and the arrival of the Japanese, resistance to the Europeans intensified. At the end of the war, the Japanese were expelled, and the European colonizers returned to Soronga, but not to Tola.

With the independence of Soronga, Tola theoretically formed part of the new nation, but in practice, it retained its regional social, economic, and political control. In 1961, however, the central government in Kildona dissolved the province of Tola and incorporated its territory into the region of West Pahia under a governor in Tava. Dissatisfaction with this move was so intense that the Tolanese proclaimed an independent Islamic Republic in 1963. This rebellion lasted until 1971, when the central government sought a political solution by giving Tola provincial status again. In 1977, Kildona granted special status to the province in the areas of religion, culture, and education.

Tola's long periods of turmoil had left their mark on the province and on its relations with the rest of the country. It was deeply suspicious of outsiders (particularly those from Hako, since that was the seat of the central government), strongly independent and fiercely proud of its heritage and ethnic identity. Although all Tolanese could speak Sorongan because that was *the* only language used in the schools, they preferred to use their native language, Tolanese, amongst themselves. The central government in Kildona had recently become concerned about giving the province priority in development projects to strengthen the ties between the province and the rest of the country.

PROGRESS OF THE PROJECT

The first year

Negotiations on the project took longer than expected, and the project actually began almost a year after it was originally scheduled to start. Hazelton selected its personnel carefully. The project manager, Frank Kennedy, had been successful in a similar position in Central America. He had also successfully cleaned up a problem situation in Lesotho. In September, Frank and an administrator arrived in Soronga, followed a month later by the major design team, bringing the total expatriate contingent to 10 families. They spent a month learning the Sorongan language but had to stay in Kildona until December because there was no housing in Maralinga. The houses had not been finished; before they could be, an earthquake destroyed the complex. Eventually, housing was rented from Australian expatriates working for another company who were moving to a complex of their own.

Hazelton was anxious to begin work, but no Sorongan project manager had been specified, and the vehicles did not arrive until late December. When the vehicles did arrive, the fuel tanks were empty and there was no fuel available. Neither was there provision in SHD's budget to buy fuel nor lubricants that year. The project would have to wait until the new fiscal year began on April 1 to have money allotted to it. Meanwhile, it would be a fight for funds.

The second year

By the beginning of the year, the equipment was on site, but the Sorongan counterpart staff still were not. Hazelton had no control over SHD staff, since it had no line responsibility. When the SHD project manager finally arrived, he was reluctant to confront the staff. Senior SHD people on the project were Hakonese, whereas most of the people at the operator level were local Tolanese. There was not only the Hakonese-Tolanese strain but an unwillingness on the part of the senior staff to do anything that would stir up this politically volatile area.

Frank was having a difficult time. He was a construction man. There were 245 kilometres of road to build and nothing was being done. It galled him to have to report no progress month after month. If the construction could start, the training would quickly follow. On top of the project problems, Frank's wife was pregnant and had to stay in Singapore, where the medical facilities were better. His frustration increased, and he began confronting the Sorongan project manager, demanding action. His behavior became counter-productive and he had to be replaced. The person chosen as his replacement was John Anderson.

John Anderson

John Anderson was a civil engineer who had worked for Hazelton for 15 years. He had a wealth of international experience in countries as diverse as Thailand, Nigeria, Tanzania, and Kenya. He liked the overseas environment for a variety of reasons, not the least of which was the sense of adventure that went with working abroad. "You meet people who stand out from the average. You get interesting points of view."

Professionally, it was also an adventure. "You run across many different types of engineering and different ways of approaching it." This lent an air of excitement and interest to jobs that was lacking in domestic work. The challenge was greater, also, since one didn't have access to the same skills and tools at home: as John said, "You have to make do."

Even though he enjoyed overseas work, John had returned to headquarters as office manager for Hazelton. His family was a major factor in this decision. As his two children reached high school age, it became increasingly important for them to be settled and to receive schooling that would allow them to enter university. John had no intention of going overseas in the near future; however, when it became evident that a new project manager was needed for Soronga, loyalty prompted him to respond without hesitation when the company called.

John had been the manager of a similar project in Nigeria where he had done a superlative job. He had a placid, easy-going temperament and a preference for operating by subtle suggestions rather than direct demands. Hazelton's top management felt that if anyone could make a success of this project, John could.

John's perception of the project

From the description of Maralinga in the original project document, John knew he would face problems from the beginning. However, when he arrived on site, it wasn't as bad as he'd expected. People were friendly, the housing was adequate, and there was access to an international school run by the Australians.

The work situation was different. The equipment that had come from Canada could not be used. Bridges to the construction sites had not been built and the existing ones could not support the weight of the machines. The bridge work would have been done before the road project started. Roads had to be widened to take the construction equipment, but no provisions had been made to expropriate the land needed. Instructions were that the road must remain within the existing right-of-way. Technically, SHD could lay claim to 15 metres, but they had to pay compensation for any crops lost, even though those crops were planted on state land. Because of these problems, the biggest pieces of machinery, such as the crusher plant, had to be taken apart and moved piece by piece. Stripping a machine down for transportation took time, money, and labor – all in short supply.

The budgeting process presented another problem. It was done on an annual basis rather than for the entire project period. It was also done in meticulous detail. Every litre of fuel and every nut and bolt had to be included. The budget was extremely inflexible, too. Money allocated for fuel could not be used for spare parts if the need arose.

When the project was initially planned, there was plenty of money, but with the collapse of oil prices, the Sorongan economy was hit hard and restrictions on all projects were quickly instituted. Budgets were cut in half. The money originally planned was no longer available for the project. Further problems arose because the project was a force account. The government bureaucracy could not react quickly, and in construction fast reactions were important. Revisions needed to be approved quickly, but by the time the government approved a change, it was often too late.

The training component of the project had more than its share of problems. Counterpart training was difficult because Sorongan managers would arbitrarily reassign people to other jobs. Other counterparts would leave for more lucrative jobs elsewhere. Among the mechanics, poor supervision compounded the problems. Those who showed initiative were not encouraged and the spark soon died.

John's arrival on site

John arrived in Soronga in March. SHD budgets were due soon after. This required a tremendous amount of negotiating. Expenses had to be identified specifically and in minute detail. By September, the process was completed, and the project finally, after more than a year, had funds to support it.

Shortly after John's arrival, the project was transferred from the maintenance section of SHD to the construction section. The Sorongan project manager changed and the parameters of the job began to change also.

SHD would not allow realignment of the road. To change the alignment would have meant getting property rights, which was an expensive, time-consuming process and inconsistent with a project that SHD saw as road improvement rather than road construction. This meant that half the design team had no work to do. Their roles had to be quickly changed. For example, the chief design engineer became costing, programming, and budgeting engineer.

The new SHD project manager was inexperienced in his post and concerned about saving money and staying within budget. Because of this, he was loath to hire more workers to run the machinery because the rainy season was coming and construction would slow down. The workers would have to be paid, but little work would be done. By October, with the rainy season in full swing, it was evident that the money allocated to the project was not going to be spent, and the project manager frantically began trying to increase activity. If this year's budget was not spent, it would be very difficult to get adequate funds for the next year. However, it was difficult to spend money in the last months because no preparatory work had been done. It took time to let tenders and hire trained staff.

The new SHD project manager was Hakonese, as was his predecessor. Neither understood the local Tolanese situation. Getting access to gravel and sand sites necessitated dealing with the local population, and this was not handled well, with the result that it took a long time to acquire land rights. The supervisors were also mainly Hakonese and could exercise little control over the workforce. Discipline was lax. Operators wouldn't begin doing any constructive work until 9:30 a.m. They would quit at 11:30 a.m. for a two-hour lunch and then finish for the day at 5:00 p.m. Drivers hauled material for private use during working hours. Fuel disappeared at an alarming rate. One morning when a water truck was inspected before being put into service, the Hazelton adviser discovered the water tank was full of fuel. No explanation as to how the fuel got there was forthcoming, and it soon vanished again.

Bridges were a problem. It had been almost two and one-half years since the original plans had been submitted, and SHD was now demanding changes. Substructures were not yet in place and the tenders had just been let. When they were finally received by midyear, SHD decided that Canadian steel was too expensive and they could do better elsewhere. The tendering process would have to be repeated, and SHD had not yet let the new tenders.

Although there was no real construction going on, training had begun. A training manager was on site, and the plan was to train the mechanics and equipment operators first. The entire program would consist of four phases. The first phase would involve 30 people for basic operator training. The second would take the best people from the first phase and train them further as mechanics. In the third phase, the best mechanics would train others. The fourth phase would upgrade skills previously learned. SHD cancelled the second phase of training because they considered it to be too costly and a waste of time. They wanted people to be physically working, not spending time in the classroom. Hazelton felt that both types of training were needed, and the cancellation raised difficulties with the financing agency, who considered the training needs paramount.

SHD, as a government agency, was not competitive with private companies in wages. It was not only losing its best engineering people to better-paying jobs elsewhere, it could not attract qualified people at the lower levels. Its people, therefore, were inexperienced and had to be taught the basics of operating mechanical equipment. Ironically, equipment on the project was some of the most sophisticated available.

SHD was directing the construction, but there didn't seem to be any plan of attack. The SHD manager was rarely on site, and the crews suffered badly from a lack of direction. Time, materials, and people were being wasted because of this. Bits and pieces of work were being started at different points with no consideration given to identifying the critical areas.

In June, there was a push to get construction underway. There was a need to give the design people something to do and a desire to get the operators and mechanics moving, as well as the equipment, which had been sitting idle for several months. Finally, there was the natural desire to show the client some concrete results. Hazelton was losing the respect of the people around them. Most people were not aware that Hazelton was acting merely in an advisory capacity. The feeling was that they should be directing the operations. Since Hazelton was not taking charge, the company's competence was being questioned.

The rainy season was due to begin in September and would last until the end of December. This was always a period of slow progress because construction was impossible when it rained. Work had to be stopped every time it rained and frequently work that had been done before the rain had to be redone.

Besides the problem of no progress on construction, some of the expatriate staff were not doing the job they had been sent out to do. Because there was little design work, the design engineer was transformed into a costing and budgeting administrator. No bridges were being built, so the bridge engineer was idle. No training was being done, so the training manager was declared redundant and sent home.

It was difficult for Hazelton to fulfil even its advisory role because SHD personnel were not telling them what they were doing next. A communication gap was rapidly opening between SHD and Hazelton. Communication between SHD in Tola and SHD in Kildona was poor, also. It appeared that the Kildona headquarters was allowing the Tola one to sink or swim on its own. Little direction was forthcoming. It didn't seem as if SHD Kildona was allocating its best people to the project, either.

The one bright spot of the year was that the project was now under the construction section of SHD rather than the maintenance section, and, thus, they could understand the situation from a construction point of view. The feeling was that things would improve because now the people in headquarters at least understood what the field team was up against and what it was trying to accomplish.

The third year

At the beginning of the year, there was little to be seen for the previous year's work.

The Hazelton staff and their Sorongan counterparts worked out of a small two-storey building in the SHD office compound in Maralinga. The Sorongans occupied the top floor and Hazelton, the bottom. A field camp trailer site had been set up in Corong, the halfway point between Maralinga and Ladawan. The plan was to move construction out from this area in both directions.

John, his mechanic supervisor, and the bridge engineer made the five-hour trip out to the site at the beginning of each week, returning to Maralinga and their families at the end of the week. The second mechanic and his wife lived on-site, whereas the erstwhile design engineer, now in charge of budgeting and administration, stayed primarily in the Maralinga office.

SHD was beginning to rethink its position on using force account labor. There were signs that in the next fiscal year it might hire a contractor to do the actual work because the force account was obviously not satisfactory. SHD also underwent another change in project manager. The third person to fill that position was due on-site in April but arrived the end of May. The new manager began making plans to move the Sorongan base of operations to Corong. The Hazelton expatriates, for family reasons, would remain based in Maralinga.

The project now also underwent its third status change. It was being given back to the maintenance section of SHD again. The budget process had to be started again. Hazelton, in its advisory role, tried to impress on the SHD staff the advantages of planning ahead and working out the details of the next year's work so that there would be funds in the budget to support it.

Construction had at last started, even though in a desultory fashion. However, Ramadan, the month of fasting for Moslems, was looming on the horizon and this would slow progress. This meant no eating, no drinking, and no smoking for Moslems between sun-up and sundown, which had obvious consequences for a worker's energy level. Productivity dropped during this period. This had not been a major problem the previous year because not much work was being done. Following Ramadan, there would be only two months to work at normal speed before construction would have to slow again for the rainy season.

John's briefing of Dan having been completed, they continued the site check. John wanted Dan to inspect the existing bridges as they arrived at them.

CASE **7**

An International Project Manager's Day (A)

Henry W. Lane and Lorna L. Wright

SITUATION

The Maralinga-Ladawan Highway Project consists of 14 expatriate families and the Sorongan counterpart personnel. Half of the expatriates are engineers from Hazelton. The other expatriates are mechanics, engineers and other technical personnel from Beauval and MBI, the other two firms in the consortium. All expatriate personnel are under Hazelton's authority. This is the fifth largest project Hazelton has ever undertaken, with a fee of $1.63 million.

You arrived in Maralinga late on March 28 with your spouse. There was no chance for a briefing before you left. Head office had said John Anderson, the outgoing project manager, would fill you in on all you needed to know.[1] They had also arranged for you to meet people connected with the project in Kildona.

On March 29, you visited the project office briefly and met the accountant/administrative assistant, Tawi, the secretary, Julip, and the office messenger/driver, Satun. You then left immediately on a three-day site check of the 245-kilometre highway with John. Meanwhile, your spouse has started settling in and investigating job prospects in Maralinga.

On your trip you stopped at the field office in Corong. Chris Williams, second mechanic and his wife, Beth, were living there. Chris was out at the timber company site to get help in recovering a grader that had toppled over the side of a ravine the night before, so you weren't able to see him. However, you met his Sorongan counterpart and he advised you that everything was going well, although they could use more manpower.

You noted that Corong did not have any telephone facilities. The only communication link, a single side-band radio, had been unserviceable for the past few weeks. If you needed to contact Chris, it would involve a five-hour jeep ride to Corong to deliver the message.

You were able to see the haphazard way the work on the road was proceeding and witnessed the difficulty in finding appropriate gravel sites. Inspecting some of the bridges you had crossed made you shiver, too. Doing something about those would have to be a priority, before there was a fatality.

You returned to Maralinga on April 1 and met some of the staff and their families. Their comments made it clear that living conditions were less than ideal, the banking system make it difficult to get money transferred and converted into local currency (their salaries, paid in dollars, were deposited to their accounts at home), and the only school it was possible to send their children to was not appropriate for children who would have to return to the North American educational system.

That evening John left for another project on another continent. It is now Tuesday morning, April 2. This morning, while preparing breakfast with your spouse, the propane gas for your stove ran out. You have tried, unsuccessfully, on your way to work to get the gas cylinder filled, and have only now arrived at the office. It is 10 a.m. You have planned to have lunch with your spouse at noon and you are leaving for the airport at 2 p.m. for a week in Kildona to visit the Beauval office, the Sorongan Highway Department (SHD) people, and the International Aid Agency (IAA) representative for discussions concerning the history and future of this project (it takes about 30 minutes to drive to the airport). This trip has been planned as part of your orientation to the job. Since the IAA representative and the senior man in the Beauval office were both leaving for other postings at the end of the month, this may be the only opportunity you will have to spend time with them.

On your arrival at the office, Julip tells you that Jim, one of the surveyors, and his wife, Joyce, are arriving at 10:30 a.m. to discuss Joyce's medical problems with you. This is the first opportunity you have had to get into your office and do some work. You have about 30 minutes to go through the contents of your in-basket and take whatever action you feel is appropriate.

INSTRUCTIONS

For the purpose of this exercise, you are to assume the position of Dan Simpson, the new project manager for the Maralinga-Ladawan Highway Project.

Please *write out* the action you choose on the Action Forms provided. Your action may include writing letters, memos, telexes, or making phone calls. You may want to have meetings with certain individuals or receive reports from the office staff.

EXHIBIT 1

SUNDAY	MONDAY	TUESDAY	WEDNESDAY	THURSDAY	FRIDAY	SATURDAY
March 24	25	26	27	28 Arrival in Maralinga	29 _____ Site check _____ with John	30
31	April 1 ──────► Return	2 (TODAY) ───	3 ─── Visit to Kildona ───	4	5	6
7 ───────	8	9 Return ──► to Maralinga	10	11	12	13
14	15	16	17	18	19	20
21	22	23	24	25	26	27
28	29	30	May 1	2	3	4

Note: You are in a Muslim area. People do not work Friday afternoons. Saturday morning usually is a workday.

For example, if you decide to make a phone call, write out the purpose and content of the call on the Action Form. If you decide to have a meeting with one of the office staff or another individual, make a note of the basic agenda of things to be discussed and the date and time of the meeting. You also need to think about establishing priorities for the various issues.

To help you think of the time dimension, a calendar follows (Exhibit 1). Also, Maralinga is 12 hours ahead of Eastern Standard Time.

Note

1 See Case 6.

Organization Chart

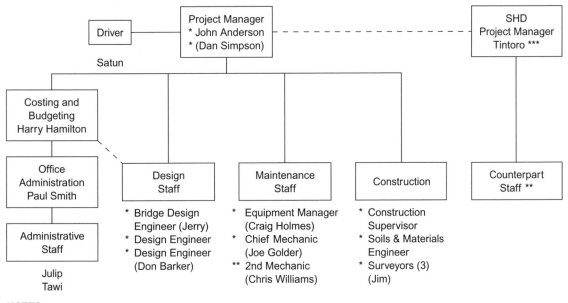

NOTES

* These people travel to Corong and other locations frequently.

** Stationed in Corong.

*** Located on the floor above Dan Simpson in the same building.

Note: The 2 expatriates responsible for the training component had been sent home. The remaining 6 expatriates called for under the contract had not yet arrived in Soronga and the 2 construction supervisors recently requested by SHD would be in addition to these 6 people.

Transportation Availability: (1) PROJECT OWNED – a) 1 Land Rover for administrative use by HQ Staff, b) 1 car shared by all the families, c) most trucks are in Corong, however there usually are some around Maralinga (2) PUBLIC – a) pedal-cabs are available for short distances (like getting to work), b) local "taxis" are mini-van type vehicles which are usually very overcrowded and which expatriates usually avoid, c) there are a few flights to Kildona each week.

PART 2

Implementing Strategy, Structure, and Systems

Today's global organizations need skilled managers. Cultural understanding and good intercultural skills are important managerial competencies. However, as a manager in the global economy you will need more than interpersonal skills. As we noted in the Introduction, you also have to understand how culture may influence your company's strategy, structure, administrative systems, and operations. The formulation and implementation of a strategy require understanding market demands and external constraints such as government policies. Managers must interpret information from the external environment, combine this interpretation with a thorough understanding of the organization's internal strengths and weaknesses, and translate the implications into appropriate organizational action that will lead to desired goals. In addition to choosing markets and manufacturing sites, for example, important organizational actions include choosing structures, work systems, and administrative mechanisms to motivate people toward the desired goals.

As we explained in Part 1, culture is the collectively held body of general beliefs and values defining the "shoulds" and the "oughts" of life that people usually cannot articulate. These "shoulds" and "oughts" are acquired through the process of *socialization*, by which common experiences create shared mental models and accepted ways of operating – the way things should be done. Since company knowledge and practices are not always systematized and documented, or made *explicit*, there is a great deal of implicit or *tacit* knowledge required to manage a company effectively.[1] Executives need to be aware of the implicit knowledge or assumptions underlying their firm's strategy, structure, systems, and practices. These practices are influenced by both organizational culture and national culture and using them, unmodified, in another country could lead to unforeseen negative consequences. Therefore, executives need to understand how their assumptions about organizing and managing may differ from those in their company's many countries of operation. This understanding can then be applied at the organizational level as well as at the interpersonal and team level of analysis using the MBI model described in Part 1.

As a company spreads beyond its home country and creates a global network, top managers need to refine their cultural "filters" through education and the acquisition of personal experience. Specifically, this should include knowledge about their different market environments, company activities in these countries, and the linkages among this network of activities. The experiences and the understood but unwritten information, as well as the explicit policies and practices shared by a top management group, create the operating and cultural filters necessary to decode, interpret, and understand context-dependent information flowing from the company's various markets and operations. With properly interpreted information, global executives can make informed strategic decisions and influence the design and implementation of culturally sensitive organization structures and systems to achieve strategic goals.[2] In short, they can develop and use a global mindset.

Most global companies have a particular organizational heritage that has evolved within the culture of their home countries. This means that a potential cultural bias may exist in their strategy, systems, and practices – "the way things are done in the headquarters' home country." For example, Lincoln Electric's renowned corporate culture of rugged individualism and piecework – with its origins in the US Midwest – shaped its early strategy for international development. When Lincoln transferred, unchanged, its US manufacturing, labor selection, compensation, and incentive systems overseas, it experienced limited success in markets that were culturally "close," or similar, to the USA – the UK and Australia – and problems in others that culturally were "distant," or less similar – Brazil and Germany. A new generation of internationally experienced top managers emerged, who understood the extent to which Lincoln Electric's operations were dependent on its American context and roots. Only at this point were the company's strategy, organization structure, and systems modified to allow for cultural differences. Then, Lincoln's international business began to recover.[3]

Executing global strategy and designing the appropriate structures and systems for use in another culture are the topics of Part 2 of this book. In the next section we elaborate on some key concepts of global strategy and how culture affects them. In the second section we consider some structural choices available to global companies, after which we focus on alliances and international joint ventures. Then we discuss the administrative systems that multinational corporations use and present the organizational architecture model, which ties together strategy, structure, and the systems in a global context. Finally, we address some important issues associated with expatriate and inpatriate managers who often are responsible for executing global strategy.

STRATEGY IN GLOBAL ORGANIZATIONS

Responding to globalization

Globalization, in business and economic terms, is often characterized as the erosion of national boundaries that has accelerated due to deregulation and technology. Trade liberalization has opened borders across which capital moves easily since the relaxing of foreign direct investment (FDI) restrictions. During the 1990s there were over a thousand changes around the world to national laws governing foreign direct investment; almost all of them had the effect of creating a climate more favorable to FDI.[4] In addition, airline travel and reliable, inexpensive communications have shrunk the globe so effectively – diminishing physical boundaries – that corporations are able to manage, control, and coordinate activities of far-ranging operations. More recently the emergence of sophisticated information services and the addition of new technologies such as the Internet have dramatically accelerated the globalization process. It is possible to do business almost anywhere through a website, as the representative of one small, family-owned Japanese company learned. She has successfully concluded sales from Boston to Saudi Arabia and Pakistan without ever going there.

Both responding to and feeding the trend of globalization, companies are "globalizing" in search of growth. Some companies continue to search for growth by expanding into new international markets and some are searching for it from innovations to be achieved by integrating and expanding their current global operations, creating what the UN has called "an international production system."[5] In this section we discuss three strategic issues in responding to globalization: new market entry modes, balancing global integration and local responsiveness, and global customers.

New market entry modes   Independent of the international growth strategies selected, companies entering new markets must decide on the appropriate business form, or entry mode, for each overseas market.[6] Entry modes establish the legal form in an overseas market; the extent to which the multinational owns the organization; the degree to which it maintains operating control; and the extent to which this new organization is part of a set of business relationships that extend beyond a one-country market.

There is a large range of entry and ownership forms. Options vary in terms of the amount of capital, other resources invested, and managerial involvement required in the host country. At one extreme, limiting a company's investment and set of activities, is the *exporting* of products or *licensing* of technology to other companies in the overseas market. There also are market-entry modes that require capital and human resources investment but permit full control of the *wholly owned businesses or subsidiaries* that can be *acquired* or developed as new, "greenfield" sites. A third set of market-entry alternatives includes hybrid modes such as a variety of *equity joint venture* and *strategic alliance* forms. An international equity joint venture involves creating a new entity owned jointly by two or more "parent" organizations to enter a market where at least one of the parent organizations is nonresident. Management responsibilities are contractually delineated. The percent of equity held by each parent generally defines who has formal strategic control. A strategic alliance is an agreement between two or more companies to engage in cooperative activities without equity involvement. For example, a strategic alliance may involve a contractual agreement to cross-sell complementary products or to engage in other activities on a cooperative basis. Passenger airlines have formed global strategic alliances to share reservation systems, complementary routes, aircraft purchasing and technical specifications, maintenance facilities and crews, ground services staff, and even pilots and cabin crews.

Costs and benefits are associated with each of these operating modes and ownership structures. The costs to be considered usually include capital, management time and commitment, impact on strategy, and the cost of enforcing agreements. Some benefits include repatriation of profits, political security, contribution to parent-company knowledge, and local distribution capability. The cases and readings in this book primarily will focus on operating issues in subsidiaries, acquisitions, and international joint ventures and alliances.

2. **Balancing global integration and local responsiveness**   Two fundamental forces influence companies operating globally: those pushing toward *global integration* and those pulling toward *local responsiveness*.[7] Forces for *global integration* push companies to minimize duplication of functions and to increase efficiencies by placing specific value-chain activities in the most suitable locations around the world. The ability to concentrate each value-chain activity in the best location has been enhanced by the erosion of national borders. This allows companies to capitalize on their competitive advantage in the particular activity and the host country's comparative advantage vis-à-vis other countries.[8] For example, the United States' Silicon Valley is considered by global technology companies to be a prime location for R&D operations because of the high concentration of professionals, educational institutions, and companies with leading-edge knowledge and expertise that nurture each other's learning. Similarly, countries in Southeast Asia have become locations of choice for manufacturing technologically intensive components because of the quality–cost–availability profile of their local labor forces. At the extreme, companies could locate each activity in a region from which the firm could best serve the rest of its global activities. This creates complex interdependencies among the firm's

multiple and often culturally diverse geographic locations and poses unique cross-cultural challenges for managers.

The requirement for *local responsiveness* appears when a company has to tailor its strategy, systems, and products to meet the needs of a specific national market. Because of different preferences for certain products and services, or different government regulations and systems, it is rarely possible, in the long term, to operate in another country exactly the same way as at home. Four elements tend to promote localization of strategy: non-tariff barriers, such as requirements to have a local partner or local standards for products; foreign-exchange shortages; cultural differences that influence consumer tastes and preferences even as some products become global; and flexible production technology that reduces the cost advantage of large-scale production while permitting greater local customization.[9] Moreover, cultural preferences that influence how people work and how they relate to each other, as well as government policies regarding human-resource practices, may favor localization of structures and systems. To achieve local responsiveness, the value-chain activities of the company are tailored to a particular country's needs and a successful company will adapt at least some elements of its operations to the local culture. At the extreme, the value-chain activities would be tailored to each locality.

In addition to balancing globalization and localization, a successful global organization engages in *global learning*, that is, the transfer and sharing of new ideas and knowledge among units.[10] A new production technology, marketing strategy, or product feature designed for one market often can be transferred to other markets. The challenge is to be able to identify synergistic links among units and to transfer knowledge and skills effectively. The proper organizational structures and systems, as well as the right individuals, play an important role in facilitating global learning.

All companies that operate globally are subject to the pressures of global integration and local responsiveness. The degree to which a company must respond to these forces depends heavily on the characteristics of the industry in which it competes and influences its multinational strategy. One common classification scheme that is based on the integration-responsiveness framework identifies four strategies: the *global*, the *multidomestic*, the *international*, and the *transnational*.[11] First, a company that follows a strategy that is highly dependent on global integration for many of its value-chain activities and that is locally responsive for few of them is following a *global strategy*. Such a company usually is characterized by a high degree of complex interdependencies among its subsidiaries and has a governance structure that is tightly and centrally controlled. Its managers have to be culturally aware and its senior management is likely to be dominated by a cadre of seasoned career overseas assignment veterans who share similar corporate values. Companies like Ericsson (telecommunications) and Sony (consumer electronics) have been identified as companies with global strategies.

At the other extreme, a firm that follows a *multidomestic strategy* is one that is minimally dependent on global integration but highly dependent on local responsiveness for many of its value-chain activities. A multidomestic strategy enables a firm to tailor its strategy, product, and operations to specific markets but does not optimize global efficiency. These organizations may operate differently in each country; in an extreme case, each country or region would have its own manufacturing, marketing, and R&D. These firms can be thought of as a confederation of loosely coupled organizations with strong local control and weak central control. The managers of multidomestic subsidiaries often function as independent "feudal lords" who may or may not be expatriate managers depending on the company's administrative heritage. Unilever, Procter & Gamble, Aegon Insurance, and KFC, while not representing the extreme end of the spectrum, tend to use multidomestic strategies.

Third, a multinational that depends minimally on global integration and minimally on local responsiveness follows an *international strategy*. Essentially, it simply replicates its home-market systems in each of its overseas subsidiaries. These companies are very centralized and their subsidiaries are simply outlets for headquarters' decisions. The product categories most suitable to such a strategy would include commodities. For example, grain businesses (AMD, Cargill) are large organizations that deal with commodity products that are traded around the world on the basis of price. Also, the ball-bearing industry to a certain extent can be seen as an industry suitable to an international strategy. For this industry there are many consumers (any manufacturer of machinery that has moving parts) and an undifferentiated product that depends on technical specifications that are applicable anywhere in the world.

Finally, a firm that is simultaneously highly globally integrated and highly locally responsive is following a *transnational strategy*. This strategy distributes the global responsibility for specific activities to the managers who manage the subsidiary to which the activity has been assigned. Each country manager may report to different persons with different worldwide activity responsibilities. The local responsiveness is achieved by managing each distributed value-chain activity with enough flexibility so that the local manager can make the essential compromises necessary to achieve as high a local market fit as possible. The transnational strategy is extremely costly to implement and requires managers who are cross-culturally and interpersonally skilled and flexible. Few – if any – truly transnational corporations exist, but many are aspiring and progressing in that direction, including Nestlé, Shell, and Matsushita.

When formulating a strategy, the ideal balance of global integration and local responsiveness and how best to implement global learning depends on many factors. Rather than present a single ideal solution (since none exists), in Part 2 we try to help you develop insights into issues involved in implementing strategies, structures, and systems to increase the chances of your success in entering new markets and managing in other countries.

3. **Global customers**   The foregoing discussion would make it appear that all the decisions to be made about operating globally were at the discretion of a company – which markets to enter, the countries in which to set up operations, and the type of strategy to follow. However, there is another factor driving firms to establish subsidiaries or enter joint ventures in international locations – the emergence of global customers and their requirements.

In the automotive industry, for example, large auto manufacturers are requiring their parts suppliers to be close to production and assembly plants to support just-in-time production systems. As a result, traditional parts suppliers are establishing joint ventures and manufacturing operations in overseas locations for their customers, such as in Canada, as in the case "Japanese-American Seating Inc.," or in Mexico.

In Reading 4, "Building Organizations Around the Global Customer," Jay Galbraith points out that in the last decade, the customer dimension has become more important to companies and many are organizing operations around their customers. In addition to the globalization of customers, the factors fueling this trend include a preference for partnerships and fewer suppliers, a desire for solutions to problems not just products, the ease of e-commerce, and the increase in the power of buyers. The rise of the global customer and the challenges they present to suppliers can be seen in the cases "Schneider Electric Global Account Management" and "Global Multiproducts."

Culture's influence on strategy

The existence of "pros" and "cons" as well as costs and benefits for each of the strategic options suggests that rational managers will weigh the tradeoffs in coming to their decision and choose the "right" course of action. However, what appears to be a rational, straightforward *modus operandi* in a manager's home market or in other international locations may not work in a new market. What a manager considers rational at home may not be so in a country whose citizens and local managers have different priorities. The "Monsanto Europe" case is an example of this. Monsanto chose a strategy for introducing genetically modified soybeans into Europe based on its experience in the United States and the lessons it learned there. It encountered significant resistance in Europe, and one has to question whether the lessons learned in the United States could be generalized to other locations.

However, a manager does not have to travel very far to experience these differences, as they can appear in his or her home environment in a joint venture relationship. For example, in the "Japanese-American Seating Inc." case, the Japanese company emphasized product quality and long-term customer relationships, while its American partner emphasized short-term profits. In addition to using the assumptions of national culture as a filter to identify and evaluate strategic options, managers also may be influenced by their organizational culture, as can be seen in the "Blue Ridge Spain" case. The "Delta" company wanted to dissolve a profitable joint venture because it did not believe in them and had been successful without using them.

Once the decision has been made to initiate international operations, to expand international activities, to use a certain entry mode, or to change mode of operations, the issues become those of execution. Someone has to travel to another country to negotiate a contract, arrange a distributorship, or work with people from another culture to make a project or joint venture a reality. Once this person leaves the office to negotiate the contract in Europe or to start up the plant in Southeast Asia, what really takes place? There are many questions to ask and issues to be faced before the business becomes a reality.

One's cultural filters and possible lack of experience with a particular country may influence the assumptions used in constructing spreadsheet analyses for new projects. Very often costs are underestimated at the start of the project and do not become apparent until later, when they outweigh the expected benefits. An experienced entrepreneur observed, "No one ever lost money on a spreadsheet. You can torture the numbers until they confess."[12] This comment attests to an apparent common tendency to make new projects or ventures look attractive by underestimating the time necessary for revenues and profits to materialize or by optimistically forecasting the initial and ongoing costs of operating internationally.

STRUCTURES: ORGANIZING FOR EFFECTIVENESS

Every company needs to decide how to divide up the work into separate tasks, and integrate it again to create coordinated performance. International organizations are among the most complex because there are many different elements to divide and coordinate. In this section, we describe typical organizational structures, discuss culture's influence on structure, explore global account management and global teams, and look at how to manage joint ventures and alliances.

Types of organizational structures

No one is best – all are valid models

Typical structures for international involvement include *international division, geographical (regional) division, product or project division, matrix,* and *networked* or *transnational.* Each of these structures has its strengths and weaknesses and would be appropriate for different situations. The two main factors that influence strategic choice of structure are the pressures for local responsiveness and the forces pushing toward global integration, as discussed in the previous section. Two additional criteria to be considered in the choice of an appropriate structure are the extent to which a company's sales and profits are derived from overseas operations and the complexity of the company's product line.[13]

In the international division structure, all business conducted outside the firm's home country is organized through one division. This form is often a starting point for firms that are beginning to internationalize and that probably have relatively little international business as a percentage of total revenues. As the overseas involvement of a firm increases, the international division structure may evolve into a geographical division structure in which all products for a particular region are grouped together. This structure is typically more suitable with a multidomestic or an international strategy. In the product or project division structure, responsibility for all markets around the world is given to specific product line or project divisions. This form tends to be adopted by multinationals that are involved in multiple product lines or businesses overseas. The matrix structure form combines regional and product emphases.

Finally, a networked organization (and sometimes what is implied by the term "transnational")[14] is emerging in some global companies. A networked organization combines many or all types of organizational units in relationships of varying degrees of ownership and relationship-intensity with the home country's headquarters. Matrix and networked forms are mostly adopted by large diversified companies and tend to be costly to implement and maintain. These forms of organization are more suitable for companies using a global strategy. The network allows a company to have a very high degree of structural flexibility. It provides all the advantages of balancing strategies in a matrix organization

Divisions do business with each other

and adds flexibility inherent in alliances with other organizations. For example, a networked organization might include global research and development in some product areas and local R&D in others, global marketing for some product lines and local marketing for others, and so on. It also might have several different types of alliances for projects having different roles in the firm's overall strategy or for product lines at varying stages of development. However, as might be predicted, a networked structure is exceptionally difficult to manage effectively.

This book does not attempt to pursue in detail an exposition of the advantages and disadvantages of each structure. There are many books and readings on the topic of international organization that comprehensively cover these issues.[15] Beyond considering the advantages or disadvantages of the various structural forms a company can use, one needs to recognize the cultural values and assumptions upon which these structures may be based.

Culture's influence on structure

Organizational structures are not free from the influence of culture. Each structure carries with it identifiable assumptions about the legitimacy of certain practices and relationships and defines the locus of authority, responsibility, and bases of power differently. Each legitimizes a different pattern of communication and interaction. In addition to "fitting" better with certain competitive situations or product characteristics, some structures may be more acceptable than others in a given culture. Both the text of Part 1 and the reading, "Cultural Constraints in Management Theories," provide insights into the impact of cultural differences on management theories and organizational structures.

André Laurent investigated the relationship between culture and organizational structure.[16] He believed that educational attempts to communicate alternative management processes and structures to managers would fail unless the "implicit management gospels" that they carried in their heads were addressed. He became convinced of this when he was trying to explain matrix organizations to French managers to whom the idea of reporting to two bosses was "so alien that mere consideration of such organizing principles was an impossible, useless exercise."[17] *— They can handle a wife + a mistress but not two bosses!*

The proposition that guided Laurent's research was that the national origin of managers significantly affected their views of what they considered proper management. His research uncovered differences in the basic conception of organization and found that these differences clustered by nationality. He demonstrated differences on four dimensions of organization: organizations as political systems, authority systems, role-formalization systems, and hierarchical-relationship systems. In another study comparing French and American managers, the results indicated that the two groups held very different views regarding structure. The US managers held an instrumental conception of structure, while the French held a social conception.[18] A comparison of these two views is presented in Table 1. Whenever you are developing or redefining organizational structures, the relevant viewpoint of the country you are in needs to be considered. The value preferences shown in Figure 10 of Part 1 provide a tool for analyzing the fit of organizational structures with cultural assumptions, including your own.

TABLE 1   Two Views of Organization

Instrumental	Social
Positions are defined in terms of task	Positions are defined in terms of social status and authority
Relationships between positions are defined as being ordered in any way instrumental to achieving organizational objectives	Relationships are defined as being ordered by a hierarchy
Authority is impersonal, rational, and comes from role or function; it can be challenged for rational reasons	Authority comes from status; it can extend beyond the function and cannot be challenged on rational grounds
Superior–subordinate relationships are defined as impersonal and implying equality of persons involved; subordination is the acceptance of the impersonal, rational, and legal order of the organization	Superior–subordinate relationships are personal implying superiority of one person over the other; subordination is loyalty and deference to the superior
Goal attainment has primacy over power acquisitions	Achievement of objectives is secondary to the acquisition of power

Source: Giorgio Inzerelli and André Laurent, "Management Views of Organization Structure in France and the USA," *International Studies of Management and Organization*, 13, nos. 1–2 (1983): 97–188.

Emerging trends in global structures: global account management and global teams

Global account management[19]   The emergence of global customers who have integrated their purchasing on a worldwide basis is driving multinational companies to consider another structural variation, global account management. Although not a new concept, it is appearing more frequently in industrial, high-technology, and some consumer goods companies. If a global customer is of sufficient importance, a supplier may decide to implement a global account management structure and to create the necessary reporting relationships on top of already existing structures and reporting lines. Although it sounds good in theory, in practice it is difficult and time-consuming to implement since it means new ways of working and a shift in responsibilities and power balances.

The key tension to manage is between the global account managers (GAMs) doing what is best for the customer and the country sales managers doing what is best for the local country organization. Three broad approaches can be identified:

1   *The balance of power lies with country sales managers.* Global account managers act as coordinators across countries, but the account ownership remains at the local level. Global account managers act as information-providers, influencers, and coordinators, but they do not have decision-making power over sales to their account.

2 *There is a "matrix organization" in which global account managers report to both their local sales manager and to a corporate executive responsible for global accounts.* This is probably the most common arrangement, seen in such companies as ABB, 3M, HP, and Intel. In cases of conflict, such as the GAM spending time building sales to the global customer in another country, it is up to the local sales manager and the corporate executive responsible for global accounts to agree on a solution. The matrix is typically not completely balanced, in that the local considerations may usually take precedence over the global, or *vice versa*.

3 *The balance of power lies with the global account managers.* This structure is currently fairly rare, but it is starting to emerge in a few companies. The logic of this structure is that global customers are more important than local sales, so the company is organized first and foremost around those customers. Examples include top-tier automotive suppliers such as Magna and Bosch and contract electronic manufacturers such as Solectron and Flextronics, because their activities are structured around a few large customers.

Emerging structural forms such as global account management put high demands on managerial sensitivity and skills. One example of developing capability with this form of organization is Schneider Electric. Schneider Electric's global account managers have to have:

- clear vision and mission statements
- empowerment, broad acceptability, and cooperation for local implementation
- an effective communication network with identified regional managers at several levels and a formalized matrix structure
- "solution-selling" competence
- cultural adaptability.[20]

At the time of writing, Paris-based Schneider Electric had grown its dedicated organization from 25 to 85 global account managers[21] and developed responses to key issues such as the effective development of global account managers, how to plan and budget for customer-specific efforts, and how to measure performance and reward results.

The implementation of a global account management structure and the systems to support it require daily use of all components of the MBI model of interpersonal and team effectiveness. Finally, it stretches the capacity of organizational designers and of more conventional managers who have to share power and be much more flexible than in the past. Although this form of network is only starting to emerge among global companies, the trends identified suggest that companies like Schneider Electric are at the leading edge of a major development. The complexity and the challenges of this structure can be seen in the case, "Schneider Electric Global Account Management."

Global team management   Teams have become a very common organizing structure for global companies. Global teams are teams of people from different parts of a multi-national organization working together to achieve a team specific-mandate that is international in scope.[22] The use of global teams has increased dramatically as companies have invested resources in technological infrastructure to connect technical expertise and local knowledge for the purpose of achieving shared global business objectives.[23]

Different types of global teams may be formed for different tasks. They may be used to develop strategies or to execute projects such as new product launches, product development, or cost reduction projects. For example, in Royal Dutch Shell the following types of global teams are used:[24]

- Project teams: Defined duration, clear deliverables.
- Management teams: Indefinite length, clear membership, high-level deliverables.
- Production/work teams: Regular and ongoing work (e.g., accounting, finance, R&D).
- Service teams: Regular and ongoing support (e.g., IT support, HR support for a global business unit).
- Action teams: Fast and fluid (e.g., emergency response teams).

Royal Dutch Shell also uses global teams to train future global leaders and to build multinational networks for knowledge sharing, innovation, an so on.

The objective is to take advantage of the expertise, experience, perspectives, and local knowledge that exists in the diverse employees of a global company. Members of global teams often represent different functional areas such as production and marketing, come from diverse cultures, and speak different native languages. They usually are located in multiple countries spread across the world in different time zones. Since they are not co-located and cannot have frequent face-to-face meetings, they usually interact "virtually" through a mediating technology such as conference calls, videoconferencing, and the Internet. For example, when Boeing designed the 777 airplane it used a global virtual design team. It had members from more than 12 countries linked together by workstations. They designed and launched an airplane with greater fuel efficiency, at less cost, and faster than teams using a paper-based design approach could have.[25]

Researchers are beginning to discover the differences between traditional, co-located teams that do most of their work face-to-face and global teams that mostly work in a virtual mode. Global teams still have to manage the *task* (what they have to do) and *social* (how they do it) processes like face-to-face teams, but the challenge is made more complex and difficult than usual by multiple time zones, geographic separation and cultural diversity. Although the concept of global virtual teams is an attractive and promising one, similar to the concept of global account management, it is not an easy one to implement successfully. Managers, team leaders, and global team members all have to have the requisite technical or business skills and "cultural acumen"[26] that are necessary in face-to-face multicultural teams. In addition, they need to understand the complexity introduced by the interaction of their task, contexts, members, time, and technology.[27] Managing this complexity to achieve satisfactory performance is the subject of the case, "The Leo Burnett Company Ltd.: Virtual Team Management."

International joint ventures and alliances

We now briefly turn our attention to the issue of alliances and international joint ventures, which are discussed in more detail in the reading, "The Design and Management of International Joint Ventures." The management of joint ventures is both a particularly important and particularly troublesome element of global strategy. Cooperative alliances, such as joint ventures, are used for many reasons. Companies may need to share financial risk, respond to government requirements, secure access to natural resources, acquire particular technical skills, gain local management knowledge and experience, or obtain access to markets and distribution systems. From a multinational's perspective, two important reasons for using joint ventures are the need to understand and have access to local markets and to have local general management knowledge, skills, and experience in the joint-venture company.

In establishing joint ventures, managers often make some common mistakes. There can be a tendency to concentrate on the end result and desired outcome and not to think carefully and critically about the *process* through which these results will be obtained. Executives need to invest in the personal relationships that must be built to create a joint venture and commit the time and effort necessary to make the venture successful. They need to think more clearly about *joint venturing*, which is a process orientation.

Another common mistake is to emphasize the "visible" inputs to the decision and the "tangible" aspects of the business. These visible inputs include the legal structure of the venture, the financial considerations of ownership and *pro forma* operating statements, and the market analyses – all the things managers (and specialists like lawyers and accountants) learned in school and deal with daily. These are important considerations that require attention, and they are necessary for success, but they are not sufficient to ensure it.

There are many operational issues beyond the legal and economic ones that may not be given enough careful forethought and may be left to be resolved as problems arise,[28] which often is too late. The "invisible," "intangible," or "non-quantifiable" components of a venture, like trust, commitment, and partners' expectations, often are overlooked or ignored, possibly because they may not be part of a manager's prior training or mindset. The situation is like an iceberg in that approximately one-seventh of it is visible above the water's surface and six-sevenths are below the surface. The result of not knowing what is hidden can be disastrous for companies as well as for ships.

Alliances are not an automatic solution to a lack of experience with or understanding of another culture, as executives sometimes think. An additional cultural interface, besides the one with the external marketplace, is created with the partner in the venture. Perhaps the most critical decision to be made in establishing an international joint venture or alliance is the choice of a partner, as J. Michael Geringer explains:

> Selecting partners with compatible skills is not necessarily synonymous with selecting compatible partners . . . Although selecting a compatible partner may not always result in a successful JV, the selection of an incompatible partner virtually guarantees that venture performance will be unsatisfactory.[29]

How does one choose a partner? Where does one look? What characteristics should a partner have? What are one's expectations? What are the potential partner's expectations? There are a number of criteria that should be considered: "complementarity of technical skills and resources, mutual need, financial capability, relative size, complementarity of strategies and operating policies, communication barriers, compatible management teams, and trust and commitment between partners."[30]

The role of relationships in strategy and international joint ventures is worthy of special comment. Often in North America, relationships are viewed as instrumental, as a means to ends, if they are thought of at all in a business context. In contrast, much of the world outside the United States and Canada values relationships in and of themselves. They form a basis of trust and linkage upon which a business activity may be built. Relationships are a major determinant of strategy, if not part of the strategy themselves. Given such striking differences in outlook on relationships, it is not surprising that partnership problems are one of the most frequently cited reasons for joint-venture failure.[31] Many of the challenges of managing international joint ventures and working with partners from other cultures can be seen in the cases "Blue Ridge Spain," "Ellen Moore: Living and Working in Korea," and "Japanese-American Seating Inc."

SYSTEMS: MANAGING THE GLOBAL ORGANIZATION

In addition to strategy and structure decisions, executing strategy globally means having to make decisions about the types of operating and administrative systems to be used and the people who will staff the international organization. Companies employ a large number of systems to manage their people and operations. These include job design, recruiting and selection, evaluation, training and development, and compensation and benefits systems. Negotiating, decision-making, and management styles are also important components of the management process. All of these systems and processes have cultural assumptions incorporated into them. Although there is some debate as to whether cultures around the world are converging or diverging and in what areas, there is no doubt that, in the realm of systems and practices preferred in a given country, culture influences preferred behavioral style and the management systems that are acceptable or even desirable. Those of one country (such as hiring of friends and relatives in many Latin countries) are often unacceptable or even ridiculed in another (such as hiring of friends and relatives in the United States and Canada). The text and readings in Part 1 provided numerous examples of how culture influenced management systems and processes, so the details will not be repeated here. Our intention now is to present an integrative framework that ties together strategy, structure, and systems with the company's people and the tasks they perform in the execution of the company's strategy.

The organizational architecture framework

Organizations are sociotechnical systems, that is to say, they have both social and technical elements. The "technical" component is the numerous technical and/or functional tasks of the business. These include acquiring inputs such as capital and raw materials, as well as using specific technology and work processes to create finished products or services. Each of the major functional areas of an organization – such as production, marketing, or finance – is a system within the larger organizational system. Each has a set of tasks and operations necessary to the functioning of the entire organization. The "social" component is the human element, the people – the individuals and groups, with their skills, needs, expectations, experience, and beliefs that carry out the tasks and operations. Managers have to align the social and technical elements of a company and solve problems that arise within and between the two in order to achieve the organization's strategic goals.

Managers use certain "tools" to organize their people, to focus them on their tasks, and to link them with other groups and departments. These relational tools provide the form and feel of the organization and channel the activities of employees at all levels. For example, the tool of structure creates reporting relationships between people at various levels of responsibility and facilitates the completion and coordination of critical tasks. It sends messages to organization members about what behavior is expected of them, on what tasks to work, toward what goals to work, with whom to work, whom to obey, and whom to direct. Structure includes such things as the division of labor as well as the recombination of specialized functions through the use of internal formal and informal networks of managers, special integrating roles for individuals, and various types of teams and task forces.

Managers also use rules, procedures, and a variety of other administrative mechanisms to align people and jobs. An example would be budgets and performance appraisals that direct behavior toward specific tasks and goals. The range of administrative devices includes selection criteria and hiring processes, training and development programs, allocation of rewards, information and control systems, and performance evaluation methods.

For the organization to be successful, there must be alignment – or "fit" – among strategy, structure, work tasks, and people, and externally between the organization and its environment. Organizational systems should help to promote this alignment. Simply stated, this means having the right people who have the right skills and attitudes, organized and motivated in the right way, producing the products and services customers want. This is easy to say, but not always easy to do.

A framework to help guide the exploration of implementing strategy in another culture is shown in Figure 1, the Organizational Architecture Model.[32]

FIGURE 1   The Organizational Architecture Model

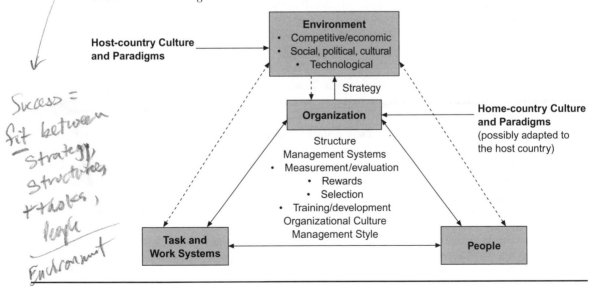

Structures and systems should be tools to help organizations and their employees succeed. There is no simple formula for choosing effective structures and systems. Judgment is required in assessing the likely impact of systems on people in jobs and in adjusting the systems to support job achievement and organizational results. Systems should be adaptable to changing conditions and workforces and not be ends in themselves. Furthermore, the "fit" that they create needs to be dynamic. This means that as strategies, competitive environments or geographic locations change, then structures, systems, and policies also need to be reevaluated and modified as necessary.

This discussion could apply to any top manager formulating and implementing strategy in his or her home market. However, an additional element of judgment is required of global managers who must work across national boundaries. Global business is distinguished from domestic business by home versus host-country cultural differences; differences in policies and operations among national governments; and the degree of integration that must take place among operating units.

Managers have to judge the impact of home-country management systems and practices in relation to host-country cultural assumptions. Managers don't necessarily give much thought to cultural influences in their domestic context, but they must learn to do so when crossing national borders. For example, in the conduct of domestic business North American companies tend to decide about strategy, structure, and systems with the use of rational, economic cost-benefit analyses. In the domestic context, it is not important for managers to understand that their analyses are based on their home country's particular set of management beliefs that may not be shared completely by managers in other countries. Decisions may be based on discussions that reference and build on implicit sets of shared cultural assumptions; all managers of the domestic companies are assumed to share these (though they don't necessarily). Yet these assumptions of common viewpoints must be challenged and questioned when a manager operates in multiple national markets.

Geert Hofstede commented that "theories reflect the cultural environment in which they were written."[33] Management concepts and practices are explained by theories regarding organization, motivation, and leadership. Therefore, theories of management systems and management practices may work well in the culture that developed them because they are based on local cultural assumptions and paradigms about the right way to manage. Hofstede also asked the question: "To what extent do theories developed in one country and reflecting the cultural boundaries of that country apply to other countries?"[34] Can structures, systems, and practices developed in one country be transferred to another where cultural assumptions and paradigms about the right way to manage may be different? If so, can they be transferred as is, or do they need to be modified?

Consider, for example, Lincoln Electric's experience with its individual-oriented, piece-rate incentive and bonus systems in factories in Europe and Brazil. Lincoln Electric's executives found that in Europe mangers were opposed to piecework and preferred more vacation time to extra income from bonuses. In Germany piecework was illegal and in Brazil bonuses paid in two consecutive years became a legal entitlement.[35] These culturally based conflicts went against the very systems that had helped Lincoln Electric become very successful in the United States.

The values underlying managerial systems, in this case reward systems, may not be obvious. It might be easier to conclude that workers were the problem instead of examining the assumptions underlying an incentive scheme. And, if the scheme is your own design, you are even less likely that to consider it a source of a problem.[36] Similarly, what are the cultural assumptions underlying practices such as empowerment, self-directed work teams, and 360-degree feedback? Numerous other examples of the impact of values on systems and management styles are provided in Part 1 in the elaboration of the Map component of the MBI model for improving interpersonal and team effectiveness. You may want to go back and review that discussion.

Management also creates the culture and climate of the organization. A set of values and philosophy will develop in every organization, whether it is created explicitly with careful forethought, or whether it happens implicitly without specific guidance and is perhaps less effective. Management's values and style can create an atmosphere of trust, problem solving, and adaptation to another country or one of mistrust, obedience, and domination.

We encourage you to use the Organizational Architecture Model as an analytic tool, but remember not to think of organizations in a static way. Organizations are dynamic. Analysis is only the beginning. It simply provides an initial outline of possible solutions and direction for action. As we pointed out earlier, the implementation process is critical. Successful implementation means finding the right combination of strategy, structure, and systems that motivate people to strive for high performance. It involves listening to, understanding, and working with people from different cultures in the organization.

A PERSPECTIVE ON HUMAN RESOURCE MANAGEMENT (HRM) SYSTEMS

It is important to recognize that even the idea of what human resource systems are and how they should be designed (or whether they can be designed) may be culturally influenced. For example, Chris Brewster has observed that the concept of human resource management, as developed originally in the United States, reflects a degree of organizational autonomy from external constraints such as government and unions that does not exist in many other countries.[37] The starting point for decisions is the firm's strategy and the goal of HRM is to fit people, practices, and systems to it in order to increase global competitiveness. As the "American model" of HRM is applied in the international arena, this autonomous orientation continues to be reflected, and although it recognizes differing host country sociopolitical and legal situations, they usually are considered simply exogenous factors that must be recognized and accommodated.

Managers in Europe, however, have much less autonomy, since workers and governments have greater influence on private organizations' human resources decisions and, thus, create significant constraints and restrict organizational decision-making autonomy. This different orientation may be more than a matter of semantics according to Brewster: "there is a need, therefore, for a model of HRM which goes beyond seeing these features as external constraints, and integrates them into the concept of HRM."[38]

Much of the international HRM literature in North America focuses on expatriate issues such as selection and training. However, when a firm operates in an overseas environment, it is not just expatriate policies that comprise the human resource management issues. There are local laws governing the hiring and firing of employees that may be unfamiliar to the firm. There could be substantial financial ramifications for firing an employee. Consistent with the culture-general orientation adopted in this book, the specifics of various laws will not be covered here. Whether it will cost two years' salary if a person is fired or six months' salary is not the issue. The laws and policies of all countries are subject to continual change. What is important is that executives recognize that such laws exist and that these laws are significant constraints on management discretion. A manager in an overseas country has to know the laws governing personnel practices.

In some countries, hiring quotas – laws requiring the hiring of people of specified ethnic or racial backgrounds – may be in force. These laws are similar in concept to the affirmative action laws in North America. Usually, these quotas have high political sensitivity and significant impact on overseas corporations that are guests in the host country. What does the manager do when the best person for the job is from a particular group, but he or she cannot hire any more people from that group? How does one manage in this situation? Does the manager try to avoid the issue, ignore it, procrastinate, actively recruit – and at what cost? How does the manager maintain cooperation and discipline in an organization when employees come from distinct subgroups that historically have been adversaries?

Where quotas exist, corporations usually are under pressure to employ local people not just at low levels, but in the higher managerial ranks as well. In a number of countries, serious localization pressures exist. What is the firm's plan for building local management capacity? How is the firm going to carry out this plan? What price is the firm prepared to pay? The firm's answers to these questions, and its localization policy, can significantly contribute to success or failure in an overseas environment.

The use of local managers has increased. In many developing countries, larger pools of better-educated management talent are appearing. In developed countries, where sufficient management talent exists, there are employment and immigration laws with which a firm must comply. In all cases, in order to attract competent local management, a firm has to offer competitive wages, benefits, working conditions, development, and advancement opportunities.

Finally, interpersonal differences and the potential for conflict exist, not just between expatriates and locals, but also between local groups – based on ethnic, tribal, linguistic, or religious differences. The citizenry of many countries is diverse in terms of culture, language, and religion. However, an outsider naively may believe that the inhabitants of a country think and behave similarly. Conflict between local people is apparent in countries of Europe, South and Southeast Asia, Africa, the Middle East, and parts of the Americas and reminds us that *intra*-country differences are also important.

Expatriates and inpatriates: keys to coordinating and integrating

In an era of global business, coordination and integration are essential contributors to successful strategy implementation in an organization of geographically dispersed activities embedded in differing cultural environments. Formal systems are employed extensively by MNCs to achieve their objectives. Numerous electronic communication and data-processing system options allow the creation of sophisticated enterprise information systems to coordinate their dispersed operations and the activities of their suppliers and customers.

However, the culturally influenced dimensions of information that provide the deepest comprehension of market-specific knowledge may not be transferable electronically. *Tacit knowledge*, which is deep-rooted and difficult to understand, explains the most important nuances of operations in a particular cultural context. This knowledge is acquired experientially and must be shared through face-to-face interactions.[39] Firms gain sustainable competitive advantage from acquiring experiences and lessons held as tacit knowledge, then sharing these insights across corporate activities. Given the dispersed nature of multinational organizations, knowledge-sharing is particularly difficult. One solution to this challenge is the use of a cadre of expatriates and inpatriates (an employee transferred from an overseas country to a corporation's home country operation or headquarters) to acquire and share this knowledge. Global companies must think about inpatriation and expatriation strategically. Inpatriation and expatriation can be used to fill positions, as a management development experience to provide managers with a global orientation or as organizational development.[40] In the organizational development role these inpatriate and expatriate managers create global relationships, inside and outside the company, and explicit and implicit operating knowledge. The relationships and knowledge then become essential to the value creation process in global operations.[41]

For a time American companies went through a period of reducing the number of expatriates they sent overseas.[42] One major reason was the expense associated with relocating them and their families. Their salaries were usually higher than those of local managers, and they usually received benefits to make an overseas move attractive. Benefits often included items like housing or a housing allowance, moving expenses, tax equalization, and schooling for children. Many of these benefits were not usually provided to local employees. In addition to lowering costs, having fewer expatriates has reduced conflict between employees and groups in the local environment and increased the development of host-country managerial and technical capabilities. The use of host-country managers continues, as does converting the status of expatriates to local employees, thereby reducing costs.

Companies also are reducing the duration of overseas assignments. Recent surveys of expatriate policies in multinational companies have found that although the number of expatriates has increased, the trend among companies is to use shorter assignments of up to one year, rather than the more traditional longer assignments of one year to three or five years.[43] The move to shorter assignments is also driven by a desire to reduce costs. Other cost conscious actions include:[44]

- establishing criteria for determining if an expatriate assignment is necessary and reviews of proposed transfers;
- finding ways to measure the return on investment of a transfer;
- more careful candidate selection to minimize early returns and failures.

Recently, we have dealt with some companies that were either increasing the number of inpatriates to headquarters or actually increasing the flow of expatriates. These inpatriate assignments were usually short term, two to three months, at headquarters for a special project. This had a double advantage of exposing the inpatriate to headquarters

Two washing learning

more $

processes, concerns, and perspective, while allowing headquarters personnel to become acquainted with cultural orientations and views of divisions from around the world. At the same time, some of these firms were establishing formal policies that required international experience as a prerequisite for consideration for promotion to senior ranks, thereby "localizing" management and eliminating many of the perks that were formerly needed as incentives for executives to accept international assignments.

What are the statistics on expatriate failure rates? There are estimates of anywhere from 20–50 percent for American expatriates. Some of the higher numbers have been called into question, but the number is still high, especially given the investment a firm makes in sending an employee and her or his family overseas.[45] There are many reasons for failure. One survey found that the two major causes were the inability to demonstrate a global mindset and poor leadership skills. An aversion to change and lack of networking skills also were problems.[46] Another survey found that the key factors of expatriate failure were partner dissatisfaction, family concerns, inability to adapt, poor candidate selection, and the job not meeting the expatriate's expectations.

Regardless of the exact rate of failure, there is a need to prepare managers for their international assignments to improve their chances of success. Global managers must develop a way of thinking and acting that is qualitatively different from the way in which managers traditionally have thought. Cross-cultural understanding and experience are essential in today's businesses. It might sound straightforward, but the process of developing globally minded managers with the requisite skills is more difficult than it appears. High-potential individuals must be carefully selected and prepared for their overseas assignments to achieve professional development and strategic objectives. In the Introduction to this book we discussed the nature of the global mindset and the necessary interpersonal skills. Here we focus on selection, training, and repatriation.

Selection

In 1973, published research showed that people were selected for international assignments based on their proven performance in a similar job, usually domestically.[47] The ability to work with overseas employees was at or near the bottom of the list of important qualifications. Unfortunately, over 30 years later the situation has not changed dramatically for the better. Very often technical expertise and knowledge are used as the most important selection criteria. Mercer Human Resource Consulting, in its 2002 Expatriate Risk Management Survey, found that companies continue to "mainly look for technical expertise followed by leadership qualities. Good organizational skills and adaptability are also sought-after qualities." Lesley Lorraine, European Principal at Mercer said:

> Expatriate assignments demand a broad set of skills, not just to survive but to succeed in challenging environments. The ability to think globally and to adapt to different cultures is key.[48]

Although technical skills and leadership and organizational skills are important, they should not be given undue weighting relative to a person's ability to adapt to and function in another culture. It does no good to send the most technically qualified engineers or finance managers to an overseas subsidiary, if they cannot function there and have to be brought home prematurely. Daniel Kealey developed a useful model for thinking about overseas effectiveness that focuses on adaptation, expertise, and interaction.[49] He states that for a person to be effective, he or she "must adapt – both personally and with his/her family – to the overseas environment, have the expertise to carry out the assignment, and interact with the new culture and its people."[50]

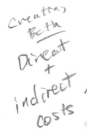

The cost of bad selection decisions is high to the corporation since the cost of an expatriate employee can be at least three times that of a domestic employee.[51] An ineffective expatriate can damage relationships in the host country and a bad selection decision also can be a high professional and personal cost to the individual expatriate.

An increasingly important decision to be considered is the international assignments of female managers. This has become an issue as more women have graduated from business schools and are in line for senior management and international careers. It is also a relevant concern both under employment equity guidelines and legislation in some countries like the United States and Canada, which encourage or require companies to promote women into positions of higher responsibility in organizations, and in the interest of ensuring that talented resources are used effectively throughout the organization.

In its survey of 181 companies (77 percent with their headquarters in the United States) with approximately 2,000 offices in 130 countries and a total of 35,150 expatriates, GMAC Global Relocation Services found that the percentage of female expatriates in 2002 had increased to 18 percent (up from 16 percent in the 2001 survey) and predicted that the female expatriate population would exceed 20 percent by 2005. In its first survey in 1993, the percentage of female expatriates was 10 percent. The reading, "Can We Send Her There? Maximizing the Success of Western Women on Global Assignments," focuses on this subject and calls into serious question some of the myths about barriers to women working internationally. The case, "Ellen Moore: Living and Working in Korea," describes the experience and challenges of a woman managing a consulting contract in Korea.

Training

The training that a person undergoes before expatriation should be a function of the degree of cultural exposure to which they will be subjected.[52] Two dimensions of cultural exposure are the degree of integration and the duration of stay. The integration dimension represents the intensity of the exposure. A person could be sent to an overseas country on a short-term, technical, troubleshooting matter and experience little significant contact with the local culture. The same person could be in another country only for a brief visit to negotiate a contract, but the cultural interaction could be very intense and might require a great deal of cultural fluency to be successful. An expatriate assigned overseas for a period of years is likely to experience a high degree of interaction with the local culture simply from living there.

The training model shown in Figure 2 suggests that, for short stays and a low level of integration, an "information-giving approach" will suffice.[53] This includes, for example, area and cultural briefings and survival-level language training. For longer stays and a moderate level of integration, language training, role-plays, critical incidents, case studies, and stress-reduction training are suggested. For people who will be living overseas for

FIGURE 2 Relationship between Degree of Integration into the Host Culture and Rigor of Cross-Cultural Training and between Length of Overseas Stay and Length of Training and Training Approach

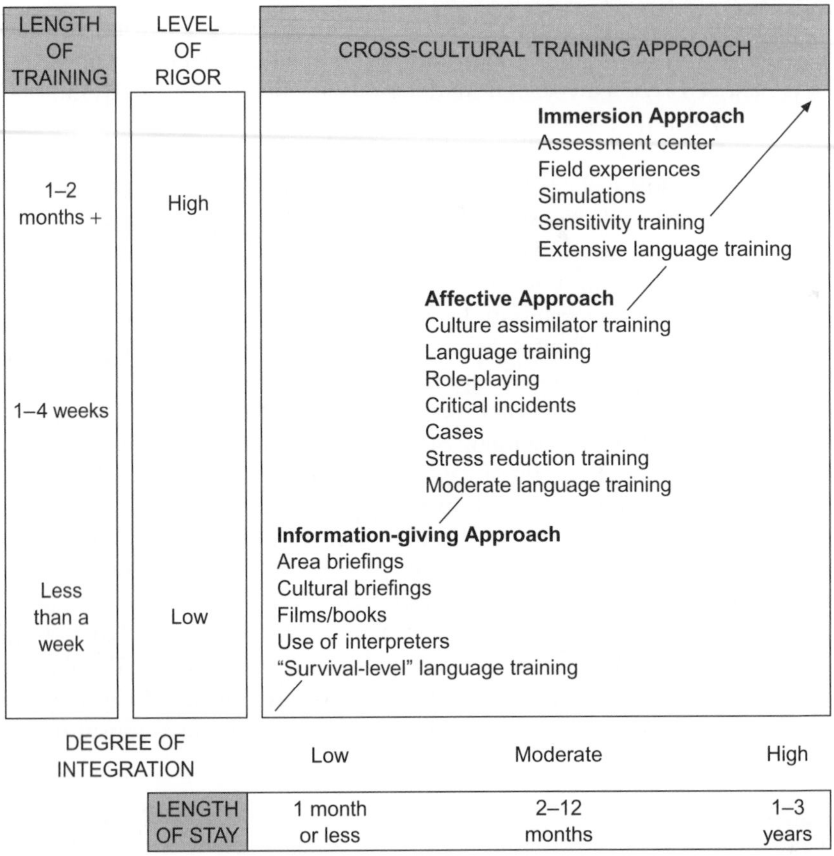

LENGTH OF TRAINING	LEVEL OF RIGOR	CROSS-CULTURAL TRAINING APPROACH
1–2 months +	High	**Immersion Approach** Assessment center Field experiences Simulations Sensitivity training Extensive language training
1–4 weeks		**Affective Approach** Culture assimilator training Language training Role-playing Critical incidents Cases Stress reduction training Moderate language training
Less than a week	Low	**Information-giving Approach** Area briefings Cultural briefings Films/books Use of interpreters "Survival-level" language training

DEGREE OF INTEGRATION		Low	Moderate	High
LENGTH OF STAY		1 month or less	2–12 months	1–3 years

Reprinted with permission of John Wiley and Sons Inc., "Expatriate Selection, Training, and Career Pathing: A Review and Critique," M. E. Mendenhall, E. Dunbar, and G. R. Oddou: *Human Resource Management*, 2b, no. 3 (1987): 340. Copyright © 1993.

one to three years and/or will have to experience a high level of integration into the culture, extensive language training, sensitivity training, field experiences, and simulations are the recommended training techniques. Effective preparation would also stress the realities and difficulties of working in another culture and the importance of establishing good working relationships with the local people.

The Canadian International Development Agency (CIDA) developed a useful approach to training for situations (see the top right-hand corner of Figure 2.) After extensive pre-departure training, expatriates are sent overseas. Shortly after they begin in their new posting, more training is provided along with their new co-workers, thus facilitating a productive integration. During the expatriates' stay overseas, periodic "refreshers" or debriefing sessions are held. Finally, the expatriates are actively involved

Side note: Always take any training your employer offers

in repatriation training both prior to and after their return home. The expatriate's spouse and family are also provided with similar training and resources.[54]

Repatriation

You can't go home again ???

Selecting the right people, training them properly, and sending them and their families to their overseas posting is not the end of the story. Reintegrating these people into the company after the overseas assignment so that the company can continue to benefit from their experience and expertise is important, and it also has proven to be a problem. Research suggests that the average repatriation attrition rate – those people who return from an overseas assignment and then leave their companies within one year – is about 25 percent.[55] GMAC Global Relocation Services found a 22 percent rate in its survey. If companies want to retain their internationally experienced managers, they will have to do a better job managing the repatriation process to include using that international experience, offering job choices upon return, recognition, repatriation career support, family repatriation support, and improving evaluations during an assignment. There are indications that some companies such as Monsanto, ABB, and Intel recognize this problem and have developed programs to address attrition issues.[56]

An international assignment may be an important vehicle for developing global managers; achieving strategic management control; coordinating and integrating the global organization; and learning about international markets and competitors, as well as about overseas social, political, and economic situations. However, the idealized goal of becoming a global learning organization will only happen if the right people are selected for overseas assignments, trained properly, repatriated with care, valued for their experience, and then used in a way that takes advantage of their unique backgrounds.

CULTURE SHOCK, THREATENING ENVIRONMENTS, AND SECURITY

The reality of culture shock

Despite a strong desire to understand and to adapt to a new environment in order to be effective as a manager, nearly everyone experiences disorientation when entering another culture. This phenomenon, called culture shock[57] or, more appropriately, acculturative stress, is rooted in our psychological processes.[58] The normal assumptions used by managers in their home cultures to interpret perceptions and to communicate intentions no longer work in the new cultural environment. Culture shock is not a shock experienced, for example, as a result of conditions of poverty. Culture shock is more the stress and behavioral patterns associated with a loss of control and a loss of sense of mastery in a situation. Culture shock, whether in normal attempts to socialize or in a business context, results in confusion and frustration. The manager is used to being competent in such situations and now finds that he or she is unable to operate effectively.

An inability to interpret one's surroundings and behave competently can lead to anxiety, frustration, and sometimes to more severe depression. Most experts agree that some form of culture shock is unavoidable, even by experienced internationalists.[59] People who repeatedly move to new cultures likely dampen the emotional swings they experience and probably shorten the period of adjustment, but they do not escape it entirely. In fact, research on intercultural effectiveness has found that those who eventually become the most effective expatriates tend to report experiencing greater difficulty in their initial adjustment. This is because those who are most sensitive to different patterns of human interaction are likely to be both disrupted by changes in these patterns and likely to become adept at new patterns.[60]

There are four modes of responding to a new environment:[61]

1   Going Native (assimilation): "acceptance of the new culture while rejecting one's own culture."
2   Being a Participator (integration): "adaptation to the new culture while retaining one's own culture."
3   Being a Tourist (separation): "maintenance of one's own culture by avoiding contact with the new culture."
4   Being an Outcast (marginalization): "the inability to either adapt to the new culture or remain comfortable with one's own culture."

The pattern experienced by people who move into a new culture usually comes in three phases: (1) the elation of anticipating a new environment and the early period of moving into it; (2) the distress of dealing with one's own ineffectiveness and as the novelty erodes and reality sets in, the realization that one has to function in a strange situation; and (3) the adjustment and effective coping with the new environment.

During the first and second periods, performance is usually below one's normal level. The time of adjustment to normal or above-average performance takes from three to nine months, depending on previous experience, the degree of cultural difference being experienced, and the individual personality. Frequently observed symptoms of culture shock are similar to most defensive reactions. People reject their new environment and the people that live there, often with angry or negative evaluations of "strangeness." Other symptoms include fatigue; tension; anxiety; excessive concern about hygiene; hostility, an obsession about being cheated; withdrawal into work, family, or the expatriate community; or, in extreme cases, excessive use of drugs and alcohol.

The vast majority of people eventually begin to accept their new environment and adjust. Most emerge from the adjustment period performing adequately and some people perform more effectively than before. A smaller percentage either "go native," which is usually not an effective strategy, or experience very severe symptoms of inability to adjust (alcoholism, nervous breakdown, and so on). These types of reactions seem to occur independently of the direction of a move. For example, North Americans going to Russia will probably exhibit patterns similar to Russians coming to North America.

Different people have different ways of coping with culture shock. Normal stress management techniques, regular exercise, rest, and balanced diet are helpful. As noted earlier, some use work as a bridge until they adjust. Usually, the work environment does have some similarities to that of one's home culture. But for the partner who does not work and who is often left to cope with the new environment on his or her own, the effects can be more severe. Language training is one very effective way of coping and provides an entry into the host culture. Education about the local history, geography, and traditions of the new culture and then exploration of the new environment also help adjustment. Whatever methods are employed, it is wise to remember that everyone experiences culture shock. Diligent preparation can only moderate the effect, not eliminate it.

Support systems are especially important during the adjustment period. One obvious source of support is the family. Doing more things together as a family, more often, is a way to cope with the pressures. Another is to realize that it is acceptable to withdraw from the new culture, temporarily, for a respite. Reading newspapers from home or enjoying familiar food is a good cultural insulator – if not carried too far. After eight months in Switzerland, an 8-year-old asked her American grandfather to bring her Cheddar cheese and a Hershey bar on a visit, even though she had grown to enjoy Swiss fondue and Swiss chocolate! It is important that the use of such temporary interruptions to one's reality be restricted to bridges to the new culture, not as permanent anchors to an old environment.

In company situations, it must be understood that the international manager in a new culture goes through these stresses. Local colleagues should not be surprised at less than perfect performance or strange behavior and can provide crucial support for the managers and their families. When one goes overseas, there are two jobs to accomplish. There is the functional or technical job – for example, the engineering, finance, marketing, or plant management responsibilities. This is obvious. However, too often it is only this job that people identify, focus on, and prepare for. The other job is cultural adaptation. If you cannot adapt successfully, you may be requested to go (or may be sent) home early – often in a matter of months. Such a manager may never get a chance to use his or her technical or functional skills.

You do not have to leave your own country to experience culture shock, as the following demonstrates. A volunteer on a project in Ghana experienced the symptoms of culture shock, even after participating in an orientation program organized by the sponsoring agency. This same person reported severe symptoms of culture shock on returning to an urban-based MBA program. However, the ultimate culture shock came upon graduating and starting work for a manufacturer located in a small, rural community in one of Canada's maritime provinces. In all three experiences, the patterns were the same, and the sharpest disorientation occurred within this person's native country, perhaps because it was least expected. It is important to note that this individual experienced a "reverse culture shock" on their return home. "Return shock" or "reentry shock" also is an adjustment phenomenon that people experience and for which they need to be prepared.[62]

Expatriate adaptation issues are the topic of the readings "Adapting to a Boundaryless World: A Developmental Expatriate Model" and "Serving Two Masters: Managing the Dual Allegiance of Expatriate Employees," as well as the case, "Marconi Telecommunications Mexico."

Corrections in CJ = Reentry =

Threatening environments

In addition to executing strategy globally under relatively "normal" conditions, executives also may find themselves in difficult environments and threatening situations. These usually reflect historical or economic events and cultural factors of a given country or region, and could pose a threat to corporate assets or to employees. Some of these situations include expropriation, currency collapse, civil war, and global terrorism.

AND Natural Disasters

In the late 1980s and early 1990s it appeared that the world was becoming an easier place in which to live and do business. China had opened up to the rest of the world; Mikhail Gorbachev introduced perestroika and glasnost; the Cold War ended, and countries in Eastern Europe were permitted to decide their own destiny; Germany was reunited; South Africa abandoned apartheid; and Iran and Iraq ended a long, bloody war. However, Tiananmen Square, Kuwait, Bosnia, Chechnya, and Chiapas took over the headlines. Even Canada narrowly escaped being split up when, in October 1995, the citizens of Quebec voted to remain in Canada by a very narrow margin.

Different challenges and opportunities had taken over by the end of the 1990s. The suddenness and depth of the Asian economic crisis in 1997 shook confidence in the economies of South Korea, Thailand, Malaysia, and Indonesia, each of which sank into a deep recession. Brazil's economy threatened to follow suit as capital markets' attitudes toward emerging economies chilled. Argentina's economy collapsed. The Indonesian government collapsed and rioters reappeared on the streets.

The first half of this decade, marked by the events of September 11, 2001, saw economic and political volatility continue worldwide. It is worth recalling that countries and regions such as China, the Soviet Union, eastern Europe, Latin America, and Indonesia at one time or another became "darlings" for investment by overseas companies. Then, when the political climates changed or the countries experienced economic problems, companies started to rethink their involvement, and some left. Executives could be tempted to say, "Well, as part of our strategy let's concentrate on places like the United States and western Europe."

We believe that global business is a long-term proposition. Companies cannot succeed by jumping in and out of countries when the going gets a little tough. Not only is it expensive, but customers and suppliers often remember when they were "deserted." Nestlé had some of its operations in South America nationalized and later resumed ownership. It then went through a second full cycle of nationalization and renewed ownership. Although the company contested and fought the actions as best it could, the attitude of senior executives was one of patience, knowing that these things happen and that, eventually, the regime would change and the assets would be returned. This company has had a real commitment to its global business and a long-term perspective, both of which have contributed to its unusual success.

Many countries could be considered difficult places in which to do business. It is important to have a realistic attitude toward these situations and to learn to live and work in a world of uncertainty and risk. The more you learn about other countries, the better you understand the risks involved. This enables better decisions to be made about entering a certain country and the steps necessary to manage the risks in that country.

The following story illustrates this well. One of the authors was having dinner with the president of a British bank's Canadian subsidiary and was describing some of his activities in East Africa to the bank president. The bank president commented about how risky it was to operate in Africa. This comment surprised the author, who understood the difficulties involved but had thought it possible to manage them. The bank president then described all the countries in South America in which the bank was operating and making money. To the author, South America had to be one of the riskiest places to operate at that time, and he said so. The bank president replied, "Not really; the bank has been there for a long time, and we understand the situation." Therein lies the moral: Familiarity with and understanding of a country provide the necessary perspective for accurately assessing risks, determining acceptable levels of risk, and managing those risks.

Companies need to have strategic and tactical plans for managing risks. Large companies can develop specialists in assessing risks to contribute to informed decision-making, and smaller ones can access specialist firms or consultants for information relevant to specific decisions. All companies are advised to listen to expatriates and locals working in the field when they provide systematic assessments of their environments required periodically as part of the normal business plan by the home office. Individual managers can add to the quality of their own decision making by reading broadly, by understanding the history of regions in which they operate, and by seeking (and paying attention to) information from international field personnel. As globalization increases, more international representation in the senior ranks of corporate headquarters personnel will also increase the ability to assess risks in specific countries. A global viewpoint, an understanding of the culture, political and social situations, and a long-term commitment to global operations are essential.

Operating globally is different from operating at home, and those differences must be understood. The costs of entering the game can be high. But the experience can be rewarding financially for the corporation, as well as personally and professionally for the manager.

Security

GMAC Global Relocation Services found in its 2002 survey that many companies had formalized programs to ensure the safety and security of their expatriates and families. Of the respondents, 44 percent reported that they received inquiries from employees about security issues, and it appears that companies are responding to these concerns to improve security, minimize international assignment turndowns, attrition, early returns, and failures. Many companies had instituted security briefings for selected countries, and some provided security briefings for all international assignments. Security systems were upgraded, evacuation procedures were put in place, and companies were updating their employee contact information – many of the issues that can be seen in the case, "Building Products International: A Crisis Management Strategy," in Part 3.

STRATEGY, STRUCTURE, AND SYSTEMS: TRANSFER, ADAPT, OR CREATE?

Organizing to do business globally requires balancing a need for achievement of efficiencies through global integration and a parallel, sometimes countervailing, need for local responsiveness, all the while ensuring that learning is taking place globally in the organization. What strategy will give the right balance between the forces of globalization and localization for a particular company? The parts of the strategy that are so important that they absolutely cannot be changed probably should be designed and managed globally to gain advantages of economies of scale or to assure protection from appropriation by competitors. Those parts of the strategy that depend on local people – as customers, employees, or allies – to be implemented effectively probably should be localized to gain advantages of local capabilities.

Executives also must decide whether existing practices, systems, and management styles can be transferred from one culture to another or whether they must be changed and adapted in some way when they appear to be in conflict with the norms of another culture. The answer is not always to change a system, even if it is different than in the host country. Sometimes people in another culture simply need to be trained to use a system (remembering, of course, that the best training format may be influenced by the culture). However, neither is the answer always to assume that training is all that is required. Each response has a proper time and place.

The decision regarding transferring, adapting, or possibly even creating a new hybrid should be the result of careful, informed judgment based on understanding the cultural biases of the systems and the cultural norms of the country in which the operations are located. Are there rules? Not really, but careful analysis can help sort out the issues and help managers solve the problem. Questions such as "How important is it that we do it identically to the way it's done at home?" can guide one's decisions. It may not be important that the procedures are exactly the same; rather, results may be more important. Just because it is the way headquarters does it, or wants it done, does not mean that it is right for a different cultural environment. What are important are the *business imperatives*, tasks that must be done well for the firm to make money.[63] Differing business imperatives and cultural accommodation requirements can be compared in the situations presented in the cases, "Japanese-American Seating Inc." and "Ellen Moore: Living and Working in Korea."

Systems and structures are tools to help managers do their job. They are culturally determined tools in their underlying assumptions about human motivation and behavior. If they become ends in themselves, they often become barriers to effective performance. This is true in one's own culture and even more so when these tools are in conflict with the values and beliefs of other cultures. The difficulty is learning to recognize one's own cultural assumptions built into the tools that may impede one from seeing that they can be changed or adapted. We remind you that the MBI Framework described in the "Cultural Orientations Framework" discussion in Part 1 provides a powerful analytic tool for testing the cultural assumptions underlying organizational systems and structures. A global organization may even find practices overseas that could be effective at home, leading to management innovation throughout the company.

The text and readings in Part 2 should guide you in developing a framework of both the choices that must be made in developing a global organization and the factors that influence those choices. The cases that follow provide opportunities to see the elements in action and to apply the understanding you have gained.

ACKNOWLEDGMENT

The authors would like to thank Professor Nick Athanassiou of Northeastern University who revised this chapter for the fourth edition and on whose work this revision is based.

Notes

1   Ikujiro Nonaka and Hirotaka Takeuchi, *The Knowledge-Creating Company* (New York, Oxford University Press, 1995).

2   Nicholas Athanassiou, "The Impact of Internationalization on Top Management Team Characteristics: A Tacit Knowledge Perspective," doctoral dissertation, University of South Carolina, 1995; and Nicholas Athanassiou and Douglas Nigh, "The Impact of Company Internationalization on Top Management Team Advice Networks: A Tacit Knowledge Perspective," *Strategic Management Journal*, 19(1) (1999): 83–92.

3   Donald F. Hastings, "Lincoln Electric's Harsh Lessons from International Expansion," *Harvard Business Review*, 77(3) (February–March 1999): 162–78.

4   *World Investment Report 2000: Cross-border Mergers and Acquisitions and Development* (New York and Geneva: United Nations, 2000): xv.

5   Ibid., p. xx.

6   P. W. Beamish, J. P. Killing, D. J. Lecraw, and A. J. Morrison, *International Management: Text and Cases*, 2nd edn. (Burr Ridge, IL: Richard D. Irwin, 1994).

7   C. A. Bartlett and S. Ghoshal, *Managing Across Borders: The Transnational Solution*, 2nd edn. (Boston: Harvard Business School Press, 1998); and C. K. Prahalad and Y. L. Doz, *The Multinational Mission: Balancing Local Demands and Global Vision* (New York: The Free Press, 1987).

8   B. Kogut, "Designing Global Strategies: Comparative and Competitive Value-Added Chains," *Sloan Management Review*, 26(4) (Summer 1985): 15–28.

9   Ibid.

10 Bartlett and Ghoshal, *Managing Across Borders*.

11 Ibid.

12 Jesus Sotomayor, Mexico City, 2003, personal communication.

13 Bartlett and Ghoshal, *Managing Across Borders*; and John M. Stopford and Louis T. Wells, Jr., *Managing the Multinational Enterprise: Organization of the Firm and Ownership of the Subsidiaries* (New York: Basic Books, 1972).

14 Bartlett and Ghoshal, *Managing Across Borders*. See also Prahalad and Doz, *The Multinational Mission*.

15 See, for example, Bartlett and Ghoshal, *Managing Across Borders*; and Prahalad and Doz, *The Multinational Mission*.

16 André Laurent, "The Cultural Diversity of Western Conceptualizations of Management," *International Studies of Management and Organization*, 13(1–2) (1983): 75–96.

17 Ibid., p. 75.

18 Giorgio Inzerilli and André Laurent, "Managerial Views of Organization Structure in France and the USA," *International Studies of Management and Organization*, 13(1–2) (1983): 97–188.

19 This section is adapted from Julian Birkinshaw and Joseph J. DiStefano, "Global Account Management: New Structures, New Tasks," Chapter 14 in Henry W. Lane, Martha L. Maznevski, Mark Mendenhall, and Jeanne McNett, *The Blackwell Handbook of Global Management: A Guide to Managing Complexity* (Oxford: Blackwell, 2004). Used with permission.

20 This list is a partial set of requirements as described by the first global account manager for the vendor (personal communication, September 1994).

21 Martin Riedel, "Implementing Key Account Management at Decentralised Customers," Master's thesis, Zurich/Altstetten, Switzerland: Private Hochschule Wirtschaft, p. 19.

22 Martha L. Maznevski and Joseph J. DiStefano, "Creating Value with Diverse Teams in Global Management", *Organizational Dynamics*, 29(1) (2000): 45–61. 2000, p. 196.

23 Henry W. Lane, Martha L. Maznevski, Mark Mendenhall, and Jeanne McNett, "Introduction to Leading and Teaming," in Lane et al., *The Blackwell Handbook of Global Management*, pp. 171–3.

24   This list was compiled by Arie Baan of Royal Dutch Shell to describe the scope of global teams at that company. Personal communication, 2004.

25   Richard Benson-Armer and Tsun-yan Hsieh, "Teamwork Across Time and Space," *McKinsey Quarterly*, 4 (1997): 19–27.

26   Mansour Javidan and Robert J. House, "Cultural Acumen for the Global Manager: Lessons from Project GLOBE," *Organizational Dynamics*, 29(4) (2001): 289–305.

27   S. G. Cohen and D. E. Bailey, "What Makes Teams Work: Group Effectiveness Research from the Shop Floor to the Executive Suite," *Journal of Management*, 23 (1997): 239–90. These authors, among many others, have identified that team effectiveness is a function of factors related to task, group, and organizational design factors, environmental factors, internal processes, external processes, and group psychosocial traits.

28   P. W. Beamish, *Multinational Joint Ventures in Developing Countries* (London: Routledge, 1988).

29   J. Michael Geringer, "Partner Selection Criteria for Developed Country Joint Ventures," *Business Quarterly*, 53(1) (1988): 55.

30   Ibid.

31   Beamish et al., *International Management*.

32   This organizational design framework and analytic model has been adapted from a number of writers on the contingency theory of organizations: James D. Thompson, *Organizations in Action* (New York: McGraw-Hill, 1967); Paul R. Lawrence and J. W. Lorsch, *Organization and Environment* (Homewood, IL: Richard D. Irwin, 1969); Jay R. Galbraith, *Designing Complex Organizations* (Reading, MA: Addison-Wesley, 1973); Jay W. Lorsch and John J. Morse, *Organizations and Their Members: A Contingency Approach* (New York: Harper & Row, 1974); Jay R. Galbraith, *Organization Design* (Reading, MA: Addison-Wesley, 1977); Jay W. Lorsch, "Organization Design: A Situational Perspective," *Organizational Dynamics* (American Management Association), 5 (1977); Jay R. Galbraith and Daniel A. Nathanson, *Strategy Implementation: The Role of Structure and Process* (St Paul, MN: West, 1978); John P. Kotter, Leonard A. Schlesinger, and Vijay Sathe, "Organization Design Tools," in *Organization: Text, Cases and Readings on the Management of Organizational Design and Change* (Homewood, IL: Richard D. Irwin, 1979). See also H. W. Lane, "Systems, Values and Action: An Analytic Framework for Intercultural Management Research," *Management International Review*, 20(3) (1980): 61–70.

33   Geert Hofstede, "Motivation, Leadership, and Organization: Do American Theories Apply Abroad?," *Organizational Dynamics*, 8(2) (Summer 1980): 50.

34   Ibid.

35   Jamie O'Connell and Christopher Bartlett, "Lincoln Electric: Venturing Abroad," Harvard Business School Case 9-398-095, p. 7.

36   The tendency to attribute success to one's own skill and to blame others for failure is not a cultural universal, however. An oriental perspective might well reverse the direction of explanation for success and failure and credit others for positive outcomes while assuming the blame for problems. The writers take a North American perspective in discussing examples in the text unless otherwise noted.

37   Chris Brewster, "Developing a European Model of Human Resource Management," *Journal of International Business Studies*, 26(1) (1995).

38   Ibid. For a comparison of these two orientations, besides the Brewster article, see Randall S. Schuler, Peter J. Dowling, and Helen De Cieri, "An Integrative Framework of Strategic International Human Resource Management," *Journal of Management*, 19(2) (1993): 419–59.

39   Athanassiou, *The Impact of Internationalization on Top Management Team Characteristics*.

40   Anne-Wil Harzing, "Of Bears, Bumble-Bees, and Spiders: The Role of Expatriates in Controlling Foreign Subsidiaries", *Journal of World Business*, 36(4): 366–79.

41   Janine Nahapiet and Sumantra Ghoshal, "Social Capital, Intellectual Capital, and the Organizational Advantage," *Academy of Management Review*, 23(2) (1998): 267–84. Ikujiro Nonaka,

"A Dynamic Theory of Organizational Knowledge Creation," *Organization Science*, 5(1) (1994): 14–37.

42 Stephen J. Kobrin, "Expatriate Reduction and Strategic Control in American Multinational Corporations," *Human Resource Management*, 27(1) (1988): 63–75. Roth Kendall, David Schweiger, and Allen Morrison, "Global Strategy Implementation at the Business Unit Level: Operational Capabilities and Administrative Mechanisms," *Journal of International Business Studies*, 22(3) (1991): 369–402.

43 *Global Relocation Trends: 2002 Survey Report*, GMAC Global Relocation Services in collaboration with the National Foreign Trade Council and SHRM Global Forum; March 2003 (www.gmacglobalrelocation.com).This survey covered 181 companies with about 2000 offices in 130 countries and a total of 35,150 expatriates. Of these companies, 77 percent had their headquarters in the United States. See also Mercer Human Resource Consulting, *2003 Survey of Expatriate Placements*, November 17, 2003. This survey covered more than 35,000 employees in over 220 multinational companies worldwide; www.mercerhr.com/pressrelease/details.jhtml/dynamic/idContent/1118245;jsessionid= 1RYYZEDUNMIGECIHAEEQOCA

44 *Global Relocation Trends: 2002 Survey Report.*

45 Anne-Wil Harzing. "Are our Referencing Errors Undermining our Scholarship and Credibility? The Case of Expatriate Failure Rates," *Journal of Organizational Behavior*, 23 (2002): 127–48.

46 Mercer Human Resource Consulting, *2002 Expatriate Risk Management Survey*, August 12, 2002; www.mercerhr.com/pressrelease/details.jhtml?idContent=1065135

47 E. L. Miller, "The International Selection Decision: A Study of Some Dimensions of Managerial Behavior in the Selection Decision Process," *Academy of Management Journal*, 16(2) (1973): 239–52.

48 Lesley Loraine, *2002 Expatriate Risk Management Survey*, Mercer Human Resource Consulting, August 12, 2002.

49 Daniel J. Kealey, *Cross-Cultural Effectiveness: A Study of Canadian Technical Advisors Overseas* (Ottawa: Canadian International Development Agency, 1990). This study was based on a sample of over 1,300 people, including technical advisors, their spouses, and host-country counterparts.

50 Ibid., p. 8.

51 Ibid.

52 Mendenhall, Dunbar, and Oddou, "Expatriate Selection."

53 Ibid.

54 M. Matteau, *Towards Meaningful and Effective Intercultural Encounters* (Hull, Canada: Intercultural Training and Briefing Centre, Canadian International Development Agency, 1993).

55 J. Stewart Black and Hal R. Gregersen, "When Yankee Comes Home: Factors Related to Expatriate and Spouse Repatriation Adjustment," *Journal of International Business Studies*, 22(4) (1991): 671–94; J. Stewart Black, Hal R. Gregersen, and Mark E. Mendenhall, "Toward a Theoretical Framework of Repatriation Adjustment," *Journal of International Business Studies*, 23(4) (1992): 737–60.

56 Charlene Marmer Solomon, "Repatriation: Up, Down, or Out?," *Personnel Journal*, 74 (1995): 28–37.

57 Some suggested readings on the topic of culture shock include: Ingemar Torbiorn, *Living Abroad: Personal Adjustment and Personnel Policy in the Overseas Setting* (Chichester, Sussex, England: John Wiley, 1982); Nancy Adler, *International Dimensions of Organizational Behavior*, 3rd edn. (Cincinnati, OH: South-Western College Publishing, 1997), Chapters 8 and 9; Kalvero Oberg, "Culture Shock: Adjustment to New Cultural Environments," *Practical Anthropology* 7 (1960): 177–82; C. L. Grove and I. Torbiorn, "A New Conceptualization of Intercultural Adjustment and the Goals of Training," *International Journal of Intercultural Relations*, 9(2) (1979).

58   Research on stress and adapting to stressful situations also suggests that there are physiological contributions as well. One reference that links physiology and culture shock is Gary Wederspahn, "Culture Shock: It's All in Your Head . . . and Body," *The Bridge* (1981): 10.

59   For these generalizations we are drawing on Torbiorn, *Living Abroad*; the research literature described by Adler in *International Dimensions*; an excellent, but unpublished paper by Clyde B. Sargent, "Psychological Aspects of Environmental Adjustment," Kalvero Oberg, "Culture Shock," *Practical Anthropologist*, 7 (1960): 177–82; and our own experience with numerous executives and students around the world.

60   Kealey, "Cross-Cultural Effectiveness."

61   Ibid., 39. This framework was developed by J. W. Berry, "Acculturation as Varieties of Adaptation," in A. Padilla (ed.), *Acculturation: Theory, Model, and Some New Findings* (Washington, DC: AAAS, 1980).

62   See Adler, *International Dimensions*, Chapter 8.

63   This statement is a good example of the North American instrumental orientation.

READING 4

Building Organizations Around the Global Customer

Jay Galbraith

Over the past decade, companies have assigned a higher priority to the customer dimension of their business operations. As a result, many companies are organizing their operations around the customer in general, and the global customer in particular. Creating these customer-facing organizational units is a challenge because these companies still have structures that are based on business units, countries and functions. This article addresses the challenge that an organization faces in creating and adding a global customer dimension. The first section deals with the increasing importance of the customer dimension. The second section describes the company's need to respond to the global customer priority. Finally, the article discusses how a company can build these new capabilities and integrate them into existing capabilities.

THE RISE OF THE CUSTOMER DIMENSION

The increasing importance of the customer is a trend in most industries. The factors causing this increase vary with the industry, but either individually or collectively, all businesses are contending with these factors. They are the:

1 Globalization of the customer
2 Preference of customers for partnerships or relationships
3 Customers' desire for solutions
4 Rise of electronic commerce
5 Steady increase in the power of the buyer.

Reprint Number 9B01TE02, *Ivey Business Journal*, September/October 2001, 66(1). Ivey Management Services prohibits any form of reproduction, storage or transmittal of this material without its written permission. This material is not covered under authorization from CanCopy or any other reproduction rights organization. © 2001 Ivey Management Services. One-time permission to reproduce granted by Ivey Management Services on 23 July 2004.

1 Globalization

Since 1985, globalization has been driven by increasing amounts of foreign direct investment. The result is that more companies, and therefore more customers, have a direct presence in more countries. Often, these global customers, who are preferred customers in many countries, object to the marginal treatment they receive from a supplier's subsidiary on entering a new country. These customers want a consistent and consistently high level of service in all countries where they buy from a supplier. Indeed, one supplier had a customer point out that 37 sales forces were calling on the firm, with 37 different standards of service. Understandably, that was unacceptable. So then, the global customer is creating pressure on suppliers to coordinate across countries and businesses to deliver better service. This desire for cross-unit coordination can also be an advantage for the supplier. ABB was an early mover into many countries, and Eastern Europe in particular. It now uses its extensive presence to host and provide services to customers as it enters new countries where ABB is already present.

Large companies B2B!

2 Customer relationships

The pressure to coordinate across existing structures is even greater when the customers want partnerships or relationships with their suppliers. Professional-services firms are finding that clients want one or two global advertising agencies, auditors, cash management/ banking suppliers, and outsourcers for information technology. In most industries, customers prefer fewer suppliers and closer, longer-term relationships with them. For suppliers, these global partnerships mean that they must coordinate activities in all countries in which the customer desires integrated services.

3 Solutions

Many customers prefer solutions or systems instead of stand-alone products. To be sure, customers still order truckloads of desktops from computer manufacturers. However, they also are ordering trading rooms or call centres. At IBM, these solutions require the integration of multiple business units in multiple countries with multiple outside suppliers, for the benefit of the customer. These solutions are not simply multiple stand-alone products that are bundled together and offered at a 10 percent discount. The customer-preferred solutions create value by packaging products and services in ways that the customers cannot easily do themselves.

They want customised service with their product purchase

Solutions therefore require an in-depth knowledge of the customer and an ability to integrate product lines. The in-depth customer knowledge is needed to identify the solutions that the customer will value. Then the supplier will need the ability to coordinate multiple profit centres from both inside and outside of the company to create the value. Neither of these capabilities comes easily. For example, real estate agencies and banks have been searching for years for a mortgage solution for time-short homebuyers. Such a solution would combine the home loan, appraisal, title, title insurance, home insurance, etc., into a single, sign-once package. Most of us are still waiting.

it called "Rent"

In addition to creating a solution, suppliers are also trying to customize them. Many companies are becoming sophisticated at identifying the most profitable customers. But while competing for the most profitable customers, companies can also "compete away" the profits. One approach to holding on to valuable customers is to customize the solutions that the customer wants. Customization requires yet more in-depth knowledge of the customer and an additional capability for integrating products and services into unique solutions.

4 Electronic commerce

Another force that is focusing attention on the customer is electronic commerce. When a company with a single brand uses its Web site as its storefront, it presents a single face to the customer. The Web site should be designed around the customers' needs and not around the suppliers' product capabilities. The site should be designed to do business the way the customer wants to do business. In order to appear as a single entity to the customer, the company needs to integrate its businesses, subsidiaries and functions and act like a single organization.

Interactivity with customers is another integrating force. Electronic connections allow the company to recognize and remember customers, to interact with them and remember more about them, and then to customize the firm's offerings based on its knowledge of the customer. Most companies, however, have not mastered integrated customer interactions. Interactivity requires the management of dialogues and content across all media the company uses to interact with the customer: Web site, e-mail, call centre, salespersons, service representatives and so on. The dialogue needs to be managed over time. The last contact with the customer needs to be remembered along with the last issue raised and how it was resolved. The resolution needs to be recorded, and then the next dialogue starts from there. All contacts and issues are to be remembered. The purpose of interactivity is to collect and integrate all data across all functions, subsidiaries and product lines in order to get a complete picture of each customer's value and needs. Only then can the company react as a single company, and be seen by the customer as a single company.

5 Buyer power

One of the main reasons that the factors mentioned above are taken seriously is that the power in the buyer-seller interaction has been shifting to the buyer. In many industries, global competition and industry overcapacity have given buyers more choice. They are now learning how to use it. Electronic commerce and information transparency have reduced the seller's knowledge advantages. So the competitive game has shifted to one of pleasing increasingly global, knowledgeable and powerful customers.

One of the responses that companies have made is to increasingly organize around the customer. Whether it is global accounts, global customer teams or customer business units, the trend is to grow a customer dimension. The customer focus is a challenge for most companies because many of them are organized around product lines called business units, countries and functions. The next section describes the capabilities needed to create a global customer dimension, while the last section describes how a company actually added, and then grew, such a global customer dimension.

DELIVER THE COMPANY TO THE CUSTOMER

Organizing around the customer requires three capabilities, and all are intended to deliver the company to the customer. To organize around the customer effectively, the company must:

1   Create a customer-centric capability
2   Perfect a lateral coordinating capability
3   Create a leadership mindset that says, "You compete with your organization."

1 Customer-centric capability

In order to create and customize solutions and appear as one organization on a customer-friendly Web site, the company needs to be customer-centric. This capability is often presented as a contrast to a product-centric capability. Table 1 shows the management mindset, culture and organizational features of a product-centric company.

A product-centric company is one that tries to find as many uses and customers as possible for its product. Sony and its Walkman are typical of such a company and product. Until recently, business units at Sony were even called Product Companies. As shown

TABLE 1   The Product-Centric Company

1   Best Product for Customer
2   Creates Value Through Cutting-edge Products, Useful Features, New Applications
3   DIVERGENT THINKING
    How Many Possible Uses of Product?
4   Manage Through Product Profit Centres, Product Reviews, Product Teams
5   MOST IMPORTANT PROCESS
    New Product Development
6   MEASURES
    • Number of New Products
    • % Revenue from Products Less Than Two Years Old
    • Market Share
7   New Product Culture – Open to New Ideas, Experimentation
8   Most Important Customer Is Advanced Customer
9   Priority-setting Around Portfolio of Products
10 Highest Reward Is Working on Next Most Challenging Product
11 Manage Creative People Through Challenges with a Deadline
12 Power to People Who Develop Products
13 On the Side of the Seller in a Transaction
14 Price to Market

[handwritten margin note: Contrast Table 1 with Table 2]

TABLE 2   The Customer-Centric Company

1	Best Solution for Customer
2	Creates Value Through Customizing for Best Total Solution
3	CONVERGENT THINKING What Combination of Products Are Best for This Customer?
4	Organized by Customer Segments, Customer Teams, Customer P&Ls
5	MOST IMPORTANT PROCESS Customer Relationships Management
6	MEASURES • Customer Share of Most Valuable Customers • Customer Satisfaction • Lifetime Value of a Customer • Customer Retention
7	Most Important Customer Is Most Profitable, Loyal Customer
8	Priority-setting Around Portfolio of Customers, Customer Profitability
9	Power to People with In-depth Knowledge of Customer's Business
10	Personalized Packages of Service, Support, Education, Consulting
11	On the Side of the Buyer in a Transaction
12	Price to Value and Risk Share

in Table 1, the profit centres, processes, measures and human resource policies are all focused on creating great products. Taken together, these policies create a culture of product excellence. Many good companies have thrived under this business model, like Hewlett-Packard, P&G and Chase Manhattan Consumer Bank. There is nothing wrong with this model when customers want to choose the best product and do the integrating themselves. But when customers want solutions and a friendly Web site, a customer-centric capability is also needed. A customer-centric capability is shown in Table 2.

A customer-centric company tries to find as many products as possible. It is based on economies of scope and on turning that scope into solutions that are valuable to the customer. The customer-centric company becomes an expert in the customer's business. It helps the customer become more effective or more competitive. Perhaps the most telling feature of a customer-centric company is that it is on the side of the buyer in the buyer-seller exchange. In order to stay on the customer's side, Amazon.com does not accept advertising from sellers. On its new e-Services Web site, the United Bank of Switzerland will offer competitive products, even those of Crédit Suisse. Thus, a customer-centric company will recommend the best product, even if it is a competitor's product, in order to earn the trust of the customer. The customer-centric company then sees these customer relationships as assets to be managed. The business model of Amazon.com and AOL has evolved to the point where they are now selling access to their customer base. A vendor must qualify, then pay a fee and/or give Amazon some of its equity, in order to access its 29 million proven Internet shoppers.

The argument above has painted the extremes of product and customer centricity. Not every company will need the extreme model of customer centricity. The main point is that in most businesses today, the forces of the business are requiring a more customer-centric orientation. This orientation is achieved by creating organizational units for global customers or customer segments, and the leadership mindsets to support them. The next section describes a variety of these global customer organizations.

2 Lateral networking capability

In order to create multiproduct solutions for global customers, a company must work through lateral networks. A simple company with a few local customers selling a single product can work through a functional hierarchy. But a company with multiple product lines in multiple countries using multiple functions must work less through hierarchy and more through networks. Indeed, a company needs a network for each strategically important dimension. Some companies like General Electric have organized around global product lines called Business Units. They have created country and functional networks to coordinate across product lines. Other companies like Nestlé have organized around country and regional profit centres. They have created product (called Strategic Business Units) and functional networks to coordinate across the geographical structure. The rise in importance of the customer dimension has created a need for a global customer network that crosses product lines, countries and functions.

Various successful but different strategies

The organization-design decision is based on matching the right kind of network with the strategic importance of the customer dimension; that is, there are different kinds of networks. Some are informal while others are formal with varying degrees of strength. The job of coordinating these networks across geographical structures will vary according to those networks' power and cost. The list of networks that follows is ordered with the simplest, cheapest and easiest to use noted first. The farther down the list a company goes, the more powerful the networks will be, and the more costly and difficult it will be to employ them. The implication is that the designers should start at the top of the list and proceed down until a network is found which matches the requirements for coordinating the customer dimension for their business.

List of Networks:

1   Informal or voluntary networks
2   Formal teams
3   Coordinator for the network
4   Matrix across the other dimensions
5   Separate customer line organization

1 Informal or voluntary networks   Informal or voluntary networks form naturally in all organizations. Management, however, can initiate them and then let them proceed under their own energy. Nestlé is an example of a company where informal networks have formed around global customers. Unlike P&G, Nestlé has not strategically focused on cross-border customers such as Carrefour or Wal-Mart. However, country managers and country account managers for Wal-Mart routinely exchange information and ideas about Wal-Mart on an informal basis. This informal exchange was judged to be sufficient until the Internet allowed more formal communication. Now the account manager in the country of the global customer's headquarters maintains a database about that customer and issues e-mails and updates about the company. Anyone dealing with the customer can add information and ideas. But while the communication has been formalized, the coordination is still informal. Each country treats the information as an input, and then acts in the best interest of its product lines and country P&L.

Formalizing communication among all people interacting with customers is one approach a company can take to show one face to the customer. Each contact is recorded and entered into a database. Others can see this running record when they deal with the customer. Each person then deals with the customer according to their function, but records all information to be used across functions.

2 Formal teams Formal teams are the next level of strength that can be applied to a customer network. This step is usually taken when a customer desires more than informal coordination. For example, global or key account teams are formed by appointing all the sales and account representatives serving a customer to one account team for that customer. These representatives from all product lines and all countries exchange information, much like Nestlé's informal networks. But they also meet regularly, prepare an account plan, and agree upon customer-specific goals. ABB started with teams for a few accounts, and within a few years it had more than 50 teams for those customers who wanted this coordinated service. The account manager in the customer's home country usually leads the team, which consists of a few core members and a larger, extended team that encompasses the salespeople from all of the customer's locations.

The customer teams can be strengthened and assume more activities when customers want partnerships along the supply chain. Wal-Mart and P&G are an example. P&G initially formed a team of its salespeople representing all the products that P&G provided to Wal-Mart. The team was expanded to include manufacturing, distribution, marketing, information technology and finance personnel. This team of about 80 people from various functions from all product lines worked to synchronize the product and order flow from P&G's factories to Wal-Mart's warehouses. Its goal was to minimize inventories and cut cycle times. Today, as Wal-Mart expands globally, this team consists of 450 people from different functions, product lines and countries.

Degussa Automotive Catalysts, which creates customer-specific, platform-specific catalysts for exhaust emissions, takes the team approach one step further and includes R&D personnel. The Degussa salespeople coordinate across borders to serve DaimlerChrysler, in the same way that ABB serves its customers. It also partners along the supply chain to synchronize its production with the DaimlerChrysler assembly lines, like P&G and Wal-Mart. But its engineers also determine DaimlerChrysler's new product needs, and coordinate with it on creating new catalysts for new automotive platforms.

These formal customer networks can vary in size from a few key account teams for salespeople, to supply-chain partnership teams of sales, logistics and other functional people, to new product-development teams that include all functions. For some companies, like Degussa, this customer-team organization is sufficient to meet the needs of its most important customer. Other companies, like Citibank, chose to take a further step of creating a full-time coordinator to manage all of the customer-team activities.

3 Network coordinator The next step in making the global customer dimension more powerful is to create a coordinator for key accounts. When companies like ABB create

50 or more teams, and customers want still more coordination, it is useful to add the Key Account or Global Account coordinator role to the informal networks and formal customer teams. The coordinator performs two important, new functions.

First, the coordinator becomes the global customer's voice on the management team. These teams usually consist of managers of product lines, geographies and functions. The coordinator gets the leadership to think in terms of a portfolio of customers, customer priorities and customer centricity. Customer teams can also appeal to the coordinator in resolving conflicts.

The second task of the coordinator is to build and manage the infrastructure to support customer teams. The formal communications were mentioned earlier. The coordinator would assume the role of managing customer information systems and communications across customer teams. She usually creates training programs for management and team members on the role and operation of key accounts. Many coordinators create a common planning system for customers. If 50 customer teams are creating plans, they are likely to create 50 planning formats. The coordinator decides on a single, common one.

Another key addition to the infrastructure is a global customer accounting system that leads to customer P&Ls. Customer profitability is a key measure in setting customer priorities. In addition, asymmetries in costs and revenues always occur across geographies. That is, the customer account manager and team in the customer's home country put in extra effort to make a sale to their customer. Often, the initiative is successful, but the customer's first purchases may be for its subsidiaries in other countries. Thus the costs are incurred in the home country and revenues are booked in other countries. A global accounting system for customers can identify these asymmetries and management can correct for them.

All of these infrastructure additions can be combined in the planning process. The countries and product lines can then set customer-specific goals for key accounts. Then, customer teams, countries and product lines will pursue an aligned set of goals.

4 Matrix organization   The next step for enhancing the power base of the global customer dimension is to form customer or customer segment-dedicated units within countries and product lines and then report to the customer coordinator. The assumption is that the customer dimension has attained a strategic importance equal to the countries and/or business units. This importance is expressed by making the customer organization an equal partner in the decision-making process. In countries where the company may not control 100 percent of the equity, joint ventures to serve multinational clients are often created between the parent company and the local subsidiary.

5 Separate customer organization   A final step is creating a separate customer-facing structure by gathering all dedicated customer-specific resources from the product lines, countries and functions. Companies serving the automotive customer, like Johnson Controls, have formed Customer Business Units. Companies like IBM formed customer-segment profit centres by gathering all relationship managers into industry groups. These global industry groups call on product profit centres for additional staffing, as the opportunities require. These separate customer-facing units are the most powerful and customer-centric form of organizing around the customer.

In summary, there are five major steps an organizational designer can take to implement a customer-centric orientation. A step-by-step approach is probably best for implementing and building the customer-centric capability. The designer may stop on any of the steps when enough customer centricity has been built to match the strength of the five customer forces described in the first section of this article.

6 The organization as competitive advantage   The third factor needed to deliver the company to the customer is a mindset among leadership that it is competing against its own organization. That is, the company's ability to deliver value to global customers depends on the organization's ability to assemble and implement a customer-centric dimension across the existing business unit, country and functional organizations. Delivering value to today's customer means managing the four dimensions of the organization.

internal entrepreneur

The creation of a four-dimensional organization runs counter to most current mindsets. Today, the preferred way is to "keep it simple" – create simple, autonomous business units which control their resources and which can be accountable for their performance.

We also believe in keeping it simple, but with the twist that we want to "keep it simple for the customer." Organizations should be designed to do business in the way that the customer wants to do business. And how do customers want to do business? They want solutions that are seamlessly integrated across the products of multiple business units and countries. But achieving this integration is difficult, and keeping it simple for the customer makes it difficult for management. But mastering that difficulty becomes a real source of competitive advantage. Most companies cannot easily integrate their profit centres with servicing a customer. And since many customers see value in this integration, competitive advantage comes from creating this value that others cannot match. Mastering the difficulty of managing four dimensions is just such an advantage.

When most people say, "keep it simple," they mean keep it simple for management. That kind of simplicity, then, means making it difficult for the customer. It is then up to the customer or some third party to do the integrating and capture the value of serving the customer. Keeping it simple for management leaves money on the table for more complex organizations to capture.

The management of Degussa Auto Catalysts recognized that their organization was their secret weapon. It partnered with their customers on developing new engines and new catalysts. It formed global customer teams across functions and countries. It created global customer profit-and-loss measurement systems. The members of the Executive Committee sat on the teams. Issues were quickly dealt with and resolved, since only one level separated the teams and the leadership. It recognized that the link between R&D and manufacturing was critical. It created an Applied Technology Group, organized by customer, to bridge the gap. It exchanged people across the Manufacturing-R&D interface. It co-located the two units and sponsored workshops to improve the process of working together. These workshops were held overnight, allowing people to get to know one another and build interpersonal networks. Management rewarded those people who were effective in this environment, and removed those who fought it. In short, Degussa management knew that it was competing with their organization as well as with their technology.

In summary, it takes a customer-centric capability, a lateral networking capability and a leadership that sees and builds its organization as a source of advantage in order to deliver the company to the global customer. But how does one build these capabilities if the company does not possess them today? In short, the capabilities are built by moving down the list of lateral coordination mechanisms. The next section traces the steps of Citibank's Global Relationship Bank.

BUILDING A CUSTOMER DIMENSION

In 1984, Citibank's commercial banking business was examining its ability to serve its multinational clients. The informal contacts between relationship managers in different countries were insufficient for servicing these customers. After some debate, Citibank resurrected the World Corporation Group (WCG) to serve a coordinating role, and created global account teams for a few interested customers.

After a couple of years, the teams had expanded from a few to a few hundred. For each team, there was a leader – a Principal Account Manager (PAM) from the customer's home country. In countries where the customer wanted more service, there was a Subsidiary Account Manager (SAM). The WCG trained all of these teams. So in several years, thousands of people were trained in customer relationships. The Nestlé team alone consisted of 60 people. The WCG also started recruiting and training the PAMs. These account managers usually stayed in the WCG.

The WCG also trained top management to manage a portfolio of customers. It developed a customer-focused planning system, and measures of customer profitability and its own share of the customer's spending. It developed customer P&Ls, and then, in 1995, it led a strategy review. In that review, Citibank articulated its customer-first strategy. Before, the priorities were country first, product second and customer third. After 1995 the priorities were customer first, product second and country third (in the developed world). The strategy recognized that Citibank was a bank (took deposits and made loans in local currencies) in over 100 countries. Its nearest competitor was a bank in only 43 countries. Citibank had the unmatchable advantage of global presence from which to serve the global customer. All it had to do was to get 100 country managers to work together.

So in 1995, Citibank created a global-customer, profit-centred organization. It eliminated country P&Ls in the developed world and grouped 1,300 customers into industry segments. It focused on delivering global products, foreign exchange and cash management to the global customer. It stopped serving domestic-only customers.

Today, this Global Relationship Bank serves over 1,700 customers. It is delivering the product-centric capabilities of Salomon, Schroeders, Smith Barney to its global customers through its customer-centric Global Relationship Bank. The *Financial Times* (July 20, 2000) suggested that the synergies between investment banking products and the global customer relationship group have earned a place for Citigroup among the bulge-bracket firms of Goldman Sachs, Morgan Stanley, and Merrill Lynch. Citibank's profits are higher than these firms, and it is trading at a higher earnings multiple. So, from a base of informal contacts in 1985, Citibank built a customer-centric, lateral capability to deliver the bank's services to the customer anywhere in the world.

The Design and Management of International Joint Ventures

Paul W. Beamish

An international joint venture is a company that is owned by two or more firms of different nationality. International joint ventures may be formed from a starting (or greenfield) basis or may be the result of several established companies deciding to merge existing divisions. However they are formed, the purpose of most international joint ventures is to allow partners to pool resources and coordinate their efforts to achieve results that neither could obtain acting alone.

International joint ventures and other forms of corporate alliances have become increasingly popular. For example, in the airline sector, virtually every major carrier has links with foreign carriers. These may be equity- or nonequity (i.e., code share, frequent flyer programs, etc.)-based and are culminating in truly global network arrangements such as Star Alliance and One World.

As Exhibit 1 illustrates, a broad range of strategic alliances exists. They vary widely in terms of the level of interaction and type. Most of the comments in this chapter focus on equity joint venture – the alliance form usually requiring the greatest level of interaction, cooperation, and investment. However, some but not all the issues are applicable to other forms of alliances. For example, IKEA, the giant Swedish furniture retailer, operates a series of nonequity buyer–supplier alliances around the world. IKEA provides component suppliers with product design, technical assistance, leased equipment, and even loans. IKEA's suppliers get new skills, direct access to a large and growing retailer, and steadier sales. This not only generates for IKEA low-cost and high-quality supply but a sense of partnership with, and loyalty to/from, suppliers.

Joint ventures have moved from being a way to enter foreign markets of peripheral interest to become a part of the mainstream of corporate activity. Virtually all MNEs are using international joint ventures, many as a key element of their corporate strategies. Merck, for example, has joint ventures with Johnson & Johnson (2001 JV sales of

EXHIBIT 1 Range of Strategic Alliances

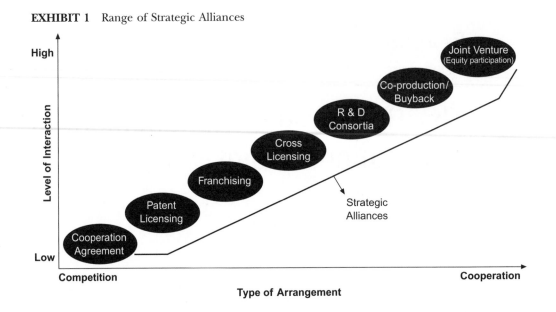

$.4 billion), Aventis Pasteur (2001 JV sales of $.5 billion), Rhône-Poulenc (2001 JV sales of $1.7 billion), and so forth. Even firms that have traditionally operated independently around the world are increasingly turning to joint ventures.

The popularity and use of international joint ventures and cooperative alliances remained strong through the 1990s. The rate of joint venture use does not change much from year to year. In general, joint ventures are the mode of choice about 35 percent of the time by US multinationals and in 40 to 45 percent of foreign subsidiaries formed by Japanese multinationals.

The popularity of alliances has continued despite their reputation for being difficult to manage. Failures exist and are usually widely publicized. Dow Chemical, for example, reportedly lost more than $100 million after a dispute with its Korean joint venture partners caused the firm to sell its 50 percent interest in its Korean venture at a loss, and to sell below cost its nearby wholly owned chemical plant. Also, after Lucent's joint venture in wireless handsets with Philips Electronics ended, Lucent took a $100 million charge at the time on selling its consumer phone equipment business. Similarly, HealthMatics, a joint venture between Glaxo Smith Kline and Physician Computer Network Inc. shut down after losing more than $50 million.

While early surveys suggested that as many as half the companies with international joint ventures were dissatisfied with their ventures' performance, there is reason to believe that some of the earlier concern can now be ameliorated. This is primarily because there is far greater alliance experience and insight to draw from. There is now widespread appreciation that joint ventures are not necessarily transitional organization forms, shorter-lived, or less profitable. For many organizations they are the mode of choice.

There now also exists an Association of Strategic Alliance Professionals (ASAP). It was created to support the professional development of alliance managers and executives to advance the state-of-the-art of alliance formation and management and to provide a forum

EXHIBIT 2 Motives for International Joint Venture Formation

	Existing Products	**New Products**
New Markets	To take existing products to foreign markets	To diversify into a new business
Existing Markets	To strengthen the existing business	To bring foreign products to local markets

for sharing alliance best practices, resources and opportunities to help companies improve their alliance management capabilities.

Why do managers keep creating new joint ventures? The reasons are presented in the remainder of this chapter, as are some guidelines for international joint venture success.

WHY COMPANIES CREATE INTERNATIONAL JOINT VENTURES

International joint ventures can be used to achieve one of four basic purposes. As shown in Exhibit 2, these are: to strengthen the firm's existing business, to take the firm's existing products into new markets, to obtain new products that can be sold in the firm's existing markets, and to diversify into a new business.

Companies using joint ventures for each of these purposes will have different concerns and will be looking for partners with different characteristics. Firms wanting to strengthen their existing business, for example, will most likely be looking for partners among their current competitors, while those wanting to enter new geographic markets will be looking for overseas firms in related businesses with good local market knowledge. Although often treated as a single category of business activity, international joint ventures are remarkably diverse, as the following descriptions indicate.

STRENGTHENING THE EXISTING BUSINESS

International joint ventures are used in a variety of ways by firms wishing to strengthen or protect their existing businesses. Among the most important are joint ventures formed to achieve economies of scale, joint ventures that allow the firm to acquire needed technology and know-how, and ventures that reduce the financial risk of major projects. Joint ventures formed for the latter two reasons may have the added benefit of eliminating a potential competitor from a particular product or market area.

Achieving economies of scale

Firms often use joint ventures to attempt to match the economies of scale achieved by their larger competitors. Joint ventures have been used to give their parents economies of scale in raw material and component supply, in research and development, and in marketing and distribution. Joint ventures have also been used as a vehicle for carrying out divisional mergers, which yield economies across the full spectrum of business activity.

Very small, entrepreneurial firms are more likely to participate in a network than an equity joint venture in order to strengthen their business through economies of scale. Small firms may form a network to reduce the costs, and increase the potential, of foreign market entry, or to meet some other focused objective. Most of these networks tend to have a relatively low ease of entry and exit and a loose structure and require a limited investment (primarily time, as they might be self-financing through fees). International equity joint ventures by very small firms are unusual because such firms must typically overcome some combination of liabilities of size, newness, foreignness, and relational orientation (often the small firms were initially successful because of their single-minded, do-it-themselves orientation).

Raw material and component supply

In many industries the smaller firms create joint ventures to obtain raw materials or jointly manufacture components. Automakers, for instance, may develop a jointly owned engine plant to supply certain low-volume engines to each company. Producing engines for the parents provides economies of scale, with each company receiving engines at a lower cost than it could obtain if it were to produce them itself.

The managers involved in such ventures are quick to point out that these financial savings do not come without a cost. Design changes in jointly produced engines, for example, tend to be slow because all partners have to agree on them. In fact, one joint venture that produced computer printers fell seriously behind the state of the art in printer design because the parents could not agree on the features they wanted in the jointly designed printer. Because all of the venture's output was sold to the parents, the joint venture personnel had no direct contact with end customers and could not resolve the dispute.

Transfer pricing is another issue that arises in joint ventures that supply their parents. A low transfer price on products shipped from the venture to the parents, for instance, means that whichever parent buys the most product obtains the most benefit. Many higher-volume-taking parents claim that this is fair, as it is their volume that plays an important role in making the joint venture viable. On the other hand, some parents argue for a higher transfer price, which means that the economic benefits are captured in the venture and will flow, most likely via dividends, to the parents in proportion to their share holdings in the venture. As the share holdings generally reflect the original asset contributions to the venture and not the volumes taken out every year, this means that different parents will do well under this arrangement. Clearly, the potential for transfer price disputes is significant.

Research and development

Shared research and development efforts are increasingly common. The rationale for such programs is that participating firms can save both time and money by collaborating and may, by combining the efforts of the participating companies' scientists, come up with results that would otherwise have been impossible.

The choice facing firms wishing to carry out collaborative research is whether to simply coordinate their efforts and share costs or to actually set up a jointly owned company. Hundreds of multicompany research programs are not joint ventures. Typically, scientists from the participating companies agree on the research objectives and the most likely avenues of exploration to achieve those objectives. If there are, say, four promising ways to attack a particular problem, each of four participating companies would be assigned one route and told to pursue it. Meetings would be held, perhaps quarterly, to share results and approaches taken and when (hopefully) one route proved to be successful, all firms would be fully informed on the new techniques and technology.

The alternative way to carry out collaborative research is to establish a jointly owned company and to provide it with staff, budget, and a physical location. Yet even here, problems may occur. In the United States, the president of a joint research company established by a dozen US computer firms discovered that the participating companies were not sending their best people to the new company. He ended up hiring more than 200 of the firm's 330 scientists from the outside.

A sensitive issue for firms engaging in collaborative research, whether through joint ventures or not, is how far the collaboration should extend. Because the partners are usually competitors, the often expressed ideal is that the joint effort will focus only on "precompetitive" basic research and not, for example, on product development work. This is often a difficult line to draw.

Marketing and distribution

Many international joint ventures involve shared research, development, and production but stop short of joint marketing. The vehicles coming out of the widely publicized joint venture between Toyota and General Motors in California, for instance, are clearly branded as GM or Toyota products and are sold competitively through each parent's distribution network. Antitrust plays a role in the decision to keep marketing activities separate, but so does the partners' intrinsic desire to maintain separate brand identities and increase their own market share. These cooperating firms have not forgotten that they are competitors.

There are, nevertheless, some ventures formed for the express purpose of achieving economies in marketing and distribution. Here, each firm is hoping for wider market coverage at a lower cost. The trade-off is a loss of direct control over the sales force, potentially slower decision making, and a possible loss of direct contact with the customer.

Somewhat similar in intent are cooperative marketing agreements, which are not joint ventures but agreements by two firms with related product lines to sell one another's products. Here companies end up with a more complete line to sell, without the managerial complications of a joint venture. Sometimes the cooperative marketing agreement can in fact entail joint branding.

Divisional mergers

Multinational companies with subsidiaries that they have concluded are too small to be economic have sometimes chosen to create a joint venture by combining their "too small" operations with those of a competitor. Fiat and Peugeot, for example, merged their automobile operations in Argentina, where both companies were doing poorly. The new joint venture started life with a market share of 35 percent and a chance for greatly improved economies in design, production, and marketing. Faced with similar pressures, Ford and Volkswagen have done the same thing in Brazil, creating a jointly owned company called Auto Latina.

A divisional merger can also allow a firm a graceful exit from a business in which it is no longer interested. Honeywell gave up trying to continue alone in the computer industry when it folded its business into a venture with Machines Bull of France and NEC of Japan. Honeywell held a 40 percent stake in the resulting joint venture.

Acquiring technology in the core business

Firms that have wanted to acquire technology in their core business area have traditionally done so through license agreements or by developing the technology themselves. Increasingly, however, companies are turning to joint ventures for this purpose, because developing technology in-house is seen as taking too long, and license agreements, while giving the firm access to patent rights and engineers' ideas, may not provide much in the way of shop floor know-how. The power of a joint venture is that a firm may be able to have its employees working shoulder to shoulder with those of its partner, trying to solve the same problems. For example, the General Motors joint venture with Toyota provided an opportunity for GM to obtain a source of low-cost small cars and to watch firsthand how Toyota managers, who were in operational control of the venture, were able to produce high-quality automobiles at low cost. Most observers have concluded that the opportunity for General Motors to learn new production techniques was more significant than the supply of cars coming from the venture.

Reducing financial risk

Some projects are too big or too risky for firms to tackle alone. This is why oil companies use joint ventures to split the costs of searching for new oil fields, and why the aircraft industry is increasingly using joint ventures and "risk-sharing subcontractors" to put up some of the funds required to develop new aircraft and engines.

Do such joint ventures make sense? For the oil companies the answer is a clear yes. In these ventures, one partner takes a lead role and manages the venture on a day-to-day basis. Management complexity, a major potential drawback of joint ventures, is kept to a minimum. If the venture finds oil, transfer prices are not a problem – the rewards of the venture are easy to divide between the partners. In situations like this, forming a joint venture is an efficient and sensible way of sharing risk.

It is not as obvious that some other industry ventures are a good idea, at least not for industry leaders. Their partners are not entering these ventures simply in the hope of earning an attractive return on their investment. They are gearing up to produce, sooner or later, their own product. Why would a company be willing to train potential competitors? For many firms, it is the realization that their partner is going to hook up with someone anyway, so better to have a portion of a smaller future pie than none at all, even if it means you may be eventually competing against yourself.

TAKING PRODUCTS TO FOREIGN MARKETS

Firms with domestic products that they believe will be successful in foreign markets face a choice. They can produce the product at home and export it, license the technology to local firms around the world, establish wholly owned subsidiaries in foreign countries, or form joint ventures with local partners. Many firms conclude that exporting is unlikely to lead to significant market penetration, building wholly owned subsidiaries is too slow and requires too many resources, and licensing does not offer an adequate financial return. The result is that an international joint venture, while seldom seen as an ideal choice, is often the most attractive compromise.

Moving into foreign markets entails a degree of risk, and most firms that decide to form a joint venture with a local firm are doing so to reduce the risk associated with their new market entry. Very often, they look for a partner that deals with a related product line and, thus, has a good feel for the local market. As a further risk-reducing measure, the joint venture may begin life as simply a sales and marketing operation, until the product begins to sell well and volumes rise. Then a "screwdriver" assembly plant may be set up to assemble components shipped from the foreign parent. Eventually, the venture may modify or redesign the product to better suit the local market and may establish complete local manufacturing, sourcing raw material and components locally. The objective is to withhold major investment until the market uncertainty is reduced.

Following customers to foreign markets   Another way to reduce the risk of a foreign market entry is to follow firms that are already customers at home. Thus, many Japanese automobile suppliers have followed Honda, Toyota, and Nissan as they set up new plants in North America and Europe. Very often these suppliers, uncertain of their ability to operate in a foreign environment, decide to form a joint venture with a local partner. There are, for example, a great many automobile supplier joint ventures in the United States originally formed between Japanese and American auto suppliers to supply the Japanese "transplant" automobile manufacturers. For the Americans, such ventures provide a way to learn Japanese manufacturing techniques and to tap into a growing market.

Investing in "markets of the future"   Some of the riskiest joint ventures are those established by firms taking an early position in what they see as emerging markets. These areas offer very large untapped markets, as well as a possible source of low-cost raw materials and labor. The major problems faced by Western firms in penetrating such markets are their unfamiliarity with the local culture, establishing Western attitudes toward quality, and, in some areas, repatriating earnings in hard currency. The solution (sometimes imposed by local government) has often been the creation of joint ventures with local partners who "know the ropes" and can deal with the local bureaucracy.

Even a local partner, however, is no guarantee of success, as the rules of the game can change overnight in such regions. This can be due to a new government coming to power, a revision of existing practice in response to a financial crisis, pressure from international funding agencies, and so forth.

BRINGING FOREIGN PRODUCTS TO LOCAL MARKETS

For every firm that uses an international joint venture to take its product to a foreign market, a local company sees the joint venture as an attractive way to bring a foreign product to its existing market. It is, of course, this complementarity of interest that makes the joint venture possible.

Local partners enter joint ventures to get better utilization of existing plants or distribution channels, to protect themselves against threatening new technology, or simply as an impetus for new growth. Typically, the financial rewards that the local partner receives from a venture are different from those accruing to the foreign partner. For example:

- Many foreign partners make a profit shipping finished products and components to their joint ventures. These profits are particularly attractive because they are in hard currency, which may not be true of the venture's profits, and because the foreign partner captures 100 percent of them, not just a share.
- Many foreign partners receive a technology fee, which is a fixed percentage of the sales volume of the joint venture. The local partner may or may not receive a management fee of like amount.
- Foreign partners typically pay a withholding tax on dividends remitted to them from the venture. Local firms do not.

As a result of these differences, the local partner is often far more concerned with the venture's bottom line earnings and dividend payout than the foreign partner. This means the foreign partner is likely to be happier to keep the venture as simply a marketing or assembly operation, as previously described, than to develop it to the point where it buys less imported material.

Although this logic is understandable, such thinking is shortsighted. The best example of the benefits that can come back to a parent from a powerful joint venture is Fuji Xerox, a venture begun in Japan in 1962 between Xerox and Fuji Photo. This is among the best known American–Japanese joint ventures in Japan.

For the first 10 years of its life, Fuji Xerox was strictly a marketing organization. It did its best to sell Xerox copiers in the Japanese market, even though the US company had done nothing to adapt the machine to the Japanese market. For example, to reach the print button on one model, Japanese secretaries had to stand on a box. After 10 years of operation, Fuji Xerox began to manufacture its own machines, and by 1975 it was redesigning US equipment for the Japanese market. Soon thereafter, with the encouragement of Fuji Photo, and in spite of the resistance of Xerox engineers in the United States, the firm began to design its own copier equipment. Its goal was to design and build a copier in half the time and at half the cost of previous machines. When this was accomplished, the firm set its sights on winning the Deming award, a highly coveted Japanese prize for excellence in total quality control. Fuji Xerox won the award in 1980.

It was also in 1980 that Xerox, reeling under the impact of intense competition from Japanese copier companies, finally began to pay attention to the lessons that it could learn from Fuji Xerox. Adopting the Japanese joint venture's manufacturing techniques and quality programs, the parent company fought its way back to health in the mid-1980s. By 1991, Xerox International Partners was established as a joint venture between Fuji Xerox and Xerox Corporation to sell low-end printers in North America and Europe. In 1998, exports to the United States grew substantially with digital color copiers and OEM printer engines. By 2002, Fuji Xerox Co. Ltd. had about $8 billion in revenues, was responsible for the design and manufacture of many digital color copiers and printers for Xerox worldwide, and was an active partner in research and development. Both the lessons learned from Fuji Xerox and the contributions they have made to Xerox have inevitably helped Xerox prosper as an independent company.

USING JOINT VENTURES FOR DIVERSIFICATION

As the previous examples illustrate, many joint ventures take products that one parent knows well into a market that the other knows well. However, some break new ground and move one or both parents into products and markets that are new to them.

Arrangements to acquire the skills necessary to compete in a new business is a long-term proposition, but one that some firms are willing to undertake. Given the fact that most acquisitions of unrelated businesses do not succeed, and that trying to enter a new business without help is extremely difficult, choosing partners who will help you learn the business may not be a bad strategy if you are already familiar with the partner. However, to enter a new market, with a new product, and a new partner – even when the probability of success for each is 80 percent – leaves one with an overall probability of success of $(.8 \times .8 \times .8)$ about 50 percent!

In recent years, there has been some discussion about whether joint ventures can be viewed as vehicles for learning. Here the modes of learning go beyond knowledge transfer (i.e., existing know-how) to include transformation and harvesting. In practice, most IJV partners engage in the transfer of existing knowledge, but stop short of knowledge transformation or harvesting. Although many multinational enterprises have very large numbers of international equity joint ventures and alliances, only a small percentage dedicate resources explicitly to learning about the alliance process. Few organizations go to the trouble of inventorying/cataloguing the corporate experience with joint ventures, let alone how the accumulated knowledge might be transferred within or between

---

EXHIBIT 3 Joint Venture Checklist

---

1 Test the strategic logic.
   - Do you really need a partner? For how long? Does your partner?
   - How big is the payoff for both parties? How likely is success?
   - Is a joint venture the best option?
   - Do congruent performance measures exist?
2 Partnership and fit.
   - Does the partner share your objectives for the venture?
   - Does the partner have the necessary skills and resources? Will you get access to them?
   - Will you be compatible?
   - Can you arrange an "engagement period"?
   - Is there a comfort versus competence trade-off?
3 Shape and design.
   - Define the venture's scope of activity and its strategic freedom vis-à-vis its parents.
   - Lay out each parent's duties and payoffs to create a win-win situation. Ensure that there are comparable contributions over time.
   - Establish the managerial role of each partner.
4 Doing the deal.
   - How much paperwork is enough? Trust versus legal considerations?
   - Agree on an endgame.
5 Making the venture work.
   - Give the venture continuing top management attention.
   - Manage cultural differences.
   - Watch out for inequities.
   - Be flexible.

---

divisions. This oversight will be increasingly costly for firms, especially as some of the bilateral alliances become part of multilateral networks.

REQUIREMENTS FOR INTERNATIONAL JOINT VENTURE SUCCESS

The checklist in Exhibit 3 presents many of the items that a manager should consider when establishing an international joint venture. Each of these is discussed in the following sections.

Testing the strategic logic

The decision to enter a joint venture should not be taken lightly. Joint ventures require a great deal of management attention, and, in spite of the care and attention they receive, many prove unsatisfactory to their parents.

Firms considering entering a joint venture should satisfy themselves that there is not a simpler way, such as a nonequity alliance, to get what they need. They should also carefully consider the time period for which they are likely to need help. Joint ventures have been labeled "permanent solutions to temporary problems" by firms that entered a venture to get help on some aspect of their business; then, when they no longer needed the help, they were still stuck with the joint venture.

EXHIBIT 4   Measuring JV Performance: The Search for Congruity

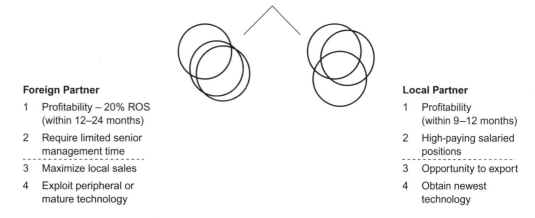

Foreign Partner

1   Profitability – 20% ROS
    (within 12–24 months)

2   Require limited senior
    management time

- -

3   Maximize local sales

4   Exploit peripheral or
    mature technology

Local Partner

1   Profitability
    (within 9–12 months)

2   High-paying salaried
    positions

- -

3   Opportunity to export

4   Obtain newest
    technology

The same tough questions a firm may ask itself before forming a joint venture need to be asked of its partner. How long will the partner need it? Is the added potential pay-off high enough to both partners to compensate for the increased coordination/communications costs which go with the formation of a joint venture?

A major issue in the discussion of strategic logic is to determine whether congruent measures of performance exist. As Exhibit 4 suggests, in many joint ventures, incongruity exists. In this example the foreign partner was looking for a joint venture that would generate 20 percent return on sales in a 1–2 year period and require a limited amount of senior management time. The local partner in turn was seeking a JV that would be quickly profitable and be able to justify some high-paying salaried positions (for the local partner and several family members/friends). While each partner's performance object-ives seem defensible, this venture would need to resolve several major problem areas in order to succeed. First, each partner did not make explicit all their primary performance objectives. Implicit measures (those below the dotted line in Exhibit 4), are a source of latent disagreement/misunderstanding. Second, the explicit versus implicit measures of each partner were internally inconsistent. The foreign partner wanted high profitability while using little senior management time and old technology. The local partner wanted quick profits but high-paying local salaries.

Partnership and fit

Joint ventures are sometimes formed to satisfy complementary needs. But when one partner acquires (learns) another's capabilities, the joint venture becomes unstable. The acquisition of a partner's capabilities means that the partner is no longer needed. If capabilities are only accessed, the joint venture is more stable. It is not easy, before a venture begins, to determine many of the things a manager would most like to know about a potential partner, like the true extent of its capabilities, what its objectives are in form-ing the venture, and whether it will be easy to work with. A hasty answer to such questions may lead a firm into a bad relationship or cause it to pass up a good opportunity.

For these reasons, it is often best if companies begin a relationship in a small way, with a simple agreement that is important but not a matter of life and death to either parent. As confidence between the firms grows, the scope of the business activities can broaden.

A good example is provided by Corning Glass, which in 1970 made a major breakthrough in the development of optical fibers that could be used for telecommunication applications, replacing traditional copper wire or coaxial cable. The most likely customers of this fiber outside the United States were the European national telecoms, which were well known to be very nationalistic purchasers. To gain access to these customers, Corning set up development agreements with companies in England, France, Germany, and Italy that were already suppliers to the telecoms. These agreements called for the European firms to develop the technology necessary to combine the fibers into cables, while Corning itself continued to develop the optical fibers. Soon the partners began to import fiber from Corning and cable it locally. Then, when the partners were comfortable with each other and each market was ready, Corning and the partners set up joint ventures to produce optical fiber locally. These ventures have worked extremely well, and their continuing success became particularly important in the late 1980s, as growth in the US market leveled off. Corning is widely acknowledged as one of the world's most successful users of joint ventures.

When assessing issues around partnership and fit, it is useful to consider whether the partner not only shares the same objectives for the venture but also has a similar appetite for risk. In practice this often results in joint ventures having parents of roughly comparable size. It is difficult for parent firms of very different size to establish sustainable joint ventures because of varying resource sets, payback period requirements, and corporate cultures.

Corporate culture similarity – or compatibility – can be a make-or-break issue in many joint ventures. It is not enough to find a partner with the necessary skills, you need to be able to get access to them and to be compatible. Managers are constantly told that they should choose a joint venture partner they trust. As these examples suggest, however, trust between partners is something that can only be developed over time as a result of shared experiences. You can't start with trust.

Shape and design

In the excitement of setting up a new operation in a foreign country, or getting access to technology provided by an overseas partner, it is important not to lose sight of the basic strategic requirements that must be met if a joint venture is to be successful. The questions that must be addressed are the same when any new business is proposed: Is the market attractive? How strong is the competition? How will the new company compete? Will it have the required resources? And so on.

In addition to these concerns, three others are particularly relevant to joint venture design. One is the question of strategic freedom, which has to do with the relationship between the venture and its parents. How much freedom will the venture be given to do as it wishes with respect to choosing suppliers, a product line, and customers? In the Dow Chemical venture referred to earlier, the dispute between the partners centered on the requirement that the venture buy materials, at what the Koreans believed to be an inflated price, from Dow's new wholly owned Korean plant. Clearly the American and Korean vision of the amount of strategic freedom open to the venture was rather different.

The second issue of importance is that the joint venture be a win-win situation. This means that the payoff to each parent if the venture is successful should be a big one, because this will keep both parents working for the success of the venture when times are tough. If the strategic analysis suggests that the return to either parent over time will be marginal, the venture should be restructured or abandoned.

Finally, it is critical to decide on the management roles that each parent company will play. The venture will be easier to manage if one parent plays a dominant role and has a lot of influence over both the strategic and the day-to-day operations of the venture, or if one parent plays a lead role in the day-to-day operations of the joint venture. More difficult to manage are shared management ventures, in which both parents have a significant input into both strategic decisions and the everyday operations of the venture. A middle ground is split management decisions, where each partner has primary influence over those functional areas where it is most qualified. This is the most common and arguably most effective form.

In some ventures, the partners place too much emphasis on competing with each other about which one will have management control. They lose sight of the fact that the intent of the joint venture is to capture benefits from two partners that will allow the venture (not one of the partners) to compete in the market better than would have been possible by going it alone.

The objective of most joint ventures is superior performance. Thus the fact that dominant-parent ventures are easier to manage than shared-management ventures does not mean they are the appropriate type of venture to establish. Dominant parent ventures are most likely to be effective when one partner has the knowledge and skill to make the venture a success and the other party is contributing simply money, a trademark, or perhaps a one-time transfer of technology. Such a venture, however, begs the question "What are the unique continuing contributions of the partner?" Shared-management ventures are necessary when the venture needs active consultation between members of each parent company, as when deciding how to modify a product supplied by one parent for the local market that is well known by the other, or to modify a production process designed by one parent to be suitable for a workforce and working conditions well known by the other.

A joint venture is headed for trouble when a parent tries to take a larger role in its management than makes sense. An American company with a joint venture in Japan, for instance, insisted that one of its people be the executive vice president of the venture. This was not reasonable, because the man had nothing to bring to the management of the venture. He simply served as a constant reminder to the Japanese that the American partner did not trust them. The Americans were pushing for a shared-management venture when it was more logical to allow the Japanese, who certainly had all the necessary skills, to be the dominant or at least the leading firm. The major American contribution to the venture was to allow it to use its world-famous trademarks and brand names.

A second example, also in Japan, involved a French firm. This company was bringing complex technology to the venture that needed to be modified for the Japanese market.

It was clear that the French firm required a significant say in the management of the venture. On the other hand, the French had no knowledge of the Japanese market and, thus, the Japanese also needed a significant role in the venture. The logical solution would have been a shared-management venture and equal influence in decisions made at the board level. Unfortunately, both companies wanted to play a dominant role, and the venture collapsed in a decision-making stalemate.

Doing the deal

Experienced managers argue that it is the relationship between the partners that is of key importance in a joint venture, not the legal agreement that binds them together. Nevertheless, most are careful to ensure that they have a good agreement in place – one that they understand and are comfortable with.

The principal elements of a joint venture agreement are listed in Exhibit 5. Most of these are straightforward and relate to topics discussed in this chapter. One item on the list that has not been discussed is the termination of the venture.

Although some managers balk at discussing divorce during the prenuptial period, it is important to work out a method of terminating the venture in the event of a serious disagreement, and to do this at a time when heads are cool and goodwill abounds. The usual technique is to use a shotgun clause, which allows either party to name a price at which it will buy the other's shares in the venture. However, once this provision is activated and the first company has named a price, the second firm has the option of selling at this price or buying the first company's shares at the same price. This ensures that only fair offers are made, at least as long as both parents are large enough to be capable of buying each other out.

EXHIBIT 5   Principal Elements of a Joint Venture Agreement

- Definitions
- Scope of operations
- Management:
    1   Shareholders and supervisory roles regarding board
    2   Executive board
    3   Arrangements in the event of deadlock
    4   Operating management
- Arbitration
- Representations and warranties of each partner
- Organization and capitalization
- Financial arrangements
- Contractual links with parents
- Rights and obligations and intellectual property
- Termination agreements
- Force majeure
- Covenants

Source: "Teaming Up for the Nineties – Can You Survive without a Partner?" Deloitte, Haskins & Sells International, undated.

Making the venture work

Joint ventures need close and continuing attention, particularly in their early months. In addition to establishing a healthy working relationship between the parents and the venture general manager, managers should be on the lookout for the impact that cultural differences may be having on the venture and for the emergence of unforeseen inequities.

International joint ventures, like any type of international activity, require that managers of different national cultures work together. This requires the selection of capable people in key roles. Unless managers have been sensitized to the characteristics of the culture that they are dealing with, this can lead to misunderstandings and serious problems. Many Western managers, for instance, are frustrated by the slow, consensus-oriented decision-making style of the Japanese. Equally, the Japanese find American individualistic decision making to be surprising, as the decisions are made so quickly, but the implementation is often so slow. Firms that are sophisticated in the use of international joint ventures are well aware of such problems and have taken action to minimize them. Ford, for example, has put more than 1,500 managers through courses to improve their ability to work with Japanese and Korean managers.

It is important to remember that cultural differences do not just arise from differences in nationality. For example:

- Small firms working with large partners are often surprised and dismayed by the fact that it can take months, rather than days, to get approval of a new project. In some cases the cultural differences appear to be greater between small and large firms of the same nationality than, say, between multinationals of different nationality, particularly if the multinationals are in the same industry.
- Firms working with two partners from the same country have been surprised to find how different the companies are in cultural habits. A Japanese automobile firm headquartered in rural Japan may be a very different company from one run from Tokyo.
- Cultural differences between managers working in different functional areas may be greater than those between managers in the same function in different firms. European engineers, for example, discovered when discussing a potential joint venture with an American partner that they had more in common with the American engineers than with the marketing people in their own company.

A very common joint venture problem is that the objectives of the parents, which coincided when the venture was formed, diverge over time. Such divergences can be brought on by changes in the fortunes of the partners. This was the case in the breakup of the General Motors–Daewoo joint venture in Korea. Relations between the partners were already strained due to GM's unwillingness to put further equity into the venture, in spite of a debt to equity ratio of more than 8 to 1, when, faced with rapidly declining market share, the Korean parent decided that the venture should go for growth and maximize market share. In contrast General Motors, itself in a poor financial position at the time, insisted that the emphasis be on current profitability. When Daewoo, without telling General Motors, introduced a concessionary financing program for the joint venture's customers, the relationship was damaged, never to recover.

A final note concerns the unintended inequities that may arise during the life of a venture. Due to an unforeseen circumstance, one parent may be winning from the venture while the other is losing. A venture established in the late 1990s between Indonesian and American parents, for instance, was buying components from the American parent at prices based in dollars. As the rupiah declined in value, the Indonesian partner could afford fewer components in each shipment. The advice of many experienced venture managers is that, in such a situation, a change in the original agreement should be made, so the hardship is shared between the parents. That was done in this case, and the venture is surviving, although it is not as profitable as originally anticipated.

In reviewing any checklist of the things to be considered when forming a joint venture, it is important to recognize that such a list will vary somewhat depending on where the international joint venture is established. Exhibit 6 summarizes 12 characteristics of

EXHIBIT 6   Summary of Differences of Joint-Venture Characteristics

	Developed Country	Developing Country	
Characteristics	Market Economy	Market Economy	Planned Economy (China)
Major reason for creating venture	Skill required	Government pressure	Government pressure
Frequency of association with government partners	Low	Moderate	Very High
Overall use of JVs versus other modes of foreign involvement	Significant (20–40%)	High (but contingent on country, industry, and technology level)	Very high (regardless of country, industry, or technology level) but declining
Usual origin of foreign partner	Other developed countries	Developed countries	Ethnic Related Locales (i.e., Hong Kong, Taiwan)
Proportion of intended JVs actually implemented	High	Relatively high	Low (under 50%)
Use of JVs with a predetermined duration	Low (except in certain industries)	Low	Previously high, but declining
Most common level of ownership for foreign MNE	Equal	Minority	Minority
Number of autonomously managed ventures	Small	Negligible	Negligible
Ownership-control relationship	Direct (dominant control with majority ownership; shared control with equal ownership)	Difficult to discern because most MNEs have a minority ownership position	Indirect
Control-performance relationship in successful JVs	Inconclusive	Shared or split	Split control
Instability rate	30%	45%	Low
MNE managerial assessment of dissatisfaction with performance	37%	61%	High

Sources: Paul W. Beamish, "The Characteristics of Joint Ventures in Developed and Developing Countries," *Columbia Journal of World Business*, Fall 1985, pp. 12–19; and Paul W. Beamish, "The Characteristics of Joint Ventures in The People's Republic of China," *Journal of International Marketing*, 1(2), pp. 29–48.

EXHIBIT 7   Japanese JV Ownership Structure, Performance, and Termination Rate

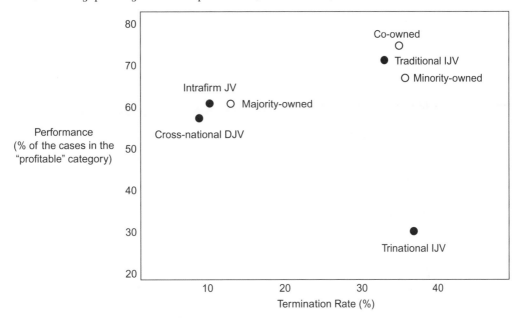

joint ventures according to whether they are established in developed versus developing countries.

Most of the descriptions of the characteristics considered are self-explanatory. Yet, more fine-grained analyses are always possible. For example, the discussion in this chapter has generally assumed a traditional equity joint venture, one focused between two firms from two different countries. Yet other types of equity joint ventures exist (see Exhibit 7), including those between firms from two different countries that set up in a third country (i.e., trinational), those formed between subsidiaries of the same MNE (i.e., intrafirm) and those formed with companies of the same nationality but located in a different country (i.e., cross-national domestic joint ventures). Further, many joint ventures have more than two partners. Interestingly, the traditional JVs (formed by Japanese MNEs) tend to simultaneously be more profitable and to have a higher termination rate than the alternative structures available.

Summary

For the reasons outlined in this chapter, international joint ventures are an increasingly important part of the strategy of many firms. They are, however, sometimes difficult to design and manage well, in part because some organizations do not treat them as "true" alliances (see Exhibit 8). The fact that some ventures are performing below their management's expectations should not be an excuse for firms to avoid such ventures. In many industries, the winners are going to be the companies that most quickly learn

EXHIBIT 8   The True Alliance versus the Pseudo Alliance

	The True Alliance	*The Pseudo Alliance*
Planned Level of Parent Input and Involvement	Continuing	One-time
Distribution of Risks/Rewards	Roughly even	Uneven
Parent Attitude Toward the JV	A unique organization with unique needs	One more subsidiary
The Formal JV Agreement	Flexible guideline	Frequently referenced rulebook
Performance Objectives	Clearly specified and congruent	Partially overlapping/ambiguous

to manage international ventures effectively. The losers will be the managers who throw up their hands and say that joint ventures are too difficult, so we had better go it alone.

In the future, will we see more or fewer international joint ventures? Certainly the reduction in investment regulations in many countries, coupled with increased international experience by many firms, suggests there may be fewer joint ventures. Yet other counter-vailing pressures exist. With shortening product life cycles, it is increasingly difficult to go it alone. And with the increase in the number of MNEs from emerging markets, both the supply and demand of potential partners will likely escalate.

SUPPLEMENTARY READING

Beamish, Paul W., and J. Peter Killing, eds. *Cooperative Strategies: European Perspectives, Cooperative Strategies: North American Perspectives*, and *Cooperative Strategies: Asian Perspectives*. San Francisco: The New Lexington Press, 1997. (Three volumes.)

——. Special Issue on Cooperative Strategies, *Journal of International Business Studies*, 27(5), 1996.

Datta, Deepak K. "International Joint Ventures: A Framework for Analysis," *Journal of General Management*, 14(2), Winter 1988.

Delios, Andrew, and Paul W. Beamish, "Joint Venture Instability Revisited: Japanese Foreign Subsidiary Survival," *Management International Review*, 2002. (Forthcoming).

Doz, Yves L., and Gary Hamel. *Alliance Advantage*. Cambridge, MA: Harvard Business School Press, 1999.

Fey, Carl, and Paul W. Beamish. "Organizational Climate Similarity and Performance: International Joint Ventures in Russia," *Organization Studies*, 22(5), 2001, pp. 853–82.

Hamel, Gary, Yves Doz, and C. K. Prahalad. "Collaborate with Your Competitors – and Win," *Harvard Business Review*, January–February 1989.

Inkpen, Andrew C. "A Note on the Dynamics of Learning Alliances: Competition, Cooperation and Relative Scope," *Strategic Management Journal*, 21(7), 2000, pp. 775–9.

Inkpen, Andrew C., and Paul W. Beamish. "Knowledge, Bargaining Power and International Joint Venture Stability." *Academy of Management Review*, 22(1), 1997.

Killing, Peter. "How to Make a Global Joint Venture Work." *Harvard Business Review*, May–June 1982, pp. 120–7.

Lane, Henry W., and Paul W. Beamish. "Cross-Cultural Cooperative Behavior in Joint Ventures in LDCs." *Management International Review*, Special Issue 1990, pp. 87–102.

Makino, Shige, and Kent E. Neupert. "National Culture, Transaction Costs, and the Choice Between JV and Wholly Owned Subsidiary," *Journal of International Business Studies*, 31(4), 2001, pp. 705–13.

Schaan, Jean-Louis. "How to Control a Joint Venture Even as a Minority Partner," *Journal of General Management*, 14(1), Autumn 1988.

Schaan, Jean-Louis, and Paul W. Beamish. "Joint Venture General Managers in Developing Countries." In *Cooperative Strategies in International Business*. Ed. F. Contractor and P. Lorange. Lexington, MA: Lexington Books, 1988, pp. 279–99.

Can We Send Her There? Maximizing the Success of Western Women on Global Assignments

Paula Caligiuri and Wayne F. Cascio

[handwritten: written 10 years ago]

The number of expatriates multinational companies (MNCs) are sending on global assignments is increasing steadily (Dobryznski, 1996; Laabs, 1993; Stroh, Dennis, & Cramer, 1994). For example, 94% of the 164 companies responding to a recent KPMG Peat Marwick LLP survey said it was important to send people on international assignments today, and a stunning 99% said it will be important by the year 2000 (McClenahen, 1997). However, the availability of people who are willing to accept global assignments is not growing at the same rapid rate. In fact, multinational companies report that finding enough of the right people with the requisite skills for global assignments is one of their greatest international human resource concerns (Stroh & Caligiuri, 1998). Even with the urgent need to broaden the global talent pool, it is still the case that only 10 to 12 percent of expatriates from Western organizations are women (Conference Board, 1992; Tung, 1997).

We believe there are three major reasons why firms should consider sending more women on global assignments: (1) multinational companies (MNCs) need competent expatriates who possess a wide-range of technical and interpersonal characteristics. Expanding the talent pool to include women provides a tactical advantage for MNCs. (2) Affording all employees who are interested in a global assignment the opportunity to be considered for one is consistent with the corporate value statements and EEO policies of many MNCs. (3) Case law (Fernandez v. Wynn Oil Co., 1981) as well as recent legislation (e.g., Civil Rights Act of 1991) make it illegal to deny a woman a global assignment on the basis of gender (Cava & Mayer, 1993).

[handwritten: It's the law!]

Journal of World Business, 33(4) (Winter 1998): 394–419. Reprinted by permission of Elsevier.

FIGURE 1   The Four Categories of Causal Agents Affecting Female Expatriates' Success

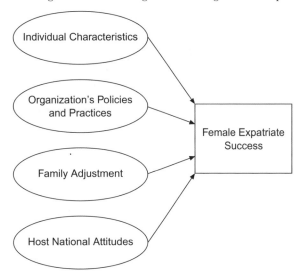

While there exist several frameworks for predicting the success of expatriates in general (McEvoy & Parker, 1995; Teagarden & Gordon, 1995), examining the strategies for maximizing female expatriates' success is appropriate because of the various sets of beliefs and expectations, both in home and host countries, about the role of women in society and in business (Fernandez & Barr, 1993). Sending a woman to a host country is likely to cause both the woman and her host national colleagues to examine those beliefs. To consider these issues in a systematic manner, this paper proposes four sets of variables for predicting a Western female expatriate's success: (1) her individual characteristics, (2) the support she receives from her organization, (3) her family, and (4) the host nationals with whom she works. We will discuss each of these four causal agents, and offer fifteen practical strategies that Western MNCs can implement to encourage the success of women on global assignments. These four causal agents are illustrated in Figure 1.

PERSONAL CHARACTERISTICS AND THE FEMALE EXPATRIATE'S SUCCESS

We describe these four causal agents in the context of Adler's "myths" surrounding female expatriates (1984a, 1984b, 1984c, 1987). The first myth addressed by Adler (1984a) concerns the most basic personal characteristic of a potential female expatriate, that is, her motivation or interest in a global assignment. Adler (1984a) tested the myth that very few women were in expatriate positions because women neither sought nor accepted international positions. She tested this assumption with a sample of more than 1,000 male and female M.B.A. students in seven top business schools. Adler (1984a) found no significant difference between men and women in their interest or desire to have an international career.

Assuming, then, that motivation to accept a global assignment is not a limiting factor, what other personal characteristics may affect the likelihood that a woman will succeed on a global assignment? From the literatures on expatriates and female managers we identified several other personal characteristics that could affect the outcome of a woman's expatriate assignment. These personal characteristics fall into three general categories: (1) technical competence, (2) self-efficacy and confidence, and (3) personality. Each will be discussed in greater detail below.

Technical competence

Technical competence is the first important personal characteristic that will affect a female expatriate's success.

While technical competence is also very important for male expatriates, it is even more critical for women who may be considered "tokens" in their global assignments. Kanter (1977) offered an operational definition of tokenism, namely, being a member of a 15% or smaller minority group. In most global contexts female expatriates would be categorized as tokens because they are not likely to have other female counterparts at their level. Indeed Kanter argues that a minority-group member (i.e., a token) has to be exceptionally competent to gain acceptance by the majority. There is support for this argument in the case of female expatriates, for female expatriates reported that "demonstrating their competence" was critical for gaining the respect of the host nationals (Adler, 1987). Other research has supported Adler's (1987) finding as well. Thus, Stone (1991) surveyed Australian, Asian, and expatriate managers to identify factors that contributed to the success of female expatriates. Australian managers ranked technical competence second, while Asian and expatriate managers ranked technical competence third (Stone, 1991). For both Asian and Australian managers, "ability to adapt" was ranked first.

Strategy 1: *MNCs should select female expatriates who demonstrate the technical or managerial skills for the position.*

Self-efficacy and confidence

Mendenhall and Oddou (1985) proposed that having a self-orientation was important for the cross-cultural adjustment of global assignees (both men and women). Self-orientation encompasses characteristics "that enable the expatriate to maintain mental health, psychological well-being, self-efficacy, and effective stress management" (Mendenhall & Oddou, 1985). Other characteristics related to "self-orientation," such as self-esteem, comfort with self, and self-confidence, have also been linked to cross-cultural adjustment (Abe & Wiseman, 1983; Black, 1988; Mendenhall & Oddou, 1988).

Self-orientation, and, more specifically, self-confidence and self-efficacy, may be especially important for women on global assignments given that they will need to believe solidly in their own competence to be successful. Both self-efficacy and self-confidence refer to one's belief regarding one's own competence or ability to overcome obstacles and succeed in a given situation (Bandura, 1982; Rosenberg, 1979). For women, having high self-efficacy and confidence is associated with success in nontraditional, powerful jobs (Ragins & Sundstrom, 1989). Further research suggests that confidence is linked with encouragement-seeking and training-seeking behaviors (Tharenou, Latimer, & Conroy, 1994) – both of which are likely to facilitate success on global assignments.

Having self-confidence during global assignments may be especially important because verbal and nonverbal signs of encouragement from host nationals may be uninterpretable due to cultural or language differences. Even when the outside signs of encouragement from others are present and interpretable, women are less likely to increase confidence in their own abilities from that encouragement (Dvir, Eden, & Banjo, 1995). Therefore, rather than encouragement coming from an outside source, women must enhance their performance by inspiring confidence from within. Again, this is important because a woman's self-confidence is related to her managerial advancement (Tharenou, Latimer, & Conroy, 1994), and her desire to remain in a group where she is a minority (Cohen & Swim, 1995). A woman facing the prospect of a global assignment is more likely to be successful if she has a high level of confidence in her ability to succeed. This leads to a second strategy:

Strategy 2: *MNCs should select women for global assignments who are self-confident in their knowledge, skills, and abilities.*

Personality characteristics

With both competence and confidence in place, women will need additional personal characteristics to be successful on global assignments. Studies examining male and female managers in a domestic context have generally concluded that there are no pronounced differences between the sexes on personality characteristics related to managerial success (Powell & Butterfield, 1979; Donnell & Hall, 1980). This picture, however, may change somewhat in a global context.

The previous section discussed one of Mendenhall and Oddou's (1985) three dimensions related to cross-cultural adjustment – self-orientation. The other two, perceptual-orientation and orientation toward others, may also be somewhat more important for woman on global assignments. With respect to the female assignee's orientation toward others, it has been noted that women tend to rely on cooperation to achieve goals, and to adopt an indirect style of communication (Tung, 1997). This trait may be particularly useful for female expatriates conducting business in high-context cultures (Asia, Latin-America), where the social values dictate indirect communication styles. The importance of cooperation in forming global strategic alliances has also been recognized (Cascio & Serapio, 1991; Tung, 1995). Thus, the ability to form relationships with host nationals as colleagues, superiors, subordinates, and clients may be integral to performing the assignment for expatriate women, and may be facilitated by certain traits that women are known to possess (Tung, 1997). Further, in a domestic context, Ragins and Sundstrom (1989) have pointed out that forming interpersonal relationships at work plays a key role in the career advancement of women. By forming relationships with superiors, subordinates, and peers women derive mentoring, support, and networking opportunities (Ragins &

Sundstrom, 1989). In an international context, orientation toward others may enable women to form such relationships, hence enabling better cross-cultural adjustment.

Given that Western women are often working in host countries that have a lower incidence of women as managers (Caligiuri & Tung, 1998), the perceptual orientation of women may be particularly important. Women, more so than men, not only need to understand cultural differences – but also the gender differences that might be present in cultures that see a more traditional (home-maker) role for women. Thus, female expatriates may be placed in situations where these cultural differences have a more direct impact on their performance on the job, and the ability to be open to differences in values, norms, and behaviors may be all the more important. Research has indicated that expatriates (both male and female) who are flexible in their attitudes toward cultural differences and are willing to learn from different cultural contexts adjust better to overseas assignments (Harvey, 1985; Abe & Wiseman, 1983; Mendenhall & Oddou, 1985). This suggests:

Strategy 3: *MNCs should select female expatriates who possess a greater perceptual-orientation (e.g., openness, flexibility).*

The second dimension, perceptual-orientation, includes personality characteristics such as nonjudgmental attitudes and openness to new cultural norms, values, and behaviors (Mendenhall & Oddou, 1985). Expatriates who adjust well cross-culturally tend to be more intellectually curious, willing to accept cultural differences, and flexible (Harvey, 1985; Abe & Wiseman, 1983; Mendenhall & Oddou, 1985). As such, we propose the following organizational strategy:

Strategy 4: *MNCs should select female expatriates who possess a positive orientation toward others (higher in sociability, high-context communicators). MNCs should also examine if the same communication style that may be deemed ineffective (i.e., unassertive) in the home culture may be appropriate for the host culture.*

THE SENDING MNC AND THE FEMALE EXPATRIATE'S SUCCESS

We now shift our focus from the characteristics a female expatriate should possess to the practices the MNC should implement. This implies four additional organizational strategies. Before discussing strategies however, it is important to consider the decision-making context of MNCs that send women on global assignments. A multinational organization, trying to blend into the host country in which it is operating, might be inclined to follow the social mores of that particular country – assuming that by doing so, it will gain a competitive advantage (Cava & Mayer, 1993; Feltes, Robinson, & Fink, 1993). Therefore, under the guise of competitive necessity, MNCs may decide not to send women to countries where women are not accepted in business settings. These MNCs assume that their businesses would suffer if they sent a woman to a country where few, if any, women occupy senior-management positions. For example, "US female expatriates may encounter resistance if they are performing traditionally male roles . . . (this) could hamper her ability to accomplish her assigned overseas mission" (Feltes et al., 1993, p. 84).

Adler (1984b) surveyed HR managers to determine the attitudes of MNCs toward sending women on global assignments. She sampled 60 HR managers from MNCs in North America and found that only 35% had selected a woman for a global assignment, compared with 80% who had selected a man. Adler (1984b) also found that 72% of these HR managers believed the number of women they would send on global assignments would increase in the future, and 82% believed that women are qualified for global assignments. She followed up with an assessment of the HR managers' beliefs regarding the barriers for women in obtaining (and presumably succeeding in) a global assignment. The HR managers believed that the prejudice of host nationals, expected problems with a dual-career marriage, and the company's reluctance (not their own) to send women on global assignments, were all potential barriers for women.

From a US legal perspective, the 1991 Civil Rights Act, the Age Discrimination in Employment Act, and the Americans with Disabilities Act protect Americans in foreign countries who are employed by American (or American-controlled) MNCs from discrimination – despite local customs or traditions (Carmell, 1997). This suggests that even if a host country "prefers" not to conduct business with women, US women cannot be unfairly denied access to jobs, training, promotions, etc., in foreign countries. In US case law, *Fernandez* v. *Wynn Oil Co.* (1981), the court held that neither stereotyped impressions of male and female roles, nor stereotyped preferences of host national customers may justify a sexually-discriminatory practice as a bona fide occupational qualification (BFOQ) under Title VII. Thus a company's allegation that its host-national customers would refuse to deal with a female corporate officer did not constitute a legitimate defense for its decision to promote only males to that position. Reversing the district court's ruling, that male gender was a BFOQ for a job performed in foreign countries where women are discouraged from pursuing business careers, the US Ninth Circuit Court of Appeals held that stereotyped gender preferences of the defendant's Latin American customers did not justify sexually-discriminatory hiring practices.

Thus, an argument cannot be made by US employers that their foreign customers "prefer" to work with men, and then subsequently use this argument as a basis for discriminating against US women. Gender, in these cases, can only be considered a BFOQ when a law of the host country limits women from doing a particular job (Cava & Mayer, 1993). Indeed, the US courts have long ruled that customer preference is not a BFOQ (*Diaz* v. *Pan American World Airways*, 1971).

Even if organizations have no desire to send women on global assignments, we have proposed at least two reasons organizations should consider doing so: The first is based on case law (in the US) and the second is that they are simply running out of potential male candidates. Therefore, we agree with other authors (Adler, 1984b; Stone, 1991) that the number of female expatriates will grow over time. What, then, can organizations do to maximize the potential of female expatriates? Building on the work of Bhatnagar (1988) we propose four specific management practices that MNCs can implement that will facilitate the success of Western female expatriates (especially those assigned to countries with more traditional views about the role of women in society and in business). These include (1) predeparture training that addresses the specific needs of female expatriates, (2) organizational support and championing, (3) in-country support and mentoring, and (4) the adoption of policies that support the fair treatment of women.

Predeparture training

Limited empirical evidence on predeparture cross-cultural training programs gener-ally supports the position that accurate exposure to a host culture, in the context of training, is related positively to the cross-cultural adjustment of both men and women (Early, 1987; Fiedler, Mitchell, & Triandis, 1971; Black & Mendenhall, 1990). For female expatriates' predeparture cross-cultural training to affect global assignment success, the training must facilitate an integration of the newly-learned behaviors into a woman's reper-toire of behavioral responses (Dinges, 1983). This may include training on the norms, values, and traditions of a host country regarding women, and deriving solutions for the potentially challenging situations that female expatriates may encounter (Feltes et al., 1993). Prior to the global assignment, MNCs should provide developmental experiences for their female expatriates (as they often do for male expatriates), such as short-term business trips and necessary domestic experiences (Adler, 1984b). In addition, they should allow potential female expatriates the opportunity to role-play or to simulate (e.g., through interactive video) a variety of difficult situations that female expatriates, in particular, may encounter (e.g., "after-hours" socializing, peer pressure for sexual favors, and, for single females, strategies for coping with the loneliness that often characterizes global assignments to "culturally distant" lands).

Cross-cultural training may also provide a realistic expectation for what is to come in the global assignment. Research suggests that realistic job previews will enhance job survival (Wanous & Colella, 1989) by helping individuals form realistic impressions about their future positions. These realistic expectations may also help to reduce anxiety dur-ing the stressful period of being a newcomer in the position (Nelson, Quick & Joplin, 1991). These ideas lead to the following organizational strategy for MNCs:

Strategy 5: *MNCs should train female expatriates on the norms, values, and traditions that the host nationals possess regarding women, and train them on deriving solutions for the potentially challenging situations they may face as women.*

Organizational support and championing

In addition to training their female expatriates, MNCs can manage the perceptions of them before and while they are on their global assignments. This may be especially important in subsidiaries of US-based MNCs where most host national managers know that US civil rights laws exist – and may assume that their female expatriate colleague fulfills an affirmative action quota. As such, MNCs should take special care to ensure that the female expatriate is "the best candidate" available, rather than simply a US EEO "requirement." Knowing that host nationals' perceptions of a Western female expatri-ate's competence may be blurred by stereotypes (confounded with some knowledge of US civil rights laws), MNCs should not only select the best manager – but also emphas-ize that she is. To demonstrate that the MNC is committed to placing the "best person" in all positions, it could send more than one female (who may be viewed as a legal "token") to a given host national location (Adler, 1984b; Feltes et al., 1993). These ideas lead to our sixth strategy.

Strategy 6: *In order to dispel the "token" image, MNCs should actively promote expatriate women as their "best qualified" candidates.*

In-country support and mentoring

Once women are in their host countries, MNCs can enhance their success through in-country support and mentoring programs. Mentors have been found to improve greatly the likelihood of success in managerial roles for women (e.g., Noe, 1988; Ragins, 1989). Mentoring relationships, "while important for men, may be essential for women," given that the barriers for success may be greater for women in organizations (Ragins, 1989).

While the barriers for women in a domestic context may still be pronounced, barriers to women's success are even more dramatic in a global context. Given that in many global assignments gaining access to potential mentors may be limited, MNCs should assign sponsors (Adler, 1984b) or in-country consultants (Feltes et al., 1993) to support women in their new roles. This suggests the following strategy for organizations:

Strategy 7: *MNCs should provide each female expatriate with an in-country support network or mentor.*

Country manager's wife!

MNC policies and organizational culture

While the previous three strategies were tactical and specific, our next recommendation involves MNCs' policies and organizational culture. In a study of almost 700 MNCs, Adler (1984c) found that the proportion of expatriates on global assignments cannot be explained by the same organizational-size variables (sales, number of countries in which a firm operates, total number of employees, and assets) for women, as it can for men. This suggests that while the proportion of male expatriates may depend on organizational size, the proportion of female expatriates depends on other factors, such as MNCs' implicit policies on women as expatriates (Adler, 1984c). Such policies could restrict women from ever obtaining a global assignment – and from succeeding once they are on one.

Adler (1984a, 1984b, 1984c) recommends that MNCs should not make any assumptions about women as expatriates (e.g., do not assume their husbands will not approve, or that they will not be accepted). We believe organizations should do more. They should actively promote policies that support women in global assignments. Promoting an organizational culture that supports women's efforts to advance and grow professionally will improve the assimilation and acculturation of these women in organizations (Hood & Koberg, 1994). Thus, we offer the following strategy for MNCs:

Strategy 8: *MNCs should have (and explicitly implement) policies worldwide regarding the fair and equal treatment of all employees, regardless of race, gender, creed, age, disability, or religion. That is, these policies should be integral parts of an MNC's worldwide culture, rather than adopted solely in the spirit of legal compliance.*

SPOUSES, CHILDREN, AND THE SUCCESS OF FEMALE EXPATRIATES

In a domestic context, discussing predictors of job success may be complete after considering the first two categories – individual characteristics and organizational practices. In a global context, however, organizations need to consider the needs of the families that will be uprooted for the sake of one person's career. Family concerns can be especially challenging for female expatriates. For example, female expatriates who are married will likely have male spouses relocating to the host country. In societies where men are considered the primary breadwinners, this is a non-traditional situation where husbands follow their wives for the sake of their wives' careers. However, with the rise of dual-career marriages (i.e., both partners are committed to their careers), this situation is becoming ever more common (Colwill & Temple, 1987; Punnett, Crocker, & Stevens, 1992; Wiggins-Frame & Shehan, 1994). To date, however, research on male expatriate spouses is virtually nonexistent (Punnett et al., 1992). Extant research on expatriate spouses has been limited primarily to samples of female, nonworking spouses (Black & Gregersen, 1991; Black & Stephens, 1989). To date, the sole research study conducted on male expatriate spouses suggests that men have some unique concerns that affect their work and social lives (Punnett et al., 1992). For female expatriate spouses, many find an intact social support network with the other expatriates' wives. A male spouse may not feel comfortable spending a significant amount of time with a group of female spouses (Punnett et al., 1992). In addition, in the dual-career situation where both partners have careers, the male partner may have a difficult time adjusting to being a nonworking spouse (Westwood & Leung, 1994). Not unique to male partners, this may be especially true in countries where host-national work-permit restrictions do not allow both partners to work in the host country (Punnett et al., 1992).

These challenges affect a male spouse's potential for cross-cultural adjustment. They are a source of concern, given that research suggests that spouses' inability to adjust to living in the host country was the most frequently cited reason for the failure (Tung, 1981; Harvey, 1985). Therefore the adjustment of an expatriate's spouse is one of the most critical determinants of whether the expatriate will complete his or her assignment (Black & Gregersen, 1991; Tung, 1981), and how successful the expatriate's performance will be while on the assignment (Black & Gregersen, 1991; Black & Stephens, 1989). These findings are not limited to US or Western expatriates. In a study of Japanese expatriates, Fukuda and Chu (1994) found that family-related problems were ranked first in explaining why expatriates terminated their assignments.

Related to this, but less often studied, is the role of children on global assignments. Again, given that women have tended to assume the traditional role of childrearing, the impact of children may affect female expatriates differentially, compared with male expatriates. Research from the literature on domestic relocation suggests that relocation may be stressful for children, but the outcome on their emotional and social functioning is not yet clear (Cornille, 1993). In the global context, adaptation may be even more extreme. Two of the most problematic areas in children's global relocation are (1) their education and (2) reestablishing social networks (Brett, 1982; Fukuda & Chu, 1994). For Japanese expatriates, education is especially a problem because of their desire to give their children a Japanese education. When students are above grade nine, finding

Japanese schools outside Japan is especially difficult. Many Japanese mothers choose to return to Japan for the sake of their children's education, thus separating the family (Fukuda & Chu, 1994).

The effect of the spouse and children's adjustment on an expatriate's performance can be explained through spillover theory (Caligiuri, Hyland, Joshi, & Bross, 1998). Spillover theory hypothesizes a reciprocal relationship between affective responses in one's work life and in one's family life. That is, such responses carry over from one domain (e.g., home life) to the other (e.g., work life) (Aldous, 1969; Barnett & Marshall, 1992; Crouter, 1984; Leiter & Durup, 1996; Piotrowski, 1979). Spillover occurs when workers carry their positive or negative emotions and attitudes from their work life into their home life (Kelly & Vyodanoff, 1985; Piotrowski, 1979), and when they carry over emotions and attitudes from their home back to the work environment (Belsky, Perry-Jenkins, & Crouter, 1985; Crouter, 1984). Studies examining the influence of work on family assume the centrality of work in establishing the conditions of family life (Kanter, 1977); however, spillover theory suggests that one's family also can affect performance while on the job. These two types of spillover may not exert equal effects. Job-to-home spillover is greater than home-to-job spillover (Galinsky, Bond, & Friedman, 1993). In the context of a global assignment, the effects of spillover from home to work and from work to home can either enhance an expatriate's performance or detract from it because the originating emotions can be positive, or negative or both (Barnett, Marshall, & Sayer, 1992; Lambert, 1990). These ideas lead to the following strategies for organizations:

Strategy 9: *MNCs should offer mechanisms to improve the likelihood that the spouses or partners of female expatriates will adjust well cross-culturally (e.g., training for spouses, male-oriented social networks, language classes).*

Strategy 10: *MNCs should offer mechanisms to improve the likelihood that the children of female expatriates will adjust well cross-culturally (e.g., day care, educational assistance, language classes).*

THE HOST NATIONALS' AND THE WESTERN FEMALE EXPATRIATE'S SUCCESS

In this last category of recommendations we focus on the people with whom female expatriates will be transacting business. Some key players in the environment where the female expatriate will be expected to do her job are the host nationals with whom she will work (e.g., clients, co-workers, superiors, subordinates). A fundamental concern is whether or not host nationals will do business with expatriate women. In her seminal research on the topic of female expatriates, Nancy Adler (1987) examined female expatriates' perceptions of whether or not host nationals are prejudiced against them. Using a sample of 52 North American female expatriates in Asia, she found that 97% of them self-reported that their assignment had been successful. She noted that other indicators besides these self-report ratings (e.g., being offered another global assignment after completion of the current one) suggested that these women were successful. Only 20% of her sample noted that "being female" was a disadvantage. As she noted, surprisingly, 42% of these expatriate women viewed their "being female" as an advantage!

Adler discovered that female expatriates perceived that they are not placed in the same "professionally limiting roles as are local women" in Asian cultures (Adler, 1993, p. 5; Adler, 1987; Jelinek & Adler, 1988). This phenomenon may be explained through the cognitive process of stereotyping subtypes: That is, the categories of distinct stereotypes for a single group (Kunda & Thagard, 1996). For example, "the elderly" may be sub-categorized as either "worried senior citizens" or "kindly grandparents" depending on the social cues (Brewer, Dull, & Lui, 1981). This subtyping would explain Adler's findings. Based on the way the female expatriates in Adler's study reported being treated, Adler concluded that these women were viewed first as foreigners and second as women (and that the second was a distant second). The salient information (being foreign) activated an entirely different stereotype from the group as a whole (being female; Kunda & Thagard, 1996). Asian host nationals, in Adler's study, may have had a substereotype of "Western working women" and a very different substereotype for "Asian working women." The reactions to these two groups may be quite different – and even inconsistent. The former may be treated very professionally, and the latter disrespectfully, by the same group of Asian host nationals.

Adler's research also found that these women were all treated as if they were (and in all likelihood they actually were) very competent. Based on these results she deduced that the host nationals perceived that "if a woman was sent by a company, then she must be exceptionally competent" (Adler, 1987). A woman sent from headquarters, in addition to being Western, may activate another substereotype (headquarters representative) to which Asian men respond very favorably. In a similar research study, female expatriates in Hong Kong believed that "if you are perceived as a competent manager and could do the job, gender was incidental" (Westwood & Leung, 1994). These women may have also benefitted from the sub-stereotyping phenomenon – while being given the opportunity to demonstrate their competence.

This line of research is encouraging for female expatriates. However, while 97% is an impressive success rate, it also seems somewhat unrealistic and not generalizable in view of anecdotal evidence suggesting that the success rate for expatriates, in general, is only about 50% (Copeland & Griggs, 1985). We also do not have a relative comparison of how well men would have performed in the same positions. In addition, the results of this research must be viewed with some caution, given that the attitudes of the host nationals were inferred; they were not assessed directly.

In a study directly assessing host nationals' preferences for expatriates, Stone (1991, p. 15) asked Asian and Australian host-national managers, and expatriate managers to respond to the following statement, "given people of equal ability, it is preferable to appoint a man to an international position." Over half the expatriates (56%) and Asian managers (53%) agreed with this statement. Over half the Australian managers disagreed with this statement (56%). When asked whether they agreed that "expatriate women managers are not appropriate for countries such as Japan and Korea" over half of the managers in all three categories agreed (Australians 64%, Asians, 53%, and expatriates 59%). Stone's (1991) findings are somewhat contrary to those of Adler (1987). However, these findings should also be viewed with caution given that they are based on a very small sample.

Izraeli, Banai, and Zeira (1980, p. 56) found similar results with a sample of European host nationals from Germany, Britain, France, Holland, and Belgium. They were asked "can a well-qualified woman successfully head and manage an MNC subsidiary?" Sixty percent of the sample responded "yes." Follow-up interviews suggested that the men in the sample responded "yes" with much hesitation. This suggests that a dichotomy (i.e., yes or no) did not allow for the variance of true feelings in the sample. Izraeli et al. (1980) report that many respondents cited reasons of the society not being prepared to accept (or recognize the competence of) a woman in a position of authority. This should be considered with caution given that the study is almost 20 years old. In addition, both the Stone (1991) study and the Izraeli et al. (1980) study incorporated several method-ological flaws, such as potentially biased samples and weak measures of the constructs.

There was agreement in the conclusions of Adler (1987), Stone (1991), and Izraeli et al. (1980), that female expatriates may find themselves victims of discrimination and sexism not only from host nationals, but also from other expatriates. Researchers have found discrimination and chauvinism against Western female expatriates by Western expatriate men. In the context of stereotyping and substereotyping, this result is interpret-able and consistent with the theory. Unlike Asians, Western men do not have a separate (and more favorable) sub-stereotype for "Western women from headquarters" given that the qualities "Western" and "from headquarters" are not salient enough to activate a substereotype. For example, in a study of Western female expatriates in Hong Kong, Westwood and Leung (1994, p. 76) noted that many women in their sample believed that "much of the sexism they encountered came from expatriate men, and not from locals . . . (except for some) older and more traditional" Chinese males. They further point out that it may be the case that Western women are better able to interpret the behaviors of Western men, and are less likely to interpret sexism in more subtle Chinese behaviors (Westwood & Leung, 1994).

At either extreme, the argument of whether or not women will be accepted as expatriate managers seems oversimplified. It is oversimplified to state that "all female expatriates have the same chance as male expatriates to succeed in every foreign situation" – because, it depends. It is also oversimplified to state that "host nationals will simply not work with women" – because it too depends. Host nationals will accept (or not accept) female expatriates as business colleagues for a variety of reasons. We propose that there are two critical factors that will interact to form the host nationals' attitudes and behaviors toward female expatriates. These are gender stereotypes and the female expatriate's power base.

Gender stereotypes

The fact that people can form an opinion to questions that ask about a person's capab-ility based solely on his or her gender suggests that stereotyping may be present. Assuming the demand characteristics were low for anonymous and confidential surveys, the more overt statements, such as those found in Stone (1991) and Izraeli et al. (1980), confirm that this is so. Gender stereotyping can take many forms, such as gender-characteristics stereotyping, gender-role stereotyping, and gender-labeling of occupations (Izraeli et al., 1980). These stereotypes can potentially limit the success of high-potential female expatriates in a global assignment. There are two reasons why stereotyping can be so damaging to the career of a female expatriate. One, a competent woman may not have her capabilities recognized or rewarded to the same extent as a man with the same talents. Two, male co-workers, superiors, and subordinates might outwardly derail a woman's drive for success. The first is more of a subtle bias, while the second is more overt discrimination.

Some gender stereotypes might not manifest themselves as overt actions against female expatriates and may play out in more subtle ways. For example, when women are in the minority of a work group they tend to be rated lower in performance than when they are in groups comprising over half women (Sackett, DuBois, & Wiggins-Noe, 1991). This is a potential problem because performance evaluations often comprise the standard by which we judge success on the job.

Some stereotypes against women as expatriates stem from the host nationals' view of what is appropriate behavior for a mother and a wife (Izraeli et al., 1980). Here, the focus is not on the job, but rather her unfulfilled duty at home. This would be the case if the female was viewed as a female first and an expatriate second. Consistent with Adler's (1987) findings, however, the perception of the female may be that she is different from a typical host-national female and therefore she may be judged by a different standard. That is, host nationals may view female expatriates in a way that is inconsistent with their views of women. In this case, the stereotype may be weakened or abandoned altogether. This leads to the following suggestion for female expatriates:

Strategy 11: *Western female expatriates should not attempt to "blend in" with host-national women (e.g., serving their male colleagues tea). That is, they should not try to change the fact that they are being viewed in a stereotypically inconsistent manner (e.g., as a foreigner and a company manager).*

Stereotypes, however, can be changed (or a sub-stereotype can be formed) – sometimes by mere exposure (Zajonc, 1968) or contact (Amir, 1969) with a successful person in the stereotyped group. Izraeli et al. (1980) found that the host nationals who were most positive about female MNC leaders were those who had exposure to a female expatriate who was successful. Izraeli's findings can be interpreted in terms of "availability heuristic" (Rothbart, Fulero, Jensen, Howard, & Birrell, 1978; Tversky & Kahneman, 1973). According to this phenomenon, the positive and salient interaction with one competent female expatriate would result in host nationals' more favorable attitudes toward female expatriates in the future. This leads to another suggestion for multinational organizations:

Strategy 12: *MNCs should give host nationals greater exposure to successful women in the organization (e.g., when host nationals visit headquarters or when female managers visit subsidiaries).*

In the United States, the organizational movement to improve the value of domestic diversity has often started with cultural awareness or cultural sensitivity training (Cox, 1994). In the international context, this training could be extended to host nationals whose exposure to "diversity" may be the female expatriates with whom they will work. It may be especially helpful to train host nationals on the appropriate behaviors for interacting with Western women on a professional level. This type of training may be helpful in making host nationals aware of their unconscious attitudes and stereotypes. However, as Cox (1994) suggests, awareness training should be used within the context of a greater initiative and not in isolation. That said, it would be unlikely that awareness training would be effective if some of the other strategies mentioned in this paper were not also addressed. This suggests Strategy 13:

Strategy 13: *MNCs should provide training to the host nationals who are going to be interacting with female expatriates.*

Stereotyping in its more overt form is demonstrated through behaviors that host nationals (or possibly other expatriates) exhibit that may reduce a female expatriate's effectiveness. For example, one study noted that a female expatriate who "attempted to exercise the authority of her position would not have the same credibility or impact" (Izraeli et al., 1980, p. 58). Following from the prior discussion of how substereotypes are formed, the host nationals may have a negative substereotype of "female expatriates" for one of two reasons. One, being "Western" does not provide enough salient information for the host nationals to alter discriminatory behavior. Or, two, the salient information from one female expatriate was so negative and salient that it created a negative substereotype in the minds of host nationals. No matter the cause, this negative stereotype will impede future business transactions between female expatriates and host nationals. This leads to the following (albeit, reluctant) implication:

Strategy 14: *If the MNC is certain that a female expatriate will need to transact business with host nationals who harbor and act upon their gender stereotypes, have a male colleague (who is respectful of the female expatriate) team up with her for a specific business situation. The crux of this strategy is that the MNC must be absolutely certain that the host's stereotypes are fixed. As was mentioned in a prior section, when in doubt, do not assume that the host nationals possess negative stereotypes toward Western women.*

Power base

Research suggests that power and status will have an impact on a group's impressions of its own abilities and other groups' abilities (Sachdev & Bourhis, 1991). This finding may be extended to individuals who would be considered minorities (female expatriates) with a host national "in group." There is the perception of high-status people that they will use "strategies involving the control of resources (power bases)" (Stahelski & Payton, 1995, p. 55). The subordinates' perceptions of their manager's status and power bases may influence the subordinates' attitudes and behaviors at work (Carson, Carson, & Roe, 1993).

In some cases, MNCs place female expatriates in positions with inherent position power. For example, if a female expatriate is a lead negotiator for a potential joint venture in which the other party is extremely interested, her gender could become quite incidental at the point of these negotiations. Her power derives from the authority she has in the situation – and her "subordinates would acknowledge and respect the power accordingly." Likewise, if a female expatriate was sent to head a subsidiary where her authority was the ultimate authority at a given location, the host nationals, by virtue of her position power, would need to take her seriously – or risk losing their jobs – as she would be recognized as holding the power bases of reward and punishment. The status of the position would lead to the perception of the power bases (Carson et al., 1993). This leads to our final suggestion for MNCs:

Strategy 15: *MNCs should give their female expatriates high position power in the host subsidiary, whenever possible.*

CONCLUSIONS AND SUGGESTIONS FOR FUTURE RESEARCH

Table 1 summarizes each of the strategies we have discussed. In addition, it suggests methods of implementing each strategy together with possible implementation problems. Table 1 suggests that four broad predictor constructs forecast the relative level of success among female expatriates – the individual characteristics of female expatriates, their treatment by host nationals, family support and adjustment, and company support. All four of these variables, operating concurrently, will likely affect the outcome of the female expatriate's assignment. It may be the case, however, that for a female expatriate, these factors are independent in affecting failure globally, yet additive in affecting her success. In other words, any one of these four causal agents could produce a highly negative environment that would reduce her chance for success, even when the other four were positive. For example, consider a situation where the entire assignment is a positive experience, yet the expatriate's husband wants to return home. On the other hand, as each of these four causal agents moves from neutral to positive in a woman's global assignment, the assignment should produce greater and greater success. For example, the company might not be very helpful, but her husband is supportive and her host-national colleagues are helpful. Each factor, independently, would make the assignment a progressively better experience. The combination of causal agents, either independent or additive, should be tested in future research.

When considering each causal agent separately, we have the least amount of direct evidence about the attitudes of host nationals toward expatriate women. This is a critical determinant of in-country success, yet much of what we think we know is based on attributions of host nationals' attitudes by third parties. However, if the field is to move beyond hunch and intuition toward predictions of success of female expatriates based on empirical data, then direct assessment of the host nationals' attitudes, along with empirical data on the remaining three predictor constructs, is necessary.

Direct assessment of the attitudes of host nationals has several advantages. First, it will allow home-country managers to dispel some of their own myths and assumptions regarding host-nationals' attitudes toward female expatriates. This should go a long way toward breaking down barriers to expatriate assignments for females. Second, it will allow us to begin to map important similarities and differences in host nationals' attitudes toward expatriate women within and between countries, and across management levels. Finally, we believe that incorporation of this information into prediction models will explain unique, incremental variability in the relative performance of female expatriates in their overseas assignments.

In conclusion, the need among MNCs for a talented pool of expatriate candidates has mandated full use of the potential of female global assignees. The strategies presented here suggest that the outcome of the assignment will likely be affected by some things

TABLE 1   Strategies, Implementation Methods and Possible Problems with Implementing the Strategies

Strategies	HR Tool, Method, or Intervention	Possible Problems with Implementing
1 MNCs should select female expatriates who demonstrate the technical or managerial skills for the position.	Selection based on demonstrated competencies. Additional technical or managerial training prior to departure, if needed	It may be difficult to find a person with **every** necessary credential who is also willing to accept the assignment. It may be difficult for the organization to anticipate every skill needed for a given global assignment.
2 MNCs should select women for global assignments who are self-confident in their knowledge, skills, and abilities.	Select expatriates based on their self-confidence in their knowledge, skills, and abilities.	An expatriate who was too self-confident may come across as arrogant to the host nationals. Finding the balance between confidence and arrogance might be challenging.
3 MNCs should select female expatriates who possess a greater perceptual-orientation (e.g., openness).	Select expatriates based on personality characteristics, such as openness and flexibility.	It may be difficult to find a person with the requisite personality characteristics who is also willing to accept the assignment.
4 MNCs should select female expatriates who possess a positive orientation toward others (e.g., sociability).	Select expatriates based on personality characteristics such as sociability.	It may be difficult to find a person with the requisite personality characteristics who is also willing to accept the assignment.
5 MNCs should train female expatriates on the norms, values, and traditions that the host nationals possess regarding women, and train them on deriving solutions for the potentially challenging situations they may face as women.	Offer predeparture culture-specific training for female expatriates.	All of the possible "difficult" situations cannot possibly be anticipated. There may not be enough lead time to conduct a thorough cross-cultural training session before the expatriate leaves on her assignment.
6 In order to dispel the "token" image, MNCs should actively promote expatriate women as their "best qualified" candidates.	Memos of introduction In-person introduction by a very senior executive A statement of qualification Any other culturally-appropriate method for establishing credibility	Some of these initiatives may be misinterpreted, depending on the cultural context. The intervention should be culture-specific.
7 MNCs should provide their female expatriates with an in-country support network or mentor.	Have a mentor back home – and a method for communication Have a mentor in-country	Communication is more difficult from a far distance.
8 MNCs should have policies worldwide regarding the fair and equal treatment of all employees.	Be sure the policy is communicated through all of the culturally appropriate channels. Train employees on the policies. Reward managers on promoting the policies.	The policies may be viewed as culturally ethnocentric if not communicated correctly.

TABLE 1 (*cont'd*)

Strategies	*HR Tool, Method, or Intervention*	*Possible Problems with Implementing*
9 MNCs should offer mechanisms to improve the likelihood that the spouses of female expatriates will adjust well cross-culturally.	Cross-cultural training for spouses Male-oriented social networks Language classes Reemployment assistance Money for professional or personal development	There is always a chance that the spouses' needs will not match what is being offered. The spouse may not use the services. The options may not be available in a given location.
10 MNCs should offer mechanisms to improve the likelihood that the children of female expatriates will adjust well cross-culturally.	Day care Educational assistance Language classes	There may not be appropriate services available for expatriate children in a given location.
11 Western female expatriates should *not* attempt to "blend in" with host national women.	Train women on how to cope with being "different" from host national women. Train women on the behaviors that could be misinterpreted (e.g., serving tea in Japan).	It may be difficult for the female expatriate to balance perceptions (i.e., not appear too masculine). It may be difficult to find role models from whom expat women can to learn culturally appropriate (and professional) behaviors.
12 MNCs should give host nationals greater exposure to successful women in the organization.	Have more professional women take short business trips to the host country to increase interactions between Western females and host nationals. Have host nationals take business trips to headquarters for the same purpose.	This strategy can always backfire if the women they interact with are not competent and professional. The host nationals may not change their attitudes toward women as a result of the interaction.
13 MNCs should provide training to the host nationals who are going to be interacting with female expatriates.	Offer the training to host nationals before the female expatriate arrives on location.	The host nationals may not change their behaviors toward women as a result of the training.
14 If the MNC is *certain* that a female expatriate will need to transact business with hosts who have gender stereotypes, partner her with a male colleague for a specific business situation.	Develop professional partnerships	The MNC must be absolutely certain that the host's stereotypes are fixed. When in doubt, do not assume that the host nationals possess negative stereotypes toward Western women – this will simply undermine her credibility.
15 MNCs should give their female expatriates high position power in the host subsidiary, whenever possible.	Succession planning into high-level expatriate positions for women	It would only be a risky strategy if the person in the position did not have the competence for the job.

out of the female expatriate's direct control (i.e., her family, company, and host national colleagues). Beyond the expatriate's own characteristics and competencies, the next most important factor appears to be the MNC's mechanisms for supporting female expatriates and their families. Multinational companies must be proactive to ensure that their female expatriates, both senior and junior, along with their families, have company backing while successfully completing their international assignments.

In this paper we offer fifteen strategies for MNCs to improve the success of female expatriates. As business becomes ever more internationally oriented, and as the sheer number of global assignments grows, finding individuals who are willing and able to uproot themselves from their native lands will put pressure on businesses to consider all members of their organizations, both male and female, for these important positions. The strategies provided in this paper should give MNCs some guidance on how to enhance the success of the women who will represent their companies in other countries.

REFERENCES

Abe, H., & Wiseman, R. L. (1983). A cross-cultural confirmation of the dimensions of intercultural effectiveness. *International Journal of Intercultural Relations*, 7: 567.

Adler, N. J. (1984a). Women do not want international careers: And other myths about international management. *Organizational Dynamics*, 13: 66–79.

Adler, N. J. (1984b). Expecting international success: Female managers overseas, *Columbia Journal of World Business*, 19: 79–85.

Adler, N. J. (1984c). Women in international management: Where are they? *California Management Review*, 26: 78–89.

Adler, N. J. (1987). Pacific basin managers: A gaijin, not a woman. *Human Resource Management*, 26: 169–92.

Adler, N. J. (1993). Competitive frontiers: Women managers in the triad. *International Studies of Management and Organization*, 23: 3–23.

Aldous, J. (1969). Occupational characteristics and males' role performance in the family. *Journal of Marriage and Family*, 31: 707–12.

Amir, Y. (1969). Contact Hypothesis in ethnic relations. *Psychological Bulletin*, 71: 319–42.

Bandura, A. (1982). Self-efficacy mechanism in human agency. *American Psychologist*, 37: 122–47.

Barnett, R. C., & Marshall, N. L. (1992). Worker and mother roles, spillover effects and psychological distress. *Women and Health*, 18: 9–36.

Barnett, R. C., Marshall, N. L., & Sayer, A. (1992). Positive-spillover effects from job to home: A closer look. *Women and Health*, 19: 13–41.

Belsky, J., Perry-Jenkins, M., & Crouter, A. C. (1985). The work-family interface and marital change across the transition to parenthood. *Journal of Family Issues*, 6: 205–20.

Benson, P. (1978). Measuring cross-cultural adjustment: The problem of criteria. *International Journal of Intercultural Relations*, 2: 12–37.

Bhatnagar, D. (1988). Professional women in organizations: New paradigms for research and action. *Sex Roles*, 18: 343–435.

Black, J. S. (1988). Work role transitions: A study of American expatriate managers in Japan. *Journal of International Business Studies*, 19: 274–91.

Black, J. S., & Gregersen, H. B. (1991). The other half of the picture: Antecedents of spouse cross-cultural adjustment. *Journal of International Business* (Third Quarter), 461–77.

Black, J. S., & Mendenhall, M. E. (1990). Cross-cultural training effectiveness: A review and theoretical framework. *Academy of Management Review*, 15: 113–36.

Black, J. S., & Stephens, G. K. (1989). The influence of spouse on American expatriate adjustment and the interest to stay in Pacific Rim overseas assignments. *Journal of Management*, 15: 529–74.

Brett, J. M. (1982). Job transfer and well-being. *Journal of Applied Psychology*, 67: 450–63.

Brewer, M. B., Dull, V., & Lui, L. (1981). Perceptions of the elderly: Stereotypes as prototypes. *Journal of Personality and Social Psychology*, 41: 656–70.

Caligiuri, P. M., Hyland, M., Joshi, A., & Bross, A. (1998). A theoretical framework for examining the relationship between family adjustment and expatriate adjustment to working in the host country. *Journal of Applied Psychology*, 83: 598–640.

Caligiuri, P. M., & Tung, R. L. (1998). Are masculine cultures female friendly? Male and female expatriates' success in countries differing in work value orientations. In G. Hofstede (Chair), Masculinity/Femininity as a Cultural Dimension. Paper presented at the International Congress of the International Association for Cross-Cultural Psychology: The Silver Jubilee Congress, Bellingham, WA.

Carmell, W. A. (1997). Application of U.S. antidiscrimination laws to multinational employers. Paper prepared for the Society for Human Resource Management, Alexandria, VA.

Carson, P. P., Carson, K. D., & Roe, W. (1993). Social power bases: A metaanalytic examination of interrelationships and outcomes. *Journal of Applied Social Psychology*, 23: 1150–69.

Cascio, W., & Serapio, M. (1991). Human resource systems in an international alliance: The undoing of a done deal? *Organizational Dynamics* (Winter), 63–74.

Cava, A., & Mayer, D. (1993). Gender discrimination abroad. *Business and Economic Review*, 40: 13–16.

Church, A. (1982). Sojourner adjustment. *Psychological Bulletin*, 9: 540–72.

Cohen, L. L., & Swim, J. K. (1995). The differential impact of gender roles on women and men: Tokenism, self-confidence, and expectation. *Personality and Social Psychology Bulletin*, 21: 876–84.

Colwill, N. L., & Temple, L. (1987). Three jobs and two people: The dual career dilemma. *Business Quarterly*: 12–15.

Conference Board (1992). *Recruiting and Selecting International Managers*. New York: Conference Board.

Cornille, T. A. (1993). Supporuit systems and the relocation process for children and families. *Marriage and Family Review*, 19: 281–98.

Copeland, L., & Griggs, L. (1985). *Going International*. New York: Random House.

Cox, T. (1994). *Cultural Diversity in Organizations*. San Francisco: Berrett-Koehler.

Crouter, A. (1984). Spillover from family to work: The neglected side of the work-family interface. *Human Relations*, 37: 425–42.

Cui, G., & van den Berg, S. (1991). Testing the construct validity of intercultural effectiveness. *International Journal of Intercultural Relations*, 15: 227–41.

Davison, E. D., & Punnett, B. J. (1995). International assignments: is there a role for gender and race in decisions? *International Journal of Human Resource Management*, 6: 411–41.

Diaz vs. Pan American World Airways, Inc. No. 30098 5th Cir. 1971.

Dinges, N. (1983). Intercultural competence. In D. Landis & R. W. Brislin (Eds.) *Handbook of Intercultural Training: Issues in Theory and Design*. Vol. 1. New York: Pergamon Press.

Dobryznski, J. H. (1996). The out-of-sight Americans: Executive pay later for their stints abroad. *International Herald Tribune*, August 18, 1, 7.

Donnell, S. M., & Hall, J. (1980). Men and women as managers: A significant case of no significant difference. *Organizational Dynamics* (Spring), 60–77.

Dvir, T., Eden, D., & Banjo, M. L. (1995). Self-fulfilling prophecy and gender: Can women be Pygmalion and Galatea? *Journal of Applied Psychology*, 80: 253–70.

Early, P. C. (1987). Intercultural training for managers: A comparison of documentary and interpersonal methods. *Academy of Management Review*, 39: 685–98.

Feltes, P., Robinson, R. K., & Fink, R. L. (1993). American female expatriates and the Civil Rights Act of 1991: Balancing legal and business interests. *Business Horizons*, 36: 82–6.

Fernandez, J. P., & Barr, M. (1993). *The Diversity Advantage.* New York: Lexington Books.

Fernandez v. Wynn Oil Co. 653 F.2d 1273 9th Cir. 1981.

Fiedler, F., Mitchell, T., & Triandis, H. (1971). The cultural assimilator: An approach to cross cultural training. *Journal of Applied Psychology*, 56: 95–102.

Fukuda, K., & Chu, P. (1994). Wrestling with expatriate family problems: Japanese experiences in East Asia. *International Studies of Management and Organizations*, 24: 36–47.

Galinsky, E., Bond, J. T., & Friedman, D. E. (1993). *National Study of the Changing Workforce.* New York: Families and Work Institute.

Hall, E. T., & Hall, M. R. (1987). *Hidden Differences: Doing Business with the Japanese.* Garden City: Anchor Press.

Harvey, M. G. (1985). The executive family: An overlooked variable in international assignments. *Columbia Journal of World Business*, 20: 84–92.

Hood, J. N., & Koberg, C. S. (1994). Patterns of differential assimilation and acculturation for women in business organizations. *Human Relations*, 47: 159–81.

Izraeli, D. N., Banai, M., & Zeira, Y. (1980). Women executives in MNC subsidiaries. *California Management Review*, 23: 53–63.

Jelinek, M., & Adler, N. J. (1988). Women: World class managers for global competition. *Academy of Management Executive*, 2: 11–19.

Kanter, R. M. (1977). *Work and Family in the United States: A Critical Review and Agenda of Research Policy.* New York: Russell Sage Foundation.

Kelly, R. F., & Vyodanoff, P. (1985). Work family role strain among employed parents. *Family Relations*, 34: 367–74.

Kunda, Z., & Thagard, P. F. (1996). Forming impressions from stereotypes, traits, and behaviors: A parallel-constraint-satisfaction theory. *Psychological Review*, 103: 284–308.

Laabs, J. (1993). Rating the international relocation hot spots. *Personnel Journal*, 72: 19.

Lambert, S. J. (1990). Processes linking work and family: A critical review and research agenda. *Human Relations*, 43: 239–57.

Leiter, M. P., & Durup, M. J. (1996). Work, home, and in-between: A longitudinal study of spillover. *Journal of Applied Behavioral Science*, 32: 29–47.

McClenahen, J. S. (1997). To go or not to go? How do you answer the call of a job abroad? *Industry Week*, January 20, 33, 36.

McEvoy, G. M., & Parker, B. (1995). Expatriate adjustment: Causes and consequences. In J. Selmer (Ed.), *Expatriate Management* (pp. 97–114). Westport, CT: Quorum Books.

Mendenhall, M., & Oddou, G. (1985). The dimensions of expatriate acculturation. *Academy of Management Review*, 10: 3947.

Mendenhall, M., & Oddou, G. (1988). The overseas assignment: A practical look. *Business Horizons*, 31: 78–84.

Moran, Stahl, & Boyer, Inc. (1988). *Status of American Female Expatriate Employees: Survey Results.* Boulder, CO.

Napier, N. K., & Taylor, S. (1995). *Western Women Working in Japan: Breaking Corporate Barriers.* Westport, CT: Quorum Books.

Nelson, D. L., Quick, J. C., & Joplin, J. R. (1991). Psychological contracting and newcomer socialization: An attachment theory foundation. *Journal of Social Behavior and Personality*, 6: 55–72.

Noe, R. A. (1988). Women and mentoring: A review and research agenda. *Academy of Management Review*, 13: 65–78.

Piotrowski, C. (1979). *Work and Family System.* New York: The Free Press. 1979.

Powell, G. N., & Butterfield, D. A. (1979). The "good manager": Masculine or androgynous? *Academy of Management Journal*, 22: 395–403.

Punnett, B. J. (1997). Towards effective management of expatriate spouses. *Journal of World Business*, 32: 243–57.

Punnett, B. J., Crocker, O., & Stevens, M. A. (1992). The challenge for women expatriates and spouses: some empirical evidence. *International Journal of Human Resource Management*, 3: 585–92.

Ragins, B. R. (1989). Barriers to mentoring: The female manager's dilemma. *Human Relations*, 42: 1–22.

Ragins, B. R. (1991). Gender effects in subordinate evaluations of leaders: Real or artifact? *Journal of Organizational Behavior*, 12: 259–68.

Ragins, B. R., & Sundstrom, E. (1989). Gender and power in organizations. *Psychological Bulletin*, 105: 51–88.

Rosenberg, M. (1979). *Conceiving the Self*. New York: Basic Books.

Rothbart, M., Fulero, S., Jensen, C., Howard, J., & Birrell, P. (1978). From individual to group impressions: Availability heuristics in stereotype formation. *Journal of Experimental Social Psychology*, 14: 237–325.

Sachdev, I., & Bourhis, R. (1991). Power and status differentials in minority and majority group relations. *European Journal of Social Psychology*, 21: 1–24.

Sackett, P. R., DuBois, C. L., & Wiggins-Noe, A. (1991). Tokenism in performance evaluation: The effects of work group representation on male-female and black-white differences in performance ratings. *Journal of Applied Psychology*, 76: 263–7.

Stahelski, A. J., & Payton, C. F. (1995). The effects of status cues on choices of social power and influences strategies. *Journal of Social Psychology*, 135: 553–60.

Stone, R. (1991). Expatriate selection and failure. *Human Resource Planning*, 14: 9–18.

Stroh, L. K., & Caligiuri, P. M. (1998). Strategic human resources: A new source for competitive advantage in the global arena. *International Journal of Human Resource Management*, 9: 1–17.

Stroh, L. K., Dennis, L. E., & Cramer, T. C. (1994). Predictors of expatriate adjustment. *International Journal of Organizational Analysis*, 2: 177–94.

Teagarden, M. B., & Gordon, G. D. (1995). Corporate selection strategies and expatriate manager success. In J. Selmer (Ed.), *Expatriate Management* (pp. 17–36). Westport, CT: Quorum Books.

Tharenou, P., Latimer, S., & Conroy, D. (1994). How do you make it to the top? An examination of influences on women's and men's managerial advancement. *Academy of Management Journal*, 37: 899–931.

Tung, R. L. (1981). Selection and training of personnel for overseas assignments. *Columbia Journal of World Business*, 16: 68–78.

Tung, R. L. (1995). Women in a changing global economy. Paper presented at the Society for Industrial and Organizational Psychology, Orlando, FL.

Tung, R. L. (1997). Canadian expatriates in Asia-Pacific: An analysis of their attitude toward and experience in international assignments. Paper presented at the meeting of the Society for Industrial and Organizational Psychology, St. Louis, MO.

Tversky, A. & Kahneman, D. (1973). Availability: A heuristic for judging frequency and probability. *Cognitive Psychology*, 5: 207–32.

Wanous, J. P., & Colella, A. (1989). Organizational entry research: Current status and future directions. In K. M. Rowland & G. R. Ferris (Eds.), *Research in Personnel and Human Resource Management* (pp. 59–120). Greenwich, CT: JAI Press.

Weeks, D. A. (1992). *Recruiting and Selecting International Managers. The Conference Board Report Number 998*. New York: Conference Board, Inc.

Westwood, R. I., & Leung, S. M. (1994). The female expatriate manager experience: Coping with gender and culture. *International Studies of Management and Organization*, 24: 64–85.

Wiggins-Frame, M., & Shehan, C. L. (1994). Work and well-being in the two-person career: Relocation stress and coping among clergy husbands and wives. *Family Relations*, 43: 196–205.

Zajonc, R. B. (1968). Attitudinal effects of mere exposure. *Journal of Personality and Social Psychology Monograph Supplement*, 9: 1–27.

Serving Two Masters:
Managing the Dual Allegiance
of Expatriate Employees

J. Stewart Black and Hal B. Gregersen

Each year hundreds of thousands of expatriate managers all over the world find themselves torn between their allegiance to the parent firm and their allegiance to the local foreign operation. To understand this tension, consider the following situation. A Dutch expatriate manager in a multinational consumer products firm is faced on the one hand, with a parent firm that wants a set of products introduced in the host country (a large developing nation) as part of its global brand image strategy. On the other hand, the host country government wants high-technology transferred into the country, not just consumer products placed on store shelves. Market research suggests that local consumers are interested in some of the core products but not others and in products not currently part of the firm's core set. The parent firm has a philosophy encouraging participative decision making, but host national employees expect managers to make decisions without burdening them.

Faced with serving two masters, many expatriate managers end up directing their allegiance too far in one direction or the other, creating serious costs and consequences for both themselves and their organizations. For example, if individuals are too committed to the local operation relative to the parent firm, it is difficult for the home office to coordinate with them. A senior Honda executive commented to us that Honda had incurred "non-trivial" costs trying to coordinate its global strategy for the new Honda Accord because some expatriate managers were too focused on the local situation. Expatriates who are overly committed to the parent firm relative to the local operation often inappropriately implement policies or procedures from the home office. The medical equipment division of a large US multinational firm recently tried to implement home office financial reporting and accounting procedures that simply did not apply to and would not work in its newly acquired French subsidiary.

FIGURE 1   Forms of Expatriate Allegiance

Allegiance to the Parent Firm	Low	Expatriates who see themselves as free agents	Expatriates who "go native"
	High	Expatriates who leave their hearts at home	Expatriates who see themselves as dual citizens
		Low	High
		Allegiance to the Local Operation	

Perhaps most important, the high competitive pressure, great geographical distances, and wide cultural diversity of global operations combined with ineffective management of expatriates can set off a vicious cycle that erodes or even destroys a firm's global competitive position:

1   Unbalanced allegiance can lead to a variety of failures during and after international assignments.
2   As managers hear about these failures, firms find it increasingly difficult to attract top international candidates.
3   Increasingly worse candidates are sent overseas, producing even worse organizational results and more failed careers.
4   This further limits the pool of willing and qualified candidates.
5   Over time the firm's overseas competitive position erodes.
6   This cycle spirals downward until it becomes nearly unstoppable.

Today's multinational firms need managers who are highly committed to both the parent firm and the local operation and who can integrate the demands and objectives of both organizations. As one senior executive put it, the bottom line question is: "How can we get expatriate managers who are committed to the local overseas operation during their international assignments, but who remain loyal to the parent firm?" Unfortunately, our research suggests that expatriate managers with high dual allegiance are a rare commodity.[1]

This is not surprising in light of studies of dual commitment in domestic contexts, such as commitment to a union and an organization (that is, United Auto Workers and General Motors) or commitment to a profession and an organization (that is, nursing and a specific hospital). These studies have found that certain factors have different effects on the two targets of commitment and that people hold different patterns of commitment. Some individuals are unilaterally committed to one organization over the other, some have low levels of commitment to both, and others have high levels of commitment to both.[2]

In this article we present a description of the patterns, causes, and consequences of expatriate dual allegiance. In brief, expatriate managers can be grouped into one of four allegiance patterns. They can be overly committed to the parent firm or the local operation, highly committed to both organizations, or committed to neither. These four basic patterns are presented in the Figure 1 matrix. Much more important than the patterns of dual allegiance are the factors that cause them and the related organizational and individual consequences. We describe the causes and consequences associated with each pattern and illustrate them with actual cases generated through numerous interviews and surveys (most managers asked that their names and firms be disguised). We also examine what firms are doing now and what they can do in the future to more effectively manage their expatriate managers.

FREE AGENTS

As an undergraduate, Paul Jackson majored in Asian studies and studied for two years in Japan. At graduation, he had intermediate fluency in Chinese and near fluency in Japanese. He immediately went on to receive a master's degree from the American Graduate School of International Management in Phoenix. He was hired by a major east coast bank and two years later was sent on a three-year assignment to Hong Kong. The expatriate package Paul and his family received made life in Hong Kong enjoyable. However, Paul felt little loyalty to the parent firm back home or the Hong Kong operation. First and foremost, Paul was committed to his career. Because he was such a hard charger, the bank invested a substantial amount of time and money into him for language and technical training. He worked hard but always kept an ear out for better jobs and pay. Two years into his Hong Kong assignment, he found a better position in another firm and took it. Four years into that company and assignment, he took a job with a different US bank and its Taiwan operation. Four years later, he took a job as vice-president and general manager for the Japan subsidiary of a large west coast bank.

When we interviewed Paul about his work history, he said: "I can't really relate to your question about which organization I feel allegiance to. I do my job, and I do it well. I play for whatever team needs me and wants me. I'm like a free agent in baseball or a hired gun in the old West. If the pay and job are good enough, I'm off. You might say, 'have international expertise, will travel.'"

Interestingly, Paul was actually part of a network we discovered of "hired-gun free agents" in the Pacific Rim. The network consisted of a group of about ten American managers hired as expatriates (not as local hires), who were either bi- or trilingual, and who had spent over half of their professional careers in Asia. This group of free agents passed along information to each other about various firms that were looking for experienced expatriate managers for their Asia operations.

Hired-gun free agents

These expatriates have a low level of commitment to both their parent firms and their local operations. They are first and foremost committed to their own "gun-slinging" careers. When asked what long-term career implications this approach might have for them, these expatriates commonly indicated that it would be very difficult for them to ever "go back home" and move up the headquarter's hierarchy in any firm. However, most did not want to for several reasons. First, they felt the experience their children received from both an educational (schools are generally international, private, and paid for by the firm) and general life perspective was far superior to what they would receive back home. Second, the expatriates would be worse off financially if they went home and had to give up the extra benefits of their expatriate packages. Third, most were confident that they would not be given a job back home with the status, freedom, and importance of those jobs they held overseas. Consequently, most of these hired guns seemed happy with their lives and careers overseas.

Firms tend to view these expatriates with some ambivalence. On the one hand, even though these hired guns receive special benefit packages, they tend to be slightly less expensive than sending expatriates from the home country. Furthermore, these expatriates have already demonstrated their specialized skills, such as language, and their ability to succeed in international settings – qualities that are often lacking in a firm's internal managerial or executive ranks. This may be especially important to US firms; on average 15–20% of their expatriate managers fail in their overseas assignments, at great cost to the firm, because they have serious problems adjusting to the foreign culture.

On the other hand, these free agent expatriates often leave the firm with little warning. Replacing them is usually costly and difficult and can have negative consequences for both the parent firm and the local operation. Sometimes these hired guns serve their own short-term career objectives at the expense of the firm's long-term interests. Also, as mentioned, few of these expatriates are willing to repatriate to the home office. This makes integrating their international experience or specific country or regional knowledge into the firm's global strategy formulation process next to impossible.

Plateaued-career free agents

Our research uncovered another type of expatriate with low levels of commitment to both the parent firm and the local operation. This type of expatriate typically comes from the ranks of home country employees rather than of hired international experts. These expatriates are generally not committed to the parent firm before leaving for the overseas assignment in part because their careers have often plateaued. They take the international assignment because they do not see themselves going anywhere in the home operations, and they hope an international stint will change things. Or they are simply attracted by the sweet financial packages common to most overseas assignments. Unfortunately, many of the factors that led to low commitment before the international assignment result in low commitment to the local operation once the manager is overseas.

Several factors can contribute to development of this type of expatriate. First, if firms simply allow candidates for overseas assignments to self-select, they open the door for this type of expatriate. As one expatriate said: "I figured I was stalled in my job [back in North Carolina], so why not take a shot at an overseas assignment, especially given what I'd heard about the high standard of living even mid-level managers enjoyed overseas." Research has shown that certain personal characteristics correlate with successful adjustment to international assignments.[3] A self-selection process leaves personal characteristics of the expatriates to chance. Second, placing a low value on international operations can increase the probability that plateaued managers will apply for overseas assignments and decrease the probability that high-potential managers will volunteer for them. In such an environment, high-potential managers know that the place to get ahead is not overseas somewhere, out of sight and out of mind, but at home. Finally, lack of pre-departure cross-cultural training can also reinforce low levels of commitment to the parent firm and the local operation. US firms may be particularly vulnerable to this factor; roughly 70% of all US expatriates receive no pre-departure cross-cultural training.[4] Lack of firm-sponsored training can contribute to the view that "the company doesn't care about me, so why should I care about it?" Lack of training can also inhibit the expatriate from understanding the foreign culture and becoming committed to the local operation.

Unlike the hired guns, many of the plateaued-career free agents are not happy in their overseas assignments. Their low level of commitment often results in little effort to adjust to the local operation and culture. At worst, they fail the assignment. A failed overseas assignment not only inhibits the individual's career advancement, it can strike severe blow to the individual's identity and self-confidence. Of course, there are also costs to the firm. Beyond the $100,000 to $250,000 it costs to bring the employee and family home and send out a replacement, the firm incurs the costs of damaged client and supplier relationships.[5] The lack of leadership during the replacement process can contribute to damaged internal and external relations. Failed assignments can also generate rumors back home that international posts are the "kiss of death" for a career, which in turn makes it more difficult to attract good candidates in the future.

Even if lack of commitment doesn't result in a failed assignment, it can still be costly to the person and the organization. Bob Brown was a typical plateaued manager for a major US aircraft manufacturer who transferred to Taiwan three years before his interview with us. Bob was not very excited about living in Taiwan and neither was his family. His wife and daughter repeatedly asked to go back home. Bob pointed out that there was really no job for him to go back to. His daughter became so distraught that she began doing extremely poorly in school. This and other pressures put a severe strain on Bob's relationship with his wife. In an interview, Bob summed it up by stating that his home life was in shambles and that work was merely a paycheck, but a fat one (his compensation and benefit package was worth about $210,000 per year).

Perhaps the parent and local firm were getting their money's worth out of Bob, but it seems unlikely. Past studies have found that of those expatriates who complete their assignments, about one-third are considered ineffective.[6] Also, it is hard to imagine that a manager whose career has plateaued back home could be paid two to three times a normal compensation package and still provide a good return on that expense. If, as we suspect, such managers cannot, then this represents a serious economic loss to firms.

To summarize, low commitment to the parent firm and the local operation seems to be found in two general types of expatriate managers – hired-gun free agents and plateaued-career free agents. Although the causes and consequences of each type are different, both types represent potentially serious costs to the individual, parent firm, and local operation, since 41% of our sample fell into this group.

GOING NATIVE

The next allegiance pattern involves having high levels of commitment to the local operation but low levels of commitment to the parent firm. These expatriates usually form a strong identification with and attachment to the country's culture, language, values, and business practices. Consequently, these expatriates are often referred to as those who "go native."

Gary Ogden had been with a large computer company for fifteen years. He was the country manager for the firm's instrument division in France and had been in Paris for about four years, his third international assignment. Of his fifteen years with the parent firm, over half had been spent overseas, including six of the last eight years. Given that this was his third international stint, it had not taken long for Gary, his wife, and their three daughters (ages six, nine, and eleven) to settle in to life in France. His girls had enrolled in regular French schools when they moved to Paris and were now fluent for their ages. Gary's French was not perfect but he was comfortable in business situations. He had spent long hours trying to understand the local business situation, and he thought that corporate was constantly requesting and demanding things that either worked against objectives for the French unit or couldn't be done effectively or sometimes at all in France. Still, Gary loved it so much in France that he had already requested an extension, even though his contract only required him to stay another six months. When asked to describe his commitment to the parent firm and the local operation, he responded, "My first commitment is to the unit here. In fact, half the time I feel as if corporate is a competitor I must fight rather than a benevolent parent I can look to for support."

Our research suggests that individuals like Gary Ogden who have spent a number of years overseas, who adjust to the local culture, and who feel at odds with corporate headquarters are the most likely to go native. As managers spend more time away from the home office, their identities seem less and less tied to the parent firm. The firm becomes both literally and psychologically distant, as compared to the local operation. Additionally, the lack of formal communication with the home office through mechanisms such as sponsors (individuals assigned to keep in touch with specific expatriates) also serves to cause or reinforce this commitment pattern. Firms that are structured in international divisions and have cadres of "career internationalists" may be particularly vulnerable to this pattern.

What are the consequences of going native in terms of expatriate allegiance? Let us consider the individual's perspective. First, Gary felt that he had effectively managed the local situation. He pointed out that his knowledge of the language, culture, and union structure had enabled him to avoid an almost certain and probably very costly strike. Unfortunately, because the strike never happened, Gary felt that corporate did not recognize his achievement. Second, because Gary knew that his career depended to some extent on the evaluations made of him back at corporate, when he had to "fight" the parent firm, he had to do it subtly: "Sometimes I would simply ignore their directives if I didn't think they were appropriate or relevant to our operations. If it's really important, eventually someone from regional or corporate will hassle me, and I'll have to respond. If it isn't important or if they think I implemented what they wanted, they just leave me alone. As long as the general results are good, it doesn't seem as if there are big costs to this approach." Gary also indicated that on occasion he had to fight corporate more overtly. Although this may have cost him back at corporate, fighting these fights and especially winning them helped him gain the trust and loyalty of the local national employees. Their greater loyalty made it easier for him to be effective in the country. Interestingly, this effectiveness often later earned him points and slack back home.

Third, when Gary was repatriated after international assignments, he disliked the lack of responsibility compared to what he enjoyed overseas and the general lack of appreciation and utilization of his international knowledge. He nearly quit the firm both times he was repatriated. His low commitment to the parent firm heightened his dissatisfaction. Gary stated that both times it was receipt of another overseas assignment that kept him from leaving the firm.

From the parent firm's point of view, one of the common problems associated with expatriates who go native is the difficulty of getting corporate policies or programs implemented at the local level. Often the intense commitment to the local foreign operation leads these expatriates to implement what they think is relevant, in a way they deem appropriate, and then to ignore or fight the rest. This can be very costly, especially when the parent firm is trying to closely coordinate activities in a wide variety of countries for the good of global corporate objectives.

Also, to the extent that low commitment to the parent firm contributes to repatriation turnover, the parent firm loses the opportunity to incorporate the knowledge and experience of these expatriates into its global strategy or to incorporate some of these individuals into their succession plans. Interestingly, our research found that most expatriates, regardless of commitment pattern, do not feel that the international knowledge and experience they gained overseas is valued by their firms (91% of US expatriates, 97% of Japanese expatriates, and 89% of Finnish expatriates). In general, firms do not seem to be utilizing these valuable resources.

Despite the negative aspects of expatriates who go native, many corporate executives recognize that these expatriates are not all bad. The high level of allegiance to the local operation generally leads these expatriates to identify with and understand the host national employees, customers, and suppliers. This understanding can translate into (1) new products and services or adapted products and services that are well targeted to the local market, and (2) managerial approaches that are suited to the host national employees.

The importance of a managerial style modified to suit host national employees must not be overlooked, especially by US firms. Although most US firms assume that good managers in New York will do fine in Tokyo or Hong Kong and consequently select expatriates based primarily on domestic track records, evidence suggests that managerial characteristics that are related to performance in the United States are not related to performance in foreign countries.[7]

This potentially positive aspect of these expatriate managers may be particularly true in firms at a multidomestic stage of globalization.[8] In most multidomestic firms, each overseas unit competes in its national or regional market independent of the firm's other organizational units in other countries. The primary information flow is within the local operation, rather than between it and the parent firm. There is a premium on understanding the local market and the host national people and culture. Expatriates with relatively high allegiance to the local operation may be particularly beneficial in this situation.

In summary, managers who have spent a lot of time away from the parent firm, who can adjust to foreign cultures, and who lack formal communication ties to the parent firm are the most likely to go native; they constituted about 15% of our sample. There are pros and cons to this pattern for both the individual and the parent firm.

Expatriates who go native often have valuable insights into the local operation, culture, and market; they can adapt procedures, products, or managerial approaches to fit the local situation. They may also be less likely to return prematurely and to invoke the serious costs associated with early returns. However, they also can frustrate global coordination efforts and may not be committed enough to the parent firm after repatriation to pass their knowledge on for country, regional, or global strategic planning.[9]

HEARTS AT HOME

The third type of expatriate manager is highly committed to the parent firm but has little allegiance to the local foreign operation. We refer to these expatriates as those who "leave their hearts at home;" they constituted about 12% of our sample. These expatriate managers identify much more strongly with the parent firm than they do with the local operation and the local country's culture, language, and business practices.

Earl Markus was the managing director of the European headquarters of a large building-supply firm's "do-it-yourself" retail division. This was Earl's first international assignment in his twenty-two years with the firm. He was married and had two children, both of whom were in college and therefore did not move with their parents to European headquarters in Belgium. Earl had worked his way up from a store manager to southwest regional manager and eventually to vice president of finance over the previous twenty-two years.

The European operations were fairly new, and Earl saw his mission as expanding the number of retail outlets from the current nine in Belgium to fifty throughout western Europe. The president and CEO of the US parent firm had assigned the CEO, Frank Johnson, to work closely with Earl during his three-year assignment.

One year into the assignment, Earl was on schedule and had opened fifteen new outlets in three countries. But he was very frustrated. He said that he had seriously considered packing up and going home more than once during the year. He claimed Europeans were lazy and slow to respond to directives. When asked about his allegiance, he said that there was no contest. He was first and foremost committed to corporate, and when the next two years were up, he was headed back home. As an example of how things had gone, Earl described the implementation of the inventory system.

About eight months into the assignment, Frank Johnson suggested that Earl implement the new computerized inventory system that had just been phased into US outlets. Frank was excited about the system's ability to reduce costs and shrinkage (i.e., theft), and he had high expectations of similar benefits for its use in Europe. For proper operation, the system required daily recording of sales and weekly random physical inventory of specific items. These reports needed to be transferred within forty-eight hours to the central office, which would generate total and store-by-store reports. The forms and procedure manuals were printed, and a two-day seminar was held for all European store managers and directors of operations and relevant staff members. Two months later, Earl inquired about how the system was operating. It wasn't. He said all he got from his managers were "lame excuses" about why the system would not work, especially in Belgium.

This case illustrates some of the main causes and consequences of expatriates' allegiance being tilted strongly in favor of the parent firm. It is not surprising that our research found a significant correlation between long tenure in the parent firm and allegiance to it. These expatriates had invested time, sweat, and heartache with the parent firm, and they expected a "return" on this investment. Over time, the expatriates' identities had intertwined with the identities of the parent firm. A high level of allegiance to the parent firm was a natural consequence.

Our research found two other factors that, in combination, contributed to this allegiance pattern. The first factor was poor adjustment to the host country and culture, in part fostered by selection processes that primarily considered domestic track records. Because these expatriates could not relate to the host country's culture and people, they could not develop a strong sense of allegiance to the local operation. The second factor was having a sponsor in the home office who was formally assigned to the expatriate to maintain a formal tie. This tie focused attention and allegiance toward the parent firm and away from the local operation.

What personal and organizational consequences resulted from this allegiance pattern? Earl Markus was frustrated; he had considered leaving the overseas assignment several times. It was his fear of negative career consequences more than anything else that kept him from going. In addition to early return costs, which we discussed in the section on free agents, organizations can also incur the cost of having ineffectual managers. These managers often try to implement and enforce programs that are inappropriate for the local operation, or they implement them in ways that offend local employees, customers, or suppliers. Earl's inventory implementation effort antagonized employees and created an adversarial relationship that hampered other programs and changes he subsequently tried to initiate.

However, just as in the case of going native, not all the consequences of leaving one's heart at home are bad. Our research found that US expatriates who had a high commitment to the parent firm during the international assignment were more likely to want to stay with the parent firm after their repatriation. Thus, to the extent that these expatriates gain valuable experience, knowledge, and skills during their international assignments, their parent firms have greater opportunities to gain future returns from them. Unfortunately, the low commitment to the local operation reduces the knowledge these expatriates can gain. Nevertheless, expatriates who leave their hearts at home can provide another advantage. They often make it easier for the home office to coordinate activities between headquarters and the subsidiary. In Earl's case, it was very easy for the corporate purchasing agent to utilize the buying power of headquarters' centralized purchasing activities for the European operations. This coordination gave the European operations access to substantial price savings.

The ability to coordinate easily with the home office may be particularly beneficial for firms at the export stage of globalization. The primary objective of most firms at this stage is to sell in foreign markets products developed and manufactured in the home country. Information flows primarily from the parent firm to the local operation. The home office plays a key coordinating role, and good coordination with the subsidiaries is important. Expatriates with relatively high commitment to the parent firm are less likely to resist following the home office's coordination efforts than expatriates with low levels of commitment to the parent.

DUAL CITIZENS

The final category consists of expatriate managers who are highly committed to both the parent *and* the local operation – dual citizens. We use the word "citizen" because it seems to reflect this group's behavior, attitudes, and emotions. These managers tend to see themselves as citizens of both the foreign country and their home country and as citizens of both the local operation and the parent corporation. They feel responsible for serving both organization's interests.

Joan Beckenridge was the director of a prominent US consulting firm's Japan office. This was Joan's second international assignment in her thirteen years with the firm. Her first assignment was a one-year special project stint in Singapore seven years before. Joan was one of three candidates considered for the job in Japan and had been selected based not only on her past performance but also on assessments by outside consultants. Because the job required a high degree of interaction with host nationals in a novel culture, Joan was given five months' notice before departing for Japan. During this time she received about sixty hours of cross-cultural training. In addition, her spouse received about ten hours of survival briefing. Four months after arriving in Japan, Joan received another forty hours of cross-cultural training. She also took advantage of hundreds of hours of language training, paid for by the parent firm.

Perhaps most important, Joan had a clear set of objectives for her assignment. The Japan office had been established to serve the Japanese subsidiaries of the firm's US clients. At this point, the office's growth was limited by the slowed pace of expansion of US client firms to Japan. Joan was charged with developing Japanese clients. This would serve two objectives. First, it would increase the office's growth potential, and second, it would make it easier to secure Japanese firms' US subsidiaries as clients, which would expand US operations.

Despite these preparations, Joan found herself frustrated in one area. Headquarters and the local operation had differing expectations regarding business and entertainment expenses. Headquarters did not realize how much time and money it took to cultivate effective relationships in Japan. Joan's Japanese business associates were fond of pointing out that their country had the highest business entertainment expenses as a percentage of sales in the world. Joan felt the tension between corporate "bean counters" who worried over entertainment expenses and local staff who floated contact opportunities that Joan could not develop. However, unlike many expatriates in similar situations, Joan had a mechanism for working out these differences. She had a high-level sponsor at corporate who was officially assigned to help her. Through this sponsor, Joan could educate corporate and bring corporate and local expectations in synch.

It was also clear from the beginning how this assignment fitted Joan's overall career path and how her repatriation would be handled. Although she was not guaranteed a specific position upon repatriation, Joan knew what her general opportunities would be if she met her objectives in Japan.

Perhaps the most important factor in Joan's effectiveness was that she had a great degree of autonomy in deciding how to achieve the assignment's objectives. She had the flexibility to deal with the inevitable conflicts and ambiguities that cropped up in the job.

When asked about her allegiance, Joan said, "I feel a strong sense of allegiance to both companies [the local operation and the parent firm]. Although they sometimes have different objectives, I try to satisfy both whenever I can." When the two organizations conflicted, Joan would work to bring them together rather than simply following one or the other.

The personal and organizational consequences of Joan's dual-citizenship orientation were primarily positive. Joan indicated that it was sometimes frustrating to be torn between parent and local needs but that the clarity of her objectives, the latitude she had to pursue them, and the relative infrequency and small magnitude of the conflicts made the work rewarding and satisfying. Joan did well in her five years in Japan and received a substantial promotion upon repatriation to a position in which her knowledge was utilized in domestic and international expansion plans. For the organization, Joan's dual-citizenship orientation helped her build solid relations with Japanese clients and government officials and helped the home office establish relationships with Japanese clients' US subsidiaries. Joan believed her dual focus also gave her a greater ability to recruit high-quality Japanese employees, which was difficult for competitors.

Thirty-two percent of our sample of US expatriate managers fit this allegiance pattern. Although it would be inaccurate to say that these expatriates never returned home early, never left the firm after repatriation, or never had adjustment or performance problems during international assignments, this group had a higher probability than the others of completing the foreign assignment, staying with the firm upon repatriation, and adjusting well to the overseas stay. These expatriate managers were much more interested than the others in understanding the needs, objectives, constraints, and opportunities of both the local operation and the parent firm. They talked of using this understanding to benefit both organizations. They could effectively implement corporate policies in the local operation and pass information from the local operation back to corporate in order to help shape strategy and policy development.

As indicated in Joan Beckenridge's case, *role conflict* played an important part in determining commitment. When the parent and local organizations had different expectations, demands, and objectives, the managers who had to negotiate these differences suffered from role conflict. The greater the role conflict, the less managers felt responsible for the outcomes and the less they felt committed to either organization. As one expatriate put it: "It's hard to feel responsible for what happens when you're being torn in opposite directions." In contrast, the greater the consistency between the two organizations, the more expatriate managers felt responsible for what happened and the more they felt committed to both organizations.

Role ambiguity produced a similar dynamic. Whereas role conflict follows from clear expectations that conflict, role ambiguity occurs when expectations from both organizations simply are not clear. Poor coordination between the parent firm and the local operation was a common source of role ambiguity. When we asked one expatriate manager how much responsibility he felt for what happened on his job, he replied: "How can I feel responsible, when I don't even know what I'm supposed to do or what's expected of me?" In contrast, the clearer the role, the more expatriates felt responsible for what happened at work and committed to both organizations.

Another factor related to dual allegiance was *clarity of repatriation programs*. Over 60% of US firms have no systematic or formal repatriation program.[10] Clear, systematic repatriation programs facilitate high levels of commitment to both organizations. Such programs seem to free expatriates from worrying about going home and allow them to focus on the job at hand. This facilitates allegiance to the local operation. Such programs also seem to communicate that the parent firm cares about their expatriates and has thought about reintegration. This creates a greater sense of obligation to the parent firm.

The most powerful factor in creating dual allegiance was *role discretion*. Role discretion is the freedom to decide what needs to be done, how and when it should be done, and who should do it. The more discretion expatriate managers have, the more they feel responsible for what happens at work and committed to the local operation. Because they generally view the parent firm as responsible for the amount of freedom they enjoy, this translates into a greater sense of commitment to the parent firm as well. Part of the reason that discretion is the most powerful factor is that most expatriate managers experience some role conflict and ambiguity. Role discretion gives the manager the freedom to define expectations and resolve conflicting ones.

Although dual citizens are desirable for any firm at any globalization stage, they are most critical for firms at the coordinated multinational stage. Such firms need information to flow back and forth between the home office and foreign subsidiaries and from one foreign subsidiary to another. They need managers who identify with both the people back home and those in the local operation. They need managers who will stay in the assignment, who will try to meet the needs of both organizations, and who will stay with the firm after repatriation so that their international experience, knowledge, and skills can be utilized.

POLICY IMPLICATIONS

Although most executives in multinational firms are aware of the issues concerning expatriate allegiance, few of the expatriates we interviewed said that their firms understood the cause and consequences of the different allegiance patterns or had systems for developing dual-citizen expatriates. However, many firms had found ways to counterbalance "lopsided" allegiance. Below we present what some of these firms are doing, and we propose steps for developing dual-citizen expatriates.

Strategy 1: Counterbalancing going native

Managers who have several years of international experience and who have successfully adjusted to foreign cultures in the past are most likely to go native. Although these managers tend to have a low commitment to the parent firm, they are also good candidates to send overseas because they lower the risks and associated costs of failed assignments and premature returns. What can firms do if their current policies tend to produce too many expatriate managers like Gary Ogden?

Limit time away from corporate   Honda brings expatriates home to Japan for a few years before they go overseas again. This method reinforces the link between the manager and the parent firm. Honda believes that it is not logical to expect career internationalists who move from one foreign assignment to the next to be highly committed to the parent firm.

Send managers with strong ties to corporate   Firms can send managers overseas who have longer tenure in the parent firm. The longer managers have been with the firm, the more they have invested in it, the more they identify with it, and the more they are committed to it. Also, long tenures build personal connections that keep individuals involved with corporate. However, this recommendation is problematic for firms such as General Electric (GE), General Motors (GM), and Ford, which increasingly use international assignments to develop younger, high-potential managers.

Establish corporate sponsor programs   GE uses sponsors to counterbalance the tendency to go native. The company assesses the expatriate's career objectives and chooses a senior manager, often in the function to which the expatriate is likely to return, who is willing to serve as sponsor. The sponsor maintains contact with the expatriate throughout the assignment, including face-to-face meetings; evaluates the expatriate's performance during the assignment; helps clarify the expatriate's career objectives and capabilities before repatriation; and provides career advice and help finding a position back at headquarters. Some divisions even commit to hiring the expatriate manager back into a specific position before the foreign assignment begins.

Executives at several firms with sponsorship programs gave us additional advice. Overall, they recommended that sponsor assignment be systematized. First, the sponsor should be senior enough relative to the expatriate to be able to provide a broad view of the organization. Second, the sponsor should receive specific guidelines about the form, content, and frequency of contacts with the expatriate. Too often the sponsor is simply assigned, and that's it. If the sponsor takes the initiative and fulfills the responsibility, things go well. Otherwise, the sponsorship is in name only. Finally, the responsibility of planning for repatriation should not rest solely with the sponsor but should be incorporated into the firm's career systems.

Provide pre-departure and post-arrival cross-cultural training   Most US firms do not provide any cross-cultural training for international assignments. While it may seem that pre-departure training would increase a tendency to identify with the host culture and thus go native, our data indicate that such training creates a sense of obligation to the parent firm stemming from the firm's demonstrated concern for the expatriate.[11] Although we only examined the impact of pre-departure training because fewer than 10% of the expatriates received post-arrival training, we suspect that a similarly positive effect could be generated by providing training after arrival if the expatriate understands that the parent firm, and not the local operation, is paying for and sponsoring the training.

Strategy 2: Counterbalancing hearts at home

Although many US executives seem unconcerned with the tendency of expatriates to leave their hearts at home, our research suggests that the consequences of this tendency are just as serious as those for going native. The lack of organizational practices in this area forces us to rely on our research for ways that firms might counterbalance the tendency of managers like Earl Markus to leave their hearts at home.

Send younger managers   The managers most likely to be highly committed to the parent firm and much less committed to the local operation are those with long tenures at the parent firm and little international experience. Thus, firms such as GE, GM, and Ford, which are increasingly sending younger managers overseas for career development, are perhaps unintentionally counterbalancing the hearts-at-home tendency.

Facilitate cross-cultural adjustment   Helping the expatriate manager adjust to the non-work environment is another powerful counterbalancing force. Ironically, many of the perks – such as company housing, car, and driver – that are given to senior expatriate executives actually isolate them and inhibit their adjustment to the environment. Family members, especially the spouse, are often more directly exposed to the foreign environment because they do not have the insulation provided by the corporate structure. Therefore, a firm's efforts to facilitate the family's adjustment can have a positive effect on the manager's adjustment.[12]

Provide cross-cultural training for the family   Ford is one of the few US firms that tries to consistently provide training and preparation for the families and especially spouses of its expatriates. Although Ford executives did not intend this training to counteract the hearts-at-home tendency, our research suggests that this is a likely consequence.

Encourage host-national sponsorship programs   Interacting with host nationals outside of work can help both families and managers adjust. Host nationals, who understand their own culture, are the best sources of instruction and especially feedback in getting along on a daily basis. However, such interaction is not always easy to develop. Firms can help by asking host national employees and their families to assist specific expatriates during the first few months. Care should be taken to match the sponsoring family's characteristics (that is, number and ages of children) with those of the expatriate family. Several Japanese auto firms actually have hired Americans who speak Japanese to help their expatriate managers and families adjust to life in the United States.

The Amos Tuck School's joint MBA program with the International University of Japan has a sponsorship program. A special employee in Japan is assigned to help US professors with logistical problems, such as housing and travel, during their stay. Several Tuck professors who spent a term in Japan expressed pleasant surprise at the willingness of both the special employee and other employees to go beyond logistical assistance and to help them navigate the cultural and business terrain. This assistance gave them important insights into the culture and people and helped them adjust to the new environment.

Strategy 3: Creating dual citizens

Although these mechanisms are useful for counterbalancing negative tendencies, the most important steps firms can take are those that create high levels of dual allegiance. Our research suggests that the primary target for fostering expatriates like Joan Beckenridge is the job.

Plan overseas jobs strategically   A firm that clearly defines the expatriate's job, reduces conflicts concerning job expectations, and gives the expatriate a fair amount of freedom in carrying out assigned tasks will foster a high level of dual allegiance. The idea is simple, but execution is complex.

One of the easiest but rarely utilized techniques for increasing role clarity is allowing the incumbent and the new manager an overlap period of several days or weeks. The more complex the job and the less experienced the new entrant, the longer the overlap. Several expatriates specifically mentioned this method as a relatively low-cost means of facilitating adjustment and effectiveness. Expatriates in Japan and Korea said that this overlap was necessary for properly introducing the replacement to employees, clients, and suppliers. Of course, sometimes there is no incumbent, and this option is not available.

Role clarification in and of itself does not necessarily reduce role conflict. In fact, clarification of job expectations can reveal previously hidden role conflicts, which most often stem from the differing expectations of the parent firm and the local operation. Thus firms must try to increase role clarity and decrease role conflict simultaneously. This requires understanding and integrating the perspectives of the parent firm and the local operation.

A firm's best intentions cannot entirely eliminate role ambiguity and conflict. This is probably why role discretion emerged as the single strongest factor in promoting high dual allegiance. Having a fair amount of freedom to decide what tasks to do, how and when to do them, and who should do them gives expatriates the flexibility to cope with ambiguity and conflict. However, too much discretion without clear objectives may make expatriates unintentionally work against the best interests of the parent firm, the local operation, or both. Firms need to consider all three job elements simultaneously.

We believe that role clarity, conflict, and discretion are best approached not as targets of manipulation but as outcomes of broader policy and strategic processes. If a firm wants to make significant, long-term, and effective changes in the expatriate manager's job, it should carefully assess the following issues:

1   Why is the expatriate being sent to this particular post? (Because there are no host nationals capable of filling the position? In order to provide developmental experience for the expatriate?)
2   How will job success be measured? What do you really want this particular person to do in this position?
3   Are the objectives of the parent firm and the local unit consistent? Are they consistent between the local unit as a whole and the individual's department?

4   How much should the parent firm coordinate and control the local operation? How much freedom and autonomy should the local unit have? Is the expatriate's level of discretion consistent with these coordination needs?

Without an assessment of these strategic issues, firms may adjust expectations in ways that are dysfunctional for the firm's overall strategy. For instance, firms may provide overlap time that serves only to clarify the severe expectation conflicts between the two organizations. Or firms may give too much freedom to expatriate managers. Consequently, such ad hoc adjustments are likely to have short-term positive results at best and severe negative results at worst. In contrast, an analysis that begins with the broader context naturally leads to appropriate job adjustments and a higher probability of a high dual allegiance.

Some readers may feel that their firms have moved beyond the coordinated multinational stage. Global firms need managers who are capable not just of dual citizenship but of world citizenship. Many firms are moving in this direction, but our data suggest that most expatriate managers are still struggling to successfully reach dual allegiance. It seems to us that the first practical step toward developing global managers for global firms is to develop managers who see themselves as dual citizens. Dual-citizen expatriates are best developed through: (1) careful selection processes; (2) cross-cultural training before and after arrival; (3) well-planned career systems that lead to clear, consistent job expectations and appropriate discretion levels; and (4) repatriation programs that effectively utilize expatriates' knowledge, skills, and experience. These steps will help expatriates more successfully serve two masters and help firms more effectively manage their expatriates.

Notes

1.   H. B. Gregersen and J. S. Black, "Antecedents to Dual Commitment during International Assignments," *Academy of Management Journal*, 35 (1992): 65–90. This article is based primarily on two international research projects. First, we did a questionnaire study of 321 US expatriate executives and managers while they were on assignment in Europe (Belgium, England, the Netherlands, and Germany) and the Pacific Rim (Japan, Korea, Taiwan, and Hong Kong). These expatriates had worked on average more than fourteen years in their US multinational firms representing a wide range of industries. We also completed in-depth interviews with more than thirty expatriates in both Pacific Rim and European countries. Second, we completed a study of expatriate commitment during repatriation for 174 Americans, 173 Japanese, and 104 Finns returning to their respective home countries after international assignments.

2.   C. V. Fukami and E. W. Larson, "Commitment to the Company and Union: Parallel Models," *Journal of Applied Psychology*, 69 (1984): 367–71; M. E. Gordon and R. T. Ladd, "Dual Allegiance: Renewal, Reconsideration, and Recantation," *Personnel Psychology*, 43 (1990): 37–69; H. B. Gregersen, "Multiple Commitments at Work and Extrarole Behavior during Three Stages of Organizational Tenure," *Journal of Business Research*, 25 (1992); and N. B. Tuma and A. J. Grimes, "A Comparison of Models of Role Orientations of Professionals in a Research-Oriented University," *Administrative Science Quarterly*, 26 (1981): 187–206.

3.   J. S. Black, "Personal Dimensions and Work Role Transitions," *Management International Review*, 30 (1990): 119–34; and M. E. Mendenhall and G. Oddou, "The Dimensions of Expatriate Acculturation," *Academy of Management Review*, 10 (1985): 39–47.

4. J. S. Black and M. Mendenhall, "Cross-Cultural Training Effectiveness: A Review and a Theoretical Framework for Future Research," *Academy of Management Review*, 15 (1990): 113–36.

5. J. S. Black, "Work Role Transitions: A Study of U.S. Expatriate Managers in Japan," *Journal of International Business Studies*, 19 (1988): 277–294; J. S. Black and H. B. Gregersen, "Antecedents to Cross-Cultural Adjustment for Expatriates in Pacific Rim Assignments," *Human Relations*, 44 (1990): 497–515; L. Copeland and L. Griggs, *Going International* (New York: Random House, 1985); and K. F. Misa and J. M. Fabricatore, "Return on Investment of Overseas Personnel," *Financial Executive*, 47 (1979): 42–6.

6. See R. L. Tung, *The New Expatriates* (Lexington, MA: Lexington Books, 1988) for a review.

7. J. S. Black and L. W. Porter, "Managerial Behavior and Job Performance: A Successful Manager in Los Angeles May Not Be Successful in Hong Kong," *Journal of International Business Studies*, 22 (1991): 99–114; and E. Miller, "The International Selection Decision: A Study of Managerial Behavior in the Selection Decision Process," *Academy of Management Journal*, 16 (1973): 234–52.

8. M. Porter, "Changing Patterns of International Competition," *California Management Review*, Winter (1986): 9–10.

9. H. B. Gregersen, "Commitments to a Parent Company and a Local Work Unit during Repatriation," *Personnel Psychology*, 45 (1992): 29–54.

10. M. G. Harvey, "Repatriation of Corporate Executives," *Journal of International Business Studies*, Spring (1989): 131–44.

11. Research consistently shows that good pre-departure training helps expatriate managers adjust to and perform well in their jobs overseas. See Black and Mendenhall, "Cross-Cultural Training."

12. See also J. S. Black and G. K. Stephens, "The Influence of the Spouse on U.S. Expatriate Adjustment in Overseas Assignments," *Journal of Management*, 15 (1989): 529–44.

Adapting to a Boundaryless World: A Developmental Expatriate Model

Juan I. Sanchez, Paul E. Spector, and Cary L. Cooper

Adjusting to an international assignment can provoke feelings of helplessness in an unprepared executive, who may have difficulty sorting out appropriate from inappropriate behavior. In fact, learning to manage in and cope with a foreign environment involves such a profound personal transformation that it has an analog in the process of human development throughout the life-span. Expatriate executives are removed from the comfortable environment of their parental culture and placed in a less familiar culture. Indeed, a management style that works at home may fail to produce the desired response abroad, or it may be even counterproductive.[1] The sudden loss of control in one's environment that results from cultural shock abruptly disrupts one's equilibrium.[2] This uneven relationship between the executive and an environment that is perceived to exceed the executive's coping resources perfectly fits the definition of stress, which threatens well-being.[3] A recent comparison of expatriate executives with a similar group that did not relocate revealed an alarming increase in the stress-sensitive hormone prolactin, reduced mental health, and an increase in cigarette and alcohol consumption in the expatriate group during the first year abroad.[4]

Rivers of ink have been dedicated to the need to develop globally minded leaders. A better understanding of the stages involved in a successful adjustment to a foreign environment should help in the development of a global mindset. A profound personal transformation, involving the formation of a multicultural identity, is necessary to buffer the stress provoked by an international assignment.

Coping with stress can be seen as a process involving two steps – primary and secondary – in the evaluation of such adverse environmental conditions as having too much work

Sanchez, Juan I., Paul E. Spector, and Cary L. Cooper, "Adapting to a boundaryless world: A developmental expatriate model," *Academy of Management Executive*, 14(2) (May 2000): 96–106. Reprinted by permission of *Academy of Management Executive*.

and uncertain job responsibilities.[5] Adverse environmental conditions function as work stressors when an individual recognizes them as stressful through the mental process known as primary evaluation. Secondary evaluation involves the selection of a coping response to deal with the stressor. The same two steps can be distinguished in coping with stress during an international assignment. First, coping requires an understanding of the new environmental conditions or stressors that demand adaptive responses from the executive.[6] Second, leverage of the new stressors demands a revision of one's old repertoire of coping responses, which may no longer be effective in the new setting.[7] Our goals in this article parallel these two steps and are to shed light on the nature of the primary stressors faced by the expatriate executive, and formulate recommendations regarding strategies that facilitate the adjustment of expatriate executives. Our recommendations are divided into two categories – those directed at expatriate executives and those directed at their employers. To provide a framework or roadmap, our review draws a parallel with the process of human development, proceeding along the developmental stages experienced by expatriate executives as they struggle to adapt to their new world. This progression is summarized in Table 1, which presents each stage, its primary stressors, and the recommended coping strategies for both executives and their employers.

EXPATRIATE SELECTION STAGE

Technical skills, family situation, relational skills, and motivational state all play a crucial role in effective cross-cultural adjustment.[8] However, 90 percent of all companies base their international selections on technical expertise while ignoring the other areas.[9] Technically qualified candidates are not always capable of easily adjusting to critical cultural differences, such as those involving social status and group dependence.[10]

Openness to the profound personal transformation that awaits the expatriate executive is perhaps the most fundamental sign of expatriate readiness. It is not surprising that courage and risk taking are among the core characteristics of successful expatriates who, knowing themselves, are willing to revisit their most deeply held assumptions.[11] Authoritarianism, rigidity, and ethnocentrism are personality aspects that impede adaptation to a foreign culture.[12] Because these are deeply ingrained personality traits that are not easily malleable, selection rather than training should be the strategy used to ensure that candidates possess these characteristics from the first day on the job. Although traditional personality inventories have not proven very effective at predicting expatriate success, available measures specifically designed to evaluate expatriate potential appear promising.[13]

A frequently reported explanation for expatriate failure has been poor adjustment of spouses.[14] Despite the key role of family-related variables in successful expatriate management, assessing the family situation without violating privacy rights is a real challenge. A practical and potentially useful strategy involves providing a realistic preview of the assignment, then instigating a self-evaluation of readiness among family members. By reflecting on the results of this evaluation, the executives can appraise their family situation and can voluntarily withdraw if the prospect is not altogether favorable.

TABLE 1 Stressors and Coping Responses in the Developmental Stages of Expatriate Executives

Stage	Primary stressors	Executive coping response	Employer coping response
Expatriate selection	Cross-cultural unreadiness.	Engage in self-evaluation.	Encourage expatriate's self- and family evaluation. Perform an assessment of potential and interests.
Assignment acceptance	Unrealistic evaluation of stressors to come. Hurried time frame.	Think of assignment as a growth opportunity rather than an instrument to vertical promotion.	Do not make hard-to-keep promises. Clarify expectations.
Pre- and post-arrival training	Ignorance of cultural differences.	Do not make unwarranted assumptions of cultural competence and cultural rules.	Provide pre-, during, and post-assignment training. Encourage support-seeking behavior.
Arrival	Cultural shock. Stressor reevaluation. Feelings of lack of fit and differential treatment.	Do not construe identification with the host and parent cultures as mutually exclusive. Seek social support.	Provide post-arrival training. Facilitate integration in expatriate network.
Novice	Cultural blunders or inadequacy of coping responses. Ambiguity owing to inability to decipher meaning of situations.	Observe and study functional value of coping responses among locals. Do not simply replicate responses that worked at home.	Provide follow-up training. Seek advice from locals and expatriate network.
Transitional	Rejection of host or parent culture.	Form and maintain attachments with both cultures.	Promote culturally sensitive policies at host country. Provide Internet access to family and friends at home. Maintain constant communication and periodic visits to parent organization.
Mastery	Frustration with inability to perform boundary spanning role. Bothered by living with a cultural paradox.	Internalize and enjoy identification with both cultures and walking between two cultures.	Reinforce rather than punish dual identification by defining common goals.
Repatriation	Disappointment with unfulfilled expectations. Sense of isolation. Loss of autonomy.	Realistically reevaluate assignment as a personal and professional growth opportunity.	Arrange pre-repatriation briefings and interviews. Schedule post-repatriation support meetings.

ASSIGNMENT ACCEPTANCE STAGE

The excessive emphasis on technical skills also seems to dominate the decision-making process that the expatriate executive and family go through before the offer is accepted. Typically, the candidate selected has technical expertise and experience related to the assignment. Therefore, the candidate does not envision being incapable of performing an assignment abroad that he or she has already done at home. Why are some managers and employers prone to overlook the cross-cultural demands of the assignment? The answer lies in the psychological perspective of work stress, which is driven by subjective appraisals of the executive's environment.[15] The objective reality of the situation does not directly provoke a stressful experience, but the subjective appraisal of the situation does. The subjective appraisal of stressors is, in essence, a judgment of person-environment fit.[16] Therefore, when an offer to take an international assignment is extended, candidates are probably unable to anticipate stressors they have not experienced before, unless they have had a prior international assignment. Ignorant of the alien environment to which they are about to be transplanted, executives might also overestimate the effectiveness of coping responses that work at home but may not work abroad. For instance, being outgoing, as it is normally understood in the US, may be perceived as being rude in other cultures, thereby provoking rather than preventing social isolation.

Consider the case of an executive with a demonstrated competence in launching start-ups who was selected to head the Asian operations of a US corporation. When considering the transfer to Asia, the executive dismissed the possibility of feeling socially isolated because he considered himself and his family outgoing and friendly, and thought they would have no problems making friends and adjusting. Six months after his arrival in Japan, the executive expressed frustration at his inability to communicate effectively with others and at his feelings of social isolation.

When weighing the pros and cons of an international assignment, the stressors to be encountered are thought to be alleviated by the prospect of career advancement once the executive returns home. Promises of immediate promotion upon return are often the main driver of an executive's decision to accept relocation.

The executive may use these promises to convince a spouse who hesitates to give up local friends, family, and perhaps a good job. However, once the executive starts the international assignment, the management representatives who were involved in selecting the executive may very well move on to other posts or other corporations. Witnessing these departures from afar, the expatriate may feel that the expectations that motivated the transfer are vanishing too. In the absence of a future payoff, the new stressors will be reappraised and may appear more unbearable than when the prospect of a red-carpet return was alive.

The offer to take an international assignment frequently comes from out of the blue. For instance, an executive previously uninterested in living abroad was motivated by a hefty relocation bonus to accept an unexpectedly sudden but nevertheless career-enhancing assignment.[17] This kind of hurried decision may lead to an unrealistic appraisal of both the stressors awaiting abroad and one's cross-cultural skills.

How should executives and their employers cope with such unanticipated circumstances? One of the answers appears to lie in the clarification of expectancies beforehand. Executives who take on international assignments hoping that an immediate promotion will materialize upon return are oblivious to the pace of change in today's business environment, where vertical career paths are no longer the norm. Instead, executives should consider international transfers as an additional growth opportunity in their career development plans.

Rather than delivering hard-to-keep, long-term promises of promotion, employers should clarify expectations and highlight the developmental growth that will result from having completed the international assignment. For example, a US executive who decided to take an assignment in Japan because it fitted into his general career plan was not guaranteed a specific promotion upon repatriation. Instead, he was made aware of what his general opportunities would be if he met his goals in Japan.[18]

PRE- AND POST-ARRIVAL TRAINING STAGE

Intercultural training can partly remedy cross-cultural insensitivity, but intercultural competence involves more than a series of country statistics and cultural gimmicks learned in a short, pre-departure training session. Making executives aware that they will face different business and social customs is not sufficient, because awareness does not necessarily bring competence in the host culture.[19]

The classic burnout symptoms of emotional exhaustion and a sense of reduced accomplishment of an American expatriate six months after he was put in charge of operations in Taiwan illustrate this point.[20] Because he was unable to obtain collaboration from local executives, he followed the recommendations of his California team. The implementation of such recommendations, however, worsened the situation he had been called to improve. Even though this executive was made aware of such cultural differences as Asians being more deferential and less straightforward in their business dealings than Americans, he had neither the interest nor the patience to participate in extended discussions of family and non-business matters with his new business acquaintances. He decided to cut his losses and gladly accepted his CEO's invitation to repatriate him.

Many corporations are becoming aware of the need to provide continued hands-on training rather than just pre-departure awareness training. An executive's pre-departure evaluation of the stressors experienced abroad may be unrealistic. Without some on-site experience in the culture, executives may overestimate their future ability to cope. In contrast to pre-departure training, post-arrival training gives expatriates a chance to evaluate their stressors after they have encountered them. A good example of this kind of on-site training is provided by the British trade giant Jardin Matheson.[21] The training format is project-based, with participants spending much of their time in their respective business areas. At regular intervals, they are brought together to discuss their experiences under the guidance of facilitators. Cultural differences are addressed when they surface in the context of working together, rather than as part of theoretical discussions regarding why Asians and Westerners behave differently.

Experiential training formats also provide an opportunity to react to cultural stressors and receive feedback about the adequacy of one's coping responses. One of these formats is the cultural assimilator, which employs descriptions of critical incidents involving stressful situations together with possible ways of coping with them.[22] With the help of a facilitator, participants discuss the consequences of their individual responses. The exchange helps reduce feelings of stress, because it reinforces the perception that they hold a reservoir of potentially effective coping responses. Foreigners trained using a Greek assimilator, for instance, felt significantly better adjusted to Greece than untrained individuals.[23]

From the employer's point of view, training is an opportunity to provide the social support that the expatriate executive needs.[24] Social support, however, can either reduce or alleviate the effects of stressors. Pre-departure training sessions, for instance, can significantly reduce stressors by providing basic information about housing, schools, foods, and transportation that may help the executives get by in the first few weeks of their assignments. Pre-departure training, however, is not likely to buffer or alleviate the cultural stressors to be faced by the expatriate executive, because cultural differences are best understood in post-arrival training sessions once they have been experienced. Although identifying the potential sources of social support is a difficult task for executives who are still unfamiliar with their host environment, training can provide the encouragement and motivation to seek the social network and activities that will make the new stressors more bearable.

ARRIVAL STAGE

Understandably, the prospect of an international assignment provokes quite a bit of excitement. However, the executive's arrival in an unfamiliar environment may soon bring almost as much frustration. Many of these frustrating times can be explained by feelings of inadequacy. In fact, the executive's sense of control, which plays a significant role in healthy adjustment, may be dramatically affected by the transfer.[25] Stressors like an excessive workload, which was not perceived as such because of the individual's sense of environmental control, suddenly turn worse because of what appears to be an uncontrollable new environment.

Feeling different, especially feeling that one is subject to differential treatment because of membership in a particular culture, can induce stress above and beyond that resulting from typical stressors such as conflict and ambiguity over perceived responsibilities.[26] If the expatriate executives attribute differential treatment to their membership in a different culture or group, their rejection of the host culture is likely to intensify. Thinking of the environment as beyond one's control induces a sense of helplessness.[27] For example, a US expatriate executive in a Central American nation felt that his written requests for equipment maintenance were ignored because he was a foreigner. Later in his assignment, he learned that such written requests were routinely ignored, and that the way to get the work done was to drop by the maintenance shop or ask a maintenance employee for help at the beginning of the work day.

Social identity theory provides a vehicle to better understand and cope with feelings of cultural rejection. Individuals are likely to experience internal conflict when concurrent identification with two or more social entities is perceived as unacceptable. For instance, a US expatriate in Mexico may feel that being an American and identifying with the Mexican culture are opposite poles of the same continuum and are therefore mutually exclusive. Feelings of frustration early in the international assignment may strengthen

FIGURE 1   Successful Evolution of Parent and Host Culture Identification

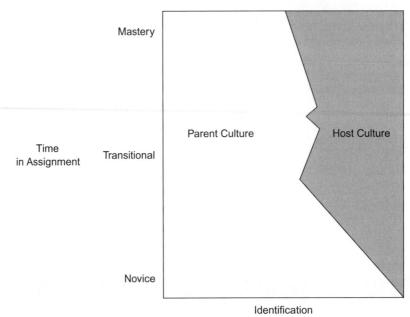

identification with the US culture to the detriment of the host culture. When the executive construes his or her identification with the two cultures in this us vs. them manner, devastating psychological consequences may follow.

Expatriate executives who reject the host culture are destined to experience continuous frustration and negative feelings as they are forced to conduct business according to local usage. Figure 1 depicts the tortuous evolution of the internal struggle between executives' identification with the host versus the parent culture. The two identifications compete for the same space. Whereas identification with the parent culture dominates in the early phases of the assignment, identification with the host culture will dominate later on. A successful adjustment implies a final identification midway between the host and parent cultures.

Understanding that identification with both cultures is possible is the safest way to prevent acculturative stress.[28] The different degrees of identification with the host and the parent culture can be summarized in four quadrants (Figure 2). The upper right quadrant represents dual identification, which is indeed possible and least stressful. A US executive on assignment in Japan indicated that his high allegiance to both the parent and the Japanese operation led him to try to bring their interests together rather than choose one over the other whenever he perceived discrepancies in their expectations and goals.[29] Reacculturation, as represented by the lower right quadrant, is significantly more stressful because one's parent culture is neglected rather than incorporated into the expatriate's new identity.

A better understanding of the host's ways should not necessarily be accompanied by a rejection of the parent culture. Executives run the risk of drifting in either direction

FIGURE 2 A Model of Expatriate Cultural Identification and Stress

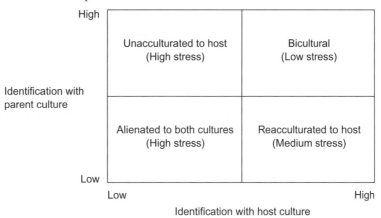

by identifying too much with one of the cultures while rejecting the other. Rather than absorbing oneself in an internal battle for self-definition, the executive should learn to view identification with the host as compatible with identification with the parent culture.

NOVICE STAGE

At the beginning of their international assignments, expatriates may make the mistake of ignoring culturally critical aspects. Why is it so difficult to make sense of and cope with the new stressors? Executives who feel stressed are likely to search their repertoire of coping responses for adequate ways to confront situations.[30] However, the choice of coping response would be determined by the effectiveness of responses used to cope with similar stressors in the past. Notions of response effectiveness are influenced by prior personal experience and culturally bound notions of response adequacy and likelihood of success. In other words, the choices of coping responses have been shaped throughout the executives' personal and cultural experience. The problem is that such responses are no longer valid in a different culture characterized by different norms and values. Thus, the experience and knowledge of social norms that the expatriate executive used to select adequate coping responses at home have lost much of their informative value.

Expatriates need to become aware of the consequences that their old repertoire of coping responses has in the host culture. Ambiguity will be overwhelming at first. Uncertainty about what is demanded will be aggravated by one's inability to decipher the meaning of a situation. Blunders can be unwittingly committed by executives who misread culturally different situations.[31] An American expatriate in Beijing dared to challenge his Chinese colleague's idea by saying, "That's a very good point, but I don't agree with you." Although this observation was respectfully made in the eyes of the American, it offended the Chinese executive, thereby straining the business deal.[32] Another US executive inadvertently offended his senior Mexican managers by asking for the junior manager's opinion in their presence.

Expatriate managers should pay attention to the functional value of the coping mechanisms employed by local executives, who make useful role models. Responses that imitate local uses can be successful, but expatriates should be sensitive to the true function of such responses, which can be rather subtle. Expatriate managers should think a bit like anthropologists trying to make sense of human behavior in a different cultural context.[33]

Coping styles have been classified as problem-solving (taking direct action to solve a problem) versus emotion-focused (taking action to make oneself feel better about a situation one cannot control).[34] Emotion-focused coping might be more characteristic of collectivistic societies, such as Asians or Hispanics, than of individualistic societies, like the US or Australia, because members of collectivistic cultures are encouraged to subordinate their personal goals to those of stable groups. However, expatriate executives in collectivistic cultures may erroneously dismiss as mere emotion-focused coping some responses that are, in fact, culturally sensitive attempts to exert control over a situation. Showing deference to superiors, not questioning formal authority in public, aligning oneself with powerful others, and attending family functions provide not mere distraction or consolation, but also unquestionable power to influence one's environment in cultures where individual subordination to a powerful group is the norm to get ahead. Executives who understand these subtleties and choose to play the game stand the best chances of coping effectively with an unfamiliar situation.

An American executive who understood the importance of family and friendship in the Middle East made a point of reminding his business contacts there of his friendship by taking their picture together at every occasion and then mailing copies to them. This action may seem a bit manipulative to some, but we can attest to the sincerity of the American expatriate, who had already internalized some of the values and customs of his Middle Eastern partners.

More straightforward coping styles involving direct attempts to control situations of the kind expected in individualistic countries like the US may be even counterproductive. A study of managerial stress in 24 countries revealed that exercising direct control over one's environment is associated with mental and physical well-being in the US, but not in many other countries.[35] Thus, expatriates who insist on employing the kind of direct control responses that have made them successful at home may only add to their stress level abroad.

Expatriates from individualistic societies should be reminded that the lengthy social interactions observed in collectivistic cultures are not a waste of time, but a necessary conduit to doing business. Executives from collectivistic cultures transplanted to an individualistic one may make the opposite mistake. For example, a southern European executive assigned to a financial institution in a US territory was used to having decisions backed by social consensus, which are the norm in the world of European labor relations. He insisted on creating task forces representing every constituent before a decision was made on nearly every human resource issue. The local executives were in turn frustrated by the slow pace of these task forces, which they considered unnecessary.

The employer should facilitate integration into a local or regional network of other expatriates, who can be an extremely valuable source of tangible and informational support in the beginning of the assignment regarding schools, shopping, obtaining a driver's license, and the like. Whereas physically distant friends and family provide simply emotional support and consolation, other expatriates provide the kind of tangible support that directly reduces stressors.

TRANSITIONAL STAGE

Executives' continued frustration may lead to identity crises when they choose to reject the parent culture by fully embracing the host culture, or vice versa.

The ability to form and maintain attachments plays a significant role in executive health in general.[36] For example, keeping in touch with the expatriate community overseas allows executives to maintain their links with the parent culture. These links can be reinforced by Internet access to family, friends, and media from the parent culture. The employer's investment in such electronic communications should provide a significant return in the form of emotional support. Even though this support cannot reduce the stressors faced abroad, it should help alleviate the strain felt by the executive.[37]

Going native by becoming too identified with the host culture may elicit a negative reaction at headquarters, because the executive's allegiance may be questioned.[38] This reversed identification phenomenon may have the same kind of negative impact on the executive's well-being that the rejection of the host culture does, because a significant part of the self is being rejected.

Expatriate executives' conflicting feelings about identification with one culture to the exclusion of the other exacerbate the normally high levels of role conflict characteristic of executive positions. Successful expatriate executives cope with these conflicting roles through constant communication. Lags in communication provoke the kind of unhealthy us vs. them attribution mentioned earlier. An American expatriate in Holland negotiated for a trip to the US every four months so he could bring the points of view of the Dutch operations to headquarters and also take headquarters' perceptions back to Holland. Physical separation and cultural differences made it difficult for the groups to understand each other's actions, and the tone of communications invariably deteriorated after three to four months.[39] The executive's trips back and forth kept negative feelings from getting too far out of hand. In essence, expatriates are forced to cope with conflicting demands imposed by their dual identification with the host and parent organizations by functioning as boundary spanners that walk the line separating the two cultures. The need to maintain this delicate equilibrium among multiple stakeholders calls for skills similar to those possessed by political diplomats.[40] The parent organization should not create additional role conflict for the expatriate with policies that are insensitive to cultural differences.

MASTERY STAGE

By the end of their assignments, successful expatriates have already developed the knowledge of cultural norms that allow them to understand their environment more fully. Over time, expats have also crafted a repertoire of coping responses adapted to their new stressors. Seasoned expatriates are capable of choosing among potential responses with a minimum of uncertainty because they have seen their choices succeed in the past. However, the developmental stages discussed here do not always follow a linear sequence, and making sense of a foreign culture will remain puzzling at times.[41] This ambiguity should not bother effective expatriates, who have already learned to cope with feelings of divided loyalty. They understand that feelings of identification with the host and the parent culture are not mutually exclusive. Instead of being frustrated, they enjoy their boundary-spanning roles of bicultural interpreters who walk between two or more cultures.

Accepting the profound personal transformation that comes with an international assignment is not easy. Fearing identity loss and unable to cope with a myriad of new stressors, nearly 40 percent of American expatriates return early.[42]

However, those who successfully complete their assignments become different people because they have experienced radically different events. Armed with the dual experience of having lived and worked both abroad and at home, expatriates are capable of seeing one culture through the eyes of the other. The ability to understand the cultural paradox that surrounds them and, most importantly, the fact that living with such a paradox does not bother them, represents the pinnacle of expatriate executive transformation. Not surprisingly, the healthiest expatriates are those who possess a strong sense of coherence and control.[43] These individuals have learned to live with and enjoy membership in more than one culture – the essence of being a global executive. A US executive working in Holland described how he had learned over the course of his assignment that being conspicuous was often frowned on in that country. He learned to be more reserved in what he said and to wear more formal clothes even when grocery shopping, so that he would not stand out as much. He and other expatriates explained that these changes did not interfere with their identification with the US, which they still genuinely felt.[44]

REPATRIATION STAGE: THE MOST STRESSFUL PART OF THE ASSIGNMENT?

Executives' repatriation can turn into the most stressful time of the entire international assignment. A survey of repatriated executives found that 33 percent were still holding temporary assignments three months after repatriation, more than 75 percent felt than their permanent post upon repatriation was a demotion from their international assignment, and 61 percent felt that they did not have opportunities to put their experience abroad to work. Perhaps the most dramatic finding was that 25 percent of the executives had quit their jobs within three months of repatriation.[45]

An expatriate banking executive working in Mexico returned to the US to find an organization whose top management had radically changed and seemed unwilling to fulfill his previous bosses' promises of upward promotion. After lingering in support roles for about a year, the executive landed a job as vice president of international banking in another financial institution. Similarly, a Mexican executive was disappointed to learn that his employer planned to repatriate him to a relatively low-level management job back home. The executive had been known to share with his coworkers in the US what he thought were his high chances of securing the general manager position in Mexico's operations. Dissatisfied with the repatriation offer, the executive quit his job and started an import-export partnership with one of the business acquaintances he had made during his assignment in the US.

Repatriation brings new stressors to executives. Feeling that others do not share their multicultural identification can create a sense of isolation. An expatriate who spent two years implementing a training program around the world characterized his repatriation as a much more traumatic event than going abroad. He complained about feelings of not belonging and about not having anyone to confide in.[46] Repatriated executives may also find themselves making an effort not to stand out by hiding the new interests and behaviors they acquired abroad. An expatriate who headed the Dutch operations of a US firm admitted that he was afraid that others might label his new manners as snobbish.

How can expatriate executives cope with these feelings of lack of fit? In a way, the repatriated executives had already coped with the feeling of not fitting in when abroad. The essence of being bicultural is being proficient in both cultures, and that includes dealing with members of one culture who, unlike the repatriated executive, are unfamiliar with the other. In short, learning to live with and not be bothered by these multiple cultural identities continues to be necessary even when executives return home.

Another dramatic change confronted by repatriated executives is the frequent loss of autonomy, augmented by possibly unrealistic expectations about being promoted upon return. The kind of bold management style that was accepted and even praised abroad may be unwelcome at headquarters. Insisting on this kind of bold style might provoke turf battles with executives from other functional areas. Employers can smooth this difficult transition by providing a sensible repatriation program that takes into account executives' interests and newly developed talents. In this sense, reentry training is at least as important as pre-departure training. Setting expectations about reentry well before it takes place is a fundamental component of this kind of training, which should begin when the expatriate is first selected and continue throughout the assignment prior to the return.[47] Pre-repatriation briefings and interviews with parent organization representatives to inform executives of available opportunities should help clarify how such opportunities fit into executives' post-repatriation career plans. After reentry, follow-up meetings are critical because they provide information regarding how executives are adjusting, whether they need additional support to cope with new stressors, and whether their coping strategies should be revised. When suitable openings are not immediately available at the parent organization, Swedish employers place expatriate executives in a multi-employer pool. Executives from this pool are loaned out to other employers who need them as a short-term solution.[48]

There are limitations to the recommendations presented here. First, the available research from which we drew is based primarily on the experiences of US expatriates working abroad. Although many of our conclusions should apply to expatriates regardless of nationality, the unique aspects of every culture should not be ignored. Similarly, about 90 percent of all expatriate managers may be male, and the recommendations presented here are therefore based on primarily male samples.[49] However, contrary to stereotypical assumptions, the case of a female executive who received equal treatment during her assignment in Japan illustrates that female expatriates need not necessarily experience more frustration than their male counterparts, even if female executives are not common in the host country.[50]

A SURVIVAL GUIDE FOR EXPATRIATE EXECUTIVES AND THEIR EMPLOYERS

Employers need to actively support the adjustment process of their expatriate executives. Cross-cultural competence-oriented training should be provided before, during, and after the assignment. In addition, the parent firm should be sensitive to the delicate balance between the interest of the parent and the host firm that executives need to maintain, listening and working with them to define and achieve common goals.

Expatriation uproots executives from a familiar environment, thereby breaking the balance between the individual and his or her ability to cope with the environment. Feelings of internal conflict are likely to be aggravated by executives' inability to decipher the meaning of culturally different situations. Even though the strain associated with such negative feelings can be partly prevented by competence-oriented intercultural training, individual predisposition and courage to cross cultural boundaries of both a physical and a psychological nature are necessary for healthy expatriate adjustment. Perhaps the most challenging of all transformations is the ability to develop a dual identification.

Otherwise, the conflicting roles experienced by expatriate executives may be exacerbated by a divided sense of social identity that views identification with the host and the parent culture as mutually exclusive. In essence, an international assignment is not only a physical adventure in a more or less remote land, but also a psychological adventure that requires the willingness to revise deeply held beliefs concerning one's own identity.

Notes

1   Selmer, J. 1999. Effects of coping strategies on sociocultural and psychological adjustment of Western expatriate managers in the PRC. *Journal of World Business*, 34(1): 41–51.
2   Cummings, T. G., & Cooper, C. L. 1998. A cybernetic theory of work stress. In C. L. Cooper (Ed.), *Theories of organizational stress*: 101–21. Oxford, U.K.: Oxford University Press.
3   Lazarus, R. S., & Folkman, S. 1984. *Stress, appraisal, and coping*. New York: Springer, 19.
4   Anderzen, I., & Arnetz, B. B. 1997. Psychological reactions during the first year of a foreign assignment: Results of a controlled longitudinal study. *Work & Stress*, 11(4): 304–18.
5   Lazarus, R. S. 1966. *Psychological stress and the coping process*. New York: McGraw-Hill.
6   Beehr, T. A., & Newman, J. E. 1978. Job stress, employee health, and organizational effectiveness: A facet analysis, model and literature review. *Personnel Psychology*, 31: 665–99.
7   Shupe, E. I., & McGrath, J. E. 1998. Stress and the sojourner. In Cooper (Ed.), op. cit., 86–100.
8   Teagarden, M. B., & Gordon, G. D. 1995. Corporate selection strategies and expatriate manager success. In J. Selmer (Ed.), *Expatriate management. New ideas for international business*: 17–36. Westport CT: Quorum.
9   Earley, P. C. 1987. Intercultural training for managers: A comparison. *Academy of Management Journal*, 30(4): 685–98.
10 Spreitzer, G. M., McCall, Jr., M. W., & Mahoney, J. D. 1997. Early identification of international executive potential. *Journal of Applied Psychology*, 82(1): 6–29.
11 Ibid.
12 Locke, S. A., & Feinsod, F. 1982. Psychological preparation for young adults traveling abroad. *Adolescence*, 17: 815–19.
13 Spreitzer, et al., op. cit.
14 Teagarden & Gordon, op. cit.

15 Lazarus, op. cit.

16 Edwards, J. R., & Cooper, C. L. 1990. The person-environment fit approach to stress: Recurring problems and some suggested solutions. *Journal of Organizational Behavior*, 11: 293–307.

17 Schell, M. S., & Solomon, C. M. 1997. *Capitalizing on the global workforce*. Chicago: Irwin.

18 Black, J. S., Gregersen, H. B., Mendenhall, M. E., & Stroh, L. K. 1999. *Globalizing people through international assignments*. Reading MA: Addison Wesley.

19 Black, J. S., & Gregersen, H. B. 1999. The right way to manage expats. *Harvard Business Review*, March–April: 52–62.

20 Schell & Solomon, op. cit.

21 Williams, G., & Bent, R. 1996. Developing expatriate managers for Southeast Asia. In D. Landis & R. S. Bhagat (Eds.), *Handbook of intercultural training*, 2nd ed.: 383–99, Thousand Oaks CA: Sage.

22 Brislin, R., Cusgner, K., Cherrie, C., & Yong, M. 1986. *Intercultural interactions: A practical guide*. Beverly Hills CA: Sage.

23 Fiedler, F., Mitchell, T., & Triandis, H. 1971. The culture assimilator: An approach to cross-cultural training. *Journal of Applied Psychology*, 55: 95–102.

24 Fontaine, G. 1996. Social support and the challenges of international assignments. In D. Landis & R. S. Bhagat (Eds.), op. cit.: 264–81.

25 Spector, P. E. 1998. A control theory of the job stress process. In Cooper (Ed.), op. cit. 153–169.

26 Sanchez, J. I., & Brock, P. 1996. Outcomes of perceived discrimination among Hispanic employees: Is diversity management a luxury or a necessity? *Academy of Management Journal*, 39: 704–19.

27 Spector, P. E., 1982. Behavior in organizations as a function of employee locus of control, *Psychological Bulletin*, 91: 482–97.

28 Sanchez, J. I., & Fernandez, D. M. 1993. Acculturative stress among Hispanics: A bidimensional model of ethnic identity. *Journal of Applied Social Psychology*, 23: 654–68.

29 Black, J. S., Gregersen, H. B., Mendenhall, M. E., & Stroh, L. K. op. cit.

30 Shupe & McGrath, op. cit.

31 Ricks, D. A. 1993. *Blunders in international business*. Cambridge MA: Blackwell.

32 Schell & Solomon, op. cit., 7.

33 Osland, J. S., & Bird, A. 2000. Beyond sophisticated stereotyping: Cultural sensemaking in context. *The Academy of Management Executive*, 14(1): 65–77.

34 Bhagat, R. S., O'Driscoll, M. P., Babakus, E., Frey, L., Chokkar, J., Ninokumar, H., Pate, L. E., Ryder, P. A., Fernandez, M. J. G., Ford, D. L., & Mahanyele, M. 1994. Organizational stress and coping in seven national contexts: A cross-cultural investigation. In G. P. Keita and J. J. Hurrell, Jr. (Eds.) *Job stress in a changing workforce*: 93–105. Washington, DC: American Psychological Association.

35 Spector, P. E., Cooper, C. L., Sanchez, J. I., et al. 1999. A twenty-four nation study of work locus of control, well-being, and individualism: How generalizable are western work findings? Manuscript submitted for publication.

36 Quick, J. C., Nelson, D. L., & Quick, J. D. 1990. *Stress and challenge at the top. The paradox of the successful executive*. Chichester U.K.: John Wiley.

37 Viswesvaran, C., Sanchez, J. I., & Fisher, J. 1999. The role of social support in the process of work stress: A meta-analysis. *Journal of Vocational Behavior*, 54: 314–34.

38 Adler, N. J. 1997. *International dimensions of organizational behavior*. Cincinnati, OH: South-Western.

39 Osland, op. cit., 118.

40 Saner, R., Yiu, L., & Sondergaard, M. 2000. Business diplomacy management: A core competency for global companies. *The Academy of Management Executive*, 14(1): 80–92.

41 Osland & Bird, op. cit.

42 Keally, D. J. 1996. The challenge of international personnel selection. In Landis & Bhagat (Eds.), op. cit., 81–105.

43 Anderzen & Arnet, op. cit.

44 Osland, J. S. 1995. *The adventure of working abroad.* San Francisco: Jossey-Bass.

45 Black & Gregersen, op. cit., 60.

46 Osland, op. cit., 171.

47 Martin, J. N., & Harrell, T. 1996. Reentry training for inter-cultural sojourners. In D. Landis & R. S. Bhagat (Eds.), op. cit.: 307–23.

48 *Sunday Telegraph.* Home truths await the returning executive. November 21, 1999.

49 Solomon, C. M. 1994. Success abroad depends on more than job skills. *Personnel Journal,* April: 51–60.

50 Black, et al., op. cit.

CASE **8**

Monsanto Europe (A)[1]

David T. A. Wesley, Francis Spital, and Henry W. Lane

> *We should diligently explore the possibilities of non-chemical methods [of pest control]. . . . Until a large-scale conversion to these methods has been made, we shall have little relief from a situation that, by any common-sense standards, is intolerable.*[2]
>
> **Environmentalist Rachel Carson, author of Silent Spring**

On November 5, 1996, the captain of *Ideal Progress* piloted the large freighter into the calm waters of Hamburg harbor. Suddenly the still autumn air was pierced by a shrill noise and large floodlights momentarily blinded the captain. The engines ground to a halt as some of the deck crew gathered around the bow to listen to the chants of their strange assailants. The captain was one of the few who understood what the commotion was about; a Greenpeace ship had come to protest the arrival of the first shipment of genetically modified soybeans from the United States.

The protesters delayed the freighter's arrival as harbor authorities guided it to the pier. For most of the crew, the event was an entertaining delay to their anticipated shore leave, but to Monsanto it had deeper implications. Nobody really knew whether *Ideal Progress* carried any genetically modified soybeans in its 67,000-ton cargo hold since

IVEY **Northeastern** U N I V E R S I T Y

David Wesley, Professors Francis Spital and Henry W. Lane prepared this case solely to provide material for class discussion. The authors do not intend to illustrate either effective or ineffective handling of a managerial situation. The authors may have disguised certain names and other identifying information to protect confidentiality.

the soybeans were mixed with conventional crops during and after harvest. Still, for Greenpeace it was an opportunity to warn Europeans that genetically modified (GM) foods were beginning to arrive on a scale hitherto unknown in Europe.

To Monsanto, *Ideal Progress* was not only the name of a ship, but also closely reflected the aspiration of the company. "Sustainable Development" through the use of genetic engineering promised to reduce the use of pesticides and curtail world hunger, two laudable goals that should have garnered support, rather than opposition. Therefore, the success of environmental agitators in Germany (where the German subsidiaries of Unilever and Nestlé, among others, pledged to avoid GM foods for the foreseeable future) was difficult to understand. Robert Shapiro, a former Northeastern University law professor and chief executive officer (CEO) of Monsanto, explained:

> New technology is the only alternative to one of two disasters: not feeding people – letting the Malthusian process work its magic on the population[3] – or ecological catastrophe. We don't have 100 years to figure that out; at best, we have decades. In that time frame, I know of only two viable candidates: biotechnology and information technology.[4]

Although other European countries remained relatively silent on the issue, Germany was one of the world's top five importers of US soybeans, and therefore a market that could not be ignored.[5] Many at Monsanto believed that the negative reaction was simply a result of incomplete information and that "once the public is informed . . . there will be widespread acceptance."[6] The next task would be to decide how best to quell opposition, while educating Germans on the benefits of GM products.

MONSANTO HISTORY

In 1901, Monsanto was founded in St Louis, Missouri, as a part-time venture to produce artificial sweetener. From the outset, the company had a multinational element. Founder John F. Queeny, an Irish immigrant without the know-how to produce the company's sole product, imported Swiss scientists and began production in direct competition with large German producers, thereby challenging their previously held worldwide monopoly.

It was not long before the company learned the importance of managing the political challenges of running a chemical company. Under pressure from the sugar industry, the US Department of Agriculture decided to investigate Monsanto Chemical Works, as it was then known, to ensure that its artificial sweetener was not poisonous. In 1911, the company sought and received the support of then president Teddy Roosevelt, who stated that he had been using the product for years "without feeling the slightest bad effects."[7]

When a trade war with Germany nearly bankrupted Monsanto, Queeny decided to diversify into other food additives. By 1916, Monsanto's catalog included such well-known products as caffeine and Aspirin. The First World War proved to be a boon to Monsanto, as its German competitors were unable to transport their products to international markets.

In the postwar years, Monsanto began to expand rapidly, purchasing other chemical producers that had not fared so well during the war. With the company's success, bank financing was easily obtained until the company's debt level well exceeded equity. When foreign competitors finally went back on line in the early 1920s, Monsanto had difficulty meeting its debt obligations. Queeny assuaged bankers with promises of a turnaround, but was barely able to forestall bankruptcy. From then on, Monsanto adopted a very conservative approach to debt financing, instead preferring to use internal funds or equity to finance growth.

Shortly after its initial listing on the New York Stock Exchange in 1927, Monsanto moved to acquire two chemical companies that specialized in rubber. Other chemicals were added in later years, including detergents. Monsanto quickly became one of the world's largest producers of commodity chemicals.

The company began to redefine itself in 1960, with the creation of the agricultural products division, the purpose of which was to produce and market pesticides developed within the company's various chemical divisions. By consolidating Monsanto's research and development efforts in this field, the company hoped to improve the level of new product development and marketing.

The 1960s also spawned what some in the company referred to as "Eco-nuts." Environmental activists were becoming especially critical of Monsanto and its catalog of toxic chemicals such as DDT (a pesticide), PCBs, Agent Orange and organic phosphates. All of these had been shown to have a direct negative impact on the environment and human health, but pesticides in particular had come under heavy criticism in the early 1960s.

Monsanto's chairman of the board at the time responded to these concerns:

> Pesticides involve the matter of tradeoffs. Their benefits far outweigh their perils. We in the pesticides business should continue to keep increasing their benefits and keep minimizing their risks.[8]

In subsequent public communications, Monsanto would argue that pesticides offered a potential solution to world hunger. "The world could never produce sufficient food without chemicals," they argued.

By the 1970s, the impact pesticides were having on the environment and human health had been well documented. Many countries, including the United States, either severely restricted or banned the use of pesticides. A new approach to pest control, known as integrated control, involved more restricted use of pesticides, along with the development of pest-resistant crops through selective breeding and the use of natural predators.

Roundup herbicide

In 1970, a glyphosate herbicide called Roundup was developed in Monsanto's research laboratories. This became the world's leading herbicide and was used on more than 100 different crops around the world. Roundup had the effect of exterminating all vegetation without discrimination. Therefore, farmers applied the herbicide to fields before crops were planted.

One advantage to farmers was that fields did not need to be plowed every year in order to remove the stubble from the previous harvest. Instead, after spraying the field with Roundup, a farmer could plant between the rows, thereby reducing labor and conserving topsoil. Roundup was also less toxic than many herbicides, largely biodegradable and would bind to soil, thereby eliminating the risk of groundwater contamination.

Roundup quickly became the company's largest contributor to agricultural sales, accounting for 40 per cent of total company operating earnings. However, in many countries, the patent for Roundup expired in 1991 and was due to expire in 2000 in the United States. As a result, Monsanto sought ways to extend the life of this highly successful product.

Genetic engineering

It was not long after the invention of Roundup herbicide that Monsanto undertook research efforts to develop genetically modified crops that could resist the herbicide in hope of increasing the value of Roundup to farmers. By the time the US Supreme Court ruled, in 1979, that genetically modified living organisms could be patented,[9] Monsanto had already begun to take a leading role in the field.[10]

The Supreme Court decision only served to increase the incentive for companies to undertake research and development (R&D) investment in this new technology. New competitors quickly began to appear on the scene, ranging from small biotech firms specializing in niche products to giants, such as DuPont. Genetically engineered produce started to reach the consumer market in the early-1980s in the form of GM potatoes and tomatoes.[11]

Biotechnology presented potential solutions to a number of problems faced by farmers. In addition to herbicide resistance, genetic engineering could make crops resistant to insects and disease, increase the nutritional content, produce crops capable of growing in less hospitable environments (such as deserts) and increase the shelf life of fruits and vegetables. Theoretically, the increased yields offered by such technologies could also help alleviate hunger in developing countries, where some 1.5 billion people lived in abject poverty.[12]

Pest-resistant crops, in particular, were held up as a solution to the *Silent Spring* scenario. Since the book's introduction in the 1960s, *Silent Spring* had become the battle cry of naturalists and environmentalists who protested the widespread and indiscriminate destruction of plant and animal life, as a result of the increased use of pesticides. Monsanto maintained that genetic engineering could become the basis for the integrated approach to pest control, since crops could be made selectively resistant to predators and disease without harming other life.

By 1984, Monsanto had begun to divest itself of commodity chemicals in order to focus more on life sciences, including biotechnology and pharmaceuticals. This was reflected in the 1985 purchase of pharmaceutical manufacturer G. D. Searle & Co., maker of the highly successful artificial sweetener known as Nutrasweet. The following year, Monsanto sold its petrochemical, paper chemical, and plastics divisions, among others.

Dick Mahoney, who was Monsanto's CEO at the time, developed a three-pronged strategy that was to carry Monsanto into the next millennium.

First, the profitability of Roundup herbicide could be sustained at least through the 1990s.
Second, agricultural biotechnology would work, would reach the market and would potentially transform agriculture.
Third, sustained research investment in [the] Searle pharmaceutical business, at a scale larger than that which Searle's revenues could support, would pay off in new products.[13]

Although Monsanto had yet to bring a single GM product to market, the company fully expected to derive nearly a third of its revenue from genetically engineered products within the next 15 years.[14] At the same time, financial analysts were wary of the new technology, citing concerns about regulatory approval and consumer acceptance, and warned investors to steer clear of biotech companies that focused on genetic engineering.[15] Philip Needleman, Monsanto's vice-president in charge of research and development, seemed unconcerned. He believed that consumer acceptance was simply a matter of getting more GM products into the hands of consumers, and that once GM foods became commonplace, people would wonder what all the fuss was about.[16]

The company's first commercial application of agricultural biotechnology was a growth hormone that stimulated milk production in cows. The hormone, known as BST, was developed in 1984, and was expected to be available to farmers in 1988. However, because of concerns about hormones entering the food supply, and the fact that world milk production already well exceeded demand, the FDA delayed approval of the product for several years while it conducted further studies. When the product finally reached the market, Needleman was proven correct, as the anticipated consumer backlash never materialized. In 1996 alone, sales of BST increased by 48 percent.

The BST case made it clear to Monsanto that regulatory bodies, not consumer acceptance, would be the greatest hindrance to the ultimate success of biotechnology products. Monsanto therefore sought to improve its understanding of, and influence with, such bodies, and to that end successfully attracted the former EPA director and the former US Secretary of Commerce to its Board of Directors.

In addition to the potential of stand-alone products, such as BST, genetic engineering also promised to extend the life of the company's most successful agricultural product, Roundup herbicides. By inserting a particular gene into seeds, crops were made resistant to the herbicide. Since Roundup Ready crops could be planted before fields were sprayed, farmers would be able to selectively spray crops when needed, and thereby reduce the amount of herbicide needed. Through "the introduction of Roundup Ready crops," noted Shapiro, Monsanto could "expect Roundup to continue generating substantial cash and earnings in the years ahead."[17]

The main factor that allowed Monsanto to capitalize on food biotechnology was a very significant drop in the cost of genetic sequencing.[18] For example, in 1974, the cost to Monsanto of sequencing only one gene approached $2.5 million. Given that a typical agricultural product, such as rice, contained approximately 40,000 genes, sequencing costs became the company's most significant barrier to developing genetically engineered products. However, in subsequent years, advances in computers and other technologies helped to significantly reduce the cost of genetic sequencing to a mere $150 per gene. Company scientists viewed this as a very significant breakthrough.

A bountiful harvest

The initial reception of GM foods in the United States was very promising. About two-thirds of all manufactured food products contained soybeans, and as more of these products began to incorporate Roundup Ready varieties, there was little or no protest. Marketing studies conducted in the United States and Japan showed overwhelming consumer approval

EXHIBIT 1   1995 Survey of US and Japanese Consumers (%)[1]

Consumer Support for Agricultural Biotechnology			
	Support	Oppose	Don't Know
Japan	82	16	2
United States	66	26	5

Consumer Willingness to Purchase				
	Very Likely	Somewhat Likely	Not Too Likely	Not at All Likely
Insect Protected				
Japan	5	54	28	3
United States	31	42	15	9
Taste Better or Fresher				
Japan	4	59	34	3
United States	20	42	23	14

1 "How Japanese Consumers View Biotechnology," *Food Technology*, July 1996.

of the high-tech foods, and it appeared that earlier concerns over public acceptance were once again unfounded (see Exhibit 1). In fact, as far as the typical US consumer was concerned, the GM issue was not an issue at all. Professor Thomas Hoban, a sociologist who conducted the US Department of Agriculture's consumer research on biotechnology, concluded:

> Biotechnology has not (and likely will not) become an issue for the vast majority of consumers. When asked either to report the greatest threat to food safety or to rate a series of food safety hazards, biotechnology is seen as the least significant issue or concern.[19]

Under the assumption that "life sciences" would give Monsanto its strategic advantage, in 1996 the company's board of directors decided to spinoff the chemical products division into a separate wholly owned subsidiary known as Solutia. Shapiro planned to recreate Monsanto's image in the public mind by disassociating the company from environmental conflict, in favor of what he called "sustainable development." Shapiro explained:

> We became a life sciences company because we were engaged in three historically separate businesses – agriculture, food ingredients and pharmaceuticals – that now have begun to share common technologies and common goals . . . the intersection of these technologies and goals defines an extraordinary set of business opportunities. . . . Few people understand the size and scope of the opportunities we're pursuing.[20]

Investors took a positive view of Monsanto's new focus, as the company's stock price more than tripled in less than two years. In 1996 alone, Monsanto shareholders were rewarded with a 62 per cent return on their investment.

By 1997, some 30 million acres of farmland, mostly in the United States and Canada, had been planted with Monsanto's genetically modified seed. Monsanto quickly engaged itself in a buying spree, acquiring biotech companies and seed distributors. In one well-publicized purchase, Monsanto paid $1 billion (23 times sales) for an Iowa-based seed company. In 1998 alone, Monsanto more than tripled its long-term liabilities to a total of $6.2 billion, outstripping equity by approximately $1.5 billion. Monsanto had clearly staked its future on biotechnology, and most investors continued to display a very high level of optimism.

EUROPEAN REACTION

> *[Biotechnology] makes me remember the first trains which crawled along the countryside. People at that time were concerned that their cows would drop dead and worse still, they were convinced that man could not survive at such high speed. They were proven wrong and now we can go from Paris to Lyon in two hours, and nobody complains about it. But from time to time a dramatic train crash will remind us that there is no such thing as zero risk.*
>
> **Emma Bonino, European Commissioner in Charge of Consumer Policy and Health Protection**

Despite the fact that the US Food and Drug Administration (FDA) and the European Union (EU) had approved the product for sale, some in the European press likened the introduction of GM foods to a number of other food safety concerns, the foremost being mad cow disease.[21] When a link was made between BSE and a similar fatal neurological disease in humans, the British government downplayed the risk and insisted that British beef was safe. This position was later reversed, but not before nearly every British consumer had been exposed.[22] "Why should these same authorities now be trusted?" some asked.

> Will the public wish to eat such genetic simulacra, knowing that they are foodstuffs that have been tinkered with by scientists, refashioned according to a relatively new technology and usually for the benefit of biochemical companies and farmers rather than consumers who will buy and eat the results?[23]

Germans, and other northern Europeans, in particular placed more importance on food purity than most other cultures. Many still shopped at bakeries and delicatessens, where mainly traditional products were sold. Even processed foods were more pure than equivalent products elsewhere in the world.[24] They did not want to see their food contaminated with genetically engineered ingredients.

Risk-averse culture

Many Americans viewed the problem of European resistance as one of risk aversion. While acknowledging the importance of the mad cow crisis in hypersensitizing consumers to food safety issues, the real issue, they argued, had more to do with culture. One top US official commented:

I joke with some of my European friends saying that the definition of an American is a risk-taking European. We immigrated here. We had faith in the future. Those who stayed behind had a little less faith in the future. They were more risk-averse.[25]

The same sentiment was echoed by advocates of GM foods in Europe. Gordon Conway, a British ecologist and president of the Rockefeller Foundation, a philanthropic organization that funded $100 million in biotech research, noted:

The US is a very hazardous place. You have hurricanes. You have tornadoes. You have rattlesnakes. You have all kinds of tick-borne fevers. You have 250 million guns. In contrast, the sole hazard in Britain is one very rare poisonous snake. That's it. Period. It's a well-manicured country. So the American population is used to living with hazards. Most Americans are more worried about getting shot than the remote chance that some GM ingredient in food is going to affect their health.[26]

In the United Kingdom, for instance, this cautious attitude was reflected in the lack of entrepreneurial optimism. Whereas in the United States, where "public attitudes encourage risk-taking," more than half of the American population was optimistic about opportunities to start a business, in the United Kingdom only 16 percent thought that good opportunities existed, despite significant government incentives.[27]

Risk versus benefit

For British consumers, the issue boiled down to one fact, that the technology had so far not produced any benefits to the consumer, but was perceived to pose a variety of risks. While Monsanto had developed products that provided consumer benefits, such as higher vitamin content or lower cholesterol, these were still being tested and were years away from commercial applications. One such product was vitamin A-enhanced rapeseed oil, one teaspoon of which provided the recommended daily intake for an average adult. This product was "designed to address the specific nutritional needs in particular areas of the world," where some 800 million people suffered from serious illnesses related to vitamin A deficiency.[28]

One Monsanto director noted, "It would have been nice if the first products could have had health benefits for the consumer instead of cost benefits to the food industry."[29]

Product labeling

Months before *Ideal Progress* left US shores, Henrik Kroner, secretary general of Eurocommerce (the official EU retail and trade association) warned Monsanto of the developing negative sentiment and requested a delay of one year to educate and prepare consumers.[30] He noted that European consumers' confidence in food safety was already at an all-time low, as a result of Mad Cow disease. His message to Monsanto was this, "If you are wise, don't ship those soybeans to Europe because you may trigger a lasting reaction. And if you must, separate and label them."[31]

Labeling advocates were also quick to point out that British biotech firm Zeneca Plant Science had earlier in the year voluntarily labeled their Flavr Savr tomatoes,[32] and consumers seemed to be responding favorably to the product.

While labeling appeared to be an easy way to calm anxiety over the new soybeans, that would have entailed separating the beans at their source. The US agricultural industry claimed to have neither the infrastructure for such an undertaking, nor the desire to incur the considerable expense required to develop that infrastructure. Instead, Roundup Ready soybeans were often mixed with conventional beans during harvest, storage and shipping. As a result, nobody could tell which were modified and which were conventional. Furthermore, as stated by Monsanto (see Exhibit 2) separating and labeling genetically modified produce would have implied that these products were different from conventional products and perhaps unsafe.

EXHIBIT 2   Monsanto Reply to Labeling Request[1]

December 16, 1996

To the Editor,
Financial Times, London

Sir,

Joe Rogaly's article "Beans and genes" did not contribute very much to the genetic engineering debate. I'm not referring to his name-calling – "mad scientist soybeans", "futuristic corporation", "Big M" – to which I won't respond, nor to his self-acknowledged cynicism (which somewhat ruined his humour just as it was starting to amuse).

I'm just disappointed that he only gave a passing reference to the fact that experts and government agencies around the world, including the US, Europe/UK, Japan, Canada, Mexico and Argentina, have concluded unconditionally that Roundup Ready soybeans (RRS) are as safe as other soybeans.

Mr Rogaly says there would be no problem if only customers could be given the option through labelling of not buying products containing RRS. However, mandatory labelling of products such as these beans, which are unchanged in composition, nutrition, function and safety, would imply that these products are different from their unmodified counterparts when they are not. Again, the same regulatory authorities as mentioned above have concluded that there is no need for special handling or labelling because these soybeans are as safe as other soybeans and because they are substantially equivalent to other soybeans. All this was reaffirmed again by the Ministry of Agriculture Fisheries and Food's food advisory committee on December 12.

We are fully aware and accept that some may have concerns and questions about RRS, which is why we and others have opened consumer hotlines and produced information leaflets to address the issues. We remain at anyone's disposal to discuss the matter.

Michael A. Scharf,
Monsanto Services International
Avenue de Tervuren 270-272, B-11150
Brussels, Belgium

1 "Experts Say Genetic Soybeans are Safe," *Financial Times*, December 18, 1996.

Misguided concern

Monsanto had heard all this before. Scaremongers had warned the company many times in the 1980s that US consumers would not buy milk from hormone-fed cows, and again that they would be reluctant to buy GM produce. Each time these dire warnings failed to materialize. Monsanto simply needed to "convince people that this is a good useful technology," Shapiro noted, and those who opposed GM foods were "at best misguided."[33]

Shapiro did not seem too concerned:

> The multinational corporation is an impressive invention for dealing with the tension between the application of broadly interesting ideas on the one hand and cultural differences on the other. Companies like ours have gotten pretty good at figuring out how to operate in places where we can make a living while remaining true to some fundamental rules. As more countries enter the world economy, they are accepting – with greater or lesser enthusiasm – that they are going to have to play by some rules that are new for them.[34]

In the company's annual report, Shapiro devoted a scant two sentences to the topic. "In some European countries," he wrote, "questions remain about the labeling and public acceptance of food products with genetically modified crops. We'll continue to work with interested parties to help resolve those questions."[35]

Growing opposition

On the other side of the Atlantic however, opposition to GM foods continued to grow. A 1997 EU-wide survey revealed that food safety had become the most important issue for European consumers, with some 68 percent of those surveyed expressing concerns about the safety of their food. As a result of such concern, the European Commission "decided to place consumer health and food safety at the center of a new political initiative." The commission responsible for implementing this initiative noted:

> Consumers are increasingly aware of the importance of safe food and the impact certain products have on health. They resist the idea of a passive role and are more and more conscious of their ability to shape the market with their buying power. They have decided to use their right of choice and quite rightly so; they demand adequate information, they want to know what they eat, what it is derived from and where it is produced.[36]

Genetically modified foods, in particular, became a focus of concern. German and Austrian consumers, while having the highest levels of awareness of food biotechnology in the world (90 percent awareness), were among the least willing to purchase GM produce (30 percent and 22 percent, respectively). In contrast, awareness in the United States had declined to 55 percent, while willingness to purchase had increased to 73 percent.[37]

Some European governments began responding to the public concerns about GM food safety by banning their import and sale (Austria and Luxembourg), while other countries imposed various restrictions. An increasingly skittish European parliament, having felt the sting of various food scandals, tried to assure Europeans that food safety was being taken seriously. Although the European Union had opposed labeling of GM foods, a new proposal known as the "Novel Foods Law," would require it, if passed. Some industry observers were skeptical of the whole notion. "Because the altered foodstuffs look exactly like the natural ones and, in most cases, will be less expensive," commented one, "many consumers don't see what the big fuss is about."[38]

THE ADVERTISING CAMPAIGN

By 1997, German opposition was well entrenched, while in the United Kingdom, most consumers were still willing to purchase modified produce. However, consumer acceptance in the United Kingdom was declining in the wake of environmental activism and negative press reports, which questioned the safety of modified produce.

Monsanto hoped to allay public fears through education. As early as 1996, the company employed targeted advertising and toll-free hotlines in both the United Kingdom and Germany, but these seemed to have little effect.

Other efforts to educate the public proved equally ineffective. An industry association known as the Familiarization and Acceptance of Crops Incorporating Transgenic Technology (FACTT) was formed by 21 European organizations with interests in biotechnology, and set out to educate British farmers and consumers about the benefits of genetically engineered crops. However, two public education events scheduled for April 1998 had to be cancelled due to a "lack of interest." A third seminar in May was also cancelled when activists threatened to vandalize trial crops and thereby disrupt the event.[39]

Field trials

More radical opponents were becoming frustrated that the British government had not taken steps to ban GM foods and began to take matters into their own hands. In one incident, the biotech industry tried to engage environmentalists in an open dialogue and invited one group (Friends of the Earth) to inspect field trials. Without authorization, Friends of the Earth published the field trial locations on the Internet. Shortly afterward, a number of environmentalists showed up at the farm dressed in white radiation suits. After a brief confrontation with a local farmer, the white-hooded invaders took to burning and uprooting crops. This, and other similar actions, hampered efforts to educate the public and resulted in the loss of valuable research data intended to address environmental and safety concerns.

While the UK government had approved applications for 152 trial crops, farmers, fearing violence and retribution at the hands of "Eco-warriors," were hesitant to co-operate with Monsanto and other biotechnology companies. Some farmers noted that GM opponents had raised "genuine concerns" and wanted these concerns answered before planting trial crops (see Exhibit 3 for a summary of environmentalist concerns).[40]

Public opposition frustrated many European biotech scientists. As a result of what appeared to be an increasing lack of opportunity in Europe, they began leaving for better paid and more respected positions in the United States.

EXHIBIT 3 Summary of Concerns by Opponents of GM Crops[1]

1. **Harm to wildlife:** Bacillus thuringiensis is a naturally occurring bacteria that organic growers use to control caterpillars and other pests. New genetically engineered plants have a toxin produced by the Bt bacterium in each and every cell, from the roots to the pollen to the chaff plowed under after harvest. Cornell University researchers made headlines when they announced laboratory research showing that monarch butterfly larvae died after eating milkweed dusted with genetically engineered corn pollen containing the BT pesticide. Milkweed, the monarch's primary food source, commonly grows alongside corn. Researchers in Europe have made similar discoveries involving ladybugs and green lacewings, both beneficial insects. Yet another study, reported in 1997 in the British publication New Scientist, indicates that honeybees may be harmed by feeding on proteins found in genetically engineered Canola flowers.

2. **Harm to soil:** Microbiologists at New York University have found that the BT toxin in residues of genetically altered corn and rice crops persists in soils for up to 8 months and depresses microbial activity. And in another study, scientists in Oregon tested an experimental genetically engineered soil microbe in the laboratory and found it killed wheat plants when it was added to the soil in which they were grown.

3. **Harm to humans:** A growing body of evidence indicates that genetic engineering can cause unintended changes to our food, making it less nutritious or even harmful.

4. **Hidden Allergens:** DNA, the cell formations from which genes are composed, directs the production of proteins. Proteins are also common sources of human allergies. When DNA from one organism is spliced into another, can it turn a non-allergenic food into one that will cause an allergic reaction in some people? The Iowa-based biotech seed company Pioneer Hi-Bred International tried to change the protein content of soybeans by adding a gene from the Brazil nut. When researchers tested the modified soybean on people with sensitivity to Brazil nuts (but no sensitivity to soybeans), they found it triggered an allergic reaction. (Based on those findings, the company shelved development of the soybean.)

5. **Antibiotic resistance:** Genetic engineers use antibiotic marker genes to help them transfer genetic coding from one life-form to another. But some scientists worry that this process could compound the increasingly serious problem of antibiotic resistant bacteria. The concern is that bacteria living in the gut of humans or animals could acquire antibiotic resistance from GMO foods eaten by the human or animal, possibly rendering treatments for such infections as meningitis and gonorrhea ineffective.

6. **Religious and Moral Considerations:** People who choose not to eat animals for religious or moral reasons face an almost impossible task with many genetically engineered foods. When genes from flounder are spliced into tomatoes or genes from chickens are added to potatoes for increased disease resistance, are those vegetables still, purely speaking, vegetables? And without mandatory labeling, how can people who object to eating any trace of meat know what they are getting?

7. **Super bugs:** With Bt constantly present in millions of acres of crops, Bt-resistant insect strains will evolve – in as little as 3 to 5 years, the biotech industry's own scientists acknowledge.

8. **Super weeds:** Plants engineered to survive herbicides, such as Canola (oilseed rape), are cross-pollinating with wild cousins, which could create herbicide-resistant weeds. Which will defeat the purpose of engineering the plants and may coax farmers into using more powerful poisons to kill weeds.

9. **Indentured farmers:** The corporations committed to genetic engineering research – many of the same companies that produce chemical pesticides – are rapidly buying up seed companies and gaining control of entire food-production systems and educational-research facilities. Farmers who use this patented technology, meanwhile, are prohibited from the self-sufficiency of saving seed and instead are forced into a costly cycle of corporate dependency.

10. **Pollen drift:** Organic farmers could lose their certification and face financial ruin if their fields are contaminated by wind-borne pollen from nearby genetically modified crops. Even non-organic farmers are at risk for problems.

1 "Ten Reasons Organic Farming is Concerned About Genetically Engineered Plants," *Organic Gardening*, January 2000.

EXHIBIT 4   Monsanto Advertisements

WORRYING ABOUT STARVING
FUTURE GENERATIONS
WON'T FEED THEM. FOOD
BIOTECHNOLOGY WILL.

THE WORLD'S population is growing rapidly, adding the equivalent of a China to the globe every ten years. To feed these billion more mouths, we can try extending our farming land or squeezing greater harvests out of existing cultivation.

With the planet set to double in numbers around 2030, this heavy dependency on land can only become heavier. Soil erosion and mineral depletion will exhaust the ground. Lands such as rainforests will be forced into cultivation. Fertiliser, insecticide and herbicide use will increase globally.

At Monsanto, we now believe food biotechnology is a better way forward. Our biotech seeds have naturally occuring beneficial genes inserted into their genetic structure to produce, say, insect – or pest-resistant crops.

The implications for the sustainable development of food production are massive: Less chemical use in farming, saving scarce resources. More productive yields. Disease-resistant crops. While we'd never claim to have solved world hunger at a stroke, biotechnology provides one means to feed the world more effectively.

Of course, we are primarily a business. We aim to make profits, acknowledging that there are other views of biotechnology than ours. That said, 20 government regulatory agencies around the world have approved crops grown from our seeds as safe.

Food biotechnology is too great a subject to leave there. Ask for a leaflet at your local supermarket, write to us, call us free on 0800 092 0401 or visit our online Comments & Questions.

We're convinced biotechnology is a responsible way to provide food for the next century. We hope you agree.

WE BELIEVE FOOD SHOULD BE
GROWN WITH LESS PESTICIDE.

Monsanto is a leading biotechnology company. We believe biotechnology is one way to cut down on the amount of pesticides used in agriculture. For instance, the tomato here is grown by fusing a naturally-occurring beneficial gene into the tomato plant, making it insect resistant. As a result, the farmer can spray substantially less insecticide onto his fields.

Some biotech crops need no insecticides at all. For others, their use is reduced by a third or more. The result is food grown in a more environmentally sustainable way, less dependent on the earth's scarce mineral resources. (We also want you to know that we produce the world's best-selling herbicide, Roundup.)

Our food crops have been approved by government regulatory agencies in over 20 countries, including Switzerland, Denmark, the Netherlands, the USA and Great Britain.

Obviously we believe in the benefits of plant biotechnology, both for the environment and for everyone who eats food grown from our seeds.

If you'd like to find out more about this subject, please ask for a leaflet at your local supermarket, call us free on 0800 092 0401 or use our online Comments & Questions form.

(THE INSECT RESISTANT TOMATO HAS NOT BEEN APPROVED IN MORE THAN 20 COUNTRIES AND IS NOT YET COMMERCIALLY AVAILABLE)

Source: Monsanto UK.

Turning back the tide

As Monsanto's position in the United Kingdom became increasingly precarious, the company decided that something had to be done to turn back the swelling tide of public opposition. Professor Thomas Hoban, the leading industry consultant on consumer opinion, suggested that educational efforts would be the best means to "facilitate acceptance." He recommended:

> The best way to reach consumers is by educating opinion leaders, including scientists and health experts, government officials, the media and food industry officials. Key messages should include the benefits and uses of biotechnology as well as the government regulations that are in place to ensure safety.[41]

On June 6, 1998, Monsanto launched an advertising campaign in the United Kingdom with the stated aim of providing consumers with "the information they need to make informed decisions," and included newspaper advertisements, a toll-free hotline, leaflets, and a consumer Web site.[42] Issues of safety and nutrition, as well as feeding the world's hungry, were central to the campaign (see Exhibit 4).

The British weeklies in which the ads appeared were those typically read by better-educated individuals from higher socio-economic backgrounds, such as government ministers, senior bureaucrats, and business leaders; the "state elites," as Monsanto referred to them. In accordance with Professor Hoban's recommendations, Monsanto hoped to influence political decision makers as a way to achieve wider acceptance of genetic engineering.

Opponents of GM foods were not impressed and reacted with campaigns of their own. Other, sometimes better respected, opponents, such as His Royal Highness, the Prince of Wales, joined traditional opponents such as Greenpeace. Two days after Monsanto's advertising campaign was announced, Prince Charles released an essay on GM crops in a leading newspaper, in which he likened modified crops to mad cow disease "and other entirely man-made disasters in the cause of cheap food."[43]

ACKNOWLEDGMENT

This case was made possible through the generous support of Darla and Frederick Bordsky through their endowment of the Darla and Frederick Brodsky Trustee Professorship in International Business.

Notes

1   This case has been written on the basis of published sources only. Consequently, the interpretation and perspectives presented in this case are not necessarily those of Monsanto Corporation or any of its employees.
2   Rachel Carson, *Silent Spring*, Riverside Press, Cambridge, 1962.
3   Malthusian Principle: A population theory advanced by Thomas Malthus in his *Essay on the Principle of Population* (1798, First Edition). Malthus criticized Britain's social welfare programs as promoting unsustainable population increases because they prevented "checks to population," such as "the want of proper and sufficient food."
4   Growth Through Global Sustainability, *Harvard Business Review*, January–February 1997.
5   Greenpeace Campaigns Against Altered Soybeans, *Journal of Commerce*, November 7, 1996.
6   Genetic Soybeans Alarm Europeans, *New York Times*, November 7, 1996.
7   Forestal, DJ, *Faith, Hope and $5000, The Story of Monsanto*, Simon and Schuster, New York, 1977.
8   Forestal, DJ, *Faith, Hope and $5000, The Story of Monsanto*, Simon and Schuster, New York, 1977.

9   The Supreme Court, 1979 Term: Patentability of Living Microorganisms, *Harvard Law Review*, November 1980.

10 Genetic Markets Tempt More Firms, *Industry Week*, July 7, 1980.

11 Test-Tube Plants Hit Pay Dirt, *Fortune*, September 2, 1985.

12 Growth Through Global Sustainability, *Harvard Business Review*, January – February 1997.

13 Letter to Shareowners, *Monsanto Annual Report*, 1996.

14 Splicing Together a Regulatory Body for Biotechnology, *Business Week*, January 14, 1985.

15 Agritech on the Move, *Financial World*, April 3–16, 1985.

16 Next Term He's in Business, *Chemical Week*, December 21, 1988.

17 Letter to Shareowners, *Monsanto Annual Report*, 1996.

18 Sequencing refers to the process by which geneticists determine the chemical structure and characteristics of a gene.

19 "Consumer Acceptance of Biotechnology in the United States and Japan," *Food Technology*, 1998.

20 Letter to Shareowners, *Monsanto Annual Report*, 1997.

21 In 1986, British livestock became contaminated with bovine spongiform encephalopathy (BSE), also known as "mad cow disease."

22 "How to Lasso a Mad Cow," *Canadian Business*, December 1996.

23 "Look What's Coming to Dinner . . . Scrambled Gene Cuisine," *The Observer*, October 6, 1996.

24 Chocolate bars were a typical example. Belgium, France, Germany, Greece, Italy, Luxembourg, the Netherlands and Spain all banned the use of cocoa substitutes in chocolate bars, while American and British chocolates regularly contained no cocoa at all, and many contained a significant number of chemical substitutes and preservatives.

25 House of Representatives Subcommittee on Risk Management, Research, and Specialty Crops, Committee on Agriculture, March 3, 1999.

26 "The Voice of Reason in the Global Food Fight," *Fortune*, February 21, 2000.

27 Report of the Director, *Annual Report of the Scottish Crop Research Institute*, 1998–1999.

28 Enhanced Rape Seed Oil Could Supply Vitamin A, *Irish Times*, September 14, 1998.

29 Firm in Pounds 1m Campaign for Genetically Altered Food, *The Daily Telegraph*, June 6, 1998.

30 Call for a Ban on Biotech Beans, *Financial Times*, October 8, 1996.

31 Genetic Soybeans Alarm Europeans, *New York Times*, November 7, 1996.

32 Flavr Savr tomatoes were modified to resist spoilage, stick better to pasta, and mix easier into sauces. Flavr Savr products were also sold for approximately 10 percent less than average price. "Future in the Can," *The Scotsman*, February 9, 1996.

33 Address to Greenpeace Business Conference, Monsanto Company Document, October 6, 1999.

34 "Growth Through Global Sustainability," *Harvard Business Review*, January – February 1997.

35 Letter to Shareowners, *Monsanto Annual Report*, 1996.

36 Speech by Commission Emma Bonino at the Opening Ceremony of EuropaBio'98 in Brussels, *Commission of the European Communities*, October 28, 1998.

37 "Consumer Acceptance of Biotechnology: An International Perspective," *Nature Biotechnology*, March 15, 1997.

38 "The Hamburg Soybean Party," *Journal of Commerce*, December 24, 1996.

39 "Threats Halt GMO Trials Open Day," *Farmers Guardian*, May 22, 1998.

40 "Monsanto Apologises Over GM Soya Bean," *Farmers Guardian*, May 22, 1998.

41 Consumer Acceptance of Biotechnology: An International Perspective, *Nature Biotechnology*, March 15, 1997.

42 Monsanto Company Announces Major U.K. Information Programme on Food Biotechnology, *Monsanto Press Release*, June 5, 1998.

43 Seeds of Disaster, *The Daily Telegraph*, June 8, 1998.

CASE 9

Vodafone: Building a Global Organization

Philip M. Rosenzweig

Vodafone, the world's largest mobile telephone network operator, was one of the great growth stories of the 1990s. Founded in the early 1980s, Vodafone first built a strong base in the UK, and then expanded abroad in the late 1980s and early 1990s. Then, under the leadership of Chief Executive Chris Gent, Vodafone engineered two bold acquisitions. In 1999, it purchased US-based AirTouch, doubling its size and adding activities in North America, Asia, and Europe. In 2000, Vodafone created a sensation by acquiring Mannesmann AG, adding large positions in Germany, Italy, and elsewhere.

By March 2000, Vodafone reported annual revenues of £7.8 billion ($12 billion). It had more than 86 million customers in 24 countries. But now that it had the largest network in the world, attention shifted to a new priority: creating an effective global organization that would capture synergies in revenue growth, cost reduction, and capital expenditures. The challenge would not be easy. Most of Vodafone's operating companies had their own brand names, distinct channel strategies, and local product strategies. Exactly how to design and manage the new organization was not clear.

A team of Vodafone managers, working closely with outside consultants, initiated a study of organization redesign in the autumn of 2000. They considered the benefits of global integration and local responsiveness for each of twenty key activities, ranging from hardware procurement to brand management to customer service. They also assessed the company's readiness for change.

In the spring of 2001, the team presented four basic design options. Top management now evaluated which of the options to approve. Beyond design, a subsequent issue had

This case was written by Professor Philip M. Rosenzweig as a basis for class discussion rather than to illustrate either effective or ineffective handling of an administrative situation.

to do with implementation. What would it take, they pondered, for Vodafone to become an outstanding global organization?

EARLY DAYS OF A GLOBAL GIANT

Vodafone traces its roots to 1982 when Racal Electronics, a British company that specialized in defense electronics, obtained the first cellular license offered by the UK government.[1] At the time, prospects for wireless telephony were uncertain. Wireless telephones were heavy and awkward – sometimes called "bricks." Most analysts believed the need for mobile telephony was limited to law enforcement, medical care, service deliveries, and other professional applications. According to a company document: "It was science fiction to think that in a few years time a mobile phone would be in the hands of millions of people worldwide."

Yet some people, including Racal executives Sir Ernest Harrison and Gerry Whent, had confidence in the new technology. They foresaw a day when people would not only talk but also transfer data over wireless networks. After obtaining the license, the Racal Telecom Division was formed with Whent as chief executive. The new division had fewer than 50 employees, based in one rented building at divisional head offices in Newbury, an hour by train west of London. They chose a name for their new network that embraced voice and data mobile communication: *Vodafone.*

From this modest beginning, the Racal Telecom Division set out to build and operate a wireless analogue network. *Building a network* meant setting up a series of base stations and switches to provide coverage across much of Great Britain. The network had to offer extensive coverage and capacity to handle high quality signals.

Operating a network meant offering services to customers. Under a UK law that was intended to stimulate competition, network operators were not allowed to sell directly to customers, but had to work through third-party service providers. Vodafone's customers therefore were UK service providers; *their* customers, in turn, were the growing numbers of end-users who wanted mobile telephony.

Launching the UK's first network

The Vodafone network was launched on January 1, 1985, with the first telephone call placed from Parliament Square to Sir Ernest Harrison's house. At that time, the best mobile telephone available was the Nokia Talkman, which weighed 4.8 kg and cost £3,000. Yet even with cumbersome hardware, the network rapidly gained popularity. By the end of 1985, Vodafone had 19,000 end-users.

By 1988, the Vodafone network accounted for a third of Racal's profits. In October 1988, 20% of the ordinary share capital of Racal Telecom Group was floated on the London and New York Stock Exchanges. In September 1991, Racal Telecom was spun off entirely and became a fully independent company, listed on the London and New York Stock Exchanges. Its name was changed to Vodafone Group Plc.

EXHIBIT 1   Vodafone Organization Design, Early 1990s

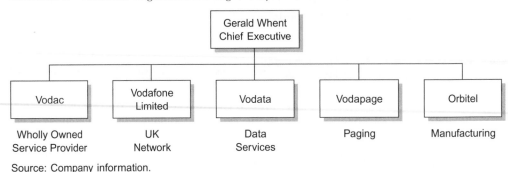

Source: Company information.

Expanding quality, services, and channels to market

Over the next years Vodafone steadily extended its UK coverage and also upgraded the quality of its network. It introduced the first GSM network in the UK in July 1992. Other digital networks soon followed, including One2One in September 1993, Cellnet in January 1994, and Orange in April 1994.

Vodafone also expanded its service offerings. A new unit, called Vodata, was created to develop and market data services. Early attempts to provide value-added services included Vodafone Recall, a voicemail service, Financial Times CityLine, and AA Road-watch. In 1994, Vodata was the first UK network operator to launch data, fax and SMS (Short Message Service) services over the digital network. The company also launched Vodapage, a paging network that covered an area that included 80% of the UK population. Yet the overwhelming amount of network use was for voice – placing person-to-person telephone calls over wireless networks rather than fixed lines.

The key to continuing growth was to get handsets – with Vodafone subscriptions – to more and more people. Network operators were prepared to subsidize the cost of handsets in order to gain monthly subscription revenues. In 1993, Vodafone opened its first retail store, called High Street Vodafone Centre, which sold handsets – along with network subscriptions. It also established its first direct distribution agreement with a major UK retailer, Comet. By the mid-1990s, Vodafone worked with more than 500 retail outlets and seven chains including John Lewis, AA stores, The Link, Talkland, and Pocket Phone.

Vodafone's organization design reflected the different parts of its business. Reporting to Gerry Whent, Vodafone's Chief Executive, were the UK network, Vodafone Limited, as well as Vodata, Vodapage, a wholly owned service provider called Vodac, and a small interest in manufacturing, Orbitel (see Exhibit 1).

VODAFONE'S INTERNATIONAL GROWTH

While expanding its domestic market, Vodafone also pursued international growth through two forms: *roaming agreements* and *investments in network operators*.

Roaming agreements, which allowed mobile phone users to use local networks when they traveled abroad, became possible as GSM emerged as an international standard. In 1991, Vodafone and Telecom Finland made the world's first international roaming call; the following year they signed the world's first international GSM roaming agreement.

Investments in network operators meant ownership positions in mobile telephone networks around the world, either through acquisition or bidding for new licenses. As the use of mobile telephones surged around the world, countries on all continents offered licenses for bid, eager to attract multinational companies who could provide financial resources, technical skills, and managerial know-how. For their part, these multinationals – including Cable & Wireless, AirTouch, Telefónica of Spain, France Télécom, BellSouth, and others – were racing to build a worldwide position, hoping to gain advantages of global scale and scope.

Vodafone used its strong earnings from the UK market to finance international investments. It obtained a small shareholding in the French network, SFR. In 1991, Vodafone added a small position in Sweden and took a large stake in a new network in Malta. In 1992, it joined other leading companies by investing in Panafon of Greece. In 1993, Vodafone joined partnerships that set up networks in Germany, South Africa, Australia, and Fiji. In 1996, it continued its overseas expansion with interests in the Netherlands and Hong Kong.

Managing global activities

Vodafone's international activities were known as *operating companies*, or OpCos. Majority-owned operating companies were called *subsidiaries*; minority-owned operating companies were called *affiliates*. Most had their own local brand name, and were run by local management, which had full profit and loss responsibility. Many also had local partners and a few were traded on local exchanges. All made their own decisions about products, channels, and technology. Their customers were overwhelmingly local residents who used the network for domestic telephone calls.

With a growing number of OpCos, Vodafone redesigned its organization structure, creating a new unit in 1997, Vodafone Group International. Led by Julian Horn-Smith, Vodafone Group International had a staff of just 12 people. Its objective was to manage the growing portfolio of international investments through representation on OpCo boards, and to secure more international business by acquisition or by license bid. It provided support for the OpCos, yet in most cases never imposed direct control. One manager recalled:

> The UK was the mother organization. It had the resources and systems to support other countries. Network design in the Netherlands and in Greece was modeled on the UK network, and so were billing systems.

THE BOOM YEARS: 1997 TO 2000

On January 1, 1997, after guiding Vodafone through 15 years of rapid growth, Sir Gerald Whent, as he had now become, retired as Chief Executive, and was succeeded by Chris Gent. With revenues outside the UK now representing well over 50% of total turnover, Vodafone shifted to a new structure that reflected a geographical split (see Exhibit 2).

EXHIBIT 2 Vodafone Organization Design, Mid-1990s

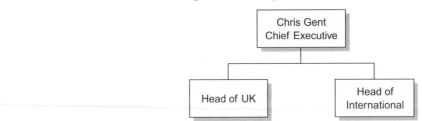

Source: Company information.

Peter Bamford became Chief Executive of UK, responsible for both Networks and Distribution. Julian Horn-Smith was head of Vodafone Group International.

Under Chris Gent's guidance, Vodafone focused even more aggressively on international growth. Vodafone subsequently acquired a GSM network in New Zealand from BellSouth. In 1999, a consortium owned 30% by Vodafone and 30% by AirTouch was awarded the license to build the second mobile network in Egypt, to be called Click GSM.

The use of mobile phones exploded in the late 1990s, as the advent of digital technology made mobile phones available to just about everyone. A virtuous cycle followed: powerful small handsets with low prices led to higher usage; growing numbers of subscribers led to even lower prices, which led to even more growth. The advent of pre-paid services further stimulated demand. Traditionally, subscribers had paid rental charges and service contracts. Handsets now came with pre-paid cards, obviating the need for time-consuming credit checks and monthly billing. With pre-paid services came a change in the mode of distribution, as any retailer or distributor could sell mobile phones along with other fast moving consumer goods.[2] In some countries, mobile phones became a fashion accessory, with young people owning several telephones of different colors and swapping them with friends.

The number of mobile phone users doubled every year during the 1990s. By 1998, the percentage of the population using mobile phones – known as penetration – exceeded 30% in 10 countries. During the first six months of 1998 alone, Europe added more than 13.3 million users, with users in France, the Netherlands, Germany, Great Britain and Portugal doubling from 1997 to 1998.[3] In 1999, Germany added 1 million subscribers per month, doubling in size from 10 million to 20 million – equivalent to the addition of a new subscriber every 2.5 seconds! Growth was just as dramatic in Asia. In Japan, despite persistent economic difficulties, the number of subscribers reached 20 million in 1998, up from just 1.3 million in 1994. Korea, China and other countries also surged. Rapid growth worldwide was expected for several years, with penetration of mobile phones expected to reach 50% in many industrialized countries by 2005.[4]

Acquisition of AirTouch, 1999

Rapid industry growth led to consolidation. In 1999, a leading US carrier, Bell Atlantic, made an unsolicited bid for another US carrier, AirTouch. AirTouch had been a partner to Vodafone in a number of investments, including Egypt. The two companies had even held informal discussions about working more closely together in the future. Once BellAtlantic made its bid for AirTouch, Vodafone responded quickly and trumped the offer.

The acquisition of AirTouch was completed on June 30, 1999. Vodafone then merged its US network with BellAtlantic and GTE to create a new company called Verizon Wireless, in which Vodafone owned 45%. It kept the other holdings, which ranged from Europe to the Pacific. The result was the largest mobile communications company in the world, with 31 million customers in 24 countries on five continents. Chris Gent stated: "Vodafone AirTouch will create an unparalleled platform for enhanced growth in what will be the unrivalled world leader in mobile communications."[5]

Redesigning the organization

The addition of AirTouch's extensive international activities prompted a redesign of the organization. The UK remained the company's single largest market, but now accounted for a much smaller share of company revenues. Now Vodafone was organized into four geographic regions (see Exhibit 3). Peter Bamford remained Chief Executive of the UK, which was treated as a region. Europe, Middle East, and Africa formed a region, with Julian Horn-Smith in charge. Arun Sarin, formerly president and COO of AirTouch, was responsible for the United States and Asia, which included Japan and Korea. Another executive, Brian Clark, was in charge of the Pacific region, comprised of Australia, New Zealand, and Fiji. Vodafone's national operating companies retained control over key decisions, and still held profit and loss responsibility.

Supplementing the four regions was a new unit with global responsibility. Tomas Isaakson, CEO of Europolitan, the Swedish operating company, was named head of Global Internet Platform Group. Since there was a strong desire to manage this new technology on a consistent basis worldwide, it made sense to place it outside of the country structures.

Mannesmann: deal and counterdeal, 2000

The acquisition of AirTouch had given Vodafone 35% of Mannesmann's D2 wireless network, the second largest in Germany. Many analysts expected Vodafone to eventually raise its stake to more than 50% – effectively taking control of D2. Vodafone and Mannesmann weren't strangers, having invested jointly in Omnitel, Italy's second largest network. The companies were also considering cooperation on future technologies, including third generation (3G). Yet Mannesmann's CEO, Klaus Esser, had different ambitions for his company, and in October 1999 made a bid to acquire Orange, the second-largest UK network. As one Vodafone executive recalled, "We could no longer be strategic partners with a company that competed with us in our own backyard, and which was thwarting our drive to be a global player. The only choice – which Chris Gent had the courage and foresight to push through – was to acquire Mannesmann."

In a move that was front-page news around the world, Vodafone made a bid for full ownership of Mannesmann, the first hostile foreign takeover in German history. A

EXHIBIT 3   Vodafone AirTouch Organization, 1999

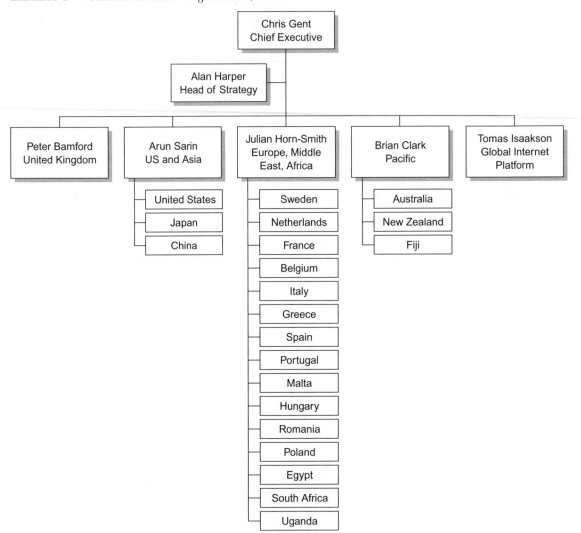

Source: Company information.

dramatic standoff followed over the next weeks. On February 4, 2000, Mannesmann's Supervisory Board broke the impasse by agreeing to Vodafone's offer. In April, the European Commission approved the deal. The final piece of the puzzle fell into place as Vodafone put Orange into a trust, from which Orange was auctioned to France Telecom.

With the acquisition of Mannesmann, Vodafone once again doubled in size. It now ranked as the largest mobile telecommunications company in the world, with more than 86 million customers in more than 24 countries. Vodafone's international activities as of March 2000 are shown in Exhibit 4. No other network operator counted so many customers or enjoyed such a broad geographic position.

EXHIBIT 4   Vodafone Operating Companies, March 2000

Country	Service	Vodafone Ownership	Population (millions)	Market Penetration (%)	Venture Customers (thousands)	Proportionate Customers (thousands)	Prepaid (%)
Europe, Middle East, Africa							
Belgium	Proximus	25	10.2	36	2,307	576	32
Egypt	Click GSM	60	67.3	2	405	243	87
France	SFR	20	59	39	7,910	1,582	37
Germany	D2	99.1	82.1	33	11,107	11,000	32
Greece	Panafon	55	10.7	40	1,773	975	62
Hungary	Vodafone	50.1	10.2	16	47	24	70
Italy	Omnitel	76	56.7	58	11,222	8,000	87
Malta	Vodafone	80	.3	12	45	36	58
Netherlands	Libertel	70	15.8	49	2,450	1,715	66
Poland	Plus GSM	19.6	38.6	11	1,692	332	26
Portugal	Telecel	50.9	9.9	52	1,795	913	72
Romania	Connex GSM	20.1	22.3	7	765	154	33
South Africa	Vodacom	31.5	43.4	11	3,069	967	68
Spain	Airtel	21.7	39.2	45	5,624	1,220	59
Sweden	Europolitan	71.1	8.9	61	885	629	19
Uganda	Celltell	36.8	22.8	0.3	23	8	87
United Kingdom							
UK	Vodafone	100	59.1	46	8,791	8,791	58
United States and Asia Pacific							
US	Verizon	Various	99.8	32	10,082	9,354	10
Australia	Vodafone	91	18.8	42	1,440	1,310	21
Fiji	Vodafone	49	0.8	3	24	12	67
New Zealand	Vodafone	100	3.7	39	473	473	67

Source: Abridged from Vodafone AirTouch Annual Report, 2000.

BUILDING A GLOBAL COMPANY

Now that Vodafone had achieved a large global position it faced a new challenge: how to transform a series of operating companies into a unified global company, able to seize the advantages of scale and scope.

At the time of its bid for Mannesmann, Vodafone outlined many of the benefits it anticipated from a large global position. Most prominent were savings from combined purchasing of mobile network hardware, software, and IT systems. Vodafone estimated these after-tax synergies at £200 million for cost savings and £200 million in capital expenditures for 2003, and £240 million in cost savings and £210 in capital expenditures for 2004. These were sizeable benefits given 2000 revenues of £7.8 billion. Vodafone also expected revenue synergies of £100 million in 2003 and £150 in 2004. Finally, it claimed that as a large global company, it would reap benefits from sharing expertise and best practices among operating companies. Vodafone noted that since the acquisition of AirTouch, it had already identified and diffused best practices, including base station efficiency (from Australia), customer relationship management (from Portugal), and leading pre-paid practices (from South Africa). The addition of D2, Omnitel and others would increase further the potential of expertise sharing, with new countries both contributing to, as well as benefiting from, other operating companies around the world.

Gaining these advantages would require a different way of organizing and managing the company. Over the course of its history, Vodafone had evolved through several different organizational firms. At first, as part of Racal Telecom Division, it was a division among several in a *product division structure*. From 1985 through 1997, Vodafone was organized by upstream networks and downstream sales and marketing – a *functional structure*. From 1997 onward, as it expanded around the world, Vodafone was organized by operating companies that reported into Regions – a *geographic structure*. Now Vodafone needed once again to consider how best to organize its activities.

The organization design team

In the summer of 2000, a team of Vodafone executives, working closely with a major consulting company, examined how best to redesign the organization.

The team began by identifying Vodafone's major activities, including these: procurement of hardware and software for networks; procurement of hardware and software for internal use; network installation and maintenance; IT and technical standards; new product development; sales channel management; brand management; customer service and support; regulatory affairs; finance (Treasury and corporate finance); finance (OpCo accounting and control); and human resource management.

One team member recalled: "For each activity, we asked: What are the benefits of taking a more coordinated approach? What are the needs for local responsiveness?" Each activity was placed in one of three categories: 1) Activities with a *high need for global integration*, often because of economies of scale or scope, or a need to provide global consistency; 2) Activities with a *high need for local responsiveness*, often because of local differences including regulations, consumer habits and tastes, levels of economic development, distribution channels, and the like; and 3) Activities with a *high need for global integration and local responsiveness*, combining elements of the first two categories.

Some of the data they considered included these:

- Worldwide, 85% of Vodafone's revenues were from individual subscribers; the remaining 15% were from corporate accounts. There were, however, significant differences among countries. In the UK and Germany, corporate and SME customers accounted for up to 35% of revenues and profits, whereas in Italy and Portugal they accounted for less than 10%.[6]
- For contract (post-paid) customers, roughly 25% of revenues were associated with international roaming – that is, outbound calls placed outside the home market. For pre-paid customers, such international roaming calls were estimated at less than 5% of revenues.
- Operating companies used a wide variety of hardware and software suppliers for network construction, including Nortel, Ericsson, Nokia, and Oracle. As noted above,

purchasing synergies could reduce costs, on an after-tax basis, by £400 in 2003 and £450 in 2004.

- Operating companies had a variety of local brands, which were well known and well respected in their markets. Yet building a single global brand was appealing, both as a way to reach new customers and to save costs on sponsorships.
- Channels differed by country. For example, Vodafone UK owned and managed many stores that sold handsets; in Italy, Omnitel relied on independent dealers.
- Each OpCo had developed its own products and services, at a considerable cost. Many of the resulting products were very similar. Products developed in one market could usually be applied in many.

Assessing readiness for change

The design team also considered the company's readiness for change. Whereas Vodafone had tight financial controls over its many international investments, it had so far exercised only loose operational control. It relied on voluntary coordination rather than direct control. Indeed, direct control had not been possible in countries where Vodafone had a minority ownership position. In some countries, Vodafone had invested along with rivals – such as Panafon of Greece, which was partly owned by France Telecom. As a consequence, Vodafone had never developed strong capabilities of global operational control.

For their part, most operating companies were used to local autonomy and might be reluctant to give it up. Many had their own boards and their own shareholders. They also tended to be among the strongest performers in their respective markets, either the largest network or second only to the state-owned network. They tended to be efficient and dynamic, and often attracted highly capable and ambitious young managers who thrived on a high degree of autonomy and independence. The entrepreneurial drive of OpCo management was a source of strength for Vodafone.

For all these reasons, it was questionable how quickly Vodafone could shift to a very different model – even if its objective analysis argued for much greater central direction. One manager recalled: "We had to look at what was a reasonable modification, given the existing operating company model."

Major design options

In early 2001, the design team presented four options to top management.

A first option, Exhibit 5a, proposed *voluntary coordination*. Operating companies would be grouped into five Regions. Region management would provide a coordinating function, but would not actively manage OpCos – each OpCo would retain all key decision-making responsibility. In addition, a set of Councils would be set up to stimulate coordination on a handful of key activities – providing, for example, systems for sharing expertise and opportunities to pool buying power – but only on a voluntary basis, represented by a dotted line. OpCos would retain their traditional autonomy and decide whether, and to what extent, to work with Councils.

EXHIBIT 5A "Voluntary Coordination"

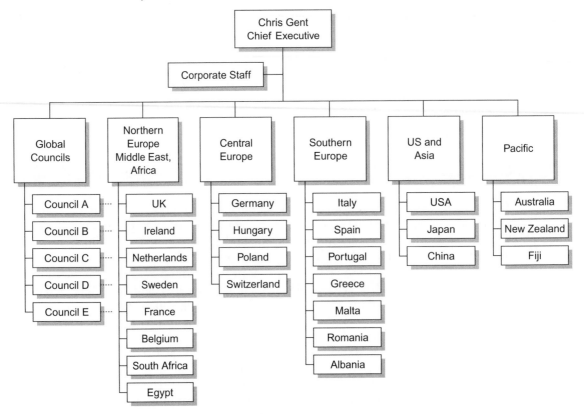

A second option, Exhibit 5b, went a step further, proposing *mandatory coordination*. Under this proposal, Councils would be responsible for optimizing their activities on a global basis; compliance by OpCos would be mandatory, not voluntary, as represented by a solid line. If Vodafone chose this approach, it would need to determine which of the twenty activities demanded formal coordination, and how many Councils to put in place. It would also need to address the nature of joint decision-making between the geographic units and the Councils – where would ultimate decision-making rest, and how would differing priorities be balanced?

A third option, Exhibit 5C, proposed strong coordination across national borders in each of three major Regions. Under this proposal, called *functional optimization*, Region management would become the key locus of managerial power, assuming a super-national role and optimizing functions for its Region. This approach promised the greatest realization of cross-border synergies, but it also imposed the greatest change on operating companies.

A fourth option, Exhibit 5d, was an *upstream-downstream hybrid* model. It organized Vodafone into upstream activities – networks – which would be coordinated globally, and downstream activities – sales and marketing – which would be managed on a geographic

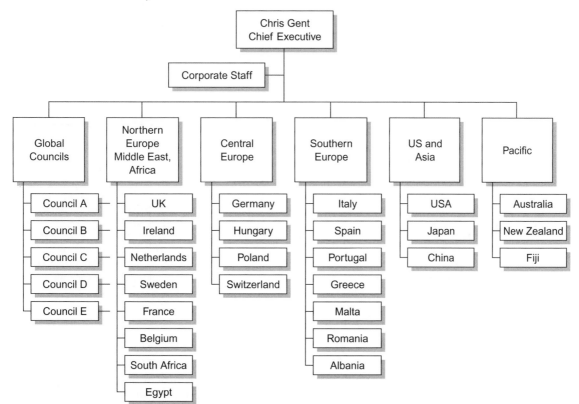

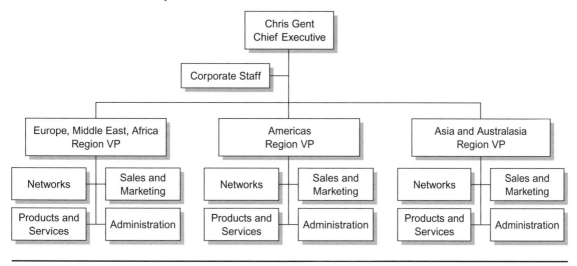

EXHIBIT 5D   "Upstream-Downstream Hybrid"

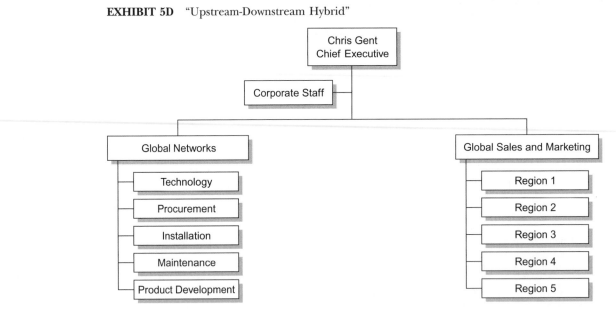

Source: Company information.

basis, responsibilities remaining with operating companies. There were some good precedents for this approach. For example, some prominent electronics companies were organized in global business divisions upstream – R&D, procurement, manufacturing was organized by television, audio, VCRs, and so forth. Downstream, in sales and marketing, distributions, customer service, activities were organized by geography. Perhaps, the design team reflected, this model would work well at Vodafone, with upstream activities – technology, procurement, installation and management of networks – managed globally, and activities that touched customers managed locally.

Looking ahead

As Vodafone managers pondered the shape of a new organization, events continued to advance briskly. 2001 was shaping up to be another year of strong growth, as 4.4 million customers were added during the first quarter. Vodafone acquired a 25% stake in Swisscom Mobile, bought control of Ireland's leading mobile communications company, Eircell, signed a strategic alliance with China Mobile (Hong Kong) Ltd, and planned increase its ownership in Japan. By the middle of 2001, Vodafone expected to have more than 93 million customers worldwide.

Notes

1   The license was initially held by Racal Millicom, a joint venture between Racal and another UK firm, Millicom. Racal always held the majority interest, and later acquired Millicom's share.

2   Price, Christopher. "Market is revitalised with lure of pre-paid packages." *Financial Times*, March 18, 1999.

3   Cane, Alan. "Millennium forecast is for 1 bn cellular users." *Financial Times*, November 18, 1999.

4   Black, George. "Promise of a 'wire-free future' heralds progress." *Financial Times*, March 11, 1999.

5   Vodafone Annual Report and Accounts, 1999 p. 4.

6   These data are case writer estimates based on industry sources. They are intended to provide the reader with typical figures, and may not necessarily be accurate for Vodafone.

C A S E **10**

Five Star Beer – Pay for Performance

Brian Golden and Tom Gleave

In June 1997, Tom McMullen (President – Alliance Brewing Group) and Zhao Hui Shen (General Manager – Five Star Brewing Co. Ltd) met to discuss the "pay for performance" systems which Zhao had been implementing at Five Star's two breweries over the past several months. McMullen needed to determine whether or not these incentive systems were properly designed to ensure that the breweries would produce higher quality beer at progressively lower costs. If not, he needed to consider how he might suggest that these and other systems be changed in order to achieve Alliance Brewing's cost and quality objectives.

FIVE STAR'S ASIMCO CONNECTION

The majority owner of Beijing Asia Shuang He Sheng Five Star Brewing Co. Ltd (Five Star) was the Beijing-based investment group, Asian Strategic Investments Corporation (ASIMCO). The primary shareholders of ASIMCO were Trust Company West, Morgan Stanley – Dean Witter Reynolds and senior management. The senior management team consisted of the following people:

Jack Perkowski (Chairman and CEO) – a former investment chief at Paine Webber (New York City) and graduate of both Yale University (cum laude) and the Harvard Business School (Baker Scholar).

Tim Clissold (President) – a physics graduate from Cambridge University who turned accountant with Arthur Anderson in the 1980s. Clissold had worked in England, Australia, China and Hong Kong for Anderson before entering London's School of Oriental and Asian Studies where he became fluent in both spoken and written Mandarin.

Michael Cronin (Chief Investment and Financial Officer) – also worked as an accountant for Arthur Anderson throughout the 1980s in Australia, the UK and Hong Kong. Previously, Cronin had worked for over five years at 3i, Europe's largest direct investment organization.

Ai Jian (Managing Director) – a Chinese native and graduate from Northwestern Polytechnical University in Xian, China. Ai's previous working experience included senior posts in the foreign relations department of China's Ministry of Foreign Trade and Economic Cooperation. He was a native Mandarin speaker and also fluent in English.

The motivations underlying ASIMCO's investment in the Chinese beer industry were twofold. First, the industry was experiencing high, sustainable growth rates. This high growth was spurred by the increasing levels of disposable incomes in China, to the point where it was expected that the Chinese beer market would become the world's largest (overtaking the USA) within the next several years. Second, the industry was highly fragmented and was undergoing a significant restructuring. This high degree of fragmentation was a consequence of China's legacy of central planning. Given its increasing adoption of market-driven mechanisms, China's central government was encouraging (or passively allowing) the rationalization of certain industries, including the beer industry. The industry consensus was that the number of breweries was expected to be reduced from over 800 to less than 600 nationwide over the next several years while managing to steadily increase overall beer volume. This meant that surviving firms would need to seek economies of scale, maintain high quality production and ensure development of strong management teams as the competition intensified.

ASIMCO's investment strategy was to identify Chinese companies that had the potential to be globally competitive and to support these firms with capital, western management skills and leading-edge technologies. The partners they sought were expected to be aggressive, profit-oriented and industry leaders. Whenever a potential opportunity was discovered, ASIMCO would marshal its skills and international resources to perform due diligence, negotiate contracts and obtain necessary approvals. ASIMCO would subsequently provide capital, western management expertise and technological know-how to the joint venture and devise an exit strategy designed to realize the value created.

ASIMCO viewed itself as an agent of change in helping to transform formerly inefficient state-owned enterprises into market-driven and export-ready competitive firms. By June 1997, ASIMCO had entered into 13 automotive parts manufacturing, two automotive parts distribution and two beer manufacturing joint ventures. The sum total of these investments, all of which were majority positions, was about US $360 million. All minority positions were held by various Chinese partners. The Five Star joint venture was ASIMCO's largest single investment in its portfolio with a total capital outlay of US $70 million for a 63 per cent stake in the company. The minority interest partner was the First Light Industry Bureau (FLIB) with a 37 per cent stake. The FLIB was a division of the Beijing municipal government and had ownership interests in many diverse

EXHIBIT 1 ASIMCO's Ownership in Brewing Joint Ventures

business activities. ASMICO's other joint venture in brewing was a 54 per cent interest in the Three Ring Beer Company, an investment valued at US $23 million. Both of the brewing joint ventures were formalized in January 1995 (see Exhibit 1).

ALLIANCE BREWING GROUP

Alliance Brewing Group (ABG) was a management services group which was specifically established to provide support to both of ASIMCO's brewery joint ventures. This gave ABG the mandate to support three different, yet related, brewing facilities. These breweries were as follows:

Brewery	Owner	Annual Capacity (tons)
Shuang Sheng	Five Star	90,000
Huadu	Five Star	180,000
San Huan	Three Ring	130,000

(Total production for the three breweries was currently running at about 250,000 tons per year.)

ABG was organized into separate corporate level support functions which included marketing, brewing and quality control, operations services, financial control and new business development. The President of ABG was Tom McMullen, an American expatriate who formerly worked in the consumer packaged goods business in the US after graduating from the Wharton School of Business (see Exhibit 2).

The overall goal of ABG was to help both brewing companies realize their return on invested capital targets. With respect to Five Star, this was expected to be accomplished through the achievement of five key objectives, which included (in order of priority) the following:

EXHIBIT 2   Alliance Brewing Group – Partial Organization Chart

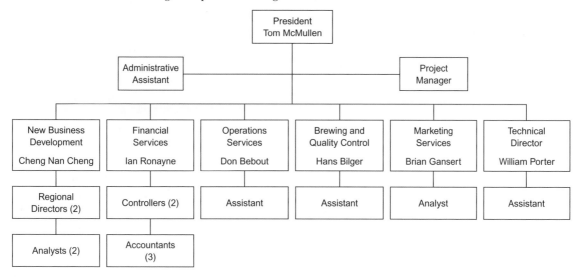

1   improved product and packaging quality.
2   reduced production costs in an effort to gain better margins.
3   the development of professional sales, marketing and distribution systems.
4   the development of a system which rewarded good performance and punished bad performance.
5   an increased understanding between Five Star's two breweries that separate production facilities did not mean separate companies. Rather, they were part of the same brewing company.

According to McMullen, one of the more meaningful signs of progress that ABG was able to make over the past year was the development of rational and integrated financial reporting systems. These new systems took more than one year to develop but eventually allowed both Chinese and expatriate managers to "talk from the same page." As evidence of the importance of the need for reliable and timely financial information, particularly with respect to the need for Chinese management to understand the importance of meeting budgeted targets, ABG had installed its own financial personnel at both of its beer companies.

FIVE STAR'S RECENT HISTORY

Five Star was one of the oldest brewing companies in China, with its origins dating back to 1915. Like most breweries in China, Five Star originally served its local markets, the main one being Beijing and the surrounding Hebei province. This focus on local markets developed as a consequence of competing interests from local governments which, in turn, led to the industry's fragmented structure. Over the years, however, Five Star was able to gain some market share in areas beyond the immediate region. This market penetration was accomplished through the establishment of licensing agreements between Five Star and other regional brewers throughout the country.

Prior to the early 1990s, the company enjoyed a majority share of the local Beijing market. This market position had developed because Five Star had a lengthy history in the region and, as a state enterprise which was wholly owned by the Beijing municipal government, was conferred special privileges. For example, in 1957, Chinese Premier Zhou Enlai decreed that Five Star was to be the exclusive beer supplied at all State banquets, thus bringing the company name to national prominence.

By the early 1990s, Five Star's market position began to deteriorate as it found itself competing in the same territories in the Beijing area with one of its largest licensees, Three Ring Beer. In 1993, Five Star entered into a licensing agreement which allowed Three Ring to produce and market Five Star beer for sale in specific territories on the northeastern outskirts of Beijing. However, Five Star soon found that Three Ring was "stealing" sales by deliberately encroaching on Five Star's exclusive territories within the core areas of the city. Three Ring was successful in securing significant market share due to its offer of lower pricing (for virtually the same products) and the lack of wholesaler and retailer loyalty. ASIMCO acquired a majority stake in both brewing companies in January 1995. This left ABG with the challenge of ensuring that the two companies refrain from directly competing with each other.

The progressive intrusion by Three Ring was compounded by the deteriorating quality of Five Star's products. It was only after it acquired ownership control that ASIMCO discovered that Five Star was experiencing greater quality difficulties than originally thought. Perhaps most disturbing of all was the consistently poor performance and apathetic attitude of Mr Xu, Five Star's former General Manager. According to Tom McMullen:

> Xu was completely lacking in competence in virtually all respects. He was simply a victim of the old state-enterprise culture which encouraged senior managers to have a minimum of initiative and innovation. He perceived himself to be a king in his castle, while ABG in general, and me in particular, were seen as interlopers. Unfortunately for him, he discovered the hard way that his position was less secure than he believed.

Admittedly, McMullen had much less control than he originally expected when he signed on with Five Star. Having worked in the US for over 20 years, McMullen was accustomed to the idea that employees could be hired, disciplined and terminated as deemed necessary. However, in China, such activities were regulated to a much greater extent and often involved political considerations. For example, the person in charge of the human resource management and training functions at Five Star was Mr Qi, resident member of the Communist Party of China. (See Exhibit 3; see also Appendix 1 – Labour Market Conditions and Human Resource Management in China.)

THE IMPERATIVE FOR QUALITY

The high degree of industry consolidation, coupled with increasing Sino-foreign joint venture activity involving numerous world famous beer companies (such as Heineken,

EXHIBIT 3   Five Star Beer Organization Chart

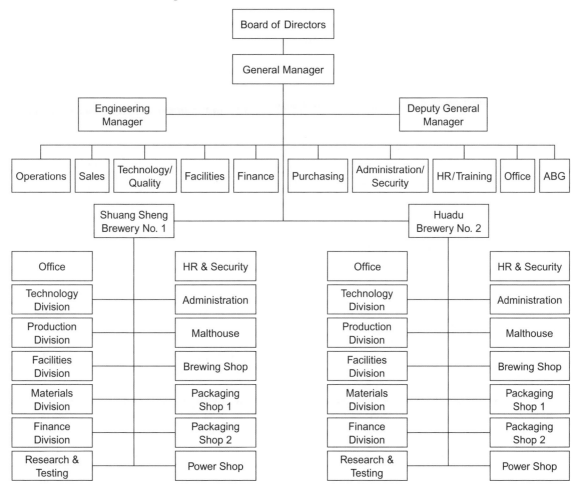

Beck's and Budweiser), meant that Five Star was beginning to experience greater competition from very capable rivals. This created a critical need for Five Star to provide higher quality beer and packaging. The common criteria by which product quality was evaluated included consistency in taste, clarity, carbonation, fill levels and labelling. The challenge of achieving consistency across all of these quality dimensions was great. Numerous documented incidences of foreign matter inside bottles, as well as unfilled or short-filled bottles and cans had been documented. Many packaging issues had also been identified and typically included poorly labelled or poorly sealed bottles and cans. One particularly poignant incident occurred shortly after the joint venture was formed and signalled to ASIMCO and ABG the need for drastically improving Five Star's quality. In this instance, a customer found a bottle which was half-full that had been released with a ripped label that was glued on sideways, despite having passed at least four inspection workers. Upon hearing the news of this episode, Tim Clissold (ASIMCO President) declared:

> It is beyond rational thought how our workers allowed this bottle to be sent out for public consumption. And when inquiries were made as to how this type of thing could happen, the line manager simply laughed with embarrassment. This is the result of the old central planning mentality in which there was no connection between reward and effort. These workers had no proper incentive or disincentive to ensure full product quality. The workers could not be fined or punished, nor were they entitled to extra wages for extra work completed.

The bottle in question was permanently displayed in ASIMCO and ABG's combined offices as a reminder of the need for ensuring diligence at every stage of the production and marketing process.

After realizing that quality issues facing Five Star were considerable, ASIMCO and ABG moved quickly to resolve the problems. ABG's professional staff was to focus on reducing costs, but a priority emphasis was placed on quality. Three key brewing professionals, the only non-Chinese to take an active role at any of the breweries, led the effort. They were:

> Don Bebout (VP – Operations Services), an American with over 19 years of experience working for Miller Brewing. He was particularly skilled in the areas of packaging and labelling.
>
> Hans Bilger (Master Brewer & ABG's Quality Manager) had a lifetime of brewing experience. In his native Germany, he grew up helping his father run a family-owned brewery before embarking for the US where he spent nearly thirty years involved in a variety of positions, both with US brewing giants and microbreweries.
>
> William Porter (Technical Director) was also an industry veteran from the US where he worked for over 20 years at such breweries as Miller, Lone Star and Pabst. Although Porter's "home" brewery was with the Three Ring brewing joint venture, he was often called upon to offer technical advice to Five Star.

These three ex-pats were each provided with dedicated assistants, all of whom were fluently bilingual. This assistance was essential since none of the three ex-pats spoke Mandarin. Among the three assistants, Zhou Yue reported directly to Don Bebout and held a graduate degree in fermentology. She had previously worked for several years at China's National Institute for Food and Fermentology. Similarly, Bi Hong, assistant to Bilger, was a genetics technologist and had also worked for the National Institute for Food and Fermentalogy. She also received 13 months of brewery training while studying in France.

A major concern of ABG's operations and quality staff was the need to achieve higher quality targets while "milking" the existing equipment. When ASIMCO took its majority stake in Five Star, the company was believed to possess some of the best equipment of any brewery in China, although some of it required refurbishing due to lack of regular maintenance. Given the recent influx of well-funded foreign brewers, Five Star appeared to be at a technological disadvantage when it came to ensuring product and packaging quality.

The need for management control and motivation

Regarding the level of management control and commitment that is necessary for ensuring consistent quality, Hans Bilger (Master Brewer) offered the following remarks:

> The skills needed to produce quality beer on a consistent basis are minimal. What you need are the monitoring procedures, the discipline to adhere to those procedures and the clear reporting of information to the appropriate people. The tasks of monitoring operations, recording data and communicating results on a regular basis are not sophisticated. The problems arise when management does not take control by ensuring that procedures are followed or that information is shared. For example, line workers are expected to regularly record the temperatures in the brewing vats. This is done often enough, but the results are frequently not communicated to the people who use this information. This is a symptom of the silo mentality around here. There really is no cross-functional coordination. And in the event that any results are communicated, you end up getting what you want to hear and not the real story, even when there is a problem. This shows that our quality problems are management-related and that the senior managers at the brewery need to become committed to quality.
>
> Quality is a way of life. It is a mindset. The senior managers at the brewery have yet to fully understand these concepts. Part of the problem could be that they are rewarded on volume output, not quality output. This is because brewing in China is a low margin business and, therefore, breweries need to pump out the volume in order to make any profits. This means that some managers are reluctant to take any measures which will impede their ability to produce as much as they can.
>
> Ideally, I would like to see Five Star have an independent quality department reporting directly to the General Manager, not to the Deputy GM and Chief Engineer as is now the case – despite what the formal organization chart suggests. Both the "Number 1" and "Number 2" breweries would have their own divisional labs which would feed their results to Five Star's quality assurance office on a regular basis. This quality assurance department would also be given policeman-like powers. Someone has to be able to say "this is not good enough," and then have the authority to take corrective action. Unfortunately, this type of arrangement goes against the strong tradition of hierarchical reporting in China.

Hiring Mr Zhao

In response to the need to replace Mr Xu, and after a thorough recruiting process, ASIMCO and ABG agreed to hire Zhao Hui Shen. Mr Zhao, formerly a factory manager at a piano manufacturing plant where he had worked for over 20 years, came highly recommended by the FLIB. Clissold was skeptical about hiring Zhao due to his obvious lack of brewing industry experience. However, Zhao won Clissold's confidence when confronted about this apparent liability by stating that, "you will not hire me to make the beer, you will hire me to manage the people who make the beer."

Zhao was expected to work impartially for the Five Star joint venture company. He was also expected to draw upon the resources of ABG in an effort to improve the overall quality and productivity of Five Star's brewing operations. Within the joint venture company, Zhao reported to the Board of Directors. The Board's membership consisted of Jack Perkowski, Ai Jian, Tom McMullen, Mr Zhao, and a representative from the FLIB.

Zhao was viewed by many others at ABG and Five Star as representing a new generation of Chinese manager. This was because he had taken a very aggressive and hands-on
approach to managing the business, a style which was a distinct departure from the
state-owned enterprise culture of the past. Zhao commented:

> You have to change the way of thinking from traditional enterprise methods. Nowadays we
> must think of management by objective. I want people to think about how they can achieve
> their goals, not how to waste time thinking of excuses for not achieving them and then
> relying on the government for money.

Zhao's performance-related pay systems

One of ABG's key objectives was to help the breweries adopt a "pay for performance"
culture. ABG believed that it must try to get people to care about their work and about
themselves, particularly since jobs were taking on an entirely new role in Chinese life.
ABG was seeking to instill a culture which would see employees take greater control over
their destinies.

When it came time (in January 1997) to begin the development of specific pay for
performance systems, Zhao requested the assistance of ABG. However, ABG was unable
to offer extensive support at that time due to limited resources and its other priorities.
In March 1997, ABG offered to assist Zhao in developing the systems, but Zhao then
declined the offer because he did not want ABG to change what he had already initiated. He did, however, offer to reveal his key objectives to ABG. This led McMullen to
acknowledge that the issue of establishing a pay for performance system may have been
a higher priority for Zhao than it was for himself.

In developing the compensation systems, Zhao believed that monetary punishment
could be used as a strong incentive for better performance, something McMullen
referred to as "using more stick than carrot." One such example of this approach involved
the bottle-filling line, where one of the key measures of quality was to ensure that all
bottles were filled to the proper level. To ensure that properly filled bottles were distributed
from the brewery, each filling line was assigned two people to manually check for empty
bottles, while four additional people were used to manually check for short-fills. When
the bottles were filled they were date-stamped and coded so that the product could be
traced to its original filling and labelling lines. In the event that a empty or short-filled
product was found in the marketplace (whether it be by Five Star's sales people, distributors or final customers), all six people on the originating filling line would be fined
a total of 500 renminbi, or about 83 Rmb each.[1] This fine would be deducted from their
salaries in which each line worker received an average compensation of about 1000 Rmb
per month, an amount which was almost double that of similar positions in Chinese
wholly owned breweries.

There was some debate in the plant as to whether or not this was an effective system.
Hans Bilger (Master Brewer) felt that this approach was too harsh. He believed that, at
a filling rate of 12,000 bottles per hour over a six-hour shift, the employees would become
too tired to identify all empty bottles or shortfills. On the other hand, Yang Xiang,
a bilingual technician working for the Operations Service group, felt that this type of

system was "to some extent fair." He felt that somebody must take responsibility for these types of errors and that it might be more effective if the line supervisors were fined, not just the line workers.

Another example of a disincentive for poor performance involved a fine levied on the brew house for poor sanitation in the rice mill under its responsibility. The beer that Five Star brewed typically consisted of 30 per cent rice grain and 70 per cent malt. A rice mill was utilized on-site to provide the appropriate supplies. A common problem in the mill was the high level of dustiness, due primarily to the lack of care in cleaning, as well as an occasionally malfunctioning dust collection system. This presented a danger of insect infestation which, apart from affecting beer quality, also posed a threat of flammable explosion. In the spring of 1997, after Bilger submitted one of his periodic inspection reports which gave the mill a failing grade, seven line workers in the mill and associated brew house were deducted 100 Rmb each from their next pay cheque. As was the case in the previous example, the affected employees also earned 1000 Rmb per month.

One of Zhao's more widely discussed systems involved the sales force. Given that Five Star was seeking to re-establish its market position within the greater Beijing area, a strong emphasis was placed on boosting sales and thus increasing market share. Although sales people began by earning a starting salary of only 600 Rmb per month, they could earn up to 10 times this amount depending upon their sales performance. Unfortunately, Mr Zhao had encountered some difficulty recruiting people who were prepared to receive compensation based largely upon their own efforts. Additionally, there were widely held suspicions among some of the ABG operations and quality staff that this particular system had invited abuse in the proper recording of sales. Although these staffers had "heard rumors" of this type activity, they had no concrete evidence. Any inquiries about the company's latest sales performance were met with "stony silence."

The implementation of Zhao's various performance-related pay schemes had given rise to a general debate among ABG's operations staff. The nature of the debate centered around which direction or approach would best motivate employees to strive for quality. The divergent views expressed by the operations staff were highlighted by the contrasting opinions between William Porter and Hans Bilger. Porter contended that cash payouts were a more effective incentive for improving performance than the recognition for a job well done. He believed that the employees would "far sooner have more renminbi in their jeans than a pat on the back." Bilger, on the other hand, suggested that pride of workmanship and the recognition of a job well done were more powerful motivators than cash rewards. His reasoning was that China was a status-conscious society where a high value was placed on securing the favorable opinion of one's peers and superiors. Despite a significant amount of spirited discussion, no clear consensus had emerged among ABG's operations staff as to whose view was more compelling.

DECISION

The next Board meeting was scheduled for mid-July 1997, at which time McMullen wished to offer the members an update on the design and implementation of the pay for performance systems at Five Star. Therefore, as McMullen contemplated how he might suggest to Zhao different ways for improving these systems, he needed to consider several important factors. First and foremost, he needed to consider the cultural, historical, social and business contexts in which Five Star and ABG found themselves. McMullen was keenly aware that the receptivity to pay for performance systems was only beginning to be slowly accepted in China. Moreover, he needed to recognize the far greater knowledge that Zhao possessed about Chinese behavioral habits and culture. Therefore, he could not presume that what would be effective in North America would be effective in China. McMullen was also intrigued by the debates which had surfaced among his own operations staff. Did the notion of "punishments" have some merit in China? Would workers respond most to cash rewards or were they more likely to be motivated by some form of recognition? The only thing which seemed clear to McMullen was that the motivation and quality problems had no easy solutions.

ACKNOWLEDGMENT

The Richard Ivey School of Business gratefully acknowledges the generous support of The Richard and Jean Ivey Fund in the development of this case as part of the Richard and Jean Ivey Fund Asian Case Series.

Note

1   The June 1997 exchange rate was about 8.28 Rmb = US $1.

APPENDIX 1 LABOR MARKET CONDITIONS AND HUMAN RESOURCE DEVELOPMENT PRACTICES IN CHINA

China's labor market in 1997 was experiencing significant structural changes as market-oriented reforms took hold. State policy efforts to establish a new social welfare system and to implement state-owned enterprise (SOE) reform have had a profound effect on labor market conditions and human resource management practices in both domestic and foreign-funded enterprises. The first national labor law came into effect in 1995 and brought with it a lower level of government intervention in human resource management (HRM) at the enterprise level and more equal treatment for domestic and foreign enterprises. It is expected that this law will eventually allow all types of firms to acquire greater control over wage setting as well as the power to hire, discipline and dismiss workers, areas which have traditionally been highly regulated by government. In the meantime, China's labor market remains under-developed: labor mobility is restricted, and HRM is a new concept. Therefore, both domestic and foreign enterprises are now operating in a highly uncertain environment which reflects a combination of the old planned economy practices with those of newer western approaches to HRM.

In 1994, China's labor force totalled 615 million, or approximately 51 per cent of the country's total population of 1.2 billion. This labor force is expected to grow by an average of 20.9 million persons per year between 1995 and 2006. Importantly, no national social welfare system has been established in China. Social welfare has traditionally been the responsibility of the SOEs, the dominant form of industrial organization in the Chinese economy since the "liberation" of 1949. However, as market forces take greater hold in China, the SOEs will find it increasingly difficult to maintain these responsibilities for delivering a wide range of social services including subsidized housing, education and health care.

Until recently, HRM in China has been defined by the tenure employment structure of the planned economy. In the old SOE system, labor was regarded as a passive input in the production process rather than a productive factor. As a result, traditional human resource management included only personnel administration activities, such as registering the recruited workers, recording increases in wages and promotions (by seniority), filing job changes, and maintaining workers' files. Although training was provided, most of it involved indoctrinating workers with the Communist Party's prevailing policies. The focus was on the use of workers rather than their career development. Compensation was not directly linked to performance and served as little incentive for better performance. From an enterprise's overall performance perspective, it is clear that these practices were not aligned with a strategy to be productive and competitive in a market-oriented economy.

Source: The Conference Board of Canada, Opportunities and Risks for Canadian Business in China, 1996.

C ASE **11**

Moscow Aerostar

Henry W. Lane and Christine Shea

BACKGROUND

The Moscow Aerostar Hotel opened for business on May 1, 1991. The hotel was a joint venture between Russia's national airline, Aeroflot, and an aerospace multinational, IMP Group Limited, based in Halifax, Nova Scotia. The relationship between the two companies began when an IMP company won a contract to service and refuel Aeroflot flights landing in Gander, Newfoundland. While on business in Moscow in 1988, Ken Rowe, IMP's Chairman and Chief Executive Officer, noticed an unfinished concrete building on Leningradski Prospect near the site of the 1980 Moscow Olympic Games. Aeroflot owned the building which originally had been designed to house athletes during the games, but had never been completed. Ken Rowe accepted the challenge of converting the unfinished building into a Western-style hotel.

> "It's been a challenging four years," admits Rowe. "Launching a joint venture in partnership with a former communist country isn't the same as working with any other country in the world. We had to overcome many obstacles, build a lot of bridges between the Russians and ourselves and navigate through some unknown waters. With the current political situation in Russia, we're coming up against something new every day!"[1]

Christine Shea prepared this case under the supervision of Professor Henry Lane solely to provide material for class discussion. The authors do not intend to illustrate either effective or ineffective handling of a managerial situation. The authors may have disguised certain names and other identifying information to protect confidentiality.

Most of the materials used to remodel the building had to be imported: electrical equipment from Spain; mechanical equipment from England, Belgium, the United States and Canada; kitchen equipment from Germany; and bathroom fixtures from Italy and Canada. Construction workers also were brought in from other countries such as Poland and Hungary. The hotel was completed only four months behind schedule – "a miracle by Russian standards."[2]

The hotel carried a four-star rating and had achieved an average occupancy rate over 80 per cent. Since it opened it had developed a reputation "as an oasis of Western efficiency in the midst of the Russian economic and political hurricane."[3] It boasted a restaurant offering full buffet breakfast, lunch, and dinner (including lobster dinners three days per week); a steak and seafood restaurant; a business office for guests complete with fax machine with satellite hookup, photocopiers and word processing services; a meeting room capable of accommodating 80 to 150 persons for meetings, press conferences or cocktail parties; a fitness room including sauna, rowing equipment, and universal gym; and a caviar and vodka bar, in addition to 417 well-appointed rooms. Room rates were 15 to 20 per cent lower than the competition (which generally had been awarded five-star ratings) and ranged from $205 per night for single occupancy including breakfast[4] to $395 per night for a triple-occupancy suite. Restaurant prices were comparable to prices at similar hotel restaurants in the West.

Achieving this standard of quality and service had not come easily. It took a talented and dedicated group of professionals to make it a reality. However, even though it already had established a positive reputation, working to maintain it continued to challenge the Aerostar's management team. Andrew Ivanyi, a Canadian, was the General Manager of the Moscow Aerostar Hotel. According to him, the development of managerial talent was one of the biggest obstacles facing the Aerostar.

The plan had been to drastically reduce the number of expatriates running the hotel within two years of opening, but after one year the number of expatriates had grown instead. Because of the low productivity resulting from having to operate with a staff which was completely inexperienced in the hotel business, the Aerostar required twice as many employees to operate than comparable hotels in the West. It had 550 Russian employees.[5] There were 20 expatriates managing the hotel when it opened and this number was to be reduced to 10 by January 1993. Instead, by June 1992, there were 22 expatriate managers. The number of employees and expatriate managers had a major impact on the budget.

RECRUITING

Recruitment of staff began with an advertisement in a Russian newspaper which had home-delivery only and was geared to young people. If the position required fluency in English for the front desk, for example, then the advertisement would be in English, which acted as an initial screen. The response to recruitment advertisements had been good and the calibre of the applicants was high. Many of the people who applied were university graduates (e.g., medical doctors, psychology professors, engineers, nurses, and lawyers). Recently, however, a decline in good applicants was prompting hotel management to consider a "hire-a-friend" campaign in which employees would be encouraged to bring in people they knew to apply for work.

Initially, the Aerostar used an Aeroflot application form which had many questions that would have been considered illegal to ask in Canada. For example, applicants had to provide their age, number of children, whether their parents belonged to the communist party, where they had worked before, what diseases they had had, and whether they had ever done military service. Many of these questions had since been removed, but some remained. They still inquired about how many children applicants had and how old they were. Children were almost sacred in Russia and it was important to know whether there was anyone at home to look after them. According to Laurie Sagle, Director of Training and Personnel, it was not uncommon for a mother to take three weeks off from work to stay at home with a child who had a simple cold. Medical certificates of absence from doctors were readily available and, just for a cold, people might take a week or two off for rest. Laurie commented that it seemed like people always wanted to rest:

> Last weekend was a four-day holiday with beautiful weather and we were outside in the parks and walking. Many of the local people stayed in their homes and rested. We had to emphasize during orientation that their hard currency bonus was based on performance and attendance. If they're not here, they're not performing.

Unlike other joint venture hotels in Moscow, the Aerostar did not rely on Russian managers to interview and select the Russian staff. Hotel policy specified that at least one, and usually two, expatriates be involved. The initial interview consisted of a 10-minute screening to see if the applicant appeared to be hireable for some job in the hotel. Interviewers checked for mastery of the English language and general grooming. If the applicant passed, a second interview was arranged on the spot since many of the applicants had no telephone. The second interview was longer and usually was conducted by a manager of a functional area. Laurie suggested that this had presented somewhat of a problem since the applicants were often very reluctant to specify which area interested them:

> Generally, they have no idea. They don't know the hotel business. They're used to being told everything. They've never been given a selection or choice before. However, you do get some who really want the front desk, for example, and those who do won't change their minds. If you don't have a job for them there, they don't want to work for you.

It was very difficult to know the right questions to ask during interviews. For example, one of the questions commonly asked in the West – "Why do you want to work here?" – did not elicit the desired response in Moscow. The usual answers included: "I want to meet foreigners" and "I want to improve my English." Questions such as: "Why should we hire you?" and "What good qualities or attributes do you have for our business?" would be followed by stunned silence since Russian people considered bragging to be rude. Asking the applicant why he or she should be hired over someone else did not help since the typical answer was that the other person would probably be a better choice. According to Laurie, the most telling replies were to the question: "What did you do in your last job?" The typical answer might be: "Oh, we had meetings, we discussed issues, we solved problems." When asked to specify what they actually did or accomplished, few people were able to answer.

Finally, I had someone who was honest and said, "Oh, I did nothing, I just sat at my desk all day." Most would say they discussed problems and when asked if anything was fixed, they would say they discussed it. It's a country that philosophizes. You could get almost no one to tell you what they did.

Another difficulty arose concerning reference checks. People were stunned when they received the call asking about an applicant, and nobody would give a bad reference even though a Russian made the call. The hotel gave up on all reference checks except those to other joint ventures in the city:

We call the personnel and training managers at the other hotels and ask them about the person: "Fired for theft" might be the reply. Let's face it, who is going to quit a job where they get paid three times the norm plus a currency bonus? Very few people quit. Most that leave are let go.

ORIENTATION

There was a five-day orientation program during which new employees were taught the concept of profit, the organization chart and what the departments do (e.g., housekeeping, stewarding, business centre), so that they would know if guests asked. They toured the hotel and had lunch in the cafeteria as a group. The rules and regulations were explained and they were given information on grooming, uniforms, receiving a salary paid in cash, and discipline issues.

Laurie explained that the hotel's expectations were made very clear during the first week of training:

I tell them that class starts at nine in the morning and if they're not here on time, the door is going to be shut. That's because time is a cultural difference we've observed; people are late all the time. Maybe it's because previously there was not a lot of work to be done, so it's not a big deal. We are trying to instill values we think are important. Punctuality is a big issue. How can we open a restaurant if the staff is not there to serve the guests? We're providing service so we have to be punctual.

The second day of training consisted of the first "Customer Service" component. Recruits were taught the hotel's two customer service standards: *Smile and Help*. Role playing and evaluations were used to show them how to smile and how to help guests by answering questions or by meeting requests. They were taught five steps for meeting a guest's requests and how they were supposed to follow up. Then they were taught general fire safety rules.

The third day included listening and communicating skills in the morning. Employees were taught how to clarify and confirm requests, and why they must listen, for example. In the afternoon, those who were going to use telephones were taught "telephone courtesy" – what to say, how to put someone on hold, how to take a proper message, what to ask and why it was important to repeat the message to make sure it had been correctly understood. Telephone courtesy courses were not offered at the hotel in Toronto where Laurie previously was the training manager, but in Russia they were needed. As Laurie said:

They have never done any of this so it's more important that they get it right at the beginning before they have a lot of guest contact.

On the fourth day, there was a review, more role playing and a written test. So far, everyone had passed, but anyone who did not achieve at least 75 per cent on the test was reviewed. In the afternoon, women received cosmetic training. They would bring their own make-up since there was no point in teaching them about make-up to which they would not have access. Laurie said:

> I tell them about some of the surveys comparing women photographed with no make-up and wearing a business suit, another with too much make-up and a business suit, and a third with the appropriate amount of make-up and a business suit. The photos were sent to a sample of CEOs who were asked to rate the women's credibility. The woman who rated highest on productivity and efficiency was the one with an appropriate amount of make-up on because she looked like she was ready for business. They find that fascinating. We tell them that if they are at the front desk with absolutely no make-up on, they may be 25 or 30 years old but look like a little girl, and it is really hard to handle a guest's problems or complaints.

In Toronto, the make-up classes were optional. But in Russia, there was nowhere to learn this information and, unfortunately, the Russian women who wore make-up wore too much. The class was held for all female employees.

Apparently, Russians were accustomed to learning by memorizing. Questions dealing with memorized facts were no problem (e.g., What does the bar offer? What's the cost of a taxi?). The problem came with questions about what to do in certain situations. Role playing had been used but had met with some difficulty since Russians were not very comfortable with that training method. Laurie said that she wanted them to practise during the training sessions because it was a safe place to do it. They were afraid of looking stupid, but she stressed that it was better to make mistakes in training than with a guest. Everyone was required to participate. At first, Laurie found it frustrating that the employees never asked questions. She encouraged them to ask questions by explaining that when they said nothing, she assumed that they were not interested and did want to be there.

On the fifth day, the employees went to the departments in which they would be working and were shown how to do the job by the supervisor.

Laurie's degree in Hotel and Restaurant Management, her diploma in Teaching and Training Adults and her experience as Training Manager at a major hotel in Toronto had not prepared her for some of the adjustments she discovered that she had to make in Moscow. In most cases, she had to completely rewrite the examples she used for her courses in Moscow. For example, one of her exercises for teaching trainees the meaning of good service consisted of asking trainees to think of a time when they were in a hotel or restaurant and received good service. In North America, people had difficulty coming up with examples of good service – precisely the point of the exercise. So, the trainer asked them to think of examples of bad service, which then led to the reverse of these examples constituting good service or hospitality. In Moscow, nobody understood the word "service." Laurie had to change the exercise to: "Raise your hand if you've ever had a guest at your house." Since Russian people loved to entertain friends and took great pride in their hospitality, everyone would raise their hand. Laurie then asked them to list some of the things they did in preparation for the evening. The answers started coming, at first tentatively and then with more assurance: "I go out and buy some Vodka!" (Everyone would laugh.) "I wear my good clothes!" "I clean the house!" "And this, what you do when you entertain guests at home", explained Laurie, "is exactly what service and hospitality are all about." And then they understood.

Laurie found that she had to incorporate social skills training into her program also in order to eliminate unacceptable behavior. For example, she described a reception catered by the hotel at which the staff were drinking while they were working:

> On New Year's Eve, we held a dinner-dance for foreigners. They bought tickets, just like at home. The staff had to work and we provided taxis home when they were done. Well, they ended up drinking all night in the back rooms. They would take someone's glass away and drink what was left in it. They felt that this was New Year's Eve and this was a party. They did not seem to realize that they were here to work. Drinking is a big thing that's culturally accepted.

SUPERVISORY TRAINING PROGRAM

Department heads selected employees from their departments for promotion to supervisor on the basis of their work performance in the department. Once an employee was promoted, he/she would be scheduled to attend the next scheduled Supervisory Orientation Supplement (SOS) and the next Supervisor Training Program.

The SOS was a general orientation during which new supervisors were given information to help them in their new jobs. They were shown how to read profit and loss statements. Their responsibilities as supervisors were explained and they were given guidance about how to discipline employees.

The Supervisor Training Program consisted of eight sessions. Two sessions were held each month and were typically attended by groups of 22 supervisors.

Session 1: Introduction

The purpose of this two-hour session was to clarify managements' expectations with respect to the supervisors' behavior during the training program. The students were expected to arrive on time for classes, do their homework, participate in class and practise what they learned in class in their daily work. The students were asked what they expected to learn from this training program and why they thought they were there. This question puzzled most of them and some of them admitted that they were there simply because their supervisors had told them to be there. Exhibit 1 lists the educational background of a typical group of supervisors.

During the introductory session, they also completed the Hersey and Blanchard situational leadership questionnaire for use in analysing and evaluating their management style during Session 2.

EXHIBIT 1   Educational Background of a Typical Group of Hotel Supervisors

Current Position at the Aerostar	Educational Background
Staff English teacher	Degree from the Pedagogical Institute of English and French
Maintenance Engineering supervisor	Degree from the Moscow Civil Engineering Institute
Security supervisor	Degree from the Highest School of the Militia and a five-year Law degree
Laundry supervisor	High School Diploma
Interpreter/Training Department administrator	Degree from the Pedagogical Institute of English and German
Switchboard supervisor	Degree from the Pedagogical Institute of English and German
Restaurant supervisor	Degree from the Pedagogical Institute of Musical Education
Bellman supervisor	Degree from the Institute of Geological Prospecting
Engineering supervisor	Degree from the Power Engineering Institute
Housekeeping supervisor	High School Diploma

Session 2: Situational leadership

During this four-hour session, the results of the situational leadership questionnaire were discussed with each participant. Laurie stressed that there was not "one best leadership style." Instead, situational leadership theory advocated the tailoring of one's leadership style to the requirements of each specific issue being addressed and each employee involved. Supervisors were taught to evaluate the competence and commitment level displayed by each of their employees on each task which they were required to perform. Supervisors were taught to rate their employees at Level 1, "Disillusioned Learner," on tasks for which they possessed low competence and low commitment; Level 2 "Enthusiastic Beginner," on tasks for which the employee possessed low competence but high commitment; Level 3, "Reluctant Contributor," on tasks for which they possessed high competence but varying levels of commitment; and Level 4, "Peak Performer," on tasks for which they possessed both high competence and high commitment. Four different leadership styles were to be used depending on the level attained by the employee on a particular task.

Session 3: Listening and communications

This was a general session on why listening is important and how to improve one's listening skills. Laurie used various activities to get these points across. One of these, for example, was the "Broken Telephone Line Game" in which each participant whispered a predetermined message to the next person and the message became garbled by the time it reached the end of the line. Another activity was to have two people sit back-to-back and have one of them instruct the other to draw something based on verbal instructions only. What was drawn was always quite different from what the communicator had intended.

Session 4: How to train employees

During this session, supervisors were taught the five steps to follow for teaching job skills: tell them, show them, let them try it, observe their performance, and praise any progress. Students practised these steps by writing job tasks which involved breaking simple jobs down into steps because, as Laurie pointed out, "you can't teach a job, you can only teach the steps."

Session 5: Giving feedback

This session was to teach the supervisors the importance of giving specific, timely and sincere feedback for the improved performance of their employees. Most of the session was spent practising and observing the effect of negative feedback, no feedback, positive but not sincere feedback, and positive and sincere feedback on performance. The exercises almost always pointed to positive and sincere feedback being associated with the highest quality work.

Session 6: Coaching theory

This was the most difficult session because it dealt with confronting employee problems. Supervisors were taught to overcome their tendency to define and solve the problem on the spot (e.g., You are late. Buy a new alarm clock and get here on time). Instead, they were to attempt to get the employee to admit that a problem existed and then, to try to engage the employee in coming up with his or her own alternative solutions to encourage more commitment to the selected solution. Supervisors were taught five steps to follow: (1) get the employee to admit that there was a problem; (2) discuss alternative behaviours; (3) decide which alternative behavior was to be selected; (4) follow up and verify that the employee was changing his/her behavior; and (5) provide recognition of any behavioral change, no matter how small.

Session 7: Coaching practice

This session began with a 10-minute review of coaching theory. The rest of the session was devoted to practising what had been learned by playing the roles of supervisors and employees dealing with realistic hotel situations.

Session 8: Exam

Two weeks after session 7, the student supervisors were given a three-hour written test and a behavioral exam on what they had learned. Finally, the supervisors were rewarded for completing the course with a certificate presented by the hotel manager at a special luncheon in the hotel restaurant.

Laurie reminisced about some of the difficulties encountered with the first group of graduates:

When the first group completed the supervisory training course, the manager and I decided that because this was our first group and because they had done so well and were so eager, we would take them to the Aerostar restaurant for lunch. Normally, they are not allowed in there. It was a fiasco! I had an inkling that it might be so and had talked about what was appropriate to have for lunch and what they could order: one appetizer, one main course and one dessert, which would be a big lunch for us. A lot of them ordered two appetizers, like a soup and shrimp. One man ordered two main courses, some of them ordered two desserts – they would have something like chocolate mousse *and* ice cream – even after we had talked to them about it! It was almost like they thought they would never get in here again, so they had to try it all. It was a "live for now, we've got it so we had better try it" behaviour. I took responsibility for it and my boss and I laughed about it later. But in the next session, I really went into detail about appropriate behavior at a business luncheon. No one had ever told them the importance of how one was perceived by a business associate!

EXPECTATIONS AND COMPENSATION

Management made it very clear that a job at the Aerostar meant more opportunities, better pay and better treatment than the employees would receive from a Russian organization, but it also meant more work than they had to do before in order to meet the higher expectations. The staff agreed that they worked harder than they ever had. Yet, Laurie felt that less was demanded of them than Western staff. There seemed to be no real work ethic. It was not uncommon for people to complain because they felt the work was physically too difficult and shift work interfered with time spent with their family. Added Laurie, "They're not even talking about children; they're talking about their parents!"

Russian employees in May 1992 were paid a ruble salary the equivalent of $25 per month which was about twice the state average. The typical salaries offered by state organizations for teachers and medical doctors would not exceed 1,500 rubles per month (or about $13). It was illegal to pay in hard currency, but each employee received a performance-based bonus in the form of a gift certificate for a hard currency shop. This bonus could be worth as much as $140 per month for some employees, or almost 10 times what the average state employee earned! In spite of this, the employees continued to demand more. When asked their opinions about the rewards they received for their work, the typical responses included:

The salary is not good, but management treats me well.

The hotel is not doing enough for me, I expected more.

In general, I am pleased with what I am earning, but, with respect to the West, it's nothing.

The bonus is not very useful, things are quite expensive at the hard currency shops.

The lack of expression of gratitude or appreciation by the Russian employees for their high rate of pay and for other things provided by hotel management was a source of frustration to management. On the first anniversary of the opening of the hotel, a banner was displayed thanking the employees for their hard work and each one was personally handed a food basket containing a bottle of French red wine, a kilo of French cheese and a pineapple. Only one employee said thank you. In fact, one employee said that he did not like red wine and asked for a bottle of white. At Christmas, the manager had food packages delivered to directors of agencies and organizations which dealt with the Aerostar. He received no thanks. Apparently, even a recent 30-per cent raise was greeted with: "Is that all? Give me more." According to Laurie:

> There are a limited number of joint ventures and good jobs here but they still don't look at what they have compared to others. The glass is always seen as half-empty, not half-full. After a while you get frustrated with that. Then you get someone who comes up and thanks you for something and you feel really good about it all again and you think, "OK, it's going to take a while but someone has appreciated something."

DEVELOPING MANAGERS

At other joint venture hotels, Russian "deputies" were paired with managers trained in the West in the hope that they would develop the skills required to do the job eventually on their own. But even that did not result in them meeting North American standards. Sending Russians to North America for training was not seen as a viable alternative because of the cost involved and the small amount of learning and skill transfer associated with the process.

Andrew Ivanyi was frustrated with the hotel staff's lack of interest in the hotel business as a career:

> The problem is that they don't see these jobs as their lifetime careers. They all want intellectual work, and manual labour unless it is taking place in a factory is not appealing to them.

In the West, promotion to line management was viewed as prestigious, but in Russia it just seemed to mean extra work. According to Laurie, there seemed to be little pride associated with a promotion to supervisor. In fact, Russian supervisors often questioned why everyone could not attend the special functions established for supervisors only or receive the rewards such as gift certificates and benefits set aside for supervisors. Lately, the benefits offered to supervisors had been changed to make them substantially more attractive than those offered to other employees. For example, the hard currency bonuses were now twice as much for supervisors as for other employees. In addition, supervisors were given their birthdays off with pay; were able to borrow video films from the hotel library for free; were reimbursed up to half of the tuition fees paid for courses directly relevant to their jobs in the hotel; were allowed to use their currency bonuses for travel outside Russia; and wore special name tags as a sign of their position. Still, with all of these attempts at trying to make supervisory positions more attractive to the hotel employees, Laurie was not sure that they were having the desired effect.

"How do we make them appreciate what they have here and want to be supervisors?" wondered Laurie.

Notes

1   Moscow Aerostar Hotel press release, March 1992.
2   *The Globe and Mail,* February 9, 1993, p. B25.
3   ibid.
4   ibid.
5   ibid.

Ellen Moore (A): Living and Working in Korea

Chantell Nicholls and Gail Ellement

Ellen Moore, a Systems Consulting Group (SCG) consultant, was increasingly concerned as she heard Andrew's voice grow louder through the paper-thin walls of the office next to her. Andrew Kilpatrick, the senior consultant on a joint North American and Korean consulting project for a government agency in Seoul, South Korea, was meeting with Mr Song, the senior Korean project director, to discuss several issues including the abilities of the Korean consultants. After four months on this Korean project, Ellen's evaluation of the assigned consultants suggested that they did not have the experience, background, or knowledge to complete the project within the allocated time. Additional resources would be required:

> I remember thinking, "I can't believe they are shouting at each other." I was trying to understand how their meeting had reached such a state. Andrew raised his voice and I could hear him saying, "I don't think you understand at all." Then, he shouted, "Ellen is not the problem!

WSI IN KOREA

In 1990, Joint Venture Inc. (JVI) was formed as a joint venture between a Korean company, Korean Conglomerate Inc. (KCI), and a North American company, Western

IVEY Chantell Nicholls and Gail Ellement prepared this case under the supervision of Professor Harry Lane solely to provide material for class discussion. The authors do not intend to illustrate either effective or ineffective handling of a managerial situation. The authors may have disguised certain names and other identifying information to protect confidentiality.

EXHIBIT 1   Organizational Structure – Functional View

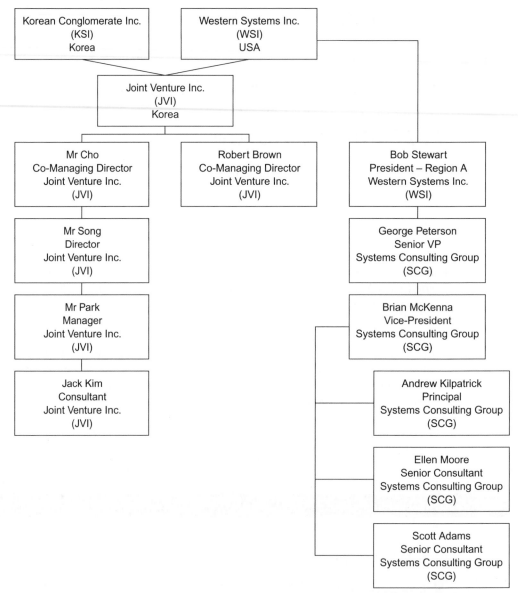

Systems Inc. (WSI) (Exhibit 1). WSI, a significant information technology company with offices world wide employing over 50,000 employees, included the Systems Consulting Group (SCG). KCI, one of the largest Korean "chaebols" (industrial groups), consisted of over 40 companies, with sales in excess of US$3.5 billion. The joint venture, in its eighth year, was managed by two Regional Directors – Mr Cho, a Korean from KCI, and Robert Brown, an American from WSI.

The team working on Ellen's project was led by Mr Park and consisted of approximately 40 Korean consultants further divided into teams working on different areas of the project. The Systems Implementation (SI) team consisted of five Korean consultants, one translator, and three North American SCG consultants: Andrew Kilpatrick, Ellen Moore, and Scott Adams, (see Exhibit 2).

EXHIBIT 2   Organizational Structure – SI Project Team

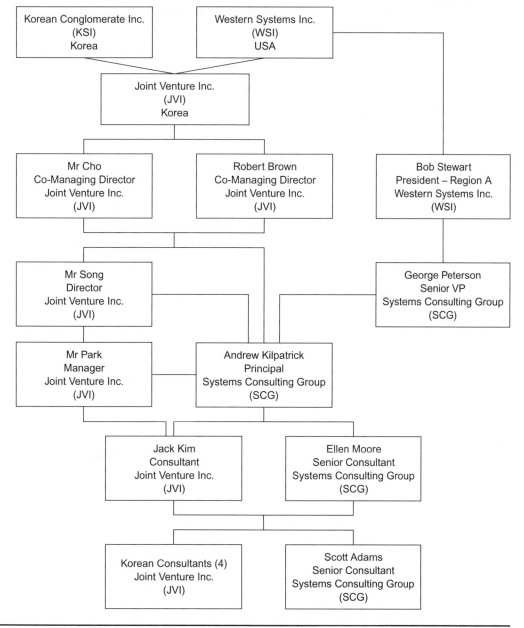

This consulting project was estimated to be one of the largest undertaken in South Korea to date. Implementation of the recommended systems into over 100 local offices was expected to take seven to ten years. The SCG consultants would be involved for the first seven months, to assist the Korean consultants with the system design and in creating recommendations for system implementation, an area in which the Korean consultants admitted they had limited expertise.

Andrew Kilpatrick became involved because of his experience with a similar systems implementation project in North America. Andrew had been a management consultant for nearly 13 years. He had a broad and successful background in organizational development, information technology, and productivity improvement, and he was an early and successful practitioner of business process reengineering. Although Andrew had little international consulting experience, he was adept at change management and was viewed by both peers and clients as a flexible and effective consultant.

The degree of SCG's involvement had not been anticipated. Initially, Andrew had been asked by SCG's parent company, WSI, to assist JVI with the proposal development. Andrew and his SCG managers viewed his assistance as a favor to WSI since SCG did not have plans to develop business in Korea. Andrew's work on the proposal in North America led to a request for his involvement in Korea to gather additional information for the proposal:

> When I arrived in Korea, I requested interviews with members of the prospective client's management team to obtain more information about their business environment. The Korean team at JVI was very reluctant to set up these meetings. However, I generally meet with client management prior to preparing a proposal. I also knew it would be difficult to obtain a good understanding of their business environment from a translated document. The material provided to me had been translated into English and was difficult to understand. The Korean and English languages are so different that conveying abstract concepts is very difficult.
>
> I convinced the Koreans at JVI that these meetings would help demonstrate our expertise. The meetings did not turn out exactly as planned. We met with the same management team at three different locations where we asked the same set of questions three times and got the same answers three times. We did not obtain the information normally provided at these fact-gathering meetings. However, they were tremendously impressed by our line of questioning because it reflected a deep interest and understanding of their business. They also were very impressed with my background. As a result, we were successful in convincing the government agency that we had a deep understanding of the nature and complexity of the agency's work and strong capabilities in systems development and implementation – key cornerstones of their project. The client wanted us to handle the project and wanted me to lead it.

JVI had not expected to get the contract, because its competitor for this work was a long-time supplier to the client. As a result, winning the government contract had important competitive and strategic implications for JVI. Essentially, JVI had dislodged an incumbent supplier to the client, one who had lobbied very heavily for this prominent contract. By winning the bid, JVI became the largest system implementer in Korea and received tremendous coverage in the public press.

The project was to begin in June 1995. However, the Korean project team convened in early May in order to prepare the team members. Although JVI requested Andrew to join the project on a full-time basis, he already had significant commitments to projects in

North America. There was a great deal of discussion back and forth between WSI in North America, and JVI and the client in Korea. Eventually it was agreed that Andrew would manage the SI work on a part-time basis from North America, and he would send a qualified project management representative on a full-time basis. That person was Ellen Moore.

At that time, Andrew received immediate feedback from the American consultants with WSI in Korea that it would be impossible to send a woman to work in Korea. Andrew insisted that the Korean consultants be asked if they would accept a woman in the position. They responded that a woman would be acceptable if she were qualified. Andrew also requested that the client be consulted on this issue. He was again told that a woman would be acceptable if she were qualified. Andrew knew that Ellen had the skills required to manage the project:

> I chose Ellen because I was very impressed with her capability, creativity, and project management skills, and I knew she had worked successfully in Bahrain, a culture where one would have to be attuned to very different cultural rules from those prevalent in North America. Ellen lacked experience with government agencies, but I felt that I could provide the required expertise in this area.

ELLEN MOORE

After graduating as the top female student from her high school, Ellen worked in the banking industry, achieving the position of corporate accounts officer responsible for over 20 major accounts and earning a Fellowship in the Institute of Bankers. Ellen went on to work for a former corporate client in banking and insurance, where she became the first female and youngest person to manage their financial reporting department. During this time, Ellen took university courses towards a Bachelor Degree at night. In 1983, she decided to stop working for two years, and completed her degree on a full-time basis. She graduated with a major in accounting and minors in marketing and management and decided to continue her studies for an MBA.

Two years later, armed with an MBA from a leading business school, Ellen Moore joined her husband in Manama, Bahrain, where she accepted a position as an expatriate manager for a large American financial institution.[1] Starting as a Special Projects Coordinator, within one year Ellen was promoted to Manager of Business Planning and Development, a challenging position that she was able to design herself. In this role, she managed the Quality Assurance department, coordinated a product launch, developed a senior management information system, and participated actively in all senior management decisions. Ellen's position required her to interact daily with managers and staff from a wide range of cultures, including Arab nationals.

In March 1995, Ellen joined WSI working for SCG. After the highly successful completion of two projects with SCG in North America, Ellen was approached for the Korea project:

> I had never worked in Korea or East Asia before. My only experience in Asia had been a one-week trip to Hong Kong for job interviews. I had limited knowledge of Korea and received no formal training from my company. I was provided a 20-page document on Korea. However, the information was quite basic and not entirely accurate.

After arriving in Korea, Ellen immediately began to familiarize herself with the language and proper business etiquette. She found that English was rarely spoken other than in some hotels and restaurants which catered to Western clientele. As a result, Ellen took advantage of every opportunity to teach herself the language basics:

> When Andrew and I were in the car on the way back to our hotel in the evening, we would be stuck in traffic for hours. I would use the time to learn how to read the Korean store signs. I had copied the Hangul symbols which form the Korean language onto a small piece of paper, and I kept this with me at all times. So, while sitting back in the car, exhausted at the end of each day, I would go over the symbols and read the signs.

The third SCG consultant on the project, Scott Adams, arrived as planned three months after Ellen's start date. Upon graduation, Scott had begun his consulting career working on several international engagements (including Mexico, Puerto Rico, and Venezuela), and he enjoyed the challenges of working with different cultures. He felt that with international consulting projects the technical aspects of consulting came easy. What he really enjoyed was the challenge of communicating in a different language and determining how to modify Western management techniques to fit into the local business culture. Scott first met Ellen at a systems consulting seminar, unaware at the time that their paths would cross again. A few months later, he was asked to consider the Korea assignment. Scott had never travelled or worked in Asia, but he believed that the assignment would present a challenging opportunity which would advance his career.

Scott was scheduled to start work on the project in August 1995. Prior to arriving in Seoul, Scott prepared himself by frequently discussing the work being conducted with Ellen. Ellen also provided him with information on the culture and business etiquette aspects of the work:

> It was very fortunate for me that Ellen had arrived first in Korea. Ellen tried to learn as much as she could about the Korean language, the culture, mannerisms, and the business etiquette. She was able to interpret many of the subtleties and to prepare me for both business and social situations, right down to how to exchange a business card appropriately with a Korean, how to read behavior, and what to wear.

ABOUT KOREA[2]

Korea is a 600-mile-long peninsula stretching southward into the waters of the western Pacific, away from Manchuria and Siberia to the north on the Asian mainland. Facing eastward across the Sea of Japan, known to Koreans as the East Sea, Korea lies 120 miles from Japan. The Republic of Korea, or South Korea, consists of approximately 38,000 square miles, comparable in size to Virginia or Portugal. According to the 1990 census, the South Korean population is about 43 million, with almost 10 million residing in the capital city, Seoul.

Korea has an ancient heritage spanning 5,000 years. The most recent great historical era, the Yi Dynasty or Choson Dynasty, enlisted tremendous changes in which progress in science, technology, and the arts were achieved. Although Confucianism had been influential for centuries in Korea, it was during this time that Confucian principles permeated the culture as a code of morals and as a guide for ethical behavior. Confucian thought was designated as the state religion in 1392 and came to underpin education, civil administration, and daily conduct. During this time, Korean rulers began to avoid foreign contact and the monarchy was referred to as the "Hermit Kingdom" by outsiders. Lasting over 500 years and including 27 rulers, the Yi Dynasty came to a close at the end of the 19th century. Today, in Korea's modem era, the nation is quickly modernizing and traditional Confucian values mix with Western lifestyle habits and business methods.

Although many Korean people, particularly in Seoul, have become quite Westernized, they often follow traditional customs. Confucianism dictates strict rules of social behavior and etiquette. The basic values of the Confucian culture are: (1) complete loyalty to a hierarchical structure of authority, whether based in the family, the company, or the nation; (2) duty to parents, expressed through loyalty, love, and gratitude; and (3) strict rules of conduct, involving complete obedience and respectful behavior within superiors–subordinate relationships, such as parents–children, old–young, male–female, and teacher–student. These values affect both social and work environments substantially.

MANAGING IN KOREA

Business etiquette in Korea was extremely important. Ellen found that everyday activities, such as exchanging business cards or replenishing a colleague's drink at dinner, involved formal rituals. For example, Ellen learned it was important to provide and to receive business cards in an appropriate manner, which included carefully examining a business card when received and commenting on it. If one just accepted the card without reading it, this behavior would be considered very rude. In addition, Ellen also found it important to know how to address a Korean by name. If a Korean's name was Y. H. Kim, non-Koreans would generally address him as either Y. H. or as Mr Kim. Koreans would likely call him by his full name or by his title and name, such as Manager Kim. A limited number of Koreans, generally those who had lived overseas, took on Western names, such as Jack Kim.

WORK TEAMS

Teams were an integral part of the work environment in Korea. Ellen noted that the Korean consultants organized some special team-building activities to bring together the Korean and North American team members:

> On one occasion, the Korean consulting team invited the Western consultants to a baseball game on a Saturday afternoon followed by a trip to the Olympic Park for a tour after the game, and dinner at a Korean restaurant that evening. An event of this nature is unusual and was very special. On another occasion, the Korean consultants gave up a day off with their families and spent it with the Western consultants. We toured a Korean palace and the palace grounds, and we were then invited to Park's home for dinner. It was very unusual that we, as Western folks, were invited to his home, and it was a very gracious event.

Ellen also found team-building activities took place on a regular basis, and that these events were normally conducted outside of the work environment. For example, lunch with the team was an important daily team event which everyone was expected to attend:

> You just couldn't work at your desk every day for lunch. It was important for everyone to attend lunch together in order to share in this social activity, as one of the means for team bonding.

Additionally, the male team members would go out together for food, drink, and song after work. Scott found these drinking activities to be an important part of his interaction with both the team and the client:

> Unless you had a medical reason, you would be expected to drink with the team members, sometimes to excess. A popular drink, soju, which is similar to vodka, would be poured into a small glass. Our glasses were never empty, as someone would always ensure that an empty glass was quickly filled. For example, if my glass was empty, I learned that I should pass it to the person on my right and fill it for him as a gesture of friendship. He would quickly drink the contents of the glass, pass the glass back to me, and fill it for me to quickly drink. You simply had to do it. I recall one night when I really did not want to drink as I had a headache. We were sitting at dinner, and Mr Song handed me his glass and filled it. I said to him "I really can't drink tonight. I have a terrible headache." He looked at me and said "Mr Scott, I have Aspirin in my briefcase." I had about three or four small drinks that night.

Ellen found she was included in many of the team-building dinners, and soon after she arrived in Seoul, she was invited to a team dinner, which included client team members. Ellen was informed that although women were not normally invited to these social events, an exception was made since she was a senior team member.

> During the dinner, there were many toasts and drinking challenges. During one such challenge, the senior client representative prepared a drink that consisted of one highball glass filled with beer and one shot glass filled to the top with whiskey. He dropped the whiskey glass into the beer glass and passed the drink to the man on his left. This team member quickly drank the cocktail in one swoop, and held the glass over his head, clicking the glasses to show both were empty. Everyone cheered and applauded. This man then mixed the same drink, and passed the glass to the man on his left, who also drank the cocktail in one swallow. It was clear this challenge was going around the table and would eventually get to me.
>
> I don't generally drink beer and never drink whiskey. But it was clear, even without my translator present to assist my understanding, that this activity was an integral part of the team building for the project. As the man on my right mixed the drink for me, he whispered that he would help me. He poured the beer to the halfway point in the highball glass, filled the shot glass to the top with whiskey, and dropped the shot glass in the beer. Unfortunately, I could see that the beer didn't cover the top of the shot glass, which would likely move too quickly if not covered. I announced "One moment, please, we are having technical difficulties." And to the amazement of all in attendance, I asked the man on my right to pour more beer in the glass. When I drank the concoction in one swallow, everyone cheered, and the senior client representative stood up and shouted, "You are now Korean. You are now Korean."

The norms for team management were also considerably different from the North American style of management. Ellen was quite surprised to find that the concept of saving face did not mean avoiding negative feedback or sharing failures:

> It is important in Korea to ensure that team members do not lose face. However, when lead-ing a team, it appeared just as important for a manager to demonstrate leadership. If a team member provided work that did not meet the stated requirements, a leader was expected to express disappointment in the individual's efforts in front of all team members. A strong leader was considered to be someone who engaged in this type of public demonstration when required.
>
> In North America, a team leader often compliments and rewards team members for work done well. In Korea, leaders expressed disappointment in substandard work, or said noth-ing for work completed in a satisfactory manner. A leader was considered weak if he or she continuously provided compliments for work completed as required.

Hierarchy

The Koreans' respect for position and status was another element of the Korean culture that both Ellen and Scott found to have a significant influence over how the project was structured and how people behaved. The emphasis placed on hierarchy had an important impact upon the relationship between consultant and client that was quite different from their experience in North America. As a result, the North Americans' understanding of the role of a consultant differed vastly from their Korean counterparts.

Specifically, the North American consultants were familiar with "managing client expectations." This activity involved informing the client of the best means to achieve their goals and included frequent communication with the client. Generally, the client's customer was also interviewed in order to understand how the client's system could better integrate with their customer's requirements. Ellen recalled, however, that the procedures were necessarily different in Korea:

> The client team members did not permit our team members to go to their offices unan-nounced. We had to book appointments ahead of time to obtain permission to see them. In part, this situation was a result of the formalities we needed to observe due to their rank in society, but I believe it was also because they wanted to be prepared for the topics we wanted to discuss.

The Korean consultants refused to interview the customers, because they did not want to disturb them. Furthermore, the client team members frequently came into the project office and asked the Korean consultants to work on activities not scheduled for that week or which were beyond the project scope. The Korean consultants accepted the work without question. Ellen and Scott found themselves powerless to stop this activity.

Shortly after arriving, Scott had a very confrontational meeting with one of the Korean consultants concerning this issue:

> I had been in Korea for about a week, and I was still suffering from jet lag. I was alone with one of the Korean consultants, and we were talking about how organizational processes should

be flow-charted. He was saying the client understands the process in a particular manner, so we should show it in that way. I responded that, from a technical standpoint, it was not correct. I explained that as a consultant, we couldn't simply do what the client requests if it is incorrect. We must provide value by showing why a different method may be taken by educating the client of the options and the reasons for selecting a specific method. There are times when you have to tell the client something different than he believes. That's what we're paid for. He said, "No, no, you don't understand. They're paying our fee." At that point I raised my voice: "You don't know what you are talking about. I have much more experience than you." Afterwards, I realized that it was wrong to shout at him. I pulled him aside and apologized. He said, "Well, I know you were tired." I replied that it was no excuse, and I should not have shouted. After that, we managed to get along just fine.

The behavior of subordinates and superiors also reflected the Korean's respect for status and position. Scott observed that it was very unusual for a subordinate to leave the office for the day unless his superior had already left:

I remember one day, a Saturday, when one of the young Korean consultants who had been ill for some time, was still at his desk. I made a comment: "Why don't you go home, Mr Choi?" Although he was not working for me, I knew his work on the other team was done. He said, "I can't go home because several other team members have taken the day off. I have to stay." I repeated my observation that his work was done. He replied: If I do not stay, I will be fired. My boss is still here, I have to stay." He would stay and work until his boss left, until late in the evening if necessary.

Furthermore, Scott found that the Korean consultants tended not to ask questions. Even when Scott asked the Korean consultants if they understood his instructions or explanation, they generally responded affirmatively which made it difficult to confirm their understanding. He was advised that responding in a positive manner demonstrated respect for teachers or superiors. Asking a question would be viewed as inferring that the teacher or superior had not done a good job of explaining the material. As a result, achieving a coaching role was difficult for the North American consultants even though passing on their knowledge of SI to the Korean consultants was considered an important part of their function on this project.

WOMEN IN KOREA

Historically, Confucian values have dictated a strict code of behavior between men and women and husband and wife in Korea. Traditionally, there has been a clear delineation in the respective responsibilities of men and women. The male preserve can be defined as that which is public, whereas women are expected to cater to the private, personal world of the home. These values have lingered into the 1990s, with Korean public life very much dominated by men.

Nevertheless, compared to the Yi dynasty era, the position of women in society has changed considerably. There is now virtual equality in access to education for men and women, and a few women have embarked on political careers. As in many other areas of the world, the business world has until recently been accessible only to men. However, this is changing as Korean women are beginning to seek equality in the workplace. Young

Korean men and women now often participate together in social activities such as evenings out and hikes, something that was extremely rare even 10 years ago.

Dual income families are becoming more common in South Korea, particularly in Seoul, although women generally hold lower-paid, more menial positions. Furthermore, working women often retain their traditional household responsibilities, while men are expected to join their male colleagues for late night drinking and eating events which exclude women. When guests visit a Korean home, the men traditionally sit and eat together separately from the women, who are expected to eat together while preparing the food.

Although the younger generation are breaking from such traditions, Scott felt that the gender differences were quite apparent in the work place. He commented:

> The business population was primarily male. Generally, the only women we saw were young women who were clerks, wearing uniforms. I suspected that these women were in the work-force for only a few years, until they were married and left to have a family. We did have a few professional Korean women working with us. However, because we are a professional services firm, I believe it may have been more progressive than the typical Korean company.

THE SYSTEMS IMPLEMENTATION TEAM

Upon her arrival in Korea, Ellen dove into her work confident that the Korean consultants she would be working with had the skills necessary to complete the job in the time frame allocated. The project work was divided up among several work groups, each having distinct deliverables and due dates. The deliverables for the SI team were required as a major input to the other work groups on the project (see Exhibit 3). As a result, delays with deliverables would impact the effectiveness of the entire project:

EXHIBIT 3 Project Time Frame

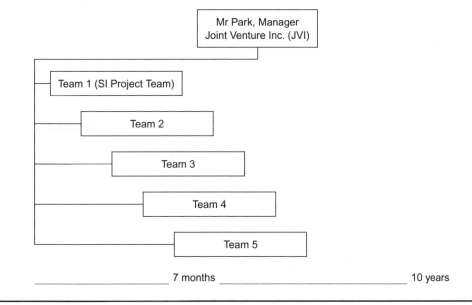

JVI told us they had assigned experienced management consultants to work on the project. Given their stated skill level, Andrew's resource plan had him making periodic visits to Korea; I would be on the project on a full time basis starting in May, and Scott would join the team about three to four months after the project start. We were informed that five Korean consultants were assigned. We believed that we had the resources needed to complete the project by December.

JACK KIM

J. T. Kim, whose Western name was Jack, was the lead Korean consultant reporting to Mr Park. Jack had recently achieved a PhD in computer systems from a reputable American university and he spoke English fluently. When Andrew initially discussed the organizational structure of the SI team with Mr Park and Jack, it was agreed that Jack and Ellen would be co-managers of the SI project.

Three weeks after her arrival, Jack informed Ellen, much to her surprise, that he had never worked on a systems implementation project. Additionally, Ellen soon learned that Jack had never worked on a consulting project:

> Apparently, Jack had been made the lead consultant of SI upon completing his PhD in the United States. I believe Jack was told he was going to be the sole project manager for SI on a daily basis. However, I was informed I was going to be the co-project manager with Jack. It was confusing, particularly for Jack, when I took on coaching and leading the team. We had a lot of controversy – not in the form of fights or heated discussions, but we had definite issues during the first few weeks because we were clearly stepping upon each other's territory.

Given Jack's position as the lead Korean consultant, it was quite difficult for Ellen to redirect team members' activities. The Korean team members always followed Jack's instructions. Scott recalled:

> There were frequent meetings with the team to discuss the work to be completed. Often, following these meetings the Korean consultants would meet alone with Jack, and it appeared that he would instruct them to carry out different work. On one occasion, when both Andrew and Ellen were travelling away from the office, Andrew prepared specific instructions for the team to follow outlined in a memo.
>
> Andrew sent the memo to me so I could hand the memo to Jack directly, thereby ensuring he did receive these instructions. Upon his return, Andrew found the team had not followed his instructions. We were provided with the following line of reasoning: you told us to do A, B and C, but you did not mention D. And, we did D. They had followed Jack's instructions. We had a very difficult time convincing them to carry out work as we requested, even though we had been brought onto the project to provide our expertise.

In July, a trip was planned for the Korean client team and some of the Korean consulting team to visit other project sites in North America. The trip would permit the Koreans to find out more about the capabilities of WSI and to discuss issues with other clients involved with similar projects. Jack was sent on the trip, leaving Ellen in charge of the SI project team in Korea. While Jack was away on the North American trip, Ellen had her first opportunity to work with and to lead the Korean consultants on a daily basis. She was very pleased that she was able to coach them directly, without interference, and advise them on how to best carry out the required work. Ellen felt that everyone worked together in a very positive manner, in complete alignment. When Jack returned, he saw that Ellen was leading the team and that they were accepting Ellen's directions. Ellen recalled the tensions that arose as a result:

> On the first day he returned, Jack instructed someone to do some work for him, and the person responded, "I cannot because I am doing something for Ellen." Jack did not say anything, but he looked very angry. He could not understand why anyone on the team would refuse his orders.

THE MARKETING RESEARCH PROJECT

A few days after Jack returned from the North American trip, the project team realized they did not have sufficient information about their client's customer. Jack decided a market research study should be conducted to determine the market requirements. However, this type of study, which is generally a large undertaking on a project, was not within the scope of the contracted work. Ellen found out about the proposed market research project at a meeting held on a Saturday, which involved everyone from the entire project – about 40 people. The only person not at the meeting was Mr Park. Jack was presenting the current work plans for SI, and he continued to describe a market research study:

> I thought to myself, "What market research study is he talking about?" I asked him to put aside his presentation of the proposed study until he and I had an opportunity to discuss the plans. I did not want to interrupt his presentation or disagree with him publicly, but I felt I had no choice.

DINNER WITH JACK

Two hours following the presentation, Ellen's translator, Susan Lim, informed her that there was a dinner planned for that evening and Jack wanted everyone on the SI team to attend. Ellen was surprised that Jack would want her present at the dinner. However, Susan insisted that Jack specifically said Ellen must be there. They went to a small Korean restaurant, where everyone talked about a variety of subjects in English and Korean, with Susan translating for Ellen as needed. After about one hour, Jack began a speech to the team, speaking solely in Korean. Ellen thought it was unusual for him to speak Korean when she was present, as everyone at the dinner also spoke English:

> Through the limited translations I received, I understood he was humbling himself to the team, saying, "I am very disappointed in my performance. I have clearly not been the project leader needed for this team." The team members were responding "No, no, don't say that." While Jack was talking to the team, he was consuming large quantities of beer. The pitchers were coming and coming. He was quite clearly becoming intoxicated. All at once,

Susan stopped translating. I asked her what was wrong. She whispered that she would tell me later. Five minutes went by and I turned to her and spoke emphatically, "Susan, what is going on? I want to know now." She realized I was getting angry. She told me, "Jack asked me to stop translating. Please don't say anything, I will lose my job."

I waited a couple of minutes before speaking, then I interrupted Jack's speech. I said, "Susan is having difficulty hearing you and isn't able to translate for me. I guess it is too noisy in this restaurant. Would it be possible for you to speak in English?" Jack did not say anything for about 30 seconds and then he started speaking in English. His first words were, "Ellen, I would like to apologize. I didn't realize you couldn't understand what I was saying."

Another thirty minutes of his speech and drinking continued. The Korean team members appeared to be consoling Jack, by saying: "Jack, we do respect you and the work you have done for our team. You have done your best." While they were talking, Jack leaned back, and appeared to pass out. Ellen turned to Susan and asked if they should help him to a taxi. Susan insisted it would not be appropriate. During the next hour, Jack appeared to be passed out or sleeping. Finally, one of the team members left to go home. Ellen asked Susan, "Is it important for me to stay, or is it important for me to go?" She said Ellen should go.

When Ellen returned to her hotel, it was approximately 11 p.m. on Saturday night. She felt the situation had reached a point where it was necessary to request assistance from senior management in North America. Andrew was on a wilderness camping vacation in the United States with his family, and could not be reached. Ellen decided to call the North American project sponsor, the Senior Vice President, George Peterson:

I called George that Saturday night at his house and said: "We have a problem. They're trying to change the scope of the project. We don't have the available time, and we don't have the resources. It is impossible to do a market research study in conjunction with all the contracted work to be completed with the same limited resources. The proposed plan is to use our project team to handle this additional work. Our team is already falling behind the schedule, but due to their inexperience they don't realize it yet." George said he would find Andrew and send him to Korea to further assess the situation.

THE MEETING WITH THE DIRECTOR

When Andrew arrived in August, he conducted a very quick assessment of the situation. The project was a month behind schedule. It appeared to Andrew that the SI team had made limited progress since his previous visit:

It was clear to me that the Korean team members weren't taking direction from Ellen. Ellen was a seasoned consultant and knew what to do. However, Jack was giving direction to the team which was leading them down different paths. Jack was requesting that the team work on tasks which were not required for the project deliverables, and he was not appropriately managing the client's expectations.

Andrew held several discussions with Mr Park concerning these issues. Mr Park insisted the problem was Ellen. He argued that Ellen was not effective, she did not assign work properly, and she did not give credible instructions to the team. However, Andrew believed the Korean consultants' lack of experience was the main problem.

> Initially, we were told the Korean team consisted of experienced consultants, although they had not completed any SI projects. I felt we could work around it. I had previously taught consultants to do SI. We were also told that one of the Korean consultants had taught SI. This consultant was actually the most junior person on the team. She had researched SI by reading some texts and had given a presentation on her understanding of SI to a group of consultants.

Meanwhile, Andrew solicited advice from the WSI Co-Managing Director, Robert Brown, who had over ten years experience working in Korea. Robert suggested that Andrew approach Mr Park's superior, Mr Song, directly. He further directed Andrew to present his case to the Joint Venture committee if an agreement was not reached with Mr Song. Andrew had discussed the issues with George Peterson and Robert Brown, and they agreed that there was no reason for Ellen to leave the project:

> However, Robert's message to me was that I had been too compliant with the Koreans. It was very important for the project to be completed on time, and that I would be the one held accountable for any delays. Addressing issues before the Joint Venture committee was the accepted dispute resolution process at JVI when an internal conflict could not be resolved. However, in most cases, the last thing a manager wants is to be defending his position before the Joint Venture committee. Mr Song was in line to move into senior executive management. Taking the problem to the Joint Venture committee would be a way to force the issue with him.

Andrew attempted to come to a resolution with Mr Park once again, but he refused to compromise. Andrew then tried to contact Mr Song and was told he was out of the office. Coincidentally, Mr Song visited the project site to see Mr Park just as Ellen and Andrew were completing a meeting. Ellen recalls Mr Song's arrival:

> Mr Song walked into the project office expecting to find Mr Park. However, Mr Park was out visiting another project that morning. Mr Song looked around the project office for a senior manager, and he saw Andrew. Mr Song approached Andrew and asked if Mr Park was in the office. Andrew responded that he was not. Mr Song proceeded to comment that he understood there were some concerns about the project work, and suggested that perhaps, sometime, they could talk about it. Andrew replied that they needed to talk about it immediately.

Andrew met with Mr Song in Mr Park's office, a makeshift set of thin walls that enclosed a small office area in one corner of the large open project office. Ellen was working in an area just outside the office when she heard Andrew's voice rise. She heard him shout, "Well, I don't think you're listening to what I am saying." Ellen was surprised to hear Andrew shouting. She knew Andrew was very sensitive to what should and should not be done in the Korean environment:

> Andrew's behavior seemed so confrontational. I believed this behavior was unacceptable in Korea. For a while, I heard a lot of murmuring, after which I heard Andrew speak adamantly,

"No, I'm very serious. It doesn't matter what has been agreed and what has not been agreed because most of our agreements were based on inaccurate information. We can start from scratch." Mr Song insisted that I was the problem.

ACKNOWLEDGMENT

The Richard Ivey School of Business gratefully acknowledges the generous support of The Richard and Jean Ivey Fund in the development of this case as part of the Richard and Jean Ivey Fund Asian Case Series.

Notes

1   For an account of Ellen's experience in Bahrain, see Ellen Moore (A): Living and Working in Bahrain, 9A90C019, and Ellen Moore (B), 9A90C020; Ivey Publishing, Ivey Management Services, c/o Richard Ivey School of Business, University of Western Ontario, London, Ontario, Canada, N6A 3K7.
2   Some of the information in the "About Korea" and "Women in Korea" sections was obtained from *Fodor's Korea*, 1993, Fodor's Travel Publications, Inc.: New York; and Chris Taylor, *Seoul – City Guide*, 1993, Lonely Planet Publications: Colorcraft Ltd, Hong Kong.

The Leo Burnett Company Ltd: Virtual Team Management

Joerg Dietz, Fernando Olivera, and Elizabeth O'Neil

On July 2, 2001, Janet Carmichael, global account director for The Leo Burnett Company Ltd (LB), United Kingdom, sat in her office wondering how to structure her global advertising team. The team was responsible for the introduction of a skin care product of one of LB's most important clients, Ontann Beauty Care (OBC). The product had launched in the Canadian and Taiwanese test markets earlier that year. Taiwanese sales and awareness levels for the product had been high but were low for the Canadian market. Typically, at this stage in the launch process, Carmichael would decentralize the communications management in each market, but the poor performance in the Canadian market left her with a difficult decision: should she maintain centralized control over the Canadian side of her team? In three days, she would leave for meetings at LB's Toronto, Canada, office, where the team would expect her decision.

THE LEO BURNETT COMPANY LTD BACKGROUND

LB, which was founded in Chicago in 1935, was one of North America's premier advertising agencies. It had created numerous well-recognized North American brand icons, including The Marlboro Man, Kellogg's Tony the Tiger, and the Pillsbury Dough Boy.

IVEY Elizabeth O'Neil prepared this case under the supervision of Professor Joerg Dietz and Fernando Olivera solely to provide material for class discussion. The authors do not intend to illustrate either effective or ineffective handling of a managerial situation. The authors may have disguised certain names and other identifying information to protect confidentiality.

By 1999, LB had expanded around the globe to include 93 offices in 83 markets. The company employed approximately 9,000 people, and worldwide revenues were approximately US$9 billion. In 2000, LB merged with two other global agencies to form b/com³ (the actual company name), one of the largest advertising holding companies in the world, but each LB office retained the Leo Burnett company name.

LB services and products

As a full-service agency, LB offered the complete range of marketing and communications services and products (see Exhibits 1 and 2). The company's marketing philosophy was to build "brand belief." The idea driving this philosophy was that true loyalty went beyond

EXHIBIT 1   LB Agency Services

Traditional core agency services included:

Account Management
Account management worked in close partnership with planning, creative, media, production and the client to craft tightly focused advertising strategies, based on a deep understanding of the client's products, goals and competition, as well as insights into contemporary consumer behavior.

Creative Services
In most LB offices, creative was the largest department. Creatives focused its visual art and copywriting talents on turning strategic insights into advertising ideas. This department was a key part of each client's brand team and often interacted with both clients and clients' customers.

Planning
Planners conducted research to gain insights about the consumer and the marketplace. They also provided valuable input to the strategic and creative agency processes in the form of the implications raised by that research, specifically combining that learning with information about a given product, the social context in which it fit and the psychology of the people who used it.

Media
Starcom was the media division for LB's parent holding company. Its role was to identify the most influential and efficient media vehicles to deliver brand communications to the appropriate audience.

Production
Production staff brought creative ideas to life with the highest quality execution in television, cinema, radio, print, outdoor, direct, point of sale, interactive or any other medium.

In addition to these core services, most offices also offered expertise in more specialized services, including:

- B2B Technology Marketing
- Direct and Database Marketing
- Health-care Marketing
- Interactive Marketing
- Multicultural Marketing
- Public Relations
- Sales Promotion and Event Marketing

EXHIBIT 2 LB Agency Products

Traditional Advertising Products

Television broadcast advertising – Usually 30-second (:30s) or 60-second (:60s) TV ads that ran during local or national television programming. This also included sponsoring specific programs, which usually consisted of a five-second announcement before or after the show, i.e., "This program is brought to you by . . ." accompanied by the visual of the sponsoring company's logo.

Radio broadcast advertising – Usually 15-, 20-, or 30-second (:15s, :20s, :30s) radio ads that were placed throughout local or national radio programming. Radio ads could include sponsoring specific programs, which usually consisted of a five-second announcement before or after the show, i.e. "This program brought to you by . . ."

Print advertising – Included black and white and color print ads in local, national or trade newspapers, journals and magazines. Magazine ads could be single-page ads or double-page spreads (two pages facing each other.)

Non-Traditional or "Below the Line" Advertising Products

Direct marketing – Normally a series of mail-out items (letters, post cards, product samples, etc.) sent to a specifically targeted population(s) called "cells", e.g., companies might send promotional mail-outs to current customers, former customers who have not shopped with the company for a period or time, and new prospective customers – each of these groups would be considered a cell.

Digital or interactive marketing – Any marketing efforts that were delivered to the consumer online or by wireless networks (e.g., hand-held wireless devices). This could include Web site design and production, banner advertising and promotions on other Web sites, e-mail marketing, and internal corporate marketing tools such as customer relationship marketing or database building tools.

Collateral – Any piece of print material that was not strictly advertising, for instance brochures, annual reports, posters, flyers, and in-store materials.

Promotions – Any marketing effort that included a time-limited offer or incentive to either purchase a product or offer personal data. Promotions could involve advertising, direct marketing, interactive marketing, product packaging, and/or outdoor marketing.

mere buying behavior. LB defined "believers" as customers who demonstrated both a believing attitude and loyal purchase behavior. The company strove to convert buyers into believers by building lasting customer affinity for the brand.

One of the most important measures of an agency's success was the quality of the creative product that was developed to connect brands to their end consumers. Each local office strove to produce outstanding creative advertising to break through the clutter of marketing messages that the general public was subjected to daily and truly reach the consumer in a memorable way. Award shows were held nationally and internationally to recognize this effort, one of the most prestigious being the annual festival in Cannes, France. With each award, individual employees (usually the art director and copy writer who had worked together to develop the ad) were recognized, as was the local agency office where they worked. These creative accolades were instrumental in helping an office win new client business. Even within the global LB network, awards were given to the local offices that produced the most outstanding creative work.

LB internal team structures

A multidisciplinary team serviced each brand. Each team had representatives from all core areas of the agency as well as members from the specialized services as appropriate for the brand. In most cases, team members had two sets of reporting lines.

First and formally, they directly reported to the supervisor of their home department (for example, account management). It was this formal supervisor who was responsible for conducting performance evaluations and assigning and managing an employee's workload.

Informally, the team members reported to a project team leader, the senior account services person, who usually was an account director or a vice-president of client services director. It was this team leader's responsibility to manage the project in question, ensure that the client was satisfied with project progress, and build and manage the overall relationship between the client and the agency. Employees on the project team would be responsible to this person for meeting project deadlines and managing their individual client relationships. This team leader would often provide input to a team member's performance evaluation, along with other agency colleagues (see Exhibit 3).

At any given time, an agency employee typically worked on two or three different brand teams, virtually all of them face-to-face teams servicing local clients.

LB typical office environment

Most LB employees were young (in their 20s and 30s) and worked about 60 hours per week. Client needs and project deadlines dictated work priorities, and the volume of work often required late nights at the office. Agency office environments were often open-concept and social. Employees spent many hours each day up and about, discussing projects with colleagues and responding to client requests. The pace was fast and the general spirit was one of camaraderie; it was common for LB employees to socialize together after a late night at the office.

LB Toronto

LB's Toronto office was founded in 1952 to service the Canadian arms of the Chicago-based clients. It was LB's first expansion beyond Chicago. In 2001, it employed a staff of approximately 200 people and billings were approximately $200 million.

LB United Kingdom

LB acquired its London, United Kingdom, office in the mid-1970s as part of an expansion into Europe. By 2001, the office had grown to over 350 employees and billings were approximately $400 million. London was also the regional LB headquarters for all European, Middle Eastern and African offices.

EXHIBIT 3 LB Agency Formal and Informal Reporting Lines

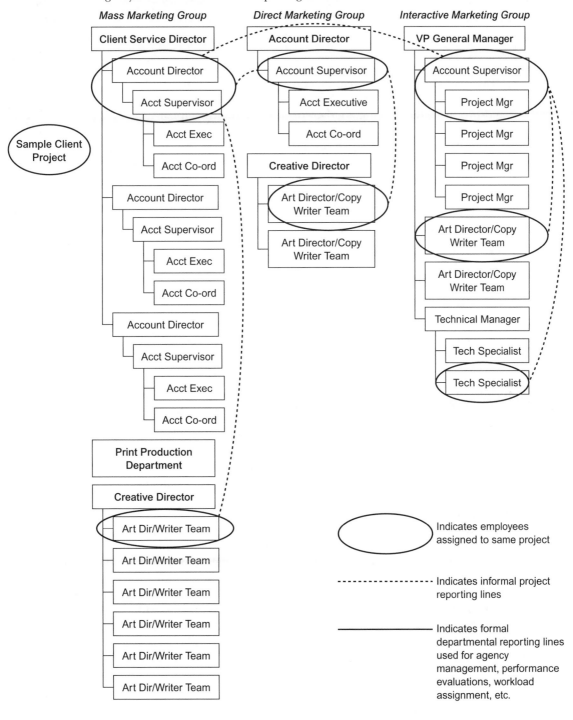

LB'S RELATIONSHIP WITH ONTANN BEAUTY CARE

Ontann Beauty Care (OBC)

OBC was a leading global manufacturer of health and beauty care products. In the late 1990s, OBC made a strategic decision to centralize the global marketing of its brands and products, designating a global team to define the global strategy for a given brand and develop the core communication materials as templates for local markets to follow. Local offices were given the responsibility for adapting the global materials and developing local "below the line" (BTL) materials which would synergize with the global vision and creative templates. Below the line materials included direct marketing, in-store materials, digital marketing, public relations and promotions (that is, everything except strict advertising). In practice, on established brands with well-defined communication templates and strong local knowledge, some local markets (at least key regional markets) were awarded more opportunity to develop their own communication material. The global team, however, retained veto power to ensure all communications were building a consistent personality and look for the brand.

Each OBC global office had as many teams as it had brands. An OBC brand team usually consisted of the global category director, the brand manager and an assistant brand manager, plus a representative from each of the various departments: marketing technology, consumer, trade/distribution, PR, sales, product development, and production.

Relationship between LB and OBC

OBC, which, like LB, was founded in Chicago, was one of LB's original clients. In 2001, as one of the top three LB clients worldwide, OBC did business with most LB offices. OBC, however, awarded its business to advertising agencies brand-by-brand. As a result, other advertising agencies also had business with OBC. Competition among advertising agencies for OBC business was strong, in particular when they had to work together on joint brand promotions.

OBC had been a client of LB's Toronto office since 1958 and of LB's London office since its acquisition in the mid-1970s. Both the Toronto and London offices initially developed advertising and communications materials for various OBC facial care brands and eventually also worked on OBC's skin care brands.

To better service OBC, LB also centralized its decision making for this client's brands and appointed expanded and strengthened global teams with the power to make global decisions. For its other clients, LB's global teams were significantly smaller, tending to consist simply of one very senior LB manager who shared learning from across the globe with a given client's senior management.

A NEW OBC BRAND: FOREVER YOUNG

In the fall of 1998, the OBC London office announced a new skin care line called "Forever Young". Product formulas were based on a newly patented process that addressed the needs of aging skin. For OBC, this brand presented an opportunity to address a new market segment: the rapidly growing population of people over the age of 50. The product line was more extensive than other OBC skin care brands. It also represented the company's first foray into premium priced skin care products. Product cost, on average, was double that of most other OBC brands, falling between drug store products and designer products. OBC intended Forever Young to be its next big global launch and awarded the Forever Young advertising and brand communications business to LB.

GLOBAL ADVERTISING AND COMMUNICATIONS TEAM FOR FOREVER YOUNG

Team formation

For LB, a successful launch of this new product would significantly increase revenues and the likelihood of acquiring additional global OBC brands. An unsuccessful launch would risk the relationship with OBC that LB had built over so many years. LB management in Chicago decided that LB London would be the global team headquarters. This decision reflected the experience that the London office had in leading global business teams and the proximity to the OBC global team for Forever Young. It was also likely that the United Kingdom would be the test market for the new product.

In LB's London office, Janet Carmichael was assigned as brand team leader for the Forever Young product line effective January 1, 1999. Carmichael was the global account director for OBC. The 41-year-old Carmichael, a Canadian, had begun her career at LB Toronto as an account executive in 1985, after completing an MBA degree at the University of Toronto. In 1987, Carmichael moved to Europe, where she continued her career with LB. She became an account supervisor in Italy, an account director in Belgium, and finally a regional and global account director in Germany before taking on a global account director role on OBC brands in the United Kingdom in 1996. She was very familiar with OBC's business and had built excellent relationships with the OBC skin care client group.

LB's initial Forever Young brand team had six members who all were employees of the London office: Carmichael as the team leader, an account director, an account executive (she formally supervised these two employees), the agency's creative director, and two "creatives" (an art director and a copy writer). Carmichael outlined a project timetable (see Exhibit 4). The LB team worked with the OBC team on consumer research, market exploration, brand creative concepts (creative), packaging samples and global copy testing throughout North America and Europe. Carmichael viewed marketing a new product to a new consumer segment in a crowded category as challenging; however, after several months of testing, LB's Forever Young brand team developed a unique creative concept that was well received by OBC.

EXHIBIT 4   Brand Development Chronology

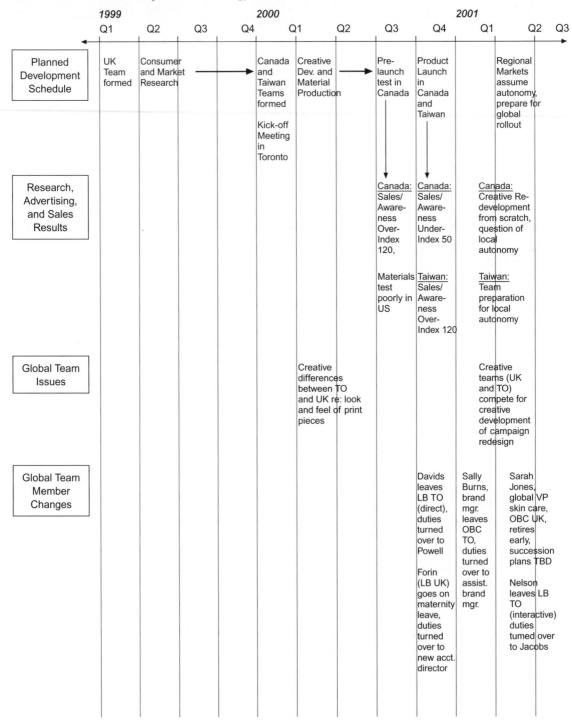

	1999 Q1	Q2	Q3	Q4	2000 Q1	Q2	Q3	Q4	2001 Q1	Q2	Q3
Planned Development Schedule	UK Team formed	Consumer and Market Research			Canada and Taiwan Teams formed Kick-off Meeting in Toronto	Creative Dev. and Material Production	Pre-launch test in Canada	Product Launch in Canada and Taiwan		Regional Markets assume autonomy, prepare for global rollout	
Research, Advertising, and Sales Results							Canada: Sales/ Aware-ness Over-Index 120, Materials test poorly in US	Canada: Sales/ Aware-ness Under-Index 50 Taiwan: Sales/ Aware-ness Over-Index 120	Canada: Creative Re-development from scratch, question of local autonomy Taiwan: Team preparation for local autonomy	
Global Team Issues						Creative differences between TO and UK re: look and feel of print pieces			Creative teams (UK and TO) compete for creative development of campaign redesign	
Global Team Member Changes								Davids leaves LB TO (direct), duties turned over to Powell Forin (LB UK) goes on maternity leave, duties turned over to new acct. director	Sally Burns, brand mgr. leaves OBC TO, duties turned over to assist. brand mgr.	Sarah Jones, global VP skin care, OBC UK, retires early, succession plans TBD Nelson leaves LB TO (interactive) duties turned over to Jacobs	

In the fall of 1999, OBC decided that the United Kingdom would be the lead market for another skin care product. Because North America was a priority for the Forever Young brand and Canada was "clean" (that is, OBC was not testing other products in Canada at that time), Canada became the new primary test market for Forever Young. In addition, Canadians' personal skin care habits and the distribution process for skin care products were more reflective of overall Western practices (i.e., the Western world) than were those in other potential test markets. Taiwan became the secondary test market for Asian consumers. These choices were consistent with OBC's interest in global brand validation.

In keeping with OBC's team structures, LB maintained the global brand team in London and, in January of 2000, formed satellite teams in Toronto, Canada, and Taipei, Taiwan, to manage material execution in their local markets. It was up to the LB Toronto and Taipei offices to determine their members in the Forever Young satellite teams. In Taipei, Cathy Lee, an account director who was particularly interested in the assignment, took the lead on local agency activities. In Toronto, Geoff Davids, an account supervisor from the direct marketing group, was assigned to lead the Toronto team. The global brand team and the two satellite teams now formed the LB side of the global advertising and communications team for Forever Young (see Exhibit 5).

Kick-off meeting

In February 2000, a face-to-face kick-off meeting took place in Toronto with the intent to bring all senior members of LB's and OBC's London, Toronto, and Taipei teams onto the same page regarding the new brand and the status of the launch process. One or two senior representatives from OBC London, Toronto, and Taipei participated in the meeting. From LB, the complete London team participated, along with Geoff Davids and a senior agency representative from the Toronto office, and Cathy Lee and a senior agency representative from the Taipei office. Carmichael and her UK team members shared their initial brand creative concepts, which had already garnered admiration throughout the LB network, and their knowledge about the product and target audience.

It was decided that Davids and Lee would serve as the main links to LB's London-based global brand team. Specifically, Davids and Lee reported to Annabel Forin, Carmichael's account director in the United Kingdom. Forin then reported to Carmichael and OBC's London team. Besides Forin, Carmichael's primary contacts would be Annabelle Manning, the global creative director at LB United Kingdom and Sarah Jones, OBC's global vice-president of skin care in London. All work produced by LB's satellite teams would require approval from LB's London team.

The creative assignments

The creative assignments for the Canadian and Taiwanese teams were slightly different from each other. Normally, the global team would produce a creative template for a brand (meaning the design of the advertising and communications materials), which would then be passed to the satellite teams to be adapted for the local market.

EXHIBIT 5 The Global Forever Young Team

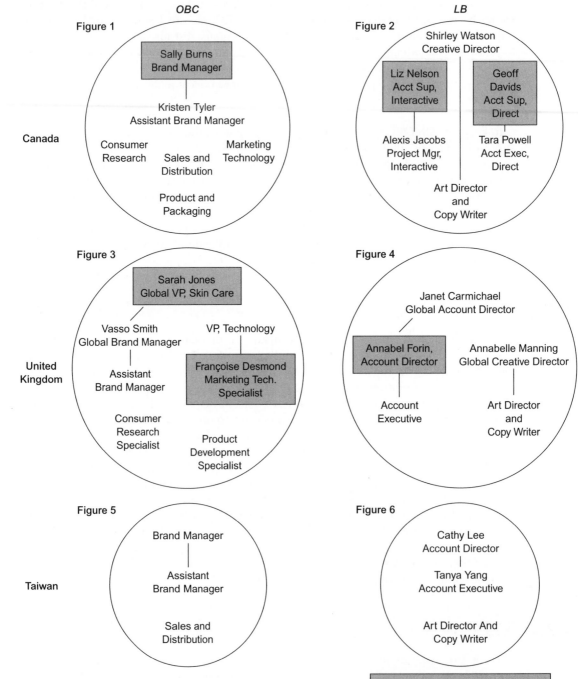

OBC

LB

Figure 1

Canada

Sally Burns
Brand Manager

Kristen Tyler
Assistant Brand Manager

Consumer
Research

Marketing
Technology

Sales and
Distribution

Product and
Packaging

Figure 2

Shirley Watson
Creative Director

Liz Nelson
Acct Sup,
Interactive

Geoff
Davids
Acct Sup,
Direct

Alexis Jacobs
Project Mgr,
Interactive

Tara Powell
Acct Exec,
Direct

Art Director
and
Copy Writer

Figure 3

United
Kingdom

Sarah Jones
Global VP, Skin Care

Vasso Smith
Global Brand Manager

VP, Technology

Françoise Desmond
Marketing Tech.
Specialist

Assistant
Brand Manager

Consumer
Research
Specialist

Product
Development
Specialist

Figure 4

Janet Carmichael
Global Account Director

Annabel Forin,
Account Director

Annabelle Manning
Global Creative Director

Account
Executive

Art Director
and
Copy Writer

Figure 5

Taiwan

Brand Manager

Assistant
Brand Manager

Sales and
Distribution

Figure 6

Cathy Lee
Account Director

Tanya Yang
Account Executive

Art Director And
Copy Writer

——— Main Reporting Lines

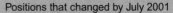

Positions that changed by July 2001

In the Taiwanese market, this would be the case. The Taiwanese LB team would be responsible for adapting the advertising materials, which would include refilming the television ad to star an Asian actress, as well as retaking photos for the print ads, again, to demonstrate product benefits on Asian skin. The brand message (meaning the text in print ads and the vocal message in television ads) would be adapted to appeal to the Taiwanese audience.

In Toronto, however, the assignment broke from this traditional format. The LB team in London would produce English television and print advertising, which would be used in the Canadian market. The LB team in Toronto would design and produce the direct marketing and Web site materials because the London office did not have strong in-house capabilities in these areas. While the Toronto office would have control of the design of these communication pieces, the UK office would require that certain elements be incorporated into the design (for example, specific photos and colors), in order for the pieces to be visually consistent with the print advertising.

EVENTS LEADING UP TO THE LAUNCH

LB's Taipei office

After returning to Taipei from the kick-off meeting, Lee formed her local team, which consisted of an account executive (Tanya Yang) and a creative team (one art director and one copy writer). In co-operation with OBC's Taipei team, Lee and her team focused first on re-creating the television ad. The ad followed the original creative idea developed in the United Kingdom but used a popular Taiwanese actress in the lead. The character differentiation was necessary to demonstrate the product's benefit to Asian skin because the original ad featured a blonde, Caucasian actress as the lead. The team moved on to adapt the brand's print advertising and direct marketing pieces and developed a public relations campaign to meet local market needs. These communication elements were visually and strategically consistent with the television ad as they incorporated photos of the same Taiwanese actress.

Throughout this process, the Taipei team regularly updated LB's and OBC's London teams about its progress. Although all work required UK approval, the Taiwanese team worked with a significant amount of autonomy because of the cultural differences present in its market. Carmichael and Manning occasionally travelled to Taiwan to meet with the team and approve its creative work, which they generally received well. In addition, the Taipei team communicated with the London offices through videoconference calls and e-mail. The LB Taipei and Toronto teams had contact with each other only during the global team videoconference meetings, held every two months.

LB's Toronto office

After the kick-off meeting, Davids, with the approval of LB's Toronto management, assigned representatives from the direct marketing group and the interactive marketing group to the brand team. This included account management (Tara Powell, account executive for direct; and Liz Nelson, account supervisor; and Alexis Jacobs, project manager for interactive) and creative staff (Shirley Watson, creative director; and one copy writer from each of the direct and interactive groups).

In co-operation with OBC's Toronto team, the LB Toronto team was responsible for developing a full communication plan for its local market. Along with running the television and print ads developed in the United Kingdom, the team would focus on producing the brand's below the line materials (i.e., direct mail, Web site). These communication elements served as the education pieces that supplemented the TV ad. Davids conducted an internal team debrief, outlining the information he had received at the kick-off meeting. From this, the team developed a communications plan that, in Carmichael's opinion, was "on-brief" (i.e., consistent with the original brand strategic direction) and included some very innovative thinking.

Next, the team began determining a creative look and feel for the direct mail pieces. The look and feel could be different from the television creative but had to be consistent across all of the paper-based (print ads, direct mail pieces and in-store materials) and online communication elements. The creatives in LB's Toronto team developed the direct marketing materials, and simultaneously the creatives in LB's UK team developed the print advertising. The two sides' creative work evolved in different directions, but each side hoped that the other would adapt their look and feel. Eventually, however, LB's Toronto team told its London counterpart to "figure it out," and they would follow London's lead. Communication between the two sides mostly flowed through Davids and Forin to Carmichael. Carmichael, however, had received a copy of the following e-mail from Watson to Davids:

> Geoff, as you know, it's always a challenge to work with someone else's art direction. I don't think the model that London chose is right for this market, and the photography we have to work with doesn't have as contemporary a feel as I would like.
>
> This would be easier if I could connect directly with Annabelle [Manning] but she's on the road so much of the time it's hard to catch her. We weren't asked for our opinion initially and, given the timing constraints at this point, we don't have much choice but to use what they've sent us, but could you please convey to Annabel [Forin] that in the future, if possible, we'd like to have the chance to input on the photography before it's taken? It will help us develop good direct mail creative.
>
> For now, though, I think we'll be able to do something with what they've sent us. Thanks.

There had been other challenges for LB's Toronto team. Davids described an incident that had occurred when his direct marketing team tried to present its creative concept to the team in the United Kingdom during a videoconference meeting:

> Our direct mail concept was a three-panel, folded piece. We sent two flat files to the United Kingdom via e-mail, which were to be cut out, pasted back-to-back [to form the front and back of the piece] and then folded into thirds. It took us *so* long to explain how to do that – somehow we just weren't getting through! Our colleagues in London cut and folded and pasted in different places, and what should have been a simple preliminary procedure took up 45 minutes of our one-hour videoconference meeting! By the time we actually got around to discussing the layout of the piece, everyone on the call was frustrated. That's never a

good frame of mind to be in when reviewing and critiquing a new layout. It's too bad our clients were on that call as well.

A greater challenge came in September 2000, when the team was behind schedule in the development of the Web site after encountering difficulties with OBC's technology standards. The budgeting for the Web site development came out of the global budget, not the local budget. This meant that the members of LB's Toronto team who were responsible for the Web site development ("interactive marketing") received directions from OBC's London team. The budgeting for direct marketing, however, came out of the local budget, and the members of LB's Toronto team, who were responsible for the development of the direct marketing materials, dealt with OBC's Toronto team. The instructions from these two OBC teams were often inconsistent. Compounding matters, the two OBC client teams repeatedly requested changes of the Web and direct marketing materials, which made these materials even more different from each other and forced the LB Toronto team into extremely tight timeframes.

Carmichael learned about this sort of difficulty mostly through the direct supervisors of the team members. She frequently received calls from LB Toronto's Interactive Marketing Group and Direct Marketing Group senior managers. Carmichael repeatedly had to explain the basic project components to these senior managers and wished that the members of LB's Toronto team would just follow the team communications protocol and forward their concerns to Davids, who would then take up matters as necessary with the UK team.

CANADIAN PRE-LAUNCH TEST

Despite these challenges, LB's Toronto team produced the materials in time for the Canadian pre-launch test in October of 2000. The pre-launch test was a launch of the complete communications program (TV ad, newspaper inserts, distribution of trial packs, direct mail, and a Web site launch) in a market whose media could be completely isolated. A small town in the interior of British Columbia, Canada's most westerly province, met these conditions. In terms of product trial and product sales as a percentage of market share, the test indexed 120 against its objectives, which had a base index of 100. Subsequently, OBC and LB decided to move immediately into research to test the advertising in the US market. The global OBC and LB teams worked with their Canadian counterparts to conduct this research, the results of which were very poor. As a result, OBC London required that LB's London and Toronto teams revised the advertising materials even before the Canadian launch.

CANADIAN NATIONAL LAUNCH

The days before the launch were panic-filled, as LB's London and Toronto teams scrambled to revise the advertising. In February 2001, the campaign was launched in Canada with the following elements:

- One 30-second TV ad;
- One direct mail piece;
- The English Web site;
- Product samples available from the Web from direct mail piece, and from an in-store coupon;
- Specially designed in-store displays;
- Trial-sized package bundles (one week's worth);
- A public relations campaign; and
- Five print ads in national magazines.

Research following the national launch showed that the brand did not perform well among Canadian consumers. It indexed 50 against a base index of 100. Because of the success of the Canadian pre-launch test, OBC and LB were surprised. The Forever Young global advertising and communications team attributed the discrepancy between the pre-launch test and national launch, in part, to the fact that the pre-launch test conditions were not replicable on a national scale. The audience penetration in the small BC town, the pre-test site, was significantly greater than it was in the national launch. OBC decided that the results of the Canadian launch were below "action standards," meaning that OBC would not even consider a rollout into the US market at the current time.

The tension levels on both LB's side and OBC's side of the Forever Young global advertising and communications team were high. LB's future business on the brand was in jeopardy. The OBC side was under tremendous pressure internally to improve brand trial and market share metrics and already planned to decentralize the local teams for the global product rollout. Despite numerous revisions to the advertising, it never tested well enough to convince OBC that a US or European launch would be successful.

A DIFFERENT STORY IN ASIA

In Taiwan, the product launch was successful. Test results showed that the brand was indexing 120 percent against brand objectives. Research also showed that Taiwanese consumers, in contrast to Canadian consumers, did not perceive some of the advertising elements as "violent." Moreover, in Taiwan, overall research scores in terms of "likeability" and "whether or not the advertising would inspire you to try the product" were higher, leading to higher sales. By June of 2001, the Taiwanese team was ready to take on more local-market responsibility and move into the post-launch phase of the advertising campaign. This phase would involve creating new ads to build on the initial success and grow sales in the market.

RECOVERY PLAN FOR CANADA

By June of 2001, LB needed to take drastic measures to develop a new Forever Young campaign in order to improve the brand's performance in the Canadian marketplace. Whereas, before the launch, there had been a clear division of responsibilities (with the United Kingdom developing the television and print advertising and Canada developing direct marketing, in-store and Web site communications), now the global LB team in London decided that it would be necessary to have all hands on deck. New creative teams from the mass advertising department in the Toronto office, as well as supplementary creative teams from the London office, were briefed to develop new campaign ideas. Each team had only three weeks to develop their new ideas, less than half of the eight weeks they would normally have, and the teams had to work independently of each other. The London and Toronto creative teams had to present their concepts to the entire global OBC and LB team at the same time. Subsequently, the results of market research would determine the winning creative concept. Squabbling between the offices began over which team would present first, which office received what compensation for the development, and whether or not overall remuneration packages were fair. Moreover, the communication between the account services members of LB's London and Toronto teams, which was the primary communication channel between the two agencies, became less frequent, less candid and more formal. The presentations took place on June 25, 2001, in Toronto. Watson, the creative director in Toronto commented:

> This process has been exciting, but we're near the ends of our collective ropes now. We have a new mass advertising creative team [who specialized in TV ads] on the business in Toronto, and they're being expected to produce world-class creative results for a brand they've only heard about for the past few days. They don't – and couldn't possibly – have the same passion for the brand that the direct marketing creative team members have after working on it for so long. I'm having a hard time motivating them to work under these tight timelines.
>
> We're even more isolated now in Toronto. Our connection to the creative teams and the global creative director in London was distant at best, and now it's non-existent. And our relationship with the local OBC client feels very remote, too. Still, we're moving forward with our work. We're trying to learn from the Taiwanese experience and are considering what success we would have with a nationally recognized actress starring in our television ads.

EVOLUTION OF THE FOREVER YOUNG GLOBAL ADVERTISING AND COMMUNICATIONS TEAM

Personnel changes

Between January and June of 2001, numerous personnel changes in the Forever Young global advertising and communications team occurred (see Exhibit 5). In LB's London office, Forin, the UK account director, had been replaced following her departure for maternity leave. In OBC's London office, Sarah Jones, the global vice-president for skin care, took early retirement without putting a succession plan in place. In LB's Toronto office, Davids, the Toronto brand team leader, had left the agency. Tara Powell, who had reported to Davids, took on his responsibilities, but she had not met most of the global team members. Liz Nelson, the account supervisor for interactive, left LB's Toronto office to return to school. Alexis Jacobs, who had managed the Web site development, took over her responsibilities. Powell and Jacobs did not have close relationships with their international counterparts. At OBC Toronto, Sally Burns, the local brand manager, who had been LB's main contact in the local market and had been with the brand since inception, left OBC. LB's and OBC's Taiwanese teams remained stable over time. Cathy Lee worked with a team that was nearly identical to her initial team.

Communications

Early on (between February and May 2000), Carmichael had orchestrated frequent face-to-face meetings to ensure clarity of communication and sufficient information sharing. In the following months, the team relied on videoconferences and phone calls, with visits back and forth between London and Toronto on occasion. Since early 2001, the team had relied increasingly on e-mails and telephone calls to communicate. In June 2001, Carmichael noted that the communication had become more formal, and she had lost the feeling of being part of a global team. She wondered if giving the LB's Toronto team more autonomy to develop the brand in their market would help the brand progress. Working together as a smaller team might improve the Toronto group's team dynamic as well. Carmichael was concerned that the current discord between LB's London and Toronto offices would negatively affect the relationship to OBC.

Budget problems

The extra creative teams assigned to the redevelopment of the brand's television advertising and the unexpected changes to the Forever Young communication materials had meant that LB's costs to staff the project had been higher than originally estimated and higher than the revenues that had been negotiated with OBC. Since OBC did not want to pay more for its advertising than had been originally budgeted, LB faced tremendous internal pressure to finish the project as soon as possible. This situation created conflict between LB and OBC in the United Kingdom, who was responsible for negotiating LB's overall fees. Because all fees were paid to the global brand office (in this case, LB's London office) and then transferred to the local satellite teams, this situation also created conflict between LB's London and Toronto teams, who had both expended additional staff time to revise the advertising materials and wanted "fair" compensation.

WHAT NEXT?

In three days, Carmichael had to leave for Toronto to sit in research sessions to test the recently presented new creative concepts. In the meetings that followed, she would present to the team her recommendation for how to move forward with the brand. Carmichael reviewed the brand events and team interaction of the past two years (see Exhibit 4) to determine the best global team structure for salvaging the Forever Young brand and maintaining the relationship between OBC and LB.

Carmichael felt torn in her loyalties. On the one hand, she was Canadian and knew LB's Toronto office well – she knew that LB's Toronto brand team worked hard, and she wished them every success. On the other hand, she had now worked in LB's London office for several years, and she had always liked the creative concept that the UK team had initially produced. If she maintained the current form of centralized control of the team, either creative concept might be chosen; however, if she decentralized team control, the Toronto team would almost certainly choose their own creative concept for the television ads. Since the creative direction chosen now would become the brand's advertising in most North American and European markets, it needed to be top calibre. Carmichael thought this posed a risk if the creative development was left to the new Toronto-based mass advertising creative team. It would be a shame to lose the UK team's original creative concept.

In making her decision on whether to decentralize the team, Carmichael considered the following:

1 Where was the knowledge necessary to create a competitive advantage for the brand in Canada? Would it be in the Canadian marketplace because they understood the market, or would it be in London because they had more in-depth knowledge of the brand?

2 Where was the client responsibility, and where should it be? Now that the London-based global vice-president of skin care was retiring, the client was considering creating a virtual global team to manage the brand, headquartered in the United States but composed of members of the original United Kingdom OBC team, in preparation for a US launch. If the client team had its headquarters in North America, should LB also structure its team this way?

3 If Carmichael decentralized the brand and gave the Toronto team greater autonomy, who would lead the brand in Toronto now that Davids had left the agency? How would the necessary knowledge be imparted to the new leader?

4 If they remained centralized, would the team make it through before it self-destructed? How much would this risk the client relationship? To what extent would it strain the already tight budget?

Carmichael had to make a decision that was best for the brand, LB and OBC.

CASE **14**

Global Multi-Products Chile

Henry W. Lane and Daniel D. Campbell

INTRODUCTION

As he drove to his office in Providencia, a modern commercial and residential area in
Santiago, Bob Thompson, Managing Director of Multi-Products Chile, was eagerly anticipating the upcoming week. He had spent a pleasant weekend with his family that had
started well on the previous Friday afternoon with what he saw as real progress at work.

He had received an e-mail from one of the sales representatives in the North branch
office reporting the minutes of the first branch sales meeting ever held in the company. Among other items, the minutes stated that the team had identified six accounts
on which they were going to work together under the Integrated Solutions program
and that they had chosen a team leader.

Thompson was surprised but delighted. The sales reps never knew what this type of
meeting could accomplish or what they could do as a group. He had not expected these
teams to function so well from the beginning. Maybe making changes in the organization would not be as difficult as he first had thought.

Upon entering his office, Thompson learned that two of his Business Unit managers were anxious to see him. The first, to whom the formally designated Integrated Solutions Manager reported, commented that he was just checking about the e-mail with Thompson and politely asked, "Have you seen the e-mail from the North? What's your opinion about the comments about Integrated Solutions? Isn't this our responsibility?"

The second Business Unit manager was more concerned and was disturbed with the tone of the e-mail: "What do you think about the note? These comments go way beyond the responsibilities of the branch people."

His earlier mood of satisfaction had turned to consternation. It appeared to him that his top executives, members of his Management Operating Committee, were suggesting a stop to his changes before they got out of hand. He found himself starting to have doubts about what he was doing. Maybe this wasn't going to be so easy after all. Should he keep pushing ahead with change when his senior management team did not appear to support it? He began to reflect on events that had led to this point.

BACKGROUND

Multi-Products Inc. was founded in the early 1900s to manufacture abrasives. The company's creation of the world's first waterproof sandpaper in the early 1920s, followed by numerous other new products, established the company's identity as an innovative, multi-product, manufacturing company. By 1998, the company manufactured and distributed over 50,000 products for a diverse range of applications. Some products were brands found in households and offices all over the world. Others became components of customer products such as computers, automobiles and pharmaceuticals. Many became the standards in their industry. All these products were the result of combining the company's core technologies in ways that solved their customers' problems.

In 1996, international sales totalled US$14.2 billion, an increase of 5.8 percent over the previous year, and income from continuing operations was US$1.52 billion, an increase of 11.7 percent over 1995. International sales represented 53 percent of total sales. Multi-Product subsidiaries operated in over 60 countries outside of the United States and were the channels to sell products into almost 200 countries.

THE COMPANY VISION

According to Bob Thompson, the global growth drivers for the company were 1) technology and innovation; 2) the supply chain; and 3) a customer focus. The 1996 annual report stated the company vision this way:

Our vision is to be the most innovative enterprise and the preferred supplier by:

- Developing technologies and products that create a new basis of competition.
- Earning our customers' loyalty by helping them grow their businesses.
- Expanding internationally, where we already generate more than half of our sales.
- Improving productivity and competitiveness worldwide.

TECHNOLOGY AND INNOVATION

In 1996, nearly 30 percent of sales came from products introduced within the previous four years. Those new products were derived from about 30 "technology platforms" where Multi-Products believed it possessed a competitive advantage. These technologies ranged from adhesives and fluorochemistry, to even newer technologies like micro-replication with potential in abrasives, reflective sheeting, and electronic displays.

These technology platforms were considered the path to the goal of developing products that would create a new basis of competition. The Chairman of Global Multi-Products had high expectations for these programs:

> We have about 30 programs under way. These products serve high-growth industries and offer the potential to generate several billion dollars of new sales by the end of this decade.

INNOVATION IN CUSTOMER SERVICE

Historically, sales efforts were by product group. Often, sales representatives from one product group built strong relationships with customers that could benefit from products from other divisions as well. As a result, in the early 1980s, in an effort to take advantage of these opportunities, the company implemented a program referred to as "Related Sales." In 1988, this program was replaced by "Customer Focused Marketing" that sought to re-orient the sales and marketing effort around the needs of customers, instead of the company's product groups.

In the early 1990s, the process was carried a step further with "Integrated Solutions." Company documents explained the program:

> Customers rely on Multi-Products not only for innovative, high quality products, but also for solutions to other important needs. We help them develop, manufacture and merchandise their products; meet occupational health and safety standards; expand globally; and strengthen their businesses in other ways. We aim to be the first choice of customers. We strive for 100 percent customer satisfaction.
>
> Multi-Products has an innovative way of doing business through which the client can easily access the [company's] products. The system has been labelled "Integrated Solutions" and voices the ideal of "one voice, one face, one company," which means that a single employee can provide you access to all products and solutions.

MULTI-PRODUCTS IN LATIN AMERICA

The company had a long history in Latin America. In 1996, it celebrated 50 years of operations in Brazil, and in 1997, the same in Mexico. The 1996 annual report explained:

> In Latin America, we operate in 16 countries. We've posted annual sales growth of 15 percent during the past five years. Throughout the area, Multi-Products is fulfilling the need

for better roads, telecommunications systems and other types of infrastructure improvement. In addition, demand for health care and consumer products is strong. We manufacture or convert[1] products in a dozen Latin American countries.

Managing Directors in the region reported to the vice president, Latin America, Africa and Canada, who, in turn, reported to the Executive Vice President, International Operations.

MULTI-PRODUCTS CHILE[2]

Multi-Products began operating in Chile in January 1976. With an initial investment of almost US$2 million, operations began in a large shed that served as the warehouse, production, and administration areas. In adherence to Chile's foreign investment legislation at the time, the company was required to establish a manufacturing operation as part of its investment.

Since its beginnings, Multi-Products Chile strove to project a presence throughout the country. The first company branch was created in Concepción in the south of the country during 1977; the second in Valparaíso near Santiago, two years later; and in 1982, a third branch was established in Antofagasta north of Santiago.

In 1992, Multi-Products Chile was asked to be formally responsible for the company's expansion in Bolivia. The local office enabled Multi-Products to directly satisfy the needs of the Bolivian market.

In 1997, the company's sales totalled approximately US$60 million with more than 8000 products. Multi-Products Chile served multiple markets with multiple technologies and products, each of them with solid positions in their category. It supplied numerous manufacturing and service sectors, such as the health and first aid area (hospitals, drugstores, dentists); the industrial sector (safety products, abrasives, reflectors, packing systems, electrical and mining products, graphic communication products); the mass consumption area (cleaning, hardware and bookstore products); office, audio-visual and automobile sectors, and the large productions areas, such as forestry and construction.

Multi-Products' reputation for innovation also was recognized in Chile. El Mercurio conducted a survey in 1998 of 117 directors and general managers of medium and large-sized companies headquartered in Chile. Multi-Products Chile was ranked sixth in response to the question: "Which are the top companies in Chile in innovative capacity and incorporation of technology?"

In 1998, the company had a staff of 270 that included 80 sales representatives, nine technical support staff, 45 people in manufacturing, and the remainder in management, administrative, and maintenance positions.

CHILE: A BRIEF HISTORY[3]

In 1970 a Marxist government was elected in Chile. Soon after elections, Salvador Allende's government began a program of "economic reform." The banking, communications, textiles, insurance and copper mining industries were nationalized. Problems were soon apparent: Chile's currency reserves were gone; business groups were dissatisfied; the US led a boycott against international credit for Chile; and strikes paralyzed the country. In 1973 inflation reached 300 percent.

In 1973, General Augusto Pinochet and the military took control of the country. Although General Pinochet's government was criticized for its human-rights record, it began to introduce market-oriented reforms such as reducing government's control of the economy, privatizing industries including those considered "strategic" and lowering import duties.

Sixteen years of military rule and a peaceful transition to a democratically elected government in 1990 that followed a similar economic path, provided the base for Chile's economic success. Chile boasted one of the best economies in the Western hemisphere: greater than seven percent average growth rates, single digit inflation, a high personal savings rate (23 percent), and a fully funded pension system.

In 1998, Chile's 14.4 million inhabitants shared a per capita GDP in excess of US$5,200, one of the highest in Latin America. While 60 percent of the country's population and economy was concentrated in the Santiago and Valparaíso region in the country's center, strong growth in the mining sector to the north, and the creation of a salmon fisheries industry to the south, had begun to decentralize economic activity.

Chilean culture

Numerous Chilean managers at Multi-Products Chile shared their opinions about Chilean culture.

> Compared with the rest of Latin America, we are formal, closer to Argentina. We are the most serious people in Latin America. We often describe other Latin American cultures as less formal and see them as paying less attention to details. We are very professional at all levels and some people think Chileans are boring.
>
> We are also polite and indirect. For example, an e-mail or Lotus Notes that might be five lines from the United States, might be two pages long, on the same subject, if written by a Chilean.
>
> Many Chileans are workaholics. We work from 8am to 8pm and we often take work home with us on weekends. However, we still have scheduling problems. Time is flexible. A meeting scheduled for 10:00 may not start until 10:20.

Another manager observed:

> Why are we, as a country, not as developed as the United States over the same period of time? Chileans are more isolated from one another. I have been living in the same place for three or four years, and I don't know my neighbors. Nothing, names, number of children, nothing. In Chile, we tend to care about ourselves, our families, and maybe our friends, but that's it.
>
> We haven't paid enough attention to implement programs that make people work together. We haven't paid enough attention to organization development or to developing a sense of community. We don't have a tradition of taking responsibility for a wider group.

Another commented on the "silo effect" stating that, in addition to age and educational background differences, recent political history had polarized society and had not encouraged trust. He commented:

> Things are starting to change slowly, but the wounds haven't healed in 10 years. This is the biggest barrier to working in teams. People didn't trust each other, don't trust each other.

Bob Thompson

Prior to going to Chile, Bob Thompson had been an executive with Multi-Products Canada. Multi-Products Canada was a mature company with a well-trained sales force backed by good technical support that Thompson felt was the company's classic model and was essential to long-term success.

However, in 1991–92, facing a flat economy and stagnating organization, Multi-Products Canada began a change process that sought to empower managers within the organization. Thompson commented:

> The message was that we just couldn't continue with that style of management. We needed to get the best out of people. We needed to be more creative. I think the change process was successful. People felt part of the company in a much deeper way. I, personally, felt very positive about it.

In Chile, his predecessors had always come from the United States; in fact, most had spent considerable time in the head office. Thompson, on the other hand, had spent his career outside of the head office and, in keeping with the Canadian subsidiary's model of management, was more comfortable with broadly shared authority. He believed in encouraging positive risk-taking and empowerment.

Multi-Products Chile had been successful, growing at about 17 percent per year which was acceptable for a subsidiary in an emerging market. Multi-Products liked to grow at between two and four times the growth-rate of the local gross domestic product and it maintained a strong focus on incrementally improving profitability.

Although there was no crisis in Multi-Products Chile when Thompson arrived in early 1996, profitability had declined and the message to him was that it could be improved. As Thompson sized up the organization, he believed it could achieve those profitability objectives. On the other hand, he could make more substantial changes to achieve the potential that headquarters felt existed in Chile.

CUSTOMER AND DISTRIBUTION CHANNEL CHANGES

The group of retailers and distributors that Multi-Products Chile had traditionally served was changing quickly. Bob Thompson commented:

> The last five years have been dramatic. Big American retailers are here or are coming. That has meant that our organization needed to change.

US superstores were rapidly changing the retail market in the country. One manager commented that in the past, local superstores might have represented 60 percent of retail sales, with small sole-proprietorships making up the rest. This superstore segment had been growing at eight to ten percent per year. In 1998, he believed superstores, local and foreign, represented over 90 percent of the business.

As the level of sophistication increased among retailers, expectations of their suppliers increased as well. Purchasing managers, due to the volume of products they were purchasing, were reluctant to deal with distributors, preferring instead to deal directly with suppliers. They also expected lower prices. Multi-Product managers commented:

> Customers are asking for direct service at lower prices. With the big US retailers, negotiation requirements have changed. We have lost power. Our products have traditionally had solid margins and I feel they were higher in the past. Before we might have averaged 80 percent margins. Now, it is difficult to have a different price from everyone else because communication systems like the Internet let people know the world price.

One manager recounted the entry of a new office products retailer into the Chilean market:

> They have been putting a lot of pressure on margins. We are assisting them to enter the market with special programs but it is costly. We have competitors, but Multi-Products has the most complete line of products. We try to add more value to the product. For example, our competitor may sell one kind of tape, where we will sell six.

Retailers were demanding more than just price discounts. They demanded a commitment to advertising support before they would place a product on their shelves. In the case of the office supplies retailer, Multi-Products paid 5 million pesos[4] for a photograph of its office products to be included in a supplementary catalogue. The catalogue would be followed up by a telemarketing campaign that was also a new concept for Chile.

Retailers also wanted more timely delivery to reduce inventories and better communication with their suppliers around ordering, billing and logistics. One manager commented:

> We had to learn to make the delivery and leave the invoice at the same time. As an industrial products company we were used to loading a big truck and sending it to the customer. In consumer products, we use smaller trucks and make more stops. We had to wait at the new, large retailers because the big, traditional consumer goods suppliers had more clout and were unloaded first.

Retailers wanted to reduce the number of Multi-Product sales representatives they were dealing with from four or five down to one. As a result, that sales person had to have access to information about all of the company's products being delivered to that retailer, even though they might originate from multiple product divisions.

The company also wanted to consolidate and had re-organized product responsibilities to achieve this. For example, where the Marketing Manager for Consumer Goods had been responsible for tape sales within his or her channel, responsibility for all tape sales, industrial and consumer, now resided with another manager in the Home and Office

Division. This meant that the Marketing Coordinators of the Home and Office and Consumer Products Division now had to work together more closely than in the past. Cross-divisional selling had become an established fact. One manager commented:

> We have to learn to work together. They have the products and product knowledge. We have the relationship with the superstores and the skill in negotiating with them. Last year 44 per cent of our division's sales were from non-consumer products to supermarkets, home centers and hardware stores.

In many instances, the company continued to use distributors, in part, because nearly 80 per cent of their product sales went to industrial users. In some industries, the number of distributors had decreased after consolidation and the sophistication of the remaining distributors was increasing. Managing the relationship with distributors had become increasingly difficult as sales representatives began selling directly to end users previously serviced by a distributor.

It was not just the retail sector that had changed, but industrial products companies as well. The mining industry used to be government-controlled but large, mining multinationals were commonplace and they operated differently. One executive commented, "Everything has been challenged. We need new skills."

NEW ROLE FOR SALES REPRESENTATIVES

Changes in the company's customer base were resulting in new responsibilities and requirements for Multi-Products' sales representatives. Generally, Chile was a fairly structured society. In business, titles conferring status in the organization were very important. The selling role was not held in the same regard as other positions, and levels of education tended to be lower. Indeed, it was often difficult for sales reps to access more senior managers in the selling process. Thompson commented that "the idea of a sales executive meeting with a client's executive does not exist commonly here."

A business unit manager described a typical sales call in the past:

> When sales representatives visited a business, they would usually sit down and have a coffee with their contact. A significant portion of their conversation would revolve around non-business-related topics such as the client's family or maybe football. The relationship was very important. Eventually, the sales representative would inspect the client's inventories and make suggestions for orders of our products.

Because of increased client sophistication and more advanced products from Multi-Products, more was required from a sales representative. Another Business Unit manager commented:

> A sales rep now needs to teach as well as to sell. In the past, they were specialists. They may have only sold simple office products. Now they need to know how to sell a multi-media projector, connect it to a notebook computer and train clients on how to use it, too! People need to be more professional in their commercial relationships and make an effort to learn. We don't sell products anymore, we sell solutions.

Instead of casual sales visits, it was not uncommon now to have a team of five or six sales people, coordinated by one single client contact, making presentations that could last two or three days. Consumer products sales reps also were now focused on visiting a given number of stores in a day and handling smaller orders faster and more frequently since there were no warehouses – just the shelves in the customers' stores. Not all the sales reps were happy with this conversion from maintaining a relationship with a store owner to being, in their view, an "ant" running all over the place.

Multi-Products Chile had started placing more emphasis on recruiting high caliber people including those for sales positions. However, most university graduates showed much greater interest in positions that appeared to offer faster mobility to executive positions such as in marketing.

INTEGRATED SOLUTIONS AND KEY ACCOUNTS IN MULTI-PRODUCTS CHILE

When Thompson arrived in Santiago, he learned that, although there was an awareness of the "Integrated Solutions" approach, little real progress appeared to have been made. He commented:

> This was our most important commercial activity globally, but it was not present in Chile. Our product line is so broad and deep, that customers were confused. "Why can't we see just one sales representative?" they would ask.
>
> The company had been organized for distribution-based selling, taking product lines to distributors. We needed to start understanding client and business applications of products . . . acting like a consultant. This approach proved new and challenging for the organization.

Sales representatives were responsible for sales of a specific product or line of products. Performance was measured on the ability of a representative to sell certain products, and there was no incentive to sell products from other areas of the company. As a result, customers who purchased a range of products from Multi-Products were forced to deal with several different sales representatives. If the customer was a multinational, it would often have to deal with a separate sales organization in each country in which it did business.

Structural changes

When Bob Thompson arrived at Multi-Products Chile, he found an organization that had been very successful with traditional distribution-based selling. The deeper Multi-Products "footprint" that he was used to, especially technical support groups, was limited. He added technical support positions along with a technical council to foster its development. As well, marketing, sales and manufacturing councils were added in time.

He also created the new position of Integrated Solutions Manager, reporting to the manufacturing products business unit manager. This person would be responsible for the implementation of Integrated Solutions in Chile and would coordinate the sales teams that would service large clients where the program was being implemented.

EXHIBIT 1 Multi-Products Chile Organization Chart

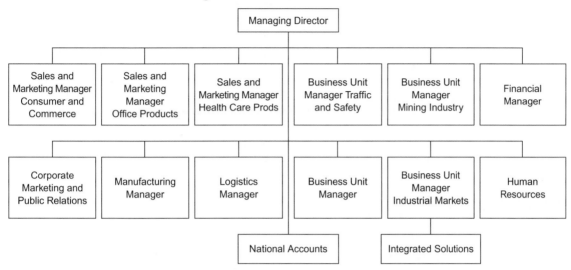

A short time later, a position of National Accounts Leader for Key Accounts was also created, reporting directly to Thompson. A new manufacturing manager was hired from Multi-Products Argentina where a more established manufacturing organization existed. See Exhibit 1 for a diagram of the revised organizational structure.

Accounts of special significance to Multi-Products Chile would now be viewed in one of two ways: Key Accounts and Integrated Solutions Targets.

Key accounts

The Key Account concept was not new to Multi-Products Chile. However, in the past, a key account was identified as a customer with the potential to purchase large quantities of the company's products. Multi-Products Chile sold directly to these customers using programs different from distributors especially in pricing structure and logistics support, but the sales effort remained similar. Multiple sales representatives from each of the product areas selling to the client would service the account. Little, or no, coordination existed between the product groups.

Now, Key Accounts were those customers whose relationship with Multi-Products took on a strategic significance beyond a buyer/supplier relationship in that Multi-Products' technology could augment the customer's business and possibly change the basis of competition. Multi-Products Chile wanted to identify strategic partnerships with its customers where activities such as research and product development could be coordinated between the organizations, creating long-term competitive advantages for both organizations.

In 1998, this process had only been initiated, and partners, as well as the specific nature of the desired relationships with these partners, were in the process of being determined. However, the criteria for selecting Key Accounts were: a) a strong relationship with

Multi-Products Chile, b) purchase potential, c) potential importance as an Integrated Solutions account, and d) an important company in Chile concerned about the environment and society and having the same values as Global Multi-Products Inc.

Multi-Products Chile was one of the first of the company's Latin American subsidiaries to create this formal Key Accounts position. The National Accounts Leader felt that his challenge was going to be to convince the other Multi-Products' companies to be consistent in their business model and prices with the Chilean company so that multinational customers could benefit from the relationship. He commented;

> This is a strategic program and will take a big change in mentality. We can't think short term, anymore. Free trade is helping to stabilize the country but we could still have big changes. This is the reason that business executives in Chile think short term.

Integrated solution targets

The real start of Integrated Solutions was in August 1997 with the collection of data about which customers would make the best targets for an initial effort. The idea was to discover those product divisions that had good relationships with clients and use the relationship to sell other products. Where the National Account Program, Key Accounts, was a strategic approach to link with a few very large accounts to create new products, Integrated Solutions was a broadly based tactical approach involving many more accounts.

Integrated Solutions represented an opportunity to sell products from multiple product groups to a client in a concerted effort. By early 1998, more than 30 customers had been identified as targets.

The next stage involved taking an "X-ray" of these companies to determine which products the company was already using. A group of specialists would map a customer's business process to find opportunities for other products that might reduce a customer's costs. This process was complicated because a single company could purchase its products directly from Multi-Products Chile, although from different product groups, as well as from a range of distributors. Once managers knew what the company was purchasing, they could measure any increase in sales to those accounts and measure that against the general market to determine if the Integrated Solutions effort was succeeding.

An individual sales representative was then selected as the leader for a specific client and would act as the single point of contact for all sales to that client, including sales outside of the sales representative's own product area. These sales representatives would then request support from other representatives as required. This leader was determined by selecting the person having the best relationship with the client, who usually was obvious.

Sales representatives and integrated solutions

Managers often described the Multi-Products Chile organization as silos, with individual product groups functioning independently of one another. One manager commented:

We used to describe the situation as feudal. There were some sales reps that supported other divisions, but there was no program to formalize the activity.

Salespeople feel they have ownership over their product areas. They would ask: "Why would I use my time opening doors for another sales rep when I can use that time to visit my own customers?"

With the implementation of Integrated Solutions, it was recognized that sales staff needed to work as a team, helping one another to sell products. Everyone had not adjusted well to working with other product divisions. Some managers demanded: "Give me the products and I will sell them and earn the commission!" One manager commented:

Not all the sales people are with the program; 15 per cent are with the program, another 60 per cent are with the program but are not leading it. The others are saying: "I will look after my own business and nothing else."

Sales people need a change in terms of mentality. They also need to develop new sales techniques and knowledge about the products. The younger people are generally more adaptable to the change.

The increased sophistication in the buying process of some of the company's clients had also caused problems. Some sales representatives felt they had less influence in the process. They had grown accustomed to pushing new products that had been created in the US. Now marketing people were often involved in the initial process of approaching retailers with new products and negotiating the terms of sale.

Compensation also became an issue, because sales representatives usually were measured against sales targets in their product areas.

Sales representative compensation

When sales representatives joined Multi-Products Chile, they were given a six-month grace period during which time their compensation was 100 per cent fixed. After that time, 40 per cent of their compensation was fixed while the remaining 60 per cent was variable or "at risk", and tied to the achievement of various targets. As a sales representative became more senior, the variable portion was reduced to 20 per cent which reduced uncertainty about pay. As one manager commented, "We Latins don't like uncertainty."

The variable compensation targets were set by the sales manager, and were designed to encourage desired activity for that period. For example, 20 per cent of the variable pay could be for the sale of new products. Other percentages could be used for sales calls on new clients, or sales of certain high-margin items. To accommodate Integrated Solutions, a sales manager could include sales of other product areas as a target within a sales representative's variable compensation. These targets were usually adjusted annually to meet the needs of the sales division.

Sales representatives could also receive additional pay in extra-compensation for exceeding their targets. For example, sales reps with 30 per cent variable compensation could earn up to 130 per cent of their salary and a senior sales rep with 20 per cent variable compensation could earn up to 120 per cent.

The sales contest

Until two years earlier, the sales contest was designed and administered by the Human Resources Department when it was transferred to Corporate Marketing. The Corporate Marketing Manager invited the Sales Council,[5] of which he was the head, to design a new program.

The new program eliminated the prizes that had been given in the past such as trips and microwave ovens which, as was clearly evident, the winners usually sold. Instead, it provided monetary rewards. If sales reps made 123 per cent of their target they would get, in effect, a bonus payment of x per cent. If the sales team of which they were a part met its objectives, they would get an additional y per cent. And, if the Business Unit met its objectives, they could receive another z per cent. In total, they could earn up to an additional $2,500.

This new sales contest presented difficulties for Bob Thompson. The Manager of Human Resources and other managers were not pleased with it. They felt that a) it was too expensive, potentially costing as much as the whole training and education budget; b) it should not have been monetarized; c) it permitted everyone to get a prize; and d) it had become part of the compensation system which was senior management's responsibility.

Thompson knew there was dissatisfaction among his managers with the new sales contest. His Human Resources Manager preferred to see changes in the plan but Thompson liked some elements of the design and since it came into effect when sales growth exceeded 23 per cent it was to a degree self-funding.

INITIATING THE CHANGE PROCESS

In late 1996, soon after Thompson's arrival, a retreat was held in Iquique, a resort area north of Santiago, for senior managers from Multi-Products Chile as well as from Multi-Products Bolivia and Peru. Prior to the managers of the three countries meeting as one group, they met individually to confirm their primary mission and goals. The Chile group appeared to struggle at working together.

One of the purposes of the retreat was to establish a general mission statement for the region created by the three countries. The discussion went poorly. Managers seemed to have trouble defining a clear mission and did not touch on broader objectives for the region. As the discussion, originally scheduled for two or three hours, entered its second day, Thompson became increasingly disappointed, not only with the group's inability to reach a conclusion, but with what appeared to him to be the quality of the discussions. Frustrated, Thompson stopped the discussion and asked the group why things were going so poorly. To his surprise, one of the Chilean managers stood up and said: "We don't trust each other."

Thompson had hired a consultant to act as a professional facilitator for the retreat. As part of his services, he later provided a report outlining his conclusions about the meeting and the group. His executive summary included the following points about the executive team:

Generally, this appears to be a strong task- and results-oriented group. They are autonomous in doing what they do and are well adjusted to standard requirements. Because of this they are able to focus on task structure and output evaluation but are less aware of group process and its importance to productivity and teamwork. At times they seem isolated and defensive. There are also some unresolved personal conflicts with no methodology about resolving those conflicts.

This information gave Thompson some idea about the nature of the Multi-Products Chile organization, and pointed out some challenges to be met as he worked to make it more responsive to the customers and markets they served.

Additionally, the company conducted company-wide employee surveys every three years. They included information from various levels of the organization, about employees' opinions on various aspects of the company such as salaries, empowerment, and safety. As a part of the data analysis, a comparison was made of the opinions of senior managers in contrast with the opinions of lower level employees on each dimension. While opinions differed on many issues, certain areas showed senior managers having a much more positive opinion than their employees (a difference of ≥ 20 percent). These included: work conditions, training, job progress, pay, safety and empowerment.

About the change process, one executive observed:

There has been resistance and conflict generated because of the changes. Maybe it has been too aggressive or too quick. People need to understand why we are changing and we are addressing this. We are in the process of changing even though not much has really changed yet.

These programs promote involvement beyond your scope of responsibility. They are long-term programs, sophisticated techniques. They won't create sales tomorrow. We are measured by our results and there is no need to change. The company is doing well. There are no rewards for thinking strategically. You can be comfortable and do well not doing these things. Thompson is doing it because he thinks it is right. It takes courage. Others do only what they are rewarded for.

CONCLUSION

Thompson's secretary interrupted his reflections to remind him that he had a meeting shortly with his human resources manager. Thompson thought to himself that, maybe, he had introduced enough change to Multi-Products Chile and that it was not necessary to go further. After all, business was good and things were going well.

Notes

1 "Converting" meant taking products originally received in bulk, and packaging or sealing them for consumption in the local market.
2 Much of this information was taken from company documents.
3 This section is adapted from *The Economist*, January 24, 1998; *Santiago; What's on*; Turiscom SA, January 1998; and *Chile Handbook*; Charlie Nurse, Footprint Handbooks, 1997.
4 In January 1998, US$1 purchased 450 Chilean pesos.
5 The composition of this council included the corporate marketing manager, and senior sales representatives from the business units.

CASE **15**

Schneider Electric Global Account Management

Joseph J. DiStefano and Anne-Valerie Ohlsson

Fritz Keller, international account manager (IAM) in Schneider Electric (Switzerland) SA, was preparing for his first account manager workshop with one of his new global accounts, Calchem, worldwide manufacturer of specialty chemicals. One of the standard challenges in introducing a new account to the advantages of the global relationship was reflected by the fact that, until a week before the meeting, Keller had been unable to persuade representatives from Calchem's head office in Basel to attend the two-day meeting in Nice. Keller believed that Calchem had never had as close a supplier relationship as he was proposing and felt uncomfortable with the idea. On the other hand, with 30% of Calchem billings originating from the US operations, one of Calchem's senior US executives had been quick to accept Keller's invitation. Then, a week before the meeting, the head of automation had accepted the invitation, and two days before the meeting, the VP of group purchasing had called to say that he would attend the second day of the two-day meeting.

After two years on the job, Fritz Keller was a strong supporter of Schneider's global account management (GAM), which he was convinced brought mutual advantages to customers and to Schneider. But the challenge with Calchem wasn't the only issue he had identified as an important concern for him and his 60 IAM counterparts around the globe. Among other things that kept him busy were:

Research Associate Anne-Valerie Ohlsson prepared this case under the supervision of Professor Joe DiStefano as a basis for class discussion rather than to illustrate either effective or ineffective handling of a business situation.

Please note that some numbers and percentages have been altered and that the names of individuals and client accounts have been disguised.

- Gaining the necessary cooperation from Schneider's local companies, which served Calchem accounts in their country's marketing structure.
- Getting timely information from Schneider's information systems, which had been established in the French headquarters to serve the large and growing number of global accounts that had been so successful in increasing Schneider's worldwide revenues.
- Finding the time to network with his IAM counterparts and getting to know important Schneider managers in key countries around the world who could make or break his promises to Calchem when special assistance was needed.
- Getting the support of his own boss to add the necessary people in Switzerland to take full advantage of the GAM opportunities of other multinationals based in Switzerland.

SCHNEIDER ELECTRIC BACKGROUND

Schneider Electric was founded in 1782 as an industrial equipment company. During its first years, the company grew rapidly, surviving both the French revolution and the Napoleonic Wars. Under the leadership of brothers Adolphe and Eugene Schneider, the company built the first French locomotive in 1836.

By 1914 the company had become one of France's most important heavy industry companies and, as such, played an important role in France's war effort during World War I. Schneider entered the electrical contracting business in 1929. During World War II many Schneider factories were either destroyed or commandeered. Following the war, and supported by the French government, the organization was restructured as a holding company. The new holding's operating units were grouped into three subsidiaries: civil and electrical engineering, industrial manufacturing and construction.

In 1969, three years after going public (the last family member passed away in 1950), Schneider merged with Empain to form the Empain-Schneider group. The merger was followed by a period of extensive acquisition and diversification, including ski equipment, fashion, publishing and travel.

The diversification strategy was not as successful as expected and, between 1980 and 1993, Schneider went through a complete reorganization. In 1993 the company merged with its former parent company, Société Parisienne d'Entreprises et de Participation. New stocks were issued to existing shareholders; operations were streamlined. Merlin Gerin (acquired in 1975) and Télémécanique (acquired in 1988) became Schneider Electric in Europe. Square D (acquired in 1991) represented Schneider's North American operations. The brands continued to be identified globally,[1] while operational synergies were obtained by shared facilities on a country or regional basis.

In a continued effort to refocus and expand, in 1996 Schneider set up the first totally French-owned company in China. In 1997 it sold Spie Batignolles, its electrical contracting subsidiary, and in 1999 it paid US$1.1 billion to acquire Lexel[2] in a move to broaden its household equipment offering. That year, the group also changed its name globally to Schneider Electric.

By 2000 Schneider Electric was one of the largest electrical manufacturers in the world, operating 150 manufacturing and marketing facilities in 130 countries. It served the electrical power, industrial, infrastructure and construction markets. Selected applications included electrical power in residential, industrial and commercial buildings, infrastructures for airports, road and rail networks, merchant marine and naval facilities and monitoring systems for power generation substations and distribution grids.

SHIFTING FROM LOCAL TO GLOBAL ACCOUNT MANAGEMENT

Communication, reliability, speed and service to local customers are what make us successful as a team. We do not win customers with the technology – it is common to all the companies in the field. We win with the relationship-building and by delivering on the relationship.

Fritz Keller, International Account Manager (Switzerland)

In 1992 Schneider Global Business Development (SGBD) was created as a worldwide sales organization, parallel to the country-based sales force. One objective was to significantly expand business with the company's global, strategic clients.

Schneider first ventured into global account management with Copiato, an American company with which it had a long-standing relationship. By developing a deeper understanding of Copiato's needs, Schneider could tailor products that better suited Copiato's market. The two companies identified mutually beneficial initiatives in product development, reduction of project cycle time, improvement of productivity, minimization of down-times, savings in maintenance costs and reduction of inventory and purchasing costs. Working together around the globe helped ensure global consistency in product offering and service quality. As an indicator of the success and quality of the relationship, Copiato and Schneider were jointly awarded the 1995 Arthur Andersen Best of the Best Award for Channel Management. Subsequently, Schneider became Copiato's first and only globally certified electrical supplier.

The global account structure developed gradually. The shift from local to global account management came with a number of challenges: global account management was expensive, pricing and contracting became far more complicated and overcoming regional differences and "parochialism" represented a significant challenge.

Other challenges were the large degree of customization the company wanted to provide the client and the shift from standardized manufacturing to client-led manufacturing. In responding to a favored customer's needs, for example, Schneider had to invest in special equipment to design the product to the client's requirements. In turn, the client made Schneider its sole supplier for that group of products. As trust developed, increasingly rich relationships followed.

The high level of communication and customer interaction necessary to make the partnership successful involved a new way of working. In the most mature relationships, Schneider and its clients designed products together, forming product-development teams with members from both organizations. This required high involvement from senior management in both organizations and high trust. (See Exhibit 1 for an example of the realignment of relationships.)

DEFINITION OF A GLOBAL STRATEGIC ACCOUNT

Schneider had set a requirement for companies that wanted to be considered as a strategic global account: the client had to offer the potential of sourcing at least 50% of

EXHIBIT 1 Evolution of Customer–Supplier Relationship

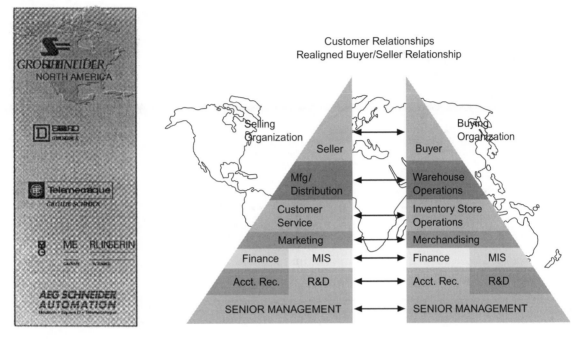

Source: Company presentation.

its global business from Schneider. This allowed Schneider to recover the startup costs of the relationship over time. As François LeBlanc, head SGBD for the past five years, noted,

> Part of the problem is that your clients are also at different levels of globalization. You have to be patient, but you must also be able to amortize your costs. That's why there is a 50% entry barrier. Within the first two years of an alliance you get really fast growth, say from 5% to 20%. But the real challenge is to obtain more than 20% of your client's total business. The only way to achieve this is to provide consistent productivity improvements to your client. Winning the next 30% or more of your client's business will take you another three years. So, if after five years you do not have 50% of that client's business, you should seriously reconsider the relationship.

In addition, the client had to meet a number of pre-established conditions set by Schneider. The client had to help Schneider understand its challenges, needs and services. It had to agree to share early project information and make purchasing commitments. Other factors Schneider considered were compatibility of goals, values, styles and time horizons. A preferred relationship also included the cost-saving benefit of neither party having to go through a bidding process for a new project.

FIGURE 1   International SGBD Network

BUILDING A STRUCTURE FOR GLOBAL ACCOUNT MANAGEMENT

The structure of Schneider's global account management could be likened to a web (see Figure 1). In the center was Schneider Electric's Paris headquarters. International account managers reported through a matrix structure: they were responsible for the global accounts through SGBD's regional structure, but they also reported to the line organization through the country heads. Headquarters coordinated global R&D, marketing, solutions and services, and provided SGBD with preferential support. The plants, located around the world, had responsibility for service contracts, time-to-market, training and maintenance. Wholesalers were in charge of pricing agreements, stocking, delivery times and technical training. The OEM/Systems Integration department managed service programs, conversion and provided technical training.

The headquarters of each global strategic account (GSA) was involved in the process. The IAM in charge of the account was based in the country of the GSA's headquarters. Together, Schneider and the client developed coordinated strategies and discussed potential reductions of overall costs.

The international account manager could obtain support from marketing resources dedicated to SGBD and from the industry expert teams in various geographical locations (e.g., Silicon Valley for the microelectronic specialists.) The IAM provided Schneider's local country correspondents (international account correspondents (IACs), or IAMs) with account information. The IACs shared this information with their local engineers and fed information back to the IAM. The engineers spent a large amount of time at the local plants of the GSAs. The GSA headquarters dealt directly with the IAM.

PERFORMANCE MEASURES AND REWARD SYSTEMS

The IAMs were reviewed every year at the annual planning and review meeting. The meeting included the IAM's corporate sponsor[3] and the cluster[4] director. The review covered three areas: key objectives (including soft, general issues such as the number of projects developed with a key account), sales forecasts and critical issues or support needed. IAM performance was measured through a globally oriented management-by-objectives system. Profits were evaluated at net-price levels to ensure that products were not given away to win the account. As LeBlanc noted:

> In countries where sensitivity to quotas and incentives is very high (such as in the US), IAMs can receive an additional 20% to 50% of their salary as bonus. In general, I consider that the amount tied to local turnover is still too high relative to global turnover. The main challenge with the reward systems is that we need to encourage both global account managers and local sales forces to look for a win-win situation.

In addition to the annual planning and review meetings, each cluster held its own annual meeting with all cluster IAMs and a number of local IACs. These meetings served the purpose of sharing information and ideas and providing industry updates. The meetings were held in a different country every year so that five to six local IACs could attend. A global SGBD meeting, including all IAMs and the SGBD central supporting team, was also held yearly.

The cost of measuring the benefits of a GSA was very high. Consequently, three to four accounts were chosen for closer scrutiny on an ad hoc, yearly basis. Corporate auditors and the corporate controller carried out an in-depth P&L analysis of these selected accounts. This independent, corporate performance measure allowed Schneider to check the validity of the approach and the margins on each GSA over years. Lou Primo, who divided his time between Paris and the US as director of international business development for SGBD, explained some of the difficulties Schneider experienced at the time:

> The issue of measurement of IAM and IAC effectiveness continues to be a difficult one for us. The same is true for measuring the worth of a GSA to Schneider Electric. While we would very much like to be able to measure these things, our current business systems are not well suited to providing data for this purpose. As a result of this lack of good business systems, we tend to take an intuitive approach to the evaluation of our IAMs, IACs and our GSAs. We rely heavily on the opinion of the country management in this regard. While we have continued to grow the number of accounts that we consider as GSAs, we have also de-listed three or four accounts which we felt did not measure up to our expectations.

A major problem in the senior and country management of Schneider Electric was the perception that large accounts often meant high volume with low margins. After several years of activity, SGBD was able to prove with actual revenue and margin figures that this was untrue. However, this perception was hard to change, and SGBD management always had to be ready to prove that global strategic accounts could yield higher-than-average margins to the overall benefit of both the account and Schneider Electric.

TRAINING

Specific skills necessary to be a successful IAM included the ability to influence without authority and the ability to work across cultures.

Schneider's global account managers were expected to exhibit the following behaviors and skills:[5]

- Clear vision and mission statements.
- Empowerment:
    - Executive global nomination
    - Reporting structure
    - Internal awareness, and
    - Cooperation for local implementation.
- Effective communication network with identified regional managers at several levels and a formalized matrix structure.
- "Solution-Selling" competence.
- Cultural adaptability.

Development activities were conducted in a variety of ways. Some centralized training was conducted at SGBD headquarters in Paris; other development occurred at client workshops. In addition to the formal training programs, the corporate sponsors and senior regional executives from SGBD worked with IAMs as on-the-job mentors. One of the gurus of GAM in Schneider, Harry Smith, who had started the Copiato account, was also renowned for his colorful coaching of IAMs, both at the client workshops he often attended and when he met with the IAMs in the field at US customer offices. Smith had taken a particular interest in Fritz Keller – he had taken Keller fishing during a visit to Smith's home in upstate New York. Smith explained why he believed in mentoring:

> The ability to network within the Schneider organization is not intuitive and there is no roadmap. Networking skills and contacts are extremely important as the IAM is a matrix manager and as such must gain support through consensus rather than edict. When an IAM networks with senior client management, senior VPs of manufacturing, engineering, purchasing, quality, finance, etc., the dialog changes as does the need set of the client. Our IAMs each have one senior Schneider manager assigned as an executive sponsor/mentor to help the IAM determine what Schneider management resource is most appropriate for each of the customer contact types identified above. Most of the time the most appropriate action for the IAM is to enable the conversation between peer members rather that conduct the meeting himself.

SCHNEIDER'S COMPETITORS AND THEIR RELATIVE STRENGTHS IN GAM

Schneider's main competitors included global players such as ABB, Alstom, Cuttler Hammer, General Electric, Rockwell and Siemens. Many of the company's main competitors embraced a project approach, rather than a solutions-oriented one. Others

EXHIBIT 2 Example of Competitor Strategy

Competitor X

Earn Trust	Set Entry Barriers	Establish Exit Barriers	Solve Problems Together
New Smart Technology Advertisements Control View Compatible Software Advertisements	Application White Papers Conversion Programs "Channel Authorization" Programs Automation Fair Exhibit & Conference Program Automation Solutions Partners ISA tradeshow Exhibit	Application Assistance Teams MIS Network Support for "Enabled Products" SPC/MIS Application Support for Software	**Integrated Manufacturing**
Broad Product Offer Ads	Nationwide Distributor Directories Free guide and conversion selectors Integrated Supply White Paper	Integrated Supply Guidelines/Programs Consortiums and Affiliations	**Integrated Logistics**
Global Advertisement	World Wide Application Service and Support Directories	Global Systems Integration Support	**Globalization**

Source: Company presentation.

pursued a "stepping-stone" approach. They developed planned sequences of advertising and promotional events tightly linked to their sales, marketing and field service plans. These events were linked to calls for action that led customers to the next milestone in a desired relationship, while explicitly seeking awareness and credibility for solving specific customer business goals. (See Exhibit 2 for an example of a competitor strategy.)

Schneider reacted to this range of strategies by developing entry and exit barriers for its clients. Entry barriers included product superiority, service superiority, networking relationships, joint long-term planning, joint product-design assistance, consignment inventory, common software systems and pricing agreements. Exit barriers included volume-based rebates, technical support, customer clubs, specialized training, formal long-term contracts, financial support and shared facilities. High switching costs made it difficult for competitors to convert their customers and for customers to convert their suppliers. (See Exhibit 3 for Schneider's competitor defense strategy.)

EXHIBIT 3   Schneider's Competitor Defense Strategy

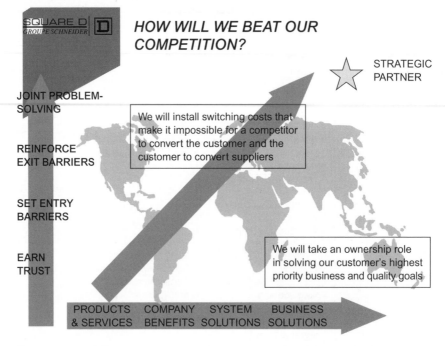

Source: Company presentation.

THE SITUATION IN 2000

By 2000 Schneider had a group of 60 international account managers, in addition to SGBD international account correspondents, in over 90 countries. The accounts were organized in four main clusters including food and beverage, automotive, pharmaceuticals and microelectronics. The center for food and beverage expertise was in France, for automotive, Germany, and pharma and microelectronics in the US. A fifth cluster included those clients who did not belong to one of the above-mentioned industries. The individual industry experts for these clusters performed two functions: As experts, their knowledge could be called upon from any country in the world, but they also managed large accounts in their clusters.

Within each country with a GSA headquarters were IAMs. In countries where the GSA had operations, Schneider designated IACs. In Austria the IAC managed six accounts belonging to four clusters. The correspondent managed sales for all six clients, but was accountable to different senior executives responsible for the different clusters who resided in different countries.

THE CALCHEM–SCHNEIDER RELATIONSHIP

Calchem developed and manufactured specialty chemicals for the paper, paint and plastics industry. The company had operations in 130 countries. Its cost structure was both power intensive and power sensitive. In the mid-1990s the company had moved away from a price-based "black boxes" approach to purchasing in order to reduce plant down-time and decrease energy costs. This focused Calchem's interest on solutions providers rather than on equipment and software providers.

The two companies shared a long-standing relationship, especially in the automation field. Calchem met the requirements defined by Schneider for its strategic accounts – global presence and a potential for over $15 million in revenue. In addition, Calchem's purchasing policy was based on technology, relationship and service before price, which mirrored the SGBD philosophy.

Prior to becoming a GSA, Calchem had purchased SFr 3 to 4 million in Schneider products (exclusively from its automation product-line). The projects and purchases were neither coordinated internationally nor across business areas. A year later, with the development of common strategies and a high degree of information sharing (coordinated by the IAM), purchasing orders amounted to SFr 10 million, with a realistic possibility for another SFr 20 to 25 million in the near future.

Convincing Calchem of the added-value of becoming a GSA was not easy. Keller recalled some of his early meetings with Calchem:

> Companies may be interested in the GAM advantages in terms of pricing deals, but they are sometimes less ready to invest the time and initial costs required to launch a global process. Yet we are actually helping the customer understand his business better by giving him a global picture of it. For example, Calchem did not know the total value of its orders with us, nor were they fully aware of the breadth of our services, product lines and solutions. The interesting thing is that some customer subsidiaries understand this better than their own headquarters. In the case of Calchem, headquarters was initially reluctant to send participants to the joint meeting in Nice, while their US subsidiary, representing 30% of the business with Schneider, jumped at the opportunity to participate.

Calchem requested status as a global strategic account at the end of 1999. Schneider and the client met several times to define needs and prepare the first single-source order. A Schneider team made up of IAMs, IACs and technical experts from the Paris headquarters visited the client's engineering centers and participated in several engineering meetings. LeBlanc, as corporate sponsor, met with senior executives from Calchem to discuss the strategic aspects of the relationship. This pairing of very senior people ensured that common goals were achieved and that the relationship was reinforced at all levels of the client organization.

THE CALCHEM–SCHNEIDER ELECTRIC WORKSHOP

Normally, company-supplier workshops were held once or twice yearly with Schneider's strategic accounts. The meetings were arranged and sponsored by Schneider. All the

EXHIBIT 4   Dos and Don'ts for IAMs and IACs

Dos and Don'ts

Do:

- Network – get to know as many Client people as you can, especially ones outside of the normal sales cycle, get their business card.
- Think of yourself as a Client Account Manager.
- Be very open and share information in the joint session.
- Think of your Client as a business ally not just a client to whom we sell product.
- Get Names.
- Copy Harry Smith on all correspondence.
- Follow-up, if you tell a Client contact that you will telephone or write or send a sample, make sure you do.
- Make sure that you spend time talking one on one with the various Client Managers, learn that they are easy to work with and welcome your advice.
- Have Fun.

Dos and Don'ts

Don't:

- Bring up orders you did not get from the Client.
- Schedule meetings with the Client – get their card and call them after the meeting.
- Make excuses about our not being able to fill an order or deliver a particular product. If something like that comes up and it probably will in the joint session, find out what the Client wants and then start to find ways to fill their order.
- Try to impress the Client with the business you are doing
- Refer to your clients as customers, customers buy goods from an attendant, clients seek the advice of a professional.

Source: Company presentation.

EXHIBIT 5   Participants in the Schneider/Calchem/Lactal Workshop

Country	Schneider SGBD	IAC for Calchem	IAC for Lactal	Calchem	Lactal	Distributor
Canada		1	1			
Switzerland		1	3	2	2	
Czechoslovakia		1	1			
Spain		1	1			
Finland		1				
France	2	1	1			
Germany		1	1			
Italy		1	2			
Mexico		1				
The Netherlands			1			
Poland		1	1			
Turkey		1				
Republic of South Africa			1			
United Kingdom		1	2			
USA	4	4	3	1	1	1
Total	6	16	18	3	3	1

Source: Company documentation.

IAMs and IACs involved with the account were invited to attend. (See Exhibit 4 for some of the dos and don'ts suggested by Harry Smith to IAMs and IACs attending the workshops.) On the customer side, country managers and heads of purchasing were also invited. As different issues emerged in the relationship, different customer executives participated in these meetings to plan ahead, solve problems and review past performance.

In the case of the upcoming Calchem meeting to be held in June 2000, the objectives for the workshop included reinforcing the relationship among Calchem's six engineering centers, the plants and Schneider on a global basis, analyzing and understanding Calchem's future needs, providing the best offering, developing new solutions and enhancing local service. (See Exhibit 5 for a list of countries and roles presented at the meeting.) Above all, the objective was to close the perception gap that prevailed in some Calchem divisions that believed, "We have a strategic alliance with Schneider, but we are the ones who make all the decisions!" Keller hoped that the two executives from Calchem would provide new information about their strategy. Since the VP for group purchasing was new to Calchem, he hoped to learn about how compatible his approach to purchasing was with Schneider's SGA philosophy.

Within Schneider's own organization the meeting also served to increase the effectiveness of cross-national teamwork among the Calchem IACs and the effectiveness of interactions with the client. In this regard, since Calchem's senior US executive was coming to the meeting, Keller had also invited a senior manager from Graybar, Schneider's main US distributor, and the country manager from Switzerland.

The meeting was expected to reinforce the message to Calchem that Schneider as a whole was strongly committed to global account management and to their needs in particular. To demonstrate this even more clearly, Smith, who worked closely with their US operations, and Primo, who oversaw all the SGBD service functions in Paris, were also making presentations at the Nice meeting. Their presence, together with attendance and participation by senior Calchem executives, would also reinforce internal commitment and understanding among the Schneider IACs in attendance. The workshop was designed to address existing issues and to highlight future challenges. For example, in this workshop, Keller knew that Smith would openly accept the blame for a design problem encountered by Calchem in the US in order to defuse the client's anger about what had been a sensitive issue in the relationship. He would also use the occasion to underscore, for both Calchem and the Schneider IACs, how the problem had been satisfactorily resolved. Keller anticipated that some of the IACs would likely disagree with his counterpart's *mea culpa* approach. That was one of the reasons he had built into the program a half-day training session on cross-cultural understanding, using a professor who had worked at other GSA-Schneider workshops.

KELLER'S CHALLENGES

This expected negative reaction from one or two of the IACs from Latin cultures reflected one of the issues facing Keller as he attempted to sell the global approach to local sale forces. As Keller put it:

The local service and sales engineers are essential to our local presence. With the GAM approach, they are afraid of losing power and independence, and tend to resist its implementation in their area. My job is to help them understand that I bring with me the resources of the whole company to support their needs.

He added:

In many projects, one or two delivering countries will benefit from the business, while other countries will provide support without benefiting from the business generated. These countries may feel that they have had costs at no advantage. However, they receive sales credits for their involvement. The country of delivery (country who gets the order), country of influence (the one who provides the equipment), country of engineering and country of destination all receive sales credits.

Primo supported this view:

Consistency of account coverage is always important with any account, but this is even more important for global strategic accounts (GSA). Global strategic accounts become very dependent upon the IAM and IAC once a strong relationship and a sense of trust are built up. This relationship-building and the gaining of the trust of the global strategic account may take several years in both the home country and in other countries. For this reason it is important to have the same people calling on the GSA over a span of years. In the major large country organizations this is usually not much of an issue. However, in smaller country organizations with higher turnover of personnel, it is sometimes hard to keep the same IAC calling on the GSA for more then a year or two.

For example, during the same week as the Calchem workshop, Keller organized a two-day workshop with Lactal, the second Swiss-based multinational qualified as a GSA. This saved travel costs since most of the IAC and SGBD attendees would be participating in both meetings. Schneider Mexico did not plan to send any participants to the Lactal workshop despite Keller's attempt to convince the Mexicans of the value of their attendance. He had tried to demonstrate the value by insisting on the importance of the Lactal account in Mexico. Although both Switzerland (as the country of the client HQ) and the US (as the provider of the equipment) would be rewarded for participating in the process, Schneider's Mexican subsidiary would receive a sales credit of 20% for further growth of the business in the country.

The biggest tensions arose with countries that did not run highly profitable organizations and therefore could not support the costs of an IAM or an IAC. LeBlanc gave the example of a European subsidiary that hosted the headquarters of two global accounts, but could not or would not support an IAM.

In this specific case, I sent the country manager an ultimatum: should he continue to resist investing in an IAM, the two accounts would be disqualified. Disqualification of an account could have serious repercussions. In most cases a country covers both a global account and that account's key suppliers. So losing an account often means losing more than one client.

He added:

> The high degree of commitment by Schneider senior management to GAM sends a clear message throughout the organization that management at all levels needs to support the concept. To assist the less profitable countries, a regional head may decide to support an IAM for a local subsidiary and carry him for a year. The four executive vice presidents for Schneider's world regions sit on SGBD's executive committee. We meet three to four times a year and address unresolved resource allocation issues such as this one. This helps IAMs like Keller to do their jobs more effectively.

Networking within Schneider was an equally important challenge for Keller, who noted:

> The main task of an international account manager is the development of a network that will enable him to bring the value of the whole company, 64,000 people, to the service of the customer. When I travel to France or the US I spend a lot of time in the engineering centers meeting engineers and software developers – the very people who are crucial in delivering a customized solution to the client. I get to know them and their capacities and they get to understand how I can connect them to customers. For example, while I was in Canada working to expand our opportunities with a Swiss-based company I am trying to add to our GSA list, I added several days to my trip to introduce myself to key Schneider manufacturing managers in the US Midwest.

Keeping up with the heavy information requirements of the GAM system was also an issue. Finding an effective process for updating and accessing information that was fast and simple required designing a new information system. In the words of Primo:

> Information systems to support the international account managers are a critical element in our success with global strategic accounts. In a networked virtual organization such as ours, the sharing and communication of information between all parties involved in support of the account is key. Development of these systems is not easy. It is vital to identify the most important pieces of information needed. This avoids overloading the account managers and others with requests for too much information. It also keeps the data bases from getting too large.

The initial system, based on Lotus Notes, was far too heavy and complicated and many account managers avoided using it as much as possible. As Keller described it:

> The account plan "main menu" includes an executive summary with general customer information about headquarters, products, organization, strategy and a consolidation of the local country files, e.g., sales to the account, contacts, locations, etc. Each IAC can read all the information, but is only able to enter information into his own country file. An important part is the discussion forum, which allows sharing of information on projects, new solutions, presentations, etc. In the SGBD headquarters, it is possible to consolidate all GSA information and analyze geographic, cluster or business unit sales development. It is a very useful internal tool, but also has some disadvantages. First, since it is primarily for internal use, it doesn't give direct added-value to the customer. Second, since many IACs are responsible for four to eight accounts in one country, the requirement to update local actions is a heavy task. It requires the IAM to provide very strong motivation to the IAC to keep the data current.

Therefore Keller developed a number of simplified paper-based solutions using various worksheets. These tools provided information that also added direct value to the customer. They included an Excel contact list that showed each of the customer's engineering centers and their locations, together with their sub-suppliers and the corresponding Schneider contacts. A project list and several presentations for IACs and local sales engineers were also available in PowerPoint format. In the early project phases, these types of information helped convince engineers and sub-suppliers of Schneider's close relationship with and knowledge about Calchem.

In addition, the SGBD network provided corporate and country presentations, information about references and applications and various directories.

Receiving support from his local boss to develop the IAM activity in Switzerland represented a further challenge to Keller. The Swiss president focused on P&L; naturally, he concentrated mainly on the Swiss business, the full range of Schneider products and services, and was therefore less prone to absorb the costs of additional IAMs, the benefits of which would be deferred. Additionally none of Calchem's 160 plants was located in Switzerland, which meant no direct revenue was credited to the Swiss P&L.

While Keller was already carrying more than his share by supporting two GSAs (as opposed to the usual "one account one IAM" approach in Schneider), he had already identified further business opportunities in Switzerland. Local sales forces were in contact with a large construction company, headquartered in Switzerland, for which Keller had identified a potential $40 million contract at three sites in Canada and the US. Keller had met the local IACs but felt that his concentrating on this additional account diluted his efforts with his two existing GSAs. To reap the benefits of this additional GSA he would need support from an additional IAM based in Switzerland. This revealed the generic problem between measurement and rewards from the country heads as profit centers based on local P&L versus the investment needed initially to generate new revenues and profit from the global account.

As he looked ahead to the excitement of the workshop in Nice, Keller also knew that he should be thinking about these challenges during the meetings, too. Some ways of dealing with the issues might well emerge from the discussions with the various people he was looking forward to seeing.

Notes

1   The brand names were retained, as in most markets there was greater customer recognition for the individual brands than there was for the Schneider brand.
2   A joint venture owned by Finland's Ahlstrom and Denmark's NKT Holding.
3   Each IAM had a senior executive from the parent corporation who was a top-level contact with the global strategic accounts associated with that IAM and who served as a mentor for the IAM. Fritz Keller's corporate sponsor was François LeBlanc, the head of the SGBD organization.
4   A cluster was a business area. For Schneider these included food & beverages, automotive, pharmaceuticals, and microelectronics.
5   Lane, H. W., J. J. DiStefano, and M. L. Maznevski. *International Management Behavior.* 3rd ed., Cambridge, USA: Blackwell Publishers, 1997: 192.

Marconi Telecommunications Mexico

Henry W. Lane, Daniel D. Campbell, and David T. A. Wesley

On January 12, 1997, Marconi Telecommunications Corporation (Martel) signed a letter of intent to purchase control of Lerida Telecom of Mexico, a leading telecommunications provider in Mexico with approximately 2,300 employees. Lerida operated 85 customer service centers throughout the country and had a full-time staff of 92 corporate sales representatives. It also had agreements with 39 distributors, including one majority-owned subsidiary of Lerida, which operated over 125 distribution locations. One year later, 14 Martel managers had been moved to Mexico.

On June 21, 1997, Martel announced that it had signed a letter of intent to purchase an interest in Communicaciones Carmona in Chile from the controlling shareholder. Two weeks later the company announced that it had signed a non-binding letter of intent to purchase a minority stake in Panamanian Cable Provider, RadioTelevisivo Panama, subject to the completion of a due diligence review and regulatory approval. The company also had minority interests in Colombia and Martel representatives were pursuing opportunities in Brazil, Venezuela and Bolivia.

Senior executives knew that one of their most pressing issues would be finding the right people to manage their Latin American operations. The plan was to build a team

IVEY Daniel D. Campbell and David T. A. Wesley prepared this case under the supervision of Professor Henry W. Lane solely to provide material for class discussion. The authors do not intend to illustrate either effective or ineffective handling of a managerial situation. The authors may have disguised certain names and other identifying information to protect confidentiality.

at Lerida and use these managers in other Latin American countries. Martel had traditionally enjoyed success when placing managers in foreign countries, but executives wondered what had been learned from the recent experience in selecting and preparing managers for Mexico, and whether the current systems and plans would support the anticipated expansion.

BACKGROUND

Marconi Telecommunications Corporation was one of Canada's most international telecommunications providers. Although Martel owned minority positions in a few companies in Europe, it primarily focused on high growth opportunities in emerging markets, principally in Latin America and in Asia. Martel's expansion into emerging markets was fuelled by opportunities and by a need for growth. The Canadian market was very competitive with a lot of domestic competition as well as competition from giant American firms like AT&T and Sprint.

In 1997, Martel operated in 12 countries with approximately 3,700 employees. It owned, developed and operated telecommunication systems such as cellular networks, PCS, paging systems, cable television, local telephone networks, long distance and fixed wireless.

Minority interests

Martel began by purchasing minority equity interests in Latin American companies. Often, a single family controlled these institutions. However, an opportunity usually came to take a majority position. This was particularly true in times of financial crisis when the companies and their principal shareholders became strapped for cash.

Another reason for taking a minority interest was the company's lack of personnel to staff the operations. Few managers were familiar with Latin America or spoke Spanish. It was Martel's practice to send a small number of managers to the companies in which it held a minority interest.

Building a competency

In 1990, anticipating Latin American expansion, Frank Kelly, who had just become the head of Latin America for Martel, each year began hiring recent graduates with appropriate backgrounds from MBA programs. In addition to their technical education and MBAs, they also had substantial Latin American backgrounds and spoke Spanish. These managers then began a four- to six-year tour of duty within the Canadian operations that exposed them to many aspects of the company's core businesses. Once they were familiar with the company's practices in Canada, it was expected that they would form the nucleus of a team that could manage a Latin American operation on behalf of Martel. By 1996, the company had hired about 12 managers with a Latin American background and had retained 10 of them.

Opportunity knocks

Mexico's Secretariat of Communications and Transportation (SCT) began to deregulate telecommunications services in Mexico in 1990 with the privatization of Teléfonos de Mexico (Telmex), the national phone company. Telmex was granted protection from competition in local service until the year 2026, but all other services, such as data communications, satellite, cellular, and long distance, were opened to domestic and foreign competition. However, the SCT still maintained strict regulatory control on pricing. In 1997, Telmex faced a significant backlog in requests for new telephone line installations. By 1998, a number of multinational providers had entered the Mexican market, such as Bell Atlantic, Southwestern Bell, MCI, and France Telecom.

The currency crisis that began in late 1994 destabilized the Mexican economy and created an opportunity to purchase Lerida at an attractive price. Management believed that they could administer the operation and, after a period of difficult negotiations, bought Lerida.

"It's a great opportunity," said John Dolan, Chairman of Martel, shortly after completing the deal. "We're really into this for the very, very, long run. It's a part of our international telecommunications network." Separately, Dolan said: "I view Mexico as having enormous opportunity. It has 100 million people and it's part of NAFTA." Although the level of penetration with respect to the number of installed lines per capita was relatively low in Mexico, the demand for new services was very strong. Demand was expected to continue growing at a much higher rate than in the United States or Canada.

Martel and Lerida finally agreed that no more than 14 managers would be sent to Mexico at any one time. Kelly felt that 14 was ideal, in part because there were not more qualified staff to send, but also because more than 14 might appear too much like a conquest. Instead, management sought to create an atmosphere of partnership. This philosophy differed from that of some of the other foreign companies that chose to transfer more expatriate managers to the companies they had purchased.

As part of the due diligence to evaluate the investment in Lerida, approximately 25 managers were sent to Mexico. The group was made up of functional teams chosen by their team leaders. Virtually all of the Canadian company's employees with Spanish language competence were included on the various teams. The remainder of the team was selected for their technical skills.

STAFFING THE NEW OPERATION

In the normal process of selecting candidates for international placement, recruiting was done both internally and externally as the company tried to identify individuals with the skills required for an overseas assignment. Internally, a system of job postings called International Opportunities was used that listed the position and the requirements. This system was designed to provide an internal source of managers for a training pool. Martel also recruited at universities and searched for external candidates.

People who had been identified through these processes were then interviewed by a panel of four managers including three from line functions and one from International

Human Resources. The successful applicants were streamed according to function (network, commercial sales) and regional pools (Latin America, Asia) and their development needs were identified. At the time seven slots were available in the management training program.

Language was a priority, but often other technical skills were major concerns as well. Most often, the external hires were individuals with limited telecommunications experience but who had an ability to function in Latin America, whereas internal hires often resulted from searches for skill requirements.

Those selected began an international orientation, based in Ottawa, that provided increased contact with international offices. Martel used a variety of methods including assignments on project teams and three-month "test" postings. Orientation lasted between three months and two years after which employees had a better sense of whether or not they were prepared for an international assignment. Some backed out at that point, but many could not wait to leave.

Sudden demand for managers

During negotiations, it did not appear that an agreement was possible and no one at Martel was expecting to complete the deal. However, at the last minute, the industrial group that owned Lerida agreed to additional concessions and a deal was reached. This sudden reversal created an unexpected and immediate demand for managers. Martel's International Human Resources (IHR) department was charged with the extremely difficult task of identifying and relocating a management team for the new company in a very short period of time. The 14 managers to be sent to Mexico were double the numbers then being prepared for that type of assignment.

Frank Kelly became president of the Mexican operations. A veteran in the telecommunications industry was selected to head up Lerida's residential services division. Two other senior, experienced Canadians were chosen to co-ordinate the cellular network and information systems and to be in charge of all commercial sales. These three executives then chose their respective teams to accompany them to Mexico.

Aside from those that had been originally hired specifically for their ability to speak Spanish and their knowledge of Latin America, individuals were chosen based on their technical expertise in areas deemed critical to the success of Lerida.

The expatriate managers assigned to Mexico fell into three broad categories: a) "traditional" managers with little or no previous international experience, b) the young "international" managers with a previous background in Latin America but without significant telecommunications experience, and c) a group that combined the traditional and the international. This latter group comprised experienced telecommunications professionals with previous international experience and/or who had emigrated from Latin America.

The "traditional" managers (6) ranged in age from 46 to 65 (average age approximately 54 years), were married with a family, Canadian, and had never worked outside of Canada before. This group comprised the senior managers with strong technical skills. The "traditional and international" group (4) were between 34 and 59 years of age (average age approximately 45 years), spoke Spanish and had previous international experience.

In contrast, the "international" managers (4) were in their early 30s, most were single, spoke Spanish fluently and had lived and worked in Latin America. Frank Kelly characterized them as world citizens who "were comfortable everywhere." They were MBAs that had completed the basic training programs through the Head Office and also held degrees in Engineering.

Human resources: process of expatriation

It was Martel's policy[1] to provide a compensation package for managers undertaking international assignments that was competitive with other major international telecommunications providers. It would allow managers to maintain, to the extent local conditions permitted, a standard of living comparable to that available in their home countries.

The policy was designed to be equal to or superior to the average of other telecommunications companies from Canada, the United States and Europe. The total compensation (salary plus benefits and allowances) was competitive. However, Jeff York, director of IHR, believed that the base salaries alone might have been less than those of competitors and this made Martel somewhat vulnerable.

The standard package of benefits covered housing, schools, compensation, relocation, automobiles, taxation and all other issues associated with the assignment. This package applied to all managers and their families. It included some additional benefits specifically for the executives being transferred to Mexico. The housing allowance was higher than normal; a security allowance was included as well as a pollution relief allowance. To claim benefits under this latter allowance, an executive and his family had to physically leave Mexico City one week-end each month during the seven worst months for pollution (November-May). An upper limit for expenses had been established and executives had to file an expense report to claim the allowance.

Although IHR was the principal point of support for employees beginning an international assignment, many other areas of the company provided services during the process. These included Relocation Services (moving, travel, hotels, selling house), Health (counselling employees and families about health risks, detailed discussions as necessary), Security (one-on-one meeting with employee to discuss country risk), and Finance (financial planning). In addition to these standard services, Martel's finance department arranged for an investment consultant to make a presentation on offshore investment opportunities not available in Canada and Martel provided an expense-paid trip to visit Mexico to see housing and schools.

It was also the general practice of the company to appoint a relationship manager for areas like Latin America to interact with the company's expatriates and to use a subsidiary company to provide on-site support. However, Martel was not able to use the services of Lerida, because the company relocated managers before it took formal control. Instead, it relied on a senior manager with many years' experience in Latin America and a local relocation company. The relocation office arranged local real estate services. However, because of the large number of managers and families moving at the same time, it was impossible to provide the same level of on-site support that had been customary with prior international transfers within the company.

To avoid unnecessary travel, employees were asked to complete a list of requirements they needed to have satisfied before they would move in order to identify potential "deal breakers". IHR had a firm view about not negotiating individual packages, according to York.

> We want to make sure there is a serious intent to go and that it is not just a vacation or fishing trip. If a person's spouse has a career and is making a big salary, we can't replace that, so let's not fool ourselves.
>
> Our policies are flexible to handle differences between countries. We can't do 200 different, individual contracts. That would be unfair, particularly if one person were a better negotiator. Occasionally, exceptions are made, but only in very rare cases.

When employees felt comfortable with the provisions being made, IHR provided them the opportunity to visit the country with their spouses to see where they would be living and to know what schools were available.

Reactions by executives and their spouses to IHR Policies generally varied by age, family status and group ("traditional", "traditional and international", "international"). Similarly, ease of adaptation to Mexico varied by group.

To go or not to go?

Generally, after being asked, managers reserved the final decision about accepting the position until they discussed it with their spouses and families. Most of the managers who were asked to move already had spent up to a month in Mexico during the due diligence. However, most of the spouses had never been to Mexico City:

> My husband came home and said that they had offered him this great job. Our daughter could go to private school and they are going to pay for the residence fees of our two other children while they studied at university. It all sounded wonderful. I think I said yes without really knowing what we were headed for.

Some managers were unhappy with the process used by IHR. Some wanted guarantees about what would be provided for them once they arrived in Mexico. Many were frustrated by what they perceived as rigidity on the part of IHR and felt that there should have been more ability to negotiate with reference to personal circumstances.

There also was some concern about the lack of career planning regarding jobs for managers when the time came for them to return to Canada. Managers cynically commented that those returning from an overseas position often found themselves regarded as surplus employees with no plan for their re-integration into the domestic organization.

The decision was more complicated for dual career families. The company's position was clear. Its obligation was to secure a work permit for the employee. The spouse might or might not be able to work. Several spouses had careers and these families had to think about whether or not the spouse would be able to find work in Mexico or even receive permission to work under Mexican immigration laws. There were concerns expressed about the loss of a second income and what the spouse could do to occupy spare time.

Among the young, "international" managers, the feeling was that the package of benefits was good, but their perception was that other companies' salaries were higher.

IHR eventually resolved most of the major obstacles. One by one, after they had found homes and suitable schools, the managers informed the company that they were prepared to move to Mexico. Most of the employees were excited by the prospect – a change, a new challenge. As one executive stated,

> I thought working in Mexico would be a wonderful opportunity. Canadian companies have a bureaucracy and hierarchy that has been built up over many years. The opportunity to advance and try something more challenging was certainly there on the international side. That was the main motivating factor.

Although most managers embraced the new job opportunity with a high level of excitement, the families shared varying levels of concern about leaving behind their communities, good friends, relatives and children who would remain in school in Canada. Those who did not speak Spanish shared additional anxiety.

Preparation

Everyone agreed that they received very little formal preparation before going to Mexico. Managers with previous experience in Mexico or other Latin American countries were not concerned by the lack of preparation. The "traditional" executives had mixed feelings about the level of preparation that they had received. Martel sponsored a one-day program offered in Ottawa. Many felt that was not sufficient. One commented,

> There just wasn't enough preparation done for moving a group this size. The program in Ottawa wasn't sufficient. We probably needed two to three days and we needed to talk with people from Mexico. There needed to be more done for the wives and children.

However, another manager viewed it differently.

> Preparation was basically nothing. I don't necessarily think that was a bad thing. You could spend five years preparing, or five days. From my standpoint, there were so many things that I wasn't prepared for that jumping into the deep end was probably as good as anything.

A manager with previous international and Mexican experience added,

> There was really no preparation by the company. Some Mexican gentleman did a one-day seminar. It was interesting but not very useful.

The spouses of the traditional managers felt a strong need for more preparation and more information. One went to the library for articles or books on living in Mexico but could not find anything recent. She talked with a friend at work that had lived there who talked about all the good times.

Another spouse commented:

The company employees had some kind of meeting to talk about houses and salaries, but the spouses were excluded from any sort of formal "orientation" that may have been done by the company.

After arrival, these spouses discovered the *New Arrival Survival Guide* published by the Newcomers Club of Mexico City:

> This book had a couple of hundred pages of good information. We never had this information. I also met the wife of a P & G executive who said that they had had an appointment with the U.S. Embassy first thing to talk about what to expect and the dangers of the country.

Language

> We had planned to begin taking Spanish lessons when we arrived. Looking back on it, we should have started the day we said "yes".

Prior to the transfer, the company hired Spanish teachers in Ottawa for employees who had the time and motivation to study the language. Employees and their families were also informed about a language school in Cuernavaca, near Mexico City. Some Martel executives, as well as their spouses, took advantage of this opportunity and spent several weeks studying at this language and cultural training centre. The centre offered intensive eight-hour days of Spanish language instruction, both one-on-one and in small groups. Classes on Mexican culture were also available.

Most of the managers attending the centre arrived with limited Spanish skills and were overwhelmed by the amount of information they were trying to absorb:

> It was very difficult to learn. There was only so much new information I could absorb. It probably would have been better if I had started the school with a base to begin with. I should have started language training in Ottawa. In Cuernavaca, I was too much in awe of everything.

After being in Mexico for awhile, most of the traditional managers and their families realized that, although there were often people available that spoke both English and Spanish, if they were going to integrate themselves into their living and working environments, they had to learn Spanish. They also began to learn that speaking only with Mexicans that spoke both English and Spanish had severe limitations. One manager commented:

> I find that I spend a lot more time with employees who are bilingual. I wasn't able to communicate directly with employees that only spoke Spanish. I often had to speak through someone who spoke both languages, but I never knew if my message was getting through the way that I intended it. I think often, it didn't.

Others had similar feelings:

> The language was the biggest issue. Anyone that tries to work down here without the language will fail or at least be frustrated for a very long time.

Some managers found themselves in situations where most, or at least key, subordinates spoke only Spanish and, therefore, had to speak Spanish immediately. At Santa Fe (the administrative center) nearly all of the employees were unilingual. Others had numerous English speakers in their departments but chose to conduct meetings in Spanish, despite the initial inconvenience. These managers learned the language quickly. Still others found the expediency of the tasks at hand too important to be slowed by a new language and often worked more closely with their English-speaking subordinates or through an interpreter. It was apparent that this practice, however, could not last:

> Over the past several months, I've noticed a change in the tolerance level of the Mexicans to work or think in a different language (English). I think their expectations are now "you have been here a year, you should know more than three words" and I can understand that perfectly.

Other managers observed:

> You are paid to manage a company. It is not possible if you don't speak the language.
>   You can't ask them to write project reports in English or to translate all their documents.
>   One of my strengths in Ottawa was an ability to communicate with people. That's gone.

Outside of the work environment, language was also a barrier when trying to meet Mexicans socially.

Arriving in Mexico

The majority of expatriates and their families went to Mexico City. The Mexico City metropolitan area was estimated to have about 22 million inhabitants making it one of the world's largest cities, maybe the largest. Although it was a fascinating city, rich in culture, history and social activities, it also had a reputation for being a very difficult place to live, due to serious pollution and crime problems.

For the executives and their spouses who had previous experience in Latin America the move was not difficult. One person had gone to Latin America 20 years earlier and had learned the language. His wife was Mexican and they had family and friends in the city. They received no preparation, got on an airplane and found a house on their own. A second spouse rented a car the day after arriving and drove outside the city to the home in which she was going to live and started preparing it for possession.

Another manager commented,

> When I moved to Mexico City I spoke the language and I had one suitcase so it was easy. The biggest problem was learning my way around the city.

He added that since both he and his wife spoke Spanish, had minored in Latin American studies, had worked in Latin America, neither had required much preparation or support. They found their own house in an old colonial section of the city.

However, the situation was very different for the traditional managers and their spouses. During the initial visits to look for housing and schools, the company hired a firm to help families as well as to look after other aspects of their relocation when they arrived in Mexico. Executives and their spouses were shuttled from place to place by representatives from the relocation company and were sheltered from many of the challenges of getting around in a new city. Even so, what they did see and experience was often a shock. One manager recalled:

> A lot of places had big security gates. That was a brand new feeling for those of us who were not accustomed to it. The least safe area in Ottawa didn't have barbed wire or guards. That was a real shock to my wife. When she saw where I was going to work and two guys with machine guns standing out front, that was a big shock.

His wife commented:

> The armed guards in front of people's driveways, in front of stores, in front of the schools that we went to look at were pretty scary. The representative from the relocation company kept saying that those people must have a lot of money or be politicians and that's why they needed armed guards. What I didn't understand was that we were going to be one of those people. In Ottawa, relatively speaking, we were just average "Joes" with a three-bedroom house and a yard.

One spouse remembered:

> We had someone holding us by the hand, driving us around most of the time. We had been to restaurants and a nice hotel that I'm sure had experience with English-speaking foreigners. Then we went to the airport to go home. We were on our own and there were so many people. We had been dropped right in the middle of Mexico. It seemed like nobody wanted to help us, and we didn't know how to ask anyway.

In the early days after moving permanently, the families of traditional managers began encountering new challenges. None felt they had a strong enough grasp of the language to live and function in Mexico on their own. The problems began the first day when they began setting up their homes, and later continued into the workplace. Not speaking Spanish and being unfamiliar with their surroundings, some of the routine activities associated with moving a household became almost insurmountable obstacles. This manager's experience was not atypical:

> My dryer had a three-pronged plug but the wall socket had only two. I needed to hire a plumber and an electrician. We had no idea how to do that at first, especially without speaking the language. I wish there could have been someone assigned to us for the first couple of days after we moved in to help with the little things.

Many of the Canadians expected the relocation company to look after a lot of the small details. Very few people were happy with the service provided to them in the early days after arrival. This manager was an exception:

> A lot of people were unhappy with the relocation company, but that really depended on what their expectations were. I wanted to know what schools were available and I wanted a

house with three bedrooms in a good area. They met those expectations. Anyone who had a bad experience had unrealistic expectations about what someone else was going to do for them.

Some managers chose to live outside Mexico City in a private, gated community to avoid the crime and pollution. However, they had a long commute early in the morning and late at night and their children attended school in the city, which negated some of the benefits.

Pollution was on the minds of the executives who lived in the city. One said that pollution was more of an issue for him than security. Another commented,

> Some days it's bad. You have to wonder what you are doing to your health. If I had little children I wouldn't be here.

A few of the "traditional and international" expatriates and their families went to live in cities other than Mexico City. Guadalajara, Mexico's second largest city, was easier to adapt to than the capital, but it had many of the problems associated with large population centers. Monterrey, on the other hand, was characterized as a "piece of cake", especially in a section called Garza Garcia:

> Everything worked. The police were not corrupt and you could call the telephone company in the morning and have your phone installed in the afternoon.

Even for executives who had prior Latin American experience and spoke the language, moving to Mexico did not always go smoothly. One family had their flight canceled in Montreal and did not arrive in Guadalajara until midnight.

> We were met by a chauffeur in a new Suburban that the company bought for us and we went to a hotel. The next morning the real estate agent met us and accompanied us to our house that, like all the homes, was surrounded by high walls. The agent forgot the garage door opener and went back to the office to get it. When she returned she asked us where our car was. It had been stolen from in front of our house on our first day in Mexico. My wife just looked at me and said, "Where have you brought us? I want to go home!"

Dual-career families

Generally, under Mexican law, spouses who were not Mexican citizens were not able to work during their stay in the country. Giving up jobs at home had been hard for some. Unable to work, and alone while their partners were at the company, the spouses took golfing lessons at the local country club and the majority studied Spanish throughout the week, but there were still a lot of hours left in the day:

> You can find lots of things to keep you busy, but finding a new purpose is difficult. I feel like my brain is becoming mush.

One executive commented that his wife always reminded him that she gave up a job and career to move to Mexico.

Even if they could work, most felt that they did not have a strong enough command of the language to function in a job. The same was true for volunteer work. In fact, several were turned down when they offered to work for a charity organization.

In one instance, IHR agreed to secure the services of an employment agency to find a position for one of the spouses. It also assisted in the process of changing her immigration status to allow her to work in Mexico. Even so, after one year, she had been unable to find employment, in part, due to a lack of Spanish language skills:

> I now know what my work really meant to me. At first, I felt like I lost my identity when I lost my job. I haven't replaced it with anything yet but now, what I first saw as a loss, I now see as an opportunity. There are probably a million things I can do, once I know Spanish a little better. It's changed from something pretty awful to something that has a lot of potential.

An ability to speak Spanish and prior experience in Latin America made a big difference in securing employment. One spouse, an American fluent in Spanish, had been a Latin American Officer in the US Peace Corps. She was hired by a US government agency in Mexico City and then went to an international foundation.

Isolation: feeling alone among 22 million people

The young managers, and those with previous Latin American experience, loved their life-styles. They had Mexican friends and adapted easily. One view was that "Socially, it's a blast."

On the other hand, the traditional managers and their spouses often had a more difficult time. One noted, "I'm not experiencing Mexico."

Outside of work-related activities, many of the Canadians found it difficult to form friendships with Mexicans. Generally, their social activities revolved around other families in the Martel team or other Canadian or American expatriates they met. The social contact they had with Mexicans was the occasional event with subordinates and their families.

Occasionally, their partner's unhappiness had an impact on the performance of some of the managers. Contributing to this unhappiness was a growing security risk, both real and perceived, that distanced the expatriates from Mexico.

Even after a year of living in Mexico, some of the families felt no more integrated into the country and culture than when they had first arrived. The spouse of one of the managers commented:

> There is a definite sense of not belonging. This isn't our home. Even just walking around, sometimes there is a sense of people looking at you like you are a foreigner. We're the minority here. Another spouse asked me "We are never going to belong here, are we? We are always going to be 'extranjeros.'" (foreigners)

However, some individuals had a different reaction:

> We were told before we came down here that it was hard to make friends with the Mexicans. I don't know if that's true. My husband has made friends with several Mexicans at work. I just don't come into contact with Mexicans as much as the others.

Many of the managers chose to live in an exclusive development outside of Mexico City called Valle de Ayora in an upscale suburb of the city known as Desierto de Leones. Desierto de Leones was the residence of Spanish aristocrats when Mexico was a colony of Spain. Walls and security gates surrounded the Valle de Ayora enclave. Armed guards at another set of gates also controlled the entrance into the general area. Because many of the families had chosen to live there, Valle de Ayora soon came to be referred to as Fort Marconi among Martel employees.

Families living there enjoyed many benefits associated with living outside of Mexico City, not the least of which were cleaner air, increased security, and quiet. However, it also increased the feelings of isolation and separation. The feeling of isolation was intensified for the spouses of Martel managers because they lacked the regular contact with other people from whom their partners benefited at work.

> A couple of weeks after I got here, I remember thinking "there's 22 million people in this city and not one of them is my friend".

Some managers rejected Valle de Ayora and chose to live in upscale neighborhoods within Mexico City. One spouse, referring to the level of isolation, commented, "I think I would go mad living in Fort Marconi."

For the traditional managers and their families, adaptation was slow but usually came:

> Even though things are getting better, some days are awful. I don't know if there will ever come a time where there won't be ups and downs, but it seems to be evening out a bit.
> You have to get on with living. A major milestone is adapting.

Security and safety

> These people have no money. They are getting desperate and its only going to get worse.

One thing everyone agreed upon and on which they shared the same viewpoint was security. Following the currency crisis in December 1994, the Mexican economy deteriorated rapidly. Inflation initially soared to more than 100 percent while wages were held relatively constant. As economic conditions grew worse, Mexico City began to experience a sharp increase in street crime. Tourists, expatriates, and Mexicans were all targets for armed robbery, pick pocketing and purse snatching.

Mexico City police offered little relief and, in fact, were often reported as the perpetrators of crime. Police routinely stopped vehicles with illegitimate charges of traffic violations in order to demand money. Most of the Martel team had been forced to pay police for alleged traffic violations, often on more than one occasion. Police would even accompany them to an automated teller machine to withdraw funds. According to one manager experienced in Mexico, "The police in Mexico City are not your friends. I go to great lengths to stay away from them."

Another executive who had previously lived in Mexico said,

Mexico is quite dangerous in some places. It is a much more dangerous place now than it was 15 years ago. If you go around the city and engage in lots of activities, you have more exposure. Some people isolate themselves.

Some of the expatriates, regardless of experience or language ability, had frightening experiences. One of the older, traditional managers had a friend murdered in another city and one of the young "international" managers was robbed at gunpoint. Another executive survived an attempted kidnapping:

I was driving home from work about 8 p.m. A car was stopped in traffic in front of me and I noticed another on an angle behind me, blocking me in. The next thing I knew, there was a noise like something was hitting the window of the car. I thought it was kids throwing stones. I looked over my shoulder and saw a gun pointed at me. I looked out the passenger window and saw another gun. When I opened the door, I was hit on the head with a gun as they tried to force me to move over and allow them into the car. I tried to move over but couldn't because my car had a center console in the front seat. Then, realizing I didn't want to go anywhere with these guys, I pushed the door open, jumped out, and then dove over the car next to mine. A shot was fired as I jumped and I heard another shot as I ran. When I finally looked back, my car was still there with the doors wide open, but the attackers were gone.

The spouse and son of one of the Canadian managers were stopped by police, dragged from the car and searched for drugs.

The company, in its country and security allowances, had taken steps to compensate employees for the level of country hardship and risk. IHR used an external consulting service to conduct an independent hardship evaluation of the countries in which the company operated. This evaluation had three components, 1) threat (personal), 2) discomfort (availability of medical services), and 3) inconvenience (availability of goods and services). It was updated twice a year. Mexico ranked 26 of 51 countries and IHR checked this ranking against other sources. Martel managers received twice the percentage allowance for Mexico compared to the US State Department. Because of the number of expatriates sent to Mexico there was an increased risk of something happening.

The company's security consultant was sent to Mexico to evaluate the situation. The consultant had travelled to most of the countries where the company had offices, and commented to employees that he had never seen anything as bad as the situation in Mexico.

On the Martel team were some very senior executives, as well as middle to upper level managers. The different ranks received different levels of security such as drivers and alarms for their houses. Many families became upset at the differences. One manager commented:

Security should not be a perk. Basic common safety should be for everybody; it shouldn't depend on rank. Some of the lower level managers had to ask "Why is that person's life more important than mine?"

The expatriates felt that they were experiencing random crime. There was no pattern of kidnapping or assaulting senior managers of multinational corporations. Employees realized, however, that managers with drivers had not had a single incident; those without drivers all had problems.

There was an internal debate at headquarters whether to provide additional money and let the employees purchase their own security services and hire a driver or to reimburse them for the actual expenses incurred. The company decided to provide additional funds that were distributed to individual employees to use as they saw fit (e.g., hire a driver). The Security Department promised to hire security consultants to advise each family on their particular security risks, but three months later that had not happened. Jeff York commented that those services were supposed to come directly from Lerida, which made it more difficult for them to control.

> A Mexican firm represented itself as being able to deliver security services in English, but it couldn't.

Company employees became more sensitive after the attempted kidnapping. Although they were upset at the security situation, they were more upset by the manner in which the situation was handled:

> If we had known about the security risks before we had come, we would probably still be here, but we would be better prepared emotionally.
>
> After blaming the company for all of the problems on earth, at one point I had to ask myself "if I was in their shoes, what could I realistically do?" Other than being on the other end of the phone and being a little more understanding, there was little more I could realistically do. Just a kind word once in a while would mean a lot.

Monterrey was felt to be a safer city than either Mexico or Guadalajara. An executive who lived in Guadalajara had multi-level security – a security system in the house, a 10,000-volt electric fence, and a neighborhood security guard.

Work and compensation

Martel had lost three employees with previous Latin American experience to companies that offered more money. Team leaders believed there was a risk of additional losses among the younger managers.

Frank Kelly felt that one of the biggest problems was the compensation system. He explained:

> It's very competitive here. The European salaries are higher than the American salaries, which are higher than the Canadians' salaries. A person could be transferred from the Miami office of the company and earn more than his Canadian boss. That's wrong.
>
> We've lost three good young executives in the last couple of months. Other companies just buy them out.

The company based its international compensation on salaries of similar managers of other Canadian multinationals with expatriate managers, but a situation had developed where there were differences between the Canadian and international market for telecommunications professionals.

In the international market place for managers, competition for talented professionals had driven salaries higher. This effect was multiplied in Latin America as international companies continued to expand rapidly throughout the region. Demand for experienced managers with Latin American experience drove salaries well beyond what a typical manager working in Canada with similar experience could expect.

> They can go work for any company in the world that does business in Latin America and double their salary.
> One year of experience here is worth 10 years anywhere else. You see so many problems that you have to solve.

Some of the Martel managers working in Latin America did not think that the compensation packages were competitive with the marketplace. The company had begun to offer additional benefits, and some came in the form of salary increases:

> The company seems to be very careful about what they will give you because they want to make sure that when you go back to Canada, they can take it all away. Additional benefits always seemed to be directly associated with working in Mexico such as athletic club memberships.

The work hours were long and there was not a lot of opportunity to take advantage of clubs:

> I've never worked harder in my life. I leave the house at 6:30. Two nights ago I got home at 11:30 and last night at 10:30. And this was not cocktail circuit stuff. Everybody is working hard. The rewards are high but the costs are high also.

However, managers felt that the challenging work was an important motivating factor. Interesting work compensated for lower salaries, at least in the short term. One of the most attractive aspects of the jobs in Mexico for the Canadian managers was the perception that they could make a difference. This was true regardless of their age, seniority or experience. Their high level of autonomy, coupled with the challenge of modernizing Lerida in this competitive market provided a level of satisfaction that many managers believed was the greatest reward for their efforts.

A senior executive thought the company did well in recognizing that it could not run Lerida from Ottawa.

> We have a lot of autonomy. It is not necessary to clear everything with Ottawa. It's my plan and I'm committed.

And it was not just the senior executives that experienced that satisfaction. One of the young managers worked with 12 people on his immediate team and had over 200 people reporting to him:

> The strength of the company is its strategy. That's what interests us. We want to implement change – that's fun. We want to be involved in decision making regarding the strategy. We are doing real value-added stuff and making a difference that you don't get back in Canada being one of thousands.

Another echoed this sentiment,

> I would love to live in Ottawa for the quality of life, but not for the job. We are living on the edge here. Home is a bureaucracy.

A REWARDING EXPERIENCE

Along with the many challenges that Mexico provided, many of the expatriates found a plenitude of new and rewarding experiences. The families enjoyed travelling, new friends, food, and culture:

> Mexico has a rich culture. We've tried to appreciate the history and culture as much as possible. The first Christmas we spent in Mexico, our children came to stay with us and we were invited for Christmas with a Mexican family which was really a highlight. We had a piñata and later enjoyed the Mexican tradition asking for *posada*.[2]

Mexican hospitality, however, was not the only benefit bestowed upon the Canadians. Martel managers began to relate to their Mexican counterparts in new ways. At one point, a group of Mexicans provided a senior Canadian manager with a comic sculpture with the caption: *To the Mexicanized Canadians from your Canadianized Mexicans.*

Many felt they had learned a great deal from their Mexican counterparts:

> I have a subordinate who really helped me in many ways. Some were attitudinal things like how to approach Mexicans in various situations. I think he realized that I had a yearning to understand the Mexican way of doing things, so he openly offered suggestions.
>
> I have a tremendous respect now for most Mexicans. They work hard. They aren't afraid to work at all. They lack some management skills and some infrastructure, yes; but hard work is never a problem.

And of course, the expatriates realized they had learned a great deal about themselves and their homes:

> At one point, I had to address all the pros and cons and make a personal decision to go or stay. On questions like security, I had to ask myself if I was really angry with the company or just frustrated as I adjusted. I finally had to identify which issues I could control and which ones I couldn't. You can't walk around unhappy all the time. I decided to stay, and things started to get better from that point.
>
> Little things don't bother me as much now.
>
> My self-definition has changed. I'm proud of Canada but I can see both sides. I'm also more self-confident and willing and prepared to tackle difficult decisions.
>
> You glamorize things back home – everything is good. But it isn't.

THE FUTURE

There was also agreement across the groups of expatriates that more development of executives was necessary:

We need to have people in the pipeline – junior and senior people. We need to identify 25 to 30 promising people at all levels and develop them to run our Latin American operations.

We need a structured, publicized development program like some of the top American companies like P&G.

The purchase of Latin American companies meant that soon Spanish would be the first language of almost one-half of Martel employees. Executives were wondering what they could learn from the Mexican experience to develop managers to run the expanding Latin American operations?

Notes

1　Expatriate Human Resource Policies, Marconi Telecommunications Corporation, February, 1997.
2　In Spanish, *posada* means guest house or inn. The traditional celebration of asking for *posada* represents the search for an inn by Mary and Joseph on Christmas eve. Guests stand outside the home and sing by candlelight, asking for lodging for the night.

CASE **17**

Blue Ridge Spain

*David T. A. Wesley, Nicholas Athanassiou, Henry W. Lane,
and Jeanne M. McNett*

Yannis Costas, European managing director of Blue Ridge Restaurants, found it difficult to control the anger welling up inside him as he left the meeting with the company's regional vice-president (VP) earlier in the day. That evening, he began to reflect on the day's events in the relative peace of his London flat. "Ten years work gone down the drain," he thought to himself, shaking his head. "What a waste!"

Costas recalled the many years he had spent fostering a successful joint venture between his company, Blue Ridge Restaurants Corporation, and Terralumen SA, a mid-sized family-owned company in Spain. Not only had the joint venture been profitable, but it had grown at a reasonably brisk pace in recent years. Without a doubt, partnering with Terralumen was a key reason for Blue Ridge's success in Spain. Therefore, Costas was somewhat dismayed to find out that Delta Foods Corporation, Blue Ridge's new owner, wanted out. Yes, there had been recent tension between Terralumen and Delta over future rates of growth (see Exhibits 2 and 3), but the most recent round of talks had ended in an amicable compromise – he thought. Besides, Delta's senior managers should have realized that their growth targets were unrealistic.

Jeanne M. McNett prepared this case under the supervision of David Wesley and Professors Nicholas Athanassiou and Henry W. Lane solely to provide material for class discussion. The authors do not intend to illustrate either effective or ineffective handling of a managerial situation. The authors may have disguised certain names and other identifying information to protect confidentiality.

They had gone over the arguments several times, and Costas tried every angle to convince his superiors to stick with the joint venture, but to no avail. To make matters worse, Costas had just been assigned the unpleasant task of developing a dissolution strategy for the company he had worked so hard to build.

BLUE RIDGE RESTAURANTS CORPORATION

Blue Ridge was founded in Virginia in 1959, and quickly established a reputation for quality fast food. In 1974, after establishing more than 500 food outlets in the United States and Canada, Blue Ridge was sold to an investment group for US$4 million.

Over the next five years, the company experienced sales growth of 96 per cent annually. However, international sales were haphazard and there was no visible international strategy. Instead, whenever a foreign restauranteur wanted to begin a Blue Ridge franchise, the foreign company would simply approach Blue Ridge headquarters with the request. As long as the franchise delivered royalties, there was little concern for maintaining product consistency or quality control in foreign markets.

In 1981, Blue Ridge was acquired by an international beverages company for US$420 million. Under new ownership, the company made its first major foray into international markets, and international operations were merged with the parent company's existing international beverage products under a new international division.

The strategy at the time was to enter into joint ventures with local partners, thereby allowing Blue Ridge to enter restricted markets and draw on local expertise, capital and labor. Partnering also significantly reduced the capital costs of opening new stores. The strategy of local partnering combined with Blue Ridge's marketing know-how and operations expertise, quickly paid off in Australia, Southeast Asia and the United Kingdom, where booming sales led to rapid international expansion.

On the other hand, there were some glaring failures. By 1987, Blue Ridge decided to pull out of France, Italy, Brazil and Hong Kong where infrastructure problems and slow consumer acceptance resulted in poor performance. Some managers, who had been accustomed to high margins and short lead times in their alcoholic beverages division, did not have the patience for the long and difficult road to develop these markets and would tolerate only those ventures that showed quick results.

These early years of international expansion provided important learning opportunities as more managers gained a personal understanding of the key strategic factors behind successful foreign entry. The success of the company's international expansion efforts helped Blue Ridge become the company's fastest growing division. When Blue Ridge was sold to Delta Foods in 1996 for US$2 billion, it was one of the largest fast-food chains in the world and generated sales of US$6.8 billion.

Delta was a leading soft drink and snack food company in the United States, but at the time of the Blue Ridge acquisition, it had not achieved significant success internationally. It had managed to establish a dominant market share in a small number of countries with protected markets in which its main competitors were shut out. For example, one competitor was shut out of many Arabic countries after deciding to set up operations in Israel.

The company's senior managers disliked joint ventures, in part because they were time-consuming, but also because they were viewed as a poor way to develop new markets.

Delta was an aggressive growth company with brands that many believed were strong enough to support entry into new overseas markets without the assistance of local partners. When needed, the company either hired local managers directly or transferred seasoned managers from the soft drink and snack food divisions.

Delta also achieved international growth by directly acquiring local companies. For example, in the late 1990s, Delta acquired the largest snack food companies in Spain and the United Kingdom. However, given that joint ventures had been the predominant strategy for Blue Ridge, and that some countries, such as China, required local partnering, Delta had no choice but to work with joint venture partners.

YANNIS COSTAS

Yannis Costas was an American-educated Greek who held degrees in engineering and business (MBA) from leading US colleges. Although college life in a foreign country had its challenges, it afforded him an opportunity to develop an appreciation and understanding of American culture and business practices. Therefore, upon completing his MBA, Costas turned-down several offers of employment from leading multinational corporations that wanted him to take management positions in his native country. Such positions, however appealing they may have been at the time, would have doomed him to a career as a local manager, he thought. He chose instead to accept a position in international auditing at Blue Ridge headquarters in Virginia, mainly because of the opportunity for extended foreign travel.

The transition from university to corporate life was a difficult one. Social life seemed to revolve around couples and families, both at Blue Ridge and in the larger community. Although Costas met some single women from the local Greek community, his heavy travel schedule prevented him from establishing any meaningful relationships. Instead, he immersed himself in his work as a way to reduce the general feeling of isolation.

Costas was fortunate to have an office next to Gene Bennett, the company's director of business development. Bennett had served as a lieutenant in the US Navy before working in the pharmaceutical industry setting up joint ventures in Latin America and Europe. He was hired by Blue Ridge specifically to develop international joint ventures. As Costas' informal mentor, Bennett passed on many of the lessons Costas would come to draw on later in his career.

It was at the urging of Bennett that Costas applied for a transfer to the international division in 1985. Three years later, Costas was asked to relocate to London, England, in order to take on the role of European regional director for Blue Ridge. In this position, he became responsible for joint ventures and franchises in Germany, the Netherlands, Spain, Northern Ireland, Denmark, Sweden and Iceland.

In 1993, Costas was transferred to Singapore where, under the direction of the president of Blue Ridge Asia,[1] he advanced in his understanding of joint ventures, market entry and teamwork. Over the next five years, Costas built a highly productive management team and successfully developed several Asian markets. He was eager to apply these new skills when he returned to London in 1998 to once again take up the role of European director (see Exhibit 1 for a summary of Costas' career).

EXHIBIT 1 Timeline

Year	Blue Ridge Restaurants	Yannis Costas
1959	Company founded in Virginia	
1974	Blue Ridge Sold for $4 million	
1975–80	96 per cent annual growth	Leaves Greece to study in United States
1981	Blue Ridge sold for $420 million	
1982	International expansion	Completes his BS in United States
1983	Begin negotiations for JV in Spain	
1984		Completes MBA and is hired by Blue Ridge; moves to Virginia
1985	JV agreement with Terralumen SA	Applies for transfer to International Division
1986	Rodrigo appointed managing director of Blue Ridge Spain	
1987	Company pulls out of France, Brazil, Hong Kong, and Italy	
1988		Promoted to European regional director; moves to London
1988–93	Spanish JV grows slower than expected	
1993	US manager sent to oversee Spanish JV	Transfer to Singapore
1995	Rodrigo replaced by Carlos Martin	
1996	Blue Ridge sold to Delta for $2 billion	
1995–98	Spanish JV grows more rapidly	
1998	5-year plan for 50 restaurants in Spain, Blue Ridge has 600 stores in Europe/ME	Costas asked to return to London
Jan. 1999		Rescues JV in Kuwait
May 1999	Södergran hired as Delta VP for Europe	
June 1999	Directors meeting for Spanish JV	
December 1999	Dryden withholds Delta payment to JV; Alvarez sells prime Barcelona property	
January 2000		Asked to develop dissolution strategy for Spain

THE SPANISH DECISION

When the decision was first made to enter the Spanish market, Bennett was sent overseas to meet with real estate developers, construction companies, retail distributors, agribusiness companies, lawyers, accountants and consumer product manufacturers in order to gather the preliminary knowledge needed for such an undertaking. Bennett soon realized that Blue Ridge would need a credible Spanish partner to navigate that country's complex real estate and labor markets.

Few Spaniards among Bennett's peer generation spoke English. However, Bennett had a basic knowledge of Spanish, a language that he had studied in college, and this helped open some doors that were otherwise shut for many of his American colleagues. Still,

Bennett knew that finding a suitable partner would be difficult, since Spaniards frequently appeared to distrust foreigners. The attitude of one investment banker from Madrid was typical:

> Many Spaniards do not want to eat strange-tasting, comparatively expensive American food out of paper bags in an impersonal environment. We have plenty of restaurants with good inexpensive food, a cozy atmosphere and personal service, and our restaurants give you time to enjoy your food in pleasant company. Besides, we don't even really know you. You come here for a few days, we have enjoyable dinners, I learn to like you, and then you leave. What kind of relationship is that?

Luckily, Bennett had a banker friend in Barcelona who recommended that he consider partnering with Terralumen.

TERRALUMEN SA

Terralumen was a family-owned agricultural company that had later expanded into consumer products. In doing so, Terralumen entered into several joint ventures with leading American companies. In recent years, Terralumen had also begun to experiment with the concept of establishing full-service restaurants.

Bennett was introduced to Francisco Alvarez, Terralumen's group vice-president in charge of restaurant operations and the most senior non-family member in the company. In time, Bennett had many opportunities to become well acquainted with Terralumen and its managers. On weekends he stayed at Alvarez's country home, attended family gatherings in Barcelona and had family members visit him in Virginia. Over the span of their negotiations, Bennett and Alvarez developed a solid friendship, and Bennett began to believe that Terralumen had the type of vision needed to be a successful joint venture partner.

After two years of negotiations, Blue Ridge entered into a joint venture with Terralumen to establish a Blue Ridge restaurant chain in Spain. Upon returning to Virginia, Bennett could not hold back his euphoria as he related to Costas the details of what he considered to be the most difficult joint venture he had ever negotiated.

BLUE RIDGE SPAIN

Alvarez hired Eduardo Rodrigo to head up the joint venture as its managing director. An accountant by trade, Rodrigo was a refined and personable man who valued his late afternoon tennis with his wife and was a professor at a university in Barcelona. He also spoke fluent English.

Before assuming his new role, Rodrigo and another manager went to Virginia to attend a five-week basic training course. Upon his return, Rodrigo's eye for detail became quickly apparent as he mastered Blue Ridge's administrative and operating policies and procedures. He knew every detail of the first few stores' operating processes and had an equally detailed grasp of each store's trading profile. As a result, Blue Ridge Spain began to show an early profit.

Profitability was one thing; growth was another. Although the Blue Ridge concept seemed to be well received by Spanish consumers, Rodrigo was cautious and avoided rapid expansion. Moreover, one of the most important markets in Spain was Madrid. Rodrigo, who was Catalan,[2] was not fond of that city and avoided travelling to Madrid whenever possible. As personal contact with real estate agents, suppliers and others was necessary to develop new stores, Blue Ridge's expansion efforts remained confined to the Barcelona area. Terralumen, becoming impatient with Blue Ridge's sluggish growth, decided to focus more resources on its consumer product divisions and less on the restaurant business.

For Costas, one of the challenges during his first assignment as European director was to convince Terralumen to focus more on the joint venture and support faster growth. Rodrigo positively opposed more rapid growth, even though Alvarez, his direct superior, voiced support for the idea. Although he had been very cordial in his interactions with his American counterparts, Rodrigo believed himself to be in a much better position to judge whether or not the Spanish market would support faster growth.

In 1993, shortly after Costas was transferred to Singapore, Blue Ridge decided to send one of its own managers to oversee the Spanish joint venture. Under pressure, Rodrigo began to ignore criticism about the company's lack of growth. On one occasion, Rodrigo decided to close the Blue Ridge offices for an entire month just as Blue Ridge's international director of finance arrived in Barcelona to develop a five-year strategic plan.[3]

Terralumen finally replaced Rodrigo with a more proactive manager who had just returned from a successful assignment in Venezuela. Under the new leadership of Carlos Martin, Blue Ridge Spain began to prosper. Soon everyone was occupied with the difficult task of acquiring new sites, as well as recruiting and training employees.

COSTAS RETURNS TO EUROPE

In late 1998, Costas was transferred from Singapore to London to resume the role of European managing director. The previous director had performed poorly and it was felt that Costas had the experience needed to repair damaged relations with some of Blue Ridge's Middle Eastern joint venture partners. By this time, Blue Ridge had more than 600 stores in Europe and the Middle East.

One of Blue Ridge's more lucrative joint ventures was in Kuwait. However, the partners were threatening to dissolve the enterprise after the previous managing director became upset that the Kuwaitis were not meeting growth targets. The partners were especially concerned when they discovered that he had begun to seek other potential partners.

Costas decided to schedule a visit to Kuwait in early January. The partners counselled against the visit since Costas would be arriving during Ramadan,[4] and therefore would not be able to get much work done. Nevertheless Costas went to Kuwait, but spent nearly all of his time having dinners with the partners. He recalled:

Most American managers would have considered my trip to be a waste of time, since I didn't get much "work" done. But it was a great opportunity to get to know the partners

EXHIBIT 2   Development Plan Agreed between Blue Ridge Restaurants and Terralumen (as of December 1998, in 000s US dollars)

	1998	2000	2001	2002	2003	2004
No. of stores	12	24	37	50	65	80
Average annual sales	700	770	847	932	1,025	1,127
Gross sales	$8,400	18,480	31,339	46,600	66,625	90,160
Cost of goods food	1,680	3,322	5,474	8,141	11,639	15,770
Cost of goods direct labor	1,680	3,323	5,641	8,374	11,646	15,766
Advertising/promotion	504	1,109	1,880	2,796	3,998	5,410
Occupancy costs	1,260	1,848	3,129	4,660	6,663	9,016
Fixed labor	840	1,478	2,507	3,728	5,330	7,213
Miscellaneous	168	277	470	699	999	1,352
Royalties to Blue Ridge US	420	924	1,560	2,330	3,331	4,508
Total costs	6,552	12,281	20,662	30,728	43,606	59,035
Contribution to G&A	1,848	6,199	10,677	15,872	23,019	31,125
Salaries and benefits	875	1,531	2,641	3,493	4,580	5,899
Travel expenses	120	240	300	375	469	586
Other	240	312	406	527	685	891
Occupancy costs	240	720	828	952	1,095	1,259
Total G&A	1,475	2,803	4,175	5,347	6,829	8,635
Earnings before interest/tax	$373	3,396	6,502	10,525	16,190	22,490
% of gross sales	4.44	18.38	20.75	22.59	24.30	24.94
Office employees (Spain)	10	20	30	35	40	45

Notes:
- This plan was agreed before Yannis Costas' appointment to Blue Ridge Europe in late 1998.
- End 2004 plan: 20 stores in Barcelona, 30 in Madrid, 30 in other cities
- Capital Investment per store $700,000 to $1 million
- Site identification, lease or purchase negotiation, permits, construction: 18 to 24 months. Key Money is a part of occupancy costs. It is a sum paid to property owner at signing; varies by site $100,000 plus. Up to 1999, many owners wanted Key Money paid off the books, often in another country.
- Store Staffing (at the average sales level):
  − One manager, two assistants full time (larger stores three to four assistants)
  − 10 to 12 employees per eight-hour shift (40 hours per week); 980 employee hours per week
- Store employees needed by end of 1999: 300; by the end of 2004: 2,250 (approx.)
- Store employee attrition: approximately 25 per cent per year
- Dividends from earnings were declared periodically and then were shared equally between partners.

Source: Company files.

and to re-establish lost trust, and the partners felt good about having an opportunity to vent their concerns.

Costas returned to London confident that he had reassured the Kuwaiti partners that Blue Ridge was still committed to the joint venture.

Costas was also happy to be working with his old friend Alvarez again, as the two began working on an ambitious plan to develop a total of 50 stores by 2002 (see Exhibit 2).[5] As Blue Ridge Spain continued to grow, stores were opened in prime locations such as the prestigious Gran Via in Madrid and Barcelona's famous Las Ramblas shopping district. Costas and Alvarez, both of whom had been involved from the beginning of the joint venture, were delighted to see how far the company had come.

EUROPEAN REORGANIZATION

Delta began to take a more direct and active role in the management of Blue Ridge. In Europe, for example, Delta created a new regional VP position with responsibility for Europe, the Middle East and South Africa. When Costas became aware of the new position, he asked whether or not he was being considered, given his extensive experience in managing international operations. The human resources department in the United States explained that they wanted to put a seasoned Delta manager in place in order to facilitate the integration of the two companies.

Although disappointed, Costas understood the logic behind the decision. He also considered that by working under a seasoned Delta manager, he could develop contacts in the new parent company that might prove favorable to his career at some future date.

In May 1999, Costas received a phone call from Bill Sawyer, Blue Ridge's director of human resources, whom Costas had known for many years.

> *Sawyer*: We hired someone from Proctor and Gamble. He's 35 years old and has a lot of marketing experience, and he worked in Greece for three years. You'll like him.
>
> *Costas*: That's great. Have your people found anyone for the VP job yet?

The line was silent, then Sawyer replied in an apologetic tone, "He *is* the new VP." Costas was dumbfounded.

> *Costas*: I thought you said you were planning to transfer a Delta veteran to promote co-operation.
>
> *Sawyer*: Nobody from Delta wanted the job, so we looked outside the company. Kinsley (president, international division) wanted a "branded" executive, so we stole this guy from P&G.

Sawyer went on to explain that Mikael Södergran, who was originally from Finland, had no background in restaurant management, but had achieved a reputation for results in his previous role as a P&G marketing manager for the Middle East and Africa. He had recently been transferred from Geneva, Switzerland to P&G European headquarters in Newcastle upon Tyne.[6] Södergran was not happy in Newcastle and saw the Delta position both as an opportunity to take on greater responsibility and to move back to the civilization of London.

"You couldn't find anyone better than *that*," Costas exclaimed. He was furious, not only for having been deceived about the need to have a Delta manager as VP, but also that he, with 10 years experience managing international operations, had been passed over in favor of someone with no experience managing operations, joint ventures or a large managerial staff. Nevertheless, the decision had been made, and Södergran was scheduled to start in two weeks.

EXHIBIT 3 Consultants' Recommendations on Blue Ridge European Expansion (Selected Markets)

	1998	2000	2001	2002	2003	2004
Stores						
Spain	12	30	65	100	135	170
France	0	10	20	55	90	130
Germany	3	15	30	65	100	150
Total	15	55	115	220	325	450
Regional managers (London)	1	15	20	22	24	26
Country staff/managers	12	40	90	180	220	250
Store employees	215	1,650	3,450	6,600	9,750	13,500

Source: Company files.

THE DIRECTORS' MEETING

It was Södergran's first day on the job when he met with Blue Ridge Spain's board of directors to discuss a recently drafted consultants' report and negotiate new five-year growth targets (see Exhibit 3). The study, which was conducted by a leading US-based management consulting firm, projected significant expansion potential for Blue Ridge in Spain, as well as in France and Germany, where Blue Ridge had no visible presence.[7] Delta also wanted to increase the royalties and fees payable from the joint venture partner in order to cover the cost of implementing new technologies, systems and services (see Exhibit 4).

Other Blue Ridge managers at the meeting included Yannis Costas and Donald Kinsley, Blue Ridge's new international president. Although Kinsley had formerly been president of a well-known family restaurant chain in the United States, this was his first international experience. Terralumen was represented by company president Andres Balaguer, Francisco Alvarez and Carlos Martin, Blue Ridge Spain's managing director.

Even before the meeting began, Delta's management team assumed that Terralumen was content to keep growth rates at their current levels and would have to be pressed to accept more aggressive targets. As expected, Martin protested that his team of 10 managers could not handle the introduction of 30 new stores a year, as suggested by the study. The meeting's cordial tone quickly dissolved when Södergran unexpectedly began to press the issue. His aggressive stance was not well received by Terralumen, who in turn questioned the ability of the consulting firm's young freshly minted American MBAs to understand the intricacy of the Spanish fast-food market. Balaguer simply brushed off the study as "a piece of American business school cleverness."

Södergran became visibly annoyed at Balaguer's refusal to consider Delta's targets. "The contract says that you are required to grow the markets," Södergran demanded. Balaguer, a tall, elegant man, slowly stood up, lifted a sheaf of papers and replied, "If this is your contract, and if we rely on a contract to resolve a partnership problem, well, here is what I think of it and of you." He walked across the room and dropped the papers

EXHIBIT 4   Blue Ridge Spain Exceptional Term Highlights

	Blue Ridge US Desired Objective	Blue Ridge Spain – Variance
Joint Venture Outlets		
Royalty	At least 4 per cent	No royalty
Fees	$20,000	$5,000
Term	10 years	5 years
Exclusivity	Avoid exclusivity	Spain, Canary Islands, Spanish Sahara, Beleares Islands
Advertising	5 per cent, right of approval	No obligations
Outlet Renewal Requirements	Renewal fee at least $2,000; Upgrading or relocation	No fee or other specific requirements
Delta Products	Required	No requirement
Development Program	Schedule for required development of territory	No requirement
Non-Competition	Restrictions on similar business	No provision
Assignment	First refusal right; approval of assignee	No provision
Sub-Franchising		
Contract privity	Blue Ridge U.S. should be a party and successor to franchisor	Blue Ridge cited; Blue Ridge succeeds on JV dissolution
Royalty	At least 4 per cent	None
Fees	$20,000	None
Joint Venture Operation		
Equity Participation	More than 50 per cent	50 per cent
Profit Distribution	At least 50 per cent	Additional 20 per cent when profits are greater than 20 per cent
Actual Management	Blue Ridge US should appoint General Manager	General Manager is from JV partner
Board Control	Blue Ridge US should have majority	Equal number of board members

Source: Company files.

into a garbage can. Then upon returning to his seat, he remarked in Spanish, "If this meeting had been conducted in my language, you would have known what I *really* think of you," in reference to Södergran.

After a long pause, Costas tried to mend the situation by pointing out that Terralumen had already committed to considerable growth, and had therefore already come some way toward Delta's expansions goals. He suggested that the two companies break to consider alternatives.

A few weeks later, Costas sent an e-mail to Södergran outlining his recommendations (see Exhibit 5).

EMERGING CONFLICTS

Costas tried his best to keep an open mind with regard to Södergran and to support him as best he could. However, as time went on, Costas began to seriously question Södergran's ability. He never seemed to interact with anyone except to conduct business.

EXHIBIT 5 Costas' Recommendations

From: Yannis Costas [Costas@deltafoods.co.uk]
Sent: Wednesday, July 7, 1999 10:16 AM
To: "Sodergran@deltafoods.co.uk"
Subject: Key Issues – Here is what I believe we should be going for in Spain.

Mikael:
Here are my recommendations for Spain.

A PRESERVE PARTNERSHIP
  • Need a "real" market success while developing markets elsewhere in Europe.
    – Fuel interest of potential partners elsewhere.
    – Keep Blue Ridge and Delta believing in European potential.
    – Market for real testing of concepts and ideas.
    – No complete reliance on UK for "successes."
B REVERSAL NOT EASY TO OVERCOME
  • May have to pay a high premium to buy out joint venture.
  • Will lose all key managers (<u>no substitutes on hand</u>)
  • If we inherit "green field"
    – Down time close to 2 years.
    – Why? From decision to opening will take approximately nine months to one year.
    – In a new market this will be longer as we have no human resource experience to draw on.
    – Potential new partners need to be convinced about why we broke up with a "good" partner.
    – Real estate market does not want to deal with foreigners or raises the price.
  • If the divorce is messy, we may be bound by the current contract for another year.
C WORK TOWARDS ACHIEVING ACCEPTABLE INTEGRATION WITH OUR DESIRABLE CONTRACT FRAMEWORK OVER CURRENT DELTA PLANNING HORIZON (5 YEARS)
  • Strong development schedule for joint venture.
  • Royalty integration over mutually acceptable period.
  • Designated "agency" for franchisees immediately, but fee flow indirectly to Blue Ridge only the amount <u>over</u> current terms with existing franchisees. Phase-in higher flow on schedule similar to royalties.
  • Accept the notion of phasing in royalties as <u>we</u> phase in systems and services (If we <u>don't</u> phase them in there won't be much of a business anyhow!)
D KEY RATIONALE
  • We may have the perfect contract, but no stores to apply it to for three years – hence no income to cover overheads. <u>SO</u> . . .
  • Accept half the current growth targets with the full expectation that by year 3 or 5, there will be a decent system for the contract's objectives to be meaningful.

On one occasion Costas suggested that they have dinner with the joint venture partners. Södergran replied, "Oh, another dinner! Why don't we get some work done instead?"

Costas became more concerned after Södergran rented a suite two floors below the company offices "in order to have some peace and quiet." Some of the regional head-quarters staff began to wonder if Södergran had taken on too much responsibility and whether he was avoiding them because of the pressure he was under. Costas also believed that Södergran was uncomfortable with him, knowing that he resented not being offered the VP position.

In October 1999, Delta sent a finance manager from the snack foods division to become the company's new VP of finance for Europe. Geoff Dryden had no overseas experience, but when he was in the United States, he had been involved in several large international acquisitions. Dryden, who was originally from North Carolina, was pleasant, well polished in his manners and dress, and very proud of his accomplishments at Delta. For him, the European assignment was an opportunity to move out of finance and, if all went well, to assume greater managerial responsibilities.

Costas, who had specialized in finance when doing his MBA, had always done his own financial projections and was not very fond of the idea of surrendering this responsibility to someone else. Still, he helped Dryden as much as needed to make accurate projections, taking into account the unique aspects of each market.

A NEW STRATEGY

Over the next six months, the joint venture board of directors met four times. In the end, Terralumen committed to half the growth rate originally proposed by Delta and agreed to make upward revisions if market conditions proved favorable. Delta's managers were clearly becoming frustrated by what they perceived to be their partner's entrenched position.

After the final meeting, Södergran and Costas met with their European staff to discuss the results. Dryden asked why they put up with it. "Why don't we just buy them out?" he asked, calling to mind Delta's successful acquisition of a Spanish snack food company. Costas reminded Dryden that not only were snack foods and restaurants two very different enterprises, but all the joint venture managers had come from Terralumen, and most would leave Blue Ridge if Delta proceeded to buy out the partners.

After the meeting, Dryden discussed the situation privately with Södergran. Noting that a major loan payment would soon be due to one of their creditors (a major Spanish bank), Dryden suggested holding back Delta's contribution, thereby forcing the joint venture company to default on the loan. If all went according to plan, the joint venture would have to be dissolved and the assets divided between the partners. This, he noted, would be much less expensive than trying to buy out their partner.

As expected, Terralumen requested matching funds from Delta, but Dryden simply ignored the request. However, unbeknownst to Dryden or anyone else at Delta, Alvarez proceeded to sell one of the company's prime real estate properties and lease back the store as a means of paying the loan.

Costas happened to be in Barcelona working on Blue Ridge Spain's marketing plan with Carlos Martin. One evening, Costas was dining with his counterparts from Terralumen when Alvarez mentioned the sale of the company's Barcelona property. Costas, who at the time was unaware of Dryden's strategy, was dismayed. Real estate values in Barcelona were expected to appreciate significantly over the short term. Selling now seemed illogical. Furthermore, Costas was surprised to discover that Alvarez had been given power of attorney to make real estate transactions on behalf of the joint venture. Alvarez explained:

> Quite a few years ago, when you were in Singapore, Blue Ridge decided to give Terralumen this authority in order to reduce the amount of travel required by your managers in the United States. Besides, as you know, it is not often that good properties become available, and when they do, we must act quickly.

On his return to London, Costas discussed the real estate transaction with Dryden, who, upon hearing the news, furiously accused Costas of "siding with the enemy." Costas was quick to remind Dryden that he had not been privy to the dissolution strategy and, besides, the whole thing was unethical. Dryden retorted, "Ethics? Come on, this is strategy, not ethics!"

Dryden was clearly surprised by the news, especially given the fact that Delta would never have given such powers of attorney to a joint venture partner. The company's lawyers could have warned Dryden, but he had not been very fond of the "old hands" at Blue Ridge's legal affairs department, and therefore had chosen to not disclose his plan. Now that his strategy had failed, an alternative plan would have to be devised.

Costas felt torn between his responsibility to his employer and his distaste for the company's new approach. This whole thing was a mistake, he believed. Costas discussed his views with Södergran:

> We cannot hope to take over the stores in Spain while simultaneously developing new markets in Germany and France. Where are we going to find suitable managerial talent to support this expansion? People in Europe don't exactly see the fast-food industry as a desirable place to grow their careers. And besides, Delta hasn't given us sufficient financial resources for such an undertaking.

Why don't we focus on France and Germany instead, and continue to allow Terralumen to run the Spanish operation? Revenue from Spain will help appease Delta headquarters while France and Germany suffer their inevitable growing pains. In the meantime, we can continue to press Terralumen for additional growth.

Södergran dismissed these concerns and instead gave Costas two weeks to develop a new dissolution strategy. Costas was furious that all his suggestions were so easily brushed off by someone who, he believed, had a limited understanding of the business.

On his way home that evening Costas recalled all the effort his former mentor, Gene Bennett, had put into the joint venture 16 years earlier, and all the good people he had had the privilege to work with in the intervening years. Just as all that work was about to pay off, the whole business was about to fall apart. Why hadn't he seen this coming? Where did the joint venture go wrong? Costas wondered what to do. Surely he had missed something. There had to be another way out.

ACKNOWLEDGMENT

This case was made possible through the generous support of Darla and Frederick Brodsky through their endowment of the Darla and Frederick Brodsky Trustee Professorship in International Business.

Notes

1 At the time, Blue Ridge Asia was one of the company's most successful operations with nearly 800 restaurants in Singapore, Malaysia, Taiwan, and Thailand.
2 Catalonia, a state in northeast Spain, had a distinct culture and language (Catalan).
3 In Spain, the month of August was traditionally set aside for vacations.

4   Ramadan is the holy month of fasting ordained by the Koran for all adult Muslims. The fast begins each day at dawn and ends immediately at sunset. During the fast, Muslims are forbidden to eat, drink, or smoke.

5   The plan to develop 50 stores was agreed to in 1998, prior to Costas' arrival.

6   Newcastle upon Tyne, United Kingdom, was an important industrial and transportation center located in northeast England (approximately 4 hours from London). It had a population of 263,000 (1991 census).

7   Large restaurant chains served only four per cent of fast food meals in Spain, compared with 15 per cent for the rest of Western Europe, and 50 per cent for the United States.

APPENDIX 1 MANAGEMENT STYLES FOR SELECTED NATIONALITIES[1]

Spain

In Spain, a strong differentiation of social classes and professional occupations exists. Business communication is often based on subjective feelings about the topic being discussed. Personal relationships are very important as a means to establish trust, and are usually considered more important than one's expertise. Established business contacts are essential to success in Spain. Therefore, it is important to get to know someone prior to conducting business transactions. Only intimate friends are invited to the home of a Spaniard, but being invited to dinner is usual.

Spaniards are not strictly punctual for either business or social events, and once a business meeting is started, it is improper to begin with a discussion of business. National pride is pervasive, as is a sense of personal honor. To call someone "clever" is a veiled insult. Only about 30 per cent of local managers speak English, while French is often the second language of choice for many older Spaniards.

Greece

Greek society employs a social hierarchy with some bias against classes, ethnic groups and religions. For Greeks, interpersonal relationships are very important when conducting business, and decisions are often based on subjective feelings. Much importance is placed on the inherent trust that exists between friends and extended families. Authority lies with senior members of any group, and they are shown great respect. They are always addressed formally.

While punctuality is important, it is not stressed. Greeks have a strong work ethic and often strive for consensus.

1   Based on *Kiss, Bow, or Shake Hands: How to do Business in Sixty Countries*, Adams Media, 1994. The descriptions do not account for individual differences within each nationality or culture.

United States

Americans are very individualistic, with more stress placed on self than on others. Friendships are few and usually based on a specific need. Personal contacts are considered less important than bottom line results. Americans have a very strong work ethic, but a person is often considered to be a replaceable part of an organization. Great importance is placed on specialized expertise. Punctuality is important.

Business is done at lightning speed. In large firms, contracts under $100,000 can often be approved by a middle manager after only one meeting. Often companies and individuals have a very short-term orientation and expect immediate rewards. Small talk is very brief before getting down to business, even during dinner meetings and social gatherings.

Finland

Finns have a strong self orientation. More importance is placed on individual skills and abilities than on a person's station in life. Decisions are based more on objective facts than personal feelings. Privacy and personal opinions are considered very important. Finns often begin business immediately without any small talk. They are very quiet and accustomed to long periods of silence, but eye contact is important when conversing. Authority usually rests with the managing director. Punctuality is stressed in both business and social events.

PART **3**

Competing with Integrity in Global Business

OVERVIEW

In Part 2 of this book we presented selected strategic and operating issues that global managers encounter. Now, we will discuss the issue of competing with integrity in global business, which encompasses corporate social responsibility and ethical behavior. Our goal is to challenge you to consider your current or future responsibilities as a business leader more broadly than simply from an economic perspective. There are human consequences linked to your decisions as well. The human and societal impacts of decisions

is it an oxymoron?

Did you take a class in Ethics? Philosophy —
until recently Not taught at US law schools
or Business schools!

should be considered at the time these decisions are being made. We have separated this topic, competing with integrity, from earlier discussions of culture and executing strategy for pedagogical purposes. We believe that issues of responsibility and ethics do not always receive the attention that they deserve and may be overlooked if combined with other topics. Highlighting the idea that executives in global corporations should compete with integrity allows more detailed analytical treatment of the issues and, hopefully, encourages development of a way of thinking about them that you, as a manager, can use.

Competing with integrity

Richard De George suggests that executives should act and compete with integrity in international business.[1] Acting with integrity is the same as acting ethically, but the word integrity does not have the negative connotation, the moralizing tone, or the sense of naiveté that the word "ethics" carries for many people. What is integrity, and how does one compete with integrity? According to De George: "Acting with integrity means both acting in accordance with one's highest self-accepted norms of behavior and imposing on oneself the norms demanded by ethics and morality."[2]

yourself and the cultural norms

Competing with integrity means that executives of multinational corporations should compete against others in a way that is consistent with their own highest values and norms of behavior. Although these values and norms are self-imposed and self-accepted, they cannot be simply arbitrary and self-serving; but neither is there a requirement to be perfect. "The imperative to act with integrity cannot insist on moral perfection. It can and does demand taking ethical considerations seriously."[3]

The ideas of ethical executive behavior and corporate social responsibility are not new. One writer has suggested that serious discussion of the topic in North America started in 1953 with the publication of *Social Responsibilities of the Businessman*.[4] That discussion turned into a debate nine years later when Milton Friedman asserted that a company's only social responsibility was to make as much money as possible for its stockholders.[5] However, discussions of social responsibility and ethical behavior in an international context usually arise only when companies are linked to activities such as bribery, employing child labor or contracting manufacturers that employ child labor, purchasing products from overseas companies that use prison labor, or moving operations to countries with less strict legislation regarding environmental protection or employment practices.

Examples come from many companies and many nations. An executive with the European Aeronautic Defense and Space Agency (EADS) was charged with corruption in a $5-billion arms sale in South Africa; an executive at Acres International (Canada) was found guilty of bribing a senior official of a project in Lesotho; Xerox admitted making improper payments to government officials in India over a period of years;[6] and the Norwegian state-run oil group, Statoil, was involved in a suspected bribery scandal with Iran in 2003. Wal-Mart, Kathie Lee Gifford, and Payless Shoes, among others, have been implicated in using sweatshops to produce shoes and apparel.[7] Nike received significant criticism for employing child labor in countries such as Cambodia and Pakistan and, as a result, suffered numerous boycotts of its products.

The environmental impact of the North American Free Trade Agreement (NAFTA) was a topic of heated discussion when Canada and the United States were debating whether

[handwritten note in left margin: People worried about NAFTA but Globalization Snuck up on them]

to participate in NAFTA. Opponents claimed that US and Canadian firms would flock to Mexico to take advantage of its less stringent environmental and labor regulations. They would reduce costs by taking advantage of lower-paid Mexican workers at the expense of displaced Americans and Canadians and by polluting the environment, since there they would not have the expenses associated with compliance with environmental laws in Canada and the United States. One can find examples of firms that have taken advantage of the lax enforcement of regulations in Mexico, as opponents of NAFTA predicted, but it has not been true of all companies.

What should a manager do when asked to pay "facilitation fees" to have a contract approved? What criteria for product safety should be fulfilled before a product goes on the market? Should a manager insist that her subordinate travel to a location that official reports say is safe, but the subordinate and his family feel is unsafe? How should a manager make the tradeoff between achieving an acceptable level of profits, helping a developing world community by providing jobs, and not using child labor or exploiting workers in other ways? These questions often seem trite on the surface, with obvious answers: don't pay bribes, make safe products, let people travel to places where they feel safe, and don't hire child labor. Or did you have different responses? In reality, of course, situations do not present themselves neatly and a manager's actions responses to those situations are complex. In this section, we clarify some of the issues around competing with integrity and provide a number of examples for readers to explore.

Areas of corporate responsibility   The areas of corporate responsibility include "the economic, legal, ethical and discretionary expectations that society has of organizations at a given point in time."[8] The first two categories, *economic* and *legal*, receive the most attention in business schools and in business. These include the responsibility to produce goods and services that society wants, make a profit, and obey the laws and regulations that govern society and business. However, companies are expected to operate and to make profits in an ethical, as well as legal, fashion. Since all of society's desired behaviors are not necessarily written down, *ethical* responsibilities include those behaviors, not embodied in laws that also are expected of businesses. Finally, there is the area of *discretionary* responsibility "about which society has no clear cut message for business."[9] As the name suggests, activities in this area are voluntary and left to executive choice and judgment.

[handwritten note in left margin: Expectations of Culture of Society]

Although there may be some ambiguity in these issues, global executives do not lack some guidance in the area of responsible and ethical behavior. Numerous international accords and sets of principles have been formulated, adopted, and endorsed in the last half-century which provide a base for the development of a transcultural standard of corporate behavior in a global economy.[10]

International accords on corporate behavior   Various accords and principles address the following issues and situations.[11][12] *[handwritten note: Read this list !]*

- *Employment practices and policies.* For example, multinationals should develop non-discriminatory employment practices, provide equal pay for equal work, observe the right of employees to join unions and to bargain collectively, give advance notice of plant closings and mitigate their adverse effects, respect local host-country job stand-ards, provide favorable work conditions and limited working hours, adopt adequate health and safety standards, and inform employees about health hazards. They should not permit unacceptable practices such as the exploitation of children, physical punishment, abuse of females, or involuntary servitude.

- *Consumer protection.* MNCs should respect host-country laws regarding consumer protection; safeguard the health and safety of consumers through proper labeling, disclosures, and advertising; and provide safe packaging.
- *Environmental protection.* MNCs should preserve ecological balance, protect the envir-onment, rehabilitate environments damaged by them, and respect host-country laws, goals, and priorities regarding protection of the environment.
- *Political payments and involvement.* MNCs should not pay bribes to public officials and should avoid illegal involvement or interference in internal politics.
- *Basic human rights and fundamental freedoms.* Multinationals should respect the rights of people to life, liberty, security, and privacy; and freedom of religion, peace-ful assembly, and opinion.
- *Community responsibility.* MNCs should work with governments and communities in which they do business to improve the quality of life in those communities.

The UN's Global Compact, which was formally launched on July 26, 2000, established a set of core values in human rights, labor standards, and environmental practice.[13] Some of the global companies that support the Compact include ABB, BP, Citigroup, Crédit Suisse, DaimlerChrysler, Deutsche Bank, Fiat, GaxoSmithKline, L'Oréal, Nestlé, Novartis, Reebok, Unilever, and the Tokyo Electric Power Company.[14] The Global Compact asks that companies embrace, support, and enact the core values within their spheres of influence. The nine core values are:[15]

*del.
A treaty et
or contract
usually with
multiple parties*

Voluntary —

- *Human rights*
  1 Businesses should support and respect the protection of internationally proclaimed human rights, and
  2 make sure they are not complicit in human rights abuses.
- *Labor*
  3 Businesses should uphold the freedom of association and the effective recognition of the right to collective bargaining,
  4 the elimination of all forms of forced and compulsory labor,
  5 the effective abolition of child labor, and
  6 the elimination of discrimination in respect to employment and occupation.
- *Environment*
  7 Businesses should support a precautionary approach to environmental challenges,
  8 undertake initiatives to promote greater environmental responsibility; and
  9 encourage the development and diffusion of environmentally friendly technologies.

Corporate social responsibility – both in terms of its definition and the management guidelines that promote it – is not only of concern to international quasi-governmental organizations such as the United Nations (UN) and the Organization for Economic Cooperation and Development (OECD) but to some private investment companies as well. For example, the Calvert Group of mutual funds in the United States and the Ethical Funds Company in Canada have pioneered socially responsible mutual funds in their respective countries and have created "screens" or criteria for choosing socially responsible companies.

In 1982, the Calvert Social Investment Fund™ was the first mutual fund to oppose apartheid in South Africa.[16] Calvert has since created the Calvert Social Index™, a benchmark for measuring the performance of large, US-based socially responsible companies. Companies must meet Calvert's criteria in the following areas:

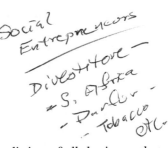

- Environment
- Workplace issues
- Product safety and impact
- Community relations and investments
- Military weapons contracting
- International operations and human rights
- Indigenous peoples' rights

The above sets of criteria may not be a comprehensive listing of all the issues that global executives might face and need to consider, but they provide a good start in thinking about them.[17]

ETHICAL ISSUES

Possibly the most difficult aspect of competing with integrity may be in the domain of ethics, which is the "moral thinking and analysis by corporate decision makers regarding the motives and consequences of their decisions and actions."[18] Ethics is the study of morals and systems of morality, or principles of conduct. The study of ethics is concerned with the right or wrong and the "should" or "should not" of human decisions and actions. This does not mean that all questions of right and wrong are ethical issues, however. There is right and wrong associated with rules of etiquette – for example, in which hand to hold your knife and fork, in the use of language and rules of grammar, and in making a computer work. Holding a fork in the wrong hand or speaking ungrammatically does not constitute unethical behavior.

The ethical or moral frame of reference is concerned with human behavior in society and with the relationships, duties, and obligations between people, groups, and organizations. It is concerned with human consequences associated with decisions and actions, not solely profits, more sophisticated technology, or larger market share. In this concern for human outcomes, it differs from other perspectives such as financial, marketing, accounting, or legal. An ethical perspective requires that you extend consideration beyond your own self-interest (or that of your company) to consider the interests of a wider community of people, including employees, customers, suppliers, the general public, and even overseas governments. It also advocates behaving according to what would be considered better or higher standards of conduct, not necessarily the minimum acceptable by law.

Our separation of this discussion of ethical decisions from strategy and operating decisions is artificial because problems in the real world do not come with neat labels attached: here is a finance problem; here is a marketing problem; and now, an ethical problem. Managers may categorize the issues by functional area or break up a complex problem into components such as those mentioned. Usually policy issues and decisions are multi-faceted and simultaneously may have financial, marketing, and production components. They also may have ethical dimensions that managers should consider. However, in considering a typical complex problem with more than one dimension, the ethical dimension may be overlooked.

If situations did come with labels on them, a person could apply the techniques and concepts he or she had learned, such as net present value to a financial problem or market segmentation to a marketing problem. What would happen if a problem labeled "ethical dilemma" arrived? A manager probably would be in a quandary because he or she most likely would not have a way of analyzing, let alone resolving, this type of problem. The decision-making tools for this type of situation probably would be missing. Business schools, traditionally, have not emphasized the teaching of ethics as rigorously as they have the teaching of finance or marketing, for example. Business students and managers generally have not been trained to think about ethical issues as they have been trained in the frameworks and techniques for functional areas of specialization. However, after numerous scandals in the United States such as Enron, Tyco, WorldCom, and Adelphia, to name a few, as well as the Parmalat scandal in Italy and other accounting scandals in Europe,[19] this likely will change as business schools move to address managerial ethics.

Ethical questions can arise in many areas of operations: the type of products produced, marketing and advertising practices, business conduct in countries where physical security is a problem, hiring and promotion practices in countries where discrimination and racism exist, requests for payments to secure contracts or sales, and payments to prevent damage to plants and equipment or injury to employees.

Responding to ethical problems – avoid or address?

How might managers respond when they encounter ethical problems such as the examples that we have just seen or work in countries where corruption is rampant and where they may encounter requests for bribes? One of the first things they may do is avoid the ethical dilemma through the process of rationalization. They may focus on some other aspect of the problem. They may transform the ethical problem into a legal or accounting problem, for instance. The reasoning seems to be that, so long as one is behaving legally or in accordance with accepted accounting practices, for example, nothing else is required. As is discussed later, compliance with laws and professional regulations is a minimum requirement for responsible managers.

Another kind of avoidance behavior is to see the problem as only one small piece of a larger puzzle and to assume that someone higher up in the organization must be looking after any unusual aspects, such as ethical considerations. Alternatively, the decision-maker might turn it into someone else's problem – perhaps a customer, supplier, or person in higher authority – with the comment, "I am following my boss's orders," or "I am following my customer's instructions." When a customer asks for a falsified invoice on imported goods for his or her records, with the difference deposited in an overseas bank, and you provide this "service," is it only the customer's behavior that is questionable?

Rationalizing one's behavior by transforming an ethical problem into another type of problem, or assuming responsibility for only one specific, technical component of the issue, or claiming it is someone else's problem, gives one the feeling of being absolved from culpability by putting the burden of responsibility elsewhere.

Who is responsible for ensuring ethical behavior? We believe that corporations have a responsibility to make clear to their employees what sort of behavior is expected of them. This means that executives in headquarters have a responsibility, not just for their own behavior, but also for providing guidance to subordinates. A number of companies have corporate codes to do just this. For example, General Electric (GE) has an integrity policy entitled *Integrity: The Spirit & Letter of Our Commitment* that covers, among other issues, ethical business practices, health, safety, and environmental protection, and equal employment opportunity. Employees sign a pledge that they will adhere to the policy. Jeffrey Immelt, CEO of GE, in his statement to employees regarding this policy, explains:

> As GE learns and grows in the 21st century, three traditions of our company become more important. Along with commitment to performance and thirst for change, we must always display total, unyielding integrity.
>
> This is a company of integrity. It's a company of standards. Our worldwide reputation for honest and reliable business conduct, built by so many people over so many years, is tested and proven in each business transaction we make.
>
> Today's GE is far more dynamic, globally directed and customer-driven than ever before. We are playing offense – trying new things to build our business success – our quality products and services; our forthright relations with customers, suppliers and each other; and, ultimately, our winning competitive record. But the GE quest for competitive excellence begins and ends with our commitment to lawful and ethical conduct. As a global company, we must create and follow a set of global rules.
>
> Each person in the GE community makes a personal commitment to follow our Code of Conduct. Guiding us in upholding our ethical commitment is a set of GE policies on key integrity issues. All GE employees must comply not only with the letter of these policies but also their spirit.
>
> I, and all GE leaders, have the additional responsibility of nurturing a culture in which compliance with GE policy and applicable law is at the very core of our business activities. It is, and must be, the way we work.[20]

However, the person on the spot facing the decision is ultimately responsible for his or her own behavior, with or without guidance from headquarters. In all the cases in this part of the book, you will be asked to develop your own stance on the issues. We encourage you to think carefully about the problems depicted in the cases and to develop reasoned positions. You may find yourself in a similar situation someday, and you will have to make a critical decision. We hope that, by working through the decisions in these cases now, you will be better able to deal with similar decisions later.

Ethical versus legal behavior

One question that always arises in a discussion of ethics is the distinction between legal and ethical behavior. If one acts legally, in accordance with the law, is that not sufficient? Not all of society's norms regarding moral behavior have been codified or made into law. There can be many instances of questionable behavior that are not illegal.[21] It would seem that acting legally is the minimum required behavior for executives. However, society relies on more than laws to function effectively in many spheres of endeavor. In business, trust is essential also. Finally, it also should be recognized that not all laws are moral.

Verne Henderson has provided a useful way to think about the relationship between ethical and legal behavior.[22] He created a matrix based on whether an action was legal or illegal and ethical or unethical, similar to that shown in Figure 1. Assuming that executives want to act legally and ethically (quadrant 4) and avoid making decisions (or acting in ways) that are illegal and unethical (quadrant 2), the decisions that create dilemmas are the ones that fall into quadrants 1 and 3. For example, consider the decision of a chemical-company manager who refuses to promote a pregnant woman to an area of the company where she would be exposed to toxic chemicals that could damage her child. The manager probably would be acting ethically, but illegally (quadrant 1). Maybe he could solve the problem by delaying the promotion, if that was possible. This simple example illustrates that a decision can be ethical but not legal; there also may be solutions that allow a win–win outcome in which the decision is legal and ethical because of the way it is made.

FIGURE 1 Framework for Classifying Behavior

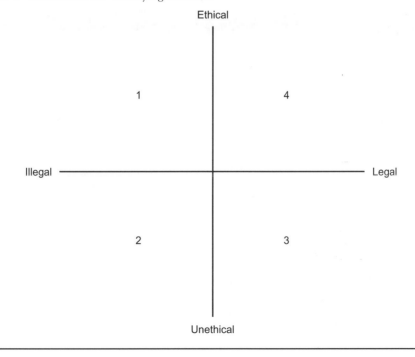

In quadrant 3, there will be situations like the marketing of infant formula in developing countries. Infant formula, which was misused in many countries with poor sanitation and polluted water and where people were illiterate and could not read directions, was blamed for the deaths of hundreds of thousands of babies each year. This activity was not illegal, but a United Nations vote regarding infant formula declared it unethical.[23] In an interesting twist to this story, studies now have shown that AIDS virus can be transmitted through breastfeeding, and the UN has estimated that one-third of all infants with HIV were infected through their mother's milk.[24] Infant formula may now be a way to combat the transmission of HIV. This example shows that society's notions of ethical behavior may change with new conditions and knowledge. Another example in quadrant 3 would be apartheid, which might have been legal in South Africa, but was not ethical.

Whose laws and values should be followed when there are conflicts? Although it might seem that we are avoiding answers, we believe that these are questions each person and company need to answer for themselves. The challenge is to find ways of operating that are consistent with local laws and high standards of conduct. We believe that this goal is attainable with thorough analysis and carefully considered action.

In situations where a win–win outcome is not possible, there is always the option of choosing not to operate in that environment. The decision to walk away and lose the business may seem naïve, but we have met and interviewed a number of executives of very successful companies that have done just that. One described how his company turned down a $50-million contract in a Latin American country because there was no way to avoid paying a bribe to a government official. Another explained that, in his experience, if a company developed a reputation for acting ethically it was not usually subjected to unethical demands.

ETHICAL FRAMEWORK[25]

Moral philosophers have developed frameworks for thinking about moral issues and for analyzing ethical problems. As we investigated various frameworks for analyzing ethical problems, we discovered that there are conflicting positions and prescriptions among them. We have heard people advocate actions representing some of the major frameworks without realizing that they are engaged in a discussion of moral philosophy. Consider the following discussion about paying a bribe:

Person X: "If we don't pay what he is asking for we will lose the contract and people back home will lose jobs. Is that ethical, when people can't feed their families?"

Person Y: "I don't care. What you are suggesting is absolutely wrong."

Person Z: "Now hold on; it doesn't seem to be against the rules there. It is different in that culture. Everyone is doing it. They need the extra money to support their families. Besides, we should not impose our system of morality on other cultures."

You may have heard or have taken part in a similar exchange. The people in the conversation above probably do not understand the weaknesses of their positions and are engaged in the type of discussion that tends to excite emotions and generate heat and argument, rather than provide insight and a thoughtful course of action.

Since you may likely take part in similar discussions (or arguments) at some time in your career, we think that knowledge of these three frameworks will be useful. The intent is to help you link some everyday reasoning and the positions you might espouse to the ethical frameworks underlying them. In the brief exchange above, one sees commonly used frameworks, which is why they were chosen for this example.

The first ethical framework is consequential or teleological, which focuses on the consequences, outcomes, or results of decisions and behavior – the loss of jobs. The second is rule-based or deontological, which focuses on moral obligations, duties, and rights. The third is cultural, which emphasizes cultural differences in standards of behavior – everyone does it here. Each represents a different moral calculus, a different ethical map. We do not claim that one or another is better or worse; the frameworks *describe* different ways in which people tend to think about ethical issues, and explain why a person who uses one framework does not see the arguments of a person who applies a different framework. Each of the approaches is discussed briefly here.

Consequential theories

Consequential theories focus on the goals, end results, and/or consequences of decisions and actions. They are concerned with doing the maximum amount of "good" and the minimum amount of "harm." Utilitarianism is the most widely used example of this type of moral framework. It suggests doing the best for the greatest number of people. Another example is acting in a way that provides more net utility than an alternative act. It essentially is an economic, cost-benefit approach to ethical decision-making. If the benefits outweigh the costs, then that course of action is indicated.

The major limitations of this approach are that it is difficult or impossible to identify and account for all the costs and benefits, and, since people have different utility curves, it is difficult to decide whose curve should be used. In real life, how do you compute this utility curve? Finally, in an effort to weigh the costs and benefits, one relies on quantitative data, usually economic data, and many important variables that should be considered are not quantifiable and, therefore, often ignored.

Rule-based theories

Rule-based theories include both absolute (or universal) theories and conditional theories. The emphasis of these theories is on duty, obligations, and rights. For example, if an employee follows orders or performs a certain task, management has an obligation to ensure that the task is not illegal or harmful to that person's health. People in power have a responsibility to protect the rights of the less powerful. These theories are concerned with the universal "shoulds" and "oughts" of human existence – the rules that should guide all people's decision-making and behavior wherever they are.

One of the best-known absolute theories is the categorical imperative of Immanuel Kant. Whereas utilitarianism takes a group or societal perspective, the categorical imperative has a more individualistic focus: individuals should be treated with respect and dignity as an end in itself; they should not be used simply as a means to an end. A person should not be done harm, even if the ultimate end is good. The criteria should be applied consistently to everyone. One of the questions to ask is: "If I were in the other person's (or group's or organization's) position, would I be willing for them to make the same decision that I am going to make for the same reasons?"

Another type of absolute approach is <u>fundamentalism</u>. In this case, the rules may come from a book like the Bible, Koran, or Torah – an authoritative, divine word that has been revealed through prophets. Difficult questions arise when considering which book or prophet to follow and whose interpretation of the chosen book to use. Priests, mullahs, or rabbis usually interpret the books, but some people worry that they may reflect the views of an elite segment of society or possibly an isolated group. There can be conflicting interpretations within the same religion as well. The rules that people follow can also be secular as well as religious, as in the case of Nazi Germany.

One shortcoming of these types of prescriptions is that they allow you to claim that you are <u>not responsible</u> for your own behavior: "I was just following orders" is a common excuse. The end result may be the same – you do not have to think for yourself or make a moral judgment, but rather you can avoid it by claiming to be following a higher authority. As this text was being revised, the "I was following orders" line of defense was being proposed by lawyers for some of the US soldiers who were facing court martial for the abuse of Iraqi prisoners in <u>Abu Ghraib</u> prison.[26] However, the war crimes trials after World War II established that following orders is not an acceptable legal defense for committing atrocities, and it probably will not be an acceptable defense for abusing prisoners of war in contravention of the Geneva Convention.

Cultural theories

With cultural approaches, <u>local standards</u> prevail. Cultural relativism is interpreted to mean that there is no single right way; in other words, people should not impose their values and standards on others. The reasoning behind the argument usually is that we should behave as the locals behave. The familiar expression tells us: "When in Rome, do as the Romans do."

We have argued throughout this book that understanding other cultures from their own point of view is critical to effective international management. However, cultural relativism is not always appropriate for resolving ethical issues. For example, the local people we are encouraged to emulate may not be the most exemplary. In your own culture, you know that people exhibit different standards of behavior. Should business people going to the United States act like the people convicted in the accounting scandal at Enron, for example, just because those people were Americans? Or should expatriate managers working in Italy follow the example set by Parmalat executives because they were Italians? Of course not!

Adopting this philosophy also can encourage denial of accountability and the avoidance of moral choice. Using arguments based on this philosophy, the morality of bribes or actions of repressive regimes, for example, do not have to be examined very closely. These theories are summarized in Figure 2.

FIGURE 2 Analytical Frameworks

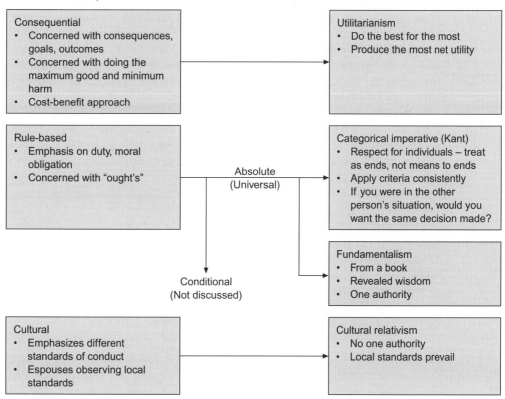

How does one choose among these conflicting approaches? There is no simple answer to this question. But we think that it is important for managers to recognize the basis for their moral and ethical decisions and to be aware, for example, if they are shifting from one theory to another as a way of avoiding tough decisions. And, if they are dealing with people who use a different moral calculus, Maps (M) of these differences provide the basis for the Bridging (B) and Integration (I) components of the MBI model to communicate across the differences and to manage them.

Intellectual and ethical development William Perry describes another perspective that managers may find useful – a process of intellectual and ethical development.[27] Although we should recognize that Perry's ideas reflect a cultural bias toward individualism and were derived from a narrow part of the US population, his ideas can help managers think about their positions on these issues.[28] The first category is *dualism*, in which a bipolar structure of the world is assumed or taken for granted. According to this perspective there is a clear right and wrong, good and bad, we and they. These positions are defined from one's own perspective based on membership in a group and belief in or adherence to a common set of traditional beliefs.

The next category, posited by Perry as a "more developed" perspective, is *relativism,* in which the dualistic worldview is moderated by an understanding of the importance of context, which helps a person to see that knowledge and values are relative. As we have seen through earlier parts of this book, different people in different parts of the world think and believe differently, and a relativistic mode of making ethical judgments recognizes this fact. As originally observed by Blaise Pascal, Geert Hofstede notes in the preface to his book, *Culture's Consequences*: "There are truths on this side of the Pyrénées which are falsehoods on the other."[29]

Is this best? →

In Perry's scheme, the third "level" of development is *commitment in relativism,* in which a person understands the relativistic nature of the world but makes a commitment to a set of values, beliefs, and a way of behaving within this expanded worldview. The goal, implicitly reflecting the individualism and mastery orientations described in Part 1, is to arrive at the point where you assume responsibility for your own actions and decisions based upon careful consideration and the application of the "essential tools of moral reasoning – deliberation and justification."[30]

Perry suggests that progression to this stage is not automatic or guaranteed and that people may become "delayed" in their development or even "stuck" in the earlier stages. People who adhere to a set of absolute rules, however, may reject this notion of a hierarchy of development. Our inclusion of Perry's ideas is not meant to judge others' choices in this regard, but rather to encourage self-awareness. We think it is important to be thoughtful about these decisions, develop self-awareness of your own logic and how it relates to others', and understand the implications of your decisions.

Some ethical issues faced by managers

Example

Ethical questions can arise in many areas of operations: the type of products produced, marketing and advertising practices, business conduct in countries where physical security is a problem, hiring and promotion practices in countries where discrimination and racism exist, requests for payments to secure contracts or sales, and payments to prevent damage to plants and equipment or injury to employees. In this section we provide a series of examples of ethical issues that managers faced. They are typical of the dilemmas managers find themselves in daily. Some are small in scale, others are very large (but may have started off small!); all demonstrate the importance of thinking through the implications of decisions beyond narrow economic transactions.

As you read these examples, try to put yourself into the situation as a decision-maker. What is legal versus ethical in this situation? Which logic – consequential, rule-based, or cultural – do you find most compelling to address this situation? What would you do? Why? Thinking through these examples and the cases in the section will help prepare you to face your own ethical dilemmas with greater insight.

Some products are controversial in themselves, such as tobacco and the abortion pill. Such products facilitate behavior that many people believe is unethical. Other products, such as soccer balls and jeans, may not create dilemmas as consumers use them, but their production raises debate. We trace the development of several types of products in this section. For each product, there are many ethical dilemmas and issues faced by many different managers.

Products

What would you do?
why?

Cigarettes

The ethical challenges of trade in tobacco products can be seen in the behavior of the US government and Philip Morris, Inc. According to the World Health Organization (WHO)[31] tobacco is the second major cause of death in the world, responsible for about 5 million deaths each year. Continuation of current smoking patterns will increase this to 10 million deaths annually by 2025, the majority of them in the developing world. One-half of the smokers today – about 650 million people – will eventually be killed by tobacco. In the United States in 2000, the Centers for Disease Control claim that tobacco was the leading preventable cause of death and the leading *actual cause of death*,[32] accounting for 435,000 deaths.[33] WHO notes that "a cigarette is the only legally available consumer product that kills through normal use."

WHO also claims that:

> The economic costs of tobacco use are equally devastating. In addition to the high public health costs of treating tobacco-caused diseases, tobacco kills people at the height of their productivity, depriving families of breadwinners and nations of a healthy workforce. Tobacco users are also less productive while they are alive due to increased sickness . . .
>
> Tobacco and poverty are inextricably linked. Many studies have shown that in the poorest households in some low-income countries as much as 10% of total household expenditure is on tobacco. This means that these families have less money to spend on basic items such as food, education and health care. In addition to its direct health effects, tobacco leads to malnutrition, increased health care costs and premature death. It also contributes to a higher illiteracy rate, since money that could have been used for education is spent on tobacco instead.

On May 21, 2003 the 192 Member States of WHO adopted the world's first public health treaty, the WHO Framework Convention on Tobacco Control (FCTC). This treaty is designed to reduce tobacco-related deaths and disease around the world. Before it goes into effect, however, countries have to sign and ratify it. Among its measures, the FCTC requires that countries impose restrictions on tobacco advertising, sponsorship, and promotion; and establish new packaging and labeling of tobacco products. Achieving agreement on the FCTC was not easy and the eventual treaty was significantly "watered down," in large measure due to the actions of George W. Bush's Administration.[34]

In a letter to President George W. Bush on April 29, 2003,[35] Democratic Representative Henry Waxman, the ranking minority member of the House Committee on Government Reform, said:

> At the most recent, and final, negotiating session, held from February 17 to February 28, 2003, the United States again attempted to weaken the tobacco control treaty on key issues. Indeed, your negotiators even opposed international efforts to restrict the distribution of free samples and to prohibit the sale of tobacco products to children.

Additionally, he stated that in previous negotiating sessions the United States had:

- opposed proposals that would require tobacco warning labels to be written in the language of the country where the tobacco products were sold;
- opposed proposals for mandatory tobacco taxes;
- opposed provisions mandating action to protect citizens from secondhand smoke;
- attempted to weaken proposals to restrict tobacco advertising;
- opposed prohibitions of the use of deceptive terms such as "light" and "low" on tobacco labels, insisting that countries first prove these terms are misleading before prohibiting their use; and
- argued that trade interests should trump [take precedence over] health issues in implementation of the treaty.

The United States, Canada, and Germany all opposed a total advertising ban, claiming that their constitutions protect freedom of speech and do not permit them to implement a comprehensive ban. NGO's proposed the adoption of a "constitutional carve-out" that allowed the FCTC to have a full ban on tobacco advertising, except for countries whose constitutions would not allow for a full ban. The United States and Germany opposed it.[36] Does freedom of speech cover cigarette advertising? Is trade more important than public health? Even if there are US Constitutional issues involving tobacco advertising bans, should the United States try to prevent other nations from banning tobacco advertising if it is permitted by their own legal systems? The treaty was eventually signed by all member states, including the United States, after it finally agreed to the inclusion of a "constitutional carve-out."

In 2003, the Government Accounting Office (GAO) found that the Foreign Agricultural Service may have violated Congress's prohibition on the US Department of Agriculture from spending any funds to promote the sale or export of tobacco products.[37] Should one part of the US government spend money to combat smoking in the United States while other parts are spending it to promote cigarette exports to other countries? One side could argue that the countries like the United States, Britain, and Japan, where the majority of big tobacco companies are located, are exporting death and disease to the developing world. The other side could counter that cigarettes are not illegal, are manufactured and sold in many countries, and therefore manufacturers would not be introducing these items for the first time. They would argue that manufacturing and selling cigarettes is not illegal, and international tobacco companies should have access to the developing world's markets.

At the company level, such as at Philip Morris, what obligations should a corporation have regarding advertising in other countries? Should the company follow the local laws, even if they are less restrictive than at home, or would there be a responsibility to advertise that cigarette smoking is hazardous to your health and include all warnings required in the United States or even elsewhere if they are stricter? Should they oppose large warning sizes because they may "infringe" on their trademarks on the packages?

All the issues regarding exporting and advertising cigarettes could be treated simply as considerations in international trade, marketing, or advertising, if one chose. Advertising cigarettes in other countries could also be treated as primarily a legal question, as the US and German governments apparently saw it. To treat complex situations and decisions as primarily trade, marketing, or legal issues without addressing the ethical implications, however, would be an oversight and a mistake.

The abortion pill

Another example of a product-safety/consumer-protection dilemma involves RU486, the so-called abortion pill. Roussel Uclaf in France developed RU486 as an alternative to surgical abortions. Clearly, there are at least two sides to this issue. One position is that RU486 would help women who chose to have an abortion and who might be at risk in unsafe surgical abortions; another point of view is that its use would be murder – killing unborn children. Against a backdrop of vehement disagreement about the morality of abortions and the pill, and a threatened international boycott, was the fact that China wanted RU486 as part of its population control program and had approved the marketing of it.[38] Should the company have marketed RU486 in China? Further complicating the decision was the fact that Hoechst Chemical was Roussel Uclaf's largest shareholder. In addition, Hoechst had a corporate creed emphasizing support for life, which had been developed in reaction to its previous role as a supplier of cyanide gas for the Nazi gas chambers, and it thought that China did not have an adequate medical infrastructure to handle the product safely.[39]

Eventually, in April 1997, when it faced a boycott by the Christian Coalition, the National Right to Life Committee, and other organizations in the United States, Hoechst Marion Roussel (HMR) decided to stop producing and distributing RU486. It gave the rights to Edouard Sakiz, former President of Roussel Uclaf and a member of the team that discovered the drug.[40]

Although HMR removed itself from the controversy surrounding RU486, the debate about abortion and RU486 continues. In September 2000 the US Food and Drug Administration (FDA) approved RU486. Proponents thought its availability in the United States would encourage more doctors to perform abortions and its opponents feared the same thing. This did not happen because RU486 is expensive and requires multiple visits by a doctor. Additionally, doctors must have the ability to perform a surgical abortion if RU486 does not work, or they must be affiliated with a hospital that is able to.[41]

Danco Laboratories, which manufactures RU486 under the name Mifeprex, in conjunction with the FDA wrote a letter to doctors stating that a number of women experienced "adverse events." Since 2001 there have been numerous reports from around the world of deaths linked to RU486.[42] On the other hand, Planned Parenthood clinics in the United States found that, "of 12,700 'medical' abortions done in one year, there was not one major complication."[43] In 2001, China banned the sale of RU486 to protect patients' safety and health after hospitals in the Beijing area reported treating women suffering from dangerous side effects.[44] What should managers in a company like Danco Laboratories or in a government agency like the FDA do? Is a letter to doctors sufficient, or are there other actions that should be taken?

Jeans, rugs, and soccer balls

All of the previous examples had public health considerations. But there are ethical issues with products that don't involve public health, such as jeans, soccer balls, and rugs, when they are manufactured in, or purchased from, countries that have been found to abuse human rights. For example, Levi Strauss stopped purchasing from subcontractors in

Myanmar and China because of practices such as using child and prison labor to manufacture products.[45] The company also has developed a set of standards called the "Global Sourcing Guidelines," which address workplace issues for its partners and subcontractors, and the selection countries for sourcing products.[46] IKEA, the Swedish furniture manufacturer and retailer, will not sell carpets unless they are certified as having been made without child labor, and some German rug-importers have launched the first "human rights label," Rugmark, which signifies that children were not used to make the rugs.[47] As of December 2002, more than 3 million carpets bearing the RUGMARK label were sold to Europe and North America.[48]

In June 1996, *Life* magazine carried an article about child labor in Pakistan, which included a photo of a 12-year-old boy sewing a Nike soccer ball which would take him most of the day and for which he would earn 60 cents.[49] Human rights activists around the world began to target Nike. Did Nike know that its contractors used bonded child labor, or should it have known? Nike claimed that it is difficult to determine ages in some countries where birth records don't exist or can be easily forged. What were executives' responsibilities? In October 2000, the British Broadcasting Corporation revealed that Nike was still employing underage women in a factory in Cambodia.[50] Nike was stung by the criticism of its continuing employment of children in Third World countries and has taken action to address its social responsibility issues. According to the company's website, in 2001:

> Nike released its first Corporate Responsibility Report in an attempt to assess and communicate the impact of how the company runs its business. The report includes a series of detailed reports of Nike's efforts at developing environmental sustainability; its efforts toward understanding and managing global labor compliance; its commitment to diversity and the company's involvement in local communities.[51]

The issue about manufacturing is not as simple as "do not use child labor." We spoke at length with a small business owner who exports rugs from Pakistan and Afghanistan. She visits her manufacturers regularly and encourages community development around the making of rugs. There are many girls as young as 8 working in her craft shops. In her words,

> If I did not hire these girls, they would not be at school. They would be in the fields. Their life expectancy would be shorter; they would be working alone. In the workshop, they sit together with women of three or more generations, they learn a skill, and they learn about their culture. Because they are in my workshop, I can provide good meals and people and materials to provide at least some education and social support for them. Am I doing the right thing? According to the press and many consumers, definitely not! But I do believe that, in this case, hiring these girls and trying to provide a better environment for them is the right thing.

Ethical issues, by definition, are not simple. Is it ever acceptable to use child labor? What are managers' responsibilities here? It is easy to find laws or guidelines to justify whichever decision you want to make. The question is, whether you understand your own rationale and the full implications of your decisions and actions.

Human rights and security   It may seem self-evident that companies should respect the human rights and security of all stakeholders. But even this issue creates controversy, often as seemingly small or isolated events grow in impact.

Shell in Nigeria

Human rights and fundamental freedoms were issues in Nigeria in November 1995 when Ken Saro-Wiwa was executed by the military government. In 1994, General Sani Abacha had declared the death penalty for "anyone who interferes with the government's efforts to 'revitalize' the oil industry."[52] The declaration was his response to striking oil workers and demands for increased revenue-sharing by local communities. Saro-Wiwa was a political activist who was campaigning on behalf of his people, the Ogoni, and against the degradation of the environment by oil spills and pollution caused by Royal Dutch Shell.[53] In 1995, Saro-Wiwa's activities were construed as "interference" and he was executed.

Initially, Shell responded defensively with full-page advertisements in major newspapers around the world explaining its position.[54] Later, under pressure from shareholders who filed a resolution at its annual meeting in 1997, it changed the tone of its response dramatically. It named Cor Herkstroter, at the time Chairman of Royal Dutch (the Dutch half of the company), to be responsible for human rights and environmental issues. Mr Herkstroter accepted the criticism that Nigeria Shell should have been more proactive in improving its environmental performance.[55] He also conducted a review of the company's business principles and added commitments to support human rights and sustainable development.

In 2002 Shell was still reporting progress and performance on environmental and social responsibility issues.[56] For example, in 2002, the company issued 5,000 copies of a new training guide on human rights dilemmas:

> The guide helps managers understand their responsibilities and identify actions they can take to support human rights. It is now part of our Business Principles training.
>
> We also developed a new human rights compliance tool for Shell companies, based on tools developed by the Human Rights and Business project of the Danish Centre for Human Rights [see www.humanrightsbusiness.org/]. First piloted in South Africa in 2001, this was revised in 2002 to give managers a practical step-by-step approach to help them avoid violating the basic human rights of employees, local communities and others directly affected by our operations. It now also covers compliance aspects by contractors and aligns with our business management processes.[57]

Apartheid in South Africa

Discrimination or racism may be deeply rooted in the history and cultures of a country and may be firmly ensconced in a country's laws, as they were in South Africa. The policies of many multinational corporations operating there lagged behind the views of the societies where their headquarters were located. Some multinationals eventually became more assertive in providing changes in their subsidiaries in South Africa. The primary pressure for this action was external, however.

One force was the emergence of pressure groups that used proxies at annual meetings to confront the issue. These were often church groups that invested in the companies in order to apply such pressure. The second was a code of acceptable behavior, the Sullivan Principles, named after the black minister who led their development. The idea was that, if companies agreed to operate in South Africa in accordance with these principles, they would earn the right to be exempt from the pressure-group tactics.

In hindsight, we have learned that these steps alone were not sufficient to bring substantial change. But unpopular policies of the South African government, political unrest, sanctions of Western countries, and an eroding economic situation finally influenced the multinationals' decisions. Many major corporations left South Africa. Some, such as Kodak, even decided not to sell their products in the country. It may well have been the case that no corporate policies directed at making change from within the system, no matter when instituted, would have been enough to end apartheid and that only by disinvesting and leaving the country did multinationals finally make a difference.[58]

Discrimination

There still are countries where discrimination against indigenous ethnic and racial groups exists but is not as obvious to the outside world as was the situation in South Africa. This removes a significant external pressure for change from a corporation, but it does not remove the ethical responsibility from executives to address diligently such issues and to take action.

Discrimination may also be based on gender. For example, people in Japan or Saudi Arabia have beliefs about the appropriate roles for women that may discourage gender equality in the workplace.[59] This creates a problem for companies that actively promote workplace equality in their home countries. In 1991, the US Congress decided that Title VII of the Civil Rights Act of 1991 protects US citizens from employment discrimination by US multinationals in their overseas operations.[60] Companies are caught in a dilemma: violate a principle and possibly a law, or risk offending people in another culture. The dilemma will not disappear by ignoring it, and corporations need to develop operating policies for managing in these environments. The "Ellen Moore" case in Part 2 shows that different perceptions of women in managerial roles can complicate choices for individuals as well as present challenges to corporate operations.

Physical security

Situations in which physical security could be a problem may present ethical issues for managers and employees. Consider a situation in which British expatriate women working in the Middle East training center of a North American-based bank found themselves. They were en route to conduct a training program in Lagos, Nigeria, and were supposed to be met by one of the bank's local staff who would assist them through customs at the airport. When the local staff member failed to appear, the women felt forced to pay bribes to bring legitimate training materials and equipment into the country. Soon after paying the money, their taxi was stopped at the darkened perimeter of the airport and machine guns were jabbed at them through the windows by uniformed men. The women were "shaken down" again and felt very vulnerable, particularly as they now had no Nigerian currency left. After repeatedly showing their documents, denying that they were violating any laws, and playing dumb about the purpose of the delay, the accusing questions, and the threatening gestures, they were finally permitted to pass. The women were deeply shaken by the experience and vowed never to travel into that country alone again.

What responsibility did the local management bear for abandoning them? And what was the ethical responsibility of the experienced managers for whom the women worked who sent them into such a situation so ill prepared? What is a manager's responsibility regarding the implementation of his or her decisions, particularly when the specific action has to be taken by another person?

Many companies currently are operating in countries where kidnappings and personal security concerns are considerations and/or where political violence and terrorism are issues.[61] For example, in Colombia between 2000 and 2004, 28 Americans were reported kidnapped in various parts of the country. The victims included journalists, missionaries, scientists, human rights workers, US government employees, businesspeople, and tourists.[62] In Mexico "express kidnappings" of Mexicans and foreigners to get quick cash from ATMs in exchange for their release have occurred in many large cities.[63] On March 11, 2004, terrorists bombed a train in Madrid, killing 191 people and injuring 2,000 others. In late May, 2004, terrorists killed 22 people in oil company office compounds and in an expatriate housing compound in Saudi Arabia and took over 40 hostages, including Americans and Europeans, while earlier in the month terrorists killed six Westerners and a Saudi in another attack.[64]

Unfortunately, having to manage crises is becoming more common in global companies. The "Building Products International" case in Part 3 puts you in the position of the Director of Human Resources who developed the crisis-management strategy for the company's Asia-Pacific Region. The company had employees in Jakarta, Indonesia at the time of the worst rioting in the region in decades and the Director of Human Resources was faced with a decision about the evacuation of various Building Products International employees, their families, and guests from Indonesia. What is a company's responsibility associated with assigning an employee to one of these countries? What should it do regarding training and protecting employees who work in these areas? What is the responsibility of individuals who agree to work there?

Bribery and corruption   One of the most common dilemmas that executives may encounter are requests for bribes or even extortion. For example, mobsters threatened Otis Elevator that they would firebomb its operation in Russia if it did not pay protection money.[65] How should this situation be handled? Otis has a code that delineates its view of right and wrong behavior that all executives sign each year. Its response was not to give in to the extortion, but to pay more for security.[66] Situations involving extortion and bribery have many facets and usually are not resolved simply.

A bribe is a payment to an individual to which they are not entitled in return for their changing a decision. The "fee" is not recorded in the official accounting statements of the receiver, nor sometimes of the payer. Rather than go to the institution, the payment usually goes directly to an individual or group of individuals. Two problems caused by bribery are corruption and tax evasion. Bribery encourages individuals to take gains for themselves rather than on behalf of their company (including employees, suppliers, and customers). These gains may be small and help the receiver's family move from poverty, but they may be large and furnish the receiver with a lifetime of luxury. Tax evasion occurs because the income is not recorded, therefore no taxes are paid on it. It many cases, tax evasion results in significant losses to the government, which prevents the money from being redistributed for services such as health and education.

Statoil in Iran

Statoil was founded in 1972 with a mandate to explore and develop Norway's offshore oil and gas reserves. Operating in Norway's harsh waters demanded a high level of innovation, which helped Statoil to become one of the world's foremost authorities in offshore production. By the end of century the company faced declining reserves at home and sought to expand through international investment.

In the years following the death of the Ayatollah Khomeini, the Iranian government decided to reopen the country to international investment. In 2001, the National Iranian Oil Company (NIOC) sought tenders to develop South Pars, an offshore oilfield that held approximately 8 percent of known world gas reserves, and 40 percent of Iran's known reserves. In October 2002, NIOC awarded Statoil a 40 percent stake in the South Pars project. Under the terms of the agreement, Statoil was to invest $300 million over four years as part of its $2.6-billion investment in the Persian Gulf.[67]

Less than one year after being awarded the contract, Statoil's future in Iran appeared to be in jeopardy. The controversy centered on alleged bribes paid by Horton Investments, on Statoil's behalf, in order to secure lucrative petroleum development contracts.

In early 2003, Statoil's internal auditors had uncovered secret payments of $5 million to Horton Investments,[68] a Turks and Caicos Islands-registered consultancy thought to be run by the son of a former Iranian president. According to Statoil, Horton Investments was hired to provide "insight into financial, industrial, legal, and social issues associated with business development in Iran."[69] But according to the Iranian government, the secret $15-million contract between Horton and Statoil was used to channel bribes to unnamed government officials.

Although occurring many years earlier and involving a company from a different country and different industry, the "Valley Farms International" case in Part 3 is eerily similar to that of Statoil and requires you to address the types of ethical problems an executive may encounter during international expansion. The Statoil and Valley Farms examples show that history may repeat itself and that executives need to be prepared for these situations. A more detailed discussion of how to manage in the face of pressure for bribes can be found in the reading, "Bribery in International Business: Whose Problem Is It?" There are many myths surrounding the issue of bribery, and this reading sheds light on the issue from different perspectives. The authors of the reading suggest that there are acceptable alternatives.

Transparency International[70]

Bribery and corruption are global problems that are not limited to public officials in a few developing countries. Executives of global corporations which have their headquarters in developed countries are affected, and some even have been implicated in scandals. Global executives should not be smug about the locus of the problem or their responsibilities. There is an old saying, "It takes two to tango." An organization that has been established to combat the problem of bribery and corruption is Transparency International.

Since it was founded in 1993, Transparency International (TI) has become the leading NGO combating national and international corruption. It was founded by people in the developed and developing world who believed that "grand corruption" was a threat to human rights, the environment, and sustainable development, and could not be ignored.[71]

TI has developed chapters in approximately ninety countries and has worked with organizations such as the OECD, the Organization of American States (OAS), the European Union, and the African Union to develop and monitor anti-corruption legislation and treaties. It analyzes corruption by measuring its occurrence through surveys, and has created resources and tools used by people around the world in the fight against corruption. These tools include the Corruption Perceptions Index, the Global Corruption Barometer, the Global Corruption Report, the Bribe Payers Index, and the latest anti-corruption information on TI's website and through the Corruption On-line Research & Information Service (CORISweb; www.corisweb.org/). Two of these tools are discussed briefly below.

TI's Bribe Payers Index (BPI) is based on surveys conducted by Gallup International Association *in* 15 emerging market countries[72] about executives' perceptions of multinational firms *from* 21 countries. The 2002 BPI was based on 835 interviews with senior executives of domestic and overseas companies, chartered public accountancies, chambers of commerce, national and overseas commercial banks, and commercial law firms. The head of TI's Research Department stated:

> The results reflect the views of expert business leaders, who are best positioned to have significant insights into issues of grand corruption and the bribery of government officials in developing countries.[73]

The 2002 BPI shows that US multinational corporations, even with the *Foreign Corrupt Practices Act*, show a propensity to bribe overseas government officials. The US score was 5.3 out of a perfect possible 10. This was similar to Japanese companies but worse than the scores for corporations from France, Spain, Germany, Singapore, and the United Kingdom.[74] The highest scores, indicating the lowest propensity to bribe overseas, were for companies from Australia, Sweden, Switzerland, Austria, Canada, the Netherlands, and Belgium.

Another index, the Corruption Perception Index score, measures the perceptions of the degree of corruption in a country as seen by business people, academics, and risk analysts. The score ranges between 10 (highly clean) and 0 (highly corrupt) for 133 countries. The entire CPI can be found on the TI web site (www.transparency.org/index.html). The top and bottom countries on this index are shown in Table 1.

Ethics: part of an international manager's daily life   With this discussion, we have tried to show that ethical dilemmas are common. All managers area likely to face ethical dilemmas in their careers. Global managers, because they operate in many different

TABLE 1   2003 Corruption Perception Index Scores for the Top and Bottom Countries[a]

Best Countries		Worst Countries	
9.7	Finland	1.8	Angola
9.6	Iceland		Azerbaijan
9.5	Denmark		Cameroon
	New Zealand		Georgia
9.4	Singapore		Tajikistan
9.3	Sweden	1.6	Myanmar
8.9	Netherlands		Paraguay
8.8	Australia	1.5	Haiti
	Norway	1.4	Nigeria
	Switzerland	1.3	Bangladesh
8.7	Canada, Luxembourg, and the United Kingdom tied for 11th		

Note:

a 10 = highly clean, 0 = highly corrupt. The United States and Ireland were tied for 18th with a score of 7.5.

contexts and with a broader spectrum of stakeholders, face particularly difficult and complex ethical dilemmas. Rather than avoid such issues, it is important to acknowledge their complexity and build insights and tools for analyzing them systematically. Develop the discipline of thinking through the impact of your decisions and actions, and learn to engage your co-workers in open discussions about ethical issues. We now turn to the final area of corporate responsibility – discretionary behavior – for which, as we said earlier, society has no clear messages.

SOCIALLY RESPONSIVE DISCRETIONARY BEHAVIOR

Companies' orientation to social responsibility has been described in many ways, but most commonly by a progression from a narrow set of responsibilities to more broadly conceived ones. For example, one such framework reflects a continuum from solely maximizing profits in the present to trusteeship of the quality of life for present and future generations:

- *social obligation* is an approach in which responsibility is limited to benefiting shareholders, compliance with laws, and doing the minimum required;
- *social responsibility* is a reactive approach to a broader group of organizational stakeholders (for example, customers, employees, suppliers); and
- *social responsiveness* is a proactive, progressive, take-the-lead approach to stakeholder and external societal interests, including environmental issues and social values.[75]

The approach chosen by a company most likely will depend on the executives' view of the relationship between business and society. Decisions about where to position a company on the spectrum are not simple or easy ones. Managers with a view that society's moral values and business objectives are inherently in conflict, or at best totally separate domains of activity, may favor a stance that resists doing more than the minimum.[76] A paradigm in which business objectives and societal values are in harmony or are complementary will more likely lead to actions deemed as progressive or as leading the way.

Social responsiveness may be viewed as a naive ideal or as good business practice that produces a positive public image, creates a competitive advantage in selling environmentally friendly products, and possibly assists in recruiting high-caliber staff looking for companies with whom they can identify.[77] Concerns about social responsiveness and good business practice are not necessarily mutually exclusive. In this section we outline two companies' approaches to social responsiveness, then briefly discuss the risks experienced by a third.

Procter & Gamble   Consumer products company Procter & Gamble (P&G) has taken a strong public stand with respect to social responsiveness. The following statement from their website articulates the social responsiveness position well:

now own Gillette

> In establishing the corporation, society gave it certain rights to encourage its success and longevity. In return, we believe a corporation has certain responsibilities to society – to the governmental entities which authorize its existence, to our employees, our shareholders, our consumers, and the communities and nations where we operate.
>
> Our most important responsibility, we believe, comes from the very purpose of a corporation – to create and build a successful business. When we're successful, we not only provide a return to our shareholders, but equally important, we provide long term employment and income for our employees, and for the many businesses that will develop and grow to support us.
>
> Fulfilling this primary responsibility is particularly important as we enter and begin growing our business in developing countries and those previously behind the Iron Curtain whose economies are undergoing fundamental change. There is a limit to what any one company can do to bring about the fundamental changes required to improve the lot of these societies, but we believe we can make the most meaningful contribution by serving as a role model for others to follow. In fact, the very presence of a successful American company helps educate the people and the government about the benefits of a free and democratic system.
>
> Going hand-in-hand with our responsibility to build a successful business is, of course, our responsibility to abide by the laws and regulations of the countries and communities in which we do business; and we do this everywhere we operate. In fact, we often go beyond what is required by law in how we treat our employees, the environment, and the communities where we live. When we see things that need changing, we work within the system of established laws and regulations of the duly constituted government.[78,79]

P&G was a founding member of the Global Sullivan Principles. Over 200 organizations including manufacturing companies, service companies, professional service firms, city governments, universities, and secular non-profit organizations endorse these principles.[80] Companies endorsing this set of principles support economic growth, social justice, human rights, political justice, and equal opportunity wherever they operate. In fiscal year 2002–3, P&G provided US $85.5 million in non-promotion cash contributions, promotion-related cash contributions, and in-kind/product contributions to numerous community projects throughout the world. This total did not include employee contributions, volunteer time, or administrative expenses, and the money went to educational, health, and human services and civic, cultural, and environmental projects.[81]

An example of P&G's discretionary activities is the HOPE Schools in Pakistan.[82] Many children in city slums and rural areas of Pakistan cannot afford to go to school or do not have access to one, resulting in high illiteracy rates in the country. P&G joined with a Karachi-based nongovernmental organization (NGO) called HOPE (Health Oriented Preventive Education) in supporting home-based schools that provide basic education to those children who otherwise could not get it. P&G funding made it possible to open 10 new schools and for 13 existing ones to continue.

P&G has found creative ways to achieve business results while supporting communities and increasing its social responsiveness. Some may argue their actions have not gone far enough, but it is a start. And the existence of a clear corporate social responsibility strategy at the company level supports ethical and responsive decision-making of managers at an individual level.

Ben & Jerry's Ice Cream   In an interview with the *New York Times Magazine*, Ben Cohen, one of the founders of Ben & Jerry's Ice Cream, defined a socially responsible business as one that "seeks to use its power to improve the quality of life within society."[83] Rather than focus only on profitability and quality like many companies, Cohen said, Ben & Jerry's tries to make an "impact on the community, on the consumer, on our employees." Ben & Jerry's, now a wholly owned subsidiary of Unilever PLC, continues to operate under a three-part mission statement emphasizing product quality, economic reward for shareholders and employees, and a social commitment. Its social mission statement is "to operate the company in a way that actively recognizes the central role that business plays in society by initiating innovative ways to improve the quality of life locally, nationally & internationally."[84] Ben & Jerry's corporate philanthropy is primarily employee-led and its purpose is to support the founding values of the company, which are economic and social justice, environmental restoration and peace through understanding, and support for Vermont communities.[85]

Ben & Jerry's, along with a few other companies with "green" reputations like Aveda and The Body Shop, was an early supporter of the CERES (formerly the Valdez) Principles, a voluntary code of corporate conduct toward the environment, covering 10 areas:[86] protection of the biosphere; sustainable use of natural resources; reduction and disposal of waste (particularly hazardous waste); wise use of energy; reduction of environmental, health, and safety risks; marketing of safe products and services; environmental damage compensation; disclosure of hazards to workers and the public; commitment of management resources to implement, monitor, and report on implementation of the principles; and an annual audit.[87] Since the early 1990s, 70 companies, large and small, have endorsed these principles, including Sunoco, American Airlines, Bank of America, Ford Motor Company, General Motors, Nike, Timberland, and the Vancouver City Savings Credit Union.[88]

As examples of this proactive attitude, Ben & Jerry's actively addresses the impact that its manufacturing operations have on global climate change by undertaking programs to reduce carbon dioxide (CO_2) emissions in its plants, and it also supported the development of the first large-scale Native American owned and operated wind turbine.[89]

When Unilever bought Ben & Jerry's there was widespread concern that it would destroy the company's open and proactive approach to corporate social responsibility. However, writing four years after the purchase, that seems not to be the case. Unilever also has a strong commitment to social responsiveness. Their purchase of Ben & Jerry's was strategic for the ice-cream market, but Unilever was also interested in learning more about social responsiveness from Ben & Jerry's.

[handwritten: Can Laws / Codes / change culture?]

Codes of conduct and responsibility   Most companies begin their journey to social responsiveness by creating a code of conduct, often one which endorses and supports an internationally negotiated code such as the CERES Principles or Global Sullivan Principles. Companies have their lawyers and communications officers develop a code, communicate it to everyone in the company with training, and then support it with policies and consequences. Developing a code of conduct is an important first step, but it must be supported with a culture of responsible decision-making and action.

It is obvious that companies can be hypocritical in their support of social responsibility. Endorsing codes of conduct such as the CERES Principles or Global Sullivan Principles is easy to do, but this act alone does not mean a company is committed to implementing them or managing by them. Statoil's alleged bribery in Iran is an example. Statoil is an endorser of the Sullivan principles but one of the principles is "not to offer, pay or accept bribes," which Statoil apparently violated.

[handwritten margin note: Walk the talk!]

Royal Dutch Shell has recently discovered an unanticipated downside to proclaiming high standards in social responsiveness. After the Nigeria and Brent Spar episodes, Shell launched a very open and public social responsiveness program which was generally well accepted. Shell tried to demonstrate that they were the most responsible oil company, and that strong business principles guided every strategic decision. In late 2003 and early 2004 Shell faced a scandal in which its most senior executives were accused of deliberately inflating estimates of the amount of reserves Shell had as assets and hiding information that would provide accurate (lower) figures. The blow to Shell and its employees was harder both internally and with the marketplace and critics because the company and its executives had held themselves up as paragons of virtue. Companies should always remember that their value statements are *values*, or guidelines for behavior and ideals to be sought after, and should not become complacent that the codes represent absolute truths.

[handwritten margin note: Fire a high level VP for Sexual Harrassment]

In developing codes of conduct executives need to consider their efficacy – do they work? Thomas Donaldson[90] found that effective codes of conduct meet three criteria:

1   Senior management has to be committed to ethical behavior and the codes of conduct; and the codes have to affect "everyday decisions and actions."
2   External or "imposed" codes are not generally effective. Companies have to develop their own and take "ownership" of their codes.
3   Various important stakeholders (employees, customers, suppliers, nongovernmental organizations) have to be involved in shaping the development and implementation of the codes.

UNIVERSALISM, RELATIVISM, AND THE "ASIAN VALUES" DEBATE[91]

It is important to acknowledge that the perspective we presented in the previous two sections on ethics and corporate social responsibility may not be universally held. For millennia there have been many fundamental differences in culture and values between what can broadly be generalized as "East" and "West." The previous brief discussion of different theories in moral philosophy provides a context for understanding the underlying ethical positions of what has been termed the "Asian values" debate. At one level it is the age-old debate in moral philosophy about universalism versus relativism. Is there a universal set of rules that should be followed, or are morals and ethics all relative, depending on the culture? Are one culture's beliefs, values, and practices superior and preferable to those of another? Whose laws, values, or ethics should be followed if and when a disagreement develops, a different course of action is proposed, or a conflict arises? Recently this theoretical debate became more tangible when it turned into an international debate about human rights and economic growth.

[handwritten: Key Question]

Asian values in recent history

In 1948, the United Nations Universal Declaration of Human Rights was signed.[92] Since that time there have been discussions and disagreements over which of the human rights specified in its 30 Articles are universal and which are culturally influenced. China, long criticized by the West for human rights violations, issued a *White Paper on Human Rights in China* in November 1991. Although it "endorsed the language of human rights and praised the development of the international human rights regime . . . [it] argue[d] that the specific contents of human rights vary with 'differences in historical background, social system, cultural tradition, and economic development.' "[93] This proclamation of cultural sovereignty was followed by other pronouncements of quasi-political bodies and prominent Asian leaders.

[handwritten: An interesting term]

In 1993, the Bangkok Declaration was signed by more than thirty Asian and Middle Eastern countries. It presented the view that universal human rights represented statements of Western values and that they were at odds with "Asian values" and not applicable to Asia. This theme later was reiterated by notable Asian leaders.

The imposition of Western values as a form of "cultural imperialism" was voiced by Singapore's Lee Kuan Yew in 1994 when he stated, "It is not my business to tell people what's wrong with their system. It is my business to tell people not to foist their system indiscriminately on societies in which it will not work."[94] In this interview he described some of the differentiators that he saw between East and West:

> The fundamental difference between Western concepts of society and government and East Asian concepts – when I say East Asians, I mean Korea, Japan, China, Vietnam, as distinct from Southeast Asia, which is a mix between the Sinic and the Indian, though Indian culture also emphasizes similar values – is that Eastern societies believe that the individual exists in the context of his family. He is not pristine and separate. The family is part of the extended family, and then friends and the wider society.[95]

Lee also commented on American society from his viewpoint as an East Asian. While admiring parts of the American system he was critical of other parts:

> As an East Asian looking at America, I find attractive and unattractive features. I like, for example, the free, easy and open relations between people regardless of social status, ethnicity or religion. And the things that I have always admired about America, as against the communist system, I still do: a certain openness in argument about what is good or bad for society; the accountability of public officials; none of the secrecy and terror that's part and parcel of communist government.
>
> But as a total system, I find parts of it totally unacceptable: guns, drugs, violent crime, vagrancy, unbecoming behavior in public – in sum the breakdown of civil society. The expansion of the right of the individual to behave or misbehave as he pleases has come at the expense of orderly society. In the East the main object is to have a well-ordered society so that everybody can have maximum enjoyment of his freedoms. This freedom can only exist in an ordered state and not in a natural state of contention and anarchy.[96]

In 1996, at the 29th International General Meeting of the Pacific Basin Economic Council, Dr Mahathir Mohamad, Prime Minister of Malaysia, continued to defend cultural relativism when he said that there was a belief among many in the West that their values and beliefs were universal.[97] Later, in 2000, echoing Lee, he said that too much democracy could lead to violence, instability, and anarchy; and that the West was using ideals such as democracy and human rights as tools to recolonize parts of Asia.[98]

In the remarks of Lee and Mahathir one can see the primary values that are in conflict in this debate:

- The East values community and family (collectivism) while the West values the individual. In the East responsibility toward family and community takes precedence over individual interests and privileges. In the East people have *duties* while in the West they have *rights*.
- The East values order and harmony while the West values personal freedom, individual initiative, and competition. In the East this is reflected in respect for age, leaders, persons of authority, hierarchy, and institutions. In the West it is reflected in democracy, the rights of individuals, and capitalism.
- The West believes in universalism while the East practices particularism. Universalism emphasizes rules, laws, and generalizations while particularism emphasizes exceptions, circumstances, and relations.[99] Particularism often is expressed in the East in practices like *guanxi* (the use of interpersonal relationships) in China, which also can be interpreted from a Western perspective as corruption or bribery.

The debate later was extended from human rights to economic development. In addition to using "Asian values" as the justification for sacrificing political and civil freedoms to maintain social stability, some Asian governments have argued that since not all Asian countries are as economically developed as the West, they cannot be expected to uphold all of the rights in the Universal Declaration. Some have claimed that "Asian values" are supportive of "paternalistic authoritarianism" (such as practiced in Singapore and Malaysia) which has fostered economic development and provided economic security for their people. However, these same values were also cited by Western observers who said they supported "crony capitalism" and contributed to the Asian financial crisis in 1997–8,[100] while other observers say these values contributed to the region's quick recovery.[101]

Not everyone in Asia agrees

Some Asian leaders and academics are critical of the way that the idea of special "Asian values" often is invoked. They point out that many "Asian values" also exist in the West, such as the importance of family and extended social networks in Latin cultures and social order in Nordic cultures. Western values are also found in Asia, as the rise of small businesses and entrepreneurship in China and India demonstrate.

Asia is not a monolithic, homogeneous area. Critics dismiss the idea that a common set of distinctively Asian principles exists, given Asia's immense cultural, religious, and political diversity. There are regional differences between East, Southeast, and South Asia and these nations have highly varying historical and religious backgrounds such as Hindu, Muslim, Confucian, Shinto, and Buddhist.

Critics also argue the debate is not so much about cultural values but about maintaining political power and an excuse for autocratic government that suppress individual rights and dissidents. Human Rights Watch and Amnesty International called China's *White Paper* a "whitewash."[102]

Not all Asians believe that human rights are an artifact of solely the Western culture. Some of those who disagree with the proponents of the "Asian values" thesis include Nobel Laureate, Amartya Sen, who has said:

> What about the specialness of "Asian values," about which so much is now being said by the authorities in a number of East Asian countries? These arguments . . . dispute the importance of human rights and press freedoms in Asian countries. The resistance to Western hegemony – a perfectly respectable cause in itself – takes the form, under this interpretation, of justifying the suppression of journalistic freedoms and the violations of elementary political and civil rights on the grounds of the alleged unimportance of these freedoms in the hierarchy of what are claimed to be "Asian values."[103]

The former president of Singapore, Devan Nair, stated, "Human rights and values are universal by any standard, and their violation anywhere is a grievous offence to men and women everywhere."[104] Wei Jingsheng, a political dissident and human rights activist exiled from China, also has argued that human rights and freedoms are universal.[105] Finally, Aung San Sui Kyi, Burmese democracy advocate and winner of the 1991 Nobel Peace Prize said, "Those who wish to deny us certain political rights try to convince us that these are not Asian values. In our struggle for democracy and human rights, we would like greater support from our fellow Asians."[106]

As we discussed in Part 1 of this book, values are guidelines to behavior. They are supported by basic assumptions about how the world works and ought to work, assumptions which cannot be proven but must be taken for granted. The Asian Values debate, like all debates about ethical issues and corporate social responsibility, cannot be "resolved" by proving one side right and the other wrong. Engaging in the debate in an informed way, however, provides managers with a richer context for understanding the impact of their own behavior, whether it is in the East, West, or any part of the world.

INTEGRITY AND ETHICAL BEHAVIOR

Some academics have commented that "academic moral theory is useless" since the debate does not lead to actionable decision criteria without embracing the beliefs of one side or the other."[107] The "Asian values" debate lends credence to that view since there does not seem to any way to cut through the debate to arrive at the "truth." One is left with having either to impose one's beliefs and values on the other through coercion or by the conflicting parties agreeing to disagree.[108]

Global executives do not have the luxury of simply debating the issue. They must make decisions and take action. How do they decide? Some decision principles may help executives make a decision.[109,110]

Good Questions (IMHO)

Ask

1 Is the practice in question less ethical than the company's usual practice, or is it just different? If it is less ethical, then the decision should be to follow the company's normal practice. James Hamilton and Stephen Knouse offer the examples of bribery and nepotism as practices that are less ethical (bribery) and, possibly, just different (nepotism).

2 Does the practice in question violate ethical minimums? If it does, then it should not be engaged in. This rule means, however, that companies must specify minimum ethical standards for its employees and also differentiate between those practices that should never be engaged in and those where informed judgment is required. The codes of conduct described earlier can be used as guides for companies in constructing their own sets of standards.

3 Does the company have leverage in the host country to follow its own practice? If it does, it should follow its own standards.

4 Do the host country's institutions have the potential for change and improvement? If so, companies may have an obligation to follow their own standards to help bring about improvement.

Thomas Donaldson also has suggested two practical decision rules. Managers may confront two types of ethical conflicts: the *conflict of relative development* and the *conflict of cultural tradition*.[111] The former recognizes that countries are in different stages of economic development and asks the question if the use of a product or practice, barring any known and unacceptable side effects, would have been considered ethical in the United States (or France, the United Kingdom, etc.) at an earlier stage of its development. The latter asks if it is possible to do business in a country without engaging in the practice or if the practice violates a core human value. These questions are pragmatic, but they still require companies and executives to define their core values and to take a position.

To assist your analysis and to promote rational discussion of ethical dilemmas, we present below a series of diagnostic questions and some recommendations. These can be applied to the case situations in the book and, we hope, can serve as a guide for you in the future. They encourage you to consider all impacts of your decisions and actions, and not to fall into the trap of transforming ethical or social responsibility decisions into decisions of some other type.

Some guidelines to consider

Our guidelines fall into four categories: preparing for future issues, understanding stakeholders, assessing options, and the manager as a human decision-maker.

Prepare for ethical and social responsibility dilemmas

1 *Develop relationships with care*

   To the extent possible, develop strong, trust-based relationships with customers and suppliers. With these relationships you will be able to assess the impact of requests your contacts make, and explain your own reasons for behaving the way you do. With strong relationships, your stakeholders are more likely to trust your actions, and less likely to push you into behaviors you believe are unethical or irresponsible. If you increase dependency on a particular customer or supplier without the time to build a relationship, be certain to retain enough power to maintain your standards.

2 *Get the best possible information*

   Take the time to get the facts, all of them. Avoid fuzzy thinking. Avoid using or being swayed by hearsay or unsubstantiated assertions. Avoid relying on statements that have no specifics to go with them, such as "Everybody is doing it," "We'll lose business if we don't do it," or "It's normal practice." When you hear statements like these, push for the analysis and details. Often, you may find that they are unsubstantiated assertions parading as analysis.

Identify the impact on stakeholders

3 *Identify all stakeholders*

   Managers have multiple interests that they must consider because they are embedded in a complex network of relationships. A company has multiple groups of stakeholders in addition to the investors in the business, and managers need to be clear about their responsibilities and obligations to all these groups since their interests, goals, and values can potentially conflict. Identifying all these relationships helps in making decisions. Who are the stakeholders that have an interest in or will be affected by the decision: shareholders, the home-country government, host-country governments, customers, suppliers, employees, unions? It is easy to ignore some of these, particularly when they are thousands of miles away and probably cannot exert any pressure on the company to behave in their interests. Ethical managers give careful consideration to these types of issues and do not avoid them or pretend they do not exist.

4 *Assess your responsibilities and obligations to stakeholders*

   What are the responsibilities and obligations to these stakeholders? Identify the responsibilities that your organization has, and do not overlook the ones that you, personally, may have to external stakeholders and/or to your own organization.

For example, take the situation of an insurance company selling life insurance in Uganda during a period of civil war.[112] Years earlier the company's operation had been nationalized by the government, and now it was having its ownership restored. The Ugandan branch was not profitable, and an economic analysis showed that it should be shut down.

But what were the company's responsibilities to its managers? These local managers had run the branch in the company's interests after it had been nationalized, and they were concerned about possible violence to field personnel and to themselves if the company closed its operations. And what were the company's obligations to its policyholders? The issue may not be whether the company should shut down, but how it should handle its responsibilities, obligations, and commitments to its employees and customers, as well as to its shareholders.

Assess and select options

5   *Identify a broad range of options*
Some options will jump up immediately, such as "Pay the bribe or don't pay the bribe," or "Hire this manufacturing company to outsource or don't enter into the contract." Are there options that have not been identified? In trying to identify possible action, avoid characterizing decisions using false dichotomies – either/or characterizations. Alternatives and options do not have to be win/lose positions. For example, the statement "We need to pay the bribe or lose the business" portrays the situation as win/lose, but it may not be. Such dichotomies often develop because the initial analysis was not as complete as it could have been. This mindset can limit the action possibilities open to the manager. Strive for a win–win situation. Is there a way to solve the problem that satisfies all parties and allows you to fulfill your obligations?

6   *Analyze assumptions behind options*
Before selecting your options, identify which assumptions are being made with each. For example, if you decide to pay a small management fee, which ethical framework are you invoking? Whose utility is being maximized? Whose values are being used? Consider multiple (including opposing) viewpoints, but examine them carefully. Weigh the costs and benefits to all stakeholders.

7   *Select an option and develop an action plan*
Sooner or later (and usually sooner!) you need to act. If you are well prepared, have analyzed the stakeholders, and identified and analyzed the options well, you are in a better position to select a good course of action. Some decision criteria to consider include: do the best for all involved stakeholders; fulfill obligations; observe laws and contracts; do not use deception; and avoid knowingly doing harm (physical, psychological, economic, or social). To be socially responsive, you should also strive for a win–win situation. Is there a way to solve the problem that satisfies all parties and allows you to fulfill your obligations? Can you go beyond this and help the communities or environment in which you are operating?

Consider your own position carefully   In conducting an arm's-length analysis, it is sometimes easy to take ourselves as people – individuals who make decisions and live with the consequences – out of the picture. Remember that there can be personal consequences associated with your decision. People have lost their jobs because someone higher in the organization needed a scapegoat, and others have gone to jail for the actions of others. Before acting, it is important to consider your role as a manager and how it is related to your role as a community member, parent, family member, or global citizen.

8 *Make decisions that are your responsibility*

Do not avoid making ethical decisions on issues that are your responsibility, for example, by passing responsibility on to someone else or waiting until the issue resolves itself (usually with bad consequences for the stakeholders involved). On the other hand, do not accept responsibility for decisions that are not yours to make. Some people will try to find a scapegoat to take the blame for a decision that may be illegal or unethical. For example, a supplier may tell you that he will go out of business if you do not help by purchasing products off the record, or an employee may ask you to approve a contract negotiation without adequate information. How do you protect yourself? You can ask for the decision or directive in writing or suggest an open meeting with other people present to discuss it.

9 *Act consistently with your own values*

Before you act, ask yourself if what you plan is in accordance with your own highest set of values and norms. Consider the "billboard" or the "light-of-day" tests. When you drive to work in the morning would you be happy to see your decision or action prominently announced on a large billboard for everyone to read and to know about? Would you be willing to discuss your actions in a meeting where you would be subject to questions and scrutiny and have to justify them? Would your actions look as reasonable in the light of day as they did when the decision was made behind closed doors?

SOME FINAL ADVICE

We close this book with a section on ethics and corporate social responsibility because we believe that informed, conscientious, and thoughtful international managers can play an important role in improving the state of our world. International business can create opportunities for economic and social development. Global institutions such as the United Nations and World Trade Organization may help by providing a framework for dialogue and action, but it is managers working day-to-day in different parts of the world who will make an impact on people in ordinary communities.

In the cases in this part of the book, you will be asked to develop your own stance on the issues. We encourage you to think carefully about the problems depicted in the cases and to develop reasoned positions. You will find yourself in a similar situation someday (if you have not already), and you will have to make critical decisions. We hope that, by working through the decisions in these cases now, you will be better able to deal with similar decisions later.

As you move through your international management career, we encourage you to maintain high standards. When in Rome don't do as the Romans do, but rather do as the *better* Romans do. Understand, respect, and enjoy cultural differences, but never use culture as an excuse for not trying to do things the right way. Finally, ask yourself, and answer honestly, if you are leading the way in the area of global social responsiveness. Are you happy with your answer? If not, you know what to do!

We think that international management is the most exciting career possible for many reasons. The opportunity to learn and act in many different contexts and to take the best from each of these to create new ways of doing business provides endless scope for

[Handwritten margin notes: "Paradox" with an X symbol; "Sometimes companies or their managers are hoping for framework or even laws!"; "Takes away the disadvantage and levels the field — allows them the freedom to do the 'right thing!'"]

achieving great things. We wish you an interesting, rewarding, and enjoyable journey in your international activities and career.

Notes

The title of Part 3 is adapted from Richard T. De George, *Competing with Integrity in International Business* (Oxford: Oxford University Press, 1993).

1 Ibid.
2 Ibid., p. 6.
3 Ibid., p. 41.
4 Howard R. Bowen, *Social Responsibilities of the Businessman* (New York: Harper & Row, 1953).
5 Archie B. Carroll, "A Three Dimensional Model of Corporate Performance," *Academy of Management Review*, 4(4) (1979): 497–505.
6 Jonathan P. Doh, Peter Rodriguez, Klaus Uhlenbruck, Jamie Collins, and Lorraine Eden, "Coping with Corruption in Foreign Markets," *Academy of Management Executive*, 17(3) (2003): 114–27.
7 "Sweat Shops – Inside a Chinese Sweatshop", *Business Week*, October 2, 2000; www.businessweek.com/2000/00_40/b3701119.htm
8 Adapted from Carroll, "A Three-Dimensional Model." Although this framework was developed in the United States with domestic concerns in mind, we believe that it can be applied in international settings.
9 Ibid.
10 William C. Frederick, "The Moral Authority of Transnational Corporate Codes," *Journal of Business Ethics*, 10 (1991): 165–77.
11 These documents include: The United Nations Universal Declaration of Human Rights (1948), The European Convention on Human Rights (1950), The Helsinki Final Act (1975), The OECD Guidelines for Multinational Enterprises (1976), The International Labor Office Tripartite Declaration of Principles Concerning Multinational Enterprises and Social Policy (1977), and The United Nations Code of Conduct for Transnational Corporations. More recently, the Caux Roundtable formulated its *Principles for Business*; the OECD developed its *Guidelines for Multinational Enterprises* (www.oecd.org); and in 1997 the Global Sullivan Principles were created.

   The Caux Round Table (CRT) (www.cauxroundtable.org/) is an international network of principled, senior business leaders working to promote a moral capitalism. It advocates implementation of its code, through which principled capitalism can flourish and sustainable and socially responsible prosperity can become the foundation for a fair, free, and transparent global society.

   In 1977, Reverend Leon Sullivan developed the *Sullivan Principles*, a code of conduct for human rights and equal opportunity for companies operating in South Africa. The Sullivan Principles are acknowledged to have been one of the most effective efforts to end discrimination against blacks in the workplace in South Africa, and to have contributed to the dismantling of apartheid. To further expand human rights and economic development to all communities, Reverend Sullivan created the Global Sullivan Principles of Social Responsibility in 1997; www.globalsullivanprinciples.org/index.htm.htm
12 Frederick, "The Moral Authority of Transnational Corporate Codes," 166–7.
13 www.iccwbo.org/home/menu_global_compact.asp
14 Ibid. See the International Chamber of Commerce website (www.iccwbo.org) for some examples of the programs that companies are following in support of the Global Compact.
15 www.iht.com/articles/8677.html

16 www.calvert.com/sri.html

17 See also Kathleen A. Getz, "International Codes of Conduct: An Analysis of Ethical Reasoning," *Journal of Business Ethics*, 9 (1990): 567–77, for a discussion of these issues.

18 Sita C. Amba-Rao, "Multinational Corporate Social Responsibility, Ethics, Interactions, and Third World Governments: An Agenda for the 1990s," *Journal of Business Ethics*, 12 (1993): 553–72, p. 555.

19 See, for example, John Plender, "Schooled by Scandal: What Auditors and Investors Still Have to Learn from Europe's Accounting Debacles," *Financial Times*, January 22, 2004: 11.

20 www.ge.com/en/commitment/social/integrity/integrity.htm

21 To see examples of this distinction in action in a large Wall Street firm in the 1980s, read Michael Lewis, *Liar's Poker* (New York: Penguin, 1989).

22 Verne E. Henderson, "The Ethical Side of Enterprise," *Sloan Management Review*, 23 (1982): 37–47.

23 Ibid.

24 Barry Meier, "Breast-feeding Wisdom in Question," *New York Times*, June 8, 1997.

25 This section draws on the following works: Jeffrey Gandz and Nadine Hayes, "Teaching Business Ethics," Working Paper No. 86-17R, October 1986, School of Business Administration, University of Western Ontario; Tad Tuleja, *Beyond the Bottom Line* (New York: Penguin, 1985); John B. Matthews, Kenneth E. Goodpaster, and Laura Nash, *Policies and Persons: A Casebook in Business Ethics* (New York: McGraw-Hill, 1985).

26 Adam Liptak, Michael Moss, and Kate Zerike, "Accused G.I.'s Try to Shift Blame in Prison Abuse," *New York Times*, May 16, 2004.

27 William G. Perry, Jr., *Forms of Intellectual and Ethical Development in the College Years: A Scheme* (New York: Holt, Rinehart & Winston, 1970).

28 In Perry's full scheme there are nine stages. The authors have chosen to use only the three major positions in the scheme.

29 Geert Hofstede, *Culture's Consequences* (Beverly Hills: Sage, 1980).

30 Jeffrey Gandz and Nadine Hayes, "Teaching Business Ethics," *Journal of Business Ethics*, 7 (1988): 659.

31 www.who.int/tobacco/about/en/

32 Defined as lifestyle and behavior such as smoking and physical inactivity that contribute to leading causes of death, including heart disease, cancer, and stroke.

33 www.cdc.gov/nccdphp/factsheets/death_causes2000.htm

34 Sabin Russell, "Ex-Clinton Official Rips White House on Tobacco Treaty," *San Francisco Chronicle*, February 13, 2003.

35 Representative Henry A. Waxman, "Administration Isolates the U.S. in International Tobacco Control Efforts," www.house.gov/reform/min/inves_tobacco/index.htm

36 www.nosmoking.ws/inb5updates.htm and htpp://petition.globalink.org/view.php?code =fctc_de

37 Senator Richard A. Durbin and Representative Henry A. Waxman, "Letter Questions USDA Promotion of Tobacco Trade," www.house.gov/reform/min/inves_tobacco/index.htm

38 China eventually banned RU486 in 2001. See Christine Hall, CNSNews.com Staff Writer, "China Bans Abortion Pill," October 22, 2001; www.cnsnews.com/ViewCulture.asp?Page=/Culture/archive/200110/CUL20011022b.html

39 Joseph L. Badaracco, Jr., "Business Ethics: Four Spheres of Executive Responsibility," *California Management Review*, 7 (Spring 1992): 64–79. See also Harvard Business School Case 9-391-050, RU486 (A).

40 "Abort, Retry, Sell?," *The Economist*, April 12, 1997: 59.

41 RU-486 Report Card, Washington Post.com, Sunday, May 5, 2002: B06; www.washingtonpost.com/ac2/wp-dyn?pagename=article&node=&contentId=A30600-2002May4&notFound=true

42   See the "RU486 Files", www.ru486.org/

43   RU-486 Report Card.

44   "China Bans Sale of RU486 Abortion Drug," *Beijing Morning Post*, October 9, 2001.

45   See "Human Rights," *The Economist*, June 3, 1995: 58–9; and William Beaver, "Levi's Is Leaving China," *Business Horizons* (March–April 1995): 35–40.

46   Beaver, "Levi's Is Leaving China."

47   "Human Rights."

48   www.rugmark.org/

49   "Hidden Child Labor in Soccer Balls Plants Contracted by Nike and Reebok," *Report of Campaign Labor Rights*, January 8, 1997; www.citinv.it/associazioni/CNMS/archivio/multinazionali/nikefabbrica.html

50   "Gap and Nike: No Sweat?," BBC News, October 15, 2000; http://news.bbc.co.uk/1/hi/programmes/panorama/970385.stm

51   www.nike.com/nikebiz/nikebiz.jhtml?page=29&item=fy01

52   Nadine Gordimer, "In Nigeria, the Price of Oil Is Blood," *New York Times*, May 25, 1997: E11.

53   "Shellman Says Sorry," *The Economist*, May 10, 1997, 65.

54   For example in the Canadian *Globe & Mail* on November 21, 1995.

55   "Shellman Says Sorry."

56   *The Shell Report 2002*; www.shell.com/home/Framework?siteId=shellreport2002-en

57   Ibid.

58   Mzamo P. Mangaliso, "The Corporate Social Challenge for the Multinational Corporation," *Journal of Business Ethics*, 11 (1992): 491–500.

59   Don Mayer and Anita Cava, "Ethics and the Gender Equality Dilemma for U.S. Multi-nationals," *Journal of Business Ethics*, 12 (1993): 701–8.

60   Ibid., 701.

61   See the U S State Department's list of Current Travel Warnings for examples of these countries: http://travel.state.gov/warnings_list.html

62   http://travel.state.gov/colombia_warning.html

63   http://travel.state.gov/mexico.html

64   http://apnews.excite.com/article/20040530/D82SJSF80.html

65   Madelaine Drohan, "To Bribe or Not to Bribe," *Globe and Mail*, February 14, 1994.

66   Ibid.

67   "Statoil Signs Iran Gas Deal," BBC News, 28 October, 2002.

68   This represented the first of three payments to Horton Investments. The contract was later annulled and no further payments were made.

69   "Statoil Still Afloat Despite Losing Man Overboard," *International Petroleum Finance*, October 8, 2003. Other sources of the Statoil story include Harald Finnvik, Diplomatic Interview, *Azerbaijan International*, Autumn 1996; "Statoil Chief Executive Quits As Board Split On Probe," *Energy Intelligence Briefing*, September 23, 2003.

70   www.transparency.org/index.html

71   *The Strategic Framework for the TI Movement*; www.transparency.org/about_ti/mission.html

72   These countries are Argentina, Brazil, Colombia, Hungary, India, Indonesia, Mexico, Morocco, Nigeria, the Philippines, Poland, Russia, South Africa, South Korea, and Thailand.

73   Ibid.

74   www.transparency.org/pressreleases_archive/2002/2002.05.14.bpi.en.html#bpi

75   See Amba-Rao, "Multinational Corporate Social Responsibility." This article discusses conceptualizations of corporate social responsibility from a number of sources, including the following, which is the primary source for the three-stage framework presented in the text: S. P. Sethi, "Dimensions of Corporate Social Performance: An Analytical Framework," *California Management Review*, 12 (1975): 58–64.

76   See John H. Barnett, "The American Executive and Colombian Violence: Social Relatedness and Business Ethics," *Journal of Business Ethics*, 10 (1991): 853–61, for a description of the three models: conflict, compartment, and complementarity.

77   Kathleen Decant and Barbara Alumna, "Environmental Leadership: From Compliance to Competitive Advantage," *Academy of Management Executive*, 8(3) (1994): 7–27.

78   www.pg.com/about_pg/corporate/community/community_submain.jhtml

79   A complete statement of P & G's values and policies can be found at www.pg.com/about_pg/corporate/sustainability/substain_catmain.jhtml

80   www.globalsullivanprinciples.org/

81   Links to the 2003 Sustainability Report can be found at www.pg.com/about_pg/corporate/sustainability/substain_catmain.jhtml;jsessionid=LUFRNYIDZL2EVQFIAJ1CZOWAVABHOLHC#

82   Ibid.

83   Claudia Dreifus, "Passing the Scoop: Ben & Jerry," *New York Times Magazine*, December 18, 1994: 38–41.

84   www.benjerry.com

85   Ibid.

86   www.ceres.org

87   Rajib N. Sanyal and Joao S. Neves, "The Valdez Principles: Implications for Corporate Social Responsibility," *Journal of Business Ethics*, 10 (1991): 883–90.

88   www.ceres.org

89   For a link to the Social and Environment Assessment 2002 go to www.benjerry.com/our_company/about_us/environment/social_audit/index.cfm

90   Thomas Donaldson, "Can Global Companies Conform to Code?" A copy can be found on his personal website, http://lgst.wharton.upenn.edu/donaldst/

91   The addition of this section was suggested by Professor Peter Steane, Macquarie Graduate School of Management, Australia. We thank him for guidance, direction, and references.

92   www.un.org/rights/50/decla.htm

93   Stephen C. Angle and Marina Svensson, 2001, www.chinesehumanrightsreader.org/reader/intros/52.html

94   Fareed Zakaria, "Culture is Destiny: A Conversation with Lee Kuan Yew," *Foreign Affairs*, 73(2) (1994): 109–26, p. 110.

95   Ibid., p. 113.

96   Ibid., p. 111.

97   www.apmforum.com/news/apmn21.htm

98   "Mahathir Warns against too Much Democracy," BBC News, 27 July, 2000; http://news.bbc.co.uk/1/hi/world/asia-pacific/853673.stm

99   Charles Hampden-Turner and Fons Trompenaars, *Building Cross-Cultural Competence: How to Create Wealth from Conflicting Values* (New Haven: Yale University Press, 2000): 13. See Chapter 1 for a detailed explanation of the universalist–particularistic dilemma.

100   Francis Fukuyama, "Asian Values and Civilization," ICAS Lecture No. 98-929-FRF. ICAS Fall Symposium, September 29, 1998, www.icasinc.org/f1998/frff1998.html

101   See, for example, Randall Peerenboom, "Beyond Universalism and Relativism: The Evolving Debates about 'Values in Asia'," Research Paper No. 02-23, UCLA School of Law, October 31, 2002.

102   See www.hrw.org/press/2001/04/china0410.htm and www.urich.edu/~vwang/ps345/art85.htm

103   Amartya Sen, "Satyajit Ray and the Art of Universalism: Our Culture, Their Culture," p. 11; http://satyajitray.ucsc.edu/articles/sen.html

104   BBC World Service; www.bbc.co.uk/worldservice/people/features/ihavearightto/four_b/casestudy_art30.shtml

105 Ibid. See also http://globetrotter.berkeley.edu/people/Wei/wei-con0.html.

106 www.globalization101.org/issue/culture/34.asp and www.dassk.com/.

107 See Peerenboom, Research Paper No. 02-23, p. 83.

108 Ibid., p. 9.

109 See J. Brooke Hamilton and Stephen B. Knouse, "Multinational Enterprise Decision Principles for Dealing with Cross-Cultural Ethical Conflicts," *Journal of Business Ethics*, 31 (2001): 77–94; and Thomas Donaldson, "Values in Tension," *Harvard Business Review* (September–October 1996).

110 Hamilton and Knouse, "Multinational Enterprise Decision Principles for Dealing with Cross-Cultural Ethical Conflicts."

111 Donaldson, "Values in Tension," pp. 58–60.

112 David Burgoyne and Henry Lane, "The Europa Insurance Company," Case 9-84-C049, London: University of Western Ontario, School of Business Administration, 1984.

Coping with Corruption in Foreign Markets

Jonathan P. Doh, Peter Rodriguez, Klaus Uhlenbruck, Jamie Collins, and Lorraine Eden

2003 (handwritten)

Pakistan (handwritten)

Russia (handwritten)

Africa (handwritten)

In 1998, incoming Pakistani Prime Minister Nawaz Sharif alleged that foreign companies investing in independent electric power projects had bribed officials from the previous Benazir Bhutto government in return for high electricity rates. He threatened to rescind the project contracts if the foreign companies did not cut their rates by more than 30 percent.[1] In Russia, several Canadian oil and mineral extraction firms were expropriated by their local joint venture partners who were able to take advantage of Russia's unpredictable court system.[2] On the African continent, legal proceedings are underway against some of the biggest European building companies for passing bribes to a local government official overseeing World Bank-financed construction projects.[3] These are among the hundreds of publicized examples of how foreign investment has been affected and disrupted by corruption.

Foreign direct investment (FDI) has grown rapidly over the past decade. Private investment in developing countries, especially in large emerging markets such as China, Brazil, Mexico, Indonesia, and Poland, has seen a particularly large increase.[4] Fueled by the broad forces of globalization and technological advancement, private investment by multinational enterprises (MNEs) in property, plant, and equipment has contributed to economic development in many emerging economies. These initiatives have also helped investors diversify portfolios and generate higher returns from fast-growing markets. Yet, beneath the veneer of benefits to both host countries and MNE investors is a troubling and persistent pattern of uncertainty and added costs associated with the risks of FDI.

Political and economic risks have received widespread attention from management practitioners and scholars, and a body of helpful managerial literature has developed

 Risk (handwritten)

Doh, Jonathan P., Peter Rodriguez, Klaus Uhlenbruck, Jamie Collins, and Lorraine Eden, "Coping with corruption in foreign markets," *Academy of Management Executive*, 17(3) (August 2003): 114–27. Reprinted by permission of *Academy of Management Executive*.

around advising firms on how best to navigate political pressure and instability.[5] One type of risk, however – the risk of government corruption – has received much less attention.[6] Although many studies detail the impact of corruption on national economies, and others have considered corruption in the context of ethics and social responsibility,[7] few efforts have been directed at assessing its impact on firms. Yet, the likelihood of investing firms confronting corruption is much higher than the chance of facing expropriation or other such events that fall into the category of political risks. This is because corruption exists (and persists) "below the radar screen" of many corporate officers, management researchers, and even government officials. The very nature of government corruption, which we define as *the abuse (or misuse) of public power for private (personal) benefit*, lends itself to a tendency to look the other way and fosters an attitude of "don't ask, don't tell." Firms are concerned that exposing corrupt behaviors will reduce profits or anger corrupt officials without changing the behavior of others. Some have suggested that corruption may even create an opportunity for international firms to overcome numerous difficulties associated with entering new foreign markets.[8] However, the costs of corruption to foreign investors, host countries, and broader societal interests are substantial. We emphasize that firms choosing to comply with or even exploit local corruption often neglect significant long-term costs.

Our focus is on FDI in developing countries. These countries have poorly developed and often ineffective institutional systems, and it is in these environments where corruption is most rampant and creates the greatest potential for distorting investment plans. While corruption is present in a variety of industries and country settings, it is more common in certain sectors. For instance, infrastructure projects are especially prone to corruption because they involve large investments and complex contracts in which corrupt payments can be easily disguised.[9]

We begin by detailing the direct and indirect costs of corruption to both host countries and foreign investors. Drawing from research on the impact of corruption on economic development, we present a framework that incorporates two important dimensions of corruption – its pervasiveness and arbitrariness. We conclude with a discussion of strategies which multinationals can pursue alone or in conjunction with governments and international organizations to stem the tide of corruption or at least reduce its worst effects.

COSTS OF CORRUPTION

Corruption can be viewed as a tax that increases costs and shifts risk from some stakeholders to others. Specifying its direct and indirect costs helps isolate the ways in which corruption affects business decision-making.

Direct costs

Bribes, kickbacks, "grease," and "speed" money are perhaps the most conspicuous types of corrupt activity. Direct costs of corruption are those costs that result from direct interaction between the firm and the government (as represented by any of its officials

TABLE 1   Direct Costs of Government Corruption

Type	Explanation
Bribes	Monetary and non-monetary payments to those with some degree of public power as a response to extortion or in exchange for some misuse of public power.
Red Tape/Bureaucratic Delay	Non-monetary and opportunity costs of dealing with corrupt officials or of complying with the illegitimate bureaucratic requirements of corrupt regimes.
Avoidance	Efforts to avoid and limit the firm's exposure to extortionary behavior by corrupt officials, including hiding output and opting out of the official economy.
Directly Unproductive Behavior	Investments in channels of influence to gain advantage in dividing up the benefits of economic activity; includes lobbying and more direct vote and influence peddling.
Foregoing Market Supporting Institutions	Costs imposed on the firm as a result of foregoing the use of courts for the enforcement of contracts, local financial operations, etc.
Engagement with Organized Crime	Monetary and non-monetary costs imposed on firms as a result of willing or unwilling engagement with organized crime.

or policy makers). Hence, bribes, bureaucratic red tape, and various categories of transaction costs are considered direct costs since they can be identified with a direct interaction or transaction between a particular firm and corrupt officials. Similarly, resources expended in an effort to avoid extortion by corrupt officials of a given firm are also a direct cost. Table 1 provides a summary of six major types of direct costs of corruption that we have identified from our research.

Bribes

Bribes cost firms and other stakeholders through monetary and non-monetary payments to those with public power. Examples of bribery are numerous. However, only a small fraction of bribes are exposed, suggesting that bribery is far more pervasive than what is reported. Consider these examples. In September 2002, Michael Woerfel, a senior employee of European Aeronautic Defense and Space Company (EADS), was charged with corruption in connection with a 1999 $5 billion arms deal with South Africa. EADS conceded that it had "helped" 30 South Africans with hefty discounts on luxury cars. In related developments, chief whip of the ruling African National Congress (ANC) Tony Yengeni was charged with corruption, fraud, and perjury.[10] Also in September of 2002, a Lesotho court found Acres International, a Toronto-based firm, guilty of passing $260,000 as a bribe to the chief executive of the project. The executive was convicted of 13 counts of bribery and of accepting more than $2 million in total bribes.[11] In July 2002, Xerox admitted in a regulatory filing that it had made improper payments of more than $500,000 "over a period of years" to government officials in India to push sales.[12]

Red tape and bureaucratic delay

Red tape and bureaucratic delay are examples of non-monetary costs that result from dealing with corrupt officials or complying with the requirements of corrupt regimes. To avoid red tape and delays in facilitating project approvals, firms often use bribes to "grease the skids."[13] This was the case when Robert King, a leading investor in Owl Securities (OSI), was convicted on five counts of conspiracy and for violating the Foreign Corrupt Practices Act by planning to bribe Costa Rican officials. The bribery was related to OSI's plan to build a new Caribbean super-port and a 124-mile dry canal through Costa Rica, designed to rival the Panama Canal.[14] Lockheed Martin agreed to a consent decree (neither admitting nor denying allegations) in which it paid nearly $25 million in fines after it was accused in 1995 of paying $1 million to an Egyptian member of parliament in order to facilitate the sale of Lockheed aircraft to the Egyptian Air Force.[15] Tehelka, an Internet news portal, captured several government officials taking bribes from undercover reporters in India. The reporters were posing as arms dealers peddling "fourth-generation" thermal hand-held cameras on behalf of a British company.[16]

Avoidance

Firms may be forced to engage in expensive efforts to avoid and limit their exposure to extortion by corrupt officials, including hiding output and opting out of the official economy. Avoiding corruption can be costly. For example, Proctor & Gamble, as part of its broader exit strategy from Nigeria, decided to close a Pampers plant rather than pay a bribe to a customs official.[17]

Directly unproductive behavior

Corruption may force firms to engage in a range of costly and unproductive behavior. This may include investment in channels of influence to gain advantage in dividing up the benefits of economic activity through lobbying, direct vote solicitations, and influence peddling.

In China, various forms of obligatory "profit sharing" with city officials in Hainan province have been reported. Employment of relatives, donations, and other "favors" are apparently an expected cost of doing business in that region. One private firm in Hainan province reported having a formal profit-sharing plan with the city officials. Firms report hiring key officials or their relatives as a way to develop political or social influence. Owners of local private firms in Wenzhous in eastern China have been known to give firm shares to senior cadres in exchange for protection from government interference.[18]

Foregoing market-supporting institutions and engaging with organized crime

Firms bear additional costs when, because of corruption, they are unable to use institutions such as courts for the enforcement of contracts. Costs increase when firms are willing (or unwilling) to engage with organized crime by paying for "protection" and other security services that would otherwise be unnecessary.

For example, many firms doing business in Russia in the post-Soviet era have been forced to take part in the underground market for "protection" by paying high fees for "security" services because the state cannot provide adequate public protection. The Canadian International Development Agency has spent $130 million to help generate Canadian business in Russia; however, many companies have claimed that projects have been stolen out from under them because of government corruption. As a result, Canadian investment in Russia has practically stopped all together, and the CIDA has virtually nothing to show for its investment.[19] This example shows how specific acts of corruption result in multiple costs; in this case, efforts to build institutions were thwarted through organized crime, which contributed to other unproductive and costly behavior.

Indirect costs

Many of the destructive costs of corruption affect firms indirectly via public-sector failure that results from missing or weak institutions, government failure to effectively use public resources, and government policies that keep the economy from growing. The indirect costs of corruption are those costs imposed on firms that cannot be specifically identified with a particular interaction between a firm and the government or its officials. These costs may result in higher prices for resources, lowered prospects for profitability, and macroeconomic instability. Indirect costs of corruption have been relatively well documented in terms of system-wide effects;[20] however, individual firms may overlook these costs because they don't recognize how such costs affect them. These indirect costs limit investment returns because they increase operating costs and decrease growth potential. Moreover, such costs may fall more heavily on some firms than others. Table 2 provides a summary of six major types of indirect costs of corruption, with a brief description of each.

Reduced investment and distorted public expenditures

Corruption has been shown to reduce the ratio of investment to GDP.[21] Corruption may also reduce public expenditures because tax revenues fall when business activity takes place outside of the official economy. Moreover, the expenditures that remain are often skewed from the most pressing needs toward projects that benefit privileged insiders. Recently, Nicaragua resorted to a national tax audit lottery to combat the problem of low tax revenues due to rampant corruption. Each month the government chooses 100 professionals at random, audits them, and publicizes the results. The government has

TABLE 2 Indirect Costs of Government Corruption

Type	Explanation
Reduced Investment	Reduced public and private investment flows. Lower rates of foreign direct investment for the formation of a robust commercial environment.
Reduced and Distorted Public Expenditures	Reduced taxes as a result of the deterrence of business activity and recourse to the unofficial economy. Selection of privately beneficial and publicly costly expenditure projects.
Macroeconomic Weakness and Instability	Reduced rates of macroeconomic growth, weak commercial environment, and greater susceptibility to financial crises.
Weak Infrastructure	Inadequate, expensive, and intermittently supplied infrastructure services such as telephony, electricity, and transportation. Weak infrastructure foments opportunities for small bribes and may indirectly reduce public trust.
Squandered/Misdirected Entrepreneurial Talent	Engagement of entrepreneurial and otherwise talented individuals into the socially unproductive avenues of advance afforded by corrupt environments.
Socio-Economic Failure	Increased poverty, income inequality, and reduced income growth for the poorest in society. Increases demands on already weak central governments.

estimated that 40 percent of all professionals are tax dodgers. The inefficient and proportionally small tax collections result in inadequate investment in infrastructure and education.[22]

Macroeconomic weakness and instability

More generally, corruption weakens institutions like courts and regulatory agencies, slowing economic growth.[23] Corruption also reduces aggregate investment through reduction in public and private investment, increasing poverty and the social ills that go along with it.[24]

Weak infrastructure

Corruption weakens public infrastructure, resulting in inadequate, expensive, and intermittently supplied services such as telephony, electricity, and transportation.[25] Weak infrastructure foments opportunities for small bribes and thereby increases direct costs of corruption. Corruption has even been shown to increase an economy's susceptibility to financial crises, such as those that occurred in Russia in the mid-1990s, Southeast Asia and Korea during 1997–1998, and in Latin America in the early 1980s and again in the mid- and late-1990s.[26]

Squandered/misdirected entrepreneurial talent

Corruption leads to squandered and misdirected entrepreneurial talent because individuals are drawn to socially unproductive avenues for advancement afforded by corrupt environments. Hence, corruption stymies the very entrepreneurial activities that could offset or mitigate some of its harshest effects.

Socio-economic failure

Finally, weaker economies, poor infrastructure, and squandered investment contribute to general socioeconomic misery. Results include increased poverty, income inequality and slow income growth for the poorest in society, increasing demands on already weak central governments, and the retarding of developmental goals such as education, literacy, and life expectancy.[27] This is perhaps the most tragic cost of corruption.

The "Haves" and the "Have-Nots"

TWO DIMENSIONS OF CORRUPTION

Our research suggests that the magnitude of both direct and indirect costs of corruption is driven by two key dimensions: the pervasiveness (or level) of corruption and its arbitrariness (uncertainty).[28]

Pervasiveness

The *pervasiveness of corruption* reflects the number and frequency of transactions (and individuals) with which (whom) the firm deals over the course of a fixed time period that involve illicit activities. Although the level of corruption is clearly difficult to measure (making a single index number inherently problematic), it captures the relative preponderance of corrupt transactions in a given country and correlates with the number of corrupt transactions that a firm expects to encounter in its normal operations. The higher the pervasiveness of corruption, the higher the direct and indirect resource costs of corruption to the firm.

Hard to Quantify!

When corruption is predictable, its effects are similar to an especially onerous tax; while damaging, companies may be able to budget for this tax as a business expense.[29] These conditions occur under well-structured, stable corruption regimes in which payment expectations are predictable and effective. Hence, firms can reasonably expect to receive the particular government-administered services in exchange for a bribe. Under such conditions, the pervasiveness of corruption could be high, but firms would still be able to operate with some degree of predictability. For example, in some countries, a standard "payment" accompanies requests to clear goods through customs.

All competitors are subject to it! No disadvantage to a single firm.

Arbitrariness

Corruption can be viewed through a second critical characteristic – *arbitrariness*. A disorganized corruption network emerges when government agents act independently and capriciously in an effort to maximize their own bribe revenue while disregarding the effects of their efforts on other officials. In such a setting, firms are uncertain of whom to pay, what to pay, and whether the payments will result in the delivery of the promised goods or services. The lack of coordination among corrupt agents works to diminish economic activity as some officials appropriate bribe revenues that would otherwise accrue to others.

These characterizations fit well with anecdotal reports by MNEs. In some countries, one bribe guarantees access to the desired property or service; in others, the size and number of bribes necessary to obtain a license or permit are uncertain and, even when paid, do not guarantee the desired right or service. For example, the *Wall Street Journal* reports that Indonesia and Russia have become nations with both pervasive and arbitrary corruption: "Before, you paid a lump sum in Jakarta and could be certain you had smoothed things out . . . Now you pay a lot of small amounts locally, and you can't be sure things will be smooth . . . It is a continuous, confusing, and discouraging process." As for Russia, "Without the structure the Communist Party provided, people didn't know who to pay, and many anarchistic bribe collectors stepped up with their hands out."[30] In such environments, corruption expectations can escalate, with each subsequent transaction demanding a higher payment.

Whereas the relationship between pervasiveness and direct costs of corruption is straightforward and positive, the arbitrariness of corruption reduces a firm's ability to estimate these costs. While pervasiveness of corruption is highly problematic, when corruption is arbitrary firms cannot anticipate the direct costs of corruption nor can they easily evaluate the impact of corruption on their operations. This aspect of corruption, however, is less obvious. Where corruption is arbitrary, firms might accept corruption and ignore the total cost of their actions, or they may avoid corrupt markets and incur opportunity costs by not entering these markets at all.

Measuring corruption's dimensions

We assessed the pervasiveness and arbitrariness of corruption based on the World Business Environment Survey (WBES) that was published by the World Bank in 1998. This survey focuses on perceptions of environmental factors facing firms. The WBES is based on a sample of 8,000 firms representing approximately 100 companies of various sizes in each of 80 developing countries. We draw the measure of the two dimensions of corruption – pervasiveness and arbitrariness – from two sets of questions on corruption in the WBES. Figure 1 represents our framework of two key dimensions of corruption and identifies five representative countries in each of four cells that reflect basic combinations of pervasiveness and arbitrariness. We chose only countries where pervasiveness of corruption, although low, is still considered a major impediment to local business. This figure shows how some countries can rank high on one measure and low on another,

FIGURE 1   The Two Dimensions of Corruption

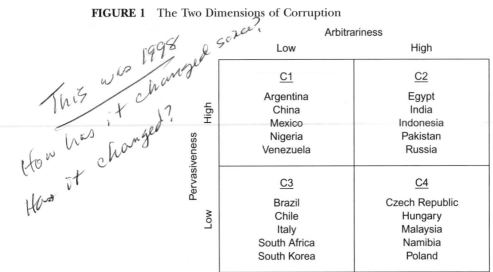

*Note: Countries have been placed in four cells in alphabetical order and do not reflect specific ordered rankings within the cells.

suggesting that corruption is a more complicated phenomenon than some companies might expect.

COPING WITH CORRUPTION: KEY STRATEGIES

Corruption, like many public policy problems, generates a negative "externality" in that individual firms may benefit, while the damage to society is substantial. Hence, a firm may not have sufficient incentives to avoid or report corruption because the "benefits" of corruption are concentrated, whereas many of the costs are diffuse. Participation in corruption may be due to competitive pressures, respect for local cultural norms, extortion, or the difficulty in monitoring individual employees. Unfortunately, if firms refuse to engage in corruption, they may consider themselves at a disadvantage vis-à-vis competitors. Nonetheless, many firms have developed strategies to respond to corruption without acquiescing to it, as summarized in Table 3.

Strategy: avoidance

Corporations face numerous challenges when considering whether to enter a market characterized by corruption. One option is to avoid the market entirely and, in so doing, eliminate the direct costs of corruption whether generated from its pervasive or arbitrary application. Often, there are other reasons to avoid markets that are corrupt, such as weak profit potential, unstable government, and slow market growth; however, these conditions may themselves result in part from corruption.

TABLE 3 Strategies for Coping with Corruption

Strategy	Cost targeted	Effective against	Advantages	Problems
Avoidance	Direct	Pervasive & Arbitrary Corruption	Bypasses problem	Forego opportunities
Adjusting Entry Mode	Direct	Pervasive & Arbitrary Corruption (different strategies for each)	Allows firm to maintain participation in market while avoiding exposure to corruption Allows firm to avoid opportunity and other costs of foregoing markets	Denies firm some advantages of entry-mode options, including acquisition of local resources Denies host country some benefits
Corporate Codes of Conduct	Direct & Indirect	Pervasive & Arbitrary Corruption	Could incorporate major MNEs around the world	Viewed as lacking "rigor" Local firms unlikely to sign on, generating differential costs/benefits
Training, Development, and Public Education	Direct & Indirect	Pervasive, but less for Arbitrary Corruption	Regional-focused programs could make progress easier For government-sponsored programs, participation could be tied to World Bank loans and aid Makes policies clear and gives employees practical examples	Training initiatives may lack "teeth" in terms of enforcement Company-sponsored initiatives affect only one company Company-sponsored initiatives may have uneven application throughout subsidiaries
Social Contributions/ Public Donations	Direct	Pervasive Corruption	Provides needed services without breaking law or ethics	May be difficult to determine when "line has been crossed" May raise expectations of continued and rising payment
Laws and Agreements	Indirect	Pervasive & Arbitrary Corruption	FCPA includes strict rules with penalties OECD agreement relatively comprehensive Some developing countries now adopting OECD principles	FCPA may disadvantage U.S. firms vis-à-vis competitors Initially covered only OECD and a few developing countries Lack of enforcement and uneven implementation in developing world creates free-rider problem

- *Pervasiveness and arbitrariness of corruption cause firms to avoid markets.* Higher pervasiveness and higher arbitrariness of corruption both reduce total investment and FDI.[31]
- *Corruption causes delays in investment.* Investment rates fall as the arbitrariness surrounding corrupt payments rises for a given level of corruption.[32] Higher degrees of ownership and specialized knowledge advantages favor delaying FDI, particularly in uncertain environments.[33] Therefore, a widespread firm-level response to corruption appears to be outright avoidance in terms of foregoing investment opportunities.

Why expose your self – choose another opportunity –

Strategy: adjusting entry mode

Individual firms will not always be willing or able to avoid investment in countries plagued by corruption. Rather, many firms attempt to offset the direct costs of corruption through selection of different entry modes and structures. For instance, in Eastern European and the former Soviet economies, the probability of an MNE investing abroad through a joint venture rather than a wholly owned subsidiary increases with the level of corruption.[34] Further, firms may employ different approaches in response to pervasive versus arbitrary corruption pressures.

We further examined how firms adjust entry modes depending on the nature of corruption, generating information that should be helpful to managers facing similar conditions. We used World Bank data on more than 400 telecommunications projects in 96 emerging and developing economies to analyze the influence of the two dimensions of corruption discussed above on entry strategies.[35] When choosing to enter a corrupt country via joint or sole venture, firms face competing pressures. On the one hand, entry via a joint venture with local partners may provide access to local networks and reduce uncertainty.[36] On the other hand, corruption weakens property rights and could allow local partners to take advantage of the foreign firm. Here is what we found:

- *Generally, foreign entrants into national markets choose joint ventures more often than wholly owned entry* as the level of corruption – both arbitrary and pervasive – increases.
- *As pervasiveness of corruption increases, market entry modes are more likely to include local partners.* As Figure 2 shows, pervasiveness has opposite effects on two subcategories of the joint-venture entry mode. The probability of choosing mixed joint ventures (that include local and international partners) grows as pervasiveness increases, but joint ventures between just international (i.e., non-local) partners become less likely as pervasiveness rises. Pervasiveness of corruption increases the preference exhibited by foreign entrants to join with local firms, suggesting that there may be benefits to including local partners as a way to mitigate risks associated with arbitrariness.
- Figure 3 shows that *joint ventures between local and foreign entrants are about as likely at low levels of arbitrariness as they are at high levels.* Foreign entrants appear to become more concerned that they may be subject to local partner opportunism as corruption becomes more arbitrary, offsetting the perceived advantages gained from partnering. Where corruption is highly arbitrary, entrants attempt to reduce risk via entry with international partners only.

FIGURE 2 Relationship Between the Probability of Joint-Venture Types and Pervasiveness

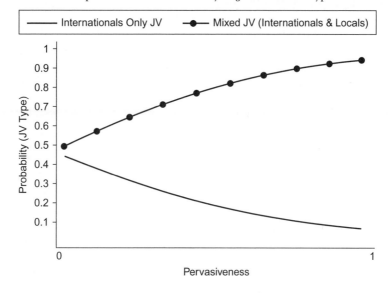

FIGURE 3 Relationship Between the Probability of Joint-Venture Types and Arbitrariness

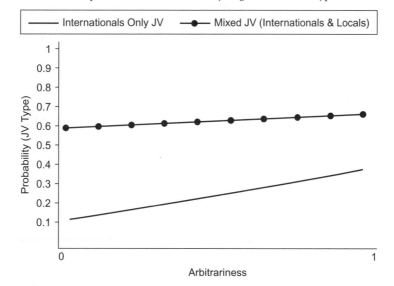

- *In addition, if both pervasiveness and arbitrariness of corruption are high, entry modes are more likely to take the form of build-own-transfer or management contracts versus build-own-operate (traditional FDI) modes.* Firms appear to reach a tipping point at which they are more inclined to transfer ownership and less willing to remain to operate their projects. In countries where both pervasiveness and arbitrariness are very high (C2 in Figure 1), virtually all projects are transferred after their completion.

Strategy: corporate codes of conduct

A complementary strategy for reducing both direct and indirect costs of corruption is the adoption of anti-bribery principles. Below we list several examples. A number of companies have developed rigorous codes and principles that guide their policies on corruption around the world, while other MNEs rely on guidelines provided by public institutions. Such approaches may be effective in environments characterized by pervasive or arbitrary corruption.

- *Shell's General Business Principles* guide corporate behavior in the area of corruption. On the specific issue of bribes, for example, the Principles state, "The direct or indirect offer, payment, soliciting, and acceptance of bribes in any form are unacceptable practices." According to Shell, each year each country chairman reports to executive management on how these business principles are being implemented, and "issues concerning corruption and bribery are always at the top of the list." Shell's goal is to help managers understand the elements of corruption and bribery and to "exercise sound judgment when faced with difficult dilemmas."[37]
- *International Chamber of Commerce (ICC) Rules Against Extortion and Bribery*. The ICC has a Standing Committee on Extortion and Bribery that promotes its "Rules Against Extortion and Bribery" in international business transactions. These rules specifically target "large-scale extortion and bribery involving politicians and senior officials." The seven basic rules address extortion, bribery and kickbacks, agents, financial recording and auditing, responsibilities of enterprises, political contributions, and company codes.[38]
- *Transparent Agents Against Contracting Entities (TRACE)*. The TRACE Standard, which is based on a review of the practices of 34 companies, applies to many types of business intermediaries, including sales agents, consultants, suppliers, distributors, resellers, subcontractors, franchisees, and joint venture partners. It is the first global business standard of its kind and is being disseminated directly by TRACE and by investment houses and pro-business organizations like the Centre for International Private Enterprise, the non-profit arm of the Chamber of Commerce. It has been well received because it sets out best practices and gives companies the confidence that they are doing as much due diligence as their corporate peers, which is an important part of a defense if an intermediary does pay a bribe.[39]
- Building from the ICC Rules, two legal experts have proposed a *Comprehensive International Corruption Code* that (1) emphasizes transparency, (2) provides guidance concerning specific practices associated with paying bribes, (3) reflects relevance to organizational environments, (4) identifies with and supports an independent entity such as an NGO or an academic center, and, perhaps most importantly, (5) can be monitored and assessed by external, independent entities.[40] This code and approach resolve the "free rider" problem by requiring many competing firms to adhere to the same standards. Further, it addresses challenges raised by both pervasiveness and arbitrariness of corruption.

*Intentional
Power –* (handwritten)

Strategy: training, development, and public education

Training and development is a natural extension of corporate codes and principles, and may help respond to both direct and indirect costs of corruption. Firms can work with governmental bodies that are eager to promote local participation in foreign-sponsored projects to help convince them to crack down on corruption. This may be effective even in countries that have highly arbitrary corruption because enforcement actions can specifically target, and ideally isolate, these cases. Unilateral efforts, as well as those supported by multinational organizations such as the UN, World Bank, or IMF, should be encouraged. Often, assistance is available from multilateral bodies that provide financial and technical support for the development of efficient government and "good governance." Below are examples of individual firm activities as well as those involving public-private collaboration.

- *Honeywell* lists "integrity and the highest ethical standards" first among its set of eight company values and unequivocally admonishes against any bribes or kickbacks in its corporate code of conduct. As a constant reminder of the code, employees are issued business-size cards containing ethically driven questions that they should ask themselves in ambiguous situations. Moreover, Honeywell flags "high risk" employees for additional corruption and bribery training. The company has established a toll-free ethics advice line run by a third-party security firm. In one specific case, Honeywell declined to bid on a major airport contract in Asia because it was asked for a bribe as a price of entry. When an investigation revealed that 11 companies paid the bribe, they were disqualified and Honeywell was awarded the contract, showing that refraining from participation in corrupt transactions may sometimes have positive competitive effects.[41]

  actually Positions Not Employees (handwritten margin note)

- *TDI Brooks International, Inc.*, a US-based oil exploration firm, openly resists corruption. The company drew attention to suspicious activities during a recent public tender clarification meeting in Mexico. TDI demonstrated that the tender included specifications and restrictions added merely to favor one particular bidder and exclude others. The company further provided evidence that the project was heavily inflated compared to a reasonable bid for the proposed work. TDI thus served as a whistleblower, suggesting corrupt interactions between managers of one of the bidding organizations and of the state-owned firm that offered the tender. Ultimately, TDI lost the specific contract to this competing bidder but, by making corruption public, initiated an investigation into corrupt practices at this state-owned firm. Subsequently, the firm has indicated that it will hire TDI for another project. Whistleblowing may be a more promising strategy in countries where arbitrariness of corruption is low and perpetrators more easily identified.

  A risky strategy (handwritten margin note)

- According to *Motorola*, a longstanding ethics program helps facilitate the understanding of bribery and corruption practices worldwide. The firm's ongoing ethics training program reportedly explores all facets of bribery and corruption, and guides employees on how to act in ethically difficult situations. Management uses actual case studies as part of its training in an attempt to give employees real-world situations, and the firm actively helps fight corruption in countries in which it operates. For example, Motorola supported training projects for internal auditors in Thailand designed to minimize corrupt behavior.

- *World Bank Anti-Corruption Knowledge Center.* Since 1996, the World Bank has supported more than 600 anti-corruption programs and governance initiatives developed by its member countries. According to the Bank, "Corruption undermines policies and programs that aim to reduce poverty, so attacking corruption is critical to the achievement of the Bank's overarching mission of poverty reduction." The World Bank's anti-corruption strategy addresses both pervasiveness and arbitrariness of corruption and builds on five key elements: (1) increasing political accountability, (2) strengthening civil society participation, (3) creating a competitive private sector, (4) institutional restraints on power, and (5) improving public-sector management.[42]

Strategy: social contributions and public donations

Some companies employ the strategy of social contributions and public donations as an alternative to both avoidance and compliance. For example, sometimes bribes are presented as agent fees or fees for public services that might not otherwise be available. Several examples are presented below. This strategy targets primarily the direct costs of corruption. These approaches, however, are unlikely to protect firms from the arbitrary application of corruption because even if a legal contribution is offered to an organization (versus individuals), other officials may demand further payments.

- *Cargill, Inc.*, an international marketer, processor, and distributor of agricultural, food, financial, and industrial products, aggressively attempts to strengthen the communities in which it operates by avoiding and speaking out against bribery and corruption as well as supporting specific causes.[43] After two Cargill offices were set on fire in India following political opposition concerning the company's entry into the sunflower seed market, the company responded by teaching Indian farmers how to improve their crop yields.[44]
- *Motorola* has permitted the payment of agent fees where they are a relatively small part of the contract. In other situations, rather than pay a fee to ensure the provision of local public services, Motorola donated equipment to the relevant government agencies. This increased the likelihood that the equipment would be used for the stated purpose.[45]
- *Hope Group* donated textbooks to 17 million students in China as a means to facilitate business relationships and reputation. In China, such relationships are considered especially important in business dealings, and this contribution also provided a substantial social benefit.[46]

Strategy: laws and agreements

Individual corporate behavior or joint activities by groups of corporations are important elements in firms' response to corruption. Ultimately, much of the burden is on governments to restrain corrupt tendencies. Firms are expected to support these efforts. Corruption has a substantial deterrent effect on FDI in host countries, especially in emerging economies, and these agreements have helped to even the playing field, at least in specific countries and regions. On the other hand, problems are created when firms from one country (like the US) are held to a different standard than others. This strategy, which obviously relies on cooperation with government agencies, targets the direct costs of corruption and is most effective at combating corruption in environments where it is pervasive but may also have some effectiveness in environments characterized by arbitrary corruption. Three examples of governmental initiatives in the area follow.

- *The Organization for Economic Cooperation and Development (OECD) Convention on Combating Bribery of Foreign Public Officials in International Business Transactions.* On November 21, 1997, negotiators from 33 countries (28 of the 29 member states of the OECD, along with Argentina, Brazil, Bulgaria, Chile, and the Slovak Republic) adopted a Convention on Combating Bribery of Foreign Public Officials in International Business Transactions. The Convention was signed by representatives of participating countries on December 17, 1997.[47]
- *US Foreign Corrupt Practices Act (FCPA).* This US law, enacted in 1977, was prompted by a series of scandals involving questionable or illegal payments by US firms to foreign government officials overseas. There were revelations that some of this money had returned to the US in the form of political contributions. The FCPA prohibits American firms from giving anything of value – such as a payment, gift or bribe – to induce a foreign government to enter into a contract or business advantage or relationship. The Act carries criminal penalties, including imprisonment for up to five years, fines of up to $100,000 for individuals, and fines of up to $2 million for companies. In 1998 the US passed legislation expanding the scope of the FCPA to bring its provisions into accord with the OECD Convention. Prior to implementation of the OECD Corruption Code, the United States was unique in having this kind of law, and in countries where corruption was widespread, the Act had made it difficult for US companies to compete. Moreover, many executives have complained that the prohibited acts are standard operating procedure in some countries, although with the OECD agreement and implementation, this is changing.[48]
- *The Organization of American States (OAS) Inter-American Convention Against Corruption:* The OAS Convention, which entered into force in March 1997, was the first multilateral anti-corruption treaty negotiated in the world. The Convention requires parties to criminalize bribery of foreign officials and to assist one another in the investigation and prosecution of such acts. The Convention also explicitly disallows the use of "bank secrecy" as a basis for denying assistance. More than 25 Western hemisphere countries are signatories to the Convention, including Argentina, Brazil, Chile, Mexico, and the United States.[49]

COPING WITH CORRUPTION: LESSONS FOR MANAGERS AND POLICY-MAKERS

Corruption has direct and indirect effects on aggregate FDI into a given economy and influences firm-level decisions about entry mode and project structure. In sum, we find that:

1 The nature of corruption is not fully appreciated and incorporated in managerial decision-making. Failure to comprehend differing types of corruption may hinder effective operation of international businesses, where resource commitments are substantial and difficult to reverse and reputation effects are long lasting.

2 While firms fully recognize the costs related to pervasiveness of corruption, arbitrariness is often disregarded in the development of proactive strategies. Whereas firms appear to adjust their entry modes when confronted by high arbitrariness, they may forego other strategies due to a mistaken perception that arbitrariness affects all firms the same, when in fact it can have significantly disproportionate impacts on firms.

3 Firms adjust and adapt their market-entry approaches to minimize exposure to partners who may attempt to exploit the corrupt environment for their own gains, yet maximize relationships with partners that can facilitate project development.

4 Firms often don't fully recognize the range of strategic alternatives to acquiescing to corrupt pressures. These strategies can help reduce costs, and some may help in deterring corruption more broadly.

5 Some strategies may be pursued by individual firms, collectives of companies, or in conjunction with governments. For example, a number of the companies mentioned above support broad, government- or industry-driven efforts to reduce corruption through membership in organizations such as the International Chamber of Commerce, while at the same time focusing on shorter-term and transaction-specific challenges that affect their day-to-day business opportunities.

Governments, independently and through international consortia, continue to struggle in their efforts to identify effective solutions to the destructive practices of corruption. At the same time, companies seeking new markets and opportunities continue to explore options that minimize the most pronounced impacts of corruption. Both governments and companies have made important steps in their efforts to stem the spread of corruption, but much more needs to be done.

We considered five strategies that show how firms can deal with corruption in a manner that preserves their strategic choices in international market entry, while protecting themselves from the costs of corruption. None of the strategies we propose comprehensively addresses corruption. At best, each reflects a partial solution. Taken together, they may provide a more comprehensive approach, particularly given the interactive and mutually reinforcing nature of firm- and government-sponsored strategies. Just as firms pursue multiple business strategies to address their objectives in international markets, so too should they consider the range of options to combat corruption.

In the interim, firms should be aware – and be wary – of their dealings in countries where corrupt practices are common. Firms would be wise to work cooperatively with each other and with government organizations to realize the substantial benefits of reduced corruption: improved firm and aggregate business performance, more effective host-nation governance, and greater and more widespread social and economic development.

ACKNOWLEDGMENTS

We would like to thank Bernie Bernard, Don Hellriegel, and Alexandra Wrage for helpful comments and acknowledge the input and guidance of Robert Ford, Celeste

Wilderom, and two anonymous reviewers on earlier versions of the article. We take responsibility for any remaining errors.

Notes

1 *Asian Wall Street Journal.* Ruling puts foreign infrastructure investors at risk, 29 March 2002: A3.

2 Webster, P. 2002. Ripped off in Russia. *Maclean's. www.mcleans.ca.*

3 *Economist.* Corruption in Lesotho: Small place, big wave. 21 September 2002: 73.

4 The World Bank, 1998. *Global development finance.*

5 See Henisz, W. J., & Williamson, O. E. 1999. Comparative economic organization – within and between countries, *Business and Politics*, 1: 261–277; Hill, C. W. L., Hwang, P., & Kim, W. C. 1990. An electric theory of the choice of international entry mode. *Strategic Management Journal*, 11: 117–128; Kobrin, S. 1979. Political risk: A review and reconsideration, *Journal of International Business Studies*, 10: 67–80; and Murtha, T. 1991. Surviving industrial targeting: State credibility and public policy competencies in multinational subcontracting. *Journal of Law, Economics and Organization*, 7: 117–143.

6 A limited but growing body of research has explored the impact of corruption on FDI, generally finding that corruption significantly reduces FDI into an economy. For a recent review, see Habib, M., & Zurawicki, L. 2002. Corruption and foreign direct investment. *Journal of International Business Studies*, 33: 291–307. These authors find that corruption reduces aggregate FDI even when controlling for political risk, cultural distance, and level-of-corruption differences between the home and host countries.

7 See D'Andrade, K. 1985. Bribery. *Journal of Business Ethics*, 4 (4): 239–248; Johnson, H. L. 1985. Bribery in international markets: Diagnosis, clarification and remedy. *Journal of Business Ethics*, 4 (6): 447–455; and Lane, H. W., & Simpson, D. G. 1984. Bribery in international business: Whose problem is it? *Journal of Business Ethics*, 3 (1): 35–42.

8 See Ahlstrom, D., & Bruton, G. D. 2001. Learning from successful local private firms in China: Establishing legitimacy. *The Academy of Management Executive*, 15 (4): 72–83; and Boddewyn, J. J., & Brewer, T. L. 1994. International business political behavior: New theoretical directions. *Academy of Management Review*, 19 (1): 119–144.

9 For a review of the particular challenges associated with securing foreign investment in infrastructure, see Vernon, R. 1971. *Sovereignty at bay: The multinational spread of U.S. enterprises.* New York: Basic Books; Doz, Y., & Prahalad, S. 1980. How MNCs cope with host government intervention. *Harvard Business Review*, March–April: 149–157; Fagre, N., & Wells, L. T. 1982. Bargaining power of multinationals and host governments. *Journal of International Business Studies*, 13: 9–23; Kobrin, S. 1987. Testing the bargaining hypothesis in the manufacturing sector in developing countries. *International Organization*, 41: 609–638; and Wells, L. T., & Gleason, E. S. 1995. Is foreign infrastructure investment still risky? *Harvard Business Review*, September–October: 44–53.

10 *The Economist.* Not quite so squeaky clean. 18 October 2001. *www.economist.com.*

11 *The Economist.* Small place, big wave. 19 September 2002. *www.economist.com.*

12 *The Economist.* When something is rotten. 25 July 2002. *www.economist.com.*

13 It should be noted that "grease payments" or "facilitating payments" are permitted under the Foreign Corrupt Practices Act if they are paid to government officials in order to induce them to undertake a routine non-discretionary task which is otherwise within their job description.

14 Cassidy, W. B. 2002. Fraud, bribery, etc. *Traffic World.* 266 (29): 8–10.

15 Scott, R. 2002. Eliminating bribery as a transnational marketing strategy. *International Journal of Commerce & Management*, 12 (1):1–17.

16 *The Economist.* Dotcom coup. 15 March 2001. *www.economist.com.*

17   *The Economist.* Special report: The short arm of the law – Bribery and business. 2 March 2002. *www.economist.com.*

18   Ahlstrom & Bruton, op. cit.

19   Webster, op. cit.

20   See Mauro, P. 1995. Corruption and growth. *The Quarterly Journal of Economics,* 110 (3): 681–712; Mauro, P. 1998. Corruption and the composition of government expenditure. *Journal of Public Economics,* 69: 263–279; World Bank. 1997. *World development report 1997: The state in a changing world.* Oxford, UK, and New York: Oxford University Press; and Herrera, A., & Rodriguez, P. 2001. *Bribery and the nature of corruption.* Papers and Proceedings, LACEA Conference, Montevideo, Uruguay.

21   Mauro, 1995, op. cit.

22   *Economist.* The revenue problem. 15 February 2003: 36. Other Latin American countries feature similarly low tax yields: Guatemala (10%), Mexico (18%) versus 30% in the US.

23   Brunetti, A., & Weder, B. 1998. Investment and institutional uncertainty: A comparative study of different uncertainty measures. *Weltwirtschaftliches Archiv,* 134: 513–533.

24   Gray, C., & Kaufmann, D. 1998. Corruption and development. *Finance and Development,* 35 (1): 7–10.

25   Mauro, P. 1997. The effects of corruption on growth, investment, and government expenditure: A cross-country analysis. In K. A. Elliot (Ed.), *Corruption and the global economy:* 83–107. Washington, DC: Institute for International Economics; Keefer, P. 1996. Protection against a capricious state: French investment and Spanish railroads, 1845–1875. *The Journal of Economic History,* 56 (1): 170–192; and Brunetti & Weder, op. cit.

26   Transparency International. 2003. *2003 global corruption report.* London: Profile Books.

27   Johnston, M. 1999. Corruption et démocratie: Menaces pour le développement, possibilités de réforme. *Revue Tiers Monde,* 161: 117–142.

28   See Rodriguez, P., Uhlenbruck, K., & Eden, L. (in press) Government corruption and the entry strategies of multinationals. *Academy of Management Review;* Shleifer, A., & Vishny, R. 1993. Corruption. *Quarterly Journal of Economics,* 108: 599–617.

29   Ibid.

30   Borsuk, R. In Indonesia, a twist on spreading the wealth: Decentralization of power multiplies opportunities for bribery, corruption. *Wall Street Journal,* 29 January 2003: A16.

31   See World Development Report, op. cit.; Wei, S.-J. 1997. Why is corruption so much more taxing than tax? Arbitrariness kills. NBER working paper No. 6255: and Campos, J. E., Lien, D., & Pradhan, S. 1999. The impact of corruption on investment: Predictability matters. *World Development,* 27: 1059–1067.

32   Campos, et al., op. cit.

33   Rivoli, P., & Salorio, E. 1996. Foreign direct investment and investment under uncertainty. *Journal of International Business Studies,* 27: 335–357.

34   Smarzynska, B., & Wei, S.-J. 2000. Corruption and the composition of foreign direct investment: Firm-level evidence. NBER Working paper No. 7969. A recent Department of Justice Advisory Opinion, however, has stated that U.S. firms would be held responsible for the business practices of the agents hired by JV partners, even if the agents were hired prior to the JV. Now, the legal burden is as great as operating alone, but the controls (through a JV partner) are virtually non-existent. In addition, while it has been suggested that some companies try to push the payment of bribes down their marketing chain to local partners, FCPA and new laws implementing the OECD Corruption Agreement state expressly that payments may not be made directly or indirectly through third parties.

35   Telecommunications is a particularly appropriate industry for this study because a significant portion of FDI in the 1990s came from telecommunication MNEs, especially investment into emerging countries with high market potential but with significant and varying corruption

levels. Further, infrastructure projects typically involve numerous government agencies, and thus corruption as defined herein is an important environmental variable. While it is true that the telecom industry has idiosyncratic characteristics that may not be applicable to some other industries, it is has been identified as the "flagship" industry for the range of international infrastructure investment – electric power development, transportation, water and sewerage – and so many other industries are reliant upon telecom services. These figures represent the findings of logistic regression analysis that includes a number of control variables at the country, industry, firm, and project levels.

36   See Zaheer, S. 1995. Overcoming the liability of foreignness. *Academy of Management Journal*, 38 (2): 341–363; Beamish, P. W. & Banks, J. C. 1987. Equity joint ventures and the theory of the multinational enterprise. *Journal of International Business Studies*, 18 (2): 1–16: Hill, et al. op. cit; and Yiu, D., & Makino, S. 2002. The choice between joint venture and wholly owned subsidiary: An institutional perspective. *Organization Science*, 13 (6): 667–683.

37   Rigby, P. 2001. Dealing with business and legal institutional risk. *Energy Business and Technology*, 3 (5): 10. *http://www.cumna.com/shell/intro.htm.*

38   Controversy incorporated. 2002. *The McKinsey Quarterly*, 4: *http://www.mckinseyquarterly.com/cotegory_editor.asp? L2=18.*

39   Major initiative launched to curb corruption in global business. TRACE. December 11. *http://www.traceinternational.org/TRACE_Press_Release_121102.doc.*

40   See Hess, D., & Dunfee, T. 2000. Fighting corruption: A principled approach: The C2 principles (Combating Corruption). *Cornell International Law Journal*, 33 (3): 595–628.

41   Business for Social Responsibility. 2002. *Corruption and bribery White Paper. http://www.bsr.org/BSRResources/White-PaperDetail.cfm?DocumentID=180.*

42   *Anticorruption. www.worldbank.org/publicsector/anticorrupt/.*

43   *Cargill citizenship report. http://www.cargill.com/citizenship.pdf.*

44   Cogman, D., & Oppenheim, J. M. 2002. Controversy incorporated. *The McKinsey Quarterly*, 4: *http://www.mckinseyquarterly.com/category_editor.asp?L2=18.*

45   Business for Social Responsibility, op. cit.

46   Alhstrom, D., & Bruton, G. D. 2001, Learning from successful local private firms in China: Establishing legitimacy. *The Academy of Management Executive*, 15 (4): 72–83.

47   *OECD anti-bribery convention summary. http://Usinfo.State.Gov/Journals/Ites/1198/Ijee/Factoecd.htm.*

48   Stackhouse, D. The foreign corrupt practices act: Bribery, corruption, recordkeeping and More. *Indiana Lawyer* 23 April 1993.

49   Business for Social Responsibility, op. cit.

Bribery in International Business: Whose Problem Is It?

Henry W. Lane and Donald G. Simpson

INTRODUCTION

No discussion of problems in international business seems complete without reference to familiar complaints about the questionable business practices North American executives encounter in foreign countries, particularly developing nations. Beliefs about the pervasiveness of dishonesty and the necessity of engaging in such practices as bribery vary widely, however, and these differences often lead to vigorous discussions that generate more heat than light. Pragmatists or "realists" may take the attitude that "international business is a rough game and no place for the naive idealist or the faint-hearted. Your competitors use bribes and unless you are willing to meet this standard competitive practice you will lose business and ultimately, jobs for workers at home. Besides, it is an accepted business practice in those countries, and when you are in Rome you have to do as the Romans do." "Moralists," on the other hand, believe that cultural relativity is no excuse for unethical behavior. "As Canadians or Americans we should uphold our legal and ethical standards anywhere in the world; and any good American or Canadian knows that bribery, by any euphemism, is unethical and wrong. Bribery increases a product's cost and often is used to secure import licenses for products that no longer can be sold in the developed world. Such corrupting practices also contribute to the moral disintegration of individuals and eventually societies."

The foregoing comments represent extreme polar positions but we are not using these stereotypes to create a "straw man" or false dichotomy about attitudes toward practices such as bribery. These extreme viewpoints, or minor variations of them, will be encountered frequently as one meets executives who have experience in developing countries. Some "realists" and "moralists" undoubtedly are firm believers in their positions, but many other executives probably gravitate toward one of the poles because they have not found a realistic alternative approach to thinking about the issue of bribery, never mind finding an answer to the problem.

The impetus for this article came from discussions with executives and government officials in Canada and in some developing nations about whether a North American company could conduct business successfully in developing countries without engaging in what would be considered unethical or illegal practices. It was apparent from these talks that the question was an important one and of concern to business executives, but not much practical, relevant information existed on the issue. There was consensus on two points: first, there are a lot of myths surrounding the issue of payoffs; and second, if anyone had some insights into the problem, executives would appreciate hearing them.

In this article, we would like to share what we have learned about the issue during the two years we have been promoting business (licensing agreements, management contracts, joint ventures) between Canadian and African companies. Our intention is not to present a comprehensive treatment of the subject of bribery or a treatise on ethical behavior. Our intention is to present a practical discussion of some dimensions of the problem based on our experience, discussions, and, in some cases, investigation of specific incidents.

THE PROBLEM IS MULTIFACETED

It can be misleading to talk about bribery in global terms without considering some situational specifics, such as country, type of business, and company. Our discussions with managers indicate that the payoff problem is more prevalent in some countries than in others. Executives with extensive experience probably could rank countries on a scale reflecting the seriousness of the problem. Also, some industries are probably more susceptible to payoff requests than others. Large construction projects, turnkey capital projects, and large commodity or equipment contracts are likely to be most vulnerable because the scale of the venture may permit the easy disguise of payoffs, and because an individual, or small group of people, may be in a strategic position to approve or disapprove the project. These projects or contracts are undoubtedly obvious targets also because the stakes are high, the competition vigorous, and the possibility that some competitors may engage in payoffs increased. Finally, some companies may be more vulnerable due to a relative lack of bargaining power or because they have no policie to guide them in these situations. If the product or technology is unique, or clearly superior, and it is needed, the company is in a relatively strong position to resist the pressure. Similarly, those firms with effective operational policies against payoffs are in a position of strength. Many senior executives have stated, with pride, that their companies have reputations for not making payoffs and, therefore, are not asked for them. These were executives of large, successful firms that also had chosen not to work in some countries where they could not operate comfortably. These executives often backed up their claims with specific examples in which they walked away from apparently lucrative deals where a payoff was a requirement.

Two other elements of the situational context of a payoff situation that vary are the subtlety of the demand and the amount of money involved. All payoff situations are not straightforward and unambiguous, which may make a clear response more difficult. Consider, for example, the case of a company that was encouraged to change its evaluation of bids for a large construction project. Some host-country agencies were embarrassed by the evaluation results since Company X, from the country providing significant financing for the project, was ranked a distant third. The agencies sought a re-evaluation on questionable technicalities. The changes were considered but the ranking remained the same. At this point pressure began to build. Phone calls were made berating the firm for delaying the project and hinting that the large follow-on contract, for which it had the inside track, was in jeopardy. No one ever said make Company X the winner or you lose the follow-on.

Although no money was to change hands, this situation was similar to a payoff request in that the company was being asked to alter its standard for acceptable business practices for an implied future benefit. The interpretation of the "request," the response, and the consequences, were left entirely to the company's management. Refusal to change may mean losing a big contract, but giving in does not guarantee the follow-on and you leave the company vulnerable to further demands. In ambiguous situations factors such as corporate policies and the company's financial strength and its need for the contract enter into the decision. In this case the company had firm beliefs about what constituted professional standards and did not desperately need the follow-on contract. Although it refused to change, another company might find itself in a dilemma, give in to the pressure, and rationalize its behavior.

Finally, payoffs range in size from the small payments that may help getting through customs without a hassle up to the multimillion dollar bribes that make headlines and embarrass governments. The payoff situations we discuss in this article are more significant than the former, but much smaller and far less dramatic than the latter. These middle-range payoffs (tens of thousands of dollars) may pose a problem for corporations. They are too big to be ignored but possibly not big enough to be referred to corporate headquarters unless the firm has clear guidelines on the subject. Regional executives or lower-level managers may be deciding whether or not these "facilitating payments" are just another cost of doing business in the developing world.

ON THE OUTSIDE LOOKING IN (THE NORTH AMERICAN PERSPECTIVE)

"It's a corrupt, payoff society. The problem has spread to all levels. On the face it looks good, but underneath it's rotten." Comments such as these are often made by expatriate business people and government officials alike. The North American executive may arrive in a Third World country with a stereotype of corrupt officials and is presented with the foregoing analysis by people-on-the-spot who, he or she feels, should know the situation best. His or her fears are confirmed.

This scenario may be familiar to some readers. It is very real to us because we have gone through that process. Two cases provide examples of the stories a businessperson may likely be told in support of the dismal analysis.

> The "New Venture": Company Y, a wholly owned subsidiary of a European multinational, wished to manufacture a new product for export. Government permission was required and

Company Y submitted the necessary applications. Sometime later one of Company Y's executives (a local national) informed the Managing Director that the application was approved and the consultant's fee must be paid. The Managing Director knew nothing about a consultant or such a fee. The executive took his boss to a meeting with the consultant – a government official who sat on the application review committee. Both the consultant and the executive claimed to remember the initial meeting at which agreement was reached on the $10,000 fee. A few days later the Managing Director attended a cocktail party at the home of a high-ranking official in the same agency. This official recommended that the fee be paid. The Managing Director decided against paying the fee and the project ran into unexpected delays. At this point the Managing Director asked the parent company's legal department for help. Besides the delay, the situation was creating a problem between the Managing Director and his executives as well as affecting the rest of the company. He initially advised against payment but after watching the company suffer, acquiesced with the approval of the parent company. The fee was renegotiated downward and the consultant paid. What was the result? Nothing! The project was not approved.

The "Big Sale": Company Z, which sold expensive equipment, established a relationship with a well-placed government official on the first trip to the country. This official, and some other nationals, assured Company Z representatives that they would have no trouble getting the contract. On leaving the country, Company Z representatives had a letter of intent to purchase the equipment. On the second trip Company Z representatives brought the detailed technical specifications for a certain department head to approve. The department head refused to approve the specifications and further efforts to have the government honor its promise failed. The deal fell through. Company Z's analysis of the situation, which became common knowledge in business and government circles, was that a competitor paid the department head to approve its equipment and that the government reneged on its obligation to purchase Company Z equipment.

While in the country, the visiting executive may even have met Company Z's agent in the "Big Sale," who confirms the story. Corruption is rampant, and in the particular case of the "Big Sale" he claims to know that the department head received the money and from whom. The case is closed! An honest North American company cannot function in this environment – or so it seems.

ON THE INSIDE LOOKING OUT (THE DEVELOPING COUNTRY'S PERSPECTIVE)

During his visit the executive may have met only a few nationals selected by his company or government representatives. He probably has not discussed bribery with them because of its sensitive nature. If the business people and the officials he met were dishonest, they would not admit it; if they were honest he probably felt they would resent the discussion. Also, he may not have had enough time to establish the type of relationship in which the subject could be discussed frankly. It is almost certain that he did not speak with the people in the government agencies who allegedly took the payoffs. What would he say if he did meet them? And more than likely he would not be able to get an appointment with them if he did want to pursue the matter further. So the executive is convinced that corruption is widespread having heard only one side of the horror stories.

Had the visitor been able to investigate the viewpoints of the nationals what might he have heard? "I would like to find a person from the developed world that I can trust. You people brought corruption here. We learned the concept from you. You want to win all the time, and you are impatient so you bribe. You offer bribes to the local people and complain that business is impossible without bribing."

Comments like these are made by local business people and government officials alike. If the visiting executive heard these comments he would be confused and would wonder whether or not these people were talking about the same country. Although skeptical, his confidence in the accuracy of his initial assessment would have been called into question. Had he been able to stay longer in the country, he might have met an old friend who knew the department head who allegedly was paid off in the "Big Sale." His friend would have made arrangements for the visitor to hear the other side of the story.

> *The "Big Sale" Revisited:* After the representatives of Company Z received what they described as a letter of intent to purchase the equipment they returned home. On the second visit they had to deal with the department head to receive his approval for the technical specifications.
>
> At the meeting they told the department head that he need not worry about the details and just sign off on the necessary documents. If he had any questions regarding the equipment he could inspect it in two weeks' time in their home country. The department head's initial responses were: (1) he would not rubber stamp anything, and (2) how could this complex equipment which was supposedly being custom made for his country's needs be inspected in two weeks when he had not yet approved the specifications.
>
> As he reviewed the specifications he noticed a significant technical error and brought it to the attention of Company Z's representatives. They became upset with his "interference" and inferred that they would use their connections in high places to ensure his compliance. When asked again to sign the documents he refused, and the company reps left saying they would have him removed from his job.
>
> After this meeting the premier of the country became involved and asked the company officials to appear before him. They arrived with the premier's nephew for a meeting with the premier and his top advisors.
>
> The premier told his nephew that he had no business being there and directed him to leave. The company officials then had to face the premier and his advisors alone. The premier asked if the company had a contract and that if it had, it would be honored. The company had to admit that it had no contract. As far as the premier was concerned, the issue was settled.
>
> However, the case was not closed for Company Z representatives. They felt they had been promised the deal and that the department had reneged. They felt that someone had paid off the department head and they were quite bitter. In discussions with their local embassy officials and with government officials at home they presented their analysis of the situation. The result was strained relations and the department head got a reputation for being dishonest.

Well, the other side of the story certainly has different implications about whose behavior may be considered questionable. The situation is now very confusing. Is the department head honest or not? The executive's friend has known the department head for a long time and strongly believes he is honest; and some other expatriate government officials have basically corroborated the department head's perception of the matter. But the business people and the government officials who first told the story seemed reputable and honest. Who should be believed? As the visiting executive has learned, you have to decide the truth for yourself.

PATTERNS OF BEHAVIOR

The preceding vignettes illustrate our position that bribery and corruption is a problem for North American and Third World business people alike. We also have observed two recurring behavioral patterns in these real, but disguised, situations. The first is the predisposition of the North American businessperson to accept the premise that bribery is the way of life in the developing world and a necessity in business transactions. The second behavioral pattern occurs in situations where payments are requested and made.

We believe that many executives visit Third World countries with an expectation to learn that bribery is a problem. This attitude likely stems from a number of sources. First, in many cases it may be true. In some countries it may be impossible to complete a transaction without a bribe and the horror stories about the widespread disappearance of honesty are valid. However, in some instances the expectations are conditioned by the "conventional wisdom" available in international business circles. This conventional wisdom develops from situations like the ones we have described. As these situations are passed from individual to individual, accuracy may diminish and facts be forgotten. This is not done intentionally but happens since it is rare that the story tellers have the complete story or all the facts. Unverified stories of bribery and corruption circulate through the business and government communities and often become accepted as true and factual. The obvious solution, and difficulty, is learning how to distinguish fact from fiction.

Another factor influencing initial expectations are the unfavorable impressions of developing countries and their citizens that are picked up from the media. Often only the sensational, and negative, news items from these countries are reported in North America. We learn of bombings, attacks on journalists and tourists, alleged (and real) *coup d'états*, and major scandals. These "current events" and the "conventional wisdom" combined with an executive's probable lack of knowledge of the history, culture, legal systems, or economic conditions of a country all contribute to the development of unfavorable stereotypes that predispose the executive toward readily accepting reports that confirm his already drawn conclusions: all Latin American or African countries, for example, are all the same and corruption is to be expected.

The stories that constitute "evidence" of corruption may be tales of bribery like the "New Venture" or the "Big Sale," or they may take other forms. The story we have heard most often has the "protect yourself from your local partner" theme. It goes like this: "If you are going to invest in this country, particularly in a joint venture, you have to find a way to protect yourself from your partner. He is likely to strip all the company's assets and leave you nothing but a skeleton. Just look what happened to Company A."

On hearing the "evidence," particularly from expatriates in the foreign country, a visiting businessperson most likely accepts it without further investigation. He has forgotten the old adage about there being two sides to every story. His conclusion and conviction are most likely based on incomplete and biased data.

Is there another viewpoint? Certainly! Many nationals have expressed it to us: "The Europeans and North Americans have been taking advantage of us for decades, even centuries. The multinationals establish a joint venture and then strip the local company bare through transfer pricing, management fees, and royalties based on a percentage of sales rather than profits. They have no interest in the profitability of the company or its long-term development."

The situation is ironic. Some local investors are desperately looking for an honest North American executive whom they can trust at the same time the North American is searching for them. Our experience indicates that this search process is neither straightforward nor easy. And while the search continues, if it does, it is difficult for the North American to maintain a perspective on the situation and remember that there are locals who may share his values and who are equally concerned about unethical and illegal practices.

In summary, we would characterize the first observed pattern of behavior as a preparedness to accept "evidence" of corruption and the simultaneous failure to examine critically the "evidence" or its source.

The second behavioral pattern appears in the actual payoff process. The request very likely comes from a low- or middle-level bureaucrat who says that his boss must be paid for the project to be approved or for the sale to be finalized. Alternatively, it may be your agent who is providing similar counsel. In either case you are really not certain who is making the demand.

Next, the payoff is made. You give your contact the money, but you never really know where it goes.

Your expectations are obvious. You have approached this transaction from a perspective of economic rationality. You have provided a benefit and expect one in return. The project will be approved or the sale consummated.

The results, however, may be very different than expected. As in the case of the "New Venture," nothing may happen. The only outcome is indignation, anger, and perhaps the loss of a significant amount of money. Now is the time for action, but what recourse do you have? Can you complain? You may be guilty of bribing a government official. And, you certainly are reluctant to admit that you have been duped. Since your direct options are limited, your primary action may be to spread the word: "This is a corrupt, payoff society."

WHY DOES IT HAPPEN?

There are numerous explanations for corruption in developing nations. First, and most obvious, is that some people are simply dishonest. A less pejorative explanation is that the cost of living in these countries may be high and salaries low. Very often a wage earner must provide for a large extended family. The businessperson is viewed opportunistically as a potential source of income to improve the standard of living. Finally, some nationals may believe strongly that they have a right to share some of the wealth controlled by multinational corporations.

Besides being familiar to many readers, these explanations all share another common characteristic. They all focus on "the other person" – the local national. Accepting that there may be some truth in previous explanations, let us, however, turn our focus to the visiting North American to see what we find. We could find a greedy, dishonest expatriate hoping to make a killing. But, let us give this person the same benefit of the doubt we have accorded the local nationals so far.

On closer examination we may find a situation in which the North American executives are vulnerable. They have entered an action vacuum and are at a serious disadvantage. Their lack of knowledge of systems and procedures, laws, institutions, and the people can put them in a dependent position. Unfamiliarity with the system and/or the people makes effective, alternative action such as they could take at home difficult. A strong relationship with a reputable national could help significantly in this situation. Quite often the national knows how to fight the system and who to call in order to put pressure on the corrupt individual. This potential resource should not be dismissed lightly. Although the most powerful and experienced MNCs may also be able to apply this pressure, most of us must be realistic and recognize that no matter how important we think we are, we may not be among those handful of foreigners that can shake the local institutions.

Time can also be a factor. Often the lack of time spent in the country either to establish relationships, or to give the executive the opportunity to fight the system contributes to the problem. Because North American businesspeople believe that time is money and that their time, in particular, is very valuable, they operate on a tight schedule with little leeway for unanticipated delays. The payoff appears to be a cost-effective solution. In summary, the executive might not have the time, knowledge, or contacts to fight back and sees no alternative other than pay or lose the deal.

SOME REAL BARRIERS

If, as we think, there are many honest business people in North America and in the developing world looking for mutually profitable arrangements and for reliable, honest partners, why is it difficult for them to find each other? We believe a significant reason is the inability of both sides to overcome two interrelated barriers – time and trust.

Trust is a critical commodity for business success in developing countries. North Americans going to invest in a country far from home need to believe they will not be cheated out of their assets. Nationals have to believe that a joint venture, for example, will be more than a mechanism for the North American to get rich at their expense. But, even before the venture is established trust may be essential if the prospective partners are ever to meet. This may require the recommendation of a third party respected by both sides.

Establishing good relationships with the right people requires an investment of time, money, and energy. An unwillingness of either party to make this investment is often interpreted as a lack of sincerity or interest. The executive trying to do business in four countries in a week (the "five-day wonder") is still all too common a sight. Similarly the successful local businessperson may have an equally hectic international travel schedule. Both complain that if the other was really serious he would find time to meet. Who should give in? In our opinion the onus is on whichever party is visiting to build into the schedule the necessary time to work on building a relationship or to find a trusted intermediary. Also both parties must be realistic about the elapsed time required to establish a good relationship and negotiate a mutually satisfactory deal. This will involve multiple trips by each party to the other's country and could easily take twelve to eighteen months.

THE COST OF BRIBERY

The most quantifiable costs are the financial ones. The cost of the "service" is known. The costs of not bribing are also quantifiable: the time and money that must be invested in long-term business development in the country, or the value of the lost business. However, there are other costs that must be considered.

1   You may set a precedent and establish that you and/or your company are susceptible to payoff demands.
2   You may create an element in your organization that believes payoffs are standard operating procedure and over which you may eventually lose control.
3   You or your agents may begin using bribery and corruption as a personally non-threatening, convenient excuse to dismiss failure. You may not address some organizational problems of adapting to doing business in the developing world.
4   There are also personal costs. Ultimately you will have to accept responsibility for your decisions and actions, and those of your subordinates. At a minimum it may involve embarrassment, psychological suffering, and a loss of reputation. More extreme consequences include the loss of your job and jail sentences.

CONCLUSION

It is clear that bribery can be a problem for the international executive. Assuming you do not want to participate in the practice, how can you cope with the problem?

1   Do not ignore the issue. Do as many North American companies have done. Spend time thinking about tradeoffs and your position prior to the situation arising.
2   After thinking through the issue establish a corporate policy. We would caution, however, that for any policy to be effective, it must reflect values that are important to the company's senior executives. The policy must also be used. Window dressing will not work.
3   Do not be too quick to accept the "conventional wisdom." Examine critically the stories of bribery and the sources of the stories. Ask for details. Try to find out the other side of the story and make enquiries of a variety of sources.
4   Protect yourself by learning about the local culture and by establishing trusting relationships with well-respected local business people and government officials.
5   Do not contribute to the enlargement of myths by circulating unsubstantiated stories.

Finally, we would offer the advice that when in Rome do as the better Romans do. But, we would add, do not underestimate the time, effort, and expense it may take to find the better Romans and establish a relationship with them.

Moral Person and Moral Manager: How Executives Develop a Reputation for Ethical Leadership

Linda Klebe Treviño, Laura Pincus Hartman, and Michael Brown

[handwritten margin note: Some cultures "value" reputation — Some value performance or success. What is success??]

Plato asked, which extreme would you rather be: "an unethical person with a good reputation or an ethical person with a reputation for injustice?" Plato might have added, "or would you rather be perceived as ethically neutral – someone who has no ethical reputation at all?" Plato knew that reputation was important. We now understand that reputation and others' perceptions of you are key to executive ethical leadership. Those others include employees at all levels as well as key external stakeholders.

A reputation for ethical leadership rests upon two essential pillars: perceptions of you as both a moral person *and* a moral manager. The executive as a moral person is characterized in terms of individual traits such as honesty and integrity. As moral manager, the CEO is thought of as the Chief *Ethics* Officer of the organization, creating a strong ethics message that gets employees' attention and influences their thoughts and behaviors. Both are necessary. To be perceived as an ethical leader, it is not enough to just be an ethical person. An executive ethical leader must also find ways to focus the organization's attention on ethics and values and to infuse the organization with principles that will guide the actions of all employees. An executive's reputation for ethical

This article is based upon the findings of a study initiated by and supported by the Ethics Resource Center Fellows Program.

leadership may be more important now than ever in this new organizational era where more employees are working independently, off site, and without direct supervision. In these organizations, values are the glue that can hold things together, and values must be conveyed from the top of the organization. Also, a single employee who operates outside of the organizational value system can cost the organization dearly in legal fees and can have a tremendous, sometimes irreversible impact on the organization's image and culture.

MORAL PERSON + MORAL MANAGER = A REPUTATION FOR ETHICAL LEADERSHIP

These ideas about a dual pillar approach to ethical leadership are not brand new. As the opening quotation suggests, the emphasis on reputation goes back to Plato. Chester Barnard addressed the ethical dimension of executive leadership sixty years ago. Barnard spoke about executive responsibility in terms of conforming to a "complex code of morals"[1] (moral person) as well as creating moral codes for others (moral manager).

another form of Culture

If Plato and Barnard had this right, why bother revisiting the subject of ethical leadership now? We revisit the subject because, in our 40 structured interviews (20 with senior executives and 20 with corporate ethics officers), we found that many senior executives failed to recognize the importance of others' perceptions and of developing a reputation for ethical leadership. To them, being an ethical person and making good ethical decisions was enough. They spoke proudly about having principles, following the golden rule, taking into account the needs of society, and being fair and caring in their decisions. They assumed that if they were solid ethical beings, followers would automatically know that. They rejected the idea that successful ethical executives are often perceived as ethically neutral. Furthermore, they assumed that good leaders are by definition ethical leaders. One senior executive noted, "I don't think you can distinguish between ethical leadership and leadership. It's just a facet of leadership. The great leaders are ethical, and the lousy ones are not."

However, a *reputation* for ethical leadership can not be taken for granted because most employees in large organizations do not interact with senior executives. They know them only from a distance. Any information they receive about executives gets filtered through multiple layers in the organization, with employees learning only about barebones decisions and outcomes, not the personal characteristics of the people behind them. In today's highly competitive business environment, messages about how financial goals are achieved frequently get lost in the intense focus on the bottom line. We found that just because executives know themselves as good people – honest, caring, and fair – they should not assume that others see them in the same way. It is so easy to forget that employees do not know you the way you know yourself. If employees do not think of an executive as a clearly ethical or unethical leader, they are likely to think of the leader as being somewhere in between – amoral or ethically neutral.

Interestingly, perceptions of *ethically neutral leadership* do not necessarily arise because the leader *is* ethically neutral. In fact, many of the senior executives we spoke with convinced us that it was impossible for them to be ethically neutral in their jobs, given the many value-laden decisions they make every day. Rather, the perception of ethically neutral

FIGURE 1   The Two Pillars of Ethical Leadership

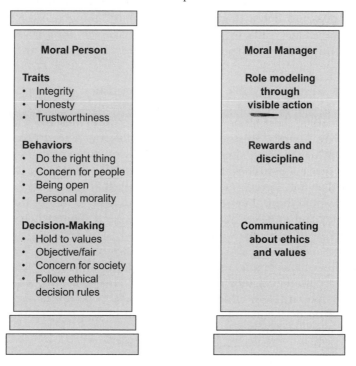

leadership may exist because the leader has not faced major *public* ethical challenges that would provide the opportunity to convey his or her values to others. As one executive noted, "They haven't had to make any decisions on the margin . . . once you're faced with [a major public ethical dilemma], you bare your soul and you're one or the other [ethical or unethical]." On the other hand, a reputation for ethically neutral leadership may exist because the leader has not proactively made ethics and values an explicit and evident part of the leadership agenda. Executives must recognize that if they do not develop a reputation for ethical leadership, they will likely be tagged as "ethically neutral." As a result, employees will believe that the bottom line is the only value that should guide their decisions and that the CEO cares more about himself and the short-term financials than about the long-term interests of the organization and its multiple stakeholders.

Figure 1 provides a summary of our study's findings.

Pillar one: moral person

Being an ethical person is the substantive basis of ethical leadership. However, in order to develop a reputation for ethical leadership, the leader's challenge is conveying that substance to others. Being viewed as an ethical person means that people think of you as having certain traits, engaging in certain kinds of behaviors, and making decisions based upon ethical principles. Furthermore, this substantive ethical core must be authentic. As one executive put it, "if the person truly doesn't believe the ethical story and preaches it but doesn't feel it . . . that's going to show through. . . . But, [a true ethical leader] walks in [and] it doesn't take very long if you haven't met him before [you think] there's a [person] with integrity and candor and honesty."

Traits   Traits are stable personal characteristics, meaning that individuals behave in fairly predictable ways across time and situations and observers come to describe the individual in those terms. The traits that executives most often associate with ethical leadership are honesty, trustworthiness, and integrity. A very broad personal characteristic, *integrity* was the trait cited most frequently by the executives. Integrity is a holistic attribute that encompasses the other traits of honesty and trustworthiness. One executive said that the average employee would say that the ethical leader is "squeaky clean." They would think "I know that if I bring an issue to him or her that I can count on their honesty and integrity on this because I've seen their standards and that one, integrity, is one that's very important to them."

Trustworthiness is also important to executives. Trust has to do with consistency, credibility, and predictability in relationships. "You can't build a long-term relationship with a customer if they don't trust you." Finally, *honesty, sincerity,* and *forthrightness* are also important. "An ethical leader . . . tends to be rather candid, certain, [and is] very careful to be factual and accurate. . . . An ethical leader does not sugarcoat things . . . he tells it like it is."

Behaviors   "Your actions speak so loudly, I can't hear what you're saying." That is the sentiment expressed by one executive. Although traits are clearly important to ethical leadership, behaviors are perhaps more so, and these include: "The way you act even when people aren't looking." "People are going to judge you not by what you say but by what you do." "People look at you and understand over time who you are personally as a result of their observations." Important behaviors include "doing the right thing," showing concern for people and treating people right, being open and communicative, and demonstrating morality in one's personal life.

First and foremost, executives said that ethical leaders *do the right thing*. One retired CEO talked about the founder of his firm, a man who "was known for his strong belief that there is only one way to do business and that's the right way."

Second, executive ethical leaders *show concern for people* through their actions. They treat people well – with dignity and respect. "I think [the ethical leader] treats everybody with dignity – meaning everybody – whether they're at the lowest level or higher levels . . . everyone gets treated with dignity and respect. I've also found that if you treat people with dignity and respect and trust, they almost invariably will respond in that fashion. It's like raising children. If you really don't trust them, they don't have much to lose by trying to get away with something. If they feel you trust them, they are going to think long and hard before they do something that will violate that trust." Several of the executives used the military example. "In the military, the troops eat before the officers. . . . Leaders take care of their troops. . . . A leader is selfless, a leader shares credit, a leader sees that contributors are rewarded."

Being open means that the executive is approachable and a good listener. Employees feel comfortable sharing bad news with the ethical leader. One executive said, "An ethical leader would need to be approachable so that . . . people would feel comfortable raising the tough issues . . . and know that they would be listened to." Another put it this way: "In general, the better leaders that I've met and know are more than willing to share their experiences of rights and wrongs, successes and failures." These leaders do not kill the messenger who brings bad news. They encourage openness and treat bad news as a problem to be addressed rather than punished.

Finally, *personal morality* is associated with ethical leadership. We asked explicitly about personal morality because our interviews with executives took place during the Monica Lewinsky scandal in the Clinton Presidency and the topic was prominent in everyone's mind. When we asked whether personal morality was linked to ethical leadership, most executives answered yes. "You can not be an ethical leader if your personal morality is in question. . . . To be a leader . . . what you do privately reflects on that organization. Secondly, to be a leader you have a greater standard, a greater responsibility than the average person would have to live up to."

Decision-making   In their decision-making role, executive ethical leaders are thought to *hold to a solid set of ethical values and principles*. They aim to be *objective and fair*. They also have a perspective that goes beyond the bottom line to include *concerns about the broader society and community*. In addition, executives said that ethical leaders rely upon a number of ethical decision rules such as the golden rule and the "*New York Times* Test." The "*New York Times* Test" says that, when making a decision, ethical leaders should ask themselves whether they would like to see the action they are contemplating on tomorrow morning's front page. This question reflects the ethical leader's sensitivity to community standards.

To summarize, the "moral person" pillar of ethical leadership represents the substance of ethical leadership and it is an important prerequisite to developing a reputation for ethical leadership because leaders become associated with their traits, behaviors, and decisions as long as others know about them. With the moral person pillar in place, you should have a reputation for being an ethical person. You can think of this as the *ethical* part of the term "ethical leadership." Having a reputation for being a moral person tells employees what *you* are likely to do – a good start, but it does not necessarily tell them what *they* should do. That requires moral managing – taking the ethics message to the rest of the organization.

Many of the executives we interviewed thought that being an ethical person who does the right thing, treats people well, and makes good decisions was necessary *and* sufficient for being an ethical leader. This is not surprising because executives know other executives personally. They have served under them, worked with them, and observed their behavior at close hand. Therefore, in their minds, an executive's ethical traits, behaviors, and decisions are automatically associated with a reputation for ethical leadership. However, some of the executives and even more of the ethics officers noted that being an ethical person was not enough. To develop a reputation for ethical leadership with employees, leaders must make ethics and values a salient aspect of their leadership agenda so that the message reaches more distant employees. To do this, they must be moral managers as well as moral persons. As one executive expressed it: "Simply put, ethical leadership means doing the right thing, and it means communicating so that everyone understands that [the right thing] is going to happen at all times . . . I think that most of the people I've been in business with adhere to the first but do less well with the second. And, in my experience, it is something that has to be reinforced constantly . . . the second part is the hardest."

Pillar two: moral manager

In order to develop a reputation for ethical *leadership*, a heavy focus on the leadership part of that term is required. The executive's challenge is to make ethics and values stand out from a business landscape that is laden with messages about beating the competition and achieving quarterly goals and profits. Moral managers recognize the importance of proactively putting ethics at the forefront of their leadership agenda. Like parents who should explicitly share their values with their children, executives need to make the ethical dimension of their leadership explicit and salient to their employees. Executives who fail to do this risk being perceived as ethically neutral because other more pervasive messages about financial success take over. One CEO put it this way: "We do some good things [turn down unethical business opportunities, develop people, champion diversity], but compare the number of times that we recognize those [ethical] achievements versus how much we recognize financial achievements – it's not close. I mean, I cringe . . . saying that . . . I'm not saying we don't work at these other things, but . . . the recognition is still very much on financial performance and . . . it's true in almost all organizations . . . And that's what's wrong. That's what's out of kilter."

Our study identified a number of ways moral managers can increase the salience of an ethics and values agenda and develop a reputation for ethical leadership. They serve as a role model for ethical conduct in a way that is visible to employees. They communicate regularly and persuasively with employees about ethical standards, principles, and values. Finally, they use the reward system consistently to hold all employees accountable to ethical standards.

Role modeling through visible action   Role modeling may seem similar to the "doing the right thing" category above. However, role modeling emphasizes *visible action* and the perceptual and reputational aspects of ethical leadership. Some ethical behaviors will go completely unnoticed while others will be noticed and will contribute to a reputation for ethical leadership. Effective moral managers recognize that they live in a fishbowl of sorts and employees are watching them for cues about what's important. "You are demonstrating by your example on and off the job, in other words, 24 hours a day, seven days a week, you're a model for what you believe in and the values." In addition, "if you're unethical . . . people pick up on that and assume because you're the leader that it's the correct thing to do . . . that not only are you condoning it, but you're actually setting the example for it."

The effective moral manager understands which words and actions are noticed and how they will be interpreted by others. In some cases, visible executive action (without any words at all) is enough to send a powerful message. One executive offered the following as an example of the power of executive action. "Some years ago, I was running one of our plants. I had just taken over and they were having some financial troubles. . . . Most of our management was flying first class. . . . I did not want . . . my first act to be to tell everybody that they are not gonna fly first class anymore, so I just quit flying first class. And it wasn't long before people noticed it and pretty soon everybody was flying coach. . . . I never put out a directive, never said a word to anybody . . . and people noticed it. They got the message. . . . People look to the leader. If the leader cuts corners, they say its okay to cut corners around here. If the leader doesn't cut corners, we must be expected not to do any of that around here."

Negative signals can also be sent by visible executive action and moral managers must be particularly sensitive to these. For example, what kind of signal does it send when your organization's ethics policy prohibits employees from accepting any kind of gift from a prospective client and then employees see a group of senior executives sitting in a client's box enjoying a professional football or basketball game? Unless the CEO is wearing a large sign that says "we paid for these tickets," the message is clear. Ethics policies do not apply equally to everyone. It becomes much easier for an employee to rationalize receiving gifts. According to one interviewee, many executives "wouldn't think twice about it because you don't intend to do anything wrong." However, employees are generally not aware of your *intent*. They see the actions and make inferences based upon them.

Communicating about ethics and values   Many executives are uncomfortable talking about ethics and wonder about those who do. In our interviews, some executives expressed concern about the leader who talks about ethics too much. "I distrust people who talk about it all the time. I think the way you do it [ethical leadership] is to demonstrate it in action . . . the more a person sermonizes about it, the more worried I am . . . sometimes you have to talk about it, but mostly you don't talk about it, you just do things." However, moral managers need to talk about ethics and values, not in a sermonizing way, but in a way that explains the values that guide important decisions and actions. If people do not hear about ethics and values from the top, it is not clear to employees that ethics and values are important. You may not feel comfortable talking about ethics if it means discussing the intricacies of Aristotle or Kant. However, talking about ethics with your employees does not mean that at all. It means talking about the values that are important to you and the organization. It is a bit like teaching children about sex. Parents can choose to avoid the uncomfortable subject, hoping that their children will learn what they need to know in school; or, they can bring an expert home who knows more than they do about the physiology of the human reproductive system. However, what parents really want their children to know about and adopt is a set of values the family believes in such as love, respect, and responsibility. To be most effective, that message must come from parents, in words and in actions. Similarly, the message about the values guiding decisions and actions in business should come from senior leaders.

The reward system   Using rewards and discipline effectively may be the most powerful way to send signals about desirable and undesirable conduct. That means rewarding those who accomplish their goals by behaving in ways that are consistent with stated values. "The most senior executive should reward the junior executive, the manager, the line people who make these [ethical] decisions . . . reinforcement is very important."

It also means clearly disciplining employees at all levels when they break the rules. A financial industry executive provided the following two examples. "If there's a situation within the corporation of sexual harassment where [the facts are] proven and management is very quick to deal with the wrongdoer . . . that's leadership. To let the rumor mill take over, to allow someone to quietly go away, to resign, is not ethical leadership. It is more difficult, but you send the message out to the organization by very visible, fair, balanced behavior. That's what you have to do."

"If someone has taken money, and they happen to be a 25-year employee who has taken two hundred dollars over the weekend and put it back on Monday, you have to . . . fire that person. [You have to make] sure everybody understands that Joe took two hundred dollars on Friday and got [fired] . . . [they must also] be assured that I did have a fact base, and that I did act responsibly and I do care about 25-year people."

Another financial industry executive talked about how he was socialized early in his career. "When I was signed . . . to train under a tough, but fair partner of the firm . . . he [said] there are things expected from you . . . but if you ever make a transaction in a client's account that you can't justify to me was in the best interest of the customer, you're out. Well that kind of gets your attention."

An airline executive said, "we talk about honesty and integrity as a core value; we communicate that. But then we back it up . . . someone can make a mistake. They can run into the side of an airplane with a baggage cart and put a big dent in it . . . and we put our arm around them and retrain them. . . . If that same person were to lie to us, they don't get a second chance . . . When it comes to honesty, there is no second chance."

The moral manager consistently rewards ethical conduct and disciplines unethical conduct at all levels in the organization, and these actions serve to uphold the standards and rules. The above reward system examples represent clear signals that will be noticed and that demonstrate clearly how employees are held accountable and how the leader backs up words with actions.

In summary, to develop a reputation for ethical leadership, one must be strong on both dimensions: moral person and moral manager. The ethical leader has a reputation for being both a substantively ethical person and a leader who makes ethics and values a prominent part of the leadership agenda.

What does ethical leadership accomplish?

The executives we talked with said that ethical leadership was good for business, particularly in the long term, and avoids legal problems. "It probably determines the amount of money you're spending in lawsuits and with corporate attorneys . . . you save a lot of money in regulatory fees and lawyer fees and settlement fees." They also said that ethical leadership contributes to employee commitment, satisfaction, comfort, and even fun. "People enjoy working for an ethical organization" and it helps the organization attract and retain the best employees. "If the leadership of the company reflects [ethical] values . . . people will want to work for that company and will want to do well." Finally, employees in an organization led by an executive ethical leader will imitate the behavior of their leader and therefore the employees will be more ethical themselves.

FIGURE 2 Executive Reputation and Ethical Leadership

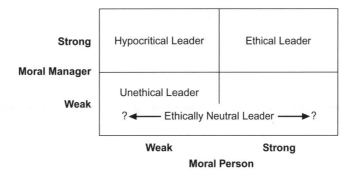

Next, we combine the two pillars of ethical leadership into a two by two matrix that can help us think about the kinds of reputation an executive can develop (see Figure 2). As noted, the combination of strong moral person and strong moral manager produces a reputation for ethical leadership. However, what happens if the leader falters in one of these areas? The matrix suggests the following possibilities: one may develop a reputation as an unethical leader, a hypocritical leader, or an ethically neutral leader.

The unethical leader A leader who is perceived to be weak on both dimensions will develop a reputation for unethical leadership. A number of executives we spoke with named Al Dunlap as a prime example of someone with a reputation for unethical executive leadership. *Business Week* recently published excerpts from John Byrne's book about Dunlap entitled *Mean Business*.[2] The article describes Dunlap as the "no-nonsense executive famous for turning around struggling companies – and sending their shares soaring in the process." However, Dunlap was also known for tirades against employees "which could reach the point of emotional abuse." "He was condescending, belligerent and disrespectful." "At his worst, he became viciously profane, even violent. Executives said he would throw papers or furniture, bang his hands on his desk, and shout so ferociously that a manager's hair would be blown back by the stream of air that rushed from Dunlap's mouth." He used the promise of huge rewards to get "employees to do things they might not otherwise do." In order to make the numbers that Dunlap demanded, creative accounting techniques were employed and "dubious techniques were used to boost sales." He also lied to Wall Street analysts. "Despite the chaos inside the company, Sunbeam's chief kept up a steady drumbeat of optimistic sales and earnings forecasts, promises of tantalizing new products, and assurances that the Dunlap magic was working." In the end, the lies could no longer cover up what was really going on. Wall Street abandoned the company and the board of directors fired Dunlap. Sunbeam was left crippled and the company continues to struggle today.

On the moral person dimension, Dunlap was found to be dishonest, he treated people horribly and made decisions based upon the financial bottom line only, disregarding the interests of multiple stakeholders in the process. On the moral manager dimension, his own behavior, communications, and the reward system were used to send a single consistent message. The bottom line was the only thing that mattered.

The hypocritical leader   A leader who is not perceived to be a strong ethical person but who attempts to put ethics and values at the forefront of the leadership agenda is likely to be perceived as a hypocritical leader who "talks the ethics talk" but does not "walk the ethics walk." In such cases, people tend to see the talk only as window dressing. They watch for actions to match the words and if there is a mismatch, the words are dismissed. As suggested above, some executives expressed concern about the leader who talks about ethics too much. In terms of the leader's reputation for ethical leadership, communicating about ethics and values, without the actions to match, is probably worse than doing nothing at all because talk without action places a spotlight on the issue that would not otherwise be there. As a result, employees become cynical and distrust everything the leader says. They also figure that they too can ignore ethical standards if they perceive that the leader does so.

The ethically neutral leader   This category generated a lot of comment. Half of the executives rejected it out of hand. The other half recognized its existence and almost all of the twenty corporate ethics officers we talked with readily acknowledged it. On the moral person dimension, it is most appropriate to say that this person is perceived to be *not clearly unethical*, but also not strongly ethical. Consider what people say about ethically neutral leaders. In terms of traits, the ethically neutral leader is seen as more self-centered than other-centered. In terms of behaviors, ethically neutral leaders are less open to input from others and they care less about people. They are less compassionate. In terms of decision making, ethically neutral executive leaders are thought to have a narrower view than do ethical leaders. They focus on financial ends more than the means that are of interest to ethical leaders. They also are more likely to base decisions upon the short-term bottom line and they are less concerned with leaving the organization or the world a better place for the future. Interestingly, much of the emphasis seems to be on what the ethically neutral leader is *not* (not open to input, not caring, not focused on means, not concerned with leaving a legacy). This is important because it means that to perceive ethical leadership, followers need evidence of positive ethical traits, behaviors, and decision processes. Lack of awareness of these positive characteristics leads to the perception that the leader is ethically neutral. Clearly, employees must be aware of these positive attributes in order for them to infer the existence of ethical leadership.

When asked to talk about ethically neutral leaders, people said virtually nothing about moral managing (role modeling, communicating, the reward system). Given that employees make sense of the messages they do get, the ethically neutral leader's focus on the short-term bottom line gets employees' attention by default. If that is what the leader is focusing on, it must be the only thing that is important. One executive said, "Ethics hasn't been on the scorecard for what's important here . . . It's kind of like quality. Quality is something that we slipped away from and someone had to say, 'It's important.' Maybe the same is true of ethics . . . we need a Deming . . . to remind us of how important it is."

Perhaps the most important outcome of ethically neutral leadership is that employees then think that ethics is not particularly important to the leader, "So they're left deciding on their own what's important in a particular situation." This means that they are acting without clear guidance about the ethics and values of the organization. The leader has not demonstrated it, has not thought through it, has not given an example of it, has not talked about it, and has not discussed it in an open forum.

CULTIVATING A REPUTATION FOR ETHICAL LEADERSHIP

Given the importance of ethical leadership, we offer the following practical steps executives can take to cultivate a reputation for ethical leadership.

Share your values: who you are as an ethical person

"Ethical leadership is not easy . . . the temptations and the rewards for unethical behavior are great. So, ethical leadership requires a discipline, a mental and personal discipline that is not easy to come by." Some senior executives arrive in their leadership positions with all of the necessary cognitive and emotional tools to be an active ethical leader. Part of the reason many of them ascend to senior leadership positions is because they have a reputation for integrity, for treating people well and for doing the right thing. They have likely had a lifetime of personal and work-related mentors and experiences that have molded and reinforced their values. By the time they reach the executive level, these values are so solid, that when challenged, the leader holds to them without question.

On the other hand, senior executive positions have a way of challenging your values in ways you may not have been challenged before. If you think that this aspect of your leadership needs work, devote energy to developing this side of yourself. Read books. Attend workshops and seminars with other senior executives who share your concerns. Work with a personal coach. Talk with your spiritual advisor about how your values can be applied in your work.

It then becomes particularly important to share this side of yourself. Find out what employees know about you and how they think of you in ethical leadership terms. You may be a strong ethical person, but your employees may have no way of knowing that. Most people do not have an accurate view of how others see them, especially when it comes to ethics. Surveys consistently find that most people think of themselves as above average and more ethical than their peers. However, the only way to honestly assess where you stand in terms of others' perceptions is to ask for candid input. A leader should "always have someone who can tell the emperor that he has no clothes." So, ask those closest to you. You can also survey your employees to find out how much they know about you as an ethical leader. Be open to what you learn and do not be surprised if employees say they simply do not know. For example, if you have not been outspoken on ethics and values issues, or you have not managed a highly public crisis that provided an opportunity for employees to learn about your values, you may be surprised to learn that employees do *not* know much about this aspect of your leadership. They may even see you as "neutral" on the ethics dimension. Talk to your communications people and your ethics officer, if you have one, about how you might successfully convey your values to employees on a regular basis. Figure out a way to open the lines of two-way communication on ethics and values issues. Ask employees to share the ethical dilemmas they face and to let you know what kind of guidance they would like from you.

Assume the role of moral manager: chief ethics officer of your organization

"Ethical leadership means that the person, the leader, who is exercising that leadership is well-grounded in a set of values and beliefs that we would view as being ethical. However, in a leadership sense . . . it means that the leader sets an example because ethical leadership doesn't just mean that leader, it means the entire organization. If there isn't an observed ethical leadership at the top, you won't find it in the organization."

As noted, moral management requires overt action on the part of the executive to serve as a role model for ethical behavior in highly visible ways, to communicate about ethics and values, and to use the reward system to hold people accountable. James Burke, former CEO of Johnson & Johnson provides an excellent example of highly visible action that gets everyone's attention. Soon after Burke assumed the presidency of Johnson & Johnson, he brought together 28 senior managers to challenge the age-old corporate credo. He asked them to talk about whether they could really live by the document that had been hanging on corporate walls for years. "If we can't live by this document then it's an act of pretension and we ought to tear it off the walls, get rid of it. If we can live with it but want to change it that's okay too, if we can agree on what the changes should be. And, we could also leave it the way it is." According to Burke, people "stayed up all night screaming at each other." When they were done, they had updated the credo. They then took it to J&J sites around the world, released a revised credo in 1979, and committed the organization to it. Less than three years later, the Tylenol poisoning occurred and lots of folks were waiting to see whether management would live up to the credo values. As every student of business ethics and corporate crisis management knows, they did, and the case is now held up as a premier example of good business ethics. Burke does not take credit for J&J's success in handling the corporate crisis. He attributes the success to the value system that had been articulated. However, clearly he was responsible for guiding the organization through the values articulation process and for making the credo prominent in the corporate culture and consciousness. As another executive put it, "all the written statements in the world won't achieve ethics in an organization unless the leader is perceived as being very serious and committed."

Following the Tylenol crisis, in 1985 Burke launched the credo survey process. All employees were surveyed regarding the company's performance with respect to the credo. Based upon the results, managers held feedback and problem-solving sessions with their employees and developed action plans to address problems. The survey process continues today on a biannual schedule under Burke's successor, Ralph Larsen, and remains a valuable way to keep attention focused on the credo and the values it represents.

To better integrate the Credo into the reward system, Larsen instigated a "standards of leadership" program which holds leaders at all levels accountable to the credo values. "At the important succession planning meetings, when upward mobility in the company is discussed, 'Credo Values' is first on the agenda. 'Business Results' is next in line. The following behaviors associated with Credo values are noted: 'Behaving with honesty and integrity. Treating others with dignity and respect. Applying Credo values. Using Credo survey results to improve business. Balancing the interests of all constituents. Managing for the long term.' "[3]

Finally, violations of Credo policy are handled swiftly and clearly. In one incident that involved infiltration of a competitor's sales meeting, President Larsen wrote the following to his management, "Our behavior should deeply embarrass everyone associated with Johnson & Johnson. Our investigation revealed that certain employees had engaged in improper activities that violated our policies. These actions were wrong and we took steps, immediately, to discipline those involved and guard against a recurrence of this kind of activity."[4]

CONCLUSION

Being an ethical leader requires developing a reputation for ethical leadership. Developing a reputation for ethical leadership depends upon how others perceive the leader on two dimensions: as a moral person and as a moral manager. Being a moral person encompasses who you are, what you do, and what you decide as well as making sure that others know about this dimension of you as a person. Being a moral manager involves being a role model for ethical conduct, communicating regularly about ethics and values, and using the reward system to hold everyone accountable to the values and standards. Ethical leadership pays dividends in employee pride, commitment, and loyalty – all particularly important in a full employment economy in which good companies strive to find and keep the best people.

Notes

1 C. Barnard, *Functions of the Executive* (Cambridge, MA: Harvard University Press, 1938 and 1968), p. 279.
2 J. A. Byrne, "Chainsaw," *Business Week*, October 18, 1999, pp. 128–149.
3 L. Foster, *Robert Wood Johnson* (State College, PA: Lillian Press, 1999), pp. 645–646.
4 Ibid., p. 646.

In Search of the Moral Manager

Archie B. Carroll

Ethics and morality are back on the front page as a result of the Ivan Boesky, General Dynamics, General Electric, E. F. Hutton, and Bank of Boston scandals. A June 1985 *New York Times* survey confirmed what earlier studies have shown repeatedly – the public gives business managers low marks for honesty.

In this era of searching for excellence, perhaps an appropriate way to phrase the theme of this article is "Searching for the Moral Manager." Pertinent questions then become:

- Are there any?
- How many are there?
- Where are they?
- Why are they so difficult to find?

IMMORAL, AMORAL, AND MORAL MANAGEMENT IN ACTION

The thesis of this discussion is that moral managers are hard to find because the business landscape is cluttered with *amoral* as well as *immoral* managers. It is easy to discuss immorality among the managerial ranks, and we'll look at some immoral managerial behavior. The real focus here, however, is on a kind of ethics – *amorality* – that has been less explored.

To lay a foundation for our discussion, let us look at examples of the three major types of more or less ethical management: immoral, amoral, and moral.

Reprinted from *Business Horizons*, March–April, 1987, by the Foundation for the School of Business at Indiana University. Used with permission.

Immoral management

Three plant managers at a big GM Chevrolet truck plant in Flint, Michigan, installed a secret control box in a supervisor's office so they could increase production by over-riding the control panel that governed the speed of the assembly line. Their action was a serious violation of the company's contract with the UAW. One plant manager explained that the bosses were putting on the pressure because of constantly missed production targets. The bosses' reaction? "I don't care *how* you do it – just do it."

Thus, with the aid of the hidden controls, the managers soon began meeting their goals and winning praise from their superiors. Once the speeding up was exposed, the UAW won $1 million in back pay.[1]

Amoral management

To advertise its Mr. PiB soft drink, Coca-Cola U.S.A. planned a promotional scheme designed to identify the "PiB girl." The contest focused on a nationwide search for a girl who most closely resembled a composite picture of five white American actresses. The composite girl would have the eyes of Susan Anton (NBC's "Golden Girl"), the mouth of Debby Boone (the singer), the hair of Pam Dawber ("Mork and Mindy"), the face shape of Melissa Sue Anderson ("Little House on the Prairie"), and the nose of Kristy McNichol (Buddy on the TV series "Family").

The contest became controversial when the principal of a black school in Chicago saw a contest entry blank. His response was not surprising: "It is immediately apparent to any sensitive person that non-Anglo contestants need not apply."

The company decided on the promotional scheme with no evil intention. The deci-sion makers simply did not see the moral issue of fairness to all races that was implicit in the choice of actresses. Fortunately, at least one major group of bottlers, the Atlanta Coke Bottlers, were quick to note that the national contest contained racial bias. By decid-ing not to participate, the Atlanta Bottlers engaged in moral management.[2]

Moral management

Polaroid's program in environmental auditing is one example of putting to work the principles of moral management. According to the corporation's director of health, safety, and environmental affairs, "For Polaroid, the *spirit* of environmental law, not just the letter, must be reflected in all of its environmental policies."[3]

Polaroid systematically searches out environmental weaknesses and strengths through company-wide audits that yield a "report card." Since 1981 the audits have helped the company to identify problems early and to prepare timely solutions. In conjunction with this, a public-issues policy committee serves as a corporate lookout, scouting dangers and opportunities that lie ahead.

FIGURE 1   Three Types of Management Ethics

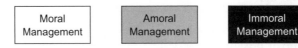

BLACK AND WHITE AND GRAY ALL OVER

In the past ten years, newspapers, television, and magazines have chronicled case after case of immoral or unethical business activity. Though some of these cases have reached scandal proportions, many have been examples of routine, garden-variety immorality. As often as not, these accounts have referred to the actions, decisions, or behavior of managers or employees as "questionable practices," a euphemism for unethical or immoral activity.

Scant attention has been given to the subtle distinctions that may be made between activities that are *immoral* and those that are *amoral*. Similarly, little attention has been given to contrasting these two forms of behavior with ethical or *moral* management. In its preoccupation with malfeasant behavior, the media may have ignored the gamut of moral management styles.

What can happen when these styles come to life through description and example? Managers will be better able to assess their own ethical styles and those of other organizational members – their supervisors, subordinates, and peers. The presumption is, of course, that managers desire a heightened ethical awareness, particularly in light of the increasingly important role that ethics plays in business, the professions, and other organizations.[4]

Another central objective is to identify more accurately the amoral management style, a style often overlooked in the rush to classify things as good or bad, moral or immoral. Finally, looking at different styles enables us to define the elements of moral judgment that must be developed if the transition to moral management is to succeed.

Figure 1 positions these three styles along a continuum, but in reality, because of the unusual nature of the amoral approach, they do not reside on a continuum. Amoral management is, in a sense, neutral and therefore is placed in between. It is no accident that moral management has a white background, immoral management a black background, and amoral management a gray background. These colors capture the tendency, in discussions of ethics, to speak of black (clearly wrong), white (clearly right), and gray (uncertain, but somewhere in between).

Let us first consider the two extremes of management style – immoral and moral management – before looking at amoral management.

IMMORAL MANAGEMENT

If "immoral" and "unethical" are synonymous, then immoral management is not only devoid of ethical principles or precepts but also positively and actively opposed to what is ethical. Management decisions, behavior, or actions do not accord with ethical principles.

This view holds that management's motives are selfish and that it cares only (or principally) about the company's gains. If management is actively opposed to what is regarded as ethical, the clear implication is that management knows right from wrong and chooses to do wrong. Thus, it is motivated by greed. Its goals are profitability and organizational success at almost any price. Immoral management does not care about others' claims to be treated fairly or justly.

What about management's orientation toward the law, considering that law is often regarded as an embodiment of minimal ethics? Immoral management regards legal standards as barriers to be overcome in accomplishing what it wants. Immoral managers will do what they can to circumvent the law.

The operating strategy of immoral management is focused on exploiting opportunities for corporate or personal gain. Corners are cut anywhere and everywhere it appears useful. Thus, the key operating question guiding management is: "Can we make money with this action, decision, or behavior?" Implicit in this question is that nothing else matters – or matters very much.

Examples of immoral management abound. The Frigitemp Corporation, manufacturers of refrigerated mortuary boxes, illustrates immoral management at the highest levels of the corporate hierarchy. In litigation, criminal trials, and federal investigations, corporate officials, including the president and chairman, admit to making millions of dollars of payoffs to get business. They took kickbacks from suppliers, provided prostitutes to customers, exaggerated earnings in reports to shareholders, and embezzled corporate funds. One corporate official said that greed was their undoing. They were so busy stealing that they got caught. Records indicate that Frigitemp's executives permitted a corporate culture of chicanery to flourish. The company eventually went bankrupt because of management's misconduct.[5]

Brown & Root, Inc., which had been building a nuclear power plant for Texas Utilities, fired a quality control inspector in 1982. It fired two other inspectors the next year. Evidence gathered by the government suggests that the employees may have been doing their jobs too well. The inspectors claim that they were discharged after resisting orders from management to overlook flaws in the plant. The Nuclear Regulatory Commission (NRC) is now conducting inquiries into the cases of dozens of inspectors who maintain that managers pressured them to ignore defects because repairs might delay construction, causing added costs and delays.[6]

The Securities and Exchange Commission (SEC) has accused Southland Corporation, a convenience-store operator and independent gasoline retailer, of paying kickbacks to big buyers of its dairy products. According to the accusation, the company disregarded minimum pricing laws in about eight states and dispensed almost $2 million in what it called "dairy discounts." A number of the major customers received monthly kickback checks in the form of anonymous cashier's checks from a bank in Utah.[7]

These are clear cases of immoral management. Executive decisions or orders are self-centered, actively opposed to what is right, focused on organizational success at whatever the cost, and cutting corners where it is useful. Such concerns as safety or fairness are disregarded.

MORAL MANAGEMENT

At the opposite extreme from immoral management is moral management. Moral management strives to be ethical in its focus on ethical norms, professional standards of conduct, motives, goals, orientation toward the law, and general operating strategy.

In contrast with the selfish motives discussed earlier, moral management aspires to succeed, but only within the confines of sound ethical precepts – that is, standards predicated upon such ideals as fairness, justice, and due process. Management's motives, therefore, might be termed fair, balanced, or unselfish. Organizational goals continue to stress profitability, but only within the confines of obeying the law and being sensitive to ethical standards. Management, therefore, pursues its objectives while simultaneously requiring and desiring profitability, legality, and morality. Moral management would not pursue profits at the expense of the law and sound ethics. Indeed, the focus here is not on the letter of the law but on the spirit as well. The law is viewed as a minimal standard of ethical behavior, and moral management strives to operate well above what the law mandates.

Moral management lives by sound ethical standards, seeking out only those economic opportunities that can be pursued within the confines of ethical behavior. When ethical dilemmas arise, the company assumes a leadership position. The central question guiding management actions, decisions, and behavior is: "Is this action, decision, or behavior fair to us and all parties involved?"

Companies in the toy industry illustrate moral management when they thoroughly test toys before releasing them for commercial production and sales. The toy industry has adopted strict standards for flammability. Other standards have been set for toxicity, safety, and durability. The safety testing process at Hasbro-Bradley, Inc., for example, eliminated nearly 2,000 toy concepts in one year before the company chose the 100 toys it planned to produce. Toys also undergo psychological testing as companies attempt to screen out toys that might have a lasting negative emotional impact on children.[8]

Organizations that engage in moral management have not done so all along. These companies – and that includes the toy industry – arrived at this posture after years or decades of rising consumer expectations, increased government regulations, lawsuits, and pressures from social and consumer activists. In many instances moral management is a pragmatic posture that evolved over time. If we hold management to a 100% historical moral purity test, then no management will fill the bill. But moral managements now see the enlightened self-interest of responding in an ethical way.

An excellent example of moral management in which the organization took the initiative in displaying ethical leadership is provided by the actions of McCulloch Corporation, a manufacturer of chain saws. Chain saws are notoriously dangerous. The Consumer Product Safety Commission estimated that in 1981 there were 123,000 medically attended injuries involving chain saws, up from 71,000 in 1976. In spite of these statistics, the Chain Saw Manufacturers Association, in what appears to be a knee-jerk, self-interested reaction against government regulations, has fought mandatory safety standards. The association claims that the accident statistics are inflated and do not offer any justification for mandatory regulations. Manufacturers support voluntary standards. However, some manufacturers say that when chain brakes, which are a major safety device, are offered as an option, they do not sell. Apparently, consumers do not have adequate knowledge of the risks inherent in using chain saws.

McCulloch became dissatisfied with the Chain Saw Manufacturers Association's refusal to support higher standards of safety and withdrew from the association in 1978. The chain brakes, which have been standard on McCulloch saws since 1975, are also mandatory for most saws produced in Finland, Britain, and Australia. The Swedish Company, Husqvarna Inc., now installs chain brakes on saws it sells in the United States. Statistics from the Quebec Logging Association and from Sweden demonstrate that kickback-related accidents fell by about 80% after the mandatory installation of safety standards, including chain brakes.[9]

McCulloch is an example of moral management. It attempted to persuade its association to adopt the higher standard that, based upon statistical evidence and sound, sensitive judgment, would greatly reduce injuries. When its attempts at persuasion failed, McCulloch took a courageous action and withdrew from the association.

AMORAL MANAGEMENT

In some respects amoral management appears to be a hybrid between the other two. However, it is not just a middle position on a continuum. Although conceptually positioned between the other two, it is different in kind. Actually there are two types of amoral management: intentional and unintentional.

Because they believe business activity resides outside the sphere to which moral judgments apply, intentional amoral managers do not factor ethical considerations into their decision making, actions, or behavior. These managers are neither moral nor immoral; they simply think that different rules of the game apply in business than in other realms of life.

Unintentional amoral managers do not think about business activity in ethical terms either, but for a different reason. These managers are simply morally casual, careless, or inattentive to the fact that their decisions and actions may have negative or deleterious effects on others. These managers lack ethical perception and moral awareness; that is, they blithely go through their organizational lives not thinking that what they are doing has an ethical dimension to it. They may be well intentioned, but they are either too insensitive or egocentric to consider the impacts of their behavior on others.

Amoral management pursues profitability as its goal, but it does not cognitively attend to moral issues that may be intertwined with that pursuit. If there is an ethical guide to amoral management, it is the marketplace as constrained by law – the letter of the law, not the spirit. The amoral manager sees the law as the boundary that marks off the playing field where business pursuits take place.

Amoral management does not bridle managers with excessive ethical structure. It permits free reign within the unspoken but understood tenets of the free enterprise system. Personal ethics may periodically or unintentionally enter into managerial decisions, but they do not preoccupy management. Furthermore, the impact of decisions on others is an afterthought – if it ever gets considered at all. To the extent that they are present, the managers' ethical mental gears are in neutral. The key management question guiding decision making is: "Can we make money with this action, decision, or behavior?" This question does not imply an active or implicit intent to be either moral or immoral.

Some examples

There are perhaps more examples of amoral management than of any other kind.

- When police departments stipulated that candidates must be at least 5 ft 10 in and weigh 180 pounds to qualify, the decision was amoral. No consideration was given that women – and men of some ethnic groups – do not, on average, attain that height and weight.
- When companies decided to use scantily clad young women to advertise autos, men's cologne, and other such products, they did not think of the degrading and demeaning characterization that eventually would come from their ethically neutral decision.
- When firms determined to do business in South Africa, their decision was neither moral or immoral. But a major unanticipated consequence has been the appearance that capitalism – and the United States – approve of apartheid.
- Nestlé's decision to market infant formula in underdeveloped, Third World countries was an amoral decision. Nestlé simply did not consider the detrimental effects of such a seemingly innocent business decision on mothers and babies in areas with impure water, poverty, and illiteracy.
- The liquor, beer, and cigarette industries have not been immoral, according to generally accepted standards, in making, advertising, and distributing their products. But they did not think about – at least not to an extent that altered their decisions – some serious moral issues: alcoholism, drunk-driving deaths, lung cancer, deteriorating health, and offensive secondary smoke.
- When Pepsico promoted corn chips on television with its "Frito-Bandito" theme, it greatly offended a group of Mexican-Americans, who put such pressure on the company that the ad campaign was dropped. Surely Pepsico did not enter into this campaign with the idea of perpetuating a stereotype. It just didn't think through the ethical consequences of its promotional campaign.

A DISTRIBUTION CURVE FOR MANAGEMENT MORALITY?

Figure 2 summarizes the major characteristics of amoral, immoral, and moral managements. Data are not available to indicate precisely what proportions of managers each represents in the total management population, but we can hypothesize a normal distribution such as that depicted in Figure 3. Based on reports of management behavior, studies of ethics, and experience in teaching ethics in executive development programs, we believe that this distribution, though the percentages are not specified, captures fairly accurately the actual proportions. However, although our hypothesis has received support in discussions with managers, for now this distribution remains untested.

To the extent that these approximate numbers capture even generally the proportion of manager types, this hypothesis is disturbing, for it suggests that the vast majority of

FIGURE 2   Approaches to Management Ethics

		Immoral Management	*Amoral Management*	*Moral Management*
Organizational Characteristics	Ethical Norms	Management decisions, actions, and behavior imply a positive and active opposition to what is moral (ethical). Decisions are discordant with accepted ethical principles. An active negation of what is moral is implied.	Management is neither moral nor immoral, but decisions lie outside the sphere to which moral judgments apply. Management activity is outside or beyond the moral order of a particular code. May imply lack of ethical perception and moral awareness.	Management activity conforms to a standard of ethical, or right, behavior. Conforms to accepted professional standards of conduct. Ethical leadership is commonplace on the part of management.
	Motives	Selfish. Management cares only about what it or the company gains.	Well-intentioned but selfish in the sense that impact on others is not considered.	Good. Management wants to succeed but only within the confines of sound ethical precepts (fairness, justice, due process).
	Goals	Profitability and organizational success at any price.	Profitability. Other goals are not considered.	Profitability within the confines of legal obedience and ethical standards.
	Orientation Toward Law	Legal standards are barriers that management must overcome to accomplish what it wants.	Law is the ethical guide, preferably the letter of the law. The central question is what we can do legally.	Obedience toward letter and spirit of the law. Law is a minimal ethical behavior. Prefer to operate well above what law mandates.
	Strategy	Exploit opportunities for corporate gain. Cut corners when it appears useful.	Give managers free rein. Personal ethics may apply but only if managers choose. Respond to legal mandates if caught and required to do so.	Live by sound ethical standards. Assume leadership position when ethical dilemmas arise. Enlightened self-interest.

managers are amoral. It suggests that, in general, ethical considerations do not get factored into management decisions, even though there is no active intent to be unethical.

It is disturbing to think that the amoral management style predominates in organizations today. Equally disturbing is an alternative hypothesis – that, for the average manager, these three styles all operate at various times under various circumstances. That is, the average manager is amoral most of the time but, because of a variety of impinging factors, slips into a moral or immoral style on occasion. Like the first hypothesis, this view cannot be empirically supported at this time, but it resembles the situational ethics argument that has been in vogue for some years.

A serious social problem in organizations today is this large middle group of well-intentioned managers who, for one reason or other, subscribe to or live out the amoral

FIGURE 3   Immoral, Amoral, and Moral Managers: A Hypothesized Population Distribution

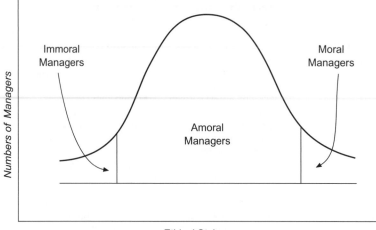

ethic. These managers are driven primarily by the profitability or bottom-line ethos that makes economic success almost the sole barometer of organizational and personal achievement. They are basically good people, but they see the competitive business world as ethically neutral. Until this group of managers moves toward the moral ethic, we will continue to see American business and organizations criticized as severely as they have been in the past two decades.

DEVELOPING MORAL JUDGMENT

At this point one might rightly ask, "What can or should be done about the prevalence of amoral management in business?" The question is easier to ask than to answer, but the direction must be toward developing moral judgment among managers.

First, managers must undergo a paradigm shift from looking at the organization as a purely economic or legal entity to one in which a multitude of responsibilities reside. Principal among these other responsibilities or perspectives is an ethical one. It is becoming increasingly obvious that society expects business to be responsive to claimants other than just the shareholders. And many of these claimant groups, whether they be employees, consumers, or community members, expect to be dealt with fairly and justly.

Second, managers must come to appreciate the key elements in making moral judgments. Powers and Vogel argue that there are six major elements or capacities that are essential in making moral judgments:[10]

1   Moral imagination;
2   Moral identification and ordering;
3   Moral evaluation;

4   Tolerance of moral disagreement and ambiguity;
5   Integration of managerial and moral competence; and
6   A sense of moral obligation.

Let us examine each of these in turn.

Moral imagination

Moral imagination refers to the ability to perceive that a web of competing economic relationships is, at the same time, a web of moral or ethical relationships. Developing moral imagination means becoming sensitive to ethical issues in business decision making, but it also means searching out places where people are likely to be hurt by decision making or behavior of managers. This moral imagination is a necessary first step, but because of prevailing methods of evaluating managers on bottom-line results, it is extremely challenging. It is essential, however, before anything else can happen.

Moral identification and ordering

Moral identification and ordering means being able to discern the relevance or non-relevance of moral factors that are introduced into a decision-making situation. Are the moral issues real or just rhetorical? The ability to see moral issues as issues that can be dealt with is at stake here. In addition to their identification, moral issues in a decision must be ranked or ordered just as economic or technological issues are. Not only must this skill be developed through experience, but it also must be finely honed through repetition. Only through repetition can it be developed.

Several decision environments in which moral identification and ordering have become important in recent years include the future of affirmative action programs, the status of employees' "right to know" what toxic chemicals they are being exposed to, the question of how to deal with whistle-blowers, and the issue of business or plant closings.[11] In each of these instances, the ability to identify and order moral issues is a key to their effective handling. To decide wrongly opens the firm up to extensive public criticism and the threat of endless lawsuits.

Moral evaluation

Once issues have been identified and ordered, the question of making evaluations or judgments enters in. This practical phase entails minimal skills – such as coherence and consistency – that have proven effective in other contexts. What managers need to develop here are:

- The importance of clear principles;
- Processes for weighting ethical factors; and

- The ability to identify what are likely to be the moral as well as economic outcomes of a decision.

The real challenge in moral evaluation is in integrating concerns for others into organizational goals and purposes. In the final analysis, the manager will not know what is the "right" answer or solution but only that moral sensitivity has been introduced into the process. There are multiple right and wrong decisions, but the important point is that amorality has not prevailed or driven the decision process.

Tolerating moral disagreement and ambiguity

One of the principal objections managers often have to discussions of ethics is the amount of disagreement generated by the volume of ambiguity that must be tolerated in thinking ethically. This disagreement and ambiguity must be accepted, however, for there is no other way.

To be sure, managers need closure and they need precision in their decisions. But the situation is never clear in moral discussions any more than it is in many traditional but more familiar decision contexts of managers – such as introducing a new product based upon limited test marketing, choosing a new executive for a key role, deciding which of a number of excellent computer systems to install, or making a strategic decision based upon instincts. All of these are precarious decisions, but managers have become accustomed to making them in spite of the disagreement and ambiguity that prevail among those involved in the decision or even within the individual.

In a real sense the toleration of moral disagreement and ambiguity is just an extension of a managerial talent or facility that is present in practically all decision situations managers face. But managers are more unfamiliar with this area because they have not had practice in it.

Integrating managerial and moral competence

Integrating managerial and moral competence underlies all we have been discussing. Few kinds of decision making are exempt from moral or social factors. The issue is whether the manager has chosen to deal with the factors.

Moral issues in management are not isolated and distinct from traditional business decision making but right smack in the middle of it. The scandals major corporations face today did not grow up apart from the companies' economic activities but were embedded in a series of decisions that were made at various times and are only the culmination of these earlier decisions. Therefore, *moral* competence is an integral part of *managerial* competence.

Managers are learning – some the hard way – that there is a significant corporate – and, in many instances, a personal – price to pay for their amorality. The amoral manager sees ethical decisions as isolated and independent of managerial decisions and competence, but the moral manager sees every evolving decision as one in which an ethical perspective must be integrated. This view to the future is an essential executive skill.

A sense of moral obligation

The foundation for all the capacities we have discussed is a sense of moral obligation and integrity. This sense is the key to the process, but is the most difficult to acquire. This sense requires the intuitive or learned understanding that moral fibers – a concern for fairness, justice, and due process to people, groups, and communities – are woven into the fabric of managerial decision making and hold the systems together. These qualities are perfectly consistent with – indeed, are essential requisites to – the free enterprise system as we know it today.

One can go all the way back to Adam Smith and the foundation of our system and find no reference to immoral or unethical practices as elements that are needed for the system to work. Our modern-day Adam Smith, Milton Friedman, has even alluded to the importance of ethics when he stated that the purpose of business is "to make as much money as possible while conforming to the basic rules of society, both those embodied in the law and *those embodied in ethical custom.*"[12]

The moral manager, then, has a sense of moral obligation and integrity that is the glue that holds together the decision-making process in which human welfare is inevitably at stake.

Figure 4 summarizes the elements of moral judgment as seen in amoral and moral managers.

MAKING MORAL MANAGEMENT ACTIONABLE

These characterizations of moral, immoral, and amoral management should provide a useful basis for managerial self-analysis. For self-analysis and introspection will be the way that managers move from the immoral or amoral ethic to the moral ethic. Numerous people have suggested management training for business ethics, a prescription with great potential. However, until senior management fully embraces the concepts of moral management, the transformation in organizational culture that is essential for moral management to blossom, thrive, and flourish will not take place.

Ultimately, senior management has the leadership responsibility to show the way to an ethical organizational environment by leading the transition from amoral to moral management, whether that is done by:

- Business ethics training and workshops;
- Codes of conduct;
- Corporate ombudsmen;
- Tighter financial controls;
- More ethically sensitive decision processes; or
- Leadership by example.

Underlying all these efforts, however, needs to be the fundamental recognition that amoral management exists and that it can be certainly, if not easily, remedied. We have outlined the symptoms and characteristics of amoral management, a morally vacuous

FIGURE 4   Moral Judgment in Amoral and Moral Managers

Amoral Managers	*Moral Managers*
Moral Imagination	
See a web of competing economic claims as just that and nothing more.	Perceive that a web of competing economic claims is, simultaneously, a web of moral relationships.
Are insensitive to and unaware of the hidden dimensions of where people are likely to get hurt.	Are sensitive to and hunt out the hidden dimensions where people are likely to get hurt.
Moral Identification and Ordering	
See moral claims as squishy, not definite enough to order into hierarchies with other claims.	See which moral claims are relevant or irrelevant; order moral factors just as economic factors are ordered.
Moral Evaluation	
Are erratic in their application of ethics, if it gets applied at all.	Are coherent and consistent in their normative reasoning.
Tolerance of Moral Disagreement and Ambiguity	
Cite ethical disagreement and ambiguity as reason for forgetting ethics altogether.	Tolerate ethical disagreement and ambiguity while honestly acknowledging that decisions are not precise but must be made nevertheless.
Integration of Managerial and Moral Competence	
See ethical decisions as isolated and independent of managerial decisions and managerial competence.	See every evolving decision as one in which a moral perspective must be integrated with a managerial one.
A Sense of Moral Obligation	
Have no sense of moral obligation and integrity that extends beyond normal managerial responsibility.	Have a sense of moral obligation and integrity that directs and holds together the decision-making process in which human welfare is at stake.

condition that can be disguised as an innocent, practical, bottom-line philosophy – something to take pride in.

Amoral management is – and will continue to be – the bane of American management until it is recognized for what it is and managers take steps to overcome it. American managers are not all "bad guys," as so frequently portrayed, but the idea that managerial decision making can be ethically neutral is bankrupt. It is no longer tenable in the society of the 1980s and beyond.

Notes

1   George Getschow, "Some Middle Managers Cut Corners to Achieve High Corporate Goals," *Wall Street Journal*, November 8, 1979: 1, 34.

2   Evan Kossoff, "Coke Bottlers Here Noticed Bias, Rejected PiB Contest," *Atlanta Journal and Constitution*, April 20, 1980: B-1.

3   "Environmental Auditing: Putting Principles to Work," *Ethics Resource Center Report*, Spring 1985: 5.

4 In a study of performance factors considered important by various levels of manage-ment, integrity is a critical factor for senior executives, while entry-level managers assign it a lower priority. The author concludes, "It may be that as managers rise to the top, they become increasingly concerned with the way they are looked up to by their peers and subordinates in the area of moral values" (Richard A. Johnson, James P. Neelankavil, and Arvind Jadhav, "Developing the Executive Resource," *Business Horizons*, 29 (1986): 32.

5 Edward T. Pound and Bruce Ingersoll, "How Frigitemp Sank After It Was Looted by Top Management," *Wall Street Journal*, September 20, 1984, p. 1.

6 Ron Winslow, "Regulators Investigate Harassing of Inspectors at New Nuclear Plants," *Wall Street Journal*, November 7, 1984, p. 1.

7 Bruce Ingersoll and Edward T. Pound, "SEC Says Southland Was Involved in Questionable Payoffs in the 1970s," *Wall Street Journal*, November 9, 1984, p. 1.

8 Pamela Hollie, "Seeking Safe Toys That Sell," *New York Times*, February 10, 1985, p. 4F.

9 Ray Vicker, "Rise in Chain-Saw Injuries Spurs Demand for Safety Standards, but Industry Resists," *Wall Street Journal*, August 23, 1982, p. 17.

10 Charles W. Powers and David Vogel, *Ethics in the Education of Business Managers* (Hastings-on-Hudson, NY: The Hastings Center, 1980): 40–45.

11 As outlined . . . by Kenneth A. Kovach and Peter E. Millspaugh, "Plant Closings: Is the American Industrial System Failing?," *Business Horizons* (March–April 1987).

12 Milton Friedman, "The Social Responsibility of Business Is to Increase Its Profits," *New York Times Magazine*, September 12, 1970: 32 (emphasis added).

NES China: Business Ethics (A)

Joerg Dietz and Xin Zhang

By April 1998, it had been almost a year since the Germany-headquartered multinational company NES AG had first submitted its application to the Chinese government for establishing a holding company in Beijing to co-ordinate its investments in China. The application documentation had already been revised three times, but the approval by the government was still outstanding. Lin Chen, government affairs co-ordinator at NES AG Beijing Representative Office, came under pressure from the German headquarters and had to find a way to obtain approval within a month.

During the past year, Chen had almost exclusively worked on the holding company application. In order to facilitate the approval process, she had suggested giving gifts to government officials. But her European colleagues, Steinmann and Dr Perrin, disagreed because they thought such conduct would be bribery and would violate business ethics. Confronted with the cross-cultural ethical conflict, Chen had to consider possible strategies that would satisfy everybody.

COMPANY BACKGROUND

NES and NES AG

NES was founded in Germany in 1881. Over the following 100 years, by pursuing diversification strategies, NES had grown from a pure tube manufacturer into one of the largest industrial groups in Germany, with sales of US$14 billion in 1997. NES built plants and heavy machinery, made automotive systems and components, manufactured hydraulic, pneumatic and electrical drives and controls, offered telecommunications services and produced steel tubes and pipes.

NES was managed by a holding company – NES AG – that implemented value-oriented portfolio management and directed its financial resources to the areas with the greatest profit potentials. In 1997, NES AG owned NES's 11 companies in four business segments: engineering, automotive, telecommunications and tubes. These companies generally operated independently and largely at their own discretion, as NES AG was interested in their profitability and not their day-to-day operations.

NES had always been committed to move along the road of globalization and internationalization. Headquartered in Germany, NES had businesses in more than 100 countries with over 120,000 employees. In the process of globalization and internationalization, NES established a business principle that demonstrated its responsibilities not only to shareholders, employees and customers, but also to society and to the countries where it operated. As an essential part of the company's corporate culture, this principle pervaded the decentralized subsidiaries worldwide and guided the decision-making and conduct of both the company and its employees.

NES China operations

NES's business in China dated back to 1889, when it built the flood barrages for the Canton River. In 1908, NES supplied seamless steel tubes for the construction of a waterworks in Beijing. Through the century, NES continued to broaden its presence. From the mid-1950s to 1997, NES supplied China with an enormous 5.2 million metric tons of steel tube and 1.6 million tons of rolled steel.

Since China opened up to foreign trade and investment in the late 1970s, NES's presence had grown dramatically. From 1977 to 1997, NES had completed more than 40 technology transfer and infrastructure projects. It had also set up 20 representative offices, six equity joint ventures and three wholly owned enterprises.

In developing business links with China, NES adhered to its business principle. Most NES enterprises in China had highlighted this principle in their codes of conduct in employment handbooks (see Exhibit 1). These codes required employees to pursue the highest standards of business and personal ethics in dealing with government officials and business customers, and to avoid any activities that would lead to the involvement of the company in unlawful practices. Instead of tendering immediate favors or

EXHIBIT 1   Excerpt from the Employment Handbook of One of the NES's Enterprises in China

Article 3 Employment and Duties

3.1   The Company employs the Employee and the Employee accepts such employment in accordance with the terms and conditions of the Employment Contract and this Employment Handbook.

3.6   The Company expects each Employee to observe the highest standards of business and personal ethics, and to be honest and sincere in his/her dealings with government officials, the public, firms, or other corporations, entities, or organizations with whom the Company transacts, or is likely to transact.

3.7   The Company does business without favoritism. Purchases of materials or services will be competitively priced whenever possible. An Employee's personal interest or relationship is not to influence any transaction with a business organization that furnishes property, rights or services to the Company.

3.8   Employees are not to solicit, accept, or agree to accept, at any time of the year, any gift of value which directly or indirectly benefits them from a supplier or prospective supplier or his employees or agents, or any person with whom the Company does business in any aspect.

3.9   The Company observes and complies with all laws, rules, and regulations of the People's Republic of China which affect the Company and its Employees. Employees are required to avoid any activities which involve or would lead to the involvement of the Company in any unlawful practices and to disclose to the proper Company authorities any conduct that comes to their attention which violates these rules and principles. Accordingly, each Employee should understand the legal standards and restrictions that apply to his/her duties.

3.10 All Employees are the Company's representatives. This is true whether the Employee is on duty or off duty. All Employees are encouraged to observe the highest standards of professional and personal conduct at all times.

Article 13 Discipline

13.1 The Company insists on utmost discipline. The Employee's misconduct or unsatisfactory performance will be brought to the attention of the responsible Head of Department or Member of the Management when it occurs and will be documented in the Employee's file.

13.2 Some offences are grounds for immediate dismissal and disciplinary procedures will apply to other offences.

13.3 Offences which are grounds for immediate dismissal include:
(i)   Breach of the Company's rules of conduct.
(j)   Neglect of duties, favoritisms or other irregularities.

Source: Company files.

rewards to individual Chinese officials and customers, NES relied on advanced technology, management know-how and top quality products and service as a source of its competitive advantage. NES emphasized long-term mutual benefits and corporate social responsibility. Since 1979, NES had trained more than 2,000 Chinese engineers, master craftsmen, technicians and skilled workers in Germany. It had also offered extensive training programs in China. Moreover, NES was the first German company to adopt the suggestion of the German federal government to initiate a scholarship program for young Chinese academics to study in Germany. As a result, NES had built a strong reputation in China for being a fair business partner and a good guest company.

NES Beijing representative office

In 1977, NES was the first German company to open its representative office in Beijing. Along with NES's business growth, the Beijing Representative Office continued to expand. In 1997, it had 10 German expatriates and more than 40 local staff in nine business units. One unit represented NES AG. This unit was responsible for administrative co-ordination and office expense allocation. The other eight units worked for the German head offices of their respective NES companies in the engineering, automotive and tube segments.

Chinese legal restrictions severely limited the activities of the Beijing Representative Office. It was allowed only to engage in administrative activities, such as conducting marketing research for the German head offices, passing on price and technical information to Chinese customers, and arranging for meetings and trade visits. Moreover, it could not directly enter into employment contracts with its Chinese employees. Instead, it had to go through a local labor service agency designated by the Chinese government and consult with the agency on almost all personnel issues including recruitment, compensation and dismissal. As a result, the German managers of the Beijing Representative Office found it difficult to effectively manage their Chinese employees. In the absence of direct employment contracts, the managers had to rely on an internal reporting and control system.

CURRENT SITUATION

Establishing a China holding company

In early 1997, NES AG had decided to establish a holding company in Beijing as soon as possible after carefully weighing the advantages and disadvantages of this decision. Establishing a China holding company was advantageous because, unlike a representative office, a holding company had its own business licence and could therefore engage in direct business activities. In addition to holding shares, a holding company could co-ordinate many important functions for its enterprises, such as marketing, managing government relations, and providing financial support. As a "country headquarters," a holding company could also unite the NES profile in China and strengthen the good name of NES as a reliable business partner in the world's most populous country. Moreover, it could hire staff directly and thus retain full control over its own workforce. In light of these advantages, NES AG expected substantial time and cost efficiencies from the China holding company.

Several disadvantages, however, potentially outweighed the advantages of a China holding company. First, Chinese legal regulations still constrained some business activities. For example, a Chinese holding company could not balance foreign exchange accounts freely and consolidate the taxation of NES's Chinese enterprises, although this might be permitted in the future. Second, the setup efforts and costs were high. To establish a holding company, NES had to submit a project proposal, a feasibility study, articles of association and other application documents to the local (the Local Department) and then to the central trade and economic co-operation departments (the Central Department) for examination and approval. Third, there was only a limited window of opportunity for NES AG. Once the China holding company had received its business licence, within two years, NES AG would have to contribute a minimum of US$30 million fresh capital to it. The Chinese regulations prescribed that this capital could be invested only in new projects, but otherwise would have to remain unused in a bank account. NES currently was in a position to invest the capital in its new projects, but the company was not certain how much longer it would be in this position.

Working team

NES AG authorized the following three individuals in the Beijing Representative Office to take up the China holding company application issue:

> Kai Mueller, 58 years old, had worked for NES in its China operations since the 1970s and had experience in several big co-operative projects in the steel and metallurgical industries. He would be the president of the holding company.
>
> Jochen Steinmann, 30 years old, was assigned to Beijing from Germany in 1996. He would be the financial controller of the holding company.
>
> Dr Jean Perrin was a 37-year-old lawyer from France who had an in-depth understanding of Chinese business laws. He would work as the legal counsel. His previous working experience included a professorship at the Beijing International Business and Economics University in the 1980s.

The trio had advocated the idea of a China holding company to NES AG for quite some time and were most happy about NES AG's decision, because the future holding company would give them considerably more responsibilities and authority than did the Beijing Representative Office.

Considering the complexity and difficulty in coping with the Chinese bureaucratic hurdles, Mueller decided in March 1997 to hire Lin Chen as a government affairs co-ordinator for the working team. Chen, a native Chinese, was a 28-year-old politics and public administration graduate who had worked four years for a Chinese state-owned company and was familiar with the Chinese way of doing business. Mueller expected that Chen would play an instrumental role in obtaining the holding company approval from the Chinese government. He also promised that Chen would be responsible for the public affairs function at the holding company once it was set up.

Chen's view of doing business in China

Chen officially joined the Beijing Representative Office in June 1997. She commented on doing business in China:

> China's economy is far from rules-based; basically, it is still an economy based on relationships. In the absence of an explicit and transparent legal framework, directives and policies

are open to interpretation by government officials who occupy positions of authority and power. In such circumstances, businesspeople cultivate personal *guanxi* (interpersonal connections based implicitly on mutual interest and benefit) with officials to substitute for an established code of law that businesspeople in the Western society take for granted.

In building and nurturing *guanxi* with officials, gifts and personal favors have a special place, not only because they are associated with respect and friendship, but also because in today's China, people place so much emphasis on utilitarian gains. In return for accepting gifts, officials provide businesspeople with access to information about policy thinking and the potentially advantageous interpretation of the policy, and facilitate administrative procedures. Co-operation leads to mutual benefits.

Although an existing regulation forbids government officials to accept gifts of any kind,[1] it remains pervasive for businesspeople to provide officials with major household appliances, electric equipment, "red envelopes" stuffed with cash, and overseas trips. There is a common saying: "The bureaucrats would never punish a gift giver." Forbidding what the West calls bribery in a *guanxi*-based society where gift giving is the expected behavior can only drive such under-the-table transactions further behind the curtain.

While sharing benefits with officials is normal business conduct in China, it is interpreted as unethical and abnormal in the West. Faced with their home country's ethical values and business rules, Western companies in China cannot handle government relationships as their Asian counterparts do. They often find themselves at a disadvantage. This dilemma raises a question for a multinational company: Should it impose the home country's moral principles wherever it operates or should it do what the Chinese do when in China, and, if so, to what extent?

Different opinions on bribery

When Chen started working in June 1997, Mueller was sick and had returned to Germany for treatment. Steinmann and Dr Perrin told Chen that NES had submitted the holding company application to the Local Department in April 1997 and that the Local Department had transferred the documents to the Central Department at the end of that month. But nothing had happened since then. Chen felt that she had to fall back to her former colleague, Mr Zhu, who had close personal *guanxi* with the Central Department, to find out first who had the authority in the Central Department to push the processing and what their general attitudes towards the application were.

In July, Chen reported her findings to Steinmann and Dr Perrin:

> The approval process at the Central Department is difficult. Because holding companies are a relatively new form of foreign investment in China, the officials are unsure whether they are a good idea for China. They have been very prudent to grant approval. Hence, we don't have much negotiating leverage, although we are a big company and have products and technologies that China needs. The officials say that they will consider a holding company's application within 90 days of its submission. They issue approval however, only when the application is deemed "complete and perfect" (in that all issues have been resolved to the Central Department's satisfaction). The Central Department is under no real obligation to approve any holding company application. They can always find some minor issues. So the approval procedure may be lengthy. The legal basis for establishing holding companies is provided by the Holding Company Tentative Provisions, Supplementary Rules and some

unpublished internal policies. This provisional and vague status allows the officials to be flexible in authorizing a holding company. In such circumstances, maintaining close connections with the responsible officials is absolutely critical.

Chen suggested:

> The quickest and most effective way to build such connections is to invite the responsible officials to dinner and give gifts. It won't cost the company too much. But what the company will gain in return – efficiency in obtaining approval and flexibility in the interpretation of the wording within the scope permitted by law – is worth much more.

Upon hearing Chen's report and suggestion, Steinmann was shocked:

> That would be bribery. In Germany bribing an official is a criminal offence for which both the briber and the bribed are punished. NES is a publicly traded company with a board of directors that reports to shareholders and monitoring authorities in Germany.
>
> We have met the criteria for setting up the holding company. What we should do now is organize a formal meeting with the officials and negotiate with them. This is the way we have done it in the past, and it has always worked. I am not aware that we ever had to use bribery. NES does not have a history of wrongdoing.

Knowing how critical it was to follow China's customary business practices in tackling such issues, Chen argued:

> Yes, it is correct. NES did not have to give gifts of this kind in the past. But don't forget: virtually all of NES's projects or joint ventures in the past were approved by agencies responsible for specific industries or local governments that were very keen on having access to NES's technology. As a result, NES always has had considerable bargaining power. It is different this time: we need to found a holding company, and we have to deal with the Central Department that we have never contacted before. Even Mueller does not have relations in this department. Moreover, our contacts at the industrial and local levels won't help much because they have very limited influence on the Central Department and, hence, the holding company application issue.
>
> Moreover, you can't equate gifts with bribes. The approval letter doesn't have predetermined "prices" and no one forces us to pay. We give gifts just to establish relationships with officials. We develop good relationships, and favorable consideration of these officials comes naturally. According to Chinese law,[2] to give gifts to government officials and expect them to take advantage of their position and power to conduct *illegal* actions is bribery. Our intent is to motivate officials to handle our application legally but without delay. I see no serious ethical problem.
>
> In some ways it's also hard to blame officials for feathering their nest because they are poorly paid. Whether they process our application quickly or slowly has absolutely no impact on their US$200 monthly income. Then, how can we expect them to give our case the green light? They are not morally wrong if they accept our gifts and don't create obstacles for us in return.
>
> Negotiation doesn't help much. Unless we have close relationships with them, they will always find some minor flaws in our documents. After all, they have the authority for interpreting the regulations. Therefore, we have to be open-minded and get accustomed to the Chinese way of doing business.

Chen hoped that Dr Perrin would support her, as she had a feeling that the French were more flexible and less ethically sensitive than the Germans. Dr Perrin, however, shared Steinmann's view. Perrin said:

> We should not give officials anything that has some value, with the exception of very small objects (pens, key holders, calendars and the like) given mainly for marketing and advertisement purposes. I also think that these officials should not accept any gifts. It's unethical and illegal. If we think it is unethical, we should combat it and refrain from it.

Nonetheless, Dr Perrin understood the importance of *guanxi* as an informal solution to Chinese bureaucracies. So he agreed that Chen could invite one of the two responsible officials to dinner through Mr Zhu and present a CD player to this official as an expression of respect and goodwill, although he thought it went too far and was approaching bribery.

On a Saturday evening in July, Chen met the official at one of the most expensive restaurants in Beijing. At the dinner, the official promised to work overtime the next day on NES's documents and give feedback as soon as possible.

The following Monday, Chen got the government's official preliminary opinion demanding a revision of 16 clauses of the application documents. Steinmann and Dr Perrin found it difficult to understand this. NES had drafted the documents with reference to those of another company, whose application had been approved by the Central Department a few months ago. Why didn't the Central Department accept the similar wording this time? Chen again contacted her former colleague Zhu, who told her:

> You should never expect to get things done so quickly and easily. It takes time to strengthen your relationships. I can ask them to speed up the procedure without changing too much of the wording. But you'd better offer them something generous to express your gratitude since they would consider it a great favor. RMB3,000 (US$360) for each of the two will be OK. Don't make me lose face anyway.

Steinmann and Dr Perrin thought it was straightforward bribery even if gifts were given through a third party. If they agreed to do so, they would run high personal risks by violating the corporate business principle and professional ethics. As controller and lawyer, they were expected to play an important role in implementing strict control mechanisms in the company and keeping the corporate conscience. Moreover, they were worried that the potential wrongdoing might damage the strong ethical culture of the Beijing Representative Office and the good corporate image among the Chinese employees of the office, although it likely would not affect the whole company because NES was so decentralized.

However, Chen thought that *renqing* (social or humanized obligation) and *mianzi* (the notion of face) were more important and that NES's business ethics and social responsibility could be somewhat compromised. In Chen's eyes, Steinmann and Dr Perrin were inflexible and lacked knowledge of the Chinese business culture. Steinmann and Dr Perrin told Chen that she needed to learn Western business rules and values in order to survive in a multinational company.

Recent developments

In August 1997, the vice-president of NES AG led a delegation to visit China. Chen arranged a meeting for the delegation with a senior official of the Central Department. It turned out just to be a courtesy meeting and did not touch upon the details of the holding company approval issue.

In November, Steinmann and Dr Perrin met the two responsible officials in hopes of negotiating with them such that the officials would allow NES to leave some clauses unchanged. But the officials insisted on their original opinion without giving a detailed explanation of the relevant legal basis. The negotiation lasted only half an hour, and Steinmann and Dr Perrin felt that it accomplished nothing.

Because of the limited window of opportunity (that is, new investment projects required an immediate capital injection), they felt that they had no choice but to modify the documents according to the officials' requirements. Modifying the documents was an administrative struggle with NES AG, because due to company-internal policies, the German headquarters had to approve these modifications. The application was resubmitted at the end of November. When Chen inquired about the application's status in December, the officials, however, said that the case needed more consideration and then raised some new questions that they said they failed to mention last time. This happened once again three months later in February 1998.

WHAT NEXT?

In April 1998, Steinmann, Dr Perrin and Chen submitted the newest revision of the application. As NES AG could not defer funding the new projects, it demanded that the Beijing working team obtained approval within a month so that NES AG could use the China holding company's registered capital of US$30 million. Otherwise, NES AG would have to re-evaluate the China holding company and might abandon it all together. In that case, Mueller, Steinmann and Dr Perrin would miss opportunities for career advancement. As for Chen, she was concerned about her job because the Beijing Representative Office would no longer need her position.

Being very anxious about the current situation, Mueller decided to come back to Beijing immediately. Chen wanted to be able to suggest a practical approach that would gain the co-operation of the bureaucrats while conforming to the German moral standards. Chen also contemplated some challenging questions. For example, what constituted bribery? When ethical values conflicted, which values should people follow? How could these differences be resolved? To what extent should a multinational company like NES adapt to local business practices? Should the future China holding company develop special ethical codes to recognize the Chinese business culture? The answers to these questions were very important to Chen, because she expected to face similar ethically sensitive issues in the future.

ACKNOWLEDGMENT

The Richard Ivey School of Business gratefully acknowledges the generous support of The Richard and Jean Ivey Fund in the development of this case as part of the Richard and Jean Ivey Fund Asian Case Series.

Notes

1 The China State Council Order No. 20 promulgated on 1988.12.01. Article 2 Any State administrative organization and its functionary shall not give and accept gifts in activities of domestic public service. The China State Council Order No. 133 promulgated on 1993.12.05. Article 7 Gifts accepted in activities of foreign public service shall be handled properly. Gifts above the equivalent of RMB200 (about US$24) according to the Chinese market price shall be . . . handed over to the gift administrative department or acceptor's work unit. Gifts of less than RMB200 belong to the acceptor or to the acceptor's work unit. P. R. China Criminal Law (revised edition) promulgated on 1997.03.14. Article 394 Any State functionary who, in his activities of domestic public service or in his contacts with foreigners, accepts gifts and does not hand them over to the State as is required by State regulations, if the amount involved is relatively large, shall be convicted and punished in accordance with the provisions of Article 382 and 383 of this law. (Article 382 and 383 regulate the crime of embezzlement.)

2 The China State Council Order No. 20 promulgated on 1988.12.01. Article 8 Any State administrative organization and its functionary who give, accept or extort gifts for the purpose of securing illegitimate benefits shall be punished in accordance with relevant state law and regulations on suppression of bribery. The P. R. China Criminal Law (revised edition) promulgated on 1997.03.14. Article 385 Any State functionary who, by taking advantage of his position, extorts money or property from another person, or illegally accepts another person's money or property in return for securing benefits for the person shall be guilty of acceptance of bribes. Article 389 Whoever, for the purpose of securing illegitimate benefits, gives money or property to a State functionary shall be guilty of offering bribes.

CASE **19**

Yahoo v. Survivors of the Holocaust[1]

Henry W. Lane and David T. A. Wesley

> *The Net interprets censorship as damage and routes around it.*
> *– John Gilmore, founder of the Electronic Frontier Foundation*

On January 29, 2001, Timothy Koogle, chief executive officer (CEO) of Yahoo Inc. (Yahoo), learned that a group of French Nazi concentration camp survivors had charged him with war crimes for allegedly justifying the Holocaust through his company's Web site, Yahoo.com. The Association of Deportees of Auschwitz and Upper Silesia filed the charges in a French criminal court after Yahoo executives refused to obey a French court order requiring the company to block access to neo-Nazi content on its US-based servers. Yahoo claimed that the court order violated US and International laws protecting freedom of speech. Holocaust survivors were angered by Yahoo's apparent support of content that demeaned their suffering and that of millions who died at the hands of Adolf Hitler's Nazi regime. If Koogle were found guilty, he potentially faced incarceration in France.[2]

IVEY ✳ **Northeastern** UNIVERSITY

COMPANY BACKGROUND

In 1995, two Stanford University students posted their Internet bookmarks on a Web site that they called Yahoo.com. The site was simple compared to other Internet search engines, but that simplicity made it popular with new users. By 1999, Yahoo had become the second most popular destination on the Net, behind America Online.

As Yahoo continued to expand its Web index, the company also began offering auxiliary services, such as news, e-mail, shopping, auctions and Web hosting. In May 1999, Yahoo acquired GeoCities for $55 million. This popular free Web hosting service was primarily supported through advertising revenues (see Exhibit 1).

In the late 1990s, the Internet had grown from a mainly English-speaking US-based information service to a multilingual global communications and commerce industry. Most analysts expected the number of online users to approach one billion within a few years. The highest levels of growth were expected in non-English speaking countries throughout Europe, Asia and Latin America. While English speakers represented a clear majority among Internet users, their majority was quickly diminishing.

EXHIBIT 1   Selected Financial Data for Yahoo and Acquired Companies

Components of the consolidated results of operations of Yahoo and the acquired companies, prior to their acquisitions by Yahoo (in thousands):

	2000	1999	1998
Net revenues			
Yahoo!	$1,104,921	$543,732	$198,981
broadcast.com	–	28,748	17,392
GeoCities	–	12,984	18,227
eGroups	5,257	3,178	32
Others	–	3,144	10,500
	$1,110,178	$591,786	$245,132
Net income (loss)			
Yahoo!	$93,156	$86,766	$30,216
broadcast.com	–	(7,617)	(14,290)
GeoCities	–	(17,249)	(19,759)
eGroups	(22,380)	(13,322)	(967)
Others	–	(767)	(8,841)
	$70,776	$47,811	$(13,641)

The following table sets forth net revenues and gross property and equipment assets for geographic areas (in thousands):

	United States	International	Total
2000			
Net revenues	$941,266	$168,912	$1,110,178
Long-term assets	119,100	62,375	181,475
1999			
Net revenues	$532,731	$59,055	$591,786
Long-term assets	88,500	4,842	93,342
1998			
Net revenues	$228,929	$16,203	$245,132
Long-term assets	45,372	1,938	47,310

TABLE 1 Yahoo Advertising and User Trends

	Q1 2001	Q4 2000	Q3 2000	Q2 2000	Q1 2000
Avg. Daily Page Views (millions)	1,100	900	780	680	625
Active Users (millions)	67	60	55	47	
Number of Advertisers	3,145	3,700	3,450	3,675	3,565
Avg. Revenue per Advertiser	$48K	$76K	$77K	$67K	$58K
Retention of Top 200 Advertisers	92%	93%	80%	98%	96%
Avg. Length of Contract (days)	285	252	235	225	230
Percentage of Non-US Revenue	18%	15%	16%	15%	14%
Percentage of Non-US Traffic	33%	29%	29%	27%	22%
Dot-com advertisers – % of Revenue	30%	33%	41%	47%	46%

Source: Deutsche Bank Alex. Brown.

Yahoo developed 24 international sites[3] in 13 languages. In each of its international markets, Yahoo built independent directories of local language Web sites and other content. By 2001, approximately 40 per cent of Yahoo users were located outside the United States, although no single international location accounted for more than 10 per cent of total company revenues.

Yahoo's international success could be traced back to early efforts, by founders David Filo and Jerry Yang, to hire qualified executives to build the company. One of their hires was Timothy Koogle, a former Motorola executive, who joined Yahoo in March 1995 as company president. After receiving his bachelor of science degree in mechanical engineering from the University of Virginia, Koogle went on to earn master of science and doctor of engineering degrees from Stanford University. In 1999, he was named one of the "Top 25 Executives of the Year" by *Business Week* for his instrumental role in building Yahoo into a $21.4 billion company. That same year, Koogle was elected company chairman. By January 2001, Koogle had accumulated stock options worth $365 million, in addition to receiving a $295,000 annual salary.[4]

As an Internet portal, Yahoo derived most of its revenues from online advertising (see Table 1). In the wake of the dot-com stock market crash in 2000, many companies cut advertising budgets in order to reduce costs. Worse still, 40 per cent of Yahoo's advertisers were other Internet companies, many of which faced bankruptcy. By the time Yahoo announced a 42 per cent decline in advertising revenues on April 11, 2001, company shares had already fallen 92 per cent.[5]

The decline of Yahoo's fortunes prompted a mass exodus of the company's leading executives in early 2001. Fabiola Arredondo, managing director of Yahoo Europe, resigned on February 15 following a sharp downturn in European advertising revenues. Savio Chow of Yahoo Asia resigned one day later. Three more Yahoo executives also quit: Mark Rubinstein, managing director of Yahoo Canada, Dennis Zhang, Yahoo's general manager in China and Jin Youm, chief executive officer (CEO) of Yahoo South Korea. Finally, on March 7, 2001, Timothy Koogle announced that he too would be replaced, albeit not on such voluntary terms as his international counterparts.[6]

YAHOO FRANCE

Established in 1996, Yahoo France, a 70 per cent-owned subsidary of Yahoo Inc., was the first major French-language Internet portal.[7] The company housed its 56 French developers and company support staff in a spacious three-storey office building in an upscale Paris suburb. Despite competition from France Telecom and other leading European media and telecommunications companies, Yahoo had grown to become the most popular portal in France, with 63 per cent of France's 7.7 million Internet users accessing the site on a daily basis.[8]

Content was organized in much the same way as the company's US parent. In fact, all of Yahoo's international sites had the same look and feel, but each tailored its content to suit local tastes. In France, sports categories focused on the Tour de France, World Cup soccer and the French Decathlon; while in the United Kingdom, these categories focused on rugby, cricket and equestrian events. The challenge was to determine what should remain uniform for global brand building and what should be adapted to suit local tastes.

YAHOO V. LA LIGUE CONTRE LE RACISME ET L'ANTISEMITISME

> As the most participatory form of mass speech yet developed, the Internet deserves the highest protection from government intrusion.
>
> – *Justice Stewart Dalzell, Panel Member, Communications Decency Act (US)*

From the start, France presented unique challenges, compared to other countries where Yahoo had local operations. Chief among these was the country's myriad regulations and a tradition of centralized bureaucracy (an artifact of the French Revolution that had been revived following Second World War by the protectionist policies of Charles de Gaulle). One example was a language law that required the use of French, even when anglicisms were commonly used among the French population. As such, computers, by law, had to be referred to as "ordinateurs" in all official and commercial documents. Another example was a labor law that made dismissing employees an extremely difficult and involved process. The head of a French business organization did not hold out much hope for the future. "Things are going to change slowly," he noted. "Some companies have moved out of France for this reason."[9]

Although Yahoo was perhaps better prepared to enter France than many other Internet companies with less international experience, no one in the company could have envisioned that Yahoo would become embroiled in the most significant legal dispute over Internet jurisdiction in history. But that is what happened. In April 2000, La Ligue Contre le Racisme et L'Antisemitisme (LICRA), together with the Union of French Jewish Students, filed suit against the US company for allowing users to post Nazi-era memorabilia for sale on Yahoo's auction site.

Yahoo executives believed that they had complied with a French law that prohibited the display or sale of items that incite racial hatred (including most historical items associated with Nazi Germany), by excluding such items from the company's French-language portal (www.yahoo.fr). For LICRA, however, Yahoo had not gone far enough. In LICRA's view, the availability of Nazi content on the company's US-based English-language site constituted a violation of French law, as the items could be displayed on computer screens in France. Yahoo also maintained more than 150 neo-Nazi Web sites through its GeoCities Web hosting service.[10]

On April 5, 2000, LICRA sent a letter to Yahoo's US headquarters in Santa Clara, California, demanding that all Nazi items be removed from the company's auction site within eight days. When Yahoo failed to comply, LICRA filed suit with the Tribunal de Grande Instance de Paris, alleging that Yahoo had violated the Nazi Symbols Act.[11]

Yahoo's lawyers argued that the French court lacked jurisdiction over a US Web site operated from the United States and directed toward US customers. The court disagreed. On May 22, 2000, it ruled that the availability of Nazi items on the company's US English-language site constituted a violation of the law because French users could access the US site. The court ordered Yahoo to block French users from accessing banned content. In the order, Presiding Judge Jean-Jacques Gomez stated:

> . . . YAHOO is currently refusing to accept through its auctions service the sale of human organs, drugs, works or objects connected with pedophilia, cigarettes or live animals, all such sales being automatically and justifiably excluded with the benefit of the first amendment of the American constitution guaranteeing freedom of opinion and expression;
>
> Whereas it would most certainly cost the company very little to extend its ban to symbols of Nazism, and such an initiative would also have the merit of satisfying an ethical and moral imperative shared by all democratic societies;
>
> Whereas it is true that the "Yahoo Auctions" site is in general directed principally at surfers based in the United States having regard notably to the items posted for sale, the methods of payment envisaged, the terms of delivery, the language and the currency used, the same cannot be said to apply to the auctioning of objects representing symbols of Nazi ideology which may be of interest to any person.
>
> Whereas, furthermore, and as already ruled, the simple act of displaying such objects in France constitutes a violation of Article R645-1 of the Penal Code and therefore a threat to internal public order.
>
> Whereas, in addition, this display clearly causes damage in France to the plaintiff associations who are justified in demanding the cessation and reparation thereof;
>
> Whereas YAHOO is aware that it is addressing French parties because upon making a connection to its auctions site from a terminal located in France it responds by transmitting advertising banners written in the French language;
>
> Whereas a sufficient basis is thus established in this case for a connecting link with France, which renders our jurisdiction perfectly competent to rule in this matter.[12]

Yahoo initially argued that the court's measures were not technically feasible since users were not identified by nationality, but by an anonymous Internet Protocol (IP) number. However, a court-convened panel of experts reported otherwise, namely that a number of startup companies had developed geolocation software for the purpose of delivering localized advertising. Such software could be adapted to selectively block 70 per cent of French users. If Yahoo were to also ask users for their nationality, the panel concluded that 90 per cent of French users could be prevented from viewing Yahoo's questionable content.[13]

On November 20, 2000, the court reconfirmed the May 22 decision, and further stated:

> We order YAHOO Inc. to comply within 3 months from notification of the present order with the injunctions contained in our order of 22nd May 2000 subject to a penalty of 100,000 Francs[14] per day of delay effective from the first day following expiry of the 3 month period;
>
> 1/ YAHOO Inc.: to take all necessary measures to dissuade and make impossible any access via yahoo.com to the auction service for Nazi merchandise as well as to any other site or service that may be construed as an apology for Nazism or contesting the reality of Nazi crimes.
>
> 2/ YAHOO France: to issue to all Internet surfers, even before use is made of the link enabling them to proceed with searches on yahoo.com, a warning informing them of the risks involved in continuing to view such sites;
>
> 3/ continuance of the proceeding in order to enable YAHOO Inc. to submit for deliberation by all interested parties the measures that it proposes to take to put an end to the trouble and damage suffered and to prevent any further trouble.[15]

Yahoo voluntarily began screening items on its auction sites worldwide to exclude some Nazi-era memorabilia,[16] but refused to screen users by nationality. Yahoo also continued to both host anti-Semitic Web sites on its GeoCities Web hosting service, and to provide Web links to similar sites hosted on third-party servers.

LICRA intended to file similar suits against Amazon and EBay. "The combat is only beginning," announced LICRA representative Marc Knobel.[17] In response, Amazon claimed that the display and sale of Nazi products wasn't "an issue" and that the company followed "all the rules of countries" in which it operated.[18]

In reality, both Yahoo and Amazon offered fresh English- and German-language copies of *Mein Kampf* on their US Web sites, as well as used copies on their German auction sites, apparently in violation of German law prohibiting the sale of the book.

That such products were used by hate groups to promote their views was undeniable. Amazon even posted white supremacist reviews for *Mein Kampf* on its Web site, one of which read:

> This is a must-read book for every self-respecting white person to understand why Hitler had to start WWII and stop communists in Russia, which were mostly of Jewish origin. . . . If Hitler hadn't stopped them, then today the whole of Europe and probably most of the world would be living under the terror of Bolshevik communists. . . . Overall, the book shows that [Adolf Hitler was] very smart.[19]

Another reviewer maintained that *Mein Kampf* was an "ingenious work straight from one of the most intelligent minds of our century."

On May 17, 2001, EBay, the most popular auction site on the Internet with more than $5 billion in annual revenues, instituted a policy prohibiting the listing of items "likely to incite violence or perpetuate hate crimes" on its Web site. A company spokesperson stated that EBay was committed to following the laws of the countries where it conducts business. "It's a matter of respecting the communities where we live and work."[20] Despite EBay's policy, hate-crime items continued to find their way onto the auction site. A June 20, 2001 search of the term "Nazi" revealed 3,694 items (about one per cent of EBay's total listings), including a mix of historical artifacts and neo-Nazi paraphernalia.

THE YAHOO COUNTERSUIT

> *In Cyberspace, the First Amendment is a local ordinance.*
> — *John Perry Barlow, Electronic Frontier Foundation*

On December 21, 2000, Yahoo filed a countersuit against LICRA with the US District Court for the Northern District of California. Yahoo argued that compliance with the French order would violate constitutionally protected free speech in the United States.[21] Yahoo also argued:

> The Orders exercise an unreasonable, extraterritorial jurisdiction over the operations and content of a US-based Web service belonging to a US citizen. The Paris Court has extraterritorially imposed on a US corporation the drastic remedy of a prior restraint and penalties that are impermissible under US law, instead of simply enforcing the French Penal Code against French citizens who break French law.[22]

According to Yahoo, the French decision violated a US federal law. The Communications Decency Act provided Internet hosts with immunity from liability for content posted by third parties (see Exhibit 2).[23] It also violated Article 19 of the International Covenant on Civil and Political Rights, Article 10 of the Convention for the Protection of Human Rights and Fundamental Freedoms, and Article 19 of the Universal Declaration of Human Rights (see Exhibit 3).

LICRA responded that the US court did not have jurisdiction over the French organizations, and that defending itself in a US court would result in an undue financial burden. District Judge Jeremy Fogel disagreed. On June 7, 2001, he declared that his court did indeed have jurisdictional authority over the French defendants. In his order, he stated:

> There can be little doubt that most people in the United States, including this court, find the display and sale of Nazi propaganda and memorabilia profoundly offensive. However, while this fact may cause one to sympathize with the Defendant's efforts before the French Court, it is immaterial to this Court's jurisdictional determination. As Yahoo! and others have pointed out, a content restriction imposed upon an Internet service provider by a foreign court just as easily could prohibit promotion of democracy, gender equality, a particular religion or other viewpoints which have strong support in the United States but are viewed as offensive or inappropriate elsewhere.[24]

Other factors that favored US jurisdiction included LICRA's use of a US marshal to serve notice on Yahoo to appear in the French court, sending a cease and desist letter to Yahoo's headquarters in Santa Clara, California and accessing the US Web site to gather evidence. The order further explained:

> If the non-resident defendant's contacts with the forum state are substantial or continuous and systematic, the defendant is subject to general jurisdiction on the forum state even if the cause of action is unrelated to the defendant's activities within the state.

EXHIBIT 2 Communications Decency Act Title 47 (Abridged)

Sec. 230. Protection for private blocking and screening of offensive material

(b) Policy

It is the policy of the United States –

(1) to promote the continued development of the Internet and other interactive computer services and other interactive media;

(2) to preserve the vibrant and competitive free market that presently exists for the Internet and other interactive computer services, unfettered by Federal or State regulation;

(3) to encourage the development of technologies which maximize user control over what information is received by individuals, families, and schools who use the Internet and other interactive computer services;

(4) to remove disincentives for the development and utilization of blocking and filtering technologies that empower parents to restrict their children's access to objectionable or inappropriate online material; and

(5) to ensure vigorous enforcement of Federal criminal laws to deter and punish trafficking in obscenity, stalking, and harassment by means of computer.

(c) Protection for "Good Samaritan" blocking and screening of offensive material

1. Treatment of publisher or speaker

No provider or user of an interactive computer service shall be treated as the publisher or speaker of any information provided by another information content provider.

2. Civil liability

No provider or user of an interactive computer service shall be held liable on account of –

(A) any action voluntarily taken in good faith to restrict access to or availability of material that the provider or user considers to be obscene, lewd, lascivious, filthy, excessively violent, harassing, or otherwise objectionable, whether or not such material is constitutionally protected; or

(B) any action taken to enable or make available to information content providers or others the technical means to restrict access to material described in paragraph (1).

(e) Effect on other laws

(1) No effect on criminal law

Nothing in this section shall be construed to impair the enforcement of section 223 or 231 of this title, chapter 71 (relating to obscenity) or 110 (relating to sexual exploitation of children) of title 18, or any other Federal criminal statute.

(2) No effect on intellectual property law

Nothing in this section shall be construed to limit or expand any law pertaining to intellectual property.

(3) State law

Nothing in this section shall be construed to prevent any State from enforcing any State law that is consistent with this section. No cause of action may be brought and no liability may be imposed under any State or local law that is inconsistent with this section.

(4) No effect on communications privacy law

Nothing in this section shall be construed to limit the application of the Electronic Communications Privacy Act of 1986 or any of the amendments made by such Act, or any similar State law.

Source: Federal Communication Commission.

Fogel also stated that, beyond the direct circumstances, the case was "ripe for adjudication" as precedent to determine future litigation against US Internet companies by foreign jurisdictions. "California has an interest in providing effective legal redress for its residents," particularly in matters that "might infringe upon the First Amendment to the United States Constitution," he argued. Furthermore:

EXHIBIT 3   International Covenants on Free Speech

International Covenant on Civil and Political Rights
UN General Assembly (1972)
Article 19

1. Everyone shall have the right to hold opinions without interference.
2. Everyone shall have the right to freedom of expression; this right shall include freedom to seek, receive and impart information and ideas of all kinds, regardless of frontiers, either orally, in writing or in print, in the form of art, or through any other media of his choice.
3. The exercise of the rights provided for in paragraph 2 of this article carries with it special duties and responsibilities. It may therefore be subject to certain restrictions, but these shall only be such as are provided by law and are necessary:
    (a)   For respect of the rights or reputations of others;
    (b)   For the protection of national security or of public order, or of public health or morals.

Convention for the Protection of Human Rights and Fundamental Freedoms
Council of Europe – Rome (1950)
Article 10 – Freedom of expression

Everyone has the right to freedom of expression. This right shall include freedom to hold opinions and to receive and impart information and ideas without interference by public authority and regardless of frontiers. This article shall not prevent States from requiring the licensing of broadcasting, television or cinema enterprises.

The exercise of these freedoms, since it carries with it duties and responsibilities, may be subject to such formalities, conditions, restrictions or penalties as are prescribed by law and are necessary in a democratic society, in the interests of national security, territorial integrity or public safety, for the prevention of disorder or crime, for the protection of health or morals, for the protection of the reputation or rights of others, for preventing the disclosure of information received in confidence, or for maintaining the authority and impartiality of the judiciary.

Universal Declaration of Human Rights
UN General Assembly (1948)
Article 19

Everyone has the right to freedom of opinion and expression; this right includes freedom to hold opinions without interference and to seek, receive and impart information and ideas through any media and regardless of frontiers.

Source: UN Office of the High Commissioner for Human Rights.

Many nations, including France, limit freedom of expression on the Internet based upon their respective legal, cultural or political standards. Yet because of the global nature of the Internet, virtually any public Web site can be accessed by end-users anywhere in the world, and in theory any provider of Internet content could be subject to legal action in countries which find certain content offensive.

Finally, LICRA unsuccessfully argued that Yahoo should have challenged the order in a French court. Fogel replied that US courts were a "more efficient and effective forum" for addressing questions of US laws and constitutional concerns. Furthermore, had Yahoo argued its case in the French court and lost, international law would have prohibited Yahoo from resubmitting its case in a US court at a later date. Yahoo's only redress would then have been to appeal the decision to a higher court in France.[25]

PURVEYORS OF HATE

The Internet is a shallow and unreliable electronic repository of dirty pictures, inaccurate rumors, bad spelling and worse grammar, inhabited largely by people with no demonstrable social skills.
— Chronicle of Higher Education, April 11, 1997

In the early 1980s, neo-Nazis and white supremacists began using computer bulletin boards to disseminate their views. Donald Black, the leader of one of the largest of these groups, had learned to use a computer while serving prison time for plotting to overthrow the government of Dominica in order to establish an Aryan state. After his release in 1985, Black launched the first white supremacist Web site. Black's "Stormfront" was one of the largest hate sites on the Internet, hosting skinheads, Ku Klux Klansmen and neo-Nazis. By 1999, Black reported more than one million hits to his Web site, with more than 2,000 Internet users accessing the site on a daily basis.[26]

The National Alliance was another of the more popular hate sites. It hosted a fictional novel titled "The Turner Diaries" in which an all-white army successfully establishes a world government and exterminates blacks, Jews and other minorities. The novel was also available in French and German, and was believed to have inspired several acts of violence, including the April 1995 bombing of the Oklahoma City federal building in which 168 people lost their lives.

Several neo-Nazi sites posted bomb-making formulas that were linked to at least 30 bombings between 1985 and 1996.[27] In April 2001, law enforcement agents uncovered a Neo-Nazi plot to destroy Boston's Holocaust Memorial, using the same explosive formula used in the Oklahoma City bombing.[28]

All told, some 800 Web sites promoted Nazism, the majority of which were physically located in the United States. Besides offering anti-Semitic literature, neo-Nazi sites also distributed computer games directed at children. These included KZ, a concentration camp simulator, and Manager, a game in which players selected victims for Nazi gas chambers.[29] More sophisticated sites offered multimedia content, including videos and rock music. Of the 50,000 white supremacist rock CDs sold annually in the United States, most were targeted toward teen listeners and included lyrics that advocated murdering blacks or committing other acts of violence.[30]

White supremacists claimed that the Internet has been very effective for recruiting new members. "We don't have money to have TV and newspaper ads," admitted one neo-Nazi Web publisher. "The Net has allowed us to reach people in a way we never could with our limited resources."[31] Some attributed the increasing popularity of such sites for the year-over-year increase in hate crimes against minorities.[32]

International outrage

Hateful speech did not enjoy the same protection in most countries as it did in the United States. Germany, France, the United Kingdom, Denmark and Canada have all brought charges against individuals and organizations for posting racist and hateful content on the Internet.

Germany was one of the first countries to vigorously prosecute publishers of electronically delivered hate propaganda. Dr Frederick Toben, an Australian citizen of German origin, operated a Web site in Australia in which he denied the Holocaust and railed against the supposed "forces of Zionist evil." Although many sites made similar claims, Toben was one of the few to direct his activities toward German users.

Toben published German-language pamphlets that advertised the site and distributed them in Germany. On December 12, 2000, Germany's highest court held that the Australian Web site was subject to German laws against denying the Holocaust, thus confirming a lower court ruling that sentenced Toben to 10 months in prison. A Georgetown University law professor, John Schmertz, explained:

> German criminal law may punish a foreign national if he publishes statements that constitute incitement of hatred among people on a foreign Internet server that is accessible to German Internet users within Germany. Such actions are considered "capable of disturbing the peace in Germany."[33]

Australian lawyer Ronald S. Huttner not only agreed with the German decision, but supported similar measures in Australia:

> In Australia we do not have any legislative equivalent of the First Amendment. On the contrary, we prefer the view that, even in the most free of democracies, the right of minorities to be protected from racial bigotry, vilification and abuse is more important than the so-called "right" of Nazis.[34]

The German interior minister, Otto Schily, criticized the United States for sheltering 90 per cent of the Web's hate content publishers. Although illegal under international law, the German government was exploring electronic countermeasures, such as spamming and denial-of-service attacks, against foreign sites that violated Germany's hate laws. In early 2001, in one of its first actions against a commercial site, German prosecutors charged Yahoo Germany for hosting *Mein Kampf* on its GeoCities Web hosting service.[35]

In the United States, anti-hate organizations, such as the Anti-Defamation League (ADL) and The Simon Wiesenthal Center, sought to combat hate and racism through education. These organizations took the position that many Internet users were unable to distinguish between legitimate Web sites, and those posting fallacious historical commentary in order to incite hatred toward minorities. They hoped to counter some of the progress made by hate groups by posting their own Web sites to expose the fallacies in Nazi propaganda.

The ADL also developed a filtering program, called the "Hate Filter," that could be downloaded by users. Whenever someone using the filter tried to access a blocked hate site, the user would be redirected to related ADL educational material. Filters were often employed by parents, schools and libraries, to counter groups intent on capturing "the minds of youngsters."[36] Critics of filters complained that they encouraged young users to access prohibited sites by bypassing the filter. Filters also blocked access to legitimate sites by historians providing information about the Second World War because these sites contained banned keywords such as "Nazi."

EXTRATERRITORIALITY

Until the 18th century, most nations maintained control over citizens and property within their borders, while lacking authority over persons or things outside their borders. When one government wished to assert its authority over another, it usually had to go to war. The Industrial Revolution and mass migrations of the 19th and 20th centuries changed that. Long before the advent of the Internet, the increased mobility of populations and the creation of multinational corporations necessitated the development of internationally accepted rules for cross-border legal disputes.

Extraterritoriality commonly referred to the practice by which one state exercised legal power over conduct that occurred in another state. Nations that exerted these powers usually did so to secure the safety and well-being of its citizens against criminal actions in foreign countries. Such would be the case when a country prosecuted foreign nationals involved in terrorist acts against its citizens. The nation initiating the case relied on the goodwill of the foreign state to enforce its judgments.

Problems of extraterritoriality occurred when both nations had an interest in the outcome of a case. The Internet vastly increased the complexity of these decisions, as content providers usually transacted, in one way or another, with individuals or organizations in multiple states simultaneously. An auction site in the United States, for example, may list an item from a seller in Japan, and then re-list that item through several online partner sites in Europe. As different jurisdictions may hold different opinions about who is actually responsible for the content, decisions over whose laws should apply remained unclear.

Prior to the Internet, businesses had to make an effort to generate sales in foreign markets. They had to set up distribution channels, advertise through local media and create local infrastructure to transact sales. Internet content providers, on the other hand, had to make an effort to *not* have their businesses accessed by foreign users. Suddenly the default market had become global and Web businesses had become subject to the laws of each country in which they transacted business. This could include a single act, such as the sale of a product to a foreign address, or a continuous presence, such as a foreign-language Web site targeted to residents of a foreign country.

The liability of the Web content provider substantially increased when the site intentionally targeted foreign users, either through the use of local languages or regionally specific content. If a Web site offered content in Malay, for example, one could be certain that it targeted Malaysian Internet users. A common interpretation of extraterritoriality suggested that the site provider could then be required to comply with Malaysian law. The US Department of Justice applied this interpretation when it convicted an Antigua-based sports gambling site of violating US gambling laws in early 2000.[37] The crux of the case rested on the fact that the gambling site knowingly accepted bets placed by US Internet customers, even though sports gambling is legal in Antigua.[38]

A few courts, however, maintained that simply having a site accessible in a given jurisdiction was sufficient for the Web content provider to be subject to the laws in that jurisdiction. In the United States, a Connecticut-based firm sued a Massachusetts firm for using its trademark on the Internet, even though both companies had similar names and could justify claim to the trademark in their respective states. The court reasoned:

The Internet, as well as toll-free numbers, is designed to communicate with people and their businesses in every state. Advertisement on the Internet can reach as many as 10,000 Internet users within Connecticut alone. Further, once posted on the Internet, unlike television and radio advertising, the advertisement is available continuously to any Internet user. [The company] has therefore, purposefully availed itself of the privilege of doing business within Connecticut.[39]

Under the Connecticut court's reasoning, any company doing business through the Internet would be subject to the laws of every jurisdiction where the Internet was accessible, even if the Web provider did not target the foreign state and did not derive any benefit from access to its site by foreign users. Increasingly, regulators in the United Kingdom and several other European Union (EU) nations began to adopt such an interpretation, namely "that if the Web site can be accessed in a particular jurisdiction, the laws of the place where the access takes place will apply and the Web site provider must comply with those local laws."[40]

Protection of free speech

The United States, however, did not extradite individuals for engaging in constitutionally protected speech, even if the activity was a clear violation of another country's law. For this reason, some experts believed that, as more countries began to enforce laws against promoting hatred, the United States would become an offshore haven for foreign hate groups. In at least one case, Ernst Zündel, a German resident of Canada, posted his anti-Semitic views on a California-based Web site in an attempt to avoid prosecution in Canada.[41]

The First Amendment's protection of speech did not prevent Internet companies from instituting an "acceptable use" policy for users. Typically, when users signed up for a service, they signed contracts that included "terms of service." Private contracts of this type were entered into between an individual and a company and therefore did not involve government protected free speech. An "acceptable use" policy could prohibit users from sending racist messages, or posting questionable content on Web pages. Internet providers relied on company employees and public users to report violations of company policy. When companies banned individuals from using their services, most customers could easily find more liberal Internet providers willing to host their activities.

International conventions on jurisdiction

The international nature of the Internet created a plethora of jurisdictional problems for legislators. Since 1968, Europeans resolved international disputes using a mechanism known as the Brussels Convention. The convention dictated that all EU nations respect and enforce civil and commercial legal decisions handed down by other EU nations. New rules approved in 2000 extended the right of consumers to sue companies in other EU nations that used the Internet to market products in multiple jurisdictions.[42]

The Hague Convention on Jurisdiction and Foreign Judgments was broader still. In the early 1990s, the Convention's 52 member nations, including the United States, sought greater co-operation in international law enforcement. Later, the treaty was expanded to include Internet disputes. If passed, the Convention would require member states to enforce commercial laws of other member states even when the actions were considered legal in local jurisdictions.[42]

ACKNOWLEDGMENT

This case was made possible through the generous support of Darla and Frederick Brodsky through their endowment of the Darla and Frederick Brodsky Trustee Professorship in International Business.

Notes

1   This case has been written on the basis of published sources only. Consequently, the interpretation and perspectives presented in this case are not necessarily those of Yahoo Inc. or any of its employees.
2   "Yahoo's Timothy Koogle," *Forbes*, January 29, 2001.
3   This figures includes localized versions of Yahoo in Argentina, Asia, Australia and New Zealand, Brazil, Canada, China, Denmark, France, Germany, Hong Kong, India, Italy, Japan, Korea, Mexico, Norway, Singapore, Spain, Sweden, Taiwan, the United Kingdom, and Ireland.
4   "Yahoo's Timothy Koogle," *Forbes*, January 29, 2001.
5   "Inside Yahoo!," *Business Week*, May 21, 2001.
6   "Out of Yahoo!'s hot seat," *Ad Age Global*, March 1, 2001.
7   SOFTBANK, a Japanese software distribution company, held a 30 per cent share.
8   "Yahoo France," *Fortune*, October 16, 2000.
9   "Yahoo France," *Fortune*, October 16, 2000.
10   The author's June 2001 search of Yahoo's GeoCities Web server using keywords such as "Aryan" and "White Pride" revealed multiple pages of links to GeoCities sites promoting hatred and violence toward minorities. (see www.geocities.com).
11   Le Nouveau Code Penal Art. R.645-2.
12   The County Court of Paris, N° RG: 00/05308 N°: 1/kl Interim Court Order, November 20, 2000. Translated by The Center for Democracy and Technology (www.cdt.org).
13   "Welcome to the Web. Passport, Please?," *The New York Times*, March 15, 2001.
14   1 French Franc = US$0.13 (July 21, 2001).
15   The County Court of Paris, N° RG: 00/05308 N°: 1/kl Interim Court Order, November 20, 2000. Translated by The Center for Democracy and Technology (www.cdt.org).
16   Excluded items included flags, uniforms and badges, but not stamps and coins.
17   "Yahoo Ordered to Bar the French from Nazi Items," *The Wall Street Journal*, November 21, 2000.
18   Ibid.
19   Review from Amazon.com. June 2001.
20   "Yahoo! Decision in France Fuels E-Commerce Sovereignty Debate," *New York Law Journal*, December 12, 2000.
21   "Yahoo! Files Suit Over French Ruling," *Mealey's Cyber Tech Litigation Report*, January 2001.
22   "Cited in First Amendment: Yahoo! v. La Ligue Contre Le Racisme et L'Antisemitisme," *Computer and Online Litigation Reporter*, January 3, 2001.
23   Communications Decency Act, 47 U.S.C. §230.
24   Yahoo! Inc., v. La Ligue Contre Le Racisme et L'Antisemitisme, Case No. 00-21275 JF, June 7, 2001.

25 "Achieving Legal and Business Order in Cyberspace: A Report on Global Jurisdiction Issues Created by the Internet," *American Bar Association*, Unpublished Draft.

26 Statement of the Anti-Defamation League on Hate on the Internet Before the Senate Committee on the Judiciary. September 14, 1999.

27 Ibid.

28 "Police: Suspect Wanted To Start Racial War," *WCVB TV*, June 21, 2001.

29 "A German and US Clash Over Efforts to Crack Down on Neo-Nazi Web Sites in the US," *International Enforcement Law Reporter*, February 2001.

30 "Web of Hate," *Salon*, October 16, 1998.

31 "Net Group Stalks LA Gunman," *Wired News*, April 11, 1999.

32 "Hate crimes reported to the FBI: 8,759 in 1996, 7,947 in 1995 and 5,932 in 1994. Web of Hate," *Salon*, October 16, 1998.

33 "German High Court decides novel issue . . . ," *International Law Update*, January 2001.

34 GigaLaw.com Discussion List, January 5, 2001 (www.gigalaw.com).

35 It's a Brave New World of On-Line Liabilities, *New York Law Journal*, May 1, 2001.

36 Statement of the Anti-Defamation League on Hate on the Internet Before the Senate Committee on the Judiciary. September 14, 1999.

37 Federal Wire Wager Act, 18 U.S.C. §1084.

38 "Yahoo! Decision in France Fuels E-Commerce Sovereignty Debate," *New York Law Journal*, December 12, 2000.

39 937 F. Supp. 161 (D. Conn. 1996) cited in "Achieving Legal and Business Order in Cyberspace: A Report on Global Jurisdiction Issues Created by the Internet," *American Bar Association*, Unpublished Draft.

40 "Thinking Twice About Your Web Site," *Corporate Risk Spectrum*, January 2001.

41 Statement of the Anti-Defamation League on Hate on the Internet Before the Senate Committee on the Judiciary. September 14, 1999.

42 "Thinking Twice About Your Web Site," *Corporate Risk Spectrum*, January 2001.

43 "Global Treaty-Threat to the Net?," *ZDNet News*, June 22, 2001.

CASE **20**

Valley Farms International (A)

Donald G. Simpson and Henry W. Lane

John Roberts, a university professor of finance, was trying to decide whether to change careers when he took a six-month leave of absence to see if he had an aptitude for international business. He accepted a short-term consulting job to conduct a feasibility study for a milk-processing plant in a country in the Middle East (which will be referred to as the "Republic").

At the time, the country's Regent was still in control, although opposition to his regime was becoming more open. When Roberts made his first trip in August, optimism for the Regent's regime was still high among Westerners and the local middle class. However, by his second trip in November, the situation was changing. There were uprisings and demonstrations, but it was considered only "temporary unrest."

Valley Farms, which was to be the supplier of cattle for the milk-processing plant project, was also supplying a small number of cattle for a demonstration farm. It had shipped eighty cattle in November, which arrived during Roberts' visit and during violent demonstrations against the Regent. The airport authorities would not allow the plane to be off-loaded, nor would they connect the power for the air conditioning. By morning, half the cattle had died before Roberts could free them. Crowds, out of control, were frantically attacking the Regent's military as well as women in Western clothing.

IVEY

Roberts, in a taxi, was caught in the demonstration. It was a frightening experience, and John commented that it was one of the few times he had been truly scared.

The feasibility study concluded that the project was economically viable, but not feasible due to the deteriorating political conditions. During the course of the study, Roberts had made the acquaintance of the owner of Valley Farm, a dairy farm and cattle auction operation that was selling a lot of cattle to countries in South America. Since the milk plant project was not going to go forward, Roberts was easily persuaded to complete his leave of absence with Valley Farms and to take on the task of organizing its burgeoning domestic and international operation.

Roberts never returned to his life as a teacher. He remained with Valley Farms as Export Manager and assumed the responsibility of arranging financing for the export sales. Eventually, a decision was made to split the export and domestic operations, and Valley Farms International (VFI) was incorporated with Roberts as one of the partners. The export operations were driven by three aspects: demand by clients for cattle, which was cyclical; the ability of the client to obtain hard currency; and the ability of Valley Farms International to find successful local agents to represent its interests. Although Roberts was prepared to travel widely to close a deal, the operation depended to a significant degree on the work of local agents. Within a short time of the incorporation, VFI had withdrawn from the South American market as Brazil's holdings of foreign currency declined rapidly. Attention turned to North Africa and the Far East. Small sales were concluded with Morocco and for three years VFI made extensive sales to South Korea. This market was saturated by 1984 and sales ended quickly.

Amazingly, however, Roberts' attention had been drawn back to the Republic. One of his old contacts in that country advised him that the Ministry of Agriculture was in the market for cattle. Yogurt, a staple in the diet of the people of the Republic, required substantial milk supplies, and the cattle population had been reduced during the worst days of the revolution. Supply sources were limited mainly to Western Europe or Canada.

In spite of the bad memories of his last involvement in the Republic, Roberts saw a good commercial opportunity. With only a general lead from his contact in the Republic as to where he might find the Ministry of Agriculture delegation, John headed off to Europe. He eventually found them in Holland and learned quickly that he was having to match wits with a group of committed young revolutionaries who behaved as if, and no doubt believed that, they were running the show and shaping the rules of the game now. Roberts' intuition, however, was that someone higher up behind the scenes was probably still pulling the strings. Two members of the group had been students in the United States and understood North Americans reasonably well; the others had not been to the United States. The leader of the group spoke no English and was a hardened revolutionary.

Following their discussions in the Netherlands, Roberts offered to fly the group of six to visit VFI and to pay their expenses while they surveyed the VFI operation. They accepted and came for a week. Roberts was kept busy showing them the dairy operation, the auction barns, and some of the farms from which cattle would be obtained and discussing the technical details of cattle selection, in which these people were not highly experienced. He also found himself discussing social responsibilities and the role of morality in one's life.

A deal was reached by the strangest of events. Throughout the week, Roberts had spent almost every waking hour touring, dining, and talking with the group in order to build trust. On Sunday, he told them he was going to church, and they were welcome to wait until his return or to go with him. To his surprise, they went and sat through the service and the informal coffee-time discussion following. Rather than being offended by their exposure to a Christian service, these religious fundamentalists were pleased to know they were dealing with a religious person.

Shortly afterward, a $6 million contract was signed with the Ministry of Agriculture. Obtaining the contract had been much easier than Roberts had expected, but no doubt implementing the contract would provide some challenges. A four-person delegation from the Republic arrived to inspect the cattle, which were to be shipped in planeloads of 200 head each. Roberts arranged for them to inspect the cattle which, at this point, were being held at different farms in the area. They did not want to see the cattle, only the papers on the cattle. To Roberts, this was not a good sign. It suggested that they were going to be more concerned with all the paper technicalities than with viewing the animals to judge their quality.

On the first morning after a cursory examination of the papers, they rejected half the available cattle. Of the half tentatively approved, they visited one small group and rejected almost all of them. One of Roberts' partners, who had been viewing their behavior incredulously, finally lambasted them for their incompetence. The members of the delegation were deeply offended and said that they were leaving for home. It took Roberts three days to calm them down. Although they agreed to stay, the following days with them seriously tested Roberts' patience. Their behavior was wildly erratic. One day they seemed to be happy with the way things were going, and the next day they would be angry. Afterwards, Roberts reflected that part of the problem was they were not confident in the job they were assigned. They took seriously the responsibility that had been given to them, but they were not sure how much to trust the word of this North American stranger.

The first shipment was made in June. A major problem developed when the cattle were tested upon arrival in the Republic. Inspectors claimed that most of the animals in the first shipment had TB and slaughtered them. Almost immediately, Roberts flew to the Republic with a veterinary doctor from the federal Department of Agriculture. Part of the problem was the manner in which the cattle were tested. Also, the cattle were being tested for a TB strain for which North Americans did not test. The testing had to be changed for future shipments. This was done and the shipments were completed to the satisfaction of both the customer and VFI, which made a good profit on the sales.

Two years later, Roberts was back in the Republic to sign a contract to deliver 10,000 cattle. As Roberts described it, negotiating in a revolutionary country was different from anything he had experienced before. The young revolutionaries who had taken over the bureaucracies were working hard to get the best deal for the government. With their bazaar-mentality upbringing, they were prepared to bargain for days at a time. Although these young bureaucrats seemed to believe honestly that they were in charge, Roberts realized that another system was at work. He needed information to understand what was going on. This information came from a contact he had made in pre-Revolutionary times, a person with earlier Canadian connections who was Westernized, capitalistic, and motivated by money.

To get negotiations started, Roberts needed his help. For a price, this man claimed he would open the gate to the powerful force behind the scenes in the Republic, that Westerners came to call "the Invisible Hand." Although Roberts knew that, according to the law of the Republic, agents were forbidden, he understood also that all serious Western companies doing business in the country had a "contact." This man had had previous contacts with Canada and knew something about how North American firms operated. The first information he had offered Roberts was accurate and useful. He had informed VFI that the Ministry of Agriculture was back in the market for cattle, and that the purchasing team was in Europe. From that time on, their conversations had been sprinkled with references to the need for some payment. These discussions were confusing to Roberts, for it was never clear exactly for what he might be paying or even to whom the money would be going.

In convoluted discussions, spread over time, he had been led to believe that "the invisible hand needed to be fed." The inference was that these were powerful people who, of course, could not be identified. However, the clear message was that without their approval Roberts' negotiations would never be treated seriously. Eventually, a figure of $300 a head (approximately 10 percent of the contract price per head) was suggested as an appropriate fee. Payment would be made upon delivery.

Thus, Roberts found himself carrying on two sets of negotiations simultaneously . . . one with the buyer and one with his contact. With the latter, he kept asking himself: "What am I buying?" As he saw it, the payment might be necessary "to get into the game . . . to begin serious negotiations with the buyers." It would be an expensive admission fee and he wondered whether or not it would be worthwhile.

CASE **21**

Enron – What Went Wrong?[1]

Bert Spector

On December 14, 2000, Houston-based Enron Corporation seemed to stand at the peak of its meteoric rise to prominence. Chief Executive Officer (CEO) Kenneth Lay announced that he would soon turn over the reins to Jeffrey Skilling. Lay and Skilling exuded both pride in the past achievements of its company and confidence in their future. Most observers agreed. At the time of the transition from Lay to Skilling, the company reported $15 billion in assets, $100 billion in revenues and 20,000 employees.

Such impressive achievements told only part of the story. Enron had done more than just succeed within the parameters of the energy industry; it had virtually redefined that industry. Embracing deregulation and free markets, adopting new technology with remarkable quickness and radically reinventing its own business model several times over, Enron seemed to stand as a paradigm of successful innovation. In 2000, *Fortune* named Enron as the "Most Innovative Company" for the fifth year in a row, and the magazine's praise did not stop there. Enron was also rated 24th on its list of "Best Companies to Work For," 29th on "America's Fastest Growing Companies," second on "Reputation of Employee Talent," and first – just ahead of General Electric – on "Reputation of Quality of Management."[2]

Almost precisely one year later, on December 2, 2001, Enron declared bankruptcy. The stunning swiftness with which Enron tumbled from one of the New Economy's most admired companies to the largest bankruptcy ever in US history up to that point, led to debates as to what had caused the collapse. Multiple theories abounded, and they all had one core idea in common: the roots of the collapse spread both deep and wide through the company's history.

ENRON CORPORATION

Enron reshapes the energy industry and itself

Kenneth Lay headed Enron since its creation from a 1985 merger between InterNorth, Inc. and Houston Natural Gas Corporation. "Spend long enough around top Enron people and you feel you are in the midst of some sort of evangelical culture," observed *The Economist*. "In a sense, you are. Mr Lay, with his 'passions for markets,' is the cult's guru." Enron employees came to view Lay as a father figure in whom they could place complete trust. Said one executive, "The employees loved him. He walked the floors. . . . He was this warm, fatherly figure. . . . They trusted him."[3]

As Lay worked to build the biggest pipeline system in the country, he focused his time and company resources on lobbying governments, especially state governments, to deregulate the energy industry.

> Early on when other natural gas companies were attempting to hold onto a regulated market, we were pushing hard to move our business upstream into unregulated businesses. We thought there'd be more opportunity here to differentiate ourselves on products and services and make a profit at it.

To achieve that goal, Enron needed deregulated energy markets, so Lay became heavily involved in state-level political campaigns, spending more than $1.9 million of Enron's money on 700 candidates in 28 states. Between 1997 and 2000, 24 states moved toward greater energy market deregulation. Up-ending the industry was an accomplishment that Lay himself viewed with pride:

> In this new world, the public utility industry will fade into memory. Competition and technological change is turning the gas and electric industry into yet another mass-marketing segment of the US and global economy.[4]

Lay also focused his energies on the promulgation of four core Enron values: communication, respect, integrity and excellence (a statement of those values can be found in Exhibit 1). He had banners hung in the company's corporate lobby proclaiming those values. "I was always in the forefront of trying to make sure that our people did in fact live and honor those values. . . ," recalled Lay. "Integrity and character are incredibly important to me."[5]

EXHIBIT 1   Enron Corporate Values

Communication
We have an obligation to communicate. Here, we take the time to talk with one another . . . and to listen. We believe that information is meant to move and that information moves people.

Respect
We treat others as we would like to be treated ourselves. We do not tolerate abusive or disrespectful treatment.

Integrity
We work with customers and prospects openly, honestly and sincerely. When we say we will do something, we will do it; when we say we cannot or will not do something, then we won't do it.

Excellence
We are satisfied with nothing less than the very best in everything we do. We will continue to raise the bar for everyone. The great fun here will be for all of us to discover just how good we can really be.

Source: Company files

Becoming a trader

A free market for natural gas allowed Enron the opportunity for its first major innovation: a "gas bank." In the late 1980s, gas prices entered a period of instability, and Enron found itself with a vast inventory of natural gas and uncertain future prices. To turn this apparent disadvantage into an opportunity, Jeffrey Skilling, who, at that time, was a McKinsey & Co. consultant working with Enron, proposed the idea of selling gas futures to customers at agreed-upon prices or price ranges. Natural gas customers, seeking a hedge against the future fluctuation of prices, could enter into a contract with Enron. They would be able to withdraw gas from the bank in the future according to the provisions set forth in a current contract. *Fortune* magazine described the trading process:

> A utility wanted gas for 30 days at a fixed price? Floating prices, but with a maximum and minimum price? A guaranteed supply of gas whenever the temperature went over 95 degrees? No problem: Enron could slice and dice the gas to a customer's specifications – and, in return, of course, could charge a little extra.

It was this notion of a gas bank that would, according to Skilling, provide Enron with the "huge breakthrough" that would allow the company to "conquer the world because we had a better idea."[6]

When Skilling left McKinsey to join Enron in 1990 as CEO of the company's gas bank division, he moved the company more decisively into trading gas futures, seeking contracts of 15 years and longer. Given the volatility of gas prices, such long-term arrangements were not without risks, so the company needed to create an ability to manage that uncertainty. Enron's risk management centered on "two simple rules: all trades must be balanced with an offsetting trade to minimize unhedged risks and each trader must report a daily profit-and-loss statement."[7]

When wholesale electricity was deregulated in 1992, Enron leaped into the market. By 1994, it was selling $10 million worth of electricity, very little of which Enron generated itself. Instead, it relied on "the arts of swaps, collars, caps, floors, and hybrids." Three years later, Enron reported revenues in electricity sales to be $4 billion, and by 2000, 95 percent of its revenues came from wholesaling energy and services.[8]

"WALL STREET IN HOUSTON"

Jeffery Skilling saw the gas bank as a model for ever-greater growth. Why not enter other non-energy markets that had never been traded before as commodities? If Enron had made money from gas and electricity futures, why could it not do the same for fiber-optic bandwidth, pollution-emission credits, even weather derivatives? Enron could move even farther afield with its trading and risk management competency, trading wood pulp, steel and television advertising. "The application [of the trading model] is almost limitless because every single business has, at its heart, markets," Skilling explained. "Enron is an incumbent player's worst nightmare."[9]

As Enron moved more decisively into the trading business, it could shed physical assets and become highly flexible and adaptive. "Jeff's theory," said a senior Enron executive, "was assets were bad, intellectual capital was good." Skilling himself disdained what he called "old economy" companies that were burdened with assets. "These big companies will topple over from their own weight," he warned.[10]

Enron's transition to pure trader was widely noted by business analysts; typically with admiration for Enron's ability to, once again, reinvent itself. *CIO Magazine* called the transformation "Enron's boldest move to date," which involved "its own version of Wall Street in Houston. . . ." *The Economist* agreed: "Enron, in effect, was abandoning its roots as an energy provider in favor of becoming a Wall Street trader that just happened to be based in Houston, Texas." A stock analyst suggested that Enron had become "a company that traded for trading's sake."[11]

Jeffrey Skilling and Andrew Fastow

Skilling, the man behind Enron's transformation, had joined McKinsey in 1979 after receiving an undergraduate degree from Southern Methodist University and an MBA from the Harvard Business School. At Harvard he was a Baker Scholar and, according to one professor, "may have been the single best student I ever had, and he did not suffer fools." Another professor found him to be passionate and relentless, adding that all the professors who had dealings with Skilling remembered him and "I don't think anybody remembered an unpleasant thing about him."[12]

When Skilling began working with Enron in 1988 – this was the point at which he introduced the gas bank idea – he was a senior partner in McKinsey's Houston-based North American Energy and Chemical Practices division. Within two years, he was CEO of the Enron Finance Corporation. "I've never not been successful in business or work," Skilling told a reporter, "Ever." Ken Lay recognized and rewarded Skilling's success by naming him president and chief operating officer (COO) (Lay retained the positions of chairman and CEO) in 1996.[13] Over the next three-and-a-half years, Enron's stock soared 350 percent to a high of $90 a share.

Skilling himself claimed General Electric's transformational leader Jack Welch as his personal role model and extolled the organizational virtues of flexibility and innovation. "You should always value the ability to move and change, because that creates options." In order to create an appropriate environment for innovation, he said, "You wanted to have an environment that weird people liked operating in. It's the weird ideas that create new businesses."[14]

Skilling took pride in surrounding himself with talent, tough-minded individuals, and none played a more important role in determining the way Enron reported its financial performance than Andrew Fastow. A graduate of Tuffs University and the Kellogg School of Management at Northwestern University, Fastow joined Enron in 1990 at age 29. Eight years later, he was chief financial officer (CFO). Said a colleague of Fastow: "What the guy knew was numbers and finance. He knew how to close a deal. No one did that better than Andy." *USA Today* noted the similarity between Fastow and Skilling: "Skilling could be cold and impersonal, but Fastow took it further – when he wasn't secluded in his office, he was arrogant and abrasive, capable of pounding his fist on the table and dressing down colleagues in front of their peers." Others talked about a kind of split personality. Said a former executive, "He was very smart and very good at what he did. He could be nice, but he could also be quite volatile and short-tempered. He didn't have a lot of patience with people who weren't as smart as him."

Skilling and Fastow helped drive Enron's performance in the 1990s, and in December 2000, Ken Lay recognized Skilling's contribution by naming him president and CEO, effective the following February. Said Lay:

> The best time for succession is when the successor is ready and when the company is well-positioned for the future. Jeff is a big part of Enron's success and is clearly ready to lead the company. With Jeff's promotion, succession is clear, our deep pool of management talent remains intact, and no other organizational changes need to be made to take the company to new levels of growth.

Ken Lay had hung a banner in Enron's corporate lobby proclaiming "The world's leading energy company." Skilling replaced that with a new banner: "The world's leading company."[15]

During his tenure as CEO, Skilling's brash style often rubbed people the wrong way, including a number of Wall Street analysts. Said one, Skilling "was famously boastful . . . and thin-skinned, declaring on a conference call that a money manager who dared ask for a balance sheet was an 'asshole.' " A colleague of Skilling offered this view: "He was always saying people don't get it."[16]

Building businesses

"To get ahead here," said Skilling, "you have to be a business builder." Human resource executive Cindy Olson agreed. "Entrepreneurs can build something of their own . . . with the luxury of a stable organization." Enron supported the idea of "cellular division" wherein entrepreneurial new businesses, especially ones that challenged established business models, would become separate divisions. Executive Lou Pai explained the reasons for this differentiation:

> A lot of times you're off running an existing business and are responsible for new business as well, you're not really as accountable for the success of the new business as long as your old business continues to do well. We want everyone building the new business to be involved 100 percent.

To enhance that sense of involvement, Enron offered "phantom equity" to the start-up teams of these new businesses. At the point where the business began to show a profit, that phantom equity could be swapped for real Enron shares. Once businesses were up and running, they became highly autonomous, selecting their own infrastructure and often raiding other units for employees.[17]

Company executives could point to a number of examples of bottom-up generators of new business ideas, including the 1999 genesis of Enron Online. "We didn't start it because the chairman said we need an e-commerce strategy," said Executive Vice-president Steve Kean. Louise Kitchen drove the initiative while heading Enron's gas trading operation in Europe. Based on previous experience with Internet trading (while she was working in Enron's Scandinavian office), she began to work on an ad hoc basis, pulling together an informal coalition of commercial, legal and technical people. She informed her immediate supervisor, John Sheriff. Chief Operating Officer Skilling remained out of the loop until the ad hoc group, which grew to 250 people, were ready to launch the online business. Sheriff finally approached Skilling in November 1999, and the COO was unenthusiastic but willing to explore the idea. Recalled Skilling:

> So John says to me, "Actually, we're almost done." I was never asked for any capital. I was never asked for any people. They had already purchased the servers. They had already started ripping apart the building. They had already started legal reviews in 22 countries by the time I heard about it.

Skilling approved, and Enron Online was up and running in less than a year. Enron's head of information technology (IT), Michael McConnell, said that online trading was revolutionary for the company, not so much because of the technology, but because of the impact it had on Enron traders: "Since Enron Online has reduced our transaction time to less than a second, our guys have to manage their businesses by the second – not just by the day as in the past."[18]

Building a trading culture

An Enron executive said a key to the company's culture was "an overweening pride, which led people to believe they could handle increasingly exotic risks without danger." The apparent success Enron enjoyed led to increasing pressure for ever-improving performance. "The driver was this unbelievable pressure to keep portraying Enron as something very, very different," said another executive, "and keep the track record going and going." The dealmakers at Enron, said a former deal maker, "thought they were so brilliant they could overcome any obstacle." Added an employee, "We were doing deals that no one had done before. We were taking risks that no one else had taken before."[19]

Lay and Skilling recognized that in order to fuel this trading culture, they would have to attract to Enron a different breed of employee from those who might otherwise find their way to Texas-based energy firms.

> We not only had to attract talent from investment banking houses, commercial banks and elsewhere, but we also had to compete against them. We also had to go up against the big consulting firms for some of the new MBAs coming out of graduate schools.

The head of an executive search firm that worked for Enron talked about this "new" type of recruit: "Enron was a real pioneer in bringing a new type of executive to the energy business. They started a trend in the energy business of attracting executives who otherwise would have gone into investment and commercial banking." What attracted these new recruits, in part, was their view of Enron "as a hip, dynamic, New Age, blue-chip company that you could join and have a good time of it."[20]

Following the vision of Lay and Skilling, these new recruits recreated the Enron culture. In Enron's world, the engineers have been replaced by theoretical physicists trained in portfolio analysis; the reliability is engineered on the trading floor, where young traders price and strike deals with customers in something like 90 seconds.

These new traders, according to Gary Hamel, "were bold, hungry, and creative. They were assigned to a territory and/or a specialty, but their real assignment was simply to find ways to make money." There were occasional examples of traders overstepping the boundaries: between 1985 and 1987, two Enron oil traders defrauded the company out of $136 million. These two employees, viewed by the company as "rogue traders" and "expensive embarrassments" to the otherwise positive culture, were promptly fired.[21]

Global expansion

As a counter-trend to Skilling's preference for pure trading, in the early 1990s, Enron began buying energy-related assets overseas. "We have created a new model based on an at-risk, entrepreneurial culture; we look for opportunity in chaos," said an Enron executive explaining the company's approach to global expansion.[22] Under the leadership of Rebecca Mark, Enron aimed first at Europe, South America and Russia, and later focused on China and India. *Newsweek* wrote of Mark:

> When she entered the utility business in the early '80s, it was populated with frumpy males in baggy suits and short-sleeved shirts with pocket protectors. Mark was a builder. . . . By the mid-'90s, she had constructed or acquired five plants in the United States and was on her way to buying or building well in excess of 15 in Europe, Asia, South America and the Middle East.[23]

Like Skilling, Mark had graduated from the Harvard Business School. Unlike Skilling, however, Mark believed in building hard assets.

In the late 1990s, Enron engaged in two large-scale overseas ventures. Azurix, Enron's subsidiary, which held its water-related assets, purchased the UK's Wessex Water for $1.9 billion. Mark brought what she referred to herself as a "missionary zeal" to her overseas expansion:

> . . . we are bringing a market mentality and spreading the privatization gospel in countries that desperately need this kind of thinking. We are in the business of doing deals. This deal mentality is central to what we do. It's never a question of finding deals but of finding the kind of deals we like to do. We like to be pioneers.

Enron also moved to build a power plant in Dabhol, in the state of Maharashtra, India. Despite a World Bank warning that such an investment in India was not viable, Enron partnered with General Electric and Bechtel to contribute $1.2 billion of the total $2.9 billion project. ("We make our own rules," said an Enron executive explaining this decision. "Most people look at the world and think too small; when we went to India, the majors said we were crazy.") The effort generated little revenue, however. A major shift in local political alignments accompanied by accusations of corruption and illegality on the part of Enron officials led the plant's sole customer, the Maharashtra State Electricity Board, to stop purchasing power. They also declined to pay past bills. Enron and its partners shut down the project in June 2001.[24]

By that time, Skilling was moving to unload Enron's international assets. In August 2000, Rebecca Mark left Enron. Skilling placed virtually the entire global holdings on the market, hoping to recover as much as possible of the $7.5 billion Enron had invested. No buyers, however, were found.[25]

Employee development

"I prefer a smart person to an asset," said Jeffrey Skilling, referring to his belief that intelligent, flexible, performance-oriented employees would provide Enron with a competitive advantage, especially when compared to asset-heavy traditional companies. Enron's human resources department sought to take advantage of that flexibility and knowledge by creating an open market for internal labor. "We have so many business units," said Executive Vice-president Cindy Olson, that "the opportunities are limitless."[26]

To maximize mobility, Enron sought to allow seamless movement across businesses and units. Common compensation and evaluation systems removed potential barriers, as did policies that allowed employees to transfer their titles as they moved. An emphasis on stock options was meant, at least in part, to keep employees focused on the overall performance of the company.[27]

In Skilling's view, knowledge had to be balanced with an emphasis on individual performance. To ensure such an emphasis, Enron employed a fixed-curve rating system. Employees were evaluated not by supervisors alone, but by a group of employees called a Performance Review Committee. Each year, units were required to identify the bottom 15 percent of their performers, and, in a system nicknamed "rank-and-yank," fire those on the bottom.[28]

Observers found both plusses and minuses in Enron's employee development system. A *Fortune* survey found Enron to be one of the most successful companies at attracting and retaining top talent in a highly competitive labor market:

> Employees are encouraged to be risk-taking career builders. College recruits spend time in several business units to see which is the best fit. As employees progress, they are pushed to manage their careers by moving around within the firm and acquiring new skills. In fact, 85 percent of the people in Enron's core business units have held at least two positions within the company. Enron also keeps a database of online resumes – updated regularly by employees – so that managers can recruit from within. As result, the company's annual turnover is a minuscule three percent, even though it hired nearly 5,000 people last year [1999].

Much internal criticism, however, was aimed at the ranking-by-committee approach. "Everyone was in it for themselves," said an executive. "People stabbed you in the back." Another complained that the review process focused entirely on the amount of revenue generated by the employee: "I never once heard a discussion about a person's teamwork or integrity or respect." Aware of such concerns, Skilling expressed support for changing the committee aspect of the ranking system.[29]

Compensation

Lay and Skilling recognized that if they were going to compete with investment houses and consulting firms for talent, they would have to offer competitive compensation packages. "Young traders just out of school were tantalized with promises of $500,000 within a year," said one observer. High salaries were matched by lavish perks: $1.5 million company parties (at one, Rebecca Mark rode in on the back of an elephant); $100 bills left on each employee's desk when the stock price reached $50. Employees felt they earned such lavishness because of their long hours and frequently gruelling travel schedules. The environment, said one executive, was, "Get it done. Get it done now. Reap the rewards." The extravagance, said another, "is what made it great to work" for Enron. Lay himself maintained that corporate spending could have a desirable motivational impact. "All these planes," he said, referring to Enron's fleet of corporate jets, "give my CEOs something to aspire to."[30]

Skilling was keen on moving Enron's compensation plan to be more rewarding of entrepreneurial behavior. "If we've broken a paradigm," an executive said, "it's the compensation paradigm. We pay people like entrepreneurs." High bonuses were paid, based on deals completed and revenue booked. Said one employee:

> The bonuses led employees to focus on pushing deals through the system, even if the deal was a bad deal. The people working on Dabhol power plant in India did very well in bonus time because they worked on a deal and got it done. Two years later, the deal went into the tank, but the system was not good at differentiating between temporary value and long-term value.

Top executives could receive sizable bonuses based on a calculated combination of dividends paid to shareholders plus improvements in the stock price. On January 11, 2001, for example, CFO Andrew Fastow received a bonus check of $350,000; on

February 5, he received a check for $1.3 million and then on February 7, he received a bonus payment of $1.4 million. Sizable bonuses were not the exclusive domain of corporate officers, though. In 2001, a 27-year-old energy trader earned an $8 million bonus on reported profits of $750 million in natural gas contracts.[31]

Increasingly, as Enron's stock price rose, the company came to rely on stock options – granting employees the right to buy shares in the future at a fixed price, typically the price of the share at the time the option is granted – as a way of rewarding executives. Skilling pointed to the reliance on stock options as a practice "used by every corporation in the world." In addition to basing rewards on company performance, stock options allowed companies to look more profitable than if they had paid executives with a salary. Granting stock options is the only form of compensation that is not reported as an expense.[32] Skilling made clear that top Enron executives were quite conscious of that advantage. "Essentially what you do is you issue stock options to reduce compensation expense," he explained, "and therefore increase your profitability." In 2000, Skilling exercised options that netted him $62.5 million.[33]

Culture of confidence

A sense of confidence and pride infused Enron's culture in a way that could be, and often was, experienced as arrogance. "The Enron way was to be brash," said an executive, "and there was an arrogance about it." Said another, "Anyone who criticized Enron – internally or externally – was taken out and flogged." If you were an Enron employee, "you thought you were better. You were smarter than everyone else."[34]

Ken Lay dismissed charges of corporate or even personal arrogance. In a June 2000 interview with *The Economist*, he compared himself and his company to Michael Milikin and Drexel Burnham Lambert. Milikin and Lambert had likewise been accused of arrogance. (Milikin had also been accused and convicted of securities fraud.) Like Enron, Lay insisted to the reporter, they were really being "very innovative and very aggressive."[35]

Aggressive accounting

Enron followed the "mark to market" rule for recognizing revenues. The fully legal practice allowed the company to book as revenue the entire projected downstream value of a deal at the time the deal was made. Thus, a deal to provide $500,000 a year in natural gas to a customer for five years would be recognized as $2.5 million at the inception of the deal.

Of course, most of Enron's trading deals were far more uncertain and ambiguous than that example. Prices and needs varied in the complex agreements struck with customers. Additionally, many of the agreements stretched out for 10 to 15 years; or, in the case of the New York State Power Authority, 33 years.[36] Would a customer exist in 10 to 15 years, let alone be willing and able to pay? Enron had just such an example of that uncertainty when the Maharashtra State Electricity Board, the sole customer of Enron's multibillion-dollar investment in India, canceled all future contracts with the Dabhol power plant and refused to pay past bills.

Rather than projecting revenue streams cautiously, Enron tended to be aggressively optimistic. For instance, in a state where power had not yet been deregulated, Enron based its projections on the assumption that power would soon be deregulated, allowing the company to raise the price. It was this aggressiveness that, while approved by Arthur Andersen, Enron's accounting firm, led to the designation of "cutting edge." Enron executive Gary Foster said that even at the time it was reporting these revenues, "we knew that we pushed the limit in our accounting practices, and that people would come in with their numbers whether we really did [achieve them] or not."[37]

Many analysts, both critics and supporters, acknowledged that openness concerning performance numbers was never Enron's strong suit. Writing in *Fortune*, Bethany McLean noted:

> . . . the company remains largely impenetrable to outsiders, as even some of its admirers are quick to admit. Start with a pretty straightforward question: how does Enron makes its money? Details are hard to come by because Enron keeps many of the specifics confidential for what it terms "competitive reasons."[38]

When Azurix, an Enron subsidiary, was trying to win a contract from the Houston Area Water Corporation to build a purification plan, the negotiations fell through because the Water Corporation's board was uneasy about Azurix's financial status. "We could never flush out of Azurix the financial documents we wanted," explained the board's chairman. "The first tell-tale sign of something being amiss is the refusal to turn over documents."[39]

When doubts were expressed about the validity of Enron's high-performance claims, company executives responded aggressively. On August 21, 2001, for example, broker Chung Wu of PaineWebber's Houston office sent a pre-dawn e-mail to clients warning about the performance of Enron's stock. Clients, Wu suggested, should "take some money off the table." Aaron Brown, Enron's manager of employee stock option plans, fired off his own e-mail to PaineWebber executives saying that he found Wu's advisory to be "extremely disturbing" and asking them to "Please handle the situation." By that evening, PaineWebber executives had fired Wu and issued a retraction, assuring clients that Enron's stock was "likely heading higher than lower from here on out. All this occurred on the same day that Ken Lay sold $4 million worth of his own personal Enron holdings.[40]

In 2000, Carl Bass, a partner at Houston office of Enron's accounting firm, Arthur Andersen, sent an e-mail to partners in the accounting firm's Chicago headquarters expressing concern over various accounting practices – how the company recognized revenues, its dealings with various off-balance sheet partnerships – and the fact that these practices had been "sustained" by the local Andersen office. Executives within Enron got wind of these concerns and lobbied, unsuccessfully on this occasion, for Andersen to "replace Carl."[41]

The collapse

It was possible to trace the collapse of Enron – at least the public manifestation of that collapse – to a Tuesday afternoon in the summer of 2001. At the close of the markets on August 14, Jeffrey Skilling who had served as Enron CEO since the previous February, unexpectedly announced his resignation. Chairman Kenneth Lay offered reassuring words: "The company is probably in the strongest and best shape it has ever been in."[42] Lay would assume the day-to-day leadership of Enron. The financial markets, however, were not reassured. The stock price, which had been as high as 90 a year earlier, now tumbled through the 30s.

Troubled by Skilling's sudden resignation and the investor scrutiny that the bombshell announcement was sure to attract, an Enron vice-president, Sherron Watkins, wrote a memo to Ken Lay expressing her concern that Enron would "implode in a wave of accounting scandals."[43] At the heart of Watkins' expressed concern was her belief that the many complex deals that Enron had constructed with off-balance sheet entities had obfuscated the true financial picture of the company. From 1999 to 2000, a period of explosive growth in Enron's stock price, CFO Andrew Fastow created hundreds of off-balance sheet partnerships. Known collectively as LJM2 and run by Fastow and fellow executive Michael Kopper, these partnerships could be used to hide debt and inflate revenues. But they rested on stock issuance, cross-collateralization and stock "trigger points." As Enron's stock price plunged, Enron faced losses in the hundreds of millions of dollars.[44]

The following week, Watkins met face-to-face with Lay. The CEO assured Watkins that he would investigate the matter, and he did in fact contact both the company's law firm as well as David B. Duncan, the senior partner of Enron's accounting firm, Arthur Andersen, in charge of the Enron account. The law firm conducted a month-long investigation and concluded there was nothing to be concerned about. Duncan pulled together an unofficial committee within Andersen to review past practices.[45]

On October 16, Enron released its third-quarter results, showing a loss of $1 billion in bad investments. And the bad news was just beginning. In a conference call with analysts the following day, Lay mentioned, in a fleeting way, an additional $1.2 billion in capital reduction stemming from unspecified problems arising from off-book partnerships run by CFO Andrew Fastow. This write-down resulted from the review conducted by Duncan, although none of these specifics was enunciated in the call. Lay was so offhanded in his handling of the announcement, in fact, that participants in the call were not sure until days later that this charge was *in addition* to the $1 billion loss announced in the quarterly report. "They were trying to sneak it by," recalled one participant.[46]

To calm investors, Lay removed Fastow as CFO, but the stock price took another hit on October 22 with an announcement by the Securities and Exchange Commission (SEC) that it had opened an investigation into certain accounting practices relating to the off-balance sheet partnerships. The stock fell to $21. On October 30, Moody's downgraded Enron's bonds to "junk" status, and the stock price plunged again. Enron employees who might have wanted to sell stock from their retirement package were prevented from doing so; the company was shifting plan administrators, and retirement accounts were temporarily frozen.

The news went from bad to worse. In the first week in November, with the stock price now in the single digits, Enron announced that it was reducing its earnings over the past four years by almost $600 million, due to the manner in which three "unconsolidated entities" had been accounted for in past financial statements (more fallout from Duncan's review of past practices) and warned that additional reductions might be forthcoming. Although Enron had borrowed $6 billion in the six weeks after the October announcement of third-quarter results, it still faced more than $31 billion in combined debt. With the stock price now below a dollar a share, with debt spiraling out of control and with no further access to capital markets, Enron filed for Chapter 11 bankruptcy on December 2, 2001.

Notes

1 This case has been written on the basis of published sources only. Consequently, the interpretation and perspectives presented in this case are not necessarily those of Enron Corporation or any of its employees.

2 See *Fortune*, Jan. 10, 2000, p. 88; Feb. 21, 2000, p. 110; Sept. 4, 2000, p. 146.

3 *The Economist.com*, June 1, 2000, p. 2; Laura Goldberg and Mary Flood, "The Rise of Ken Lay As Dramatic As His Fall," *HoustonChronicle.com*, Feb. 3, 2002, p. 1, John Schwartz, "As Enron Purged Its Ranks, Dissent Was Swept Away," *New York Times*, Feb. 3, 2002, p. C1.

4 Lay is quoted in *Fortune*, June 23, 1997, p. 87; and Kenneth L. Lay, "Coming Soon To Your Home and Business: The New Energy Majors," in G. William Dauphinais and Colin Price, eds., Straight From the CEO: The World's Top Business Leaders Reveal Ideas That Every Manager Can Use (New York: Simon & Schuster, 2000), p. 255. See also *New York Times*, March 27, 2002, p. A20; Kurt Eichenwald, "Audacious Climb to Success Ended in a Dizzying Plunge," *New York Times On the Web*, Jan. 13, 2002, p. 7; Greg Farrell and Chris Woodyard, "Three Powerful Men Forged Enron's Path," p. 2B.

5 Gruley and Smith, "Keys to Success Left Kenneth Lay Open to Disaster," p. A5.

6 Brian O'Reilly, "The Power Merchant," Fortune (April 2000), p. 154. Skilling is quoted in *USA Today*, Jan. 28, 2002, p. 3B and Gary Hamel, Leading the Revolution, (*Boston: Harvard Business School Press*, 2000), p. 221.

7 Kathleen M. Eisenhardt and Donald N. Sull, "Strategy As Simple Rules," *Harvard Business Review* (January 2001), p. 114.

8 *Economist.com*, Feb. 26, 1998, pp. 1–2; *Fortune*, April 17, 2000, p. 156; *Fortune.com*, March 5, 2001, p. 2.

9 Skilling is quoted in *The Industry Standard.com*, Aug. 14, 2001, p. 2.

10 The Enron executive is quoted in *Business Week Online*, Dec. 17, 2001, p. 1. Skilling is quoted in Bethany McLean, "Why Enron Went Bust," *Fortune.com*, Dec. 24, 2001, p. 2.

11 Koch, "Reinvent Now: 100 Leaders For the Next Millennium," p. 2. The analyst is quoted in *McLean*, "Why Enron Went Bust," p. 3. See also the *Economist.com*, Nov. 29, 2001, p. 2.

12 Quoted in Marie Brenner, "The Enron Wars," Vanity Fair, April 2002, p. 190 and John Schwartz, "As Enron Purged Its Ranks, Dissent Was Swept Away," *New York Times*, Feb. 3, 2002, p. C1.

13 Skilling is quoted in John Schwartz, "Darth Vader. Machiavelli. Skilling Set Intense Pace," *New York Times On the Web*, Feb. 7, 2002, pp. 2–3.

14 Farrell and Woodyard, "Three Powerful Men Forged Enron's Path," p. 3B; Thomas A. Stewart, "Taking Risk to the Marketplace," *Fortune.com*, March 6, 2000, p. 1; Schwartz, "As Enron Purged Its Ranks, Dissent Was Swept Away," p. C1.

15 Ken Lay is quoted in "Skilling Named Enron CEO," *FinancialTimes.com*, Dec. 14, 2000, p. 1. The banner change is reported in the *Economist.com*, June 28, 2001, p. 2.

16 Bethany McLean, "Enron's Power Crisis," *Fortune.com*, Sept. 17, 2001, p. 1; John Schwartz, "Darth Vader. Machiavelli. Skilling Set the Pace," *New York Times On the Web*, Feb. 7, 2002, p. 2.

17 Skilling and Olson quoted in Nicholas Stein, "Winning the War To Keep Top Talent," *Fortune.com*, May 29, 2000, p. 4. Pai quoted in *Hamel, Leading the Revolution*, p. 271.

18 Skilling is quoted in *Hamel, Leading the Revolution*, p. 216. McConnell is quoted in *Economist.com*, June 28, 2001, p. 4. On Enron Online, see also *Economist.com*, June 28, 2001,

p. 2 and Nicholas Stein, "The World's Most Admired Companies," *Fortune.com*, Oct. 2, 2000, p. 2.

19 *Economist.com*, June 1, 2000, p. 1; McLean, "Why Enron Went Bust," p. 2; *Washington Post*, Jan. 27, 2002, p. A1; "Enron's Aggressive Risk-Taking Culture That Eventually Led to Its Demise, National Public Radio's All Things Considered, Feb. 6, 2002.

20 Lay is quoted in *Fortune*, June 23, 1997, p. 87. Ron Lumbra of Russell Reynolds Associates is quoted in *Houston Chronicle*, Dec. 9, 2001, p. A1.

21 *Economist.com*, Feb. 26, 1998, p. 1; *Hamel, Leading the Revolution*, p. 213; Corey Kilgannon, "Coincidences From a Case 15 Years Old," *New York Times On the Web*, March 5, 2002, pp. 2–3.

22 Quoted in Andrew Inkpan, Enron and the Dabhol Power Company (American Graduate School of International Management/Thunderbird, 2002), p. 2.

23 Johnnie L. Roberts and Evan Thomas, "Enron's Dirty Laundry," *Newsweek*, March 11, 2002, p. 25.

24 *New York Times*, March 7, 2002, p. C7. Mark is quoted in V. Kasturi and Krishna G. Palepu, Enron Development Corporation: The Dabhol Power Project in Maharashtra, India (A). (Boston: Harvard Business School Publishing, 1997), p. 1. The Enron executive is quoted in Inkpen, Enron and the Dabhol Power Company, p. 2.

25 Laura Goldberg and Tom Fowler, "The Myth of Enron," *Houston Chronicle.com*, Jan. 26, 2002, p. 2; *New York Times*, March 9, 2002, p. B3.

26 Skilling is quoted in Thomas A. Stewart, "Taking Risk to the Marketplace," *Fortune.com*, March 6, 2000, p. 1; Olson is quoted in Nicholas Stein, "Winning the War To Keep Talent," *Fortune.com*, May 29, 2000, p. 2.

27 Stewart, "Taking Risk to the Marketplace," p. 2.

28 Matthew Boyle, "Performance Reviews: Perilous Curves Ahead," *Fortune.com*, May 28, 2001, p. 1.

29 Stein, "Winning the War To Keep Talent," p. 4; *Houston Chronicle*, Dec. 9, 2001, p. A1; Joshua Chaffin and Stephen Fidler, "The Enron Collapse," *Financial Times*, April 9, 2002, p. 30.

30 Brenner, "The Enron Wars," p. 196; Schwartz, "As Enron Purged Its Ranks, Dissent Was Swept Away," p. C1; Neela Banerjee, "At Enron, Lavish Excess Often Came Before Success," *New York Times*, Feb. 26, 2002, p. C1. Lay is quoted in *Brenner*, "The Enron Wars," p. 195.

31 The executive is quoted in Hamel, Leading the Revolution, p. 271; *Houston Chronicle*, Dec. 9, 2001, p. A1. Information on Fastow's bonuses as documented by company records, is reported in Kurt Eichenwald, "Enron Paid Huge Bonuses in '01; Experts See a Motive for Cheating," *New York Times on the Web*, March 1, 2002, p. 2. On John Arnold's bonus, see David Barboza, "Enron Trader Had a Year to Boast of, Even If . . ." *New York Times*, July 9, 2002, p. C1.

32 If stock options were counted as an expense, profitability of many large corporations would be reduced substantially. A study by the Federal Reserve estimated that between 1995 and 2000, the average earnings growth rate for S&P 500 companies would have been reduced by 25 percent if stock options had been reported as expenses. When the option is exercised, the issuing company declares a tax deduction based on the difference between the option price and the exercise price. The exercise of stock options by all Enron executives in 2000 accounted for a $390 million tax break for the company.

33 Skilling is quoted in "Transcript of Senate Commerce Committee Hearing on Enron," p. 41. On his 2000 stock option income, see "Stock Option Excess," *New York Times*, March 31, 2002, Section 4, p. 8.

34 All quotes are from the *Houston Chronicle*, Dec. 9, 2001, p. A1.

35 Lay is quoted in *The Economist.com*, June 1, 2000, p. 2.

36 *Hamel, Leading the Revolution*, p. 214.

37 Gruley and Smith, "Keys to Success Left Kenneth Lay Open to Disaster," p. A5.

38   Bethany McLean, "Is Enron Overpriced?" *Fortune.com*, March 5, 2001, p. 1.

39   Quoted in *Houston Chronicle*, Dec. 9, 2001, p. A1.

40   Quotes from Richard A. Oppel, Jr., "The Man Who Paid the Price For Sizing Up Enron," *New York Times*, March 27, 2002, pp. C1, C4.

41   "Documents Show Company's Partner Lost Enron Work after Criticizing Energy Firm," *Boston Globe*, April 3, C2.

42   "Enron CEO Jeffrey Skilling Unexpectedly Resigns," *FinancialTimes.com*, Aug. 14, 2001, p. 1.

43   The full text of this memo is provided in *Fortune.com*, Jan. 16, 2001, pp. 1–6.

44   In August 2002 Michael Kopper pleased guilty to charges of conspiring to commit fraud and money laundering in connection to these partnerships. Federal investigators made clear that the Kopper plea bargain was only the beginning in the prosecution of other Enron executives.

45   It is this committee that, on October 23 – a day after the S.E.C. announced that they had opened an investigation into "certain related party transactions" – commenced the destruction of thousands of Enron-related documents. That destruction led, eight months later, to the conviction of Andersen on federal charges of obstruction of justice.

46   "Analysts Vent Anger at 'Hidden' Enron Charge," *FinancialTimes.com*, Oct. 18, 2001, p. 1.

CASE **22**

Facing a Crisis: Lars Kruse Thomsen Starts his New Job (A)

Joseph J. DiStefano and Colleen Lief

As he bounded up the stairs to his new office, Lars Kruse Thomsen was under no illusions about the challenges that lay ahead of him. He knew from an earlier fact-finding trip and the parent company's admonition to preserve market share at all costs that Poland was House of Prince's number one problem. Yet, at this moment, the first day of his new job as director of sales and marketing, he felt ecstatic. The international assignment he had worked so hard to obtain was now his. As he pushed back the door, he could barely believe his eyes. Instead of a well-appointed executive office, Thomsen found only a desk; otherwise nothing, not even basic office equipment or supplies. There was no computer, telephone, paper or pencils. He was both surprised and disappointed.

The empty office embodied all the problems he had heard existed in Warsaw: turf battles reigned, problems were ignored, no one took responsibility for anything outside of their own little fiefdom. The erratic, authoritarian business model that had characterized the company for so many years left no one feeling responsible. So no one had acted to prepare Thomsen's office. Thomsen vowed to himself:

> One thing is clear – I will need to shake the foundation of how this place works, or rather, doesn't work! In the future, new employees will be welcomed with flowers and business cards. A new era of performance and accountability is about to take hold. Things are going to change.

Research Associate Colleen Lief prepared this case under the supervision of Professor Joseph J. DiStefano as a basis for class discussion rather than to illustrate either effective or ineffective handling of a business situation.

Note: Some names have been disguised.

HOUSE OF PRINCE BACKGROUND

House of Prince – Denmark

House of Prince A/S (HoP) manufactured and sold a variety of tobacco products and was a 100% subsidiary of Skandinavisk Tobakskompagni A/S (ST), both located near Copenhagen, Denmark. In 1961 three established Danish tobacco companies, including one founded in 1750, had come together to form ST. By the 21st century ST consisted of six group companies engaged in tobacco, retailing and trading activities in Norway, the Netherlands and Denmark. The House of Prince subsidiary accounted for 37% of ST's sales and included the flagship international cigarette brand, Prince. HoP accounted for 95% of cigarette sales in Denmark.

In addition to its home market, HoP operated wholly owned subsidiaries in Sweden, Latvia, Estonia, Lithuania, Russia and the Czech Republic. In Poland the organizational pattern was a little different – HoP held only a 51% stake in House of Prince Poland SA (HoP-Poland). HoP embarked on an international expansion strategy in the early 1990s to open promising new markets close to home.

House of Prince – Poland

HoP's foray into the newly emerging Polish market began in 1992 when it joined the Polish government in a 50/50 joint venture to acquire a formerly state-owned tobacco company in Łódź. Like most multinationals entering Poland at this time, HoP led with its top brand – Prince. Although this strategy was not successful, HoP still believed in the potential of the Polish market. In 1995, after withdrawing from the joint venture, it bought 51% of Alliance Cigarette Factory in Krakow, which had 3% to 4% market share and 400 employees, and set out to build a large national player. Two Polish investors owned the remaining 49%. One of the investors, Tadeusz Makowski, had started Alliance from nothing and built it solely on the strength of his energy and personality. After the HoP acquisition Makowski served as the managing director (MD) of HoP-Poland. A management board and a supervisory board oversaw the running of the company. The heads of production, sales/marketing, and finance/administration sat on the management board with Makowski. The supervisory board consisted of the two Polish shareholders and three senior managers from HoP in Denmark. Although the Danish owners had a majority ownership position and 60% of the supervisory board seats, the original purchase agreement stipulated that motions could only be approved by a minimum 67% margin. Therefore, the minority shareholders could block any proposal they found unacceptable.

With this second attempt at capturing the Polish market, HoP ceded the reins of the company to Makowski, who had enjoyed sparkling success thus far. HoP now had established local products in its portfolio to support its Prince brand. Developing local brands that catered to the tastes of Polish smokers carved out a market niche for the company.

EXHIBIT 1   Polish Cigarette Industry Sales (billions of pieces)

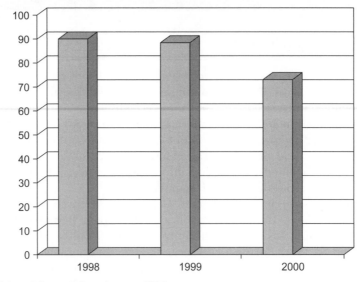

Source: HoP Internal Presentation, January 2002.

BUILDING MARKET SHARE AND GROWING PROFITS: 1995–2000

Operating environment

Poland was probably the most vibrant marketplace for tobacco products in Eastern Europe. Its per capita consumption of 2,500 cigarettes per year,[1] far outstripped that of any other country in the region. Since privatization, cigarette production in Poland had been on an upward trend, culminating in a high of 90.2 billion pieces in 1998. Each successive year brought lower (official)[2] sales levels, which hit 73.1 billion pieces in 2000 (see Exhibit 1 for details).

All the major global tobacco companies were present in Poland: Philip Morris (US), Reemtsma (Germany, and recently purchased by Imperial Tobacco), British American Tobacco (UK), Altadis (France), HoP and Japan Tobacco.[3] The country was unusual among emerging markets in that 80% of cigarette sales were of domestic brands. This phenomenon surprised the global players, which saw Poland as another country ripe for conversion to their established brands and did not consider the local brands to be competition for their superior products and marketing techniques. Poles, however, preferred brands with some local connection or that recalled a more prosperous time in their history. They also demanded value for money. The international producers ultimately responded by developing many locally produced brands targeted specifically at the Polish market. So although 80% of consumption was of local brands, these were dominated by global players.

Market Share by Competitor: 2000[4]

Philip Morris (PM)	33%
Reemtsma	20%
British American Tobacco (BAT)	15%
HoP-Poland	13%
Altadis	11%
Others	8%
Total	**100%**

Excise taxes on tobacco products in Poland had risen dramatically since 1995. They were a significant revenue source for the Polish government, accounting for 6%[5] of the federal budget in the late 1990s. Taxes on the most popular segment rose 200% per 1,000 cigarettes between 1995 and 2000 (from Z1 24 to Z1 72). The steep rise in excise taxes, along with a revamp of the tax system, was also part of a coordinated effort to prepare Poland for European Union (EU) membership in 2005. The dramatic increase in taxes contributed to significantly raising the cost of cigarettes to consumers and to shifting industry dynamics.[6] The new excise tax structure narrowed the band between different product segments and generally increased the price of cigarettes in Poland – by an average of 28.6% from 1996 to 2001.

Brand and product strategies

Four main product segments were found in the Polish market as of 2000.[7]

Segment	Market share	Top sellers
70 mm International:	54%	Fajrant (PM), Mocne (Reemtsma), Fox (Altadis)
Top Tier	19%	Marlboro (PM)
Lower End		L&M (PM), West (Reemtsma)
King Size (Domestic)	22%	Sobieski (BAT), Mars (Reemtsma), Cristal (HoP)
Non-filtered	5%	Various local players
Total	**100%**	

The international brands were expensive and the non-filtered segment constituted a fraction of the market, so much of the competition among the titans lay in the short (70mm) and king size domestic segments. The 70mm segment was important for HoP, in particular, as it represented more than half of company sales and also formed the centerpiece of Makowski's strategy for HoP-Poland from 1996 to 2000. When Makowski first joined forces with HoP, the focus had been on marketing HoP's international brand, Prince. But significant sales never materialized for Prince, and Makowski decided to follow his instinct of pursuing a strategy diametrically opposed to that of every other major tobacco company. Makowski's experience told him that Polish smokers wanted good quality cigarettes at low prices and that high volumes would be his reward. Prices could be raised incrementally over time and escape the notice of the devoted consumer. Greater market share meant greater leverage with wholesalers, who were so critical to overall success.

Makowski believed a good cigarette at a good price would be a "self-seller" and should be launched as a 70mm product to capture the bulk of the domestic market. He did not believe in building brands or the market research behind them. In Makowski's world, it was HoP's job to design the best product for the least money and toss it into the market-place. Consumers would decide the winners and losers. Variants and brand extensions would be developed from the winners, the losers would be withdrawn. But in practice they never were. Alexander Telje, business development manager for HoP-Poland, remembered, "The company was good at bringing kids into the world, but bad at bring-ing them up!"

Telje was unaccustomed to this casual view of marketing. In all his years of working at Coca-Cola in Eastern Europe before he joined HoP, he had never witnessed such a commodity orientation to selling fast-paced consumer goods. This unfocused approach resulted in HoP offering as many as 55 different brand variations. Since ideas were developed on Makowski's whim, new products were conceived and set in motion in a matter of hours or days. The flexibility and breadth of productive capacity required were significant and, as volumes grew sharply between 1995 and 1999, necessitated huge out-lays for plant and equipment.

Cigarettes in Poland were distributed through three channels: wholesale, retail and key accounts (grocery stores and gas stations/convenience stores). Most product moved to the marketplace through wholesalers. Although there were over 1,000 wholesale firms in HoP-Poland's franchise, 35 accounted for 70% of sales through this channel. The company's retail channel consisted of 50,000 different touch points (180,000 for the industry as a whole). However, at this time, HoP ignored key accounts as a distribution channel, even though they were gaining stature with its competitors largely due to the advertising ban enacted in 1999. Key accounts constituted 5% of industry revenue in 1999. The ban limited the forum for product promotion and new product introduction, and meant that retail outlets would be the primary vehicles for interacting with the public in the future. Hypermarkets and gas station/convenience stores were new to the Polish market and were gaining popularity. In the past, cigarettes had been more expensive at more convenient venues such as these. However, following the passing of a law in 2000 which decreed that the price of cigarettes must be printed on the package, these outlets became ever more popular as a convenient and cost-effective source of cigarettes for consumers.

Makowski believed that his overarching strategy of building market share was the only way to level the playing field with wholesalers and would ultimately enrich them both. Makowski's approach to his constituents worked. HoP's market share had risen to 14% by 1999. The MD's autocratic and instinctive approach allowed HoP-Poland to respond quickly to nuances in the market, and its pricing strategy appealed to cost-conscious consumers. HoP's success with Makowski's strategy led to a high degree of confidence inside the firm. One of the managers noted that it bordered on arrogance. The success strongly reinforced the MD's belief that building market share through lower priced, quality products was the key to market success.

The rise in market share thrilled the Danish owners. Having 95% of the market in Denmark, they were accustomed to being number one and, therefore, operated in a mainly defensive manner. Stability was HoP's chief concern domestically. But growth was constrained by a drop in the number of Danish smokers, a declining population and an already dominant position at home. The engine of future expansion had to be sought elsewhere. The former Soviet economies emerging from years of centralized planning offered a large base of consumers and a generally entrepreneurial heritage. The vagaries of the dynamic and rapid evolution of the Polish market ran contrary to decades of corporate history. Experience told them to rely on a limited portfolio of strong brands. Therefore, when Makowski failed to produce a strong brand identity in Poland, they became concerned over the weakness of the product family and by the fact that the company's low price strategy was beginning to show signs of driving down overall price levels. But, in view of his success, they decided to leave him alone for the time being.

ORGANIZATIONAL DESIGN: 1998–2000

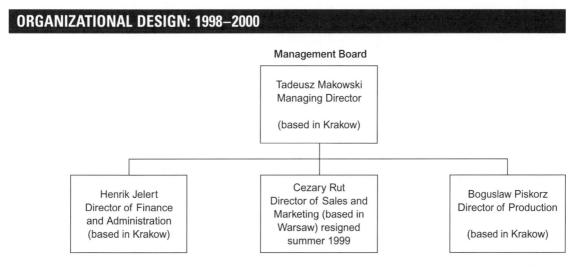

Between 1998 and 2000 the MD, supported by three other directors – Henrik Jelert (finance and administration), Boguslaw Piskorz (production) and Cezary Rut (sales and marketing) – spearheaded day-to-day operations. Jelert, a Dane who spoke fluent Polish, had been on the management board of the company since the beginning and aspired to a general management position. The total number of employees grew from 623 in 1998 to 1,072 in 2000. Rut had a staff of 305 and 5 direct reports (see Exhibit 2 for the sales and marketing organization chart).

Systems

Since, practically speaking, HoP-Poland was being run by one individual who operated by intuition, generating accurate customer and market data was neglected. Decisions were made on an ad hoc basis and information was not viewed as vital to the mission of the organization. All the MD needed to know, he had in his head. So, basic systems of financial reporting and human resource management were limited. Wide dissemination of financial data was prohibited, and managers were usually unaware of how their own

EXHIBIT 2   Sales and Marketing Department, February 2001

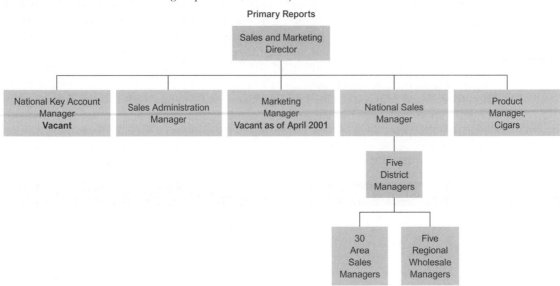

Source: Company information.

divisions performed. The little information that functional heads received was jealously guarded as a source of power or self-protection.

People

Some employees at HoP-Poland lacked a feeling of ownership and accountability. Their Communist past had left a legacy of controlled, structured and risk averse thought. Makowsi's authoritarian, non-participative management style only further frustrated their entrepreneurial tendencies. An act as simple as walking down the hall could spell trouble. Makowski was known to call people into a conference room to get their opinion on whatever happened to be the topic of the hour. Staff would be provoked for their opinion on issues far outside of their field of knowledge, and then would frequently be derided or fired for giving the wrong answer. In this high unemployment era, no one could afford the luxury of innovation or problem solving. Everyone "adapted to the king's philosophy," according to Telje. Jelert noted that many simply chose to "hide" when Makowski was around. Another described the MD as "a neurotic demagogue."

Given Makowski's distrust of brand building, research and even his own employees, neither HoP's name recognition nor the sales and marketing staff were developed. The marketing budget was often expropriated to pay for the latest wholesale discount or loyalty program. The lack of a brand orientation and the fact that Makowski handled important wholesaler relationships personally caused HoP-Poland to seek out the least skilled, least expensive sales force it could find. Product knowledge, relationship building and advanced sales techniques were not valued. Even the most basic sales training was seen as unnecessary. The sales staff were not assigned personal sales goals, nor did they receive formal appraisals, since they essentially functioned as shelf stockers. Given the dearth of accurate sales and market data, the sales force could not measure or improve its performance. In many newly privatized companies in Poland, pay for performance systems formed the basis of sales force compensation plans, but this was not the case at HoP-Poland where the bonus plan became another manifestation of the MD's distrust. Jelert remembered:

> Often the MD would promise that if you did "X," you would get a "Y" bonus. Then, just before the payout was due, he would say "Sorry!" You couldn't trust anything he said. He said you couldn't trust the numbers, so why pay for them!

The lack of training, goals and incentives for the sales force, and the absence of a thoughtful marketing plan, left the company vulnerable to the demands of a dynamic market and to attacks from competitors.

Policy

As market share began to fall in 1999–2000, wholesalers were becoming increasingly sophisticated and were beginning to adjust to changing market conditions. In theory, HoP-Poland's policy was to maintain the same terms for all wholesalers regardless of size. But in reality, Makowski did one-off deals, trying to placate important wholesalers with larger credit limits and generous payment terms. The gap between policy and practice alienated the wholesalers who were not so favored.

To reduce the heavy reliance on the wholesale market, Makowski targeted the retail sales network, planning to visit every retail outlet in the country on a regular basis. Such an effort required a significant expansion of sales staff. So he instructed the newly formed human resources group, under the direction of Jelert, to hire the cheapest workers it could find and turn them into HoP salespeople.

Jelert watched these negative events unfold in 2000 and saw the possibility of his becoming Makowski's successor. He sensed that the Danish owners were becoming increasingly annoyed at the way Makowski was squandering the market share he had built up over the last five years, from 3% in 1995 to 14% in 1999. Everyone knew the company was now losing ground. Share was down to 13% and the company was launching too many brands to form an identity with the public. Grom and Grot had been successfully introduced in the 70mm segment in 1998 and now were feeling the effects of 1999 price increases. King size Dark suffered a similar fate. Further, news of the MD's increasingly erratic behavior continued to make its way to Copenhagen. The supervisory board members had personally witnessed Makowski propose a budget in his role as MD, and then vote against it in his role as shareholder! Jelert did not like Makowski, nor did he approve of the way he operated. Jelert recalled:

> He did little to run the company. He left operating the company to me and the VP of production. He was only interested in product development and distribution through more sales staff and hands-on managing the day-to-day price policy.

EXHIBIT 3   Market Share by Segment

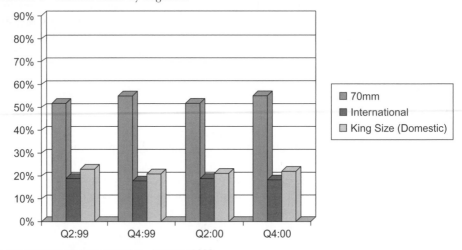

Source: HoP internal presentation, January 2002.

Jelert thought that there was an opportunity to become MD, especially since he had already been operating beyond the finance and accounting functions for several years.

THE COMPETITION RETALIATES

Philip Morris breaks with its past

The competitive landscape became more and more crowded in the lower price categories, led by HoP's pacesetting behavior in the 70mm and king size segments (refer to Exhibit 3). The industry was stuck in an unprofitable and overcrowded position, with no visible way out. Consumers' preference for 70mm local brands was being met at prices so low that tobacco companies could barely afford to sell them. So in late 1999 and early 2000, HoP-Poland instituted a series of rapid and substantial price increases in its most popular brands, Grom and Grot in the 70mm segment and Dark in the king size.

This situation presented Philip Morris with the opportunity to establish its dominance in the whole Eastern European market. All of the major tobacco companies were active in Poland and it appeared that Philip Morris began to view the country as "battleground Europe." The industry skirmishes taking place across the region could be determined in one conclusive battle. The narrowing range of cigarette prices instigated by the change in the excise tax system also seemed to benefit Philip Morris. As the gap between its international brands – Marlboro at the top end and L&M at the low end – and domestic products became smaller, consumers would be inclined to try, and ultimately prefer, them to the local 70mm and king size varieties. Since the price differential would be negligible in a future scenario of a higher, narrower band of national cigarette prices, Philip Morris could effectively internationalize the Polish market – something it had failed to do thus far. Greater market share would also give the company muscle in its dealings with wholesalers.

The price war starts: June 2000

The opening salvo in the price war sounded when Philip Morris launched 70mm Fajrant[8] as a direct challenge to HoP-Poland's Grom and Grot brands. HoP-Poland had led the market toward low price competition but Philip Morris' actions would keep it there. Fajrant was launched at a price below existing 70mm levels, forcing competitors to match the low price or suffer the consequences. The pricing and tax environment provided a mechanism for strategically isolating the Marlboro brand. Philip Morris could risk interim losses knowing that, after the dust settled, Marlboro's position would be enhanced through a flight to quality. Marlboro's global cachet was unparalleled and provided an opportunity to consolidate Philip Morris' regional position through lower prices in Poland. No one thought, though, that the price war could last. It was too damaging to continue for long.

THE SITUATION DETERIORATES: JUNE 2000–SEPTEMBER 2000

HoP-Poland hesitated in following Philip Morris in lowering prices in June 2000 (refer to Exhibit 4 for price changes by segments). That delay cost HoP dearly in lost market share. By the time the company reacted, Fajrant was leading the pack. The thinking behind the price war struck right at the heart of HoP-Poland's approach to the business. Its position as low-price leader no longer existed, so its strategy was now floundering. With no brand recognition and no capable marketing force, HoP-Poland was at the mercy of its competitors. Its market share fell rapidly from a high of 14% to 13%. Pricing among product segments continued to compress. Given the market dynamics and with no end

EXHIBIT 4   Average Price by Segment (zlotys per pack)

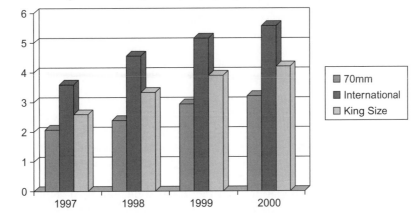

Source: HoP internal presentation, January 2002.

to the price war in sight, headquarters in Denmark began to get nervous. It was facing a precipitous decline in hard-won market share with no obvious way of limiting the fall. Net revenue was down 36% in the three months ending September 2000 from the same period the previous year. Profits, which were already modest, were dropping quickly (60% from September 1999 to September 2000).

The balance sheet showed the effects of both erratic marketing habits and the loss of market share. Inventory expanded 153% from FYE 6/99 to FYE 6/00 and fixed assets rose by 108% over the same period. The bank loans required to support higher inventory and fixed asset levels grew by 227% at FYE 6/00. Seasonal fluctuations and a 15% reduction in Q1:01 (9/00) inventory resulted in a 10% drop in bank loans in Q1:01 (9/00) but fixed assets increased slightly, by 2%, during the interim period.

Another factor was driving prices and profits down. In response to the jump in excise taxes – accounting for nearly 44%[9] of the average cost of a pack of cigarettes in 2000 – smuggling activities in Poland had increased dramatically. Against a backdrop of declining economic prosperity and an overall rise in cigarette prices, smuggling thrived. Jelert estimated that smuggling had reached 18% to 20% of the total market, and official cigarette consumption statistics confirmed a 17% drop from 1999 to 2000.

Only Philip Morris was thought to be making money in this environment. The cushion provided by Marlboro and a rumored favorable tax treatment allowed it to escape the losses prevalent in the rest of the industry. HoP-Poland found itself in dire straits. Copenhagen was forced to consider the degree of its commitment to Poland. In the end, the opportunities presented by 10 million[10] smokers convinced HoP to stay in the country. But it became clear that the current approach had, as Telje described, "completely bombed."

THE MANAGING DIRECTOR GOES

Millennium

The situation reached dramatic proportions over the summer of 2000. As in the past, HoP-Poland decided to introduce a new brand to find a way out of difficulties. Although Millennium was conceived as a king size novelty product leveraging the turn of the century excitement in the year 2000, Makowski invested a lot of money in package design and product positioning. The cost of the packaging alone would have required Millennium to be priced at the high end of the market, close to the international brands. Such a high price point for a HoP-Poland product ran contrary to everything Makowski believed about the market. The supervisory board was faced with the choice of launching Millennium at a high price that practically ensured failure, or launching it at a price so low the company would not even recover its costs. Neither prospect seemed appealing so the board decided to cut its losses and halt the launch of Millennium.

However, the supervisory board was unaware that Makowski had bypassed the purchasing department and already placed a huge packaging order. Makowski defied a direct decision by the board and launched Millennium at the low price he had originally envisioned. This was not the first time Makowski had taken matters into his own hands. In 1997 the supervisory board had voted against launching two brands over the Christmas holiday. While everyone was away on vacation, the MD had launched them anyway. This time his insubordination proved too much for the board, who removed him as MD in September 2000. But Makowski retained his role on the supervisory board, given his 24.5% ownership stake.

Vacancies

HoP-Poland now faced a real challenge, especially as key vacancies had gone unfilled – the key account manager and marketing manager positions were open, and the company had not had a sales and marketing director since Rut left one and a half years earlier. At that time, the clash between Danish and Polish approaches was manifested by the disagreement over whether to offer a menthol variant to the Prince brand in Poland. Poles in the sales force had advocated selling a menthol Prince cigarette to appeal to Polish tastes. But when the Danish management refused to consider this change, Rut had left the company. Now, with the MD gone a power vacuum existed. Rank and file employees and even managers were unaccustomed to taking responsibility for or controlling their own functional areas, much less pitching in to fill the void created by vacancies.

Despite the lack of accurate data, HoP managers in Copenhagen knew the problems engulfing its Polish operation. They may have been unaware of the depth of the crisis but it was evident that an immediate solution was required. Ideally they believed it was important to have a Pole as president, in order to maintain market knowledge and to deal with increasing health activism and EU membership issues. But in the short run some oversight by Copenhagen was necessary to protect the parent's investment. Leo Soerensen, senior vice president of the HoP Group and based in Copenhagen, became the new MD of HoP-Poland. But HoP-Poland faced a direct threat from the competition and the results of its business model. The viability of the enterprise was in question.

Soerensen was helped in this task by Telje, who had started as business development manager a couple of months earlier. In fact, Telje had originally been slated to leave his job with Coca-Cola in Eastern Europe and join HoP in September 2000, but had received an urgent call to start as soon as possible when the parent company realized the seriousness of the situation. Telje acted as a liaison between Copenhagen and Warsaw. However, since he was based in Denmark, the time he could spend in Poland amounted to only three or four days per week. Managing all Eastern European subsidiaries took up Soerensen's time and limited his presence in Poland to one day a week. No permanent leaders meant no decisions. Valuable opportunities were lost during this period.

Telje and Soerensen, with help from Jelert, who had a deeper knowledge of the organization and culture, set about trying to stop the bleeding in Poland. This was a tall order for two managers who were not a constant presence in the company. In November Telje presented management in Denmark with a plan that emphasized brand development, transformation of the sales force through training and the implementation of a bonus system. A revamped plan, including a structured training program for the sales force and, for the first time, basic standards for sales calls and performance, was then rolled out to employees. The plan also introduced a sweeping structural change to the organization. Wholesale and retail activities were merged and led by Jan Wisnewski. He began to feel the overwhelming responsibility that rested on his shoulders. He directed the entire company's sales efforts throughout Poland in an increasingly competitive environment and with intermittent management input.

Another critical issue to attack early was the undermining influence of what was known as the "KGB." Because Makowski did not trust anyone, especially the sales force, he had established a group to be his eyes and ears in the field. Jelert recalled:

> For him, field reps were like machines, except machines can't cheat you! Makowski had created a control department, but its real function was to do surreptitious security checks on the field sales force. Off the record, it was nicknamed KGB, as their methods seemed so similar. People lost their jobs based on their secret reports; it was really ugly. The first thing we did after Makowski left was to fire those four guys.

LARS KRUSE THOMSEN

Background experience

In many ways, Thomsen's background provided a foundation for the challenges that lay ahead. He was born in Denmark, but because his father was an officer in the merchant fleet, he spent his childhood traveling the world, including 10 nations in Africa, Singapore, the US, Argentina and many countries in Europe. After graduating with a marketing degree from business school in Denmark, Thomsen spent four years in marketing and brand management in Copenhagen, first at a newspaper group, then for Carlsberg A/S. There he actively sought an international assignment, which would take him out into the field. When an international posting did not materialize, Thomsen accepted a marketing manager position at HoP. For the next four years, Thomsen managed brand strategy and positioning for the company's flagship Prince brand in Copenhagen. His staff of two worked on analysis, research, advertising and design issues.

As one of HoP's promising young managers, Thomsen was offered the opportunity to go to IMD – International Institute for Management Development in Lausanne, Switzerland. Thomsen joined the MBA program at IMD in January 2000. By the time he graduated at the end of the year, he was fully conversant in the latest management approaches and practices, and HoP management offered him a choice between a start-up operation in another Eastern European country or taking on the sales and marketing director role in Warsaw. Thomsen visited Poland to try to measure the depth of the challenges there. Although they appeared to be substantial, the opportunity to make a highly visible impact proved irresistible. Poland accounted for a significant proportion of HoP's international production, and making a real difference there could be crucial to his career.

Expectations going in

When Thomsen started in February 2001, he entered a power vacuum. Although his greeting reflected the downside of having no one at the helm, Thomsen began to see the unexpected opportunities. He would be less hamstrung than most new managers and could have an immediate impact by filling vacant positions with individuals who embodied a spirit of competitiveness and professional competence. On his earlier visit to Warsaw, Thomsen had met Wisnewski, who held the pivotal role of national sales manager. Thomsen was not convinced that Wisnewski was equal to the formidable task that lay before them. There was talk, too, that Makowski had promised Wisnewski the board seat that was now Thomsen's. This tension set up an interesting dynamic, the outcome of which Thomsen could only speculate on.

From his initial briefing in Copenhagen, Thomsen knew what was expected of him: increase sales and prices, enhance the stature of brands in Poland and defend market share, which had dipped to 10%, at all costs. He knew loyal customers were hard to win the first time and nearly impossible to get back. With these exhortations in mind, Thomsen outlined the following goals for himself: maintain headquarters support and the CEO's ear, clearly define his role within the organization, create a strong sales and marketing team, revamp the sales force and build an effective and competent marketing department with the ability to develop brands.

Starting work

Within two weeks of his arrival in Poland, the difficulty of the task facing Thomsen had crystallized. He was attending his first management board meeting in Krakow at which the litany of problems besetting the company was reviewed. Wisnewski, although in charge of the company's sales efforts in all of Poland, suddenly sprang from his chair, as Thomsen recalled, and exclaimed, "I'm glad this is not my problem!" From then on, Thomsen knew he would be fighting this battle alone and could not rely on subordinates for help. He was not sure if the reasons were cultural differences or the many years of struggling to survive under erratic management, or both. Not even the senior managers reporting to Thomsen acknowledged problems or sought solutions. His staff generally seemed technically skilled, but they lacked other, intangible qualities. Language further complicated teamwork. Although English was the official language of HoP-Poland, miscommunication was rampant, as employees possessed varying levels of capability in the language and were often loathe to admit if they did not understand each other.

"I kept asking myself, What is the most important problem?" said Thomsen of those first days. In search of an answer, he posed this question to six senior managers. He was surprised and dismayed when he received six completely different answers. There was no agreement among the company's top officers on what most threatened its future. The divergence of responses reflected the silo mentality that had flourished, and indeed had been necessary for survival, under the old regime. But the more he discovered about how the company functioned, the more he realized that lack of commercial transparency deserved a large part of the blame. "How can managers have a global view of problems, if basic financial and performance information is kept secret?" he thought. He also discovered that the 3-D (Distribution, Display, Dominance) handheld computer information system that the sales force used reported remarkably similar sales results for the entire sales team.

With limited input from his staff, Thomsen quickly developed his own set of priorities. There were "fires breaking out all over. No matter what rock I looked under, I found scorpions."

The first month: Operation Brain Drain

He began to sense that another force was causing the reticence to share ideas and formulate solutions. The only way to protect one's livelihood under the previous MD had been to form alliances among peers. Although their attitude was hidden underneath a respectful and polite surface, Thomsen observed, "Middle management is sticking together against me, like I'm a passing fad." Jelert characterized the philosophy as follows:

> People in this country have learned from history . . . don't get too friendly too fast. And, Lars is a foreigner here on a three-year contract. The sales managers think, "We will be here after he leaves." So, if "Team up" or "Shut up" are the choices, the "Shut up" will win.

As if the internal problems were not serious enough, Thomsen was quickly dealt another blow. The price war that had started almost nine months earlier was escalating. In early 2001, HoP attempted once again to raise prices in the 70mm segment, but competitors did not follow suit. HoP was forced to retreat. Philip Morris then attacked another segment, taking aim at BAT's enormously popular Sobieski king size (domestic) brand. Philip Morris dropped the price of L&M, its low-end offering in the international segment, by about 11% to match the price of a pack of Sobieski. The divergence of price among the three main segments narrowed further. With this move, Marlboro continued to be the highest priced product in the market, but the rest of the field was huddled in a dangerously unprofitable cluster at the bottom. Marlboro was a category in itself and would stand defiantly against all challengers. So Philip Morris was free to target the 70mm and king size segments that provided strength to its competitors. If Philip Morris could destroy the long-term competition in these segments, it could establish its dominance in Poland and Eastern Europe. At this point, Thomsen thought:

> Super options I've got – choose between plague and cholera! If we maintain prices on our 70mm varieties, market share will quickly erode. If we lower prices, margins and profits, which are already suffering, will deteriorate further and perhaps drive the company out of business. What a great way to start a new job in a new country!

Against this backdrop, Thomsen launched "Operation Brain Drain" in February 2001. He gathered together his team for what he hoped would be a brainstorming, teambuilding and problem solving session. Through a series of PowerPoint slides outlining general ideas, Thomsen hoped to provoke some good ideas from the group and to gain their commitment to participate actively (refer to Exhibit 5 for a summary of his presentation). Thomsen tried to rally his managers behind the cause of saving the company and believed that through establishing teams with tight deadlines and high expectations, he could both get good ideas and build some cohesion across the silos of the past.

EXHIBIT 5   "Operation Brain Drain" Summary

- Attempted to convey sense of crisis, urgency: "Present situation is the most critical in the history of HoP-Poland"
- Short-term "quick and dirty" fixes sought
- Established work teams to attack retail and wholesale product portfolio problems
- Set rapid time line for idea generation
- Asked participants to "Be open-minded" and to "Break out of existing . . . ways and habits"

But neither the meeting nor the days that followed produced anything like what he had expected. Indeed, from what he could gather from his assistant, his attempt to involve his subordinates had exactly the opposite effect from what he had intended! Thomsen scared people with his questions and demands and expectation of speed. Reflecting on the failure of this approach and similar disappointments in his informal attempts to engage his subordinates, Thomsen concluded, "My typical soft Scandinavian orientation toward people and process has gotten me labeled as weak."

Jelert agreed with Thomsen, noting:

> Lars came in and was a wonderfully naive Scandinavian with a year of Swiss learning about how things are supposed to be! He got screwed backwards and forwards and within a few weeks his house got robbed! What a way to learn!

Bruised by these initial experiences in the first month, Thomsen was determined to get on top of the problems. Now he needed to review his situation and decide on priorities for dealing with both the internal and external problems.

Notes

1 Poland Tobacco and Products Annual Report 2000, Global Agricultural Information Network Report, USDA Foreign Agricultural Service, May 10, 2000.
2 Official sales figures are affected by the high degree of cigarette smuggling, which has increased as a result of high government taxes on cigarettes.
3 Japan Tobacco withdrew in late 2001.
4 House of Prince Internal Presentation, January 2002.
5 Poland Tobacco and Products Annual Report 2000, Global Agricultural Information Network Report, USDA Foreign Agricultural Service, May 10, 2000.
6 Poland Tobacco and Products Annual Report 2000, Global Agricultural Information Network Report, USDA Foreign Agricultural Service, May 10, 2000.
7 House of Prince Internal Presentation, January 2002.
8 *Fajrant* is the Polish word for the moment when the workday is over.
9 House of Prince Internal Presentation, January 2002.
10 Poland Tobacco and Products Annual Report 2000, Global Agricultural Information Network Report, USDA Foreign Agricultural Service, May 10, 2000.

CASE **23**

Dealing with Crisis: Lars Kruse Thomsen Moves to Solve Problems (B)

Joseph J. DiStefano and Colleen Lief

After one month of gaining a better understanding of the crisis he faced, and the reasons for it, Thomsen had presented "Operation Brain Drain" as a way to provoke his managers to action, to elicit from the team members contributions that he guessed lay dormant. But the response to his team-oriented call to action was inertia and fearfulness. He was shocked by the difference between his expectations and the reality in HoP-Poland. He sensed that the staff could competently carry out orders when given, but independent thought and innovation were not among their strengths. The inability to anticipate problems and create solutions extended to the most senior levels.

Shortly after Thomsen first arrived in Poland, he spent three days in Krakow. He asked for presentations from managers on their functional areas. He viewed this as a way of kick starting his own understanding of the situation, of "tapping into prepared knowledge to accelerate learning," so he could quickly get up to speed on the primary issues facing the company. As each manager entered the room, Thomsen remembered:

> Invariably they sat down, slapped their hands on the table and said, "So, what do you want to know?" No one had briefed them. No one had thought enough to wonder what I might want to know!

Research Associate Colleen Lief prepared this case under the supervision of Professor Joseph J. DiStefano as a basis for class discussion rather than to illustrate either effective or ineffective handling of a business situation.

Note: Some names have been disguised.

The impact of these experiences on Thomsen's thinking was not subtle. Although his staff could not agree on the most pressing matters facing HoP-Poland, its major organizational and market challenges became glaringly obvious to him through such disappointing encounters.

For its part, headquarters in Denmark gave general guidance on what it perceived as the most urgent problems. HoP management expected Thomsen to maintain hard-won market share at all costs. His mission was also to increase sales and profits and introduce new brands with higher contribution margins. Thomsen said:

> I guess they had the confidence that I would find problems myself and solve them. It was such a mess over here that no matter what I did, it would be progress.

FROM "LARS" TO "THOMSEN"

With little direction from either senior management in Denmark or subordinates, Thomsen began slicing his way through to the heart of the company's myriad problems and making organizational changes. He instituted "shock therapy" by refusing to accept problems or requests for decisions without a considered analysis and recommendation of a solution. Forcing a results orientation onto managers would be key to freeing Thomsen to address the many looming issues crowding his agenda. "Expectations had to be high and clear," reflected Thomsen, in order to communicate both the urgency and importance of changing the company's course. A forceful, take-charge taskmaster was rapidly replacing the thoughtful, consensus-building Scandinavian in him. For a time, "Lars" had to move over and let "Thomsen" take control. The difficult tasks that lay before him required a steely persistence and a tougher exterior. Thomsen felt this kind of macho behavior was expected in the culture, but it also had the unwelcome side effects of loneliness and isolation. Another unexpected feature of his new situation was the required shift from doing to facilitating others' success.

> I would look at something and think, "I could do that better myself. Instead of wasting time on this meeting, why don't I just do it?" But, if you do it, you lose out on the facilitation of 10 other projects, which at the end of the day means you are losing. You are also taking away the mandate and attacking the competence of the people who should have done it.
>
> The ability to delegate to and drive managers, as opposed to doing everything yourself was a frustration. For years, I had been thriving on producing, thinking and managing projects. But this was the biggest of all traps here. The tradeoff was that, the moment I went into managing a project myself, I would not be able to supervise and facilitate many other projects done by others. I would lose out every time I tried to micro-manage. And not getting into the details was a challenge because of my own set of values. I didn't feel productive in the traditional sense. This process of facilitating managers meant challenging things, being the one who's championing increased quality, asking the right questions, putting it into the context that they didn't consider. Finding this role took some time, I think, because I had the bad conscience of not producing anything.

The original utopian slide show was followed up with two more initiatives that contrasted sharply with the participative, invitational mode of "Operation Brain Drain." These activities focused on sales force performance ranking and a new organizational design for the sales and marketing department. Thomsen had quickly observed that although the HoP-Poland sales force outnumbered those of its peers, it was still fourth in the market. There were rumors of unreliability in the 3-D (Distribution, Display, Dominance) handheld computer information system the sales force used. And the educational and experience level of important front-line sales representatives was worryingly inadequate. So, a new day had dawned and the dirty work of retooling the entire HoP-Poland sales organization would begin. The first step of ranking the entire sales force, from the top down, began in March 2001 and in April a new organizational structure that would help the company focus on its mission was introduced. The emphasis was on efficiency, speed, responsibility, initiative and teamwork—concepts that were alien to the Polish operation.

PERSPECTIVES FROM COLLEAGUES

At the same time that Thomsen inspired fear and uncertainty in his subordinates, his colleagues were, in Telje's words, delighted to "see light at the end of the tunnel when Lars arrived." The other expatriates who had been at the company for a while were ready with advice. Jelert said:

> I told him he can't expect these people to be proactive. It just isn't a matter of the usual reluctance to act until you know your new boss. They have learned that whenever a new person comes in they sack everyone below. Their instinct is to duck down and avoid trouble. Their first reaction is to try to look like they are performing. So, not a lot of creative feedback or information or ideas are likely.

Most thought the timing for change was right. Thomsen could have done nothing to reinvent the company if the former MD were still at the helm. In fact, the power vacuum and vacancies that existed actually helped Thomsen. He needed to introduce change agents into the mix right away, and the marketing manager and key account manager vacancies provided the perfect opportunity. Jelert said:

> The vacancies above and below him meant that Lars needed to make decisions himself . . . that actually helped him, though it might not have felt that way at the time.

In the end Thomsen's direct reports, too, sensed the sea changes in the company's situation and in the industry that now threatened to engulf them. The former era had passed and no one could deny that the company was in real trouble. Most managers ultimately accepted that change was inevitable and necessary and stood ready to implement the severe measures that would be required.

WHAT TO DO NOW?

Thomsen had a big-picture idea of how the sales organization should work, but few specific personnel changes in mind. However, introducing key change agents who could, as Thomsen said, "act as facilitators, not generals" would be pivotal to success and to diluting the existing organizational culture. Thomsen examined his department from the top down and bottom up and knew he had his work cut out for him.

Thomsen saw four areas that needed to be addressed right away, if the company was to survive the price war: 1) development of a market support (intelligence) department, 2) improvement in sales force efficiency, 3) adequate training of sales representatives, and 4) implementation of a brand-building program. The market intelligence function was intended to challenge the status quo through the use of facts and data. The free flow of accurate data was essential to tracking, measuring, reporting and rewarding higher levels of performance. Training and equipping the sales force for excellence and efficiency were essential in this new environment where only strong brands survived. The "push strategy" espoused by the former regime was no longer viable, and the sophistication and independence of the consumer could no longer be ignored.

Regular meetings between Thomsen and his department heads became common and were the primary weapon against the pervasive silo mentality. The pace of the work accelerated in concert with the urgency of the task facing HoP-Poland. This was not the time for subtle change. Dramatic solutions that could be quickly deployed were critical. Increasingly, management of trade channels was seen as a key area for improved performance due to the limitations imposed by the advertising ban enacted in 1999. As Torben Svendsen, head of the company's market support department, put it:

> The only option for reaching consumers was in-store communication. We needed a quick, unique message for this context.

NEW PRESIDENT: JUNE 2001

Despite the pressure caused by Soerensen's time constraints since November 2000, HoP-Poland took special care to find the right person for the MD role. Neither political considerations nor nepotism clouded the company's view. HoP-Poland retained a headhunter and in June 2001, Jaroslaw Szlendak assumed the post of MD. His background in distribution, wholesaling and sales, first at his own company and then at Kimberly-Clark and an investment fund, provided a solid foundation for this new challenge.

Although Szlendak was trained as a physicist under the old educational system, he soon applied his intellect to business. In 1991 he started a distribution company in Lublin with some friends with $20,000 in capital. He honed his skills as sales and marketing director and head of supplier strategy. When the company was ultimately sold, sales and staff had grown tremendously. Szlendak then moved to Warsaw and assumed the position of sales director at Kimberly-Clark. Soon, however, his interest in having a stronger academic base for managing could no longer be denied. He earned a masters degree at the University of Warsaw and an MBA from the Warsaw School of Economics/ University of Minnesota. His last challenge before joining HoP-Poland was turning around companies purchased by an investment fund. In this work, he gained experience in developing export markets and product lines and restoring troubled companies to health.

His expertise in turnaround situations would be put to the test right away, as the company faced serious and urgent difficulties on a variety of fronts. His many years of experience in the trenches of sales and distribution organizations quickly alerted him to irregularities and inefficiencies at the company. Szlendak not only uncovered a relaxed approach to work but also serious attempts to defraud the company. As Thomsen remembered:

> Jaroslaw knows all the dirty tricks. With his arrival, I no longer felt alone.

For his part, Szlendak was shocked at what he found at HoP-Poland. Based on his interview in Denmark, he formed one picture of the Polish operation in his mind. But what he discovered was radically different and much more dire. He found:

> Very limited communication and coordination between the departments, a partition of the company through silos, a lingering loyalty to the former managing director, a staff which still didn't feel safe to express ideas, and sales managers who were being manipulated by their employees. They tried to pit Polish against Danish, Krakow against Warsaw. People said they were open to change but they were actually afraid of it.

Although Thomsen and Szlendak were very different personalities, they shared a passion for many of the same things: dramatic action, quick responses to threatening circumstances, building a team of capable managers – and saving the company. Their complementary approaches to shaking up the company worked well. In addition to his role as primary interface with Denmark, Szlendak led the rationalization effort in the rest of the company. Thomsen concentrated on the sales organization, sparring with Szlendak, who from previous experience had a very well developed sense of "organizational caveats."

Having rapidly uncovered incompetence in the crucial purchasing department, Szlendak replaced the purchasing manager and, thereby, assumed much of the blame for the "bloodbath" which ensued. Szlendak reduced the non-sales infrastructure costs of HoP-Poland by 10% over the next few months. Thomsen believed he had found a kindred spirit in his colleague, as now he was the one being pushed for more effectual, decisive action by Szlendak. When Thomsen proposed a plan for reducing costs or increasing sales, Szlendak would ask why it could not be done sooner, better, more dramatically. An era of radical change, which might just save the company, had now arrived at HoP-Poland. Thomsen and Szlendak worked together on the *coup de grâce*. Through a major round of lay-offs, a new sales organization would be carved out by July 2001 (see Exhibit 1). An intelligent restaffing of the sales force could lead the company forward and help it to emerge from the price war victorious.

ACCURATE, RELEVANT INFORMATION: PREREQUISITE FOR CHANGE

In recognition of the importance of quality information, a crucial first step in the reorganization process was the establishment of the market support department headed by Svendsen. He had arrived in Poland in 1999 and had been able to stay out of Makowski's line of fire in his position as Prince brand manager. Once Makowski had made his exit, Svendsen assumed a more prominent role in helping determine how to get the company out of its morass. He became the brand manager for the highly successful Cristal menthol product and worked with Telje and Soerensen in rolling out the revamp plan. Now that Thomsen had arrived, there was a quorum of like-minded professionals dedicated to saving the company.

EXHIBIT 1   Sales and Marketing Department (July 2001)

Source: Company information.

Thomsen quickly recognized the necessity of generating accurate, up-to-the-minute data and sharing it with those responsible for the numbers – everyone. But the chief of this new effort needed to be someone beyond reproach, accepted by the majority of employees and well versed in the company's finances. Thomsen decided Svendsen was the man for the job:

I knew I needed to give him enough stripes to be the chief whip of the organization.

Svendsen's mandate was to drive the implementation of a performance culture through the development of standards and metrics. The corporate culture worked against him initially. But without a reliable, trusted source of sales and market information, HoP-Poland could not institute sales goals, performance measurement, appraisals, relevant training or a bonus system.

PAY FOR PERFORMANCE

Svendsen led the effort to institutionalize free and open data sharing throughout all layers of the organization. However, the primary source of information at HoP-Poland remained the 3-D system. The quality of the information from the handheld computer devices used by sales representatives had to be reliable and trustworthy. Despite worries about the "KGB" history associated with the past, Thomsen, Szlendak and Svendsen strongly believed that a control function was the only way to ensure the validity and accuracy of the data that formed the basis for performance standards, targets and the bonus system. Everything hinged on transparency and the perception of fairness.

The reinstatement of a control mechanism immediately caused the sales force to panic and envision a reincarnation of the "KGB." But, ultimately, the new control unit came to be accepted as an impartial, normal component of a professional sales operation. This was the result of a deliberate combination of coaching and control on transparent terms. In other words, the field control added value to the representatives' performance and was perceived as doing so. Once the quality of the data was ensured, other necessary systems were built on this foundation. Regular evaluations of performance were supported by a training plan designed to raise performance steadily higher. Once programs for measurement and goal setting had been established, a real, quantifiable bonus plan was next on the drawing board. Although the November 2000 plan had introduced a 20% performance bonus, the sales force still relied primarily on salary. Management pushed for implementation of a system offering even greater rewards for excellence. Ultimately, employees could earn 40% of their salary as a performance bonus.

SUMMER 2001 REORGANIZATIONS

In July 2001 the company launched a massive reorganization that removed a significant number of people from HoP-Poland's employment rolls. The five district managers who reported to Thomsen were instructed to compile a list of those recommended for lay-off. Jelert asked his human resource (HR) staff to develop an independent, objective view of where cuts should take place, to ensure that the most qualified, motivated people were retained.

In two of the five districts, no material differences were found between the HR and managers' lists. The lay-off lists compiled by the other three managers, however, were filled with people who lay outside of their sphere of influence and were either considered enemies or irrelevant to maintaining their existing power structure.

In light of the company's contracting market share and generally lower sales levels, Thomsen intuitively believed that the sales staff and, therefore, the sales management team were too large and unwieldy for current market realities. Furthermore, the unification of the retail and wholesale businesses that Telje and Soerensen had instituted in fall 2000 was not working. Given the dramatically different business conditions, players and requisite strategies in the two segments, Thomsen sought to separate the retail and wholesale functions and restructure the sales organization with the purpose of getting the focus back on wholesale and increasing the efficiency of the field force. These hard facts dictated that two district managers needed to go, along with 60 to 70 sales representatives in the summer of 2001. The goal was to have a fully functioning sales force by December 2001. The net effect of rationalizing and hiring reduced the total number of employees in the sales and marketing department from 305 to 230.

The new field force manager

One of the old guard, though, appeared amenable to change and had begun to see the need for a reasoned response to the forces threatening the company's future. Pawel Wichur was promoted from district manager to field force manager in charge of a staff of 175 in Thomsen's new leaner sales organization. This position represented the culmination of nine years of experience on the front lines with the company which had been his only employer.

In 1993 Wichur had answered a newspaper advertisement seeking sales representatives for HoP-Poland's predecessor company. He remembered the Prince brand from visits to Sweden. Wichur was hired and began work as the only retail HoP-Poland representative in Krakow. His responsibilities included placing promotional materials, developing a retail distribution network and hiring a small staff to assist him. Product offerings were limited to Prince and a couple of its variants. Once HoP joined forces with Alliance, Wichur obtained a whole line-up of local brands, although still not a Prince menthol variant, for which he had been lobbying. He believed a Prince menthol would better appeal to Polish tastes and would offer an alternative to the modestly successful Prince brand.

Wichur's in-the-trenches experience made him valuable to Thomsen. For his part, Wichur welcomed Thomsen's pragmatic approach to sales and saw his arrival as an opportunity to gain the resources necessary to market cigarettes. For the first time, he felt free to discuss problems and issues with senior management and empowered to influence product decisions and strategy. Wichur became adept at translating the rhetoric of fundamental strategic change into real world implementation. He raised the bar for performance through his own dogged determination to return HoP-Poland to viable competition for the world's premier tobacco companies.

His dedication became key to energizing a demotivated staff who had lived through large scale hiring followed by firings. In Wichur's view, three successive rounds of lay-offs were necessary, but engendered fear and uncertainty among employees for months. After the lay-off of the other two district managers, Wichur felt ambivalent:

> The difference between them and me was that sometimes they had voiced really critical observations. Everyone had comments, but they were too critical for the new times.

He thought his colleagues had been judged without having had a chance to demonstrate what they could do. They were also his friends. Wichur did some soul searching and decided that the chance to build an effective sales team, a good working atmosphere and allegiance to his only employer were enough to make him stay at HoP-Poland.

Other important changes

In parallel with his and Thomsen's *coup de grâce* in the sales organization, Szlendak was working to improve the rest of the company. Large quantities of obsolete inventory and equipment were written off and the production facility moved from four shifts to three.

Not everyone responded positively to the rapidly changing environment. It felt as if the company had changed overnight from one where colleagues could linger over coffee to one demanding an overwhelming, draining pace. Although a rising unemployment rate provided a powerful incentive, remnants of a wistful, backward-looking sentiment remained just under the surface. Senior staff could not conceal the pride they felt that the old regime had rejected "Western" norms in its unconventional and temporarily successful approach.

HIRING REPLACEMENTS FOR KEY POSITIONS

After getting rid of dead wood and filling key roles with just the right insiders, Thomsen needed to strengthen his team and build enthusiasm for the new strategic approach through the careful introduction of external change agents. Thomsen hired Lucyna Lisiewska, an experienced key account specialist who worked first for United Biscuits and later for Danone, to lead the charge on growing the key account portfolio at HoP-Poland. Key accounts figured prominently in the new strategy to ensure the company's viability and as such were to be expanded and enhanced.

Emphasizing the key account segment represented a radical shift from a volume orientation to brand building in the company. Although the profit anticipated from even a highly successful key account campaign would be minimal, the advertising ban meant that in-store promotion was one of the few remaining avenues for customer interaction and new product introduction. Lisiewska's mandate was to improve the flow of competitor information, chain coverage and feedback from sales efforts. Although key account sales people were not included in the new bonus system implemented for the rest of the sales force, employees wanted to be a part of the team. Retail chains were of growing importance and key accounts were a critical element in HoP-Poland's plans for this business. As Lisiewska's staff increased to 12 (largely through the merger with the cigars and pipe tobacco operation), her ambitions to raise the profile of her group within the organization also grew. Because of the relatively small size of the existing key account business, Lisiewska felt that her department was often overlooked. She soon set a goal of doubling the proportion of company sales contributed by key accounts from 3% to 6% or 7%.

Arek Rochala was another key hire. Brought to HoP-Poland in July 2001 from competitor Altadis, Rochala took on the challenge of building a marketing team from the ground up as the company's marketing manager. Since the previous management had not believed in brand development and, therefore, the need for marketing, the company did not have an effective marketing infrastructure. Together with Thomsen and Svendsen, Rochala carried forward a marketing plan that incorporated staff performance standards, assessment of the product portfolio and the redesign and relaunch of the majority of the company's brands to optimize their position in the marketplace. The next step was to obtain talented brand managers who shared the company's strategic outlook and could lead the charge on HoP-Poland's new brand philosophy. Once inside the organization, Rochala assigned brand manager portfolios and delegated responsibility for their success. Although brand managers were given a free hand to achieve sales goals, Rochala ensured a consistent marketing approach through regularly scheduled meetings.

The new managers from outside were drawn to HoP-Poland by the *esprit de corps* and energy of senior management. Rochala, who had launched the Fox brand during his time with Altadis, saw the chance for promotion and a lack of political complications in coming to HoP-Poland. He, like Lisiewska, was also impressed with Thomsen's pragmatic approach, market orientation and ambitious goals for the company. Lisiewska had worked with a major multinational. When first contacted by a headhunter about the key account manager job, she rebuffed his overtures. She recalled:

First, when I heard cigarette company–House of Prince – I wasn't very happy with the prospect of working there. But, step-by-step, after an interview with Lars, HR and the former finance director,[1] I felt that I'd like to work for this company because of their professional manner and the challenge. I would get the chance to build something and that was exciting to me. I really wanted to make a contribution to the company's success.

HELP FROM OTHERS AND TRAINING BEGINS

Svendsen and Thomsen created an environment in which managers grew steadily more comfortable about coming forward with problems. In this new phase in the company's history, problems did not attract trouble. Instead, senior managers gave attention and resources to help solve them.

Steve Dobson, an external consultant who worked closely with daughter companies within the HoP Group, played an instrumental role in preparing the company's sales staff to face off against the competition. His rich experience in Eastern Europe and HoP supplemented Thomsen's global marketing perspective.

Dobson began work in Poland in April 2001. His participative style helped salve the wounds of the sales and marketing department. Not only were there many changes to adjust to within the organization, but sales people had also grown accustomed to being outgunned and overrun in the marketplace. The naturally competitive tendencies of the marketers meant that they welcomed Dobson's real world and inclusive approach.

In designing a program for Poland, he integrated the work already done by the HR trainers with proven techniques he had employed elsewhere. By November 2001, basic and advanced selling courses were rolled out and formed the cornerstone of staff education.

REACTIONS OF OTHERS

Old habits die hard. Almost one year after the company started reinventing itself, many things had changed and many had stayed the same. The introduction of carefully chosen internal and external change agents, in concert with a pragmatic brand building philosophy, produced a radically different organization. Many who were initially resistant to change embraced it, once they saw the benefits. Adaptability also seemed to be a generational issue, as older workers retained more of the legacy of communism.

In some respects, the massive lay-offs negated the progress inherent in the more open, performance-oriented culture that Thomsen introduced. In an era of projected 16% unemployment,[2] people were apt to keep their heads down to avoid trouble, and job insecurity played into those fears. A dynamic environment attracted those secure in their education and experience, but proved intimidating to some of the old guard. A segment of employees romanticized the past by chalking up the hectic pace and many demands of the new era to Thomsen's reorganization. But Thomsen believed that the price war and the economic downturn were more likely at fault. Joergen Tang, the new director of finance and administration, gave an example of the resistance and fear encountered in the interactive budgeting process. He remembered:

They think they will be executed if their budgets are not adhered to. But it's changing and I get positive surprises every week.

Culture can serve as an impediment to clear communication. HoP-Poland had only four expatriates, none of whom spoke Polish and, therefore, were not privy to feelings of concern or satisfaction among the staff. As Tang reflected:

When people can't communicate with you, they feel uneasy and endangered.

For his part, Thomsen felt:

"Thomsen" can become "Lars" again. Now the "bastard" could be softer.

He felt he had grown closer to his staff now that the "bloodbath" was over, although – paradoxically – he thought that this was what had contributed to this sense of closeness. He was free now to relax a little with those who remained, as the bulk of the dirty work was done. The hands-on, critical evaluation of each individual's strengths and weaknesses had brought Thomsen closer to his direct reports. In a very real sense, they were handpicked.

Yet Thomsen also recognized that the many direct confrontations and his ongoing efforts to raise performance standards had left him with an image far from the one characterized by the Scandinavian approach he had applied when he first came to Poland. As Thomsen's assistant, Barbara Rusniok, put it:

Some are still scared to enter Lars' office because they are afraid of the many detailed questions that he asks. At times, they see him as someone who makes a big storm out of a little detail. Yet, they respect his contributions and the fact that he is willing to pay the personal price for change.

SZLENDAK AND THOMSEN

Szlendak and Thomsen felt good about their work together that had yielded positive changes at HoP-Poland. They had complementary personalities and brought their individual strengths to bear in this crisis situation. Szlendak said:

Lars has done tremendous work in implementing professional standards. He did a lot to establish a reasonable structure and many processes are ongoing, including the development of new working standards, key performance indicators, an efficient organizational structure, a training program, a performance evaluation system and a reliable reporting mechanism.

Thomsen felt similarly:

Szlendak is strong on wholesale, which happens to be my weakest point. He is not as strong on marketing, which is my whole base. We are very good at complementing each other's competencies. He is used to building a business from scratch and turning over every zloty, every dollar. He's driven by fast change and is very action oriented. It is largely due to him that operational costs are down significantly compared to last year. He runs at 200 miles an hour.

On reflection, although many of his original perceptions of the situation in Poland were correct, one problem that did not turn out as he expected was Jan Wisnewski. Thomsen originally feared that, driven by the frustration of being denied a board seat, Wisnewski would try to derail his reorganization efforts. Although Wisnewski never seemed to accept the gravity and importance of his position as national sales manager, Thomsen thought he might actively attempt to incite a revolt or, at the very least, get in the way of his success. Instead Wisnewski exhibited neither outward resistance to, nor enthusiasm for, Thomsen's strategic overhaul of the company and, in late 2001, left HoP-Poland.

Perhaps the most startling results to date have been reflected in Thomsen himself. His approach to problem resolution and interactions with peers and subordinates has become more direct and assured. He has also become highly motivated by challenge. He commented:

> I like being surrounded by things that need to be changed. I thrive on this. It was the ultimate change management challenge. And it's not over.

WHAT TO DO NEXT?

The absence of notable improvement in wholesale had been a matter of continuing concern to Thomsen and Szlendak, given wholesale's importance to the company overall. Wholesalers remained a very powerful force in the market and, with time, their sophistication in dealing with manufacturers had grown markedly.

Although there were two price rises in the year since Thomsen arrived, the increases merely accommodated the higher excise taxes decreed by the government. Producers received no benefit from the price increases and so continued to be subjected to the damaging effects of the price war. There was no end in sight. Poland's tobacco excise tax accounted for roughly 44%[3] of the purchase price of a pack of cigarettes in 2001. The uphill march of cigarette prices and desperate competitor grabs for market share looked likely to increase, as Poland continued in its quest to reach the 57% excise tax rate required by the EU. Ongoing market pressures would only intensify and accentuate shortcomings in HoP-Poland's wholesale organization and market intelligence capabilities. Alternative sources of competitor and market data were needed to enhance the company's responsiveness and enable it to be proactive in addressing marketplace issues.

With the difficult task of culling and selecting staff behind it, the company's attention could be turned to improving the quality and training of staff and reducing the level of fear caused by lay-offs. Surveying the future, Szlendak said:

> We need to reach breakeven by growing volume with drastic direct and operational cost reduction, strengthen market position by brands development, protect market share through emphasis on penetration strategy and numerical distribution growth, apply customer relationship management solutions with more "us" and less "me."

Finally resolving the quagmire of ownership and control issues, which had hampered the company for so long, was perhaps the most important long-term element to tackle. The structure of the joint venture agreement, which gave majority ownership to HoP but denied it the right to exercise control, had been the genesis of the many disputes and difficulties that plagued the company. The fact that Poland had been a corporate leader in product development meant that this situation could have much wider implications for HoP. Because of the Polish market's large-scale rejection of foreign brands, HoP-Poland was forced to develop an array of low-cost local brands. Copenhagen would be prevented from offering these products in any of its nearby markets, since it did not own the brands outright. Buying out the Polish shareholders could resolve the issue of who was in charge in Poland and could also provide an entire product line to the other HoP subsidiaries in the Baltics. Although the parties have engaged in talks over the years, the Polish shareholders wanted a purchase price 50% to 60% higher than a KPMG valuation of the company. So the dance continued.

As Thomsen reviewed the past year, he wondered where he should put his greatest efforts in the future and what he should do next. He had managed to build an enthusiastic team of capable professionals, drawing from both HoP-Poland ranks and those of talented local sales professionals. Significant inroads had been made in developing a brand culture and performance-oriented environment in the company, and financial performance was beginning to improve.

The company had turned the corner and its viability was no longer in short-term danger. But much remained to be done to bring the company's performance fully in line with its potential. Most critical to Thomsen was still the integration of the sales and marketing functions, speed to market and, last but not least, the development of the wholesale function. What should he do to ensure his and the Polish operation's success?

ENTERING 2002

During the next half year, the change process continued with less radical but still rapid and intense steps toward the future. In January, a new sales director entered the arena, carefully selected for his pragmatic approach and eagerness for change, and Wichur left the company to work as sales director in another industry.

The wholesale organization was strengthened as its coverage of clients expanded significantly, supported by an advanced database that tracked and targeted brand rotation and distribution. The field force, now developed and fully functioning, was reintegrated with the wholesale operation. Following Svendsen's return to Copenhagen, the market support department was integrated with marketing. While these moves brought about a synthesis of the company's sales effort, it also reduced Thomsen's management team from six to three and thereby contributed to swifter market actions, greater alignment with business objectives and a reduction in silo mentality. This reduction in management staff was enabled by the earlier implementation of the focused six-person management team, which established basic standards of performance and organizational transparency. Although the leaner team now consisted of relative newcomers, the change culture remained strong.

The competitive landscape had shifted once again, as Japan Tobacco announced its withdrawal from the Polish market, with a subsequent sell-down of inventory at reduced prices. Imperial Tobacco consolidated its position in the market through its acquisition of Reemtsma.

Notes

1   Jelert left in September 2001 to become president of a formerly state-owned company in Warsaw.
2   Business Central Europe, *The Annual*, 2001.
3   House of Prince Internal Presentation, January 2002.

CASE **24**

Building Products International –
A Crisis Management Strategy (A)

Joseph J. DiStefano and Donna Everatt

It was Friday, May 15 and Nick Alanzo, director of human resources, Asia-Pacific for Building Products International, had let his dinner grow cold during the closing banquet of the company's regional annual meeting in Korea. His mind was elsewhere, and he was exhausted with keeping up his attendance at various meetings and events during the three-day conference while concurrently monitoring the situation in Jakarta, where BPI had extensive operations. In the preceding three days, Jakarta had erupted in "an orgy of violence," as the *Washington Post* referred to it. Hourly updates on CNN showed coverage of the violence as it unfolded and its aftermath – streets littered with the smoldering, burned-out carcasses of cars and buildings, plumes of black smoke emanating from the hardest-hit areas of the city, and frightened victims and residents panicking and fleeing from danger. These and other disturbing images were splashed on the front pages of the *Asian Wall Street Journal* and the *International Herald Tribune*.

Alanzo had lost his appetite as a result of several difficult decisions, including not only the myriad of issues involved in the logistics of a probable evacuation of BPI employees from Jakarta, but also the question of which employees to evacuate. BPI's

three senior managers were expatriates (expats) whereas BPI's four middle managers were Indonesian citizens of Chinese origin. BPI's 15 supervisors were a mixture of Chinese and indigenous Indonesians (or "Prebumi"). The remaining 228 employees were exclusively Prebumi (see Exhibit 3). Experts believed that expats and Indonesians of Chinese origin would be exposed to greater risk during the social strife in Indonesia than the Prebumi. Alanzo also had to decide whether to authorize the return back to Jakarta of those managers attending the conference who were demanding to return to Indonesia to protect and rescue their families. Complicating his decision was the fact that he was receiving inconsistent information as he scrambled to piece together an assessment of the situation in Jakarta. Alanzo had overseen the development of a crisis management strategy for Jakarta, and he knew that in its implementation, time was of the essence. He had to act fast if he wanted to protect BPI employees and their families during the worst rioting Asia had seen for decades.

BUILDING PRODUCTS INTERNATIONAL

Headquartered in Detroit, Building Products International (BPI) was a multinational conglomerate, operating in over 100 countries, with significant investments in multiple businesses in Indonesia, throughout Asia and the world. BPI's market strengths were its advanced technology and process knowledge, combined with its global manufacturing, service and marketing capabilities. In 1997, its bi-centennial year of operations, BPI saw a double-digit increase over its 1996 sales to US$2.7 billion, and an after-tax income of over US$175 million. A good portion of these revenues was generated from its Asian operations, of which Indonesia represented one of the top three divisions, in terms of revenues as well as size and scope of operations.

BPI's Indonesian operations consisted of the manufacture and distribution of tools and machinery for the construction industry. Manufacturing operations were concentrated in Indonesia's large urban centres, with the largest site located in the outskirts of Jakarta, where the vast majority of BPI's 250 employees worked. Over the years, an extensive sales and marketing network had been established in Indonesia, which distributed BPI products and after-sales service to far-flung regions throughout Indonesia's expansive area.

Given that its global operations were widely dispersed throughout so many countries, the company developed a highly decentralized organizational structure which became an integral part of the culture of the company. This decentralized structure allowed a high degree of local autonomy, which, in turn, resulted in increased operating flexibility and customer responsiveness throughout the many diverse regions where BPI operated (see Exhibit 1). However, this type of organizational structure posed certain challenges, which Alanzo explained:

> Sometimes, it's very hard to get people to work together – to coalesce. By and large, managers will not follow central mandates unless they originate from the top one or two executives in the organization. Thus, it takes a lot to get "buy-in" and to have everyone move together in the same direction unless you are clearly aligned with their local interests. Often, department heads can be myopic.

EXHIBIT 1 BPI Organizational Chart

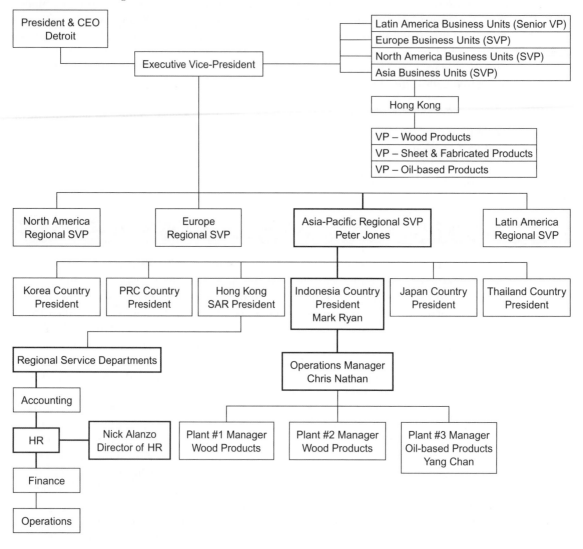

REGIONAL CRISIS MANAGEMENT AT BPI

Responsibility for the development of a regional crisis management program fell under the jurisdiction of the human resources (HR) department. Alanzo had been BPI's director of human resources for the Asia Pacific region for the last two years, after having held a similar position in the US for several years. He had joined BPI directly after obtaining his MBA from an American university almost 15 years ago.

Alanzo explained that the development of a crisis management policy typically fell under the umbrella of HR responsibilities for several reasons. First, the HR division would be the most effective within the organization to coordinate a multi-divisional strategy. Moreover, much of the information that would be required during an emergency resided in HR files. Finally, it was necessary for someone at the regional office to take responsibility for the development of a crisis management program and it seemed, almost by default, that HR ended up with the responsibility. Alanzo had attended and spoken at several crisis management seminars over the past couple of years and had more knowledge on the subject than anyone else at BPI.

In the development of a regional crisis management plan, Alanzo recognized that, as part of doing business in Asia, it was necessary for BPI to assess country risk in the region on an annual basis. Alanzo described his analysis of the situation in Jakarta:

> Our concern with Indonesia began about a year and a half to two years ago. There were signs on the horizon – relatively small-scale student uprisings had occurred and there was some question as to how the military would react and whether they were the harbinger of more widespread social unrest. We did some scenario planning and asked ourselves "What if" in Indonesia. That scenario planning included the development of a template for an evacuation plan, and we sat down with security experts and talked through how we should deal with a crisis, should one occur.

BPI had initiated discussions with the global security firm, Aegis International, based in Washington and it was decided that in the event of a crisis in Indonesia, BPI would call upon Aegis' services. Aegis had agreed to commit a complement of eight staff to BPI on a 24-hour a day basis during the crisis period. Under normal circumstances, Aegis would also supply BPI with monthly updates on various Southeast Asian countries where BPI operated and would augment these reports with flash updates if a particular region began to heat up. Their duties during a crisis management phase would include: management of a crisis centre in the US; operation of a crisis centre on-site; convoy support of employees; liaison with local authorities; collection of tactical intelligence in the region; management of evacuation flights; coordination with BPI staff, employees and dependents; coordination of immigration issues; liaison with airport authorities; escort services for movements within the city; inspection of and security for residents; liaison with BPI HR and executive personnel in Hong Kong and the US; management of local problems; and coordination of exit formalities.

The plan which BPI and Aegis developed addressed many of the logistical issues which were expected to arise during a crisis situation. It also covered detailed elements of a crisis management and evacuation plan ranging from how local managers were to brief their employees, to how to coordinate the transfer of expatriate managers and their dependents and guests to safe-houses, to how to secure the manufacturing site and transfer important documentation off-site. Alanzo explained the local manager's roles and responsibilities in the context of BPI's crisis management program:

> The plan was communicated to each of the local managers throughout the region so that they could understand the actions of central control during the crisis and would know what to expect. Moreover, in the event of interruptions to communication, the managers

could implement the plan to the best of their ability, take "appropriate action," and make decisions according to a range of options as laid out in the plan, using their best judgment. Nonetheless, during periods of normal communication, the plan dictated that a local manager should acquiesce to commands from the person in charge in regional office, most likely myself.

We did not fully develop a contingency plan for every possibility, as that would have added several layers of detail, requiring vast amounts of time and resources. The development of the initial crisis management template had proven to be a very time-consuming process for me and my staff, as it was in addition to our regular responsibilities.

According to Alanzo, although BPI had forged an initial relationship with Aegis and developed a thorough template for an evacuation plan, it "pretty much sat on the shelf, although we dusted it off from time to time and reminded our country managers of their roles and responsibilities as they related to the plan."

THE EVACUATION PLAN

As was common with many crisis management plans, one of the first major components of the plan was to sequester BPI's expatriate staff into large foreign hotels, designated as "safe-houses". This was a common practice during a crisis and it made sense to Alanzo for several reasons. First, the foreign hotels offered a degree of security through professionally trained staff – families were more vulnerable in individual houses with little or no security. Army personnel could often be found stationed outside of large international hotels, because the local governments were concerned with keeping foreign businessmen and tourists safe since the local economy would suffer acutely once foreigners were harmed. According to Alanzo, high-rise hotels also had the psychological advantage of being imposing, more so than individual homes. Importantly, by congregating employees in a few select locations, they could be evacuated at a moment's notice. Also, it was easier to monitor their employees if they were contained in one area. Finally, Alanzo had hoped that a sense of togetherness would help the employees feel more secure and comfortable knowing they were not alone. During this process, the services of Aegis would be called upon, and they would coordinate the evacuation through their field operations and their headquarters in the US, using their established network throughout Indonesia.

The question of which employees were to be evacuated was an issue that would be decided on an individual basis. However, BPI policy dictated that, generally speaking, all expatriate managers and their dependents were to be evacuated. When to evacuate was another issue, and it was generally agreed that discussions with managers in the field were to be the determining factor, augmented with media reports as well as advisories from the US embassy based in the city in question. Alanzo was fairly certain that under the terms of BPI's insurance contract, Embassy advisories issued from each employee's Embassy (i.e., the American Embassy for American employees) would justify BPI's evacuation of expatriate employees from Jakarta. Further, such advisories would activate coverage for the evacuation costs of the employees and their dependents and guests (see Exhibit 2). BPI, however, had a policy that allowed greater flexibility. Alanzo explained:

EXHIBIT 2 Endorsement – Emergency Repatriation and Relocation Extension

Issued to: Building Products International, Co.

This endorsement effective on 08/12/95 at 12:01 a.m. standard time for part of Certificate No. A91 – 298933352

It is agreed that Section IV – Item 4 (Additional Coverage) shall be amended to include Insured Losses hereinafter defined and sustained by the Named Insured or an Insured Person (RELATIVE or GUEST) in connection with EMERGENCY REPATRIATION and RELOCATION necessitated by:

I.   The officials of the RESIDENT COUNTRY issuing, for reasons other than medical, a recommendation that categories of persons which include insured persons, RELATIVES or GUESTS should leave the country in which such persons are temporarily resident and/or;
II. An insured person, RELATIVE OR GUEST being expelled or declared "persona non grata" on the written authority of the recognized government of the country of temporary residence, and/or;
III. The wholesale seizure, confiscation or expropriation of the property, plant and equipment of the Named Insured.

For the purposes of this endorsement, Insured Losses shall be deemed to mean:

I.   Costs incurred by the Named Insured or an Insured Person, RELATIVE or GUEST for passage to the nearest place of safety or to the RESIDENT COUNTRY;
II. Reasonable accommodation costs incurred by the Named Insured or an Insured Person, RELATIVE or GUEST;
III. Economy class fares on any licensed common carrier operating from a published timetable incurred by the Named Insured or an Insured Person, RELATIVE or GUEST for the RELOCATION of said individuals;
IV. The SALARY paid by the Named Insured to an Insured Person at the rate in effect immediately prior to the INSURED EVENT. Said SALARY to be reimbursable for a maximum of three months following the EMERGENCY REPATRIA-TION, or until the date of RELOCATION, whichever comes first.

CONDITIONS:
It is agreed that, as respects coverage provided hereunder for EMERGENCY REPATRIATION, the Named Insured and/or Insured Persons, RELATIVES or GUESTS shall be indemnified solely for the costs of transportation by economy fares unless unavailable, clearly impractical or unless travel by any other class of service is essential to ensure the safety of an Insured Person, RELATIVE or GUEST.

DEFINITIONS
For the purposes of this endorsement, the following definitions should apply:

I.   INSURED EVENT means the Emergency Repatriation and Relocation of an Insured Person, RELATIVE or GUEST.
II. RELOCATION means the return of the Insured Person, RELATIVE or GUEST who has been the subject of an EMERGENCY REPATRIATION to the country from which he/she had been repatriated.
III. EMERGENCY REPATRIATION means the return of an Insured Person, RELATIVE or GUEST to his/her resident country.
IV. RESIDENT COUNTRY means the country of which an Insured Person, RELATIVE or GUEST is a national.

EXCLUSIONS
It is further agreed that coverage shall not apply to Insured Losses sustained by the Named Insured or an Insured Person, RELATIVE or GUEST by the Named Insurer or an Insured Person, RELATIVE or GUEST attributable to:

I.   Violation by the Named Insured or an Insured Person, RELATIVE or GUEST of the laws and regulations of the country in which the EMERGENCY REPATRIATION and RELOCATION takes place.
II. The failure of the Named Insured or Insured Person, RELATIVE or GUEST to properly procure and maintain immigration, work, residence or similar type visas, permits or documents.
III. A debt, insolvency, commercial failure or repossession of any property by a title-holder or any other financial cause.
IV. The failure of the Named Insurer or Insured Person, RELATIVE or GUEST to honor any contractual obligations or bond or to adhere to any condition(s) in a license.

At any point, if an expatriate or members of his or her family stated their desire to depart prior to a perceived need on the part of regional headquarters in Hong Kong, company policy dictated that their wish was to be respected – without question.

In order to facilitate an emergency evacuation, the senior expatriate managers in each country had an emergency fund of several thousand US dollars, kept in a safe place in their homes. However, Alanzo had concerns regarding travel documentation. BPI lacked specific details, such as passport numbers, for employees or any visiting relatives and friends, which might be required in an emergency to ensure a hassle-free exit from Indonesia.

Moreover, Alanzo had no way of knowing for certain whether the employees, their visiting friends or relatives had kept their visas current (which required renewal on a two-month basis). Generally, expats in Indonesia traveled outside the country on a regular basis (i.e., to BPI headquarters in Hong Kong), permitting an additional two-month stay upon their return to Indonesia. If they had not kept their visas up to date, it could delay the departure of the entire group, or at the very least, result in increased stress for those having problems with immigration authorities – and for Alanzo.

By May, Alanzo's staff had begun the process of updating BPI employee's HR files with passport, immigration and visa information as well as emergency contact numbers. The impetus for Alanzo to begin this process was several flash reports from Aegis that a crisis in Indonesia could erupt given enough provocation. In 1997, the region al financial crisis provided just that. However, by the time the crisis erupted in Indonesia and the country became unstable, the employee files were far from complete.

THE POLITICAL, ECONOMIC, AND SOCIAL SITUATION IN INDONESIA – A HISTORICAL VIEW

The shape of Indonesian politics last took a cataclysmic turn over 30 years ago in October 1965, following a leftist coup attempt against President Sukarno, the republic's first leader. This insurrection sparked the killing of tens of thousands of alleged communists by rightist gangs, reportedly encouraged by military commanders. By 1966, an estimated 500,000 people had been killed and President Sukarno was forced to transfer key political and military power to then General Suharto, who had led the military defeat of the leftist coup.

With the crucial backing of the military, Suharto advocated policies of economic rehabilitation and development, transforming Indonesia into highly diversified manufacturing and export-driven economy, from an inefficiently operating agricultural base. Per-capita income rose from US$70 in 1966, to almost US$1,000 in 1996, with an accompanying decline in poverty rates to an estimated 11 percent, from 60 percent over the same period.

The 1980s saw further economic reforms and the liberalizing of trade and finance sectors in Indonesia, expanding foreign investment and deregulation. The resultant boom in trade and investment was reflected in the growth of Indonesia's economy, averaging seven percent from 1985 to 1996. Suharto, his friends and family benefited greatly from this impressive economic expansion, controlling an empire estimated in the range of US$20 billion, covering many industries including hotels, transportation, banks and automobiles by 1998.

The country's economic prosperity, however, did little to improve the political freedoms of the average Indonesian. Over the '60s, Suharto's security forces routinely crushed uprisings by jailing activists for speaking out against the government, and rumors of torture and murder were substantiated with gruesome facts. Despite the corruption and human rights abuses, Suharto maintained his power for over three decades.

However, the President's grip began to loosen with Thailand's devaluation of the baht in July 1997, causing the value of the rupiah to drop precipitously – almost 80 percent. Foreign investors fled and the domestic bankruptcy rate increased dramatically. As with many other regional economies, weaknesses in Indonesia's banks were exposed, and 16 had their operations suspended. Indonesia's food distribution system was inefficient, meaning that the majority of food had to be imported, and even then it was difficult and expensive to get food to outlying areas or avoid the black market activities in the urban centers.

As the country negotiated with the International Monetary Fund (IMF) over the terms of its US$43 billion bailout package in early 1998, riots began to erupt over rising food and basic commodity prices, gradually intensifying despite police efforts to quell them.

In March 1998, Suharto was re-elected to a seventh term by the People's Consultative Assembly, a legislative body largely assembled by the President himself, spiked with key military figures. Student protests ensued and calls for Suharto to relinquish his post grew louder by the day. By May, the situation had turned violent. No longer were the gatherings comprised of students calling for reform; by that time, starving Indonesians, with nothing to lose, began a wave of rioting and looting which reached levels of violence not seen in Indonesia for several decades. The ethnic Chinese in Indonesia were the primary targets of the looting and violence.

THE ETHNIC CHINESE IN INDONESIA

Although the ethnic Chinese comprised only three percent of Indonesia's population, they were a key driver of the Indonesia economy. The Chinese had been a part of Indonesia's history for several centuries, as they fled China to escape persecution and established a niche for themselves as traders and entrepreneurs. When the Dutch arrived in Indonesia 400 years ago, they established a semi-apartheid state that segregated the population into three groups – the Europeans, the foreign Orientals, and the indigenous. The Dutch employed a selected group of Chinese as trading partners, creating the foundation of patronage that many believed still existed in 1998. The few wealthy Chinese who had become extremely rich through their close association and system of patronage with the Suharto government, his ministers and generals, were often accused by indigenous Indonesians of using Indonesia to get rich while investing their capital abroad. Indonesians did not always make a distinction between this select group of wealthy Chinese owners, and the shopkeepers on the streets of Jakarta who held a commanding control of the retail sector. Although the ethnic Chinese were a minority in Indonesia, their business activities were an integral part of Indonesia's middle class.

This economic dominance continued despite affirmative action and various government programs which had restricted the rights of the Chinese minority for decades. Chinese-language reading materials and characters were banned in Indonesia, as were public celebrations of the Chinese New Year. Moreover, Chinese were not permitted to be involved in politics in Indonesia. Their employment in the civil service was restricted, as was their entrance to Indonesian universities. Although they were free to practise their religion – Christianity or Buddhism – religion acted to further separate the ethnic Chinese from Prebumis (or native Indonesians). Indonesia was the largest Muslim nation in the world – almost 90 percent of Indonesians were Muslim.

The dominance of a few dozen ethnic Chinese families who had amassed incredible wealth through the system of patronage with the Suharto government had resulted in a public image of the ethnic Chinese as rich opportunists. Moreover, by 1998, the ethnic Chinese were Indonesia's most powerful economic group, controlling about 70 percent of Indonesia's private wealth and much of its retail and banking sectors. With ever-increasing ranks of Indonesians continuing to fall below the poverty line and several thousand losing their jobs each day, the temptation to use the Chinese as scapegoats was growing to ever more dangerous levels.

THE FIRST SIGNS OF TROUBLE

By early May, Alanzo was receiving weekly updates, augmented with flash reports from Aegis, regarding the situation in Indonesia and had discussed the information with several managers in the field. By May 6, Alanzo became aware of the most dramatic wave of violence seen in the past few months, with riots and looting breaking out in Medan, in Northern Indonesia, and tens of thousands of students demonstrating throughout the country. According to the news reports Alanzo was receiving, IMF-dictated price increases – part of a recovery program which ended subsidies for basic commodities mandated as a condition of the bailout funds – were the impetus for the protests. Indonesians saw the price of gasoline rise 70 percent in one day, accompanied by dramatic increases in the price of electricity and transportation. These austerity measures, which harshly affected the average Indonesian, were not the type of "economic reform" that the students had been calling for – they considered the abolishing of the corruption, collusion, and nepotism which characterized the Suharto regime a more appropriate response to the country's woes. Alanzo believed at this point that the economic hardship imposed by these measures meant that the protests would swiftly gain momentum. Nonetheless, he was assured by his managers in the field that the media were "over-reacting" and that the demonstrations that day, although on a larger scale, were similar to many seen in the past in Indonesia. Alanzo was nonetheless concerned about the situation and questioned whether the field managers had a sense of false confidence due to their experience in Jakarta, resulting in a sense of complacency. By mid-May, Alanzo's fears seemed much more justified.

THREE DAYS IN MAY

Wednesday May 13 – 2:40 p.m.

Alanzo had just arrived in Korea for BPI's annual regional meeting. The meeting was attended by all heads of business units and regional senior executives, including the president and the CFO of Asia-Pacific, as well as a number of executives from the US headquarters, including BPI's COO.

Over lunch, Alanzo had heard rumors from other attendees at the conference that Jakarta was in a state of emergency. Although over recent weeks police had fired rubber bullets and tear gas into crowds, apparently live rounds of ammunition were now being used in a more heavy-handed crack-down by Suharto's security forces and the military. This resulted in the first student deaths in nearly three months of demonstrations on campuses across the country. Alanzo heard that this bloody outbreak of violence resulted in the death of at least six students and the wounding of dozens more. He also heard reports that the demonstrations had involved crowds of over 5,000 but when he contacted managers in the field, he was still reassured that there was no clear and present danger to BPI employees who avoided the "isolated insurrections."

Given Alanzo's familiarity with operations throughout Indonesia, as well as his exposure to crisis management planning, BPI's executive group in Korea came to the consensus that Alanzo should be responsible during the crisis for closely monitoring the situation, and responding as he felt the situation warranted. This was a contentious issue as Mark Ryan, the country president for Indonesia, as well as his direct subordinate, Chris Nathan, reported to Peter Jones, the Asia-Pacific regional SVP (see Exhibit 1). Alanzo understood the need to show a great degree of diplomacy and protect the established and entrenched normal reporting lines. Therefore, although he was in charge, he was very careful to solicit opinions and encourage the participation of other managers in the decision-making process.

Alanzo's first step was to initiate communications with Chuck Conrad, his contact at Aegis. Conrad and Alanzo immediately began planning for an operations control center in Jakarta, to be staffed 24 hours a day by several Aegis employees.

Although the afternoon business reviews at the conference were conducted as planned, Alanzo was outside the conference rooms on his cell phone for the majority of the meetings, attempting to gather information from managers in the field, the US Embassy and Conrad, with a view to piecing together an understanding of the events as they unfolded. Alanzo formally disseminated a summary of this information immediately to the management complement still within Indonesia, to the managers that had gathered at the conference, and to BPI's head office in Detroit.

Alanzo noted that "the informal communications were the most complicated and time-consuming." Later that night, Alanzo's room in the hotel had become an operation control center. He fielded calls from every stakeholder in each region, including the regional managers in Korea, the regional president, the manager on-site in Jakarta, the wives in Jakarta of the managers in Korea who wanted to get in touch with their husbands (and vice-versa), the US head office, Aegis' staff, and the US embassy in Jakarta.

As his research uncovered the serious and swift nature of the unfolding events in Jakarta and the speed with which they could deteriorate, Alanzo began to appreciate the magnitude of the situation. As he retired for evening, he found it difficult to sleep as his mind kept running to the myriad of organizational details that would be required over the next few days with the prospect of evacuation of several BPI employees and their families.

Thursday, May 14 – 6:00 a.m.

After a disturbed night of half-sleep, Alanzo awoke to a call from Conrad alerting him of a US Embassy advisory indicating that the 8,000 Americans living in Jakarta, as well as those in Surabaya, Indonesia's second-largest city, should "depart the country as soon as possible" and that the US Pacific Command had begun making plans for an emergency military evacuation of US citizens which they were prepared to invoke should the situation further deteriorate. According to Conrad, a flotilla of US warships was positioned off the coast of Thailand and was standing by to assist. According to Conrad, this meant that the situation in Jakarta had deteriorated significantly. He explained:

> Aegis developed evacuation plans separate from the Embassy evacuation plan. This is because the Embassy must take into consideration the political implications and potential to further destabilize the region by ordering an evacuation. An evacuation of the US Embassy signals that the current government is no longer viable, or can't handle the situation. Therefore, an Embassy will delay the decision to evacuate as long as possible. We generally use the Embassy plan for contingency purposes only.

While drinking several cups of strong black coffee, Alanzo pored over Associated Press reports which reported that major US companies in Indonesia had begun moving their expatriate employees into downtown hotels for possible evacuation. This prompted Alanzo to make similar arrangements for expatriate employees and their families (see Exhibit 3). Aegis' team in Jakarta planned to escort them to an internationally managed hotel in downtown Jakarta.

Alanzo was somewhat relieved that he had taken this step. Throughout the day, he heard steady reports from Conrad and various media sources that Jakarta had erupted in a series of violent riots, resulting in the destruction of hundreds of stores, malls, and offices, sending panic-stricken residents fleeing for the airport or the relative safety of downtown hotels.

To augment the media reports, Alanzo was on the phone all day with Ryan and Aegis control center. He also attempted to contact field managers, although he often was very frustrated by his efforts to reach them because they were busy attempting to operate their business units in an environment of anarchy. When he did reach them, he was somewhat surprised by their complacency in the face of what Alanzo considered to be a clear and present danger – they were not overly concerned with the events in Jakarta, and felt that they were at a safe distance outside Jakarta, sufficient to avoid the worst of the chaos. Thus, they stayed on-site and prepared to suspend and secure operations should the need arise, while assuring Alanzo that there was little reason to be overly concerned.

EXHIBIT 3 Personnel Profile

Name	Ethnicity	Nationality	Position
Indonesian Senior Managers*:			
Mark Ryan	N/A	American	Country Manager
Chris Nathan	British	British	Operations Manager
Christopher Wright	Australian	Australian	Purchasing Manager
Field Managers:			
Stan Lin	Chinese	Indonesian	Personnel Manager
Yang Chan	Chinese	Indonesian	Head of Forestry Division
2 Plant Managers	Chinese	Indonesian	Plant managers, Plants A & B
Supervisors:			
Wei Fong	Chinese	People's Republic of China	Supervisor
Alan Li	Chinese	Indonesian	Supervisor
4 supervisors	Chinese	Indonesian	Various supervisory capacities throughout BPI Indonesian operations
9 supervisors	Indonesian	Indonesian	Various supervisory capacities throughout BPI Indonesian operations
Workers:			
228 employees	Indonesian	Indonesian	Factory and forestry workers crews, support services, ground workers, maintenance crews, and assistants to supervisors and managers

* (all in attendance at the annual global conference in Singapore)

They did, however, concede that the Chinese staff members would be wise to adopt a low profile over the next few days.

In the meantime, some of the spouses who were sharing hotel rooms had been discussing the situation in Jakarta. These discussions, augmented by various disturbing rumors circulating throughout expatriate informal communication networks in Jakarta, had increased their sense of urgency for evacuation. They were conveying these concerns to their husbands in Korea, which meant that the pressure to act was increasing and Alanzo felt pressed from every direction.

Although no one was able at that point to establish the death toll in Jakarta, Alanzo had heard reports from witnesses that the Chinatown section in North Jakarta was particularly devastated. This prompted businesses in other parts of the city to erect signs outside of their businesses reading "Prebumi" to avoid being mistaken for a Chinese business. Alanzo watched the news that night with great anxiety as he listened to reports of closure of schools and businesses, disrupted transportation services, and delays and cancellations at the airport due to mass rioting along the main artery to the airport. Alanzo had heard reports of victims, whose cars had been stopped by the rioting crowds on the way to the airport, pulled from their vehicles and beaten and robbed. Chinese and expatriates were the primary targets as they were the wealthy segments of the population and the most likely to be fleeing. In newscasts from Jakarta, plumes of black smoke could be seen rising from several sections of the city which looked as if it was being shelled.

By Thursday night, all expatriate BPI employees and their families had been moved from their respective homes, and were ensconced in the hotel. However, this gave Alanzo only partial relief. As he watched CNN's coverage of Thursday's events on the nightly news, Alanzo became aware that the prospect of evacuating these, and perhaps other BPI employees, was quickly becoming a reality. This kept him up late into the night, but by 3:00 a.m., he lay down to try to get some rest.

Friday May 15 – 11:50 a.m.

Friday morning, with the annual meeting coming to an end, Alanzo made his return booking for the first flight to Hong Kong the next morning. By this point, he had made the decision to begin with the evacuation of various BPI staff, but some difficult issues remained.

Beyond the challenging logistical decisions such as how exactly the employees should be evacuated, Alanzo felt the burden of making other difficult decisions, such as whom to evacuate, and whether to facilitate the re-entry of the managers who wished to return to Jakarta to aid their families. During the past several days, several of the expatriates and Chinese management with Alanzo in Korea who had family in Jakarta made requests of Alanzo to arrange for their return to their families. It was clear that those in Indonesia were in great danger and naturally the managers wanted to return, regardless of the personal danger they would face. Alanzo could certainly understand their desire to return – he himself had a wife and two young children. However, in his opinion, logic was against authorizing their return. First, personal danger to the managers would be great and likely increasing. Moreover, their return would compound the organizational logistics of the evacuation exponentially, further adding to the risks to their families. However, many of the managers had been in contact with their Indonesian managers, and the field reports they were receiving portrayed a much less serious perspective than that conveyed through the media. Thus, they were clamoring to be let back in.

Alanzo also faced other difficult decisions, such as to whom to provide emergency assistance. He thought to himself:

> Should I offer safe refuge for all of BPI's 250 employees in Indonesia? If so, the cost could be enormous. And who would end up paying those costs? Would it come from the unit's budget, regional expense budget, or even that of BPI general emergency fund? Moreover, the ramifications of offering refuge to some employees and not others could be enormous, both in terms of morale and morality.
>
> Even if I were to decide that only certain employees were to be offered refuge, which factors should serve as the basis for my decision? An employee's years of service? Their service record? Their ethnicity? Their position seemed like a good place to start but where do I draw the line? Should I evacuate only those who explicitly stated their desire to leave? My own moral perspective impacts my decision, of course, but I also have to consider my actions and their implications as a director of BPI. I'm caught between a rock and hard place, but someone has to make the difficult decisions in this situation. I've taken on that

EXHIBIT 4   Initial Aegis Estimate of Indonesian Repatriation Project

Expense	Amount (US$)
Fees incurred to activate Jakarta evacuation plan	4,600
Professional services fee*	35,000
Hotel (safe-house accommodation)	6,790
Air tickets	12,750
Meals	690
Land Travel	372
Security patrols at executive residences	980
Exit fees and immigration facilitation	900
Air travel incurred by Aegis staff	2,530
Telephone, fax (local and international)	874
Miscellaneous	2,500
TOTAL	**67,986**

* professional services including: management and staffing of regional crisis center and US-based coordination; convoy support of employees within Jakarta; liaison with local authorities; coordination of evacuation flight services; security escorts; liaison with BPI employees in the field, at the regional and head offices; local emergency supplies coordination; etc.

N.B. Insurance coverage was "first dollar" coverage (i.e., no deductible), with the expectation that most expenses as listed would be covered fully.

responsibility and I accept that. The most important thing at this point is the safety of BPI employees. The other stuff I can work out later.

The events of the past few days had so consumed Alanzo that he was exhausted by the time Friday's closing banquet started. He excused himself right after dinner, and returned to his hotel room to pack for his return to Hong Kong the following day. He knew he would need a good night's sleep to get the strength to face several difficult decisions which he had to make. During the night, Alanzo slept fitfully, as he woke up and jotted down more notes in preparation for the next day.

ACKNOWLEDGMENT

The Richard Ivey School of Business gratefully acknowledges the generous support of The Richard and Jean Ivey Fund in the development of this case as part of the Richard and Jean Ivey Fund Asian Case Series.

Index